BEHAVIORAL INTERVENTIONS IN SCHOOLS

SECOND EDITION

APPLYING PSYCHOLOGY IN THE SCHOOLS BOOK SERIES

Assessing Bilingual Children in Context: An Integrated Approach
   Edited by Amanda B. Clinton

Autism Spectrum Disorder in Children and Adolescents: Evidence-Based Assessment and Intervention in Schools
   Edited by Lee A. Wilkinson

Behavioral Interventions in Schools: Evidence-Based Positive Strategies, Second Edition
   Edited by Steven G. Little and Angeleque Akin-Little

Empowered Families, Successful Children: Early Intervention Programs That Work
   Susan Epps and Barbara J. Jackson

Empowered Learning in Secondary Schools: Promoting Positive Youth Development Through a Multitiered System of Supports
   Cynthia E. Hazel

Enhancing Relationships Between Children and Teachers
   Robert C. Pianta

Health-Related Disorders in Children and Adolescents: A Guidebook for Understanding and Educating
   Edited by LeAdelle Phelps

Healthy Eating in Schools: Evidence-Based Interventions to Help Kids Thrive
   Catherine P. Cook-Cottone, Evelyn Tribole, and Tracy L. Tylka

Implementation of Mental Health Programs in Schools: A Change Agent's Guide
   Susan G. Forman

Psychoeducational Assessment and Intervention for Ethnic Minority Children: Evidence-Based Approaches
   Edited by Scott L. Graves, Jr. and Jamilia J. Blake

School-Based Mental Health Services: Creating Comprehensive and Culturally Specific Programs
   Bonnie Kaul Nastasi, Rachel Bernstein Moore, and Kristen M. Varjas

School-Centered Interventions: Evidence-Based Strategies for Social, Emotional, and Academic Success
   Dennis J. Simon

Self-Regulated Learning Interventions With At-Risk Youth: Enhancing Adaptability, Performance, and Well-Being
  Edited by Timothy J. Cleary

Single-Case Intervention Research: Methodological and Statistical Advances
  Edited by Thomas R. Kratochwill and Joel R. Levin

Testing Accommodations for Students With Disabilities: Research-Based Practice
  Benjamin J. Lovett and Lawrence J. Lewandowski

Treatment Integrity: A Foundation for Evidence-Based Practice in Applied Psychology
  Edited by Lisa M. Hagermoser Sanetti and Thomas R. Kratochwill

Universal Screening in Educational Settings: Evidence-Based Decision Making for Schools
  Edited by Ryan J. Kettler, Todd A. Glover, Craig A. Albers, and Kelly A. Feeney-Kettler

Working With Parents of Aggressive Children: A Practitioner's Guide
  Timothy A. Cavell

Working With Parents of Noncompliant Children: A Guide to Evidence-Based Parent Training for Practitioners and Students
  Mark D. Shriver and Keith D. Allen

BEHAVIORAL INTERVENTIONS IN SCHOOLS

Evidence-Based Positive Strategies

SECOND EDITION

Edited by
Steven G. Little and Angeleque Akin-Little

AMERICAN PSYCHOLOGICAL ASSOCIATION
Washington, DC

Copyright © 2019 by the American Psychological Association. All rights reserved. Except as permitted under the United States Copyright Act of 1976, no part of this publication may be reproduced or distributed in any form or by any means, including, but not limited to, the process of scanning and digitization, or stored in a database or retrieval system, without the prior written permission of the publisher.

The opinions and statements published are the responsibility of the authors, and such opinions and statements do not necessarily represent the policies of the American Psychological Association.

Published by
American Psychological Association
750 First Street, NE
Washington, DC 20002
www.apa.org

APA Order Department
P.O. Box 92984
Washington, DC 20090-2984
Phone: (800) 374-2721; Direct: (202) 336-5510
Fax: (202) 336-5502; TDD/TTY: (202) 336-6123
Online: http://www.apa.org/pubs/books
E-mail: order@apa.org

In the U.K., Europe, Africa, and the Middle East, copies may be ordered from
Eurospan Group
c/o Turpin Distribution
Pegasus Drive
Stratton Business Park
Biggleswade, Bedfordshire
SG18 8TQ United Kingdom
Phone: +44 (0) 1767 604972
Fax: +44 (0) 1767 601640
Online: https://www.eurospanbookstore.com/apa
E-mail: eurospan@turpin-distribution.com

Typeset in Goudy by Circle Graphics, Inc., Reisterstown, MD

Printer: Sheridan Books, Chelsea, MI
Cover Designer: Naylor Design, Washington, DC

Library of Congress Cataloging-in-Publication Data

Names: Little, Steven G. editor. | Akin-Little, Angeleque, editor.
Title: Behavioral interventions in schools : evidence-based positive
  strategies / edited by Steven G. Little and Angeleque Akin-Little.
Description: Second edition. | Washington, DC : American Psychological
  Association, 2019. | Series: Applying Psychology in the Schools Book
  Series | Includes bibliographical references and index.
Identifiers: LCCN 2018043207 (print) | LCCN 2018059513 (ebook) | ISBN
  9781433830716 (eBook) | ISBN 143383071X (eBook) | ISBN 9781433830143
  (hardback) | ISBN 1433830140 (hardcover)
Subjects: LCSH: Behavior modification. | Problem children—Behavior
  modification. | Problem children—Education. | Behavioral assessment. |
  BISAC: PSYCHOLOGY / Psychotherapy / Child & Adolescent. | PSYCHOLOGY /
  Psychopathology / Autism Spectrum Disorders. | PSYCHOLOGY / Movements /
  Behaviorism.
Classification: LCC LB1060.2 (ebook) | LCC LB1060.2 .B443 2019 (print) | DDC
  370.15/28—dc23
LC record available at https://urldefense.proofpoint.com/v2/url?u=https-3A__lccn.loc.gov_
  2018043207&d=DwIFAg&c=XuwJK26h77xqxpbZGgbjkdqHiCAgI8ShbCmQt4lrFlM&r=
  jxDmcfdMwrJ1f_jnNnialA&m=HA33sYoHattYOaAVsuY5v4V8HX9pecQFzcwGwTkiVUc&s=
  y5Kg0Gkh7NvpTNHI04DiDMdMXZJLb4YTcrdmaSGLmeU&e

British Library Cataloguing-in-Publication Data
A CIP record is available from the British Library.

Printed in the United States of America

http://dx.doi.org/10.1037/0000126-000

10 9 8 7 6 5 4 3 2 1

This book is dedicated to the students and professionals
who will use the information contained herein
to improve the lives of children and their families.
We wish in every way a light- and love-filled life.

CONTENTS

Contributors xiii

Series Foreword xvii
Michelle M. Perfect

Acknowledgments xix

Introduction 3
Steven G. Little and Angeleque Akin-Little

I. Foundations of Behavioral Interventions 13

Chapter 1.   Narrative Reports and Recordings for Behavioral Problem–Solving in Schools 15
Christopher H. Skinner

Chapter 2.   School-Wide Positive Behavioral Interventions and Supports: A Systems-Level Application of Behavioral Principles 35
Brandi Simonsen and George Sugai

Chapter 3.	Classroom Management 61	

Joseph H. Wehby and Kathleen Lynne Lane

Chapter 4. Reductive Procedures: Positive Approaches to
Reducing the Incidence of Problem Behavior 77
Steven G. Little and Angeleque Akin-Little

Chapter 5. Generalization and Maintenance 97
Jamie L. Pratt, Garry D. Wickerd, and Mark W. Steege

Chapter 6. Effect of Extrinsic Reinforcement on "Intrinsic"
Motivation: Separating Fact From Fiction 113
Angeleque Akin-Little and Steven G. Little

Chapter 7. Applied Behavior Analysis in Education:
The Role of the Board Certified Behavior Analyst 133
Mark D. Shriver

Chapter 8. Behavioral Interventions for Academic Performance:
A Summary of the Literature 143
Robin S. Codding, Kourtney R. Kromminga, and
Kristin Running

Chapter 9. Adults as Change Agents: Applications of
Behavioral Consultation 171
William P. Erchul, Ann C. Schulte, Austin H. Johnson,
and Cathleen A. Geraghty

II. Working With Children With Autism Spectrum Disorder 189

Chapter 10. Autism Spectrum Disorder: Screening and Diagnosis 191
Steven G. Little, Angeleque Akin-Little, and
Geri M. Harris

Chapter 11. Overview of Applied Behavior Analysis and
Early Intervention for Autism Spectrum Disorder 205
Caitlin Irwin and Judah B. Axe

Chapter 12. Discrete Trial Training: A Structured Learning
Approach for Children With ASD 227
Jeff Sigafoos, Amarie Carnett, Mark F. O'Reilly, and
Giulio E. Lancioni

Chapter 13.	Classroom Pivotal Response Teaching 245
	Rianne Verschuur, Bibi Huskens, and Laurie McLay

Chapter 14.	Verbal Behavior Intervention in Autism Spectrum Disorders 263
	Elizabeth R. Lorah, Matt Tincani, and Ashley Parnell

Chapter 15.	Video-Based Interventions for Children With Autism Spectrum Disorder 285
	Steven G. Little, Lauretta K. Montes, John Spangler, and Angeleque Akin-Little

Chapter 16.	TEACCH and Other Structured Approaches to Teaching 299
	Laurie McLay, Sarah Hansen, and Amarie Carnett

III. Cognitive Behavior Therapy 323

Chapter 17.	What Is Cognitive Behavior Therapy? 325
	Raymond DiGiuseppe, Rachel Venezia, and Roseanne Gotterbarn

Chapter 18.	Cognitive Behavior Therapy With Children 351
	Mark D. Terjesen, Tamara Del Vecchio, and Nora Gerardi

Chapter 19.	Application of Alternatives for Families: A Cognitive Behavioral Therapy to School Settings 375
	Carrie B. Jackson, Laurel A. Brabson, Amy D. Herschell, and David J. Kolko

Chapter 20.	Trauma-Focused Cognitive Behavior Therapy 393
	Steven G. Little and Angeleque Akin-Little

Index 403

About the Editors 421

CONTRIBUTORS

Angeleque Akin-Little, PhD, BCBA–D, President, Akin-Little & Little Behavioral Psychology Consultants, Malone, NY

Judah B. Axe, PhD, BCBA–D, Associate Professor, Department of Education, Department of Behavior Analysis, Simmons College, Boston, MA

Laurel A. Brabson, MS, Doctoral Student, Department of Psychology, West Virginia University, Morgantown

Amarie Carnett, PhD, Assistant Professor, Department of Educational Psychology, University of Texas at San Antonio

Robin S. Codding, PhD, BCBA–D, Associate Professor of School Psychology, University of Minnesota, Minneapolis

Tamara Del Vecchio, PhD, Professor, Department of Psychology, St. John's University, Queens, NY

Raymond DiGiuseppe, PhD, Professor, Department of Psychology, St. John's University, Queens, NY

William P. Erchul, PhD, ABPP, Professor and Director, School Psychology Program, Graduate School of Education, University of California, Riverside

Cathleen A. Geraghty, PhD, Assistant Professor of Teaching, Graduate School of Education, University of California, Riverside

Nora Gerardi, PsyD, Psychology Post-Doc, Cognitive & Behavioral Consultants, LLC, White Plains, NY

Roseanne Gotterbarn, PhD, Lecturer, Department of Health and Behavioral Sciences, Teachers College, Columbia University, New York, NY

Sarah Hansen, PhD, Assistant Professor of Early Childhood Special Education, Department of Learning Sciences, College of Education and Human Development, Georgia State University, Atlanta

Geri M. Harris, PhD, Walden University, Houston, TX

Amy D. Herschell, PhD, Associate Professor, West Virginia University, Morgantown, and the University of Pittsburgh School of Medicine, Pittsburgh, PA

Bibi Huskens, PhD, BCBA, Psychologist and Senior Researcher, Dr. Leo Kannerhuis Center for Autism, Doorwerth and SeysCentra, Malden, the Netherlands

Caitlin Irwin, MS, BCBA, Doctoral Student, Adjunct Professor, Department of Behavior Analysis, Simmons College, Boston, MA

Carrie B. Jackson, MS, Doctoral Student, Department of Psychology, West Virginia University, Morgantown

Austin H. Johnson, PhD, BCBA–D, Assistant Professor, Graduate School of Education, University of California, Riverside

David J. Kolko, PhD, Professor, University of Pittsburgh School of Medicine, Pittsburgh, PA

Kourtney R. Kromminga (McNallan), MEd, Doctoral Student, School Psychology, University of Minnesota, Minneapolis

Giulio E. Lancioni, PhD, Professor, Department of Neuroscience and Sense Organs, University of Bari, Bari, Italy

Kathleen Lynne Lane, PhD, BCBA–D, CF–L1, Department of Special Education, University of Kansas, Lawrence

Steven G. Little, PhD, BCBA–D, Coordinator, Program in Applied Behavior Analysis, Walden University, Malone, NY

Elizabeth R. Lorah, PhD, BCBA–D, Associate Professor, University of Arkansas, Fayetteville

Laurie McLay, PhD, Senior Lecturer, School of Health Sciences, University of Canterbury, Christchurch, New Zealand

Lauretta K. Montes, PhD, Hayden Consultation Services, Inc., Camarillo, CA

Mark F. O'Reilly, PhD, BCBA–D, Audrey Rogers Myers Centennial Professor in Education, Department of Special Education, The University of Texas at Austin

Ashley Parnell, MSEd, BCBA, University of Arkansas, Fayetteville

Jamie L. Pratt, PsyD, BCBA–D, Assistant Professor, School of Education and Human Development, University of Southern Maine, Gorham

Kristin Running, MEd, Doctoral Student, School Psychology, University of Minnesota, Minneapolis

Ann C. Schulte, PhD, Professor Emerita, Department of Psychology, North Carolina State University, Raleigh

Mark D. Shriver, PhD., BCBA–D, Professor, Psychology, Munroe-Meyer Institute, University of Nebraska Medical Center, Omaha

Jeff Sigafoos, PhD, Professor, School of Education, Victoria University of Wellington, Wellington, New Zealand

Brandi Simonsen, PhD, Department of Educational Psychology, University of Connecticut, Storrs

Christopher H. Skinner, PhD, School Psychology Professor, The University of Tennessee, Knoxville

John Spangler, MS, Phoenix, AZ

Mark W. Steege, PhD, NCSP, BCBA–D, Professor and Associate Dean, School of Education and Human Development, University of Southern Maine, Gorham

George Sugai, PhD, Department of Educational Psychology, University of Connecticut, Storrs

Mark D. Terjesen, PhD, Associate Professor, Department of Psychology, St. John's University, Jamaica, NY

Matt Tincani, PhD, BCBA–D, Professor, Temple University, Philadelphia, PA

Rachel Venezia, MA, Doctoral Fellow, Psychology Department, St. John's University, Queens, NY

Rianne Verschuur, MSc, Doctoral Student, Radboud University, Nijmegen; Psychologist, Dr. Leo Kannerhuis Center for Autism, Doorwerth, the Netherlands

Joseph H. Wehby, PhD, Department of Special Education, Peabody College of Vanderbilt University, Nashville, TN

Garry D. Wickerd, PhD, NCSP, BCBA, Assistant Professor, School of Education and Human Development, University of Southern Maine, Gorham

SERIES FOREWORD

Outside of their homes, children spend more time in schools than any other setting. From tragedies such as Sandy Hook and Columbine to more hopeful developments such as the movement toward improved mental health and academic achievement, there is an ongoing need for high-quality writing that speaks to ways in which children, families, and communities associated with schools worldwide can be supported through the application of sound psychological research, theory, and practice.

For the past several years, the American Psychological Association (APA) Books and Division 16 (School Psychology) have partnered to produce the Applying Psychology in the Schools Book Series. The mission of this series is to increase the visibility of the science, practice, and policy for children and adolescents in schools and communities. The result has been a strong collection of scholarly work that appeals not only to psychologists but also to individuals from all fields who have reason to seek and use what psychology has to offer in schools.

Behavioral Interventions in Schools, first published in 2009, described key, evidence-based strategies for preventing and intervening to address emotional and behavioral problems in the classroom. In the years since, the need for such interventions has only grown. As in the 2009 edition, the contributors to this book are outstanding scholars who write accessibly on a range of topics, including behavioral assessment, positive behavioral supports and classroom management strategies, and procedures for reducing behavioral excesses. New to this edition are chapters that offer an in-depth look at assessments and interventions for students with autism spectrum disorder, which has become a major focus of behavioral intervention in schools in recent years. This new emphasis makes this book even more appealing than the first edition, and a strong contender for use in graduate level classes.

Since its initiation, many individuals have made significant contributions to this book series. We would like to acknowledge the dedication of past series editors Sandra L. Christensen, Catherine Christo, Jan Hughes, R. Steve McCallum, David McIntosh, LeAdelle Phelps, Linda Reddy, Susan Sheridan, Christopher H. Skinner, David Shriberg, and Melissa Pearrow. We also thank Linda Malnasi McCarter and the editorial team of APA Books for their editorial work and support, as well as all of the people at APA Books who have worked behind the scenes to bring this book to fruition. Finally, we thank the editors and the chapter coauthors for their inspired vision and writing in the second edition of *Behavioral Interventions in Schools*.

The leadership of Division 16 welcomes your comments about this volume, as well as your ideas for other topics that you would like to see explored in this series. To share your thoughts, please visit the Division 16 website (http://www.apadivsions.org/division16).

—Michelle M. Perfect, PhD
Series Editor

ACKNOWLEDGMENTS

The editors are extremely grateful to all of the contributing authors. Each and every one of you made our job incredibly easy. We were gratified that you agreed to work on what we feel is an important book for psychologists, particularly school psychologists. You were prompt with your submissions and revisions, and you wrote excellent manuscripts. We gave you the opportunity to structure the chapters the way you saw fit—you are the experts, after all—and you did not let us down. We thank everyone from the American Psychological Association (APA) who helped with this project. You have all been very kind to us neophytes as we traversed the new territory of editing a book. We would like to give a special thank you to Linda McCarter from APA Books, who provided great encouragement and gently led us through this process with prompt, detailed responses to any questions. Tyler Aune was also a great help in formulating the final versions of the chapters. In the end, this book would not have happened without contributions from everyone. We thank all of you for joining us in this process. We feel the end product is something of which we can all be proud.

BEHAVIORAL INTERVENTIONS IN SCHOOLS

SECOND EDITION

INTRODUCTION

STEVEN G. LITTLE AND ANGELEQUE AKIN-LITTLE

In 2009, the first edition of *Behavioral Interventions in Schools: Evidence-Based Positive Strategies* was published, and we thank Melissa Bray and Tom Kehle for their contributions to that book. The reception we received for that book exceeded our expectations. In 2009, with school psychologists still reacting to learning disability eligibility criteria changes with regard to the Individuals With Disabilities Education Act of 2004 (Pub. L. 108-446), as well as the advent of response-to-intervention models, we thought it important for school psychologists to focus on both academic and classroom behavior. We hope that book served that purpose.

Today, 10 years since the publication of the first edition, it is still selling, and we are still receiving positive comments. However, as we began to consider a second edition of this book we tried to focus on the direction of psychology in the schools since 2009 and how we would like to see it progress in the future. We also have had some important experiences since the first edition, derived from the opportunity we had to work and live in New Zealand. Steve served as director of the Educational (School) Psychology Programme at Massey University, and Angeleque worked for the New Zealand Ministry of Education. We noticed that New Zealand had much less emphasis on psychoeducational assessment than what we had seen in the United States. New Zealand schools used mostly a problem-solving model and put less emphasis on identification of disabilities. In teaching school psychology at the postgraduate level, we noted that the courses were yearlong and integrated a larger amount of, and more diverse, content. For example, the interventions class covered the full range of behavioral interventions, from specific applied behavior analysis (ABA)–oriented interventions to cognitive behavior therapies (CBT). No single coursebook covered both types of intervention; therefore, we thought this book should.

During this time there has also been a tremendous increase in the number of students being diagnosed with autism spectrum disorder (ASD). We have also seen a great deal of variability in the quality of school programming for students with ASD. In addition to being trained as school psychologists and licensed as psychologists, we are both also Board Certified Behavior Analysts at the doctoral level (BCBA–D) and have had the opportunity to serve as consultants in this area. We have noticed that ABA services are more and more likely to be designed and implemented by BCBAs trained in behavior analysis, education, or speech and not by school psychologists, who lack such credentials. At the same time, we believe that school psychologists need to work more closely with students with ASD because the depth of their training makes them the ideal professionals to design and supervise these services. That is why we have added to this edition an entire section devoted to ASD and treatment options for working with this population.

We also believe that school psychologists need to become full-service psychologists in the schools. In addition to training in ABA, for use in both regular and special education settings, we need to be able to address the emotional needs of all students. CBT is the approach to psychotherapeutic intervention that has the greatest amount of empirical support. We have therefore devoted another section of this book to CBT and its applications, including working with children who have experienced trauma. Although a book such as this cannot fully train someone in these approaches, we hope it will spur an interest in readers to expand their knowledge and skills so that each and every person reading this book will grow in his or her practice and school psychology can grow with them. For example, Steve attended training in rational emotive behavior therapy conducted at the Albert Ellis Institute in New York City. The skills he acquired during this training not only have helped in his work with children and adolescents, but they have also been valuable when working with parents and teachers, in helping them better meet the needs of their children.

A FOCUS ON BEHAVIOR

As with the first edition, this book maintains a strong emphasis on behavior and behavioral interventions. Given that its foundations lie in the philosophical movement of positivism, a focus on behavior has had a strong impact in psychological and educational intervention methodology. The modern term *behaviorism* was initially coined by Watson in 1914 (Alberto & Troutman, 2013) and included a focus on direct observational data. Skinner's work in operant conditioning and the use of his theoretically derived principles to change human behavior became much more prominent in the 1950s and 1960s with the advent of behavior modification and applied behavior analysis. Early work, such as Ogden Lindsley's (1990) successful application of operant methods to the behaviors of psychotic children and adults at his Harvard Behavior Research Laboratory, Bijou's (1957) work with reinforcement and extinction in young children, Lovaas and colleagues' work with children with ASD (Lovaas, Freitag, Gold, & Kassorla, 1965), and Patterson and Brodsky's (1966) work with antisocial children, provided the initial empirical support for this technology.

We now have decades of empirical research supporting the efficacy of behavioral interventions in the classroom. This includes work with token economies by Ayllon and Azrin (1968); Birnbrauer, Wolf, Kidder, and Tague (1965); and O'Leary and Drabman (1971); Barrish, Saunders, and Wolf's (1969) Good Behavior Game; Iwata and colleagues' research in functional analysis (Iwata, Dorsey, Slifer, Bauman, & Richman, 1982); and Litow and Pumroy's (1975) seminal work in group contingencies. All have helped firmly established the continued efficacy of behavioral approaches.

During the past 3 decades, research has continued to provide evidence for the efficacy of behavioral and cognitive behavioral interventions with children and adolescents. Casey and Berman (1985) conducted a meta-analysis on the effects of child and adolescent psychotherapy. Their results indicated an overall effect size of 0.71, but behavioral interventions were found to be more effective than nonbehavioral interventions, with effect sizes of 0.91 and 0.40, respectively. Similar results were found by Weisz, Weiss, Alicke, and Klotz (1987), who obtained a mean effect size of 0.79 for psychotherapy, with behavior therapy ($d = 0.88$) again being found more effective than nonbehavioral interventions ($d = 0.44$). Stage and Quiroz (1997) conducted a meta-analysis to examine interventions designed to decrease disruptive behavior in public education settings. Their results yielded a mean effect size of −0.78, indicating a reduction in disruptive behavior of a magnitude approaching Cohen's (1977) definition of a large effect size. Behavioral interventions such as group contingencies ($d = 3.41$; Little, Akin-Little, & O'Neill, 2015), self-management ($d = 0.93$; Briesch & Briesch, 2016), ABA for adaptive behavior in children with autism ($ds = 0.68–2.91$; Peters-Scheffer, Didden, Korzilius, & Sturmey, 2011), and token economies ($d = 0.82$; Soares, Harrison, Vannest, & McClelland, 2016) also have strong support in the meta-analytic literature. Meta-analyses have also supported the efficacy of cognitive behavioral interventions. Hoogsteder et al. (2015) conducted a meta-analysis on the effectiveness of individually oriented CBT for severe aggressive behavior in adolescents and found a mean effect size of 1.14. Scaini, Belotti, Ogliari, and Battaglia (2016) found an effect size of 0.99, supporting the efficacy of CBT intervention with children and social anxiety disorder, whereas Arnberg and Öst (2014) found an effect size of 0.66 after examining CBT as an intervention for children with depressive symptoms.

Thus, we designed this book keeping in mind the abundance of empirical support for behavioral and cognitive behavioral interventions, coupled with the need for school psychologists and other personnel to be equipped with knowledge of these interventions. In other words, we wanted to create a book that informs its readers by providing information on evidence-based positive behavioral strategies for use in schools. We also felt it was important to provide the content in a concise, easy-to-read, and understandable format. Hence, we have chapters that are written so that a person somewhat new to behavioral interventions will be able to use the techniques presented immediately and with ease at the same time that more experienced practitioners could have a helpful resource to guide their practice. Of course, there may be instances in which readers may need to seek out other sources for more details on specific methodologies, implementation techniques, and so on; however, the chapters are designed for readers to be able to use the information immediately.

EVIDENCE-BASED PRACTICE

In August 2005 the American Psychological Association (APA) adopted a policy with regard to evidence-based practice in psychology. The purpose of this was, and is, to promote effective psychological practice by using evidence derived from clinically relevant research (APA, 2005). Evidence-based guidelines have created the necessity for practitioners to use interventions (including primary and secondary prevention programs) that have clinically proven effectiveness. The aim is to improve the quality and efficacy of interventions, delivered efficiently and economically, as measured by objective criteria. Proponents of the evidence-based movement seek to incorporate research-supported techniques into interventions; however, psychologists and others working with children and adolescents recognize the challenges in doing this (APA Task Force on Evidence-Based Practice for Children and Adolescents, 2008). Each chapter in this book is predicated on the principles of evidence-based interventions. Empirically supported principles of psychological assessment, case formulation, and intervention are integrated with issues and concerns faced by psychologists and other professionals who work with children and adolescents in educational contexts (APA, 2005).

POSITIVE AND PREVENTIVE APPROACHES TO BEHAVIORAL INTERVENTIONS

Emotional and behavioral problems of students in the classroom have been deemed a major concern for teachers, administrators, and the public (Hardman & Smith, 2003; Macciomei, 1999). Without effective behavior management, a positive and productive classroom environment is impossible to achieve. The most effective model for producing behavior change and preventing the development of maladaptive behavior is the behavioral model (Wielkiewicz, 1995). In addition, and as discussed above, research indicates that behavioral approaches are very effective in developing effective instructional strategies. However, resistance to the use of behavioral procedures in the classroom has come from a variety of sources, and some individuals have been particularly harsh in their criticism of the use of positive reinforcement (e.g., Kohn, 1993).

As psychologists, we are involved in interventions now more than ever, and a book such as this is needed to provide all kinds of practitioners with a summary of empirically valid and ecologically sound intervention strategies that recognize primary, secondary, and tertiary prevention. To effectively cover the breadth of behavioral interventions related to school behavior it was necessary to maintain a certain level of brevity in our discussions. The chapters, however, should provide practitioners, students, and trainers with a resource that aids in identifying and understanding the foundations of appropriate interventions and gives direction as to where additional details can be found. No book can describe, in complete depth, the multitude of problems faced in schools today, but we believe this one gives readers as complete and comprehensive an understanding as possible.

OVERVIEW OF THIS BOOK

We have structured the book into three major parts: (I) Foundations of Behavioral Interventions, (II) Working with Children with Autism Spectrum Disorder, and (III) Cognitive Behavior Therapy. We strove to recruit the top researchers in each area, and we believe we have put together a very impressive array of authors from around the world. A PsycINFO search of authors conducted in July 2018, as we were beginning the book's development process, indicated that the chapter authors collectively have published a total of 2,140 journal articles, book chapters, and books. We are also very proud of the international diversity of our authors. In addition to the United States, authors hail from New Zealand, The Netherlands, and Italy. Given this diversity, some chapters may include slightly different terminology, but we believe these are minor and should not confuse any reader.

An understanding of the foundations of behavioral interventions is necessary for any intervention to be implemented with integrity and efficacy. Part I, then, focuses on foundations. It includes chapters on behavioral assessment, positive behavioral supports, classroom management, reductive procedures, generalization and maintenance, an overview of the extrinsic reinforcement–intrinsic motivation issue. The chapters in this part present information integral to readers in the use of behavioral interventions in the school setting. Chapter 6, although it does not present a specific intervention, discusses an issue important to the effective application of behavioral interventions. Many educational professionals have been exposed to an antibehavioral bias from a theoretical standpoint, believing that the use of behavioral techniques will decrease intrinsic motivation (see Kohn, 1993). The authors of Chapter 6 attempt to clarify this issue and provide further support for the proper use of positive, evidence-based behavioral techniques.

Part II contains chapters on working with children with ASD. This part includes chapters on screening and diagnosis, an overview of ABA, discrete-trials training, pivotal response training, verbal behavior interventions, video-based interventions, and structured teaching approaches. The chapters in Part II present the major types of behavioral interventions with children with ASD that will give all readers a comprehensive overview of behavioral approaches to evidence-based interventions for children with ASD.

The chapters in Part III focus on another competency area we believe is essential for any full-service psychologist in the schools: CBT. Splett, Fowler, Weist, McDaniel, and Dvorsky (2013) discuss the role of school psychologists in advancing school mental health programs and services. School psychologists are in a key position to develop, advance, and implement mental health services in the schools and desire that role and function (Fagan & Wise, 2007), but they are not always given that opportunity (Friedrich,

2010). One of Splett et al.'s recommendations to enhance school psychologists' involvement in school mental health was to "ensure that content courses provide sufficient knowledge needed to provide continuum of SMH services" (p. 251). We believe that including chapters such as these provides the knowledge needed to begin this process.

The target audiences for this book are practicing school psychologists, school psychology students, and other psychologists who work with children. All children in the United States and Canada receive compulsory education. Even if intervention services are not taking place primarily in the schools, practitioners cannot ignore the role of the school and the importance of coordinating interventions with the school. The fact is, much of what is discussed in this book is applicable in multiple environments, including schools, homes, residential facilities, and any place children reside or are educated. It is our sincere hope that other audiences (e.g., teachers, administrators, parents) also have the opportunity to avail themselves of the information provided in this book. To maximize the efficacy of interventions; teachers, parents, and school administrators all must be involved with psychologists in effective implementation. We believe this book will be particularly useful to traditional and special education teachers and school administrators as well as counselors and social workers.

Behavioral and cognitive behavioral interventions clearly work. Many data support this contention. In this book we have attempted to bring together a sampling of the world's leading researchers in behavioral interventions in school psychology, behavior analysis, and education. As we have discussed, although the target audience is psychologists, we believe this book can also benefit all who work with children and adolescents in an educational context. The chapters provide details of behavioral interventions, grounded in science (e.g., evidence based), in a simple and easy-to-use format, to provide the very best educational environment for children and adolescents. We truly believe this is what that population deserves and that these techniques are best to ensure a positive outcome.

REFERENCES

Alberto, P. A., & Troutman, A. C. (2013). *Applied behavior analysis for teachers* (9th ed.). Upper Saddle River, NJ: Pearson Prentice Hall.

American Psychological Association. (2005). *Policy statement on evidence-based practice in psychology*. Retrieved from http://www.apa.org/practice/guidelines/evidence-based-statement.aspx

American Psychological Association Task Force on Evidence-Based Practice for Children and Adolescents. (2008). *Disseminating evidence-based practice for children and adolescents: A systems approach to enhancing care*. Washington, DC: American Psychological Association.

Arnberg, A., & Öst, L. G. (2014). CBT for children with depressive symptoms: A meta-analysis. *Cognitive Behaviour Therapy, 43*, 275–288. http://dx.doi.org/10.1080/16506073.2014.947316

Ayllon, T., & Azrin, N. (1968). *The token economy: A motivational system for therapy and rehabilitation*. New York, NY: Appleton-Century-Crofts.

Barrish, H. H., Saunders, M., & Wolf, M. M. (1969). Good behavior game: Effects of individual contingencies for group consequences on disruptive behavior in a classroom. *Journal of Applied Behavior Analysis, 2*, 119–124. http://dx.doi.org/10.1901/jaba.1969.2-119

Bijou, S. W. (1957). Patterns of reinforcement and resistance to extinction in young children. *Child Development, 28*, 47–54.

Birnbrauer, J. S., Wolf, M. M., Kidder, J. D., & Tague, C. E. (1965). Classroom behavior of retarded pupils with token reinforcement. *Journal of Experimental Child Psychology, 2*, 219–235. http://dx.doi.org/10.1016/0022-0965(65)90045-7

Briesch, A. M., & Briesch, J. M. (2016). Meta-analysis of behavioral self-management interventions in single-case research. *School Psychology Review, 45*, 3–18. http://dx.doi.org/10.17105/SPR45-1.3-18

Casey, R. J., & Berman, J. S. (1985). The outcome of psychotherapy with children. *Psychological Bulletin, 98*, 388–400. http://dx.doi.org/10.1037/0033-2909.98.2.388

Cohen, J. (1977). *Statistical power analysis for the behavioral sciences* (Rev. ed.). New York, NY: Academic Press.

Fagan, T. K., & Wise, P. S. (2007). *School psychology: Past, present, and future* (3rd ed.). Bethesda, MD: National Association of School Psychologists.

Friedrich, A. (2010). *School-based mental health services: A national survey of school psychologists' practices and perceptions* (Unpublished doctoral dissertation). Department of Psychological and Social Foundations, University of South Florida. Retrieved from http://scholarcommons.usf.edu/etd/3549

Hardman, E. L., & Smith, S. W. (2003). Analysis of classroom discipline-related content in elementary education journals. *Behavioral Disorders, 28*, 173–186.

Hoogsteder, L. M., Stams, G. J. J. M., Figge, M. A., Changoe, K., van Horn, J. E., Hendriks, J., & Wissink, I. B. (2015). A meta-analysis of the effectiveness of individually oriented cognitive behavioral treatment (CBT) for severe aggressive behavior in adolescents. *Journal of Forensic Psychiatry & Psychology, 26*, 22–37. http://dx.doi.org/10.1080/14789949.2014.971851

Individuals with Disabilities Education Act, 20 U.S.C. § 1400 (2004).

Iwata, B. A., Dorsey, M. F., Slifer, K. J., Bauman, K. E., & Richman, G. S. (1982). Toward a functional analysis of self-injury. *Analysis and Intervention in Developmental Disabilities, 2*, 3–20. http://dx.doi.org/10.1016/0270-4684(82)90003-9

Kohn, A. (1993). *Punished by rewards: The trouble with gold stars, incentive plans, A's, praise, and other bribes*. Boston, MA: Houghton Mifflin.

Lindsley, O. R. (1990). Precision teaching: By teachers for children. *Teaching Exceptional Children, 22*, 10–15. http://dx.doi.org/10.1177/004005999002200302

Litow, L., & Pumroy, D. K. (1975). A brief review of classroom group-oriented contingencies. *Journal of Applied Behavior Analysis, 8*, 341–347. http://dx.doi.org/10.1901/jaba.1975.8-341

Little, S. G., Akin-Little, A., & O'Neill, K. (2015). Group contingency interventions with children—1980–2010: A meta-analytic study. *Behavior Modification, 39*, 322–341. http://dx.doi.org/10.1177/0145445514554393

Lovaas, O. I., Freitag, G., Gold, V. J., & Kassorla, I. C. (1965). Experimental studies in childhood schizophrenia: Analysis of self-destructive behavior. *Journal of Experimental Child Psychology, 2*, 67–84. http://dx.doi.org/10.1016/0022-0965(65)90016-0

Macciomei, N. R. (1999). Behavior problems in urban schoolchildren. In N. R. Macciomei & D. H. Ruben (Eds.), *Behavior management in the public schools: An urban approach* (pp. 1–17). Westport, CT: Praeger.

O'Leary, K. D., & Drabman, R. (1971). Token reinforcement programs in the classroom: A review. *Psychological Bulletin, 75*, 379–398. http://dx.doi.org/10.1037/h0031311

Patterson, G. R., & Brodsky, G. (1966). A behaviour modification programme for a child with multiple problem behaviours. *Journal of Child Psychology and Psychiatry, 7*, 277–295. http://dx.doi.org/10.1111/j.1469-7610.1966.tb02253.x

Peters-Scheffer, N., Didden, R., Korzilius, H., & Sturmey, P. (2011). A meta-analytic study on the effectiveness of comprehensive ABA-based early intervention programs for children with autism spectrum disorders. *Research in Autism Spectrum Disorders, 5*, 60–69. http://dx.doi.org/10.1016/j.rasd.2010.03.011

Scaini, S., Belotti, R., Ogliari, A., & Battaglia, M. (2016). A comprehensive meta-analysis of cognitive-behavioral interventions for social anxiety disorder in children and adolescents. *Journal of Anxiety Disorders, 42*, 105–112. http://dx.doi.org/10.1016/j.janxdis.2016.05.008

Soares, D. A., Harrison, J. R., Vannest, K. J., & McClelland, S. S. (2016). Effect size for token economy use in contemporary classroom settings: A meta-analysis of single-case research. *School Psychology Review, 45*, 379–399. http://dx.doi.org/10.17105/SPR45-4.379-399

Splett, J. W., Fowler, J., Weist, M. D., McDaniel, H., & Dvorsky, M. (2013). The critical role of school psychology in the school mental health movement. *Psychology in the Schools, 50*, 245–258. http://dx.doi.org/10.1002/pits.21677

Stage, S. A., & Quiroz, D. R. (1997). A meta-analysis of interventions to decrease disruptive behavior in public education settings. *School Psychology Review, 26*, 333–368.

Weisz, J. R., Weiss, B., Alicke, M. D., & Klotz, M. (1987). Effectiveness of psychotherapy with children and adolescents: A meta-analysis for clinicians. *Journal of Consulting and Clinical Psychology, 55,* 542–549. http://dx.doi.org/10.1037=0022-006X.55.4.542

Wielkiewicz, R. M. (1995). *Behavior management in the schools: Principles and procedures* (2nd ed.). Boston, MA: Allyn & Bacon.

I
FOUNDATIONS OF BEHAVIORAL INTERVENTIONS

1

NARRATIVE REPORTS AND RECORDINGS FOR BEHAVIORAL PROBLEM–SOLVING IN SCHOOLS

CHRISTOPHER H. SKINNER

Interest in behavioral assessment in educational settings has been attributed to a variety of factors (Shapiro, 2011). Laws have required educators to evaluate behavioral plans, and a recent focus on positive behavioral supports and response-to-intervention models has enhanced the application of behavioral assessment procedures in school settings (Fairbanks, Sugai, Guardino, & Lathrop, 2007; Gresham, 2005; Individuals With Disabilities Education Improvement Act, 2004). Many of these initiatives have a similar goal of identifying and remedying problem behaviors before they become so severe that more intensive strategies are required (Sandomierski, Kincaid, & Algozzine, 2007; Severson, Walker, Hope-Doolittle, Kratochwill, & Gresham, 2007).

Others have linked the interest in developing and validating behavioral assessment procedures to dissatisfaction with more traditional strategies that focus on identifying stable, within-student constructs that may explain or

http://dx.doi.org/10.1037/0000126-002
Behavioral Interventions in Schools: Evidence-Based Positive Strategies, Second Edition, S. G. Little and A. Akin-Little (Editors)
Copyright © 2019 by the American Psychological Association. All rights reserved.

label problems but do not always lead to more effective interventions (e.g., Shapiro, 1987). The increase in students with autism and the growth of behavior analysis as a profession have also spurred an interest in and acceptance of behavioral procedures (Axelrod, McElrath, & Wine, 2012; Matson & Neal, 2009). Finally, conceptual and applied advances associated with functional behavioral assessment and the contribution these data make to the development and validation of effective, efficient, and contextually sound interventions has enhanced researchers' and practitioners' interest in behavioral assessment principles and procedures (Lane et al., 2007).

BEHAVIORAL ASSESSMENT CONCEPTS

In the first article of the first issue of *The Journal of Behavioral Assessment*, Hartmann, Roper, and Bradford (1979) described the difference between behavioral and traditional assessment across assumptions, implications, use of data, and characteristics. Although it is beyond the scope of this chapter to comprehensively review that article, several concepts are critical to our understanding of how behavioral assessment procedures can be applied in educational settings. After these critical concepts are described, the remainder of the chapter focuses on the narrative data gathered via informant reports and naturalistic direct observation and how these data are used in collaborative behavioral problem–solving processes in educational settings.

Behaviors Are Critical

One of the most important concepts underlying behavioral assessment is that behaviors, in and of themselves, are an appropriate target for measurement and intervention. This assumption differs from views that behaviors are merely indicators of some other, within-student problem (e.g., an indicator of a diagnostic category that is seen to cause the behavior problem) and is one reason behavioral assessment is considered to be more direct and less inference-laden than most other models (Shapiro, 1987). Regardless, this assumption does not imply that unobservable behaviors (e.g., thoughts, feelings) and other constructs (e.g., intelligence, interest, personality traits) are not important; rather, it merely states that human behavior is an appropriate target for assessment.

Behaviors Vary Naturally

There is a saying that you cannot dip your toe into the same river twice. If the behavior of interest is toe dipping and the environment is the river, then behaviorists would agree with the implication that environments, like rivers, are constantly changing. From a behavioral perspective, the primary problem with this statement is that it is incomplete. Behavioral assessment assumes that you cannot dip your toe (the behavior) the exact same way in the same river. Although behaviorists have often been characterized using derogatory terms, the assumption that behaviors are naturally unstable is hopeful and positive as it suggests that behaviors can be learned and modified.

Behavior–Environment Interactions

If behaviors vary naturally, it would be difficult to repeatedly measure a specific behavior. However, behaviorists have always focused on the role of behavior–environment interactions. Specifically, the focus has been on how the environment selects behaviors that are more likely to be repeated. Just as two parents produce children who are not identical to each other, repeated behaviors are not identical, but they vary. In this manner, incidental behavior–environment interactions can alter or modify behaviors (Skinner, 1966).

When discussing undesired behaviors, behaviorists focus on environmental events that maintain behaviors and make them more likely to reoccur, but perhaps not in the same form. Consequently, behaviors that are very different (e.g., daydreaming vs. throwing a book) may be similar in that they may serve the same function (e.g., escaping a demand to do math work). Thus, two very dissimilar behaviors may be treated the same way when they are part of a functional response class. Regardless, knowing the function of a behavior can help psychologists to purposefully arrange behavior–environment interactions that decrease undesired behaviors and enhance desired behavior (Gresham, Watson, & Skinner, 2001). Carr's (1993) contention that behaviorists are more interested in variables that influence, cause, or maintain behaviors than they are in the behaviors themselves is reflected in the recent emphasis on developing functional assessment procedures that allow the formation of a hypothesis regarding what may be maintaining behavior in their natural environment.

Intraindividual Analysis

Because each person has a different history of environment–behavior interactions, behaviorists do not assume that an intervention that works for one person will work for a similar person who displays similar behavior problems. The focus on enhancing their understanding of each individual's behavior–environment interactions has lead behaviorists to form hypotheses based on an individual's behavior and accompanying environmental events in their natural environment (Hartmann et al., 1979). Thus, behavior analysts have developed single-subject design procedures that use intra-individual analysis to develop procedure and repeated measures to evaluate and validate interventions (Kazdin, 2011).

BEHAVIORAL ASSESSMENT AND BEHAVIORAL PROBLEM–SOLVING

Gresham et al. (2001) succinctly described the goals of functional behavioral assessment during a problem-solving process designed to address undesired behaviors. Specifically, the goal is to accurately describe conditions, both general and specific, when undesired behaviors are more likely to occur. Additionally, a functional assessment will describe the problem behavior along with desired alternative replacement behaviors. Finally, a successful functional assessment will specify environmental events that follow the problem behavior and are serving to maintain or reinforce it. Functional and behavioral assessment allows the development of interventions that are consistent with empirically supported behavioral principles and procedures, are supported by behavioral assessment data (Kern & Dunlap, 1999), and are contextually valid (Foster & Skinner, 2011; Skinner, 2013).

With their focus on idiosyncratic learning histories and environment–behavior instability, a behavioral model of assessment is not designed to suggest a specific empirically validated intervention, with the intent to implement the intervention in the exact same manner as it was applied during validation studies. However, behavioral assessments can provide evidence that more general procedures or strategies may help address a presenting problem. Selecting these general strategies and shaping them into specific interventions must also take into account specific idiosyncratic factors (e.g., for one child, peer attention is a reinforcer; for another, it is a punisher). Behavioral assessment data can provide an indication of idiosyncratic or child-specific factors that should be taken into account when selecting general strategies and developing specific interventions and selecting appropriate intervention components.

Classroom contextual factors (e.g., a teacher with 30 children vs. a teacher and teaching assistant with 12 children) must also be considered when shaping a general strategy into a specific classroom intervention. Skinner (2013) indicated that developing evidenced-based interventions that are supported by functional behavioral assessment data is necessary, but not sufficient, as even interventions with strong scientific support (i.e., strong conceptual support and evidence of both internal and external validity) may not be effective unless they can be implemented in the current classroom context (e.g., by this teacher and in this teacher's context). Consequently, a general understanding of the current class context can often allow a practitioner to better select general strategies and develop or adapt interventions that can be successfully applied in a specific classroom.

A variety of behavioral assessment procedures can be used to obtain this information. including informant reports (e.g., interviews, checklist and rating scales, self-monitoring) and direct observation (e.g., antecedent–behavior–consequence analysis, systematic time sampling). It is beyond the scope of this chapter to describe all of these procedures. Rather, this article focuses on how narrative data (e.g., informant reports and narrative descriptions of direct observations) can play a crucial role in a collaborative behavioral problem-solving process. Those interested in more scientific, empirically verifiable behavioral assessment procedures are encouraged to review literature on systematic direct observation, which is often needed when attempting to contribute to the scientific literature, and analogue experimental analysis procedure, which can help identify the function of undesired behaviors when more efficient procedures have proven ineffective.

Several factors support a focus on teacher reports (i.e., interviews) and narrative recordings taken during direct observations. First, school systems that develop and apply problem-solving service delivery models are primarily interested in solving the problem, and the goal is to solve the problem rapidly. Thus, problem-solving models like Bergan's (1977) behavioral consultation, which includes developing systematic behavioral assessment procedures that are verifiable, sensitive enough to detect small changes in behavior, and establish empirical and verifiable goals, often require too much time and resources. A second reason for focusing on teacher reports and non-empirical recording procedures is overanalysis. One reason that problem-solving approaches fail is that too much time and energy is spent on assessment or analysis—paralysis by analysis. Another reason problem-solving efforts fail is insufficient assessment and analysis (Dougherty, 2014).

So how to know when you have sufficient data to begin the process of intervention development and implementation? Kern and Dunlap (1999) indicated that knowing when you have sufficient data to support general strategies requires judgments that must be made by both the teacher and consultant (e.g., school psychologist, behavior analyst, student support team). In many instances, teacher interviews and direct observation data may prove sufficient to allow both teachers and consultants to agree that they have specified the inappropriate behavior(s) and desired appropriate behavior(s) and have identified the function of the inappropriate behavior in the classroom. The next step, which requires and understanding of the current classroom context and the individual student, is to develop an efficient and effective intervention that can be applied in the current classroom.

GENERAL UNDERSTANDING OF THE PROBLEM: REFERRAL AND INITIAL INTERVIEW

When students present with behavior problems, various systems have been developed to address those problems. These systems often begin with a teacher referral, which is followed by an interview, both of which are informant reports. Informant reports are considered an indirect behavioral assessment procedure because they rely on retrospective narrative reporting. Thus, the primary limitation of informant reports is that they are difficult or impossible to empirically verify (Shapiro, 1987). However, the strengths associated with these reports are numerous, and it is difficult to imagine a consultant conducting a collaborative problem-based behavioral assessment without making extensive use of teacher interviews. In fact, Bergan's (1977) behavioral consultation model is based on a series of teacher interviews.

Many school systems have forms that require the referring agent to describe the presenting problem, in writing, using narrative descriptions. The primary purpose of most referral forms is to trigger additional services. One advantage of these narrative behavior descriptions is that they may indicate when a behavioral problem–solving process is warranted and when it is not. For example, a report of a student displaying inappropriate behaviors that represent a clear and present danger to self or others requires immediate direct action as opposed to the application of a time-consuming problem-solving process (Jacob, Decker, & Hartshorne, 2011). Another example would be a student who has recently lost a parent and concomitantly began to display much different behavior. In this instance, grief-counseling services may be more appropriate (Winokuer & Harris, 2015).

Teacher Interview

Assuming the problem is appropriately addressed via a collaborative behavioral problem–solving process, the next behavioral assessment procedure applied is typically an interview. Almost all treatment models make use of interviews, but many focus on interviewing the person with the presenting problem. Behavioral models assume that environment–behavior interactions are maintaining problem behaviors and that manipulating these interactions can be used to change behaviors. Consequently, they interview educators (e.g., teachers) who are likely to have the ability to alter these environmental events.

A variety of semistructured behavioral interviews have been developed and include Bergan's (1977) Problem Identification, Problem Analysis, and Plan Evaluation Interviews, Watson and Steege's (2003) Behavioral Stream Interview, and Edwards (2002) Functional Assessment Informant

Record—Teacher. Additionally, many school systems have developed their own semi-structured interviews. Regardless, because an initial interview can influence the remainder of the collaborative problem-solving process, it is important for the consultant to focus on two distinct, but critical, goals. One goal is to establish an effective working relationship with the referring agent (e.g., the teacher). A second goal is to for the consultant to gain a better understanding of the presenting problem, the general context (classroom), and specific variables that may be influencing or maintaining the behavior in an efficient manner.

Where to Interview

There are numerous reasons a teacher interview should take place in the classroom when class is not in session. Teaching is incredibly demanding, and it would be disrespectful to expect an educator to complete a behavioral interview while teaching. Being in the classroom allows the consultant to gain a better understanding of the physical layout of the classroom, including where specific activities take place, where the target student typically sits, and where the teacher's desk is located. Gaining a better understanding of the classroom environment can influence the problem-solving practice. For example, entering a classroom and seeing that the arrangement of the target student's and the teacher's desks does not allow the teacher to observe the student easily could have implications related to the function of the behavior.

Conducting an initial interview in the classroom can enhance the efficiency and quality of communications. For example, when outside the classroom, a teacher may have trouble describing an independent, group-oriented contingency that involves each student being instructed to move a marker (e.g., a clothespin) up or down a ladder contingent on his or her behavior. However, when in the room, the teacher can point to the materials and quickly describe the procedure. Additionally, the teacher is likely to have easy access to records and permanent products that may be useful.

There are numerous recommendations for forming effective working relationships with teachers. Any teacher who volunteers to devote his or her time and energy to attempting to remedy a presenting problem must be encouraged and treated with respect and dignity. Thus, the initial interview requires much listening, reflecting, and clarifying, which takes time. Additionally, an initial interview allows the consultant to address teacher expectations and describe the problem-solving process. It is not unusual for teachers to expect referrals for behavior problems to be addressed via some type of talk therapy. Briefly describing the problem-solving process can correct teacher misconceptions that could hinder the remainder of his or her efforts (Dougherty, 2014).

Collecting Narrative Data

Functional behavioral assessments should specify (a) the problem behaviors, (b) desired replacement behaviors, (c) general and specific events that precede the problem behavior, and (d) events that follow the problem behavior and are serving to reinforce and maintain the behavior. There are numerous challenges associated with gaining this information, and behavioral interviews are ideally suited to addressing these challenges. The primary advantage of interviews is the flexible give-and-take between the teacher and consultant, which allows an efficient way to gain a more complete understanding of the problem and its context via questioning, confirming, and clarifying (Bergan, 1977; Watson & Steege, 2003). Further, teacher reports are likely to be based on many hours of observing and working with the child. Consequently, they are able to provide more accurate behavioral information (e.g., specify behavior and relevant environmental events) than any "expert" who has spent little time with the child in the classroom (Shapiro, 2011).

The initial interview typically begins by focusing on problem behavior dimensions and general context. The most obvious dimension is the shape or topography of a behavior. However, some behaviors are appropriate or inappropriate depending on duration, rates, and intensity. Finally, context is critical, and some behaviors are inappropriate in some context or situations but not in others. For example, calling out an answer is not appropriate during a typical teacher-led recitation session, but speaking without permission may be appropriate during other classroom activities (e.g., cooperative learning activities). Even when speaking without permission is both permitted and desirable, a student may speak too softly or too loudly, indicating an intensity problem.

A student talking so much that others do not have an opportunity to participate can be considered a rate, ratio, or duration problem. Many behaviors that are more continuous or less discrete are duration problems. For example, being out of seat frequently may not be considered a problem when a student fidgets around her assigned seat, frequently coming out of her seat for brief moments then returning to the seat (high rate but low duration behavior). Alternatively, during 20 minutes allotted for independent seatwork, a student may only leave his seat once, but it is problematic because he is out of seat for 15 of the 20 minutes. In this case, out of seat is a duration problem but not a rate problem. Latency problems that are often a concern and include the time students spend between a stimulus being presented and their responding. For example, one concern is the student who receives a direction and takes a long interval to begin following that direction.

Many of the challenges associated with defining problem behaviors can be addressed most efficiently via an interview process. The give-and-take allows the psychologist to elicit and confirm information that enhances understanding of the relevant behavior dimensions (e.g., topography, rate, intensity, duration, latency) and contextual factors that contribute to the specific behaviors being considered problematic. Regardless, there are several common challenges associated with gaining a more thorough understanding of a behavior problem via a behavioral interview.

One challenge is that referrals are often made for a broad class of behaviors. Descriptions of such behavior include the student being disrespectful, disruptive, or "all over the place." Other descriptions of inappropriate behaviors associate the behavior with diagnostic categories (e.g., "he is hyper," "he is Aspergery"). These descriptions, although not behavioral, do provide a good start and through the interview process, broad descriptions can be reduced to more precise dimensional (topography, rate, latency, duration, intensity) descriptions. Prompts such as "tell me what he is doing when he is being hyper or disrespectful" can enhance understanding of the behavior.

Although reducing broad descriptions to behavioral terms is useful, in some instances, it can result in a list of numerous, precisely defined problem behaviors. For example, during a teacher interview, the process of specifying problem behaviors of a child initially described as "hyper" may yield numerous possible target behaviors, including calling out, leaving seat, and failure to follow directions. When faced with numerous problem behaviors, there are several options.

Interviews allow psychologists to work with educators to prioritize target behaviors. A variety of guidelines have been proposed for prioritizing target behaviors, but one supersedes all others: If the behavior presents a clear and present danger to self or others, it must be addressed immediately and not through a time-consuming, collaborative behavioral problem–solving process. Some guidelines for prioritizing other target behaviors include targeting behaviors that (a) interfere with learning across objectives, (b) are most likely to get the student placed in a more restrictive environment, (c) are judged to be easiest to change before going on to a subsequent behavior, (d) that cause the most disruption to the classroom environment, and (e) reliably precede other inappropriate behaviors (Shapiro, 2011). The key to prioritizing target behaviors is that the process requires teacher judgments, and interviews are an efficient strategy for gathering such data.

Another strategy when faced with a variety of target behaviors is to include all of the behaviors as targets under a more general term. For example, calling out and out-of-seat behavior could be labeled as disruptive behaviors. If both behaviors are part of a functional response class (e.g., both are reinforced by teacher attention), then treating them simultaneously is appropriate. However, if each behavior serves a different function, this strategy may not be effective.

Multiple behavior problems could also be addressed by altering the focus of the interview from problem behaviors to desired behaviors. For example, consider a student who is frequently out of seat, talking without permission, and pestering others primarily during time allotted for independent seatwork. One approach could be to focus on increasing the time the student spends on task (e.g., oriented toward his independent seatwork) or the amount of work completed correctly (Fudge et al., 2008; Popkin & Skinner, 2003; Quillivan, Skinner, Hawthorn, Whited, & Ballard, 2011). One advantage of this strategy is that it may reduce the number of target behaviors, but the biggest advantage may be its focus on the problem-solving process on increasing appropriate replacement behavior (Sprague, Sugai, & Walker, 1998). This strategy may be acceptable to teachers because most educators enter their profession to encourage and develop student behavior, not suppress it.

Informant reports are not always effective in specifying unusual idiosyncratic behavior. For example, some students make unusual hand movements or odd noises that are difficult to describe or demonstrate. When this occurs, direct observation is typically warranted.

Alternative Replacement Behaviors

As Gresham et al. (2001) indicated, a sole focus on problem behaviors is not sufficient. We have already alluded to collecting data on desired behaviors. In many instances, teachers have an easier time specifying desired behavior. However, there are several factors that must be considered when selecting desired replacement behaviors. First, it must be determined whether the student can perform the desired replacement behavior, and in many instances, teachers can provide this information via interview. If students cannot perform a desired replacement behavior, then there are several options including shaping or teaching the desired replacement behavior, choosing another appropriate behavior that is in their repertoire, or providing accommodations that allow the student to perform the desired behavior. It is beyond the scope of this chapter to discuss all the processes and procedure associated with teacher and accommodating undesired behaviors.

When students can perform the desired replacement behavior, the problem-solving process can be conceptualized in term of Herrnstein's (1961) matching law, which requires the consideration of the undesired behavior relative to the desired behaviors across at least four factors (Skinner, Wallace, & Neddenriep, 2002). One factor is the amount of effort required to perform the desired behavior relative to the problem behavior. When given the choice of two or more behaviors and all else is equal, organisms choose to engage in the behavior that requires less effort (Billington, Skinner, & Cruchon, 2004; Friman & Poling, 1995). Consequently, it is more challenging to increase a desired high-effort behavior than a desired low-effort behavior. Even with scientific instruments, measuring effort is difficult; however, a teacher's judgment regarding relative effort should be considered during the interview process.

The other relative factors to consider are reinforcer quality, rate, and immediacy. When choosing between two behaviors and all else is equal, students are more likely to choose to engage in the behavior that yields (a) more immediate reinforcement, (b) the higher quality reinforcers, or (c) a greater rate of reinforcement (e.g., Neef, Shade, & Miller, 1994). This behavior principle is useful when desired behaviors require much effort and when teachers have difficulty controlling reinforcers for undesired behaviors. For example, it is not unusual to find a student, sometimes referred to as a "class clown," whose disruptive but funny behaviors are reinforced by peer attention. Clearly, it is difficult for teachers to control peer attention, and even their own attending behavior (e.g., laughing) that is delivered contingent on unexpected funny comments. However, educators could still address this problem of uncontrolled immediate attention by providing delayed, high-quality reinforcers contingent on desired alternative behaviors (see Skinner, Waterson, et al., 2002).

Events Surrounding the Problem Behavior

Up to this point, the focus has been on assessing behaviors, but an equally important goal is to identify conditions under which a behavior is likely to occur and consequences that may be serving to reinforce the desired behavior. Thus, during the initial interview it is common to solicit information that describes a sequence of events. Events that occur prior to the behavior (e.g., motivating operations and antecedent stimuli) can sometimes be manipulated in a manner that decreases inappropriate behavior. For example, researchers have shown that academic assignment can be altered in numerous ways that decrease the probability of inappropriate behaviors, while increasing the probability of student engaging in desired behaviors. Some strategies include interspersing brief academic tasks among more time-consuming tasks, allowing students to select among several tasks, and altering response requires so that they require less effort (Skinner, Wallace, et al., 2002). Many teachers have difficulty with classroom management, and it is not unusual for teachers to indicate that there is no way to teach specific students when they cannot even get them to attend to brief directions or instructions (Saifer, 2003). Other antecedent alteration procedures include using prompts to obtain students' attention (Fudge et al., 2008).

From a functional perspective, soliciting information on what follows problem behaviors can allow the formation of a hypothesis regarding what may be reinforcing those behaviors. Descriptions of these events and conditions can be gained by merely asking what is generally (e.g., independent seatwork) or specifically (e.g., "I told the student to return to his seat and raise his hand") occurring before the inappropriate behavior and what occurs after the behavior. In general, the goal of asking what follows the behavior is to identify positive reinforcers or what stimuli are delivered contingent on the behavior (e.g., attention) or negative reinforcement or what stimuli is removed contingent on the behavior (e.g., academic tasks).

Because more immediate reinforcers are more powerful than delayed reinforcers (Neef et al., 1994), events that occur immediately after behaviors may be reinforcing those behaviors. Thus, asking the teacher to report what happens immediately after the student engages in the problem behavior is supported by evidence-based behavioral principles. However, what occurs immediately after a behavior may not be reinforcing it. The actual reinforcer may be a high-quality delayed reinforcer. For these and other reasons, most functional assessment procedures are said to allow hypotheses formation regarding the possible function of the behavior, as opposed to drawing a conclusion.

NATURALISTIC DIRECT OBSERVATION

No assessment procedures should be conducted without a specific purpose or goal. In many instances, having the consultant carry out a direct observation can be used to clarify or specify problem and desired behaviors, conditions, and events; when they are more and less likely to occur; and events that follow the behavior. Thus, any follow-up observations should be conducted to address these specific goals. However, even when a teacher and consultant finish an interview by agreeing that they have meet these goals, there are several reasons that a naturalistic direct observation (i.e., observing in the classroom while class is in session) should still be conducted before moving to intervention development and implementation.

One reason to observe is that you don't know what you don't know. Because behavior analysts tend to focus on within-student behavior, it is possible to have accurate information but not enough information. For example, after an initial interview, the consultant may conduct a direct observation that suggests that many students in the classroom are displaying behavior problems that could be address with a class-wide procedure that is more acceptable to the teacher and students (see Fudge, Reece, Skinner, & Cowden, 2007; Skinner & Skinner, 2007).

A second reason to conduct an observation is evaluating the feasibility of different interventions. Too often, as general strategies are discussed, well-meaning teachers overcommit. When discussing multiple strategies that are empirically support, conceptually sound, and consistent with behavioral assessment data, instead of selecting one strategy, teachers may excitedly advocate for doing everything. Although their commitment is sincere, it may not be feasible for them to install and maintain all these various strategies, while completing all their other duties (Skinner, 2013). Even when one strategy is selected, several classroom-specific factors that can adversely affect an intervention application.

Skinner (2013) identified several factors that influence the context validity of specific classroom interventions that are relevant in some classrooms and not others. One threat is a failure to grasp an understanding of the skills, training, and resources needed to install an intervention. Observing a classroom can provide the consultant with a general idea of teacher strengths and available resources. Other concerns are related to intervention complexity and required precision. Classrooms are dynamic and complex; interventions that require many steps or teachers to frequently make rapid decisions and react are difficult to implement consistently and correctly. In many classrooms such interventions may have limited utility and observing the classroom during typical activities can provide a consultant with a general impression of whether such an intervention is appropriate. When they are not appropriate, the consultant can consider whether a general strategy can be applied in a manner that fits this specific classroom (e.g., apply the general strategy using less complex intervention procedures). Another alternative is to select a different strategy that does not require as much precision to be effective (Saecker et al., 2008).

Another factor to consider is possible side effects. It is difficult to anticipate all possible negative side effects. Consequently, observing the classroom can alert the psychologist to general strategies and specific procedures that may have an adverse influence on classmates, teachers, the target student, or the overall classroom climate (Skinner, Cashwell, & Dunn, 1996). Similarly, observing the room can identify the positive side effects that may encourage the application of a general strategy or some specific procedures. Other concerns are available teacher time and the possibility of adapting or tweaking procedures that are already being used. Again, directly observing the classroom can alert the psychologist to procedures and systems that are currently in place. Finally, factors associated with maintaining interventions should be considered. Some interventions can be applied and sustained, while others require so many resources that sustaining them is difficult. Observing the classroom can prevent the development of an intervention that is conceptually sound but not feasible in the current environment. Consequently, observing and recording observations should almost always be conducted before meeting with a teacher to select general strategies and develop an intervention.

When the goal is either to confirm or more carefully specify the problem behavior, observers should again use narrative records to attempt to develop a definition of the problem behavior and relevant dimensions that can be agreed on. In many instances, directly observing the behavior (e.g., seeing hand flapping, hearing a child make odd clicking noise) is the most efficient way to accomplish this goal. If desired alternative behaviors are not established during the initial interview, then observing and describing what peers are doing can help provide options (Shapiro, 2011). When several behaviors are identified, directly observing and recording sequences of behavior and behavior–environment interactions may help prioritize target behaviors (e.g., target the first behavior in a chain of inappropriate behaviors).

Directly observing events that occur before and after problem behaviors can be used to confirm or identify possible functions. One narrative procedure that may be useful is often referred to as antecedent–behavior–consequence (A-B-C) recording. An example of an A-B-C recording is shown in Table 1.1. When taking A-B-C recordings, it is often best to record from left to right. Specifically, the observer should record what happens immediately after the target behavior (leaving seat), then the activity that occurred before the target behavior. The target behavior may or may not have to be recorded. If the behavior is already defined, one might merely place a mark indicating its occurrence. As the title of this recording method implies, the procedure is designed to identify what events may serve as reinforcers that are maintaining the target behavior. Despite this title, it is important for the observer to record events that occur after the behavior without consideration of whether those events would be typical reinforcers. After all, one reason many problem behaviors exist is that educators may have had

TABLE 1.1
An Example of Antecedent–Behavior–Consequence (A-B-C) Recording

Antecedent	Behavior	Consequence
After working on independent seatwork in math for several minutes	Jane leaves her seat and approaches another child and verbally interacts with her	Teacher reprimands Jane and tells her to go back to her seat

difficulty identifying reinforcers for those behavior because the reinforcers are atypical.

Considerations Regarding Observations

There are several reasons that direct observations may provide misleading data. One is related to sampling. The observer is only in the classroom for a limited amount of time. Consequently, he or she may not have the opportunity to observe the problem behavior. Second, because behavior–environment interactions vary, the observer may accurately record events and behaviors that are atypical. Thus, observers should always ask teachers to confirm their information (e.g., "Was that what the behavior typically looks like?").

Another concern is reactivity, which is behavior bought about by the presence and behavior of the observer. Although reactivity is difficult to predict and control, there is evidence that the rationale for the observation and the conspicuousness of the observer can influence reactivity (Johnson & Bolstad, 1973). Skinner, Rhymer, and McDaniel (2000) recommended that at the end of an interview, the consultant should both schedule and plan direct observation sessions. Planning should include prompting the teacher on how to explain the observer's presence. The teacher should never specify why the observer is there (e.g., "We have an observer here who is working with me to reduce John's inappropriate vocalization"). Rather, the teacher should provide a general reason for the observer's presence (e.g., "Someone is here to observe our class"). Additionally, to reduce conspicuousness, it may be best not to tell the students the observer's name or title. Observers can also reduce their conspicuousness by avoiding interacting with any children and the teacher. Students may be less likely to approach the observer when the observer appears to be busy. While in the classroom, observers should appear to be busy engaged in other activities (e.g., writing information on a data collection sheet).

Before observing, the teacher and observer should decide where the observer is going to sit. Because it is hard for an observer to be inconspicuous when directly facing the students, it is best for observers to sit to all students back or side. Additionally, observers should avoid being oriented toward the target student or any student for sustained periods of time. It is better for the observers to shift their orientation, while using their eyes to maintain contact (e.g., looking sideways).

Again, because reactivity may influence student behavior, when finished with the session, observers should confirm that the observation session was reflective of typical classroom events. Although efforts can be made to reduce student reactivity, there are legitimate concerns related to teacher reactivity. The teacher knows the rationale for the observation. Thus, the best that can done is to merely request that the teacher behave in a typical manner.

WHAT'S NEXT: OTHER ASSESSMENT PROCEDURES AND INTERVENTION DEVELOPMENT

After completing a direct observation, observers typically meet with the teacher in an attempt to specify, confirm, or adapt behavior specifications, functional hypotheses, and descriptions or events preceding target behaviors. If, after the observation, the consultant and teacher still cannot agree that they have met their goals, additional behavioral assessment procedures can be applied. When an observer did not have the opportunity to observe target behaviors or the teacher reported that the student or the class's behavior were atypical during the observation session, another naturalistic observation may be scheduled. A variety of checklist and rating scales (see Briesch, Chafouleas, & Riley-Tillman, 2016) have been developed with items that provide tight descriptions of behaviors and allow teachers to rate those behaviors across dimensions (e.g., rates, percentage, time spent). Additionally, such direct behavior reports may prove to be an efficient way to evaluate intervention effects. Others have developed rating scales that are designed to indicate function (for early examples, see Durand, 1988, and Lewis, Scott, & Sugai, 1994). Such instruments may prove useful in helping to clarify reinforcing events.

Collaborative behavioral problem–solving in classroom environments may be best accomplished when at least one problem solver has a thorough understanding of empirically validated behavioral concepts, classroom environments (in general), and the specific classroom environment, target child, and problem behavior. Fortunately, many educators have and are receiving enhanced training in behavioral concepts and procedures (e.g., school psychologists and special educators who have or are in the process of completing requirements to become board certified behavior analysts). This is a positive development because successful behavioral problem–solving requires dealing with uncertainty and making informed judgments and decision.

This chapter has described how to efficiently gather data designed to guide intervention development. The next steps—strategy selection and intervention development, installation, and maintenance—are difficult and may be more likely to succeed when a respectful and professional relationship has been established that allow teachers to freely report information, disagree with the consultant, and take on a primary role in making decisions regarding interventions. Interviews and naturalistic direct observation can allow the collection of important behavioral assessment data while helping to establish this required professional relationship.

REFERENCES

Axelrod, S., McElrath, K. K., & Wine, B. (2012). Applied behavior analysis: Autism and beyond. *Behavioral Interventions, 27,* 1–15. http://dx.doi.org/10.1002/bin.1335

Bergan, J. R. (1977). *Behavioral consultation.* Columbus, OH: Charles E. Merrill.

Billington, E. J., Skinner, C. H., & Cruchon, N. M. (2004). Improving sixth-grade students perceptions of high-effort assignments by assigning more work: Interaction of additive interspersal and assignment effort on assignment choice. *Journal of School Psychology, 42,* 477–490. http://dx.doi.org/10.1016/j.jsp.2004.08.003

Briesch, A. M., Chafouleas, S. M., & Riley-Tillman, T. C. (2016). *Direct behavior rating: Linking assessment, communication, and intervention.* New York, NY: Guilford Press.

Carr, E. G. (1993). Behavior analysis is not ultimately about behavior. *The Behavior Analyst, 16,* 47–49. http://dx.doi.org/10.1007/BF03392608

Dougherty, A. M. (2014). *Psychological consultation and collaboration in school and community settings* (6th ed.). Belmont, CA: Brooks/Cole, Cengage Learning.

Durand, V. M. (1988). The Motivation Assessment Scale. In M. Hersen & A. Belack (Eds.), *Dictionary of behavioral assessment techniques* (pp. 309–310). Elmsford, NY: Pergamon.

Edwards, R. P. (2002). A tutorial for using the Functional Assessment Informant Record—Teachers (FAIR–T). *Proven Practice: Prevention and Remediation Solutions for Schools, 4,* 31–38.

Fairbanks, S., Sugai, G., Guardino, D., & Lathrop, M. (2007). Response to intervention: Examining classroom behavior support in second grade. *Exceptional Children, 73,* 288–310. http://dx.doi.org/10.1177/001440290707300302

Foster, L. N., & Skinner, C. H. (2011). Evidence supporting the internal, external, and contextual validity of a writing program targeting middle school students with disabilities. *Evidence-Based Communication Assessment and Intervention, 5,* 37–43. http://dx.doi.org/10.1080/17489539.2011.593848

Friman, P. C., & Poling, A. (1995). Making life easier with effort: Basic findings and applied research on response effort. *Journal of Applied Behavior Analysis, 28,* 583–590. http://dx.doi.org/10.1901/jaba.1995.28-583

Fudge, D. L., Reece, L., Skinner, C. H., & Cowden, D. (2007). Using multiple classroom rules, public cues, and consistent transition strategies to reduce inappropriate vocalization: An investigation of the Color Wheel. *Journal of Evidence-Based Practices for Schools, 8,* 102–119.

Fudge, D. L., Skinner, C. H., Williams, J. L., Cowden, D., Clark, J., & Bliss, S. L. (2008). Increasing on-task behavior in every student in a second-grade classroom during transitions: Validating the color wheel system. *Journal of School Psychology, 46,* 575–592. http://dx.doi.org/10.1016/j.jsp.2008.06.003

Gresham, F. M. (2005). Response to intervention: An alternative means of identifying students as emotionally disturbed. *Education and Treatment of Children, 28,* 328–344.

Gresham, F. M., Watson, T. S., & Skinner, C. H. (2001). Functional behavioral assessment: Principles, procedures, and future directions. *School Psychology Review, 30,* 156–172.

Hartmann, D. P., Roper, B. L., & Bradford, D. C. (1979). Some relationships between behavioral and traditional assessment. *Journal of Behavioral Assessment, 1,* 3–21. http://dx.doi.org/10.1007/BF01322415

Herrnstein, R. J. (1961). Relative and absolute strength of response as a function of frequency of reinforcement. *Journal of the Experimental Analysis of Behavior, 4,* 266–272.

Individuals With Disabilities Education Improvement Act of 2004, Pub. L. No. 108-446, § 1400 et seq.

Jacob, S., Decker, D. M., & Hartshorne, T. (2011). *Ethics and law for school psychologists* (6th ed.). Hoboken, NJ: Wiley.

Johnson, S. M., & Bolstad, O. D. (1973). Methodological issues in naturalistic observation: Some problems and solutions. In L. A. Hamerlynck, L. E. Handy, & E. J. Mash (Eds.), *Behavior change: Methodology, concepts, and practices* (pp. 7–68). Champaign, IL: Research Press.

Kazdin, A. E. (2011). *Single-case research designs* (2nd ed.). New York, NY: Oxford Press.

Kern, L., & Dunlap, G. (1999). Developing effective program plans for students with disabilities. In D. Reschly, D. Tilly, & J. Grimes (Eds.), *Special education in transition: Functional assessment and noncategorical programming* (pp. 213–232). Longmont, CO: Sopris West.

Lane, K. L., Rogers, L. A., Parks, R. J., Weisenbach, J. L., Mau, A. C., Merwin, M. T., & Bergman, W. A. (2007). Function-based interventions for students who are nonresponsive to primary and secondary prevention efforts: Illustrations at the elementary and middle school levels. *Journal of Emotional and Behavioral Disorders, 15,* 169–184. http://dx.doi.org/10.1177/10634266070150030401

Lewis, T. J., Scott, T. M., & Sugai, G. (1994). The Problem Behavior Questionnaire: A teacher-based instrument to develop functional hypotheses of problem behavior in general education classrooms. *Assessment for Effective Intervention, 19,* 103–115.

Matson, J., & Neal, D. (2009). *History and overview. Applied behavior analysis for children with autism spectrum disorders.* New York, NY: Springer.

Neef, N. A., Shade, D., & Miller, M. S. (1994). Assessing influential dimensions of reinforcers on choice in students with serious emotional disturbance. *Journal of Applied Behavior Analysis, 27,* 575–583.

Popkin, J., & Skinner, C. H. (2003). Enhancing academic performance in a classroom serving students with serious emotional disturbance: Interdependent group contingencies with randomly selected components. *School Psychology Review, 32*, 282–295.

Quillivan, C. C., Skinner, C. H., Hawthorn, M. L., Whited, D., & Ballard, D. (2011). Using a cell phone to prompt a kindergarten student to self-monitor off-task/disruptive behavior. *Journal of Evidence-Based Practices for Schools, 12*, 131–146.

Saecker, L., Sager, K., Williams, J. L., Skinner, C. H., Spurgeon, S., & Luna, E. (2008). Decreasing teacher's repeated directions and students' inappropriate talking in an urban, fifth-grade classroom using the Color Wheel procedures. *Journal of Evidence-Based Practices for Schools, 9*, 18–32.

Saifer, S. (2003). *Practical solutions to practically every problem: The early childhood teachers manual* (Report No. PSO31176). Marion, IN: Indiana Wesleyan Center for Educational Excellence. (ERIC Document Reproduction Service No. ED475175)

Sandomierski, T., Kincaid, D., & Algozzine, B. (2007). Response to intervention and positive behavior support: Brothers from different mothers or sisters with different misters? *Positive Behavioral Interventions and Supports Newsletter, 4*(2), 1–4.

Severson, H. H., Walker, H. M., Hope-Doolittle, J., Kratochwill, T. R., & Gresham, F. M. (2007). Proactive, early screening to detect behaviorally at-risk students: Issues, approaches, emerging innovations, and professional practices. *Journal of School Psychology, 45*, 193–223. http://dx.doi.org/10.1016/j.jsp.2006.11.003

Shapiro, E. S. (1987). *Behavioral assessment in school psychology*. Hillsdale, NJ: Erlbaum.

Shapiro, E. S. (2011). *Academic skills problems: Direct assessment and intervention* (4th ed.). New York, NY: Guilford Press.

Skinner, B. F. (1966). The phylogeny and ontogeny of behavior: Contingencies of reinforcement throw light on contingencies of survival in the evolution of behavior. *Science, 153*, 1205–1213. http://dx.doi.org/10.1126/science.153.3741.1205

Skinner, C. H. (2013). Contextual validity: Knowing what works is necessary, but not sufficient. *The School Psychologist, 67*(1), 14–21.

Skinner, C. H., Cashwell, C., & Dunn, M. (1996). Independent and interdependent group contingencies: Smoothing the rough waters. *Special Services in the Schools, 12*, 61–78. http://dx.doi.org/10.1300/J008v12n01_04

Skinner, C. H., Rhymer, K. N., & McDaniel, C. E. (2000). Naturalistic direct observation in educational settings. In E. S. Shapiro & T. R. Kratochwill (Eds.), *Conducting school-based assessments of children and adolescents* (pp. 21–54). New York, NY: Guilford Press.

Skinner, C. H., & Skinner, A. L. (2007). Establishing an evidence base for a classroom management procedure with a series of studies: Evaluating the Color Wheel. *Journal of Evidence-Based Practices for Schools, 8*, 88–101.

Skinner, C. H., Wallace, M. A., & Neddenriep, C. E. (2002). Academic remediation: Educational application of research on assignment preference and choice. *Child & Family Behavior Therapy, 24*, 51–65. http://dx.doi.org/10.1300/J019v24n01_04

Skinner, C. H., Waterson, H. J., Bryant, D. R., Bryant, R. J., Collins, P. M., Hill, C. J., . . . Fox, J. (2002). Team problem solving based on research, functional behavioral assessment data, teacher acceptability, and Jim Carey's interview. *Proven Practices: Prevention & Remediation Solutions for Schools, 4*, 56–64.

Sprague, J., Sugai, G., & Walker, H. (1998). Antisocial behavior in schools. In T. S. Watson & F. M. Gresham (Eds.), *Handbook of child behavior therapy* (pp. 451–474). New York, NY: Plenum Press. http://dx.doi.org/10.1007/978-1-4615-5323-6_23

Watson, T. S., & Steege, M. W. (2003). *Conducting school-based functional behavioral assessments: A practitioner's guide*. New York, NY: Guilford Press.

Winokuer, H. F., & Harris, D. L. (2015). *Principles and practice of grief counseling* (2nd ed.). New York, NY: Springer.

2

SCHOOL-WIDE POSITIVE BEHAVIORAL INTERVENTIONS AND SUPPORTS: A SYSTEMS-LEVEL APPLICATION OF BEHAVIORAL PRINCIPLES

BRANDI SIMONSEN AND GEORGE SUGAI

School-wide Positive Behavioral Interventions and Supports (PBIS) is a preventive, positive, and systemic framework or approach to affect meaningful educational and behavioral change. PBIS was first introduced into federal legislation in 1997, with the amendments to the Individuals With Disabilities Education Act (IDEA). IDEA was an important legislative act that reinforced the importance of a positive behavioral approach to meeting the needs of individuals with disabilities and significant problem behaviors (Carr et al., 2002). As authorized under IDEA, the Office of Special Education Programs (OSEP) established the National Technical Assistance Center on PBIS (TA Center on PBIS).

Preparation of this chapter was supported in part by a grant from the Office of Special Education Programs, U.S. Department of Education, Center on Positive Behavioral Interventions and Support (Grant H H326S03004; http://www.pbis.org). Opinions expressed herein are those of the authors and do not necessarily reflect the position of the U.S. Department of Education, and such endorsements should not be inferred. For more information, contact Brandi Simonsen (brandi.simonsen@uconn.edu).

http://dx.doi.org/10.1037/0000126-003
Behavioral Interventions in Schools: Evidence-Based Positive Strategies, Second Edition, S. G. Little and A. Akin-Little (Editors)
Copyright © 2019 by the American Psychological Association. All rights reserved.

In addition, PBIS has become an important component of other federally funded school and mental health grant initiatives. For example, Project Prevent Grant Program funded local education agencies to increase their capacity to address and prevent pervasive school violence. The School Climate Transformation Grants (SCTG) Program provided funding to local and state education agencies to develop and implement multitiered behavioral frameworks that improve behavioral outcomes and learning conditions for all students. The Project Advancing Wellness and Resilience Education (AWARE) Grant Program supported local and state education capacity to address behavioral health concerns. The TA Center on PBIS was charged with providing supportive technical assistance to these grant programs.

After 2 decades of research, the evidence from rigorous group and single case design studies clearly document that when implemented with fidelity, PBIS results in (a) reduced major disciplinary infractions and aggressive behavior; (b) improved academic achievement, concentration, prosocial behavior, and emotional regulation; (c) enhanced perception of organizational health and safety; (d) reduced teacher-reported bullying behavior and peer rejection; and (e) improved school climate (Algozzine, Wang, & Violette, 2011; Bradshaw, 2015; Bradshaw, Koth, Bevans, Ialongo, & Leaf, 2008; Bradshaw, Koth, Thornton, & Leaf, 2009; Bradshaw, Mitchell, & Leaf, 2010; Bradshaw, Pas, Goldweber, Rosenberg, & Leaf, 2012; Bradshaw, Reinke, Brown, Bevans, & Leaf, 2008; Bradshaw, Waasdorp, & Leaf, 2012; Burke, Hagan-Burke, & Sugai, 2003; Goldweber, Waasdorp, & Bradshaw, 2013; Horner, Sugai, & Anderson, 2010; Horner et al., 2009; McIntosh, Chard, Boland, & Horner, 2006; McIntosh, Horner, Chard, Dickey, & Braun, 2008; Nelson, Johnson, & Marchand-Martella, 1996; Simonsen et al., 2012; Sørlie & Ogden, 2015; Waasdorp, Bradshaw, & Leaf, 2012; Wang & Algozzine, 2011).

PBIS has received a great deal of attention and is built on a long and rich history of applied behavioral theory, research, and practice. In this chapter, we describe the behavioral roots of PBIS; specifically, we (a) present an overview of PBIS; (b) introduce and define key behavioral principles that underlie PBIS; (c) illustrate how the behavioral principles are implemented with all (school-wide), some (targeted group), and few (individual) students; and (d) summarize recent enhancements to the implementation of the PBIS framework.

OVERVIEW OF POSITIVE BEHAVIORAL INTERVENTIONS AND SUPPORTS

The features, practices, and processes of PBIS have been described in detail (Horner & Sugai, 2015; Horner, Sugai, & Fixsen, 2017; Lewis & Sugai, 1999; OSEP Center on PBIS, 2015a; Safran & Oswald, 2003;

Sugai, Horner, et al., 2000). In this section, we provide a brief overview of PBIS: (a) three-tiered continuum of support, (b) critical elements, and (c) implementation.

Three Tiers of Support

PBIS interventions are organized into a three-tiered prevention framework (OSEP Center on PBIS, 2015a; Walker et al., 1996) that provides a working logic for organizing the outcomes, data management, practices, and systems along a continuum of support for all students (see Figure 2.1). Tier 1 (primary or universal) support is available to all students and provided by all staff members across all school environments (i.e., classroom and nonclassroom settings). When implemented with fidelity, most students will benefit from Tier 1 supports. For example, preliminary descriptive data (collected across 2,979 elementary schools, 889 middle and junior high schools, and 390 high schools implementing PBIS) suggest that when Tier 1 support is in place, approximately 84% of students will receive one or fewer office discipline referrals for major rule violations during a school year (Horner, 2016).

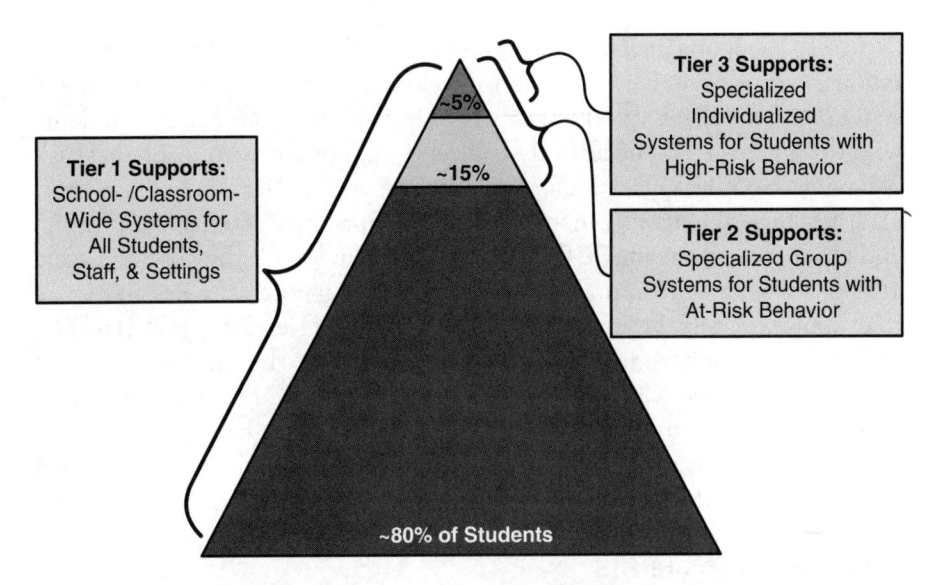

Figure 2.1. Three-tiered continuum of supports. Adapted from "Positive Behavioral Interventions and Supports (PBIS) Implementation Blueprint: Part 1—Foundations and supporting information," by Office of Special Education Programs Technical Assistance Center on Positive Behavioral Interventions and Supports, 2015 (https://www.pbis.org/blueprint/implementation-blueprint). In the public domain.

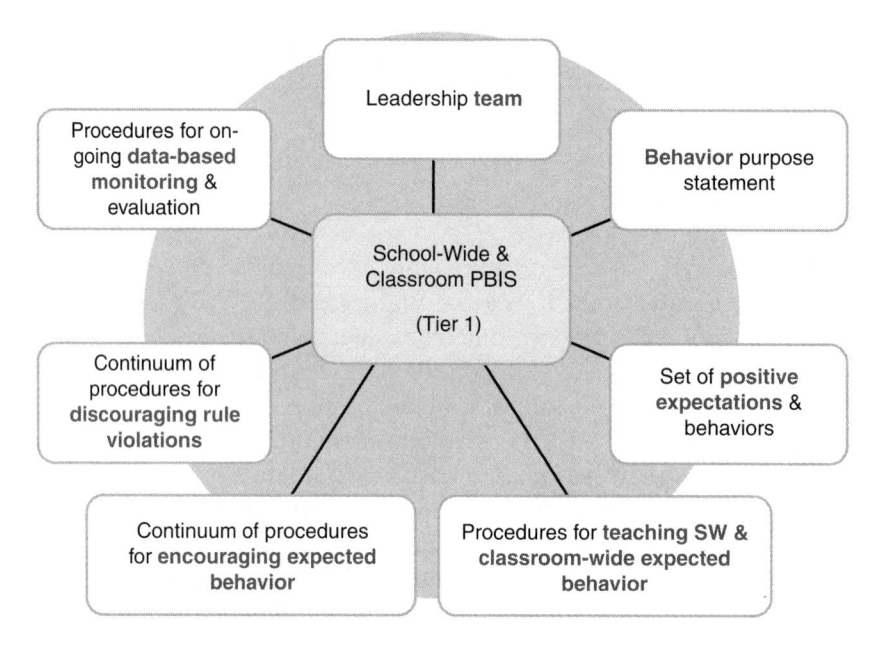

Figure 2.2. Elements of Tier 1 support. SW = school-wide. Data from Office of Special Education Programs Technical Assistance Center on Positive Behavioral Interventions and Supports (2015a).

Tier 1 supports include establishing and teaching positively stated expectations, increasing active supervision, developing a school-wide reinforcement system, and investing in other supports depicted in Figure 2.2. For students who do not respond successfully to Tier 1 support or who display at-risk behavior challenges, Tier 2 support is implemented. Tier 2 support is characterized by systematically increasing the prompts, instructions, monitoring, and reinforcement available for appropriate behavior. Of the approximately 16% of students who do not respond to primary support, schools can expect that approximately 11% will require and receive Tier 2 support (Horner, 2016). Finally, for students who do not respond to the first two layers of support (approximately 5%), Tier 3 support is designed to meet the needs of each student. Individualized, high intensity, function-based, and positive behavior intervention plans; person-centered planning; and services identified and coordinated through wrap-around process are elements of Tier 3 support.

Critical Elements of PBIS

Schools implementing PBIS identify relevant and culturally equitable outcomes, use culturally valid data to guide the selection and implementation of evidence-based and culturally relevant practices, and establish culturally knowledgeable systems to sustain implementation and evaluation activities (Fallon, O'Keeffe, & Sugai, 2012; Lewis & Sugai, 1999; Sugai, O'Keeffe, & Fallon, 2012; Vincent, Randall, Cartledge, Tobin, & Swain-Bradway, 2011). Figure 2.3 illustrates the interrelationship among these four critical elements of PBIS (outcomes, data, practices, and systems), and the following sections describe each element.

Outcomes are observable and measurable goals that are locally determined; based on and validated by collection and analysis of local data; considerate of cultural and regional demographics and customs; related to state, district, and federal priorities; and feasible within the allocated time frame.

Data are collected to determine the present level of performance (i.e., baseline) of all, some, or individual students at Tiers 1, 2, and 3, respectively. Thus, data are used to (a) prioritize need areas; (b) select outcomes that are observable, measurable, and specific; and (c) evaluate progress toward outcomes. Data also guide the selection practices across the three levels of intervention. Given the importance of data for decision-making and evaluation, PBIS schools capitalize on data sources that are readily available (e.g., extant data) and invest in a data management system that allows efficient input

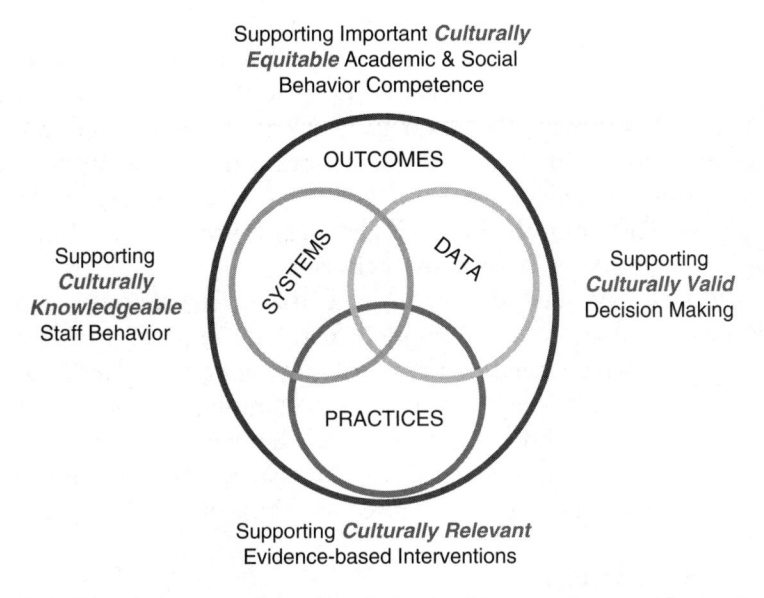

Figure 2.3. Critical elements of Positive Behavioral Interventions and Supports. Adapted from "Positive Behavioral Interventions and Supports (PBIS) Implementation Blueprint: Part 1—Foundations and supporting information," by Office of Special Education Programs Technical Assistance Center on Positive Behavioral Interventions and Supports, 2015 (https://www.pbis.org/blueprint/implementation-blueprint).

and creates flexible and meaningful visual displays (e.g., graphs or tables) to facilitate decision-making (e.g., Simonsen & Sugai, 2007).

Systems are the organizational and process structures and activities designed to support staff and ensure sustained implementation of PBIS. One of the key structures within PBIS is teaming. Teams are formed at the state, district, and school levels to oversee and guide implementation of Tier 1, 2, and 3 supports. For example, the school-level team includes (a) a school administrator, who ensures that the team is given priority, status, and resources, and (b) a select group of staff members who are chosen to be representative of the grade levels, disciplines, and types of staff within the school. For each team, members meet regularly, have clearly defined roles and responsibilities, and are held accountable by a documented action plan. In addition, school staff members engage in professional development and staff reinforcement activities that are designed to initiate, maintain, and increase implementation of practices. In sum, systems-level activities focus on the needs and supports of those staff members who are responsible for accurately and consistently implementing effective practices to achieve PBIS outcomes.

Practices, then, are the interventions selected, developed, and implemented to support students. Social skills instruction and contingency management (e.g., systematic reinforcement) are typical components of most PBIS interventions. Selected practices should be preventative, evidence based, indicated by data, aligned with identified outcomes, clearly supported by systems, and positive. In addition, these practices are adapted to accommodate the unique characteristics (e.g., language, culture, ethnicity, family) of students who are intended to benefit from and staff members who are responsible for their implementation. Positive practices are designed to teach (establish stimulus control, discussed subsequently) and increase (reinforce), rather than solely decrease (punish), behavior.

Within a continuum of support logic, the effort (intensity, frequency, duration, specialization, differentiation, teaming) required to address the learning and behavior needs increases when moving from Tier 1 to Tier 2 to Tier 3 (see Figure 2.4). This logic has important implications for ensuring that Tier 1 practices and supports are being implemented effectively and with fidelity to enable the delivery of specialized supports needed for students with serious behavior challenges that require Tier 2 or Tier 3 supports.

Implementation of PBIS

As of July 2018, more than 26,000 schools across all 50 states have received training and technical assistance in implementing PBIS from the OSEP Center on PBIS (http://www.pbis.org). In addition, many more schools

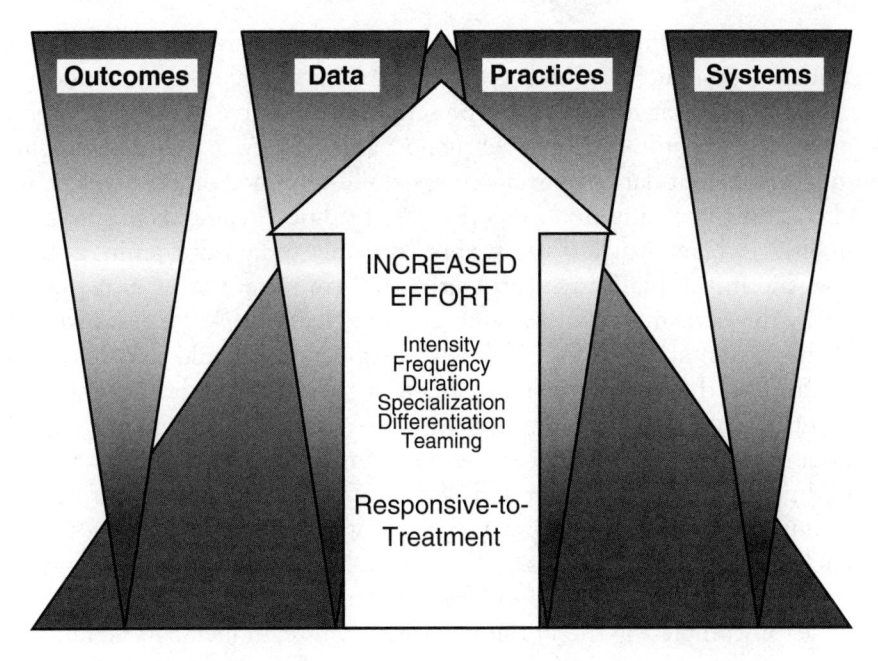

Figure 2.4. Continuum logic of data, practices, systems, and outcomes.

and districts are estimated to have adopted PBIS practices and processes that have not been supported by the Center, and international interest has grown (e.g., Australia, Canada, Cayman Islands, Denmark, Jamaica, Netherlands, New Zealand, Norway, Spain, South Korea, Sweden, Taiwan). To facilitate implementation across states, regions have established networks to maximize local implementation capacity (e.g., Mid-Atlantic PBIS, Midwest PBIS, Northeast PBIS, Northwest PBIS). Similarly, international groups are also forming networks (e.g., Australia, Canada, PBS Europe, Hong Kong, SWPBS Nederland, Taiwan; http://apbs.org/network-preview.html) affiliated with the Association for Positive Behavior Support.

Typical training and technical assistance activities span 3 or more years and are designed to promote the careful adoption, accurate and sustained implementation, and controlled expansion or scaling of the full continuum of PBIS support. Across these years, school teams are guided through a series of capacity-building stages, for example: (a) meet readiness requirements, (b) participate in intensive team and school-wide systems development, (c) develop and implement with fidelity primary practices and support systems, (d) develop and implement with fidelity secondary and tertiary practices and support systems, and (e) participate in regular booster professional development events for sustaining and enhancing implementation efforts and outcomes.

Before receiving training or assistance, schools are required to meet readiness requirements, which typically include formal commitments and agreements from at least 80% of the school staff, active involvement of a school administrator, district level support and priority, a 3- to 4-year commitment, efficient data management system, established school-level team, and coaching or facilitation support. After readiness requirements are met, school-level teams participate in approximately 6 days of training spread across the initial planning year. During the training, the team members identify the outcomes, data, systems, and practices that will be involved in their implementation of PBIS. The team members then build an action plan detailing how they will (a) share information gained during the training with the entire school staff, (b) perform the tasks required to ensure a successful rollout of the primary system (e.g., establishing a small number of positively stated rules, designing student and staff reinforcement systems) during the upcoming year, and (c) monitor progress toward identified outcomes. The "coach" or facilitator serves a follow-up link or prompt between training events and team implementation of action plan activities.

After completing the initial planning year, team members facilitate a *rollout* or formal introduction by all staff members of primary support within their school. During the initial implementation year, school teams continue to participate in training activities (approximately three days across the year) and receive support through coaching networks. Activities emphasize, for example, data-based enhancements of practices, school-wide fidelity and fluency of implementation, and acknowledgments for data-based demonstrations of success and progress. In subsequent years, teams continue to receive training and technical assistance to sustain their implementation of primary systems and establish Tier 2 and Tier 3 systems. In addition, various states and regions have established advanced professional development activities to promote further professional growth. These activities may be available to schools across all stages of implementation but are specifically designed to support schools that have been implementing for 4 or more years. Examples of implementation workbooks, activities, practices, and other resources are available at state (e.g., Florida, Michigan, Minnesota, New Jersey, Wisconsin) and regional websites (Mid-Atlantic, Midwest, Northeast) and at the OSEP TA Center on PBIS website (http://www.pbis.org).

Across all levels of training, school teams are presented with user-friendly and applied information that is directly based on early behavioral theory (i.e., the work of B. F. Skinner), years of applied behavior analytic research and practice (e.g., studies published in the *Journal of Applied Behavior Analysis* and the *Journal of Positive Behavioral Interventions*), and other applications of behavioral theory (e.g., organizational behavior, industrial-organizational psychology). Therefore, to understand PBIS, the basic tenets and principles of behavioral theory also must be acknowledged, understood, and given priority.

KEY BEHAVIORAL PRINCIPLES THAT UNDERLIE PBIS

Behaviorism is the theory and applied behavior analysis (ABA) is the applied science that underlies PBIS. In this section, we describe the behavioral principles that serve as the foundation and guidelines for the development and implementation of the practices and systems of PBIS: (a) basic tenets of behavioral theory and (b) behavioral principles in the context of the three-term contingency.

Basic Tenets of Behavioral Theory

Behaviorism is a theory-based and empirical approach to studying behavior (e.g., Alberto & Troutman, 2006; Cooper, Heron, & Heward, 2007; Vargas, 2013). Unlike other fields of study within psychology, behaviorism does not focus on mental and emotional states that cannot be directly observed; instead, observable and measurable events are used to more objectively predict, explain, and modify behavior (e.g., Skinner, 1953). Early behaviorism emphasized experimental work designed to describe, understand, and confirm the principles and mechanisms that could be used to expand the theory, explain observed behavioral phenomena, and refine interventions and treatments for individuals with behavioral problems.

From this early work, researchers and practitioners developed awareness that behavioral theory had applications to problems being experienced by humans in everyday life (e.g., supporting individuals who engage in challenging behavior, mental health supports, juvenile justice) and an extension of behaviorism emerged: ABA. In a seminal article published in the first volume of the *Journal of Applied Behavior Analysis*, Baer, Wolf, and Risley (1968) defined ABA as a science that addresses real (applied) behavior problems (e.g., decreasing aggressive behavior of an individual), in a systematic and objective manner, by (a) applying conceptually sound behavioral interventions and (b) analyzing the effect of those interventions on the target behaviors of an individual to ensure that a meaningful, socially significant, and enduring behavior change occurs.

From ABA, we have learned that all behaviors (desired and undesired) are learned by and functional for (i.e., operate on and are responsive to the environment) an individual (Baer et al., 1968; Cooper et al., 2007; Vargas, 2013). The basic unit of analysis for describing, understanding, and affecting occurrences of behavior is the three-term contingency, which is characterized as an antecedent–behavior–consequence (ABC) sequence (e.g., Alberto & Troutman, 2006).

Behavioral Principles in the Context of the Three-Term Contingency

The ABC or three-term contingency demonstrates that behavior does not occur in a vacuum or independent of environmental factors. Specifically, behavioral occurrences are described as "occasioned" and "maintained" by environmental events; that is, the presence (or absence) of specific antecedent stimuli (e.g., conditions, activities, objects, events) sets the occasion or opportunity for specific consequence conditions (i.e., punishment or reinforcement) if a specific behavior is emitted (or not) in the presence of the antecedent stimuli.

The development, implementation, and evaluation of behavioral intervention are guided by the three-term contingency. Interventions are designed to (a) change antecedent stimuli such that they trigger (occasion) desired (appropriate) behaviors and do not trigger undesired (problem) behaviors, (b) teach appropriate behavior(s) that more efficiently and effectively lead to reinforcement than problem behavior, and (c) modify consequence stimuli such that appropriate behaviors are more likely to result in reinforcement and inappropriate behaviors less likely. In the following subsections, we discuss the specific principles and procedures used to modify the antecedents, behaviors, and consequences (see Figure 2.5).

Strategies for Modifying Antecedent Stimuli

In each ABC sequence, a specific antecedent (discriminative stimulus, or S^D) triggers or occasions a specific behavior, or response. The S^D is described as "signaling" an increased likelihood of a specific consequence (reinforcement)

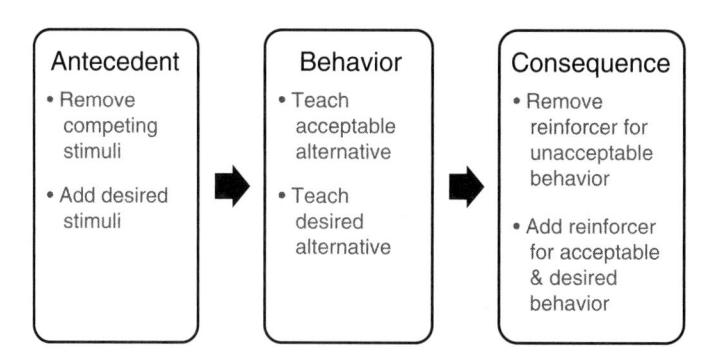

Antecedent	Behavior	Consequence
• Remove competing stimuli • Add desired stimuli	• Teach acceptable alternative • Teach desired alternative	• Remove reinforcer for unacceptable behavior • Add reinforcer for acceptable & desired behavior

Figure 2.5. Instructional manipulations within ABC (antecedent–behavior–consequence) Contingency.

if the behavior is emitted in its presence and of a different consequence (neutral or punishment) if the behavior is emitted in its absence. In more applied or lay terms, individuals learn that if "A" is present and they do "B," then "C" will follow.

Therefore, to effect a desired change in behavior, antecedent stimuli should be modified in two key ways. First, the presentation or availability of antecedent stimuli that occasion desired behavior should be increased or enhanced. For example, if teacher attention is a desired (positively reinforcing) consequence and if a student has received teacher attention for engaging in appropriate behavior in the past, then the presence of a teacher (signaling the availability of teacher attention) is more likely to occasion appropriate student behavior. So, to occasion more desired student behavior, an intervention plan would include manipulations that increase teacher presence, for example, closer and more frequent teacher proximity, increased teacher-initiated interactions, or more teacher-directed instruction. Another way to enhance an antecedent stimulus is to add prompts to the environment that draw students' attention to the S^D and remind them of the desired behavior, for example, teacher statements (e.g., "I like talking with *respectful* students"), posted rule-reminders (e.g., "Raise your hand before answering or asking"), or modeling gestures (e.g., teacher raises a hand while asking a question).

Second, the stimuli that trigger or occasion undesired behavior should be eliminated or modified; that is, remove or alter stimuli that typically signal reinforcing consequences for displays of undesired behavior. For example, if slowdowns and collisions in a crowded stairway occasion verbal and physical aggression (e.g., maintained by peer attention), then modifying antecedent stimuli might include instituting a staggered hallway dismissal to reduce crowding, or adding "stay to the right" arrows on the floor to decrease collisions.

By altering antecedent stimuli, the objective is to increase the likelihood of appropriate behavior and prevent (decrease the likelihood of) problem behavior. For antecedent strategies to be effective, individuals must already have (a) the behavior in their behavioral learning history and (b) been trained to perform the behavior under the specific antecedent conditions. Thus, antecedent strategies are only useful when an individual has learned how and when (i.e., stimulus control) to emit and not emit the behavior.

Strategies for Teaching Behavior

When a behavior is not already within an individual's repertoire or when a behavior has not been learned under the desired conditions, stimulus control must be established, that is, teach. Whether learning an academic or a behavior skill, teaching is about establishing lasting behavior change through four phases of learning: (a) acquisition—accurate (> 90% correct) responding, (b) fluency—accurate responding at acceptable rates, (c) maintenance—accurate responding at acceptable rates over time, and (d) generalization—accurate and adapted responding at acceptable rates over time and under a variety of stimulus conditions. When an individual has not demonstrated accurate displays of a behavior under desired instructional stimulus conditions, the focus of instruction is on skill acquisition. This phase emphasizes stimulus control, which is established by (a) providing reinforcement contingent on accurate displays of a target behavior in the presence of specific antecedent conditions (i.e., S^D) and (b) either withholding reinforcement or providing an error correction for displays of the target behavior when the specific antecedent conditions are not present or for displays of other behaviors in the presence of the specific antecedent conditions. Stimulus control is evident when the desired response occurs more often (or exclusively) in the presence of the S^D than in its absence.

To facilitate skill acquisition, an explicit and systematic instructional approach is adopted: define, model, practice, assess, and reinforce. With academic skills, like reading, math, and social studies, this explicit or "direct instruction" approach (Engelmann & Carnine, 1982; Kameenui & Simmons, 1990) is characterized as a "model–lead–test" (or "I do, we do, you do") approach. A similar approach is adopted for teaching social behaviors or skills. In addition to an explicit instruction, *shaping* (i.e., differentially reinforcing successive approximations of a desired behavior) is used to teach simple (single-step) behaviors and *chaining* (i.e., breaking a task down into component parts and reinforcing the learner for completing more and more steps in succession) is used to teach complex (multistep) behaviors (e.g., Alberto & Troutman, 2006).

After the skill has been acquired, the focus of instruction moves toward increasing the fluency with which the behavior is performed. High levels of accuracy are maintained, and reinforcement is provided systematically and contingently as more acceptable rates or consistency of performance are demonstrated. Again, shaping is emphasized along with repeated practice.

At the maintenance phase, skill practice is continued; however, instructional supports are faded, and schedules of reinforcement are leaned or thinned to approximate what might be available in the natural or non-instructional environment. The goal is to establish maintained rates of responding by shifting control from instructional to naturally occurring prompts and consequences. If expected schedules of reinforcement are not available to maintain behavioral occurrences, self-management strategies can be taught (e.g., self-manipulation of antecedent and consequence events) to provide what is needed.

Ultimately, teaching is not successful if the newly acquired skill is not used and maintained in noninstructional settings and conditions, that is, where the skill has not been taught and practiced. To program for generalized responding, instruction shifts to teaching with a full range of examples and nonexamples (i.e., antecedent and consequence conditions) such that a "general case," rule, or concept is established (Horner, Bellamy, & Colvin, 1984; Wolery, Bailey, & Sugai, 1988). As in maintenance, the instruction continues to emphasize approximating consequence conditions that characterize the natural or generalization settings, but increased attention is placed on teaching a representative sample of the stimulus conditions that exist outside the instructional context (Engelmann & Carnine, 1982; Kameenui & Simmons, 1990).

In sum, when an individual does not know how to perform a behavior, the focus of instruction is on skill acquisition (teaching the "B" part of the A-B-C chain). Once an individual emits the behavior accurately, the focus of instruction is on building the A-B portion of the chain or establishing stimulus control. When an individual knows how and when to perform a desired behavior but does not perform it with the expected frequency, rate, or intensity, instructional focus shifts to modifications of consequences, or the C part of the three-term contingency.

Strategies for Modifying Consequences

In behavioral theory, consequence manipulations may have one of three associated effects on a behavior: (a) *none*—consequence manipulation is associated with no predictable effect on occurrence of behavior in future, (b) *increase*—manipulation of consequence stimuli is associated with an increased likelihood that a behavior will occur in the future (reinforcement), or (c) *decrease*—consequence manipulation is associated with a decrease in likelihood that a behavior will occur in the future (punishment). In general, two types of manipulations are considered: (a) give or present (positive) and (b) remove or take (negative). Thus, four types of consequences can be characterized by two manipulations (positive or negative) and two effects (increase or decrease) on the future probability of behavior.

Positive reinforcement describes a condition in which a stimulus is *presented* contingent upon emission of a behavior and is associated with an *increase* in probability of future behavior occurrences. For example, a student is working quietly on a sheet of math problems and the teacher gives verbal praise (e.g., "I like how you are working quietly"). If the student is more likely to work quietly in the future, then the contingent presentation of verbal praise is positive reinforcement.

Negative reinforcement describes a condition in which a stimulus is *removed* contingent on emission of a behavior and is associated with an *increase* in probability of future behavior occurrences. For example, because another student is working slowly on her math problems, the teacher "nags" at the student to work faster, stop talking, and keep her eyes on her own work. The student works faster to reduce the amount of teaching nagging. If the student is more likely to work quietly and faster in the future, then the contingent removal of teacher nagging is negative reinforcement.

Positive punishment is used to describe a condition in which a stimulus is *added* contingently upon the emission of a behavior and is associated with a *decrease* in the likelihood of future occurrences of the behavior. For example, a child throws blocks and the caregiver gives a reprimand (e.g., "No. We do not throw blocks"). If future occurrences of block throwing decrease, then positive punishment describes the situation.

Negative punishment describes a condition in which a stimulus is *removed* contingent on emission of a behavior and is associated with a *decrease* in the future probability of that behavior being emitted. For example, a different child is throwing blocks, and the caregiver takes the blocks away. If future occurrences of block throwing decrease, negative punishment is used to describe the situation. Caution should be taken whenever punishment procedures are used. The literature is replete with considerations when using punishment-based interventions, for example, (a) always include and emphasize strategies that are based on positive reinforcement, (b) never use punishment-only procedures, (c) use effective punishment procedures and fade their use as quickly as possible, (d) plan for side effects (e.g., aggression, escape, withdrawal), (e) monitor fidelity of implementation and behavior effects continuously, (f) use the most effective and least aversive, (g) do no harm, and (h) emphasize teaching of prosocial alternative behaviors (Alberto & Troutman, 2006; Cooper et al., 2007; Wolery et al., 1988).

In addition to the four main types of consequences, extinction may be used. *Extinction* occurs when reinforcing consequences that have been shown to maintain a behavior are withheld and is associated with a decrease in future occurrences of that behavior. Extinction procedures can be difficult to implement alone in an applied setting because (a) all reinforcement must be identified and withheld consistently and completely upon emission of the targeted response and (b) temporary increases in the frequency, rate, or intensity of the response (extinction burst) can be experienced before decreases are observed. For example, a student repeatedly talks out during teacher-directed instruction. In the past, the teacher has responded to these talk-outs by giving immediate attention (e.g., called on the student, redirected the student to another task, asked the student to wait and try again later). Realizing that talking out has been positively reinforced by teacher attention, the teacher decides to implement an extinction procedure. Specifically, the teacher decides to withhold attention each time the student talks out. Initially, the student talks out more frequently in a louder tone of voice (extinction burst). If the teacher consistently and contingently withholds attention every time the student talks out, then that behavior will eventually decrease in frequency.

Behavior reduction procedures, like punishment or extinction, should always be combined with constructive strategies that teach and strengthen occurrences of appropriate alternative behaviors (e.g., raise hand for 5 seconds, and if necessary try again later). Combinations of positive reinforcement and extinction (i.e., differential reinforcement) can take a variety of forms (e.g., differential reinforcement of an alternative behavior). For example, the teacher may remove attention each time a talk-out occurs, but immediately presents attention each time the student seeks teacher attention appropriately (e.g., raises hand, approaches teacher's desk appropriately). These basic consequence procedures can be used to manipulate environmental stimuli to increase occurrences of desired, or decrease occurrences of undesired, behavior in the future. In a school setting, students often have stimuli presented (e.g., praise, tokens, points, grades, items, activities) or removed (e.g., homework pass) in an effort to increase desired behavior. Similarly, students often have stimuli presented (e.g., office discipline referrals, verbal reprimands) or removed (e.g., detention from fun activities, recess taken away) in an effort to decrease undesired behaviors. Regardless of intent, school staff can use observations of student behavior to determine whether they are actually reinforcing desired behavior and punishing or extinguishing undesired behavior. For example, a principal may assign (give) a student in-school suspension for engaging in disruptive behavior, thinking that positive punishment is being applied. However, if disruptive behavior continues or increases, the principal's consequence procedure is more likely to be positive (presentation of adult attention) or negative (removal from an aversive classroom environment) reinforcement.

BEHAVIORAL PRINCIPLES APPLIED THROUGHOUT TIERS OF PBIS

Most ABA applications have involved individuals who present behavioral challenges (behavior deficits and/or excesses) and require individualized behavior intervention plans. ABA principles and interventions can be extended easily to organizations, like classrooms and schools, and to the behavior of a variety of individuals within those settings, that is, students, teachers, administrators, and other school personnel. The behavior of the individual remains a primary consideration; however, applications are extended to groups of individuals in a consistent and efficient manner. The three-term contingency remains central to PBIS applications, and behavioral principles (e.g., reinforcement, stimulus control, punishment) guide the development, implementation, and evaluation of PBIS implementations. As Sugai and Horner (2006) described, "Organizations do not 'behave.' Instead, individuals within the organization engage in behavior. The greater the extent to which these behaviors move the organization toward a common goal, the stronger the organization" (p. 248).

PBIS is the systems-level approach that organizes the application of basic behavioral principles on the behavior of individuals within an organization (i.e., classroom, school) in the previously described three-tiered continuum of behavior support: Tier 1 for all students, Tier 2 for smaller groups of students whose behaviors are not responsive to Tier 1 interventions, and Tier 3 for individual students whose behaviors are not responsive to Tier 1 and Tier 2 interventions. Across each intervention tier, school staff members implement strategies that involve modifying antecedent and consequence conditions and teaching of prosocial behaviors. The ultimate goals are to redesign teaching and learning environments to (a) eliminate triggering antecedent stimuli and maintaining reinforcing stimuli for undesirable behaviors, (b) establish strong stimulus control for (i.e., teach) prosocial desirable behaviors, and (c) increase availability and presentation of triggering antecedent stimuli and maintaining (reinforcing) consequence stimuli for desirable behavior. The greater extent to which common outcomes, verbal behaviors, and overt routines can be established, the greater the integrity and effectiveness of the organization, that is, school-wide and classroom behavior support. Examples of PBIS practices and interventions across the three-tiered continuum of support are described in the following sections.

Behavioral Principles Applied in PBIS Tier 1

At Tier 1, interventions are implemented by all staff members for all students across all classroom and school settings. Changes are made to the larger environmental conditions to occasion (antecedent strategies) and reinforce (consequence strategies) desired, rule-following behaviors. Schools implementing PBIS emphasize systematically teaching rule-following behaviors within each school routine and setting (stimulus control). For example, visual prompts (e.g., posters, pictures) are added to key settings (e.g., classroom, cafeteria, hallway, playground, and common areas). A small set of general school-wide behavioral expectations are established and taught. Often, schools approach this practice by building a school-wide rule matrix that highlights specific behavior examples that are relevant to each school setting and general school wide expectation. Sound teaching and behavioral principles are applied by selecting positive school-wide rules or expectations (e.g., *Being Responsible, Being Respectful, Being Safe, Being a Learner*), emphasizing context (e.g., *hallway, classroom, bus, assembly, cafeteria*), and identifying specific behavioral examples that are linked to context (e.g., *walk to the right in hallway, share equipment on playground, sit in your seat on the bus until you get to school, return your tray to the stack and litter to the trash can*). Figure 2.6 presents an example of a teaching matrix illustrating verbal labels (*Respecting Others, Self, Environment, and Learning*), location or context (*Classroom, Lunchroom, Bus, Hallway, Assembly*), and sample behaviors (e.g., *listen to speaker, return lunch trays, arrive on time*).

Tier 1 PBIS also emphasizes providing regular, contingent, and effective positive reinforcement. Although the critical component is that adults provide specific positive feedback (praise) contingent on desired student behavior, many schools also implement a token economy for all staff, students, and settings. Following student displays of expected or desired behavior, staff members present social and token reinforcers, which are linked to later social and backup reinforcers. Individual students, whole classrooms, entire grade levels, and/or the whole student body can receive a positive reinforcer based on cumulative performances. School administrators and PBIS leadership team members also provide positive reinforcers for staff members who accurately adhere to teaching and intervention protocols. Tokens are faded as naturally occurring stimuli (e.g., verbal praise, social gestures, self-statements) acquire more positively reinforcing value (conditioned).

	Classroom	Lunchroom	Bus	Hallway	Assembly
Respect Others	Use inside voice	Eat your own food	Stay in your seat	Stay to right	Arrive on time to speaker
Respect Environment & Property	Recycle paper	Return trays	Keep feet on floor	Put trash in cans	Take litter with you
Respect Yourself	Do your best	Wash your hands	Be at stop on time	Use your words	Listen to speaker
Respect Learning	Have materials ready	Eat balanced diet	Go directly from bus to class	Go directly to class	Discuss topic in class w/ others

Figure 2.6. Teaching matrix example.

In addition, Tier 1 PBIS includes a continuum of consequences for rule violations. The goal of any consequence should be to (a) decrease the likelihood of future rule violations and (b) provide the student with necessary skills to meet expectations (and receive reinforcement) in the future. This continuum of consequences begins with the least intrusive/aversive for minor rule violations (e.g., reminder and reteaching, extinction, differential reinforcement, conference) and progresses to more intrusive/aversive strategies for moderate (e.g., brief verbal reprimands, response costs, short timeouts) and severe (e.g., in-school detention, out-of-school detentions) violations. It is important to note that behavior reduction procedures are not arbitrarily repeated or intensified for students whose behaviors do not decrease. Instead, decision rules are applied to determine when the next intervention tier should be considered (i.e., responsiveness to intervention).

Behavioral Principles Applied in PBIS Tier 2

In Tier 2, interventions are focused on increasing structure and prompting, intensifying instruction, increasing the frequency and intensity of reinforcement, or some combination of the these (Crone, Horner, & Hawken, 2004). Typically, schools will adopt one or two standardized behavioral interventions to be implemented at the secondary level (e.g., targeted social skills instruction or check-in/check-out). The logic is that students whose behaviors are unresponsive to Tier 1 interventions (school-wide and class-wide) require more intensive and specialized behavioral strategies; however, the same basic intervention can be applied to all students in a similar or group-based manner, making implementation more efficient, relevant, and cost-effective than attempting more costly and complicated individualized programming for each student.

In general, Tier 2 interventions are characterized as having (a) regular and frequent daily behavior assessment (by self or others), (b) direct alignment with the school-wide behavioral expectations, (c) regular and frequent daily positive reinforcement for displays of appropriate behavioral expectations, (d) group-based contingencies that involve positive reinforcers for whole classrooms based on individual student or group performance, (e) behavior reporting to and positive reinforcement opportunities by parents, and (f) routine progress review and intervention adjustments based on student responsiveness.

Behavioral Principles Applied in PBIS Tier 3

In Tier 3, individualized interventions are developed for each student based on student-specific information. These students are identified for Tier 3 interventions because specific behaviors are unresponsive to interventions at Tiers 1 and 2 or occur at such high intensity and risk that immediate supports are indicated. At the crux of this intervention tier is a function-based approach to behavioral assessment and behavior support planning (Crone & Horner, 2003; Sugai, Lewis-Palmer, & Hagan-Burke, 2000). Specifically, trained staff members conduct a functional behavioral assessment to identify typical antecedent and consequence conditions that occasion and maintain, respectively, undesired behavior. In other words, the assessment data identify the "function" or type of reinforcement that maintains the undesired behavior (positive or negative reinforcement).

Trained staff use information about function to guide the development of a positive behavior intervention plan that specifies (a) changes to the antecedent conditions, (b) strategies for teaching replacement behaviors that are more efficient and effective than the problem behavior at meeting the same function, (c) strategies for providing function-based reinforcement contingent on displays of the replacement behavior (i.e., the identified positive or negative reinforcement currently maintaining the undesired behavior), (d) strategies for reinforcing successive approximations of the ultimate desired behavior (i.e., the expected behavior for the identified antecedent conditions that may not meet the same function as the undesired behavior), and (e) strategies for preventing reinforcement of the undesired behavior (i.e., put the undesired behavior on extinction).

Behavior support planning at Tier 3 requires individuals with specialized behavioral competence (e.g., special educator, school psychologist, behavioral counselor) who can work as a team that includes family members to develop comprehensive, positive, thorough, and effective function-based behavior intervention plans. The need for this level of specialized support is evidenced by the student's behavior being relatively unresponsive to intervention attempts at the primary and secondary tiers.

PBIS ENHANCEMENTS

Over the past 10 years, the PBIS framework has been enhanced by important research and evaluation work, especially in the areas of implementation, school climate, school mental health, equity and culture, positive and proactive classroom behavior management, family engagement, and international implementation and cultural adaptation. These enhancements have demonstrated the utility and responsiveness of the prevention based three-tiered continuum to contemporary school issues. Table 2.1 presents a sample of resources, identified by the contribution and contributor, for key enhancement areas.

TABLE 2.1
Recent PBIS Enhancements

Enhancement area	Contribution (contributors)
Implementation	Tiered Fidelity Inventory (Algozzine et al., 2014)
	PBIS Implementation Blueprint (OSEP Center on PBIS, 2017)
	Multi-Tiered Systems of Support (McIntosh & Goodman, 2016)
	Capacity Development (Horner, Sugai, & Fixsen, 2017; Sugai, Simonsen, Freeman, & La Salle, 2016)
	Scaling Best Practice (Horner et al., 2014)
School climate	School Climate and PBIS (La Salle, Meyers, Varjas, & Roach, 2015; OSEP Center on PBIS, 2016)
	School Climate Survey Suite (La Salle, McIntosh, & Eliason, 2016)
	National Climate Change (Sugai, Freeman, Simonsen, La Salle, & Fixsen, 2017)
School mental health	Interconnected Systems Framework (Barrett, Eber, & Weist, 2015)
	School Mental Health and Tiered Systems of Support (Stephan, Sugai, Lever, & Connors, 2015)
Equity and culture	Culture and Behavior Analysis (Sugai, O'Keeffe, & Fallon, 2012)
	Equity in School Discipline (McIntosh, Ty, Horner, & Sugai, 2013)
Classroom behavior management	Supporting and Responding to Behavior (OSEP Center on PBIS, 2015b)
	Classroom Management (Scott, 2017; Simonsen & Myers, 2015)
Family engagement	Alignment, PBIS, and Family Engagement (Weist, Garbacz, Lane, & Kincaid, 2017)
International implementation	Association of Positive Behavior Supports (http://www.apbs.org)
	Norway (Sørlie & Ogden, 2015)

Note. OSEP = Office of Special Education Programs; PBIS = Positive Behavioral Interventions and Supports.

CONCLUSION

Over the past 20 years, PBIS has established its utility and effectiveness as a school-wide intervention approach, in part because of a solid tradition of basic and applied research and practice that is grounded in sound behavioral theory and applied behavior analysis. PBIS is a system-wide intervention approach focused on practices and systems that give schools the capacity to adopt, learn, organize, and implement evidence-based behavioral interventions with fidelity and durability. Specifically, schools implement a continuum of behavior support that includes Tier 1 support for all students across all settings, Tier 2 support for a targeted group of students who display at-risk behavior and require additional support to be successful, and Tier 3 support for individual students who display high-risk behavior and require individualized support to be successful.

In addition to these *practices*, schools implementing PBIS identify relevant *outcomes*, collect *data* to measure progress and guide intervention decisions, and establish *systems* to ensure sustained implementation of adopted practices. PBIS is not a new approach, but instead the demonstrated application and extension of sound behavioral theory, principles, and practices that had beginnings at the individual level in non–education-related settings.

Unlike traditional behavioral approaches that focus on supporting individuals who present significant problem behavior repertoires, PBIS addresses the needs of all students by emphasizing prevention (Biglan, 1995): (a) preventing the development or acquisition of problem behavior; (b) preventing the occurrence and intensifying of existing problem behavior; (c) teaching prosocial behavior that is more efficient, effective, and relevant than problem behavior; and (d) redesigning teaching and learning environments that promote more prosocial behavior.

Finally, given a tradition of continuous research, evaluation, and demonstration, the PBIS framework aligns and integrates with contemporary school concerns, including school mental health, school climate, positive and proactive classroom behavior management, equity, and family engagement. Implementation of the framework continues to expand across the United States and internationally and to adapt to local culture and context.

REFERENCES

Alberto, P. A., & Troutman, A. C. (2006). *Applied behavior analysis for teachers* (7th ed.). Upper Saddle River, NJ: Pearson.

Algozzine, B., Barrett, S., Eber, L., George, H., Horner, R., Lewis, T., . . . Sugai, G. (2014). *SWPBIS Tiered Fidelity Inventory* (version 2.1). OSEP Technical Assistance Center on Positive Behavioral Interventions and Supports. Retrieved from https://www.pbis.org/Common/Cms/files/pbisresources/SWPBIS%20Tiered%20Fidelity%20Inventory%20%28TFI%29.pdf

Algozzine, B., Wang, C., & Violette, A. S. (2011). Reexamining the relationship between academic achievement and social behavior. *Journal of Positive Behavior Interventions, 13,* 3–16. http://dx.doi.org/10.1177/1098300709359084

Baer, D. M., Wolf, M. M., & Risley, T. R. (1968). Some current dimensions of applied behavior analysis. *Journal of Applied Behavior Analysis, 1,* 91–97.

Barrett, S., Eber, L., & Weist, M. (Eds.). (2015). *Advancing education effectiveness: Interconnecting school mental health and school-wide positive behavior support.* OSEP Technical Assistance Center on Positive Behavioral Interventions and Supports. Retrieved from https://www.pbis.org/common/cms/files/pbisresources/Final-Monograph.pdf

Biglan, A. (1995). Translating what we know about the context of antisocial behavior into a lower prevalence of such behavior. *Journal of Applied Behavior Analysis, 28,* 479–492. http://dx.doi.org/10.1901/jaba.1995.28-479

Bradshaw, C. P. (2015). Translating research to practice in bullying prevention. *American Psychologist, 70,* 322–332. http://dx.doi.org/10.1037/a0039114

Bradshaw, C. P., Koth, C. W., Bevans, K. B., Ialongo, N., & Leaf, P. J. (2008). The impact of school-wide positive behavioral interventions and supports (PBIS) on the organizational health of elementary schools. *School Psychology Quarterly, 23,* 462–473. http://dx.doi.org/10.1037/a0012883

Bradshaw, C. P., Koth, C. W., Thornton, L. A., & Leaf, P. J. (2009). Altering school climate through school-wide positive behavioral interventions and supports: Findings from a group-randomized effectiveness trial. *Prevention Science, 10,* 100–115. http://dx.doi.org/10.1007/s11121-008-0114-9

Bradshaw, C. P., Mitchell, M. M., & Leaf, P. J. (2010). Examining the effects of schoolwide positive behavioral interventions and supports on student outcomes: Results from a randomized controlled effectiveness trial in elementary schools. *Journal of Positive Behavior Interventions, 12,* 133–148. http://dx.doi.org/10.1177/1098300709334798

Bradshaw, C. P., Pas, E. T., Goldweber, A., Rosenberg, M. S., & Leaf, P. J. (2012). Integrating school-wide positive behavioral interventions and supports with Tier 2 coaching to student support teams: The PBIS*plus* model. *Advances in School Mental Health Promotion, 5,* 177–193. http://dx.doi.org/10.1080/1754730X.2012.707429

Bradshaw, C. P., Reinke, W. M., Brown, L. D., Bevans, K. B., & Leaf, P. J. (2008). Implementation of school-wide positive behavioral interventions and supports (PBIS) in elementary schools: Observations from a randomized trial. *Education & Treatment of Children, 31,* 1–26. http://dx.doi.org/10.1353/etc.0.0025

Bradshaw, C. P., Waasdorp, T. E., & Leaf, P. J. (2012). Effects of school-wide positive behavioral interventions and supports on child behavior problems. *Pediatrics, 130,* e1136–e1145. http://dx.doi.org/10.1542/peds.2012-0243

Burke, M. D., Hagan-Burke, S., & Sugai, G. (2003). The efficacy of function-based interventions for students with learning disabilities who exhibit escape-maintained problem behaviors: Preliminary results from a single-case experiment. *Learning Disability Quarterly, 26,* 15–25. http://dx.doi.org/10.2307/1593681

Carr, E. G., Dunlap, G., Horner, R. H., Koegel, R. L., Turnbull, A. P., Sailor, W., . . . Fox, L. (2002). Positive behavior support: Evolution of an applied science. *Journal of Positive Behavior Interventions, 4,* 4–16. http://dx.doi.org/10.1177/109830070200400102

Cooper, J. O., Heron, T. E., & Heward, W. L. (2007). *Applied behavior analysis* (2nd ed.). Upper Saddle River, NJ: Prentice Hall.

Crone, D. A., & Horner, R. H. (2003). *Building positive behavior support systems in schools: Functional behavioral assessment.* New York, NY: Guilford Press.

Crone, D. A., Horner, R. H., & Hawken, L. S. (2004). *Responding to problem behavior in schools: The behavior education program*. New York, NY: Guilford Press.

Engelmann, S., & Carnine, D. (1982). *Theory of instruction: Principles and applications*. New York, NY: Irvington.

Fallon, L. M., O'Keeffe, B. V., & Sugai, G. (2012). Consideration of culture and context in school-wide positive behavior support: A review of current literature. *Journal of Positive Behavior Interventions, 14*, 209–219. http://dx.doi.org/10.1177/1098300712442242

Goldweber, A., Waasdorp, T. E., & Bradshaw, C. P. (2013). Examining the link between forms of bullying behaviors and perceptions of safety and belonging among secondary school students. *Journal of School Psychology, 51*, 469–485. http://dx.doi.org/10.1016/j.jsp.2013.04.004

Horner, R. (2016). *Discipline prevention data*. Eugene: OSEP Center on Positive Behavior Interventions and Supports, University of Oregon.

Horner, R. H., Bellamy, G. T., & Colvin, G. T. (1984). Responding in the presence of nontrained stimuli: Implications of generalization error patterns. *Journal of the Association of the Severely Handicapped, 9*, 287–295.

Horner, R. H., Kincaid, D., Sugai, G., Lewis, T., Eber, L., Barrett, S., . . . Johnson, N. (2014). Scaling up school-wide positive behavioral interventions and supports: Experiences of seven states with documented success. *Journal of Positive Behavior Interventions, 16*, 197–208. http://dx.doi.org/10.1177/1098300713503685

Horner, R. H., & Sugai, G. (2015). School-wide PBIS: An example of applied behavior analysis implemented at a scale of social importance. *Behavior Analysis in Practice, 8*, 80–85. http://dx.doi.org/10.1007/s40617-015-0045-4

Horner, R. H., Sugai, G., & Anderson, C. M. (2010). Examining the evidence base for school-wide positive behavior support. *Focus on Exceptionality, 42*, 1–14.

Horner, R. H., Sugai, G., & Fixsen, D. L. (2017). Implementing effective educational practices at scales of social importance. *Clinical Child and Family Psychology Review, 20*, 25–35. http://dx.doi.org/10.1007/s10567-017-0224-7

Horner, R., Sugai, G., Smolkowski, K., Eber, L., Nakasato, J., Todd, A., & Esperanza, J. (2009). A randomized, wait-list controlled effectiveness trial assessing school-wide positive behavior support in elementary schools. *Journal of Positive Behavior Interventions, 11*, 133–145. http://dx.doi.org/10.1177/1098300709332067

Individuals With Disabilities Education Act (IDEA) Amendments of 1997. Public L. No. 105-17. 111 Stat.37 (1997).

Kameenui, E. J., & Simmons, D. C. (1990). *Designing instructional strategies: The prevention of academic learning problems*. Columbus, OH: Merrill.

La Salle, T. P., McIntosh, K., & Eliason, B. M. (2016). *School climate survey suite administration manual*. Eugene: OSEP Technical Assistance Center on Positive Behavioral Interventions and Supports, University of Oregon.

La Salle, T. P. L., Meyers, J., Varjas, K., & Roach, A. (2015). A cultural-ecological model of school climate. *International Journal of School & Educational Psychology, 3*, 157–166. http://dx.doi.org/10.1080/21683603.2015.1047550

Lewis, T. J., & Sugai, G. (1999). Effective behavior support: A systems approach to proactive school-wide management. *Focus on Exceptional Children, 31*, 1–24.

McIntosh, K., Chard, D. J., Boland, J. B., & Horner, R. H. (2006). Demonstration of combined efforts in school-wide academic and behavioral systems and incidence of reading and behavior challenges in early elementary grades. *Journal of Positive Behavior Interventions, 8*, 146–154. http://dx.doi.org/10.1177/10983007060080030301

McIntosh, K., & Goodman, S. (2016). *Integrated multi-tiered systems of support: Blending RTI and PBIS*. New York, NY: Guilford Press.

McIntosh, K., Horner, R. H., Chard, D. J., Dickey, C. R., & Braun, D. H. (2008). Reading skills and function of problem behavior in typical school settings. *The Journal of Special Education, 42*, 131–147. http://dx.doi.org/10.1177/0022466907313253

McIntosh, K., Ty, S. V., Horner, R. H., & Sugai, G. (2013). School-wide positive behavior interventions and supports and academic achievement. In J. Hattie & E. M. Anderman (Eds.), *International guide to student achievement* (pp. 146–148). New York, NY: Taylor & Francis/Routledge.

Nelson, J. R., Johnson, A., & Marchand-Martella, N. (1996). Effects of direct instruction, cooperative learning, and independent learning practices on the classroom behavior of students with behavioral disorders: A comparative analysis. *Journal of Emotional and Behavioral Disorders, 4*, 53–62. http://dx.doi.org/10.1177/106342669600400106

Office of Special Education Programs Technical Assistance Center on Positive Behavioral Interventions and Supports. (2015a). *Positive Behavioral Interventions and Supports (PBIS) Implementation Blueprint: Part 1—Foundations and supporting information*. Eugene: University of Oregon.

Office of Special Education Programs Technical Assistance Center on Positive Behavioral Interventions and Supports. (2015b, October). *Supporting and responding to behavior: Evidence-based classroom strategies for teachers*. Eugene: University of Oregon.

Office of Special Education Programs Technical Assistance Center on Positive Behavioral Interventions and Supports. (2016, September 14). *School climate: Academic achievement and social behavior competence*. Eugene: University of Oregon.

Office of Special Education Programs Technical Assistance Center on Positive Behavioral Interventions and Supports. (2017). *Positive Behavioral Interventions and Supports (PBIS) Implementation Blueprint: Part 2—Self-assessment and action planning*. Eugene: University of Oregon.

Safran, S. P., & Oswald, K. (2003). Positive behavior supports: Can schools reshape disciplinary practices? *Exceptional Children, 69*, 361–373. http://dx.doi.org/10.1177/001440290306900307

Scott, T. M. (2017). *Teaching behavior: Managing classrooms through effective instruction.* Thousand Oaks, CA: Corwin. http://dx.doi.org/10.4135/9781506337883

Simonsen, B., Eber, L., Black, A., Sugai, G., Lewandowski, H., Sims, B., & Myers, D. (2012). Illinois statewide positive behavior interventions and supports: Evolution and impact on student outcomes across years. *Journal of Positive Behavior Interventions, 14,* 5–16. http://dx.doi.org/10.1177/1098300711412601

Simonsen, B., & Myers, D. (2015). *Classwide positive behavior interventions and supports: A guide to proactive classroom management.* New York, NY: Guilford Press.

Simonsen, B., & Sugai, G. (2007). Using school-wide data systems to make decisions efficiently and effectively. *School Psychology Forum, 1,* 46–58.

Skinner, B. F. (1953). *Science of human behavior.* New York, NY: Macmillan.

Sørlie, M., & Ogden, T. (2015). School-wide positive behavior support—Norway: Impacts on problem behavior and classroom climate. *International Journal of School & Educational Psychology, 3,* 202–217. http://dx.doi.org/10.1080/21683603.2015.1060912

Stephan, S. H., Sugai, G., Lever, N., & Connors, E. (2015). Strategies for integrating mental health into schools via a multitiered system of support. *Child and Adolescent Psychiatric Clinics of North America, 24,* 211–231.

Sugai, G., Freeman, J., Simonsen, B., La Salle, T., & Fixsen, D. (2017). National climate change: Doubling down on our precision and emphasis on prevention and behavioral sciences. *Report on Emotional and Behavioral Disorders in Youth, 17,* 58–63.

Sugai, G., & Horner, R. H. (2006). A promising approach for expanding and sustaining school-wide positive behavior support. *School Psychology Review, 35,* 245–259.

Sugai, G., Horner, R. H., Dunlap, G., Hieneman, M., Lewis, T. J., Nelson, C. M., . . . Ruef, M. (2000). Applying positive behavioral support and functional behavioral assessment in schools. *Journal of Positive Behavior Interventions, 2,* 131–143. http://dx.doi.org/10.1177/109830070000200302

Sugai, G., Lewis-Palmer, T., & Hagan-Burke, S. (2000). Overview of the functional behavioral assessment process. *Exceptionality, 8,* 149–160. http://dx.doi.org/10.1207/S15327035EX0803_2

Sugai, G., O'Keeffe, B. V., & Fallon, L. M. (2012). A contextual consideration of culture and school-wide positive behavior support. *Journal of Positive Behavior Interventions, 14,* 197–208. http://dx.doi.org/10.1177/1098300711426334

Sugai, G., Simonsen, B., Freeman, J., & La Salle, T. (2016). Capacity development and multi-tiered systems of support: Guiding principles. *Australasian Journal of Special Education, 40,* 80–98. http://dx.doi.org/10.1017/jse.2016.11

Vargas, J. S. (2013). *Behavior analysis of effective teaching* (2nd ed.). New York, NY: Routledge.

Vincent, C. G., Randall, C., Cartledge, G., Tobin, T. J., & Swain-Bradway, J. (2011). Toward a conceptual integration of cultural responsiveness and schoolwide positive behavior support. *Journal of Positive Behavior Interventions, 13*, 219–229. http://dx.doi.org/10.1177/1098300711399765

Waasdorp, T. E., Bradshaw, C. P., & Leaf, P. J. (2012). The impact of schoolwide positive behavioral interventions and supports on bullying and peer rejection: A randomized controlled effectiveness trial. *Archives of Pediatrics & Adolescent Medicine, 166*, 149–156. http://dx.doi.org/10.1001/archpediatrics.2011.755

Walker, H. M., Horner, R. H., Sugai, G., Bullis, M., Sprague, J. R., Bricker, D., & Kaufman, M. J. (1996). Integrated approaches to preventing antisocial behavior patterns among school-age children and youth. *Journal of Emotional and Behavioral Disorders, 4*, 194–209. http://dx.doi.org/10.1177/106342669600400401

Wang, C., & Algozzine, B. (2011). Rethinking the relationship between reading and behavior in early elementary school. *The Journal of Educational Research, 104*, 100–109. http://dx.doi.org/10.1080/00220670903567380

Weist, M. D., Garbacz, S. A., Lane, K. L., & Kincaid, D. (2017). *Aligning and integrating family engagement in positive behavioral interventions and supports (PBIS): Concepts and strategies for families and schools in key contexts.* Center for Positive Behavioral Interventions and Supports (funded by the Office of Special Education Programs, U.S. Department of Education). Eugene: University of Oregon Press.

Wolery, M. R., Bailey, D. B., Jr., & Sugai, G. M. (1988). *Effective teaching: Principles and procedures of applied behavior analysis with exceptional students.* Boston, MA: Allyn & Bacon.

3

CLASSROOM MANAGEMENT

JOSEPH H. WEHBY AND KATHLEEN LYNNE LANE

Across the United States, K through 12 students come to school with a range of academic, behavior, and social skills. For example, some students have prerequisite academic skills coupled with strong self-determined and interpersonal skills needed to engage in the academic task at hand while successfully negotiating relationship with teachers, other authority figures, and peers (Shogren, Wehmeyer, & Lane, 2016). In contrast, some students have been exposed to a range of risk factors, resulting in splintered academic skills and behavioral excesses and deficits that impede instruction (Walker, Irvin, Noell, & Singer, 1992).

It is the responsibility of all educators to welcome, support, and educate all students, including those who are "ready to learn" as well as those at heightened risk for learning and behavioral challenges (Every Student Succeeds Act [ESSA], 2015). Clearly meeting students' multiple needs—academic, behavioral, and social—is a formidable task. Yet with the introduction of

---

http://dx.doi.org/10.1037/0000126-004
Behavioral Interventions in Schools: Evidence-Based Positive Strategies, Second Edition, S. G. Little and A. Akin-Little (Editors)
Copyright © 2019 by the American Psychological Association. All rights reserved.

tiered systems of support theoretically grounded in applied behavior analysis, school systems are increasingly prepared to meet students' various needs (Horner & Sugai, 2015; Lane, Oakes, Cantwell, & Royer, 2016). A range of tiered systems are in place, such as response to intervention models (Fuchs, Fuchs, & Compton, 2012); Positive Behavior Interventions and Supports (PBIS; Horner & Sugai, 2015); multitiered systems (blending academic and behavioral objectives); and comprehensive, integrated, three-tiered models (Ci3T; blending academic, behavior, and social objectives; Lane, Oakes, & Menzies, 2014). In each tiered systems, a cascade of supports are available to students, including primary (Tier 1) preventions efforts for all, secondary (Tier 2) intervention for approximately 15% of a student body, and tertiary (Tier 3) interventions reserved for students with the most intensive intervention needs.

Ideally, tiered systems comprise evidence-based strategies, practices, and programs at each level of prevention (Cook & Tankersley, 2013). Data from reliable, valid screening tools are used in partnership with other data (e.g., treatment integrity data to make certain intended practices are in place) to connect students with interventions of the appropriate intensity. In each of these systems, the role of classroom management is critical as decades of inquiry have established that academic and behavioral performance are not separate, mutually exclusive entities (Hinshaw, 1992; Lane, 2004; Wehby, Tally, & Falk, 2004). Namely, how teachers teach influences how students behave and how students' behavior influences how teachers teach.

As part of most primary (Tier 1) prevention efforts, school-site teams draw upon the 30 years of teacher expectations literature to establish clear expectations for all key school settings (e.g., classrooms, hallways, buses; Lane, Carter, Common, & Jordan, 2012). Teachers explicitly teach these expectations, provide opportunities for students to practice meeting expectations, and acknowledge students' meeting expectations (e.g., PBIS ticket paired with behavior-specific praise). The intent of these models is to create positive, productive, safe environments for all learners. Yet many teachers work in contexts that do not subscribe to tiered models of prevention. Nonetheless, all teachers are charged with establishing effective, safe learning involvements for students.

Even when students are aware of desired expectations, whether school-wide or classroom expectations (eliminating acquisition deficits), some students may still not meet established expectations. In these instances, students exhibit performance deficits. Essentially, they know the expectations, but the contingencies in place are not sufficiently motivating for students to demonstrate desired expectations. As such, it is imperative for all educators to be well-versed in practical, effective, respectful strategies for (a) preventing challenging behaviors from occurring and (b) responding when challenges arise (Lane, Menzies, Ennis, & Oakes, 2015; Moore, Wehby, Oliver, & Chow, 2017).

Fortunately, volumes have been written about the relation between classroom structure, student decorum, and academic engagement (e.g., Cipani, 2008; Evertson & Weinstein, 2006; Kerr & Nelson, 2002). For example, when classroom structure is characterized by physical arrangements allowing for cooperative learning, independent work, material storage, and transitions coupled with clear operating procedures and well-defined teacher expectations, then classrooms function smoothly. Establishing classroom structure in which classroom events are as predictable as possible is a key goal of any classroom management system (Paine, Radicchi, Rosellini, Deutchman, & Darch, 1983; Walker, Ramsey, & Gresham, 2004). Efficient, effective classroom structures are especially important for students with or at risk for emotional or behavioral disorders (EBDs) who struggle to negotiate the classroom context effectively. When classroom environments are predictable, teacher expectations are understood and reinforced consistently, instructional tasks are on point for students' developmental and instructional levels, and teacher–student interactions are positive, then student engagement is maximized, and interfering behavior problems are minimized (Lane, Wehby, & Cooley, 2006; Walker et al., 2004; Wehby, Symons, Canale, & Go, 1998). It is essential for all teachers—general and special educators alike—to be empowered with effective, efficient PBIS strategies to enhance their classroom management skills.

PURPOSE

In this chapter, we present three low-intensity, proactive strategies that teachers can implement during instruction to facilitate high levels of student engagement and positive decorum and to minimize challenging behaviors that impede instruction. Whereas many consequent-based interventions (e.g., time-out from reinforcement, verbal or gestural redirects) are available for use in response to undesirable behaviors (e.g., when a student is off task or argumentative), antecedent-based approaches can be invoked before challenging behaviors occur. Specifically, we present the following strategies: (a) incorporating instructional choices, (b) increasing students' opportunities to respond (OTRs), and (c) precorrection. We describe each strategy and discuss supporting evidence when used with students with or at risk for learning and behavior challenges. We conclude with a brief discussion of the benefits of empowering teachers with these antecedent-based, teacher-delivered strategies for preventing problems from occurring.

LOW-INTENSITY STRATEGIES TO SUPPORT INSTRUCTION AND MANAGE BEHAVIOR

Incorporating Instructional Choices

Instructional choice is an antecedent-based strategy involving a relatively simple shift educators can incorporate into their instructional practices. Instructional choice involves creating opportunities for students to independently select one or more options and then providing students with the option they selected (Jolivette, Stichter, & McCormick, 2002). Choice-making skills and opportunities are a core component of self-determined behaviors that many individuals contend are related to quality of life for all students—including those with an EBD (Algozzine, Browder, Karvonen, Test, & Wood, 2001; Shogren, Faggella-Luby, Bae, & Wehmeyer, 2004).

Educators can offer a range of instructional choices that can be broadly categorized into two main types: *across-activities* and *within-task activities* (Rispoli et al., 2013). Across-activity choices provide students with opportunities to select among different tasks taking place simultaneously. For example, students might be able to select the order in which they complete the assigned tasks (e.g., choosing which task they would like to do first), or they might choose from a menu of options to demonstrate what they learned at the end of a unit (e.g., writing a story, creating a YouTube video, make a diorama). Within-activity choices keep the task or activity fixed, yet provide students with opportunities to select instructional materials or environmental contexts. For example, the task may be to read a chapter in a book, and students might be given an opportunity to read the chapter on an electronic device or in a hard-bound book (instructional materials) or read it independently at their desk or with a reading partner in the library (environmental context). Choice-making interventions are designed to decrease the aversive nature of a given task by incorporating student-identified preferred activities or stimuli into established instructional tasks (Dunlap, Kern-Dunlap, Clarke, & Robbins, 1991; Jolivette, Wehby, Canale, & Massey, 2001).

Incorporating instructional choices is feasible—requiring limited time, materials, or monetary resources—and they are often-used strategies for enhancing self-determined behaviors for students with EBDs (Kern & State, 2009; Lane, Menzies, et al., 2015). There are various theories as to why instructional choices are effective (Morgan, 2006). For example, Kern and State (2009) noted that there is "something innate in all of us that makes us like to have choices" (p. 4). Some have contended that instructional choice is effective because it allows student to access preferred tasks. Other work suggests that offering choices of nonpreferred activities has resulted in lower rates of challenging behavior (Kern, Mantegna, Vorndran, Bailin, &

Hilt, 2001). Still other theories suggest that providing instructional choices enables students to avoid what they do not want to do at a given time (Kern & State, 2009).

Several studies illustrate applications of instruction choice in a range of contexts and with a variety of students, consistently suggesting a functional relation between the introduction of instructional choices and decreases in disruption and increases in engagement (e.g., Dunlap, Kern-Dunlap, Clarke, & Robbins, 1991; Dyer, Dunlap, & Winterling, 1990; Parsons, Reid, Reynolds, & Bumgarner, 1990). For example, Dunlap and colleagues (1991) illustrated the impact of choice-making with a 12-year-old girl with an emotional disturbance in a self-contained classroom for students. She completed four assignments (math, science, social studies, and handwriting) in two conditions: choice and no choice. In the choice condition, the student chose the order in which tasks were completed. In the no choice condition, the teacher randomly assigned order of completion. Findings indicated higher levels of engagement and lower levels of disruption in the choice condition compared with the no choice condition.

Dunlap et al. (1994) found similar results in a subsequent choice-making studies. Using an ABAB reversal design conducted in a self-contained classroom during independent seat work (English and spelling), the investigators established a functional relation between the introduction of instructional choices (e.g., students chose from a menu of academic tasks related to their educational objectives) for two 11-year-old boys. Results indicated both students demonstrated higher task engagement levels and lower disruption levels relative to the no choice conditions in which the teacher assigned daily lessons.

Instructional choice has also been examined in inclusive settings. For example, Skerbetz and Kostewicz (2013) explored academic choice with five 13-year-old eighth-grade students with EBDs educated in an inclusive setting. Specifically, the study took place in a general education classroom during a brief vocabulary development section of English and language arts. The authors used an ABAB withdrawal design to test the introduction of instructional choice on several student outcomes: task engagement (percentage of intervals engaged), task accuracy (percentage correct), and completion time (time to complete a task). During the choice condition, students selected one task from a packet with four assignments: (a) cloze sentences and multiple-choice items, (b) sentence writing, (c) fill in the blanks and yes/no items, and (d) word maps. During the no choice condition, the teacher assigned tasks. Treatment integrity was assessed by researchers using videotapes, indicating 100% integrity. Results suggested students were more academically engaged, completed more work, and were more accurate in the choice versus no choice conditions. In addition to demonstrating positive student outcomes, social validity data indicated that students enjoyed being offered choices, and teachers reported being willing to incorporate instructional choices in the future.

In a recent systematic review of the evidence base for instructional choices in K through 12 settings, Royer, Lane, Cantwell, and Messenger (2017) found that offering instructional choices resulted in increases in desired academic behavior and decreases in challenging behaviors. Of the 26 studies they reviewed, 12 met at least 80% of the quality indicators established by the Council for Exceptional Children (2014) offering evidence of methodologically rigorous studies from which to draw these conclusions. We do not believe that there is sufficient evidence to establish instructional choice as an evidence-based strategy due to the small number of participants in the reviewed studies as well as the modest effect sizes. As such, additional inquiry is needed to meet this rigorous standard. However, other systematic reviews such Shogren and colleagues' (2004) meta-analysis of single-subject research studies using choice-making intervention for problem behavior found positive outcomes. The review by Shogren et al. (2004) identified 13 studies involved 30 participants, with results indicating that offering choices resulted in significant and sustained reductions in the occurrence of problem behaviors.

In sum, providing instructional choices is an effective, feasible, antecedent-based intervention for increasing engagement and decreasing disruption. Intervention studies suggest positive outcomes for a range of students including middle-school boys with severe behavior problems living in residential settings (Cosden, Gannon, & Haring, 1995), students with developmental disabilities (Dyer et al., 1990), and students with autism (Moes, 1998). In addition to shaping behaviors that facilitate instructional processes, providing instructional choices supports students in acquiring self-determined behaviors that may ultimately improve students' quality of life (Shogren et al., 2004).

Opportunities to Respond

Increasing OTRs is another effective, efficient strategy for supporting academic success, also contributing to a positive, productive classroom climate (Trussell, 2008). This strategy enables students to learn new information, review previously taught material, and build skill fluency, while increasing academic engagement and decreasing challenging behaviors. OTRs are a behavior analytic technique grounded in the notion that when instructional pacing is optimized, students are more likely to be engaged and consequently less likely to be disruptive than when pacing is not optimized (Sutherland & Wright, 2013). Instructional pacing ideally needs to be brisk enough to keep students interested, but not so rapid that students are overwhelmed and unable to participate—a delicate balance indeed (Kounin, 1970).

The OTR strategy is designed to provide students frequent opportunities in a fixed period of time (e.g., 15 minutes) to respond to teacher prompts about targeted academic material. Often OTRs are best used when students have a basic understanding of the concepts to be addressed. In brief, an OTR includes three steps. First, the teacher determines the content or skills to be addressed. Second, the teacher develops a set of questions or prompts to guide the practice session. Finally, the teacher leads an instructional session with a high rate of questioning (at least three questions per minute), rapid student responding, and immediate teacher feedback (Sutherland & Wehby, 2001; Sutherland & Wright, 2013). During the instructional session, the teacher explains to students how they will respond. For example, students may be asked to respond in unison or individually and using a range of responses (e.g., whiteboards, electronic devises, thumbs-up or thumbs-down, response cards, or verbally; Schnorr, Freeman-Green, & Test, 2016; Sutherland & Wright, 2013). After teaching the students how they will respond, the teacher provides the prompt (e.g., a question, "This question is for everyone, What is . . . ?"), offers wait time (e.g., gesturing with fingers to count down from five), asks student to respond (e.g., "Hold up your cards with your response"), and provides feedback (e.g., "That is correct, the answer is . . .").

During this instructional period, teachers provide a brisk pace, offering students a high number of prompts (also referred to as cues or questions) to which students respond as described. The teacher continues until he or she has offered an adequate number of questions to for students to practice the concepts. Some teachers will sort the questions into two groups, those answered correctly and those answered incorrectly during the activity, which can be used to inform future instruction (Messenger et al., 2017).

Similar to instructional choices, increasing OTRs has been used in a range of settings. For example, Sutherland, Alder, and Gunter (2003) used increased OTRs to improve academic outcomes of students with EBDs being education in a special day class of nine students (8–12 years old). In this study, the researchers worked with the teacher to estimate the teacher's current level of OTRs per minute and then shared a graph of baseline levels. Next, the researchers briefly discussed the benefits of using OTRs and explained the steps involved. They set a goal of three OTRs per minute and provided instruction on how to graph his rate of daily OTRs. Results of this ABAB design indicated that increases in OTRs resulted in higher levels of teacher praise, higher levels of student engagement, lower rates of disruptive behavior, and more accurate student responding relative to baseline conditions. The intervention required little training and demonstrated the most pronounced impact on student engagement and disruptive behavior.

In another study, Haydon, Mancil, and Van Loan (2009) examined whether the use of OTRs would improve the disruptive behavior of a fifth-grade girl educated in a self-contained elementary classroom. The teacher participated in a 30-minute training to learn how to use the OTR strategy. Specifically, he reviewed the definition and purpose of OTRs, watched video clips of how to use the OTR strategy, and practiced delivering questions to obtain a rate of at least three questions per minute. In this study, the teacher did the following: cued students to reply to the questions, provided enough wait time for all students to respond, presented the next questions to students, and offered feedback following their responses. The teacher increased his OTR rate to at least three questions per minute, with students responding chorally. During the intervention conditions, the target student's performance improved as evidenced by increased task engagement, decreased disruptive behavior, and increased response accuracy.

As discussed previously, there is a clear link between academic engagement and problem behavior in classrooms. Namely, classrooms with higher rates of academic instruction are often classrooms with the lowest rates of challenging behavior (Gunter & Denny, 1998). Unfortunately, decades of descriptive research have established students exhibiting high levels of challenging behaviors often receive low levels of instruction (Carr, Taylor, & Robinson, 1991). For example, Wehby et al. (1998) indicated that students exhibiting high rates of aggressive behavior were likely to receive less than half of the instruction time offered to students with low rates of aggressive behavior in the same classroom. Given the inverse relation between academic instruction and challenging behavior, many researchers and practitioners have focused on empowering teachers with low-intensity, feasible strategies to increase academic engagement and thereby decrease challenging behaviors. Increasing OTRs is an ideal strategy for accomplishing this goal and can be used to adjust pacing during whole group, small group, and individual instruction (Gunter & Denny, 1998; Sutherland et al., 2003).

In a systematic review of the OTR literature, Sutherland and Wehby (2001) identified six studies that examined the impact of increasing OTRs on a variety of misbehavior that occurs in classrooms. Results of this review indicated increases in OTRs—a relatively simple strategy—typically yielded higher levels of engagement that, in turn, lead to lower levels of undesirable behavior. In addition, it is important to note that several techniques are available for supporting teachers in installing and sustaining the use of OTRs. For example, self-evaluation and performance feedback are established methods of increasing the use of targeted instructional behaviors (Sutherland et al., 2003; Sutherland & Wehby, 2001; Sutherland, Wehby, & Copeland, 2000). In some studies, present levels of OTRs have been recorded using direct observation techniques and shared with teachers, with a goal of establishing existing and desired OTR levels during a specified period of time (e.g., 15 minutes).

In sum, the use of OTRs is an effective, efficient strategy for supporting engagement and decreasing challenging behaviors. Using relatively simple, straightforward procedures, teachers are able to assess the frequency of their instructional practices (including OTRs) and monitor the shifts in student performance.

Precorrection

Precorrection is another easy-to-use, effective strategy that teachers can incorporate into their instructional repertoire. Precorrection involves determining predictable contexts typically resulting in challenging behavior and offering students supports, prompts, and reinforcement for engaging in desired behaviors (Crosby, Jolivette, & Patterson, 2006). For example, rather than raising one's voice to students when they run in the hallway or take far too long to transition between activities in a science lab, teachers can remind them of the expectation before taking students into the hallway or starting lab activities. In these instances, the desired behavior is prompted, and students can receive reinforcement for meeting expectations, preventing these problems from happening.

Colvin, Sugai, and Patching (1993) introduced a set of step-by-step procedures for using the precorrection strategy. First, teachers determine the context in which challenging behaviors often occur. Second, they define the expected behavior, which is often included in a school-wide expectation matrix in schools implementing school-wide PBIS. Third, they modify the context by adjusting teacher behavior (e.g., reteaching expectations just before students move into the challenging context) or making environmental changes (e.g., posting expectations or other discriminative stimuli in the setting of interest). Fourth, teachers afford students opportunities to practice expected behaviors (e.g., practicing walking in the hallway with quite voices and in an orderly manner). Fifth, teachers acknowledge students for meeting expectations, using behavior-specific praise (often paired with a ticket or other token). Sixth, teachers develop a prompting plan to remind students to perform the desired behaviors. Seventh, teachers establish a plan to monitor plan effectiveness—including measuring the extent to which the intervention is put in place as planned (treatment integrity) as well as student performance. These seven steps are comprehensive and include adjustment to antecedents and consequences to prevent challenging behaviors from occurring and prompt desired behavior.

We note that precorrection is different from correction. *Correction* entails letting an individual student (or group of students) know that an error has occurred, providing corrective statements explaining how to perform the desired response, offering opportunities to perform the task, and providing reinforcement for correct performance (Colvin et al., 1993). In contrast, precorrection is proactive in that the focus is on anticipating potential circumstances (e.g., settings, time of day, or activities) that could—or often do—result in challenging behaviors. Whereas correction is consequence-based strategy, precorrection involves antecedent and consequence adjustments. Some benefits of precorrection relative to correction is that the teacher prevent the undesirable behavior from happening and foster more positive teacher–student interactions, which is particularly important for students with and at risk for an EBD (Lane, Menzies, et al., 2015).

Precorrection has been used effectively to decrease problem behaviors in a range of settings. For example, Stormont, Smith, and Lewis (2007) partnered with two teachers and one teaching assistant working in two Head Start centers to increase their use of precorrection and behavior-specific praise statements. Researchers collected data on teacher and student behaviors. They used event-recording procedures to collect data on teacher's use of behavior-specific praise, precorrection statements, and reprimand statements. They also assessed students' problem behavior. As part of the intervention, teachers learned how to use precorrection statements by reviewing expectations with students before they joined small group lessons and increasing the use of behavior-specific praise during groups when students met expectations. The training was brief, requiring a 30-minute individual meeting with each student. Using a multiple-baseline across teachers design, results indicated two of the three teachers increased their use of the precorrection strategy (with the third teacher already using precorrections during baseline). All teachers increased their use of behavior-specific praise statements and decreased the use of reprimands. Teachers' social validity data were positive, indicating that they viewed the intervention as effective and were likely to use this intervention in the future.

Precorrection has also been used successfully in noninstructional settings as well. Lewis, Colvin, and Sugai (2000) used precorrection coupled with active supervision to improve elementary students' playground behavior. In this study, the precorrection strategy involved first identifying undesirable behavior exhibited during recess and determining the more desirable behaviors. They printed expectations, reviewed them with students, and then provided precorrection statements before students went to recesses. The active supervision involved a 15-minute meeting and 10-minute follow-up session, during which playground supervisors were instructed to walk around the playground, visually scan all areas, and interact with students. A multiple-baseline design across recess periods indicated that although there was little change in supervisor's playground monitoring behavior, there was a decrease in student problem behavior during structured and unstructured activities as a result of the precorrection strategy. In this case, student behavior changed substantially in response to the posting of rules and reminders of playground expectations.

Precorrection, like instructional choice and OTRs, has been used successfully with a range of students and in a variety of settings. In a recent systematic review of the evidence base for precorrection in K through 12 settings, Ennis, Royer, Lane, and Griffith (2017) found that using precorrection resulted in positive changes in desired behaviors. Of the 10 studies included in the reviews, half met at least 80% of quality indicators established by the Council for Exceptional Children (2014). These methodologically sound studies involved more than 20 students, supporting the use of precorrection.

In sum, precorrection is an effective, efficient strategy that can be used instead of punishment procedures (e.g., raising our voice or withholding recess) to prevent challenging behaviors from occurring. This strategy fosters more positive, productive relationships between teachers and students and provides a respectful way of preventing challenging behaviors from occurring. After determining when precorrection is needed, teachers have flexibility in determining how to provide precorrections (e.g., gentle reminders regarding expected behavior for an activity or a brief series of questions such as, "Joe, what side of the hallway will our class walk on when we go to the assembly?").

CONCLUSION

In this chapter, we introduced three low-intensity, proactive, feasible strategies that teachers can implement during instruction: incorporating instructional choices, increasing opportunities to respond, and using precorrection. Each strategy is easy to implement, requires little time, and contributes to positive teacher–student interactions. When implemented with integrity, these three practical strategies have demonstrated success in increasing students' engagement and minimize challenging behaviors that impede instruction (Lane, Falk, & Wehby, 2006). Whereas consequence-based interventions such as verbal redirects and time-out from reinforcement may be effective in shaping student behavior, the strategies presented here offer respectful, antecedent-based approaches that can be invoked before challenging behaviors occur. Such strategies empower teachers to better serve a range of students with learning and behavior challenges, including students with EBDs, who often struggle on many fronts (e.g., academically, behaviorally, socially).

Educators are charged with the formidable task of meeting students' academic, behavioral, and social needs, with each student having various competencies in these areas (ESSA, 2015). Some educators work in tiered systems offering effective, efficient structures for assisting students who require more than primary (Tier 1) prevention efforts, and others do not. Yet, regardless of the school context, all teachers need to be equipped to meet the increasingly diverse needs of today's pre-K through 12 student body. The strategies presented here are intended to empower teachers with effective, efficient, low-intensity supports (Lane, Menzies, et al., 2015; Wehby et al., 1998). As discussed, when incorporated with integrity into teachers' instruction repertoires, these strategies facilitate instruction and minimize disruption of the educational environment due to challenging behaviors.

It is critical for teacher preparation programs and technical assistance providers to offer high-quality professional learning opportunities to support educators in building fluency in these and other low-intensity supports, thus increasing the likelihood of school success (Lane, Menzies, et al., 2015). We encourage interested readers to consider a range of resources for offering professional learning (e.g., practice guides, web-based resources) according to adult learner preferences (Lane, Carter, Jenkins, Dwiggins, & Germer, 2015).

REFERENCES

Algozzine, B., Browder, D., Karvonen, M., Test, D. W., & Wood, W. M. (2001). Effects of interventions to promote self-determination for individuals with disabilities. *Review of Educational Research, 71*, 219–277. http://dx.doi.org/10.3102/00346543071002219

Carr, E. G., Taylor, J. C., & Robinson, S. (1991). The effects of severe behavior problems in children on the teaching behavior of adults. *Journal of Applied Behavior Analysis, 24*, 523–535. http://dx.doi.org/10.1901/jaba.1991.24-523

Cipani, E. (2008). *Classroom management for all teachers: Plans for evidence-based practice* (3rd ed.). Columbus, OH: Pearson Merrill Prentice Hall.

Colvin, G., Sugai, G., & Patching, B. (1993). Precorrection: An instructional approach for managing predictable problem behaviors. *Intervention in School and Clinic, 28*, 143–150. http://dx.doi.org/10.1177/105345129302800304

Cook, B., & Tankersley, M. (Eds.). (2013). *Effective practices in special education.* Boston, MA: Pearson.

Cosden, M., Gannon, C., & Haring, T. G. (1995). Teacher-control versus student-control over choice of task and reinforcement for students with severe behavior problems. *Journal of Behavioral Education, 5*, 11–27. http://dx.doi.org/10.1007/BF02110212

Council for Exceptional Children. (2014). *Council for Exceptional Children standards for evidence-based practices in special education.* Arlington, VA: Author.

Crosby, S., Jolivette, K., & Patterson, D. (2006). Using precorrection to manage inappropriate academic and social behaviors. *Beyond Behavior, 16*, 14–17.

Dunlap, G., dePerczel, M., Clarke, S., Wilson, D., Wright, S., White, R., & Gomez, A. (1994). Choice making to promote adaptive behavior for students with emotional and behavioral challenges. *Journal of Applied Behavior Analysis, 27*, 505–518.

Dunlap, G., Kern-Dunlap, L., Clarke, S., & Robbins, F. R. (1991). Functional assessment, curricular revision, and severe behavior problems. *Journal of Applied Behavior Analysis, 24*, 387–397. http://dx.doi.org/10.1901/jaba.1991.24-387

Dyer, K., Dunlap, G., & Winterling, V. (1990). Effects of choice making on the serious problem behaviors of students with severe handicaps. *Journal of Applied Behavior Analysis, 23*, 515–524.

Ennis, R. P., Royer, D. J., Lane, K. L., & Griffith, C. (2017). A systematic review of precorrection in PK–12 settings. *Education and Treatment of Children, 40*, 465–495.

Evertson, C. M., & Weinstein, C. S. (2006). *Handbook of classroom management: Research, practice, and contemporary issues.* Mahwah, NJ: Erlbaum.

Every Student Succeeds Act of 2015, 20 U.S.C. 6301 et seq. (2015).

Fuchs, D., Fuchs, L. S., & Compton, D. L. (2012). Smart RTI: A next-generation approach to multilevel prevention. *Exceptional Children, 78*, 263–279. http://dx.doi.org/10.1177/001440291207800301

Gunter, P. L., & Denny, R. K. (1998). Trends and issues in research regarding academic instruction of students with emotional and behavioral disorders. *Behavioral Disorders, 24*, 44–50. http://dx.doi.org/10.1177/019874299802400104

Haydon, T., Mancil, G. R., & Van Loan, C. (2009). Using opportunities to respond in a general education classroom: A case study. *Education & Treatment of Children, 32*, 267–278. http://dx.doi.org/10.1353/etc.0.0052

Hinshaw, S. P. (1992). Externalizing behavior problems and academic underachievement in childhood and adolescence: Causal relationships and underlying mechanisms. *Psychological Bulletin, 111*, 127–155. http://dx.doi.org/10.1037/0033-2909.111.1.127

Horner, R. H., & Sugai, G. (2015). School-wide PBIS: An example of applied behavior analysis implemented at a scale of social importance. *Behavior Analysis in Practice, 8*, 80–85. http://dx.doi.org/10.1007/s40617-015-0045-4

Jolivette, K., Stichter, J. P., & McCormick, K. M. (2002). Making choices—Improving behavior—Engaging in learning. *Teaching Exceptional Children, 34*, 24–29. http://dx.doi.org/10.1177/004005990203400303

Jolivette, K., Wehby, J. H., Canale, J., & Massey, N. G. (2001). Effects of choice-making opportunities on the behavior of students with emotional and behavioral disorders. *Behavioral Disorders, 26*, 131–145. http://dx.doi.org/10.1177/019874290102600203

Kern, L., Mantegna, M. E., Vorndran, C. M., Bailin, D., & Hilt, A. (2001). Choice of task sequence to reduce problem behaviors. *Journal of Positive Behavior Interventions, 3*, 3–10. http://dx.doi.org/10.1177/109830070100300102

Kern, L., & State, T. M. (2009). Incorporating choice and preferred activities into classwide instruction. *Beyond Behavior, 18,* 3–11.

Kerr, M. M., & Nelson, C. M. (2002). *Strategies for addressing behavior problems in the classroom* (5th ed.). Columbus, OH: Merrill Prentice Hall.

Kounin, J. S. (1970). *Discipline and group management in classrooms.* New York, NY: Rinehart and Winston.

Lane, K. L. (2004). Academic instruction and tutoring interventions for students with emotional/behavioral disorders: 1990 to present. In R. B. Rutherford, M. M. Quinn, & S. R. Mathur (Eds.), *Handbook of research in emotional and behavioral disorders* (pp. 462–486). New York, NY: Guilford Press.

Lane, K. L., Carter, E. W., Common, E., & Jordan, A. (2012). Teacher expectations for student performance: Lessons learned and implications for research and practice. In B. G. Cook, M. Tankersley, & T. J. Landrum (Eds.), *Classroom behavior, contexts, and interventions: Advances in learning and behavioral disabilities* (Vol. 25, pp. 95–129). Bingley, England: Emerald. http://dx.doi.org/10.1108/S0735-004X(2012)0000025008

Lane, K. L., Carter, E. W., Jenkins, A., Dwiggins, L., & Germer, K. (2015). Supporting comprehensive, integrated, three-tiered models of prevention in schools: Administrators' perspectives. *Journal of Positive Behavior Interventions, 17,* 209–222. http://dx.doi.org/10.1177/1098300715578916

Lane, K. L., Falk, K., & Wehby, J. H. (2006). Classroom management in special education classrooms and resource rooms. In C. M. Evertson & C. S. Weinstein (Eds.), *Handbook of classroom management: Research, practice, and contemporary issues* (pp. 439–460). Mahwah, NJ: Erlbaum.

Lane, K. L., Menzies, H. M., Ennis, R. P., & Oakes, W. P. (2015). *Supporting behavior for school success: A step-by-step guide to key strategies.* New York, NY: Guilford Press.

Lane, K. L., Oakes, W. P., Cantwell, E. D., & Royer, D. J. (2016). *Building and installing comprehensive, integrated, three-tiered (Ci3T) models of prevention: A practical guide to supporting school success* [Interactive eBook]. Phoenix, AZ: KOI Education.

Lane, K. L., Oakes, W. P., & Menzies, H. M. (2014). Comprehensive, integrated, three-tiered models of prevention: Why does my school—and district—need an integrated approach to meet students' academic, behavioral, and social needs? *Preventing School Failure, 58,* 121–128. http://dx.doi.org/10.1080/1045988X.2014.893977

Lane, K. L., Wehby, J. H., & Cooley, C. (2006). Teacher expectations of students' classroom behavior across the grade span: Which social skills are necessary for success? *Exceptional Children, 72,* 153–167. http://dx.doi.org/10.1177/001440290607200202

Lewis, T. J., Colvin, G., & Sugai, G. (2000). The effects of pre-correction and active supervision on the recess behavior of elementary students. *Education and Treatment of Children, 23,* 109–121.

Messenger, M., Lane, K. L., Common, E., Oakes, W. P., Menzies, H. M., Cantwell, E. D., & Ennis, R. P. (2017). Empowering teachers with low-intensity strategies to support student engagement: Increasing opportunities to respond for students with internalizing behaviors. *Behavioral Disorders, 42*, 170–184.

Moes, D. R. (1998). Integrating choice-making opportunities within teacher-assigned academic tasks to facilitate the performance of children with autism. *Journal of the Association for Persons With Severe Handicaps, 10*, 183–193.

Moore, T. C., Wehby, J. H., Oliver, R., & Chow, J. C. (2017). Teachers' reported knowledge and implementation of research-based classroom and behavior management strategies. *Remedial and Special Education, 38*, 222–232. http://dx.doi.org/10.1177/0741932516683631

Morgan, P. L. (2006). Increasing task engagement using preference or choice-making: Some behavioral and methodological factors affecting their efficacy as classroom interventions. *Remedial and Special Education, 27*, 176–187. http://dx.doi.org/10.1177/07419325060270030601

Paine, S. C., Radicchi, J., Rosellini, L. C., Deutchman, L., & Darch, C. B. (1983). *Structuring your classroom for academic success.* Champaign, IL: Research Press.

Parsons, M. B., Reid, D. H., Reynolds, J., & Bumgarner, M. (1990). Effects of chosen versus assigned jobs on the work performance of persons with severe handicaps. *Journal of Applied Behavior Analysis, 23*, 253–258.

Rispoli, M., Lang, R., Neely, L., Camargo, S., Hutchins, N., Davenport, K., & Goodwyn, F. (2013). A comparison of within- and across-activity choices for reducing challenging behavior in children with autism spectrum disorders. *Journal of Behavioral Education, 22*, 66–83. http://dx.doi.org/10.1007/s10864-012-9164-y

Royer, D. J., Lane, K. L., Cantwell, E. D., & Messenger, M. (2017). A systematic review of the evidence base for instructional choice in K–12 settings. *Behavioral Disorders, 42*, 89–107. http://dx.doi.org/10.1177/0198742916688655

Schnorr, C. I., Freeman-Green, S., & Test, D. W. (2016). Response cards as a strategy for increasing opportunities to respond: An examination of the evidence. *Remedial and Special Education, 37*, 41–54. http://dx.doi.org/10.1177/0741932515575614

Shogren, K. A., Faggella-Luby, M. N., Bae, S. J., & Wehmeyer, M. L. (2004). The effect of choice-making as an intervention for problem behavior: A meta-analysis. *Journal of Positive Behavior Interventions, 6*, 228–237. http://dx.doi.org/10.1177/10983007040060040401

Shogren, K. A., Wehmeyer, M. L., & Lane, K. L. (2016). Embedding interventions to promote self-determination within multitiered systems of supports. *Exceptionality, 24*, 213–224. Advance online publication. http://dx.doi.org/10.1080/09362835.2015.1064421

Skerbetz, M. D., & Kostewicz, D. E. (2013). Academic choice for included students with emotional and behavioral disorders. *Preventing School Failure, 57*, 212–222. http://dx.doi.org/10.1080/1045988X.2012.701252

Stormont, M. A., Smith, S. C., & Lewis, T. J. (2007). Teacher implementation of precorrection and praise statements in Head Start classrooms as a component of a program-wide system of positive behavior support. *Journal of Behavioral Education, 16,* 280–290. http://dx.doi.org/10.1007/s10864-007-9040-3

Sutherland, K. S., Alder, N., & Gunter, P. L. (2003). The effect of varying rates of opportunities to respond to academic requests on the classroom behavior of students with EBD. *Journal of Emotional and Behavioral Disorders, 11,* 239–248. http://dx.doi.org/10.1177/106342660301100040501

Sutherland, K. S., & Wehby, J. H. (2001). The effect of self-evaluation on teaching behavior in classrooms for students with emotional and behavioral disorders. *The Journal of Special Education, 35,* 161–171. http://dx.doi.org/10.1177/002246690103500306

Sutherland, K. S., Wehby, J. H., & Copeland, S. R. (2000). Effect of varying rates of behavior-specific praise on the on-task behavior of students with EBD. *Journal of Emotional and Behavioral Disorders, 8,* 2–8. http://dx.doi.org/10.1177/106342660000800101

Sutherland, K., & Wright, S. A. (2013). *Students with disabilities and academic engagement: Classroom-based interventions.* In K. L. Lane, B. G. Cook, & M. Tankersley (Eds.), *Research-based strategies for improving outcomes in behavior.* Boston, MA: Pearson.

Trussell, R. P. (2008). Classroom universals to prevent problem behaviors. *Intervention in School and Clinic, 43,* 179–185. http://dx.doi.org/10.1177/1053451207311678

Walker, H. M., Irvin, I. K., Noell, J., & Singer, G. H. S. (1992). A construct score approach to the assessment of social competence: Rationale, technological considerations, and anticipated outcomes. *Behavior Modification, 16,* 448–474. http://dx.doi.org/10.1177/01454455920164002

Walker, H. M., Ramsey, E., & Gresham, F. M. (2004). *Antisocial behavior in school: Evidence-based practices.* Belmont, CA: Wadsworth.

Wehby, J. H., Symons, F. J., Canale, J. A., & Go, F. J. (1998). Teaching practices in classrooms for students with emotional and behavioral disorders: Discrepancies between recommendations and observations. *Behavioral Disorders, 24,* 51–56. http://dx.doi.org/10.1177/019874299802400109

Wehby, J. H., Tally, B. B., & Falk, K. B. (2004). Identifying the relation between the function of student problem behavior and teacher instructional behavior. *Assessment for Effective Instruction, 30,* 41–51. http://dx.doi.org/10.1177/073724770403000104

4

REDUCTIVE PROCEDURES: POSITIVE APPROACHES TO REDUCING THE INCIDENCE OF PROBLEM BEHAVIOR

STEVEN G. LITTLE AND ANGELEQUE AKIN-LITTLE

It is the intent of this chapter to present an overview of empirically supported and socially valid procedures to reduce the incidence of problem behavior in the classroom and summarize supplemental positive approaches to complement and build on these reductive procedures. Specifically, this chapter has three major objectives: (a) to discuss the concept of behavioral momentum and relate Newton's second law of motion to behavioral functioning; (b) to summarize the most recent research on reductive procedures, particularly time-out; and (c) to provide school personnel with evidence-based approaches to the use of reductive procedures that emphasize the positive, proper, and proactive aspects.

BEHAVIORAL MOMENTUM AND NEWTON'S SECOND LAW OF MOTION

The concept of behavioral momentum provides a structure for understanding the effective use of reductive procedures. Nevin (2002) drew on physics in explaining the metaphor of behavioral momentum. Applications of this theory have been used to explain reinforcer rates in individuals with developmental disabilities (Dube, McIlvane, Mazzitelli, & McNamara, 2003), verbal fluency in children with autism spectrum disorder (ASD; Kelly & Holloway, 2015), academic achievement for students with behavior disorders (Belfiore, Lee, Scheeler, & Klein, 2002), reading persistence in adolescents with emotional and behavioral disorders (Vostal & Lee, 2011), behavior of children with conduct disorder (Strand, 2000), transferring stimulus control when working with a student with autism (Ray, Skinner, & Watson, 1999), and the duration and velocity of successful serves in high school girls volleyball (Wanzek, Houlihan, & Homan, 2012). Specifically, in physics a moving body possesses both mass and velocity, with the velocity of the object remaining constant under constant conditions. To change the velocity of the object, it is necessary to exert an external force in inverse proportion to its mass. In terms of student inappropriate behavior, the baseline level of that behavior is considered to be the initial velocity, and the resistance to change of that response rate is its mass—that is, the lesser the change in response rate as a function of intervention, the greater the behavioral mass and the greater the strength of the intervention needed to produce change in behavior. The goal of intervention is believed to be not just a function of decreasing the momentum of the undesirable behavior but also to increase the momentum of the alternate, more desirable behavior.

Gresham (2005) drew on the metaphor of behavioral momentum in discussing factors related to resistance to intervention. These include (a) severity of behavior (initial velocity), which is related to the amount of reinforcement the behavior is receiving before intervention; (b) chronicity of behavior; and (c) generalization of behavior change (i.e., the problem of behavior change not generalizing outside of the intervention environment). Generalization is a problem when the intervention focuses primarily on reducing the momentum of the undesirable behavior and not attempting to increase the momentum of an alternative, more positive behavior. Indeed, it is unethical to leave a behavioral vacuum by focusing only on the reduction of the problematic behavior; appropriate behavior must also be taught. Gresham's factors also include (d) tolerance of behavior, arguing that the more the behavior disrupts others, the more likely people in the environment will take steps to reduce its occurrence; and (e) treatment strength. In general, all other things being equal, the greater the momentum of the problem behavior, the stronger the treatments will have to be to increase the likelihood of producing behavior change in the desirable direction.

For the purpose of this chapter, we also draw on another analogy to physics that relates to the concept of behavioral momentum and helps conceptualize patterns of disruptive behavior in the classroom. Newton's second law of motion states that the net force acting on an object equals the product of the mass and the acceleration of the object. In other words, force is believed to equal mass times acceleration ($F = MA$). We can conceptualize force as analogous to the magnitude of the behavior and mass, as in behavioral momentum theory, the behavior's resistance to change. What behavioral momentum theory fails to clearly articulate is the acceleration of the behavior. In studies investigating the behavioral concept of chaining (Cooper, Heron, & Heward, 2007), when a behavioral sequence leads to a reinforcer, each response in the sequence acts as a conditioned reinforcer for the preceding response. We know that if a behavior (positive or negative) is occurring on a regular basis in the classroom, it is leading to some form of reinforcement for that student. If we can identify the steps in the chain leading to the undesirable behavior, we can disrupt the acceleration and, therefore, the force of the behavior. The conceptualization of time-out, as discussed later in this chapter, relies heavily on this concept.

REDUCTIVE PROCEDURES AND REINFORCEMENT

The use of punishment procedures, although widely practiced, is independently insufficient to improve a student's behavior (Sarafino, 2011). In addition, punishment procedures may lead to undesirable associations with the punishing agent (teacher or parent), the environment in which the punishment occurs (e.g., classroom), or appropriate behaviors that may be temporally related to the undesirable behavior (e.g., classwork, homework). This has led many people to recommend the use of reinforcement-based procedures as one method to reduce the incidence of undesirable behavior (Alberto & Troutman, 2013). It has also been recommended that the use of pretreatment functional analysis can increase the likelihood of the use of reinforcement-based procedures by developing an understanding of the factors maintaining the inappropriate behavior (Wadsworth, Hansen, & Wills, 2015; Wilder, Harris, Reagan, & Rasey, 2007). The four levels of reductive procedures to be discussed include (a) differential reinforcement of low rates of behavior (DRL), (b) differential reinforcement of other behavior (DRO), (c) differential reinforcement of incompatible behavior (DRI), and (d) differential reinforcement of alternative behavior (DRA).

Differential Reinforcement of Low Rates of Behavior

Under this schedule, reinforcement is contingent on a response being emitted fewer than a predetermined number of times after a specified minimum time period has elapsed. DRL has been demonstrated to be effective in reducing problem behavior, but it requires continuous effort by the teacher (Austin & Bevan, 2011), and its utility in the classroom may be limited. This may explain why there are few recent examples of the use of DRL in an educational context. Laprime and Dittrich (2014) used a social story, discrimination training, and DRL with response cost to decrease vocal stereotypy in a preschooler diagnosed with ASD. Eccles and Pitchford (1997) used DRL with noncompliance in a multielement plan with a 6-year-old boy with severe behavior problems and noted sufficient improvement in 12 weeks. The only other school-based study published after 1995 is an application of DRL targeting a 13-year-old girl with psychogenic cough (Watson & Heindl, 1996).

Differential Reinforcement of Other Behavior

DRO is the most researched differential reinforcement procedure and is sometimes referred to as differential reinforcement of zero responding. With DRO, reinforcement occurs after a specified period of time in which there are no occurrences of the target behavior. When using a DRO schedule, it is best to start off with a relatively short time period determined based on baseline rate of behavior and then gradually increase the interval required to earn reinforcement until the behavior is occurring rarely, if at all, and the reinforcement given is minimal (Little, Akin-Little, & Cook, 2009).

DRO can be either whole interval or momentary. In whole-interval DRO (wDRO), the target behavior must not be exhibited during the entire interval. In momentary DRO (mDRO) behavior is sampled at the specific moment the interval ends, and reinforcement is given if the target behavior is not evident at that time. Vance, Gresham, and Dart (2012) used DRO to decrease problem behavior for students whose problem behaviors were hypothesized to be functionally related to peer attention. Nuernberger, Vargo, and Ringdahl (2013) found DRO to be successful in reducing repetitive behavior in a teenager with ASD. Conyers, Miltenberger, Romaniuk, Kopp, and Himle (2003) found wDRO with edible reinforcement to be more effective in reducing mild disruptive behavior in a preschool classroom than mDRO or wDRO with token reinforcers. In addition, DRO procedures have been found to be effective in eliminating body rocking in a boy with autism (Shabani, Wilder, & Flood, 2001), reducing disruptive behavior (e.g., Conyers et al., 2003), aggression (Hegel & Ferguson, 2000), and a variety of self-injurious behaviors (Lindberg, Iwata, Kahng, & DeLeon, 1999). Perhaps most encouraging are the enhanced effects found when combining DRO procedures with extinction (Neidert, Iwata, & Dozier, 2005; Wilder, Chen, Atwell, Pritchard, & Weinstein, 2006).

Differential Reinforcement of Incompatible Behavior and Differential Reinforcement of Alternative Behavior

DRI involves reinforcing a response that is opposite, or incompatible, with the target behavior. For example, sitting and standing cannot occur at the same time. DRA, in contrast, involves reinforcing a positive behavior that is not necessarily incompatible with the target behavior. We have combined our discussion of these schedules as research based on functional analyses has found that DRA is more effective when using a replacement behavior that is functionally equivalent rather than just incompatible (Vollmer & Iwata, 1992).

DRA schedules also appear to have the greatest applicability in the classroom of all the differential reinforcement schedules. The primary purpose of students being in schools is the acquisition of academic competencies. If teachers are concerned about student disruptive and inattentive behavior, the most logical alternative behavior to reinforce would be academic performance. This is particularly true if the function of a student's inappropriate behavior is to garner teacher attention. The logical way to proceed with intervention would be structured ignoring (extinction) of the student's inappropriate behavior with attention (praise) being provided for appropriate academic behaviors. Reinforcement of academic behavior has been consistently demonstrated to contribute to increases in on-task behavior and decreases in disruptive behavior (Little & Akin-Little, 2014). Although reinforcement of academic behavior has demonstrated efficacy, teacher attention for appropriate academic behaviors may be even more effective, and it is relatively easy for teachers to implement (Maag, 2001). DRA has also been found to be effective in reducing problem behavior (Mace et al., 2009), reduction in challenging behavior and increase in replacement behavior (Flynn & Lo, 2016), and increases in social interaction (Harper, Iwata, & Camp, 2013). However, treatment challenges unique to DRA need to be considered (Vollmer, Roane, Ringdahl, & Marcus, 1999). For example, if the implementer is not paying close attention, he or she could potentially provide reinforcement to the student, even though there are some occurrences of the problem behavior. Or the implementer could withhold reinforcement even though there are some occurrences of the alternative behavior. The point here is that DRA can be a powerful intervention if implemented consistently and accurately.

Extinction

Extinction has been defined as "the discontinuing of a reinforcement of a previously reinforced behavior (i.e., responses no longer produce reinforcement): the primary effect is a decrease in the frequency of the behavior until it reaches a pre-reinforced level or ceases to occur" (Cooper et al., 2007, p. 695). It is important to recognize that although extinction may be an effective procedure to reduce or eliminate the incidence of maladaptive behaviors, it does not aid in the development of appropriate prosocial behaviors. The most effective use of extinction is in combination with one of the differential reinforcement procedures described earlier, particularly DRA or DRI (Kazdin, 2012).

Research suggests that treatment with operant extinction may result in adverse side effects (Waller & Mays, 2007). Foremost is the extinction burst, an increase in the frequency of the target behavior when an extinction procedure is initially implemented (Cooper et al., 2007). Lerman and Iwata (1995) found that an extinction burst occurred in approximately one third of the cases when extinction was the sole intervention. When combined with other treatment components such as differential reinforcement, the incidence of an extinction burst can be reduced substantially. It is important, however, if implementing an extinction procedure with teachers or parents that they be apprised of the possibility of an extinction burst and given encouragement that this is a temporary phenomenon.

In schools, extinction is used primarily to decrease the frequency of behaviors maintained by teacher attention, but it is also important to consider extinction when behaviors are controlled by negative reinforcement (i.e., escape or avoidance). For example, in the classroom, a child may become disruptive to escape a specific activity (e.g., math assignment) or an aversive environment (e.g., the classroom itself). If the student is not allowed to escape or avoid, we would expect the incidence of the disruptive behavior to eventually decrease. This should be particularly effective if combined with reinforcement for appropriate academic activities and performance. To use extinction effectively, it is important to understand the function that a behavior performs (Gresham, Watson, & Skinner, 2001). Once the function of a behavior is identified, it is much easier to design an intervention to reduce the problem behavior and increase positive behavior (Witt, Daly, & Noell, 2000). A recent meta-analysis found that functional behavior assessment (FBA)–based interventions were associated with large reductions in problem behaviors compared with non–FBA-based interventions (Hurl, Wightman, Haynes, & Virues-Ortega, 2016). Extinction has been used to decrease many maladaptive behaviors including disruptive or aggressive behavior (Richman, Wacker, Asmus, Casey, & Andelman, 1999), idiosyncratic ritual and compulsive behaviors in individuals with autism (Wolff, Hupp, & Symons, 2013), and off-task behavior (Stahr, Cushing, Lane, & Fox, 2006).

PUNISHMENT

The use of the term *punishment* can be controversial, especially in the context of public education (e.g., Hyman & Snook, 1999). For example, a Google search using the key words "school punishment" yielded more than 16 million hits. A review of the first few sites indicated all contained arguments, both pro and con, on the use of punishment in schools, including corporal punishment. The definition of punishment is simply a stimulus that (a) immediately follows a response and (b) decreases the future frequency of that type of behavior in similar conditions (Cooper et al., 2007). Maag (2001) suggested that educators may adopt the use of punishment because it is easy to administer, it works quickly to suppress behavior, and encouragement of punishment (i.e., discipline) is part of our cultural ethos. It is important that psychologists working in the schools recognize these issues when suggesting behavioral interventions to teachers. It is also important to recognize that some educators' may evidence disdain for reinforcement-based techniques (Akin-Little, Eckert, Lovett, & Little, 2004). Therefore, if punishment is the initial recommendation, it may strengthen the teacher's existing bias in favor of punishment and lower the acceptability of reinforcement-based procedure. Also, it is important to understand each student for whom punishment will be used because in some cases, the intention to punish a behavior may result in the behavior being inadvertently reinforced (e.g., removal of student from class for disruptive behaviors when the function of the problem behavior was to avoid doing academic work). Although the following punishment procedures are offered, it is recommended that they be used sparingly and only in the context of a more comprehensive behavior management program that includes positive reinforcement.

Response Cost

Response cost, defined as a procedure for reducing inappropriate behavior through withdrawal of specific amounts of reinforcer contingent on the behavior's occurrence (Alberto & Troutman, 2013), is a versatile procedure with few negative side effects. It is particularly adaptable to a token reinforcement system in which students can earn token reinforcers for appropriate behaviors and lose tokens for misbehavior. Kazdin (2012) noted that token systems have been applied advantageously in settings such as group homes, psychiatric facilities, and schools. Hackenberg (2009) went as far as saying that token economies "stand as among the most successful behaviorally-based applications in the history of psychology" (p. 258), and Glynn (1990) wrote that "token economies are among the most well-validated and effective behavioral treatments" (p. 383) for everything from severe psychiatric disorders to behavior in regular education classrooms. Further, Kazdin emphasized the utility of a response cost procedure within a token economy by stating that the loss of tokens can be more effective than loss of any single reinforcer that serves as a backup reinforcer in the token system.

Response cost procedures can also be implemented without a token economy system being in place in the classroom. A teacher who "fines" a child with the loss of free time or recess would be an example of a response cost procedure. Alberto and Troutman (2013) offered a guide to setting up a response cost procedure in the classroom. They recommended asking the following questions: (a) Have reinforcement-based procedures been considered first? (b) Does the student have access to a pool of reinforcers from which to deduct payment? (c) Are there clear rules for appropriate behavior, and are the penalties for violation of these rules clear? (d) Has the magnitude of the penalty relative to the infraction been considered? (e) Is there a way in which the student can earn back the reinforcer? and (f) Is there adequate reinforcement available to the student? If these conditions are met, then a response cost procedure may be appropriate. Some of the behaviors in which response cost procedures have been shown to be effective include reducing problem verbal and physical behavior (Nolan & Filter, 2012), off-task behavior (Pelios, MacDuff, & Axelrod, 2003), classroom disruptive behavior (Conyers et al., 2004; Musser, Bray, Kehle, & Jenson, 2001), and tics in youth with Tourette's syndrome (Capriotti, Brandt, Ricketts, Espil, & Woods, 2012).

Overcorrection

Overcorrection involves penalizing an undesirable behavior by having the student perform some other behavior (Kazdin, 2012). Alberto and Troutman (2013) described two types of overcorrection. Restitutional overcorrection consists of correcting the environmental effect of the student's misbehavior, not only to its original condition but to a better condition. For example, if a student is caught writing on his or her desk, the teacher may require the child not only to erase or clean their writing but all writing on the desk. This can be a particularly effective form of punishment for vandalism, littering, or other behavior that has a clear environmental outcome. While meeting the definition of punishment because of its ability to reduce behavior, MacKenzie-Keating and McDonald (1990) argued that it differs from punishment in its social validity and educative value. They proposed that the term *overcorrection* be eliminated and that the term *restitution training* would be more appropriate.

Regardless of the terminology used, restitutional overcorrection has been demonstrated to be effective in reducing a wide variety of behaviors (Alberto & Troutman, 2013).

Positive-practice overcorrection is cited much more frequently in the psychological literature and consists of repeatedly practicing the appropriate behavior, sometimes in an exaggerated or overly correct form. It has been found to be effective in reducing the incidence of a variety of behaviors, including levels of motor stereotypy in children with ASD (Peters & Thompson, 2013), vocal stereotypy (Anderson & Le, 2011), and bruxism (Watson, 1993). Although not technically reductive in nature, it has also been used successfully with a variety of academic behaviors, such as mathematics fluency (Rhymer, Dittmer, Skinner, & Jackson, 2000) and oral reading (Singh & Singh, 1986).

Time-Out

Time-out is a procedure used to discipline children for misbehavior by removing access to reinforcing stimuli, events, or conditions for a brief period of time (Warzak, Floress, Kellen, Kazmerski, & Chopko, 2012). It is one of the most popular (Everett, 2010) and possibly most misunderstood forms of behavior management used, and there is little question concerning its efficacy (Sterling Turner & Watson, 1999). Everett (2010) found that special education teachers depended heavily on time-out, and Barkin, Scheindlin, Ip, Richardson, and Finch (2007) found that 42% of parents reported using time-out. Other studies have found that 88% of special education teachers (Ruhl, 1985) and 85% of school psychologists (Shapiro & Lentz, 1985) used time-out procedures. Time-out has been found to be an effective procedure with many different behaviors, populations, and environments (Costenbader & Reading-Brown, 1995; Everett et al., 2007; Jenson, Sloane, & Young, 1988; Kazdin, 2012; Sterling et al., 1999; Warzak et al., 2012; Yell, 1994). Despite its effectiveness and popularity, "teachers probably use time-out ineffectively as often as effectively" (Goldstein, 1995, p. 249).

Research on time-out is based on the two general categories to which time-out is usually divided: (a) exclusionary and (b) nonexclusionary. Exclusionary (isolation) time-out involves removing the individual from the environment in which reinforcement is occurring and is the most frequently used and cited time-out procedure (Costenbader & Reading-Brown, 1995). Nonexclusionary time-out involves withholding reinforcement from the child without removing him or her from the classroom. The biggest difference between the two is that exclusionary time-out attempts to remove the child from all forms of reinforcement contingent on the undesired behavior, and nonexclusionary time-out usually involves the removal of social reinforcement from a specific behavior that has previously been reinforced.

Although time-out has been used effectively in the classroom for a variety of problem behaviors, several barriers to effective implementation exist (Martens, Witt, Daly, & Vollmer, 1999). One such barrier is teachers' understanding of time-out and their history of success with the procedure. Data from a survey that questioned regular education teachers' understanding and use of time-out (Little, 1997) indicated that although the vast majority of respondents reported having used time-out in their classroom (91.1%) and found time-out to be an acceptable behavior management procedure (85.7%), a significant number of teachers had little understanding of the type of behaviors for which time-out was most appropriate or what constituted time-out. Building on the work of Noell and Witt (1998) and Martens et al. (1999), it appears best to approach implementation of time-out in the classroom with the assumption that implementation skills must be systematically taught to the teacher (for specific suggestions, see Sterling Turner & Watson, 1999).

A Different Conceptualization of Time-Out

Little et al. (2009) proposed a different way to conceptualize time-out that may have greater utility in the classroom. Most of the research on time-out has conceptualized the process as a punishment procedure (i.e., the removal of the individual from access to positive reinforcement for a specific period of time). This presents methodological as well as ethical concerns. An alternative conceptualization to the use of time-out in the classroom may help facilitate teachers' understanding of time-out and improve treatment integrity in situations where it is implemented. It may be best to conceptualize time-out not as punishment but as an impediment to behavioral momentum and acceleration. A chain represents a series of responses that tend to be performed in a particular order. In the behavioral literature, this has usually been discussed in the context of training a new response (Alberto & Troutman, 2013). However, just as a new response can be taught by building sequences of behaviors (chaining), existing responses can be reduced in frequency by interfering with the sequence. It seems unlikely that the student's behavior of concern manifests itself initially in the manner in which the teacher attends. It is more likely that other, less obtrusive behaviors appear, and when they do not attract the teacher's attention, they serve as the trigger for the next, more obtrusive behavior in the sequence. It is possible that there are many steps in the behavioral sequence before the behavior reaches the level to which the teacher attends.

Take the example of a student who exhibits disruptive behavior. A functional assessment has determined that this behavior is maintained through teacher and peer attention. It is entirely possible that the behavior of concern is at the end of a behavioral chain. If we can identify the antecedents to the disruptive behavior in the chaining sequence, we may be able to stop the behavior from accelerating, thus effectively eliminating the force of the behavior. Using the F = MA analogy from physics, we can attempt to reduce the acceleration of the behavior to close to zero. We have therefore effectively eliminated the force (i.e., magnitude) of that behavior, at least at that particular time. If, over time, we have interrupted the chain sufficiently, the reinforcement that occurs at the end of the chain will no longer be associated with the behaviors at the beginning of the chain. We may then have effectively extinguished the problem behavior. The focus is then on reinforcing a functionally equivalent behavior (e.g., on-task, academic behaviors) so that the probability of the inappropriate behavior returning is minimal. We have, in effect, decreased the behavioral momentum of the disruptive behavior and increased the momentum of appropriate classroom behavior. We know that short-duration time-out can be effective (Chelonis, Bastilla, Brown, & Gardner, 2007; Marlow, Tingstrom, Olmi, & Edwards, 1997), but additional research is necessary to fully understand the mechanisms through which it is effective.

POSITIVE, PROPER, AND PROACTIVE

Resistance to the use of operant procedures to change behavior has come from a variety of sources, and some individuals have been particularly harsh in their criticism of the use of positive reinforcement (e.g., Kohn, 1993; for a discussion, see Akin-Little et al., 2004). Because of the inherent ethical and methodological problems with punishment and the apparent acceptability of punishment procedures among educators, the use of punishment and alternative reductive procedures must be carefully considered before making recommendations to teachers. We therefore recommend considering the following three words in designing interventions to reduce the occurrence of maladaptive behavior: (a) *positive*, (b) *proper*, and (c) *proactive*.

Positive

The focus should always be on positive aspects of student behavior and on strengthening those behaviors. There is little doubt that positive reinforcement-based procedures have been proven efficacious in increasing and maintaining appropriate academic and social behaviors as well as contributing to the reduction of maladaptive behaviors (Alberto & Troutman, 2013; Cooper et al., 2007). We should also be guided by the principle of least restrictive alternative in which positive approaches should receive first consideration. It seems clear then that when given alternatives for the reduction of maladaptive behavior; ethical, research-based psychologists should consider positive interventions first.

Proper

Proper refers to interventions that are both research-based and socially valid. Although the methods we employ have gone through changes over the years, one thing has remained invariant: Scientific validation of our techniques is essential. In fact, this could be seen as the defining characteristic of behavioral approaches. We cannot assume that a technique is effective just because it is widely used or sounds good. We must have data that support the efficacy of the procedure. Nevertheless, this does not guarantee the effectiveness of an intervention. Even a well-designed, empirically supported plan will not be effective if not implemented with integrity.

Proactive

If we can prevent the occurrence of behavior problems we have no need to even worry about reductive procedures. It is also easier to prevent behavior problems than deal with them reactively (Maag, 2001; Sugai & Horner, 2008). This leads us to a discussion of our last consideration, being proactive. One alternative to traditional use of reductive procedures and other disciplinary techniques is the use of positive behavioral supports (PBS; Simonsen & Sugai, 2009). PBS uses problem-solving strategies to improve student behavior by building on strengths and has been found to improve the learning environment of the school and, more specifically, the classroom (Simonsen & Sugai, 2009). A better learning environment improves student achievement and student attendance (Anderson-Ketchmark & Alvarez, 2010; Lepage, Kratochwill, & Elliott, 2004).

It is also important that consultation with teachers not always be in response to a specific child with a specific problem behavior. Changing teachers' approach to classroom management and reinforcing positive, preventive teacher behaviors should be an aspect of all school psychologists' routines. Maag (2001) offered five easy-to-implement recommendations for teachers.

1. *Catch students being good.* Teachers and parents too often focus on the negative aspects of student behavior. Although it has been recommended that there be a 5:1 ratio between parents' and teachers' positive and negative verbalizations, Armstrong

and Field (2012) found a baseline rate of 1:1 between parents' positive and negative verbalizations. Jenson, Olympia, Farley, and Clark (2004) called the classroom a "sea of negativism" (p. 69) and reported that teachers are also more likely to attend to students' inappropriate behaviors than to respond to positive behaviors using praise and other positive techniques. It is important for teachers to attend to and reinforce appropriate social and academic behavior, especially with students with existing behavior problems.

2. *Think small*. Shaping is an important concept to convey to teachers. A student who is having difficulty behaving in a manner consistent with the rules and expectations in the classroom is unlikely to change his or her behavior rapidly. Shaping involves the reinforcement of successive approximations of the desired behavior. Teachers need to focus on and be willing to recognize small improvements in behavior because that is the only way they will arrive at large-scale behavior change.

3. *Have a group management plan*. It is easier to manage specific students with behavior problems when the entire class is well behaved (Maag, 2001). One way to increase the likelihood of a well-behaved class is through the use of a class-wide behavior management plan. Kehle, Bray, Theodore, Jenson, and Clark (2000) and De Martini-Scully, Bray, and Kehle (2000) offered a multicomponent intervention that could be adaptable to an entire class. Using a contingency contract, their intervention comprises precision requests, antecedent strategies, positive reinforcement, and response cost. It was reported that this intervention has been successful with both regular and special education students. In addition, Skinner, Skinner, and Burton (2009) provided a detailed explanation of the use of group-oriented contingencies in the classroom.

4. *Prevent behavior problems*. Teachers should be encouraged to take steps to ensure a positive class climate. Maag (2001) suggested that this can be accomplished by (a) establishing classroom rules and reinforcing students for obeying the rules, (b) having students academically engaged at least 70% of the day, (c) not letting children with challenging behaviors sit next to one another, and (d) having teachers move around the room as much as possible to monitor student behavior and reinforce appropriate behavior. Wehby and Lane (2009) discussed proactive strategies for classroom manage which include

(a) proximity, (b) high rates of opportunities to respond, (c) high probability requests, and (d) choice making.

5. *Use peer influence favorably.* Peers, through their smiles, comments, gestures, and so on, have a tremendous influence on classroom behavior (Müller, Hofmann, Fleischli, & Studer, 2016). Attempts at eliminating these behaviors through punishment is unlikely to be effective, so teachers should be encouraged to use these behaviors to their advantage. One way to effectively use peer influence is through the use of group contingencies (see Skinner et al., 2009).

REFERENCES

Akin-Little, K. A., Eckert, T. L., Lovett, B. J., & Little, S. G. (2004). Extrinsic reinforcement in the classroom: Bribery or best practice? *School Psychology Review, 33,* 344–362.

Alberto, P. A., & Troutman, A. C. (2013). *Applied behavior analysis for teachers* (9th ed.). Upper Saddle River, NJ: Pearson Prentice Hall.

Anderson, J., & Le, D. D. (2011). Abatement of intractable vocal stereotypy using an overcorrection procedure. *Behavioral Interventions, 26,* 134–146. http://dx.doi.org/10.1002/bin.326

Anderson-Ketchmark, C., & Alvarez, M. E. (2010). The school social work skill set and positive behavior support: A good match. *Children & Schools, 32,* 61–63. http://dx.doi.org/10.1093/cs/32.1.61

Armstrong, A. B., & Field, C. E. (2012). Altering positive/negative interaction ratios of mothers and young children. *Child & Family Behavior Therapy, 34,* 231–242. http://dx.doi.org/10.1080/07317107.2012.707094

Austin, J. L., & Bevan, D. (2011). Using differential reinforcement of low rates to reduce children's requests for teacher attention. *Journal of Applied Behavior Analysis, 44,* 451–461. http://dx.doi.org/10.1901/jaba.2011.44-451

Barkin, S., Scheindlin, B., Ip, E. H., Richardson, I., & Finch, S. (2007). Determinants of parental discipline practices: A national sample from primary care practices. *Clinical Pediatrics, 46,* 64–69. http://dx.doi.org/10.1177/0009922806292644

Belfiore, P. J., Lee, D. L., Scheeler, C., & Klein, D. (2002). Implications of behavioral momentum and academic achievement for students with behavior disorders: Theory, application, and practice. *Psychology in the Schools, 39,* 171–179. http://dx.doi.org/10.1002/pits.10028

Capriotti, M. R., Brandt, B. C. Ricketts, E. J. Espil, F. M., & Woods, D. W. (2012). Comparing the effects of differential reinforcement of other behavior and response-cost contingencies on tics in youth with Tourette syndrome. *Journal of Applied Behavior Analysis, 45,* 251–263. http://dx.doi.org/10.1901/jaba.2012.45-251

Chelonis, J. J., Bastilla, J. E., Brown, M. M., & Gardner, E. S. (2007). Effect of time-out adult performance of a visual discrimination task. *The Psychological Record*, 57, 359–372. http://dx.doi.org/10.1007/BF03395582

Conyers, C., Miltenberger, R. G., Maki, A., Barenz, R., Jurgens, M., Sailer, A., . . . Kopp, B. (2004). A comparison of response cost and differential reinforcement of other behavior to reduce disruptive behavior in a preschool classroom. *Journal of Applied Behavior Analysis*, 37, 411–415. http://dx.doi.org/10.1901/jaba.2004.37-411

Conyers, C., Miltenberger, R., Romaniuk, C., Kopp, B., & Himle, M. (2003). Evaluation of DRO schedules to reduce disruptive behavior in a preschool classroom. *Child & Family Behavior Therapy*, 25, 1–6. http://dx.doi.org/10.1300/J019v25n03_01

Cooper, J. O., Heron, T. E., & Heward, W. L. (2007). *Applied behavior analysis* (2nd ed.). Upper Saddle River, NJ: Pearson Education.

Costenbader, V., & Reading-Brown, M. (1995). Isolation timeout used with students with emotional disturbance. *Exceptional Children*, 61, 353–363. http://dx.doi.org/10.1177/001440299506100404

De Martini-Scully, D., Bray, M. A., & Kehle, T. J. (2000). A packaged intervention to reduce disruptive behaviors in general education students. *Psychology in the Schools*, 37, 149–156. http://dx.doi.org/10.1002/(SICI)1520-6807(200003)37:2<149::AID-PITS6>3.0.CO;2-K

Dube, W. V., McIlvane, W. J., Mazzitelli, K., & McNamara, B. (2003). Reinforcer rate effects and behavioral momentum in individuals with developmental disabilities. *American Journal on Mental Retardation*, 108, 134–143. http://dx.doi.org/10.1352/0895-8017(2003)108<0134:RREABM>2.0.CO;2

Eccles, C., & Pitchford, M. (1997). Understanding and helping a boy with problems: A functional approach to behavior problems. *Educational Psychology in Practice*, 13, 115–121. http://dx.doi.org/10.1080/0266736970130206

Everett, G. E. (2010). Time-out in special education settings: The parameters of previous implementation. *North American Journal of Psychology*, 12, 159–170.

Everett, G. E., Olmi, D. J., Edwards, R. P., Tingstrom, D. H., Sterling-Turner, H. E., & Christ, T. J. (2007). An empirical investigation of time-out with and without escape extinction to treat escape-maintained noncompliance. *Behavior Modification*, 31, 412–434. http://dx.doi.org/10.1177/0145445506297725

Flynn, S. D., & Lo, Y. (2016). Teacher implementation of trial-based functional analysis and differential reinforcement of alternative behavior for students with challenging behavior. *Journal of Behavioral Education*, 25, 1–31. http://dx.doi.org/10.1007/s10864-015-9231-2

Glynn, S. M. (1990). Token economy approaches for psychiatric patients: Progress and pitfalls over 25 years. *Behavior Modification*, 14, 383–407. http://dx.doi.org/10.1177/01454455900144002

Goldstein, S. (1995). *Understanding and managing children's classroom behavior*. New York, NY: Wiley-Interscience.

Gresham, F. M. (2005). Response to intervention: An alternative means of identifying students as emotionally disturbed. *Education and Treatment of Children, 28,* 328–344.

Gresham, F. M., Watson, T. S., & Skinner, C. H. (2001). Functional behavioral assessment: Principles, procedures, and future directions. *School Psychology Review, 30,* 156–172.

Hackenberg, T. D. (2009). Token reinforcement: A review and analysis. *Journal of the Experimental Analysis of Behavior, 91,* 257–286. http://dx.doi.org/10.1901/jeab.2009.91-257

Harper, J. M., Iwata, B. A., & Camp, E. M. (2013). Assessment and treatment of social avoidance. *Journal of Applied Behavior Analysis, 46,* 147–160. http://dx.doi.org/10.1002/jaba.18

Hegel, M. T., & Ferguson, R. J. (2000). Differential reinforcement of other behavior (DRO) to reduce aggressive behavior following traumatic brain injury. *Behavior Modification, 24,* 94–101. http://dx.doi.org/10.1177/0145445500241005

Hurl, K., Wightman, J., Haynes, S. N., & Virues-Ortega, J. (2016). Does a pre-intervention functional assessment increase intervention effectiveness? A meta-analysis of within-subject interrupted time-series studies. *Clinical Psychology Review, 47,* 71–84. http://dx.doi.org/10.1016/j.cpr.2016.05.003

Hyman, I., & Snook, P. (1999). *Dangerous schools: What we can do about the physical and emotional abuse of our children.* San Francisco, CA: Jossey-Bass.

Jenson, W. R., Olympia, D., Farley, M., & Clark, E. (2004). Positive psychology and externalizing students in a sea of negativity. *Psychology in the Schools, 41,* 67–79. http://dx.doi.org/10.1002/pits.10139

Jenson, W. R., Sloane, H. N., & Young, K. R. (1988). *Applied behavior analysis in education: A structured teaching approach.* Englewood Cliffs, NJ: Prentice Hall.

Kazdin, A. E. (2012). *Behavior modification in applied settings* (7th ed.). Long Grove, IL: Waveland Press.

Kehle, T. J., Bray, M. A., Theodore, L. A., Jenson, W. R., & Clark, E. C. (2000). A multi-component intervention designed to reduce disruptive classroom behaviors. *Psychology in the Schools, 37,* 475–481. http://dx.doi.org/10.1002/1520-6807(200009)37:5<475::AID-PITS7>3.0.CO;2-P

Kelly, L., & Holloway, J. (2015). An investigation of the effectiveness of behavioral momentum on the acquisition and fluency outcomes of tacts in three children with autism spectrum disorder. *Research in Autism Spectrum Disorders, 9,* 182–192. http://dx.doi.org/10.1016/j.rasd.2014.10.007

Kohn, A. (1993). *Punished by rewards: The trouble with gold stars, incentive plans, A's, praise, and other bribes.* Boston, MA: Houghton Mifflin.

Laprime, A. P., & Dittrich, G. A. (2014). An evaluation of a treatment package consisting of discrimination training and differential reinforcement with response cost and a social story on vocal stereotypy for a preschooler with autism in a preschool classroom. *Education & Treatment of Children, 37,* 407–430. http://dx.doi.org/10.1353/etc.2014.0028

Lepage, K., Kratochwill, T., & Elliott, S. (2004). Competency-based behavior consultation training: An evaluation of consultant outcomes, treatment effects, and consumer satisfaction. *School Psychology Quarterly, 19*, 1–28. http://dx.doi.org/10.1521/scpq.19.1.1.29406

Lerman, D. C., & Iwata, B. A. (1995). Prevalence of the extinction burst and its attenuation during treatment. *Journal of Applied Behavior Analysis, 28*, 93–94. http://dx.doi.org/10.1901/jaba.1995.28-93

Lindberg, J. S., Iwata, B. A., Kahng, S., & DeLeon, I. G. (1999). DRO contingencies: An analysis of variable-momentary schedules. *Journal of Applied Behavior Analysis, 32*, 123–136. http://dx.doi.org/10.1901/jaba.1999.32-123

Little, S. G. (1997, April). Teacher's use, understanding, and acceptability of time-out. Paper presented as part of symposium *Behavioral School Psychology: Time-Out Revisited* (S. G. Little, Chair) at the annual meeting of the National Association of School Psychologists, Anaheim, CA.

Little, S. G., & Akin-Little, A. (2014). Linking assessment and intervention. In S. G. Little & A. Akin-Little (Eds.), *Academic assessment and intervention* (pp. 27–30). New York, NY: Routledge.

Little, S. G., Akin-Little, A., & Cook, C. R. (2009). Classroom application of reductive procedures: A positive approach. In A. Akin-Little, S. G. Little, M. A. Bray, & T. J. Kehle (Eds.), *Behavioral interventions in schools: Evidence-based positive strategies* (pp. 171–188). Washington, DC: American Psychological Association. http://dx.doi.org/10.1037/11886-011

Maag, J. W. (2001). Rewarded by punishment: Reflections on the disuse of positive reinforcement in schools. *Exceptional Children, 67*, 173–186. http://dx.doi.org/10.1177/001440290106700203

Mace, F. C., McComas, J. J., Mauro, B. C., Progar, P. R., Taylor, B., Ervin, R., & Zangrillo, A. N. (2009). The persistence-strengthening effects of DRA: An illustration of bidirectional translational research. *The Behavior Analyst, 32*, 293–300. http://dx.doi.org/10.1007/BF03392192

MacKenzie-Keating, S. E., & McDonald, L. (1990). Overcorrection: Reviewed, revisited and revised. *The Behavior Analyst, 13*, 39–48. http://dx.doi.org/10.1007/BF03392516

Marlow, A. G., Tingstrom, D. H., Olmi, D. J., & Edwards, R. P. (1997). The effects of classroom-based *time*-in/*time*-out on compliance rates in children with speech/language disabilities. *Child & Family Behavior Therapy, 19*, 1–15. http://dx.doi.org/10.1300/J019v19n02_01

Martens, B. K., Witt, J. C., Daly, E. J., & Vollmer, T. R. (1999). Behavior analysis: Theory and practice in educational settings. In C. R. Reynolds & T. B. Gutkin (Eds.), *The handbook of school psychology* (3rd ed., pp. 638–663). New York, NY: Wiley.

Müller, C. M., Hofmann, V., Fleischli, J., & Studer, F. (2016). Classroom peer influence from the entire class, dominant students, and friends. *Journal of*

Cognitive Education and Psychology, 15, 122–145. http://dx.doi.org/10.1891/1945-8959.15.1.122

Musser, E. H., Bray, M. A., Kehle, T. J., & Jenson, W. R. (2001). Reducing disruptive behaviors in students with serious emotional disturbance. *School Psychology Review, 30*, 294–304.

Neidert, P. L., Iwata, B. A., & Dozier, C. L. (2005). Treatment of multiply controlled problem behavior with procedural variations of differential reinforcement. *Exceptionality, 13*, 45–53. http://dx.doi.org/10.1207/s15327035ex1301_6

Nevin, J. A. (2002). Measuring behavioral momentum. *Behavioural Processes, 57*, 187–198. http://dx.doi.org/10.1016/S0376-6357(02)00013-X

Noell, G. H., & Witt, J. C. (1998). Toward a behavior analytic approach to consultation. In T. S. Watson & F. M. Gresham (Eds.), *Handbook of child behavior therapy* (pp. 41–57). New York, NY: Plenum. http://dx.doi.org/10.1007/978-1-4615-5323-6_3

Nolan, J. D., & Filter, K. J. (2012). A function-based classroom behavior intervention using non-contingent reinforcement plus response cost. *Education & Treatment of Children, 35*, 419–430. http://dx.doi.org/10.1353/etc.2012.0017

Nuernberger, J. E., Vargo, K. K., & Ringdahl, J. E. (2013). An application of differential reinforcement of other behavior and self-monitoring to address repetitive behavior. *Journal of Developmental and Physical Disabilities, 25*, 105–117. http://dx.doi.org/10.1007/s10882-012-9309-x

Pelios, L. V., MacDuff, G. S., & Axelrod, S. (2003). The effects of a treatment package in establishing independent academic work skills in children with autism. *Education and Treatment of Children, 26*, 1–21.

Peters, L. C., & Thompson, R. H. (2013). Some indirect effects of positive practice overcorrection. *Journal of Applied Behavior Analysis, 46*, 613–625. http://dx.doi.org/10.1002/jaba.63

Ray, K. P., Skinner, C. H., & Watson, T. S. (1999). Transferring stimulus control via momentum to increase compliance in a student with autism: A demonstration of collaborative consultation. *School Psychology Review, 28*, 622–628.

Rhymer, K. N., Dittmer, K. I., Skinner, C. H., & Jackson, B. (2000). Effectiveness of a multi-component treatment for improving mathematics fluency. *School Psychology Quarterly, 15*, 40–51. http://dx.doi.org/10.1037/h0088777

Richman, D. M., Wacker, D. P., Asmus, J. M., Casey, S. D., & Andelman, M. (1999). Further analysis of problem behavior in response class hierarchies. *Journal of Applied Behavior Analysis, 32*, 269–283. http://dx.doi.org/10.1901/jaba.1999.32-269

Ruhl, K. (1985). Handling aggression: Fourteen models teachers use. *Pointer, 29*, 30–33. http://dx.doi.org/10.1080/05544246.1985.9944691

Sarafino, E. P. (2011). *Applied behavior analysis: Principles and procedures in behavior modification*. New York, NY: Wiley.

Shabani, D. B., Wilder, D. A., & Flood, W. A. (2001). Reducing stereotypic behavior through discrimination training, differential reinforcement of other behavior, and self monitoring. *Behavioral Interventions, 16,* 279–286. http://dx.doi.org/10.1002/bin.96

Shapiro, E. S., & Lentz, F. E., Jr. (1985). A survey of school psychologists' use of behavior modification procedures. *Journal of School Psychology, 23,* 327–336. http://dx.doi.org/10.1016/0022-4405(85)90045-7

Simonsen, B., & Sugai, G. (2009). School-wide positive behavior support: A systems-level application of behavioral principles. In A. Akin-Little, S. G. Little, M. A. Bray, & T. J. Kehle (Eds.), *Behavioral interventions in schools: Evidence-based positive strategies* (pp. 125–140). Washington, DC: American Psychological Association. http://dx.doi.org/10.1037/11886-008

Singh, N. N., & Singh, J. (1986). A behavioural remediation program for oral reading: Effects on errors and comprehension. *Educational Psychology, 6,* 105–114. http://dx.doi.org/10.1080/0144341860060201

Skinner, C. H., Skinner, A. L., & Burton, B. (2009). Applying group-oriented contingencies in the classroom. In A. Akin-Little, S. G. Little, M. A. Bray, & T. J. Kehle (Eds.), *Behavioral interventions in schools: Evidence-based positive strategies* (pp. 157–170). Washington, DC: American Psychological Association. http://dx.doi.org/10.1037/11886-010

Stahr, B., Cushing, D., Lane, K., & Fox, J. (2006). Efficacy of a function-based intervention in decreasing off-task behavior exhibited by a student with ADHD. *Journal of Positive Behavior Interventions, 8,* 201–211. http://dx.doi.org/10.1177/10983007060080040301

Sterling Turner, H., & Watson, T. S. (1999). Consultant's guide for the use of time-out in the preschool and elementary classroom. *Psychology in the Schools, 36,* 135–148. http://dx.doi.org/10.1002/(SICI)1520-6807(199903)36:2<135::AID-PITS6>3.0.CO;2-3

Strand, P. S. (2000). A modern behavioral perspective on child conduct disorder: Integrating behavioral momentum and matching theory. *Clinical Psychology Review, 20,* 593–615. http://dx.doi.org/10.1016/S0272-7358(99)00010-0

Sugai, G., & Horner, R. H. (2008). What we know and need to know about preventing problem behavior in schools. *Exceptionality, 16,* 67–77. http://dx.doi.org/10.1080/09362830801981138

Vance, M. J., Gresham, F. M., & Dart, E. H. (2012). Relative effectiveness of DRO and self-monitoring in a general education classroom. *Journal of Applied School Psychology, 28,* 89–109. http://dx.doi.org/10.1080/15377903.2012.643758

Vollmer, T. R., & Iwata, B. A. (1992). Differential reinforcement as treatment for behavior disorders: Procedural and functional variations. *Research in Developmental Disabilities, 13,* 393–417. http://dx.doi.org/10.1016/0891-4222(92)90013-V

Vollmer, T. R., Roane, H. S., Ringdahl, J. E., & Marcus, B. A. (1999). Evaluating treatment challenges with differential reinforcement of alternative behavior. *Journal of Applied Behavior Analysis, 32,* 9–23. http://dx.doi.org/10.1901/jaba.1999.32-9

Vostal, B. R., & Lee, D. L. (2011). Behavioral momentum during a continuous reading task: An exploratory study. *Journal of Behavioral Education, 20*, 163–181. http://dx.doi.org/10.1007/s10864-011-9129-6

Wadsworth, J. P., Hansen, B. D., & Wills, S. B. (2015). Increasing compliance in students with intellectual disabilities using functional behavioral assessment and self-monitoring. *Remedial and Special Education, 36*, 195–207. http://dx.doi.org/10.1177/0741932514554102

Waller, R. J., & Mays, N. M. (2007). Spontaneous recovery of previously extinguished behavior as an alternative explanation for extinction-related side effects. *Behavior Modification, 31*, 569–572. http://dx.doi.org/10.1177/0145445507300935

Wanzek, J. S., Houlihan, D. D., & Homan, K. J. (2012). An examination of behavioral momentum in girl's high school volleyball. *Journal of Sport Behavior, 35*, 94–107.

Warzak, W. J., Floress, M. T., Kellen, M., Kazmerski, J. S., & Chopko, S. (2012). Trends in time-out research: Are we focusing our efforts where our efforts are needed? *The Behavior Therapist, 35*, 30–33.

Watson, T. S. (1993). Effectiveness of arousal and arousal plus overcorrection to reduce nocturnal bruxism. *Journal of Behavior Therapy and Experimental Psychiatry, 24*, 181–185. http://dx.doi.org/10.1016/0005-7916(93)90047-Z

Watson, T. S., & Heindl, B. (1996). Behavioral case consultation with parents and teachers: An example using differential reinforcement to treat psychogenic cough. *Journal of School Psychology, 34*, 365–378. http://dx.doi.org/10.1016/S0022-4405(96)00022-2

Wehby, J. H., & Lane, K. L. (2009). Proactive instructional strategies for classroom management. In A. Akin-Little, S. G. Little, M. A. Bray, & T. J. Kehle (Eds.), *Behavioral interventions in schools: Evidence-based positive strategies* (pp. 141–156). Washington, DC: American Psychological Association. http://dx.doi.org/10.1037/11886-009

Wilder, D. A., Chen, L., Atwell, J., Pritchard, J., & Weinstein, P. (2006). Brief functional analysis and treatment of tantrums associated with transitions in preschool children. *Journal of Applied Behavior Analysis, 39*, 103–107.

Wilder, D. A., Harris, C., Reagan, R., & Rasey, A. (2007). Functional analysis and treatment of noncompliance by preschool children. *Journal of Applied Behavior Analysis, 40*, 173–177. http://dx.doi.org/10.1901/jaba.2007.44-06

Witt, J. C., Daly, E., & Noell, G. H. (2000). *Functional assessment: A step-by-step guide to solving academic and behavioral problems*. Longmont, CO: Sopris West.

Wolff, J. J., Hupp, S. C., & Symons, F. J. (2013). Brief report: Avoidance extinction as treatment for compulsive and ritual behavior in autism. *Journal of Autism and Developmental Disorders, 43*, 1741–1746. http://dx.doi.org/10.1007/s10803-012-1721-7

Yell, M. L. (1994). Timeout and students with behavior disorders: A legal analysis. *Education and Treatment of Children, 17*, 293–301.

5

GENERALIZATION AND MAINTENANCE

JAMIE L. PRATT, GARRY D. WICKERD,
AND MARK W. STEEGE

It has always been the task of formal education to set up behavior which would prove useful or enjoyable *later* in the student's life.
—B. F. Skinner

Schools are tasked with the mission of preparing students for future success. Whether success is defined in terms of preparedness for a personally meaningful life, employment, or continued education, educators clearly maintain a responsibility to facilitate the acquisition of skills that may be applied outside the school environment. The Every Student Succeeds Act (ESSA) of 2015 legislates this responsibility through provisions that ensure schools use evidence-based instructional strategies to prepare all students for successful employment and/or postsecondary education (U.S. Department of Education, 2016). Alignment with the mission of the educational system and adherence to ESSA therefore requires educators to implement evidence-based strategies to increase the likelihood that skills acquired in the context of a classroom generalize to other environments and maintain over time. In other words, the "train and hope" approach (see Stokes & Baer, 1977) is no longer acceptable, and educators maintain a responsibility to explicitly program for generalization and maintenance.

---

http://dx.doi.org/10.1037/0000126-006
Behavioral Interventions in Schools: Evidence-Based Positive Strategies, Second Edition, S. G. Little and A. Akin-Little (Editors)
Copyright © 2019 by the American Psychological Association. All rights reserved.

GENERALIZATION AND MAINTENANCE EXPLAINED

Effective instruction achieves *generality*: behavior change that is apparent across multiple contexts, spreads to a variety of related behaviors, and persists over time (Baer, Wolf, & Risley, 1968). From this perspective, school-based interventions are useful and meaningful only to the extent that they produce behavior change that yields positive outcomes for students across their lives. To increase the likelihood that school-based interventions effect these lasting changes, educators must be well-versed in the concepts of *stimulus generalization*, *response generalization*, and *temporal generalization*.

Stimulus Generalization

Stimulus generalization occurs when a behavior is emitted at different times, in different places, and/or in the presence of different people (Mayer, Sulzer-Azaroff, & Wallace, 2014). In other words, stimulus generalization refers to the demonstration of learning in situations that differ from the instructional context. For example, stimulus generalization may be observed when a student who practices appropriate social greetings with peers in the classroom subsequently emits an appropriate social greeting when encountering a peer at a family event.

Understanding the process of stimulus generalization requires familiarity with antecedent stimulus classes, which refer to groups of objects or events that share certain features and occasion similar responses (Cooper, Heron, & Heward, 2007; Mayer et al., 2014). For example, the written word *stop* includes a standard arrangement of letters and yields common effects on behavior (e.g., saying the word *stop* when reading aloud or pressing the brakes of a vehicle when observing a stop sign). The written word *stop* may be displayed using highly varied fonts and font sizes, but all written versions of the word form a stimulus class based on common features and functions. In this example, stimulus generalization would be a critical outcome of an instructional procedure designed to teach sight word recognition of "stop." That is, the skill would be functional only to the extent that students learned to emit the same response to varied members of that textual stimulus class (e.g., *stop* in a book, on the classroom door, or on a street sign).

The likelihood of stimulus generalization may be increased by delivering instruction across a wide array of conditions that include varied members of the relevant stimulus class (Stokes & Osnes, 1989). For example, students may be taught to request assistance from multiple peers and adults or to wash their hands using a variety of sinks. Stimulus generalization also may be enhanced by ensuring that students contact reinforcement for behaviors across novel stimulus conditions. Consider, for example, the likelihood that a student's "colorful" joke-telling will generalize to all peers if multiple peers (i.e., members of a stimulus class who share features such as age and size) consistently respond with high-quality social reinforcement (e.g., rip-roaring laughter).

Response Generalization

Response generalization is a type of generalization that occurs when the effects of intervention spread to other classes of behavior (Mayer et al., 2014). In other words, response generalization refers to the occurrence of behaviors that are similar, but not identical, to behaviors that were explicitly taught and reinforced. Response generalization occurs, for example, when a student who learns a social problem-solving model subsequently uses that approach with modifications appropriate for the situation. Another example of response generalization may be observed when a student who learns to greet others by saying "hello" begins emitting similar, untrained greetings such as "hi" or "hey."

Understanding the process of response generalization requires familiarity with response classes, which refer to sets of behaviors that produce the same reinforcing consequences (Mayer et al., 2014). In the previous example, greetings such as "hi" and "hello" typically result in social attention and therefore form a single response class. Various behaviors that produce access to definitions for unfamiliar vocabulary words (e.g., asking a teacher, referencing a dictionary, or searching online) are another example of a response class. Although reinforcement typically strengthens all members of a response class, effective instruction explicitly aims to promote response generalization by expanding the range of behaviors that comprise a response class. One strategy to promote this type of response generalization involves modeling a variety of acceptable responses during instruction (Stokes & Osnes, 1989).

Temporal Generalization

Temporal generalization, which is more commonly referred to as response maintenance, is the final primary form of generalization. Response maintenance refers to the endurance of behavior change over time, after intervention has been discontinued (Cooper et al., 2007). For example, response maintenance would be demonstrated by students who learned effective study habits in a high school course that they continued to practice throughout college. Similarly, a school-based intervention designed to strengthen social skills may be described as promoting maintenance if students continued to demonstrate the targeted skills during follow-up assessments scheduled months after the intervention ended.

One procedure for promoting maintenance is schedule thinning. Continuous schedules of reinforcement (i.e., reinforcing every occurrence of the target behavior) typically are recommended during initial instruction, whereas intermittent schedules of reinforcement (i.e., reinforcing only some occurrences of the target behavior) typically are recommended for promoting sustained responding over time (Cooper et al., 2007; Mayer et al., 2014). Schedule thinning procedures are used to transition from continuous to intermittent schedules of reinforcement by gradually increasing (a) the number of responses required before a reinforcer is delivered or (b) the interval of time between reinforcer deliveries (Cooper et al., 2007). Consider the example of a math intervention designed to teach single-digit addition. An effective strategy may be to deliver praise to students after each correct response on the initial items. Once the students demonstrate the skill consistently, though, the teacher may thin the schedule of reinforcement by delivering praise after variable and gradually increasing numbers of correct responses. In this example, shifting quickly to an intermittent schedule of reinforcement may increase the likelihood that students will continue to respond correctly after programmed praise is discontinued (Mayer et al., 2014).

PROGRAMMING FOR GENERALIZATION

Educators responsible for teaching academic and functional skills, including behaviors intended as replacements for challenging behaviors, may experience occasions when generalization occurs unexpectedly. For example, after reading a book to a young student and teaching the name of a pictured animal, an owl, the student may spontaneously say the word *owl* when seeing a picture of that animal in a different book. The teacher in this scenario did not intentionally arrange the environment to increase the probability of generalization but may promote continued generalization by reinforcing the target response (i.e., saying the word *owl*) when it occurs appropriately outside of the instructional context.

Generalization does not reliably occur automatically, however, and best practice entails actively programming for generalization, rather than passively expecting it to occur (Stokes & Baer, 1977). Fortunately, the behavior analytic literature highlights diverse technologies for promoting generalization. In 1989, Stokes and Osnes codified the existing knowledge about generalization, and many of the strategies they presented are summarized in this chapter with contemporary examples and supporting research evidence. These generalization strategies are organized into three categories to mirror the natural flow of instruction: (a) the *planning phase*, which involves the selection of target behaviors; (b) the *instructional phase*, which involves direct implementation of interventions; and (c) the *transfer phase*, which involves bridging the gap between the instructional and natural environments. A planning worksheet (see Figure 5.1) is also provided to facilitate the application of these generalization strategies within the educational setting.

Planning Phase Strategies

Select Behaviors With Natural Maintaining Contingencies

For an intervention to yield enduring positive outcomes for students, the behaviors targeted for strengthening must be effective in natural environments. In accordance with the *relevance of behavior rule*, only behaviors that will be reinforced outside of the instructional context should be selected as intervention targets; otherwise, an intervention with contrived reinforcement contingencies may need to remain in place indefinitely (Ayllon & Azrin, 1968; Baer, 1999).

From this perspective, the first step in planning for generalization and maintenance involves selecting target behaviors that are relevant, socially significant, and likely to produce reinforcement after intervention ends. This may be accomplished by (a) conducting direct observations of students in the natural environment to identify age-appropriate behaviors and naturally occurring consequences and (b) involving students and other stakeholders in decision-making to select target behaviors that are socially acceptable and valued (Mayer et al., 2014). McGee and Daly (2007) demonstrated this approach when teaching conversational skills to three preschool-age children with autism. Specifically, they selected target social phrases for instruction by collecting questionnaire data from preschool teachers and gathering language samples from typically developing preschool-age children.

Consider another illustrative example involving a student with limited English proficiency who recently immigrated to the United States. The student initially may receive instruction on social greetings within a small group setting, but the goal would be for the student to display this skill across a variety of everyday school contexts (e.g., during lunch and recess). Before delivering instruction, the teacher could observe and record the types of greetings exchanged by similarly aged students to identify targets that are likely to be perceived as acceptable and result in naturally occurring social reinforcement. This approach to intervention planning may promote generalization by increasing the likelihood that the student's greetings will be maintained by natural contingencies of reinforcement.

Generalization Planning Worksheet

Target Behavior to Increase:

Given the target behavior, consider the following questions to identify and design individualized interventions that are likely to promote generalization and maintenance.

Planning Phase: Considerations for selecting behaviors for generalization	
To what extent will the behavior produce reinforcement in the natural environment?	
To what extent is the behavior useful and practical in the natural environment?	
To what extent does the behavior produce consequences that are valuable to the student?	

Instructional Phase: Considerations for instructional delivery that increase the probability of generalization	
To what extent does the student exhibit the behavior fluently and independentlly?	
To what extent does instruction include multiple examples?	
To what extent does the instructional setting mirror the natural environment?	
To what extent are context, people, directions, and other features of instruction varied?	
To what extent is instruction delivered across relevant environments?	

Transfer Phase: Considerations for improving generalization applied in the natural environment	
To what extent is reinforcement delivered unpredictably?	
To what extent will reinforcement be faded?	
To what extent is the student asked to perform the behavior in the natural environment?	
To what extent is the student taught to recruit reinforcement from others?	
To what extent are others detecting and reinforcing the target behavior?	
To what extent have self-management strategies been considered?	

Figure 5.1. Generalization planning worksheet.

Choose Functional Behaviors

Generalization and maintenance also may be promoted by selecting target behaviors that consistently produce access to valuable reinforcers. Functional behavioral assessment seeks to identify the variables that evoke and maintain interfering behaviors and therefore guides the selection of appropriate replacement behaviors. In other words, knowledge of the function of interfering behaviors allows educators to design interventions that teach students alternative ways to access valuable reinforcers. Durand (1999), for example, conducted functional assessments to identify the reinforcers maintaining interfering behaviors exhibited by five students with severe disabilities and then implemented a functional communication training program to teach those students to request the same reinforcers using assistive communication devices. These students subsequently evidenced reductions in interfering behaviors and displayed generalized increases in communication across novel people and settings. Durand proposed that the approach of teaching functionally equivalent communication skills that could be understood by novel people enabled the students to recruit valuable reinforcers in their natural environments. In other words, generalization may be promoted by selecting target skills that are effective across multiple contexts and produce access to reinforcers that are valuable to the student.

Instructional Phase Strategies

Teach to Mastery

Unless target behaviors are taught to a level of mastery recognizable in generalized settings, students may not contact reinforcement for those behaviors and therefore may not demonstrate generalization (Baer, 1999). *Teaching to mastery* means delivering instruction until the target response reliably and accurately occurs with the appropriate topography, magnitude, latency, frequency, and duration needed to produce reinforcement (Cooper et al., 2007). To identify the necessary topographical and dimensional qualities of a target behavior, educators should observe typical responses that produce reinforcement in the natural environment. Observations about the acceptable range of physical response forms and intensities (topography and magnitude), typical delays to initiating the target response (latency), the desirable response rate (frequency), and the expected length of time for the target response (duration) are critical for determining mastery criteria. Instruction then may be delivered until students are able to emit fluent responses that meet predetermined topographical and dimensional criteria.

Consider the case of a student who learns to solve addition and subtraction problems in the classroom. To ensure that the student achieves a level of mastery that will produce reinforcement in other settings, the student needs to practice until the topography and other dimensional properties of adding and subtracting match those expected in natural settings. For example, to calculate a bank account balance, the student would need to add and subtract accurately, legibly, and fluently. Teaching addition and subtraction skills to mastery levels at school increases the probability that the student will efficiently calculate a correct account balance in other settings, such as at a store or bank.

Teach Sufficient Exemplars

Perhaps the most reliable way to promote generalization is to teach many examples across people, settings, and behaviors. Stimulus generalization is most likely when the target behavior is practiced with multiple people and across varied settings, using diverse instructional materials, and response generalization is most likely when multiple examples of the target behavior are taught (Stokes & Osnes, 1989). For example, designing a social skills intervention likely to promote generalized behavior change may require modeling several examples of the target social skill, presenting multiple examples of scenarios in which to apply the skill, role-playing the skill with different people, and arranging opportunities to practice the skill in varied environments.

Reeve, Reeve, Townsend, and Poulson (2007) illustrated the application of multiple exemplar training in a study designed to promote generalized helping behavior among children. The researchers used video modeling, prompting, and reinforcement to teach a variety of helping behaviors (e.g., cleaning and picking up) in the presence of varied stimuli (e.g., statements about the area being messy or someone else starting to clean/pick up). After the children mastered several types of helping behavior across a variety of training scenarios, they demonstrated an increase in helping behavior toward novel people in novel environments. Educators may adopt a similar approach by teaching many examples of the target skill and prompting students to display those skills across varied situations.

General case programming is a systematic approach to delivering instruction that promotes generalized performance by attending to the sufficiency of exemplars. As outlined by O'Neill (1990), general case programming involves defining the range of situations in which the target skill is expected to be demonstrated, identifying the variability in the universe of relevant stimuli and responses, selecting instructional examples that reflect the full range of stimulus and response variability, delivering carefully sequenced instruction using multiple examples and nonexamples, and then testing for accurate generalization. Tekin-Iftar and Birkan (2010) used the general case approach to teach food preparation skills to three children with autism. They began by identifying the relevant universe of food items and kitchen tools, assessing the range of stimulus and response variations (e.g., some blenders required pressing a button, whereas others required turning a knob), and then developing task analyses to teach representative exemplars. This general case approach, combined with the use of evidence-based prompting strategies, successfully facilitated the children's acquisition of generalized food preparation skills. Neef, Lensbower, Hockersmith, DePalma, and Gray (1990) also provided evidence for the effectiveness of the general case approach when they taught laundry skills to four individuals with developmental disabilities. Relative to instruction with a single washing machine and dryer set, instruction using several washing machines and dryers (selected via general case analysis) resulted in the emission of fewer errors when operating novel appliances. In sum, the generalized case approach emphasizes the importance of teaching multiple examples of the target skill using materials or other stimuli that adequately represent the variation a student would encounter in the natural environment.

Program Common Stimuli

Basic research suggests that the greater the similarity between the instructional setting and the natural environment, the greater the likelihood of generalization (Mayer et al., 2014). Therefore, another method for promoting generalization involves arranging for the instructional setting to mirror the conditions expected in the natural environment using a two-step process: (a) identify the relevant stimulus conditions in the natural environment and (b) incorporate those stimuli into the instructional context (Cooper et al., 2007). For example, to design a program to teach students with developmental disabilities to participate safely in dental examinations by programming for common stimuli, it would be necessary to begin by observing an actual dental examination to identify the sequence of activities and the relevant stimuli present (e.g., medical scrubs, masks, dental tools, background music, a reclining chair, and specific instructions delivered by the dentist). Subsequently, students could be taught to comply with the steps in a simulated dental examination facilitated by teachers wearing medical uniforms, using common dental tools, delivering typical instructions, and following the standard procedures expected during actual examinations.

Adopting a slightly different approach, Mesmer, Duhon, and Dodson (2007) applied the strategy of programming for common stimuli to promote the generalization of academic engagement. Specifically, the researchers implemented an intervention designed to increase students' rates of accurate math completion, and they facilitated generalization from the special education classroom (instructional setting) to the regular education classroom (generalization setting) by introducing some common, salient stimuli across both environments (e.g., goal statements, timers, thumbs-up symbols). In sum, when it is not feasible to deliver instruction in the natural environment, educators may use simulations and program for common stimuli to increase the likelihood that students will exhibit target skills outside of the instructional context.

Teach Loosely

Teaching loosely involves varying as many noncritical (functionally irrelevant) dimensions of the instructional context as possible and accepting a wide range of responses as correct (Stokes & Baer, 1977). This approach prevents students from displaying highly restricted skills only in response to a narrow range of stimulus conditions (e.g., responding accurately to a receptive language task when asked to "point" but not when asked to "show me") and therefore increases the probability of generalization.

Incidental teaching approaches use the tactic of teaching loosely to promote generalized improvements in verbal skills (Hart & Risley, 1980). Incidental teaching of language occurs in rich, natural environments, and instructional trials are initiated when a child communicates motivation for a reinforcer; accordingly, the stimuli present and the verbal responses that produce reinforcement are naturally "loose." Educators also may build looseness into their teaching by varying the context of instruction (e.g., teaching in different rooms, varying the seating arrangements within the classroom, changing the time of day for instruction, and altering the size and composition of instructional groups) and presenting instructions using varied language (e.g., varying an instruction to walk by saying "Walk with me please," "Come with me," and "Let's walk"; Mayer et al., 2014). Educational programs that arrange for students to receive instruction from multiple adults, use a variety of instructional methods, and take advantage of incidental learning opportunities therefore exemplify the practice of teaching loosely.

Use Sequential Modification

A less efficient but more guaranteed approach to ensure that students demonstrate generalized skills is to use systematic sequential modification: the process of teaching and reinforcing target behaviors across each relevant setting until durable performance is observed (Mayer et al., 2014). Consider, for example, a scenario in which an educator implements an intervention to increase social commenting behavior exhibited by a student during a morning snack period but does not observe generalized responding across settings. The teacher subsequently could use instructional strategies to increase social commenting behavior during afternoon snack time and continue sequentially implementing the intervention across other relevant contexts (e.g., lunch, recess, homeroom) until an acceptable level of generalized responding is observed. Instructional programs that supplement simulations with in situ training opportunities also utilize the sequential modification approach (Mayer et al., 2014). For example, Johnson et al. (2006) used a behavioral skills training model to teach abduction-prevention skills to a group of children, and they reported the highest levels of skill performance in real-world situations for children who participated in both simulated and in situ instruction.

Transfer Phase Strategies

Use Indiscriminable Contingencies and Schedule Thinning

Specific instructions and consistent, immediate reinforcing consequences may facilitate the acquisition of new skills; however, these strategies may inadvertently thwart efforts to achieve generalization (Mayer et al., 2014). Stokes and Osnes (1989) attributed this to the effects of predictability. In other words, when individuals are able to accurately predict when engagement in a target behavior will produce reinforcement, they are likely to exhibit highly discriminated responding (i.e., emitting the behavior only in the presence of stimuli that signal the current availability of reinforcement), rather than durable and sustained responding. Consider, for example, a student who learns that task engagement produces reinforcement only in the presence of a teacher roaming around the classroom. The predictability of the contingencies in the classroom may result in on-task behavior when the teacher wanders the classroom and off-task behavior when the teacher sits at the desk and diverts attention toward other activities. In this scenario, highly discriminated responding is less desirable than generalized responding, and an effective strategy would be to alter the predictability of the contingencies by asking the teacher to reinforce on-task behavior intermittently, at variable intervals of time and after varying delays, while randomly modifying the antecedent conditions (e.g., sometimes delivering reinforcement while seated at the desk, sometimes during direct instruction, and sometimes when walking around the classroom). Cariveau and Kodak (2017) used a similar strategy when they implemented a randomized, relatively indiscriminable, group contingency to promote high, sustained levels of academic engagement among elementary school students during reading and writing classes.

To apply this tactic, educators who deliver rich, continuous schedules of reinforcement to facilitate the acquisition of new skills should consider thinning these schedules by gradually increasing response requirements or delays (or both) to reinforcement as soon as the skill is established (Cooper et al., 2007). For example, to establish an appropriate communication response (e.g., asking for a break) as a replacement for interfering behavior, it initially may be necessary to reinforce each request immediately. However, gradually switching to a variable schedule of reinforcement (e.g., reinforcing only the first request after a variable duration of time elapses) and/or increasing the delay to honoring the request (e.g., requiring completion of additional work before allowing the break) may promote more enduring behavior change.

Request Generalization and Recruit Reinforcement

Baer (1999) noted that individuals interacting with students outside of instructional settings must be "woken up" to behaviors targeted for generalization. Three simple tactics increase the chances that others will notice and reinforce target behaviors. First, educators should explicitly ask students to emit the target behavior in natural environments. This simple request facilitates generalization by cueing students to demonstrate target behaviors outside the instructional environment (Stokes & Baer, 1977). Second, educators should teach students to request reinforcement through recruitment training. Recruitment training teaches students to emit a response that brings attention to their behavior (Alber & Heward, 1997). Recruitment training responses typically include students saying "How am I doing?" or "Does this look right?" (Craft, Alber, & Heward, 1998). Third, educators should inform individuals in the generalization setting to watch for target behaviors. It is easier for others to attend to and reinforce a behavior when they are primed to notice it. A simple case example illustrates these three strategies. To promote generalization of on-task behavior from school to home, a teacher may explicitly ask the student to practice on-task behavior at home and to recruit reinforcement by asking, "Am I on-task?" Additionally, the teacher may prompt caregivers to intentionally look for and reinforce on-task behavior at home. Overall, by helping others notice and reinforce target behaviors, these three tactics significantly increase the likelihood that target behaviors will occur and persist in natural environments.

Teach Mediation Strategies

Self-generated mediation strategies allow students to become the facilitators of generalized behavior change (Kazdin, 2012; Miltenberger, 2015). After teaching a target behavior, educators may use this method by (a) teaching students a strategy for transferring the behavior from one situation to another and (b) encouraging students to use this strategy in novel situations to self-direct the occurrence of the target behavior. Self-mediation strategies include carrying physical stimuli (e.g., activity schedules, visual task analyses, checklists) that provide reminders about expected behaviors, reciting self-instructions, and utilizing self-management strategies (Mayer et al., 2014;

Stokes & Osnes, 1989). One self-management approach, self-monitoring, requires students to observe and record occurrences of their own target behaviors and typically produces increases in desired behaviors with corresponding decreases in interfering behaviors. As a strategy for generalization, self-monitoring typically is used in concert with self-administered consequences to transfer the occurrence of a desired target behavior to anticipated generalization situations.

To understand the application of self-mediation strategies, consider the example of a high school student who readily engages in extended, subject-related discussions with a history teacher but rarely contributes to class discussions. To increase the student's level of participation during class discussions, the school psychologist could help the student develop a self-management procedure involving (a) a definition of contributing to class discussions, (b) identification of a goal to contribute to class discussions a minimum of five times per period, (c) a chart for recording each contribution to class discussions, and (d) a corresponding reinforcement schedule and menu. Mediation strategies such as this one are powerful tools to help students recognize, record, and reinforce their own behaviors in generalization settings where support from others may be improbable, atypical, or potentially unnecessary.

Blending Strategies

The aforementioned generalization strategies should not be viewed as mutually exclusive; in fact, the most effective approach to promote generalization may involve blending multiple strategies. For example, to teach a student appropriate ways to request adult attention, a combination of strategies may be necessary to facilitate stimulus, response, and temporal generalization. In the intervention planning phase, generalization tactics may include observing typical peer behavior to identify the types of requests that are likely to be considered acceptable and produce reinforcement in natural environments. Then, during intervention, generalization strategies may include teaching several examples of appropriate requests (e.g., tapping an adult on the shoulder, saying "excuse me," and raising a hand), practicing the requests with multiple adults across a variety of stimulus conditions (e.g., during group instruction and in the cafeteria), using both role-play and in situ approaches to instruction, systematically thinning the schedule of reinforcement during instruction, asking the student to practice the skill independently, encouraging other adults in the school to reinforce appropriate requests, and providing the student with visual cue cards to prompt the use of the skill throughout the day. To assist educators in planning for generalization and maintenance by blending multiple evidence-based strategies, a planning worksheet is provided (see Figure 5.1) in this chapter.

CONCLUSION

The ultimate success of any intervention is the degree to which it helps learners achieve generalized and enduring improvements in socially significant behaviors. Behavior change is of limited value to the learner if it does not last over time, is not emitted in appropriate contexts, or occurs in restricted forms when varied or expanded topographies are appropriate (Cooper et al., 2007). Rather than waiting for generalized responding to occur by chance, best practice entails actively applying a blend of evidence-based strategies to promote generalization and maintenance of socially appropriate behaviors. Well-designed interventions that explicitly program for generalization strengthen a repertoire of behaviors that are useful within and across diverse contexts and thereby result in overall improvements in quality of life.

REFERENCES

Alber, S. R., & Heward, W. L. (1997). Recruit it or lose it! Training students to recruit positive teacher attention. *Intervention in School and Clinic, 32*, 275–282. http://dx.doi.org/10.1177/105345129703200504

Ayllon, T., & Azrin, N. H. (1968). *The token economy: A motivational system for therapy and rehabilitation.* New York, NY: Appleton-Century-Crofts.

Baer, D. M. (1999). *How to plan for generalization* (2nd ed.). Austin, TX: Pro-Ed.

Baer, D. M., Wolf, M. M., & Risley, T. R. (1968). Some current dimensions of applied behavior analysis. *Journal of Applied Behavior Analysis, 1*, 91–97.

Cariveau, T., & Kodak, T. (2017). Programming a randomized dependent group contingency and common stimuli to promote durable behavior change. *Journal of Applied Behavior Analysis, 50*, 121–133.

Cooper, J. O., Heron, T. E., & Heward, W. L. (2007). *Applied behavior analysis* (2nd ed.). Upper Saddle River, NJ: Merrill/Prentice-Hall.

Craft, M. A., Alber, S. R., & Heward, W. L. (1998). Teaching elementary students with developmental disabilities to recruit teacher attention in a general education classroom: Effects on teacher praise and academic productivity. *Journal of Applied Behavior Analysis, 31*, 399–415. http://dx.doi.org/10.1901/jaba.1998.31-399

Durand, V. M. (1999). Functional communication training using assistive devices: Recruiting natural communities of reinforcement. *Journal of Applied Behavior Analysis, 32*, 247–267. http://dx.doi.org/10.1901/jaba.1999.32-247

Hart, B., & Risley, T. R. (1980). In vivo language intervention: Unanticipated general effects. *Journal of Applied Behavior Analysis, 13*, 407–432.

Johnson, B. M., Miltenberger, R. G., Knudson, P., Egemo-Helm, K., Kelso, P., Jostad, C., & Langley, L. (2006). A preliminary evaluation of two behavioral skills training procedures for teaching abduction-prevention skills to schoolchildren. *Journal of Applied Behavior Analysis, 39,* 25–34.

Kazdin, A. E. (2012). *Behavior modification in applied settings* (7th ed.). Belmont, CA: Wadsworth.

Mayer, G. R., Sulzer-Azaroff, B., & Wallace, M. (2014). *Behavior analysis for lasting change* (3rd ed.). Cornwall-on-Hudson, NY: Sloan.

McGee, G. G., & Daly, T. (2007). Incidental teaching of age-appropriate social phrases to children with autism. *Research and Practice for Persons With Severe Disabilities, 32,* 112–123. http://dx.doi.org/10.2511/rpsd.32.2.112

Mesmer, E. M., Duhon, G. J., & Dodson, K. G. (2007). The effects of programming common stimuli for enhancing stimulus generalization of academic behavior. *Journal of Applied Behavior Analysis, 40,* 553–557. http://dx.doi.org/10.1901/jaba.2007.40-553

Miltenberger, R. G. (2015). *Behavior modification: Principles and procedures* (6th ed.). Belmont, CA: Wadsworth/Thomson Learning.

Neef, N. A., Lensbower, J., Hockersmith, I., DePalma, V., & Gray, K. (1990). In vivo versus simulation training: An interactional analysis of range and type of training exemplars. *Journal of Applied Behavior Analysis, 23,* 447–458.

O'Neill, R. E. (1990). Establishing verbal repertoires: Toward the application of general case analysis and programming. *Analysis of Verbal Behavior, 8,* 113–126. http://dx.doi.org/10.1007/BF03392852

Reeve, S. A., Reeve, K. F., Townsend, D. B., & Poulson, C. L. (2007). Establishing a generalized repertoire of helping behavior in children with autism. *Journal of Applied Behavior Analysis, 40,* 123–136. http://dx.doi.org/10.1901/jaba.2007.11-05

Stokes, T. F., & Baer, D. M. (1977). An implicit technology of generalization. *Journal of Applied Behavior Analysis, 10,* 349–367.

Stokes, T. F., & Osnes, P. G. (1989). An operant pursuit of generalization [republished article]. *Behavior Therapy, 20,* 337–355. http://dx.doi.org/10.1016/S0005-7894(89)80054-1

Tekin-Iftar, E., & Birkan, B. (2010). Small group instruction for students with autism: General case training and observational learning. *The Journal of Special Education, 44,* 50–63. http://dx.doi.org/10.1177/0022466908325219

U.S. Department of Education. (2016). *Every Student Succeeds Act (ESSA).* Retrieved from http://www.ed.gov/essa

6

EFFECT OF EXTRINSIC REINFORCEMENT ON "INTRINSIC" MOTIVATION: SEPARATING FACT FROM FICTION

ANGELEQUE AKIN-LITTLE AND STEVEN G. LITTLE

The use of rewards or reinforcement is common in schools. Teachers frequently use some sort of reward system for academic output and appropriate behavior (e.g., stickers given for completed classwork, pizza coupons given for reading books, tokens given for appropriate classroom behavior), and decades of empirical research support the efficacy of reinforcement-based procedures in the classroom (e.g., Barrish, Saunders, & Wolf, 1969; Beavers, Iwata, & Lerman, 2013; Birnbrauer, Wolf, Kidder, & Tague, 1965; Mann-Feder & Varda, 1996; O'Leary & Drabman, 1971; Swiezy, Matson, & Box, 1992).

However, some educators and psychologists have expressed concern over the use of reward contingency systems in classrooms (Deci, Koestner, & Ryan, 1999a, 1999b, 2001; Gneezy, Meier, & Rey-Biel, 2011; Kohn, 1993, 1996). The perceived problem is the belief that extrinsic reinforcers may have a detrimental effect on a student's intrinsic motivation to perform a task once the reinforcer for that task is withdrawn. These writers posited that if reinforcement is used, an individual's perceptions of competence and self-determination will lessen, thereby decreasing, possibly forever, that individual's intrinsic motivation to perform the task. Teachers and teacher education students are frequently told that the use of extrinsic reinforcement kills creativity (Hennessey, 2015; Tegano, Moran, & Sawyers, 1991). Further, many teacher education programs emphasize intuition and insight to facilitate learning. In the resulting teaching practices (e.g., discovery learning, constructivism), the teacher does not impart knowledge; rather, the focus is on teacher arrangement of the environment to help students "discover" knowledge in the absence of external reinforcement. This pedagogical instruction is in direct conflict with the available data that support the use of external reinforcers in the classroom and the efficacy of direct instruction (Alberto & Troutman, 2013).

In 1994, Cameron and Pierce conducted a meta-analysis on the effect of external reinforcement on intrinsic motivation, and it generated intense debate on this topic (Cameron & Pierce, 1996; Kohn, 1996; Lepper, 1998; Lepper, Keavney, & Drake, 1996; Ryan & Deci, 1996). Subsequently, two additional meta-analytic studies were conducted (Cameron, Banko, & Pierce, 2001; Deci et al., 1999a) with contradictory results. Cameron and Pierce (1994) and Cameron et al. (2001) found no detrimental effect or detrimental effects only under certain proscribed conditions, whereas Deci et al. (1999a) found negative effects. Further, others have attempted to provide illumination for contradictory findings by examining findings of the detrimental effect from a more behavioral, scientific perspective (Akin-Little, Eckert, Lovett, & Little, 2004; Akin-Little & Little, 2004; Carton, 1996; Dickinson, 1989; Flora, 1990; Mintz, 2003).

DEFINITIONS OF INTRINSIC AND EXTRINSIC MOTIVATION

Deci and Ryan (1985) defined an *intrinsically motivated behavior* as one for which there exists no recognizable reward except the activity itself (e.g., reading). That is, behavior that cannot be attributed to external controls is usually attributed to intrinsic motivation. However, according to Flora (1990), no behavior occurs without an identifying external circumstance:

> A complete scientific explanation of behavior does not require reference to constructs which are, in principle, unobservable. . . . A complete scientific account for any behavior of any organism may be obtained with a *complete* description of the functional interdependency of the behavior–environment interaction. (p. 323)

Many behavioral researchers (e.g., Akin-Little et al., 2004; Dickinson, 1989) have criticized continued attempts to identify the construct of "intrinsic motivation," suggesting that such efforts impede the goal of the scientific study of behavior. Creating internal constructs that depend on inferences in their explanations may obstruct the discovery of the true function of behavior through more scientific, measurable, and observable means.

In general, if the dichotomy between intrinsic and extrinsic motivation is accepted, intrinsic motivation is assumed to be of greater value (Delaney & Royal, 2017; Fair & Silvestri, 1992). This belief is due in large part to the Western conceptualization of the human as autonomous and individualistic. In this view, humans are driven toward self-actualization, and any occurrence that impinges on self-determination causes dissonance. Further, the use of extrinsic reinforcement is seen as controlling or limiting self-discovery, creativity, and the capacity for humans to reach fulfillment (Eisenberger, Pierce, & Cameron, 1999; Hennessey, 2015). Interestingly, when this tenet is examined in relation to the use of punishment, punishment is perceived as less of a threat to autonomy because humans may choose how to behave to avoid punishment (Maag, 1996).

Not surprisingly, a debate has resulted surrounding the intrinsic–extrinsic distinction. Several critics (e.g., Akin-Little & Little, 2004) have produced data that illuminate the problems associated with identifying intrinsically motivated behaviors. Other theories have been proposed that purport to explain behavior that appears to occur in the absence of any extrinsic motivation. However, these behaviors may, in fact, be due to anticipated future benefits (Bandura, 1977) or intermittent reinforcement (Dickinson, 1989). Zimmerman (1985) stated that cognitive definitions of intrinsic motivation are definitions "by default" (p. 118). That is, behavior that cannot be attributed to external controls is usually attributed to intrinsic motivation.

According to Deci and Ryan's (1985) definition, intrinsic motivation is evidenced when people participate in an activity because of the internal enjoyment of the activity and not because of any perceived extrinsic reward. Intrinsic motivation enables people to feel competent and self-determining. Intrinsically motivated behavior is said to result in creativity, flexibility, and spontaneity. In contrast, extrinsically motivated actions are characterized by pressure and tension and are believed to result in low self-esteem and anxiety. Horcones (1987) stated that intrinsic consequences occur in the absence of programming by others. They are natural and automatic responses inevitably produced by the structural characteristics of the physical environment in which humans exist. Extrinsic consequences, conversely, are those that occur in addition to any intrinsic consequences and are most often programmed by others (i.e., the social environment, researchers, teacher, applied behavior analysts). On the basis of this differentiation, Mawhinney, Dickinson, and Taylor (1989) subsequently defined intrinsic and extrinsic motivation as follows: "Intrinsically controlled behavior consists of behavior controlled by unprogrammed consequences while extrinsically controlled behavior consists of behavior controlled by programmed consequences" (p. 111).

THEORIES AND INVESTIGATIONS OF REINFORCER–REWARD EFFECTS

Cognitive Evaluation Theory

Deci and Ryan's (1985) cognitive evaluation theory is based on the assumption that self-determination and competence are innate human needs. Cognitive evaluation theory states that events facilitate or hinder feelings of competence and self-determination depending on their perceived informational, controlling, or amotivational significance. Deci and Ryan divided rewards into two categories: *task-contingent* rewards and *quality-dependent* rewards. Task-contingent rewards are given for participation in an activity, solving a problem, or completing a task. Quality-dependent rewards involve the "quality of one's performance relative to some normative information or standard" (p. 74). Task-contingent rewards are hypothesized to detrimentally affect intrinsic motivation by decreasing self-determination (i.e., reward is viewed as a controlling event attempting to determine behavior thereby decreasing self-determination and, consequently, intrinsic motivation). Quality-dependent rewards are also believed to act to decrease intrinsic motivation by reducing one's feelings of self-determination. However, quality-dependent rewards also serve to increase feeling of competence, according to Deci and Ryan (i.e., reward is viewed as an informational event indicating skill at a certain task, leading to an increase in feelings of competence that serves to increase intrinsic motivation). Therefore, it is never clear whether the decremental effect to self-determination or the incremental effect to competence will be stronger when examining quality-dependent rewards. Thus, for Deci and Ryan, quality-dependent rewards may not decrease intrinsic motivation. The detrimental effect of greatest concern, then, is in circumstances involving task-completion rewards. Eisenberger and Cameron (1996) further divided task-completion rewards into the subcategories of performance-independent rewards that individuals receive simply for participation in an activity and completion-independent rewards given when an individual has finished a task or activity. Cognitive evaluation theory would suggest that an individual's intrinsic motivation would be most detrimentally affected upon reception of tangible, anticipated rewards. Additionally, according to this theory, verbal rewards may be informational and therefore increase intrinsic motivation. Events may also be perceived as amotivational, indicating an individual's lack of skill, which reduces one's cognitions of competence and, subsequently, intrinsic motivation.

In 1988, Rummel and Feinberg conducted a meta-analysis assessing cognitive evaluation theory. They concluded that controlling, extrinsic rewards do have a damaging effect on intrinsic motivation, providing support for the theory. Basic problems with cognitive evaluation theory, however, were also identified. First, faulty reasoning was used because rewards were identified as controlling, informational, or amotivational after the performance had been measured. Second, feelings of competence and self-determination, central to the theory as agents for change in intrinsic motivation, are not measurable. The assumption is made that changes are occurring because changes in behavior are observed. The constructs of self-determination, competence, and even intrinsic motivation are inferred from the very behavior they supposedly cause (Cameron & Pierce, 1994). The theory contains no explanation for why the disquiet associated with a decrease in self-determination would reduce intrinsic motivation. As Eisenberger and Cameron (1996) wrote, "based on the theory's premise, one could alternatively argue that reduced self-determination would, for example, reduce preference for the reward or instigate anger at the person delivering the reward" (p. 1156).

Results of a meta-analysis performed by Cameron and Pierce (1994) partly serve to refute cognitive evaluation theory. Deci and Ryan (1985) stressed the importance of measurements of attitude, theorizing that interest, enjoyment, and satisfaction are central emotions to intrinsic motivation. How a person feels about an activity is reflected behaviorally as time spent on task. The results of the Cameron and Pierce meta-analysis, however, suggest that reward (and subsequent withdrawal) tends not to affect attitude. They further found that attitude seems to be affected positively when verbal rewards are used and when rewards are contingent on a precise level of achievement.

Other researchers (Cameron & Pierce, 1994; Eisenberger & Cameron, 1996; Eisenberger et al., 1999) have suggested that CET is not a useful or viable theory and that any decrements in behavior are better explained through learned helplessness or general interest theory. In learned helplessness, the decrement in intrinsic motivation is said to be due to the single reward delivery paradigm used by most studies in this area. General interest theory suggests that intrinsic motivation is driven by more than just self-determination and competence needs. Eisenberger et al. (1999) proposed that rewards must be examined for both the content and the context of tasks. Rewards that communicate task performance can satisfy needs, wants, and desires, which can increase intrinsic motivation while rewards that convey the task is extraneous to needs, wants, and desires may serve to decrease intrinsic motivation. The symbolic function of rewards is then what is important along with personality and cultural influences.

Overjustification Hypothesis

Lepper, Greene, and Nisbett (1973) divided preschool children into three groups: expected reward, unexpected reward, and no reward. Children in the first group were promised and received a good-player award contingent on their drawing with magic markers. Children in the second group received an award but were not promised it beforehand, and children in the third group did not expect or receive an award. In subsequent free-play sessions, children from the expected-reward group were observed to spend less time drawing than the other two groups.

In an attempt to explain their results, Lepper et al. (1973) offered the *overjustification hypothesis*. According to this hypothesis, if a person is already performing an activity and receiving no extrinsic reward for that performance, introduction of an extrinsic reward will decrease intrinsic interest or motivation. This occurs because the person's performance is now overjustified, resulting in the person's perception that his or her level of intrinsic motivation to perform the activity is less than it was initially. According to this theory, the person subsequently performs the activity less once the reinforcement is removed (Lepper, 1983; Williams, 1980).

Lepper et al.'s (1973) results have been replicated (e.g., Deci & Ryan, 1985; Greene & Lepper, 1974; Morgan, 1984); however, research with more school-like tasks and older students suggest that an undermining effect of reward does not occur if the students are told they have achieved a preset standard and the task is at a challenging level for them (Pittman, Boggiano, & Ruble, 1983). The use of rewards has actually been shown to increase intrinsic motivation by studies in which rewards were administered contingent on performance (e.g., Lepper, 1983), rewards provided information about the students' competence (e.g., Lepper & Gilovich, 1981; Rosenfield, Folger, & Adelman, 1980), and rewards were given to students not optimally motivated toward desirable educational goals (Morgan, 1984). Moreover, researchers have consistently found that verbal rewards tend to increase intrinsic motivation, whereas tangible rewards may decrease intrinsic motivation (Cameron & Pierce, 1994). Reductions of intrinsic motivation have not been found with traditionally behavioral studies using a single-subject, repeated-measures design (Akin-Little & Little, 2004; Cameron & Pierce, 1994; Mintz, 2003). Additionally, when long-term effects of extrinsic rewards have been examined, no decrement in behavior has been observed (Halpern et al., 2015; Jackson, 2010).

Behavioral Investigations

Flora (1990) stated that "[behavioral] psychology is supposedly the study of individual behavior, not the study of group means" (p. 338). This statement succinctly illustrates the importance of within-subject designs in behavioral research. Behaviorally oriented researchers assert that cognitive researchers studying the effects of extrinsic reward using between-groups designs have used measurement phases that are too short to detect temporal trends or transition states (Cameron & Pierce, 1994). Within-subject designs, however, measure behavior over a number of sessions, thereby alleviating this shortcoming. Unlike between-groups paradigms, the within-subject design takes measurements of time on task over a number of sessions for each phase. After baseline (B) data are collected, reinforcement is introduced, and measurements are again taken repeatedly. Finally, a withdrawal of reinforcement occurs (i.e., baseline II, BII), and measurements of time on task are taken again. Time on task is taken as a measurement of intrinsic motivation, and the difference in time on task between pre- and postreinforcement (i.e., B I and II) is cataloged as intrinsic motivation where differences are attributed to external reinforcement. Behavioral investigations have also traditionally included a follow-up phase during which measures of behavior are taken 2 to 3 weeks after the conclusion of the experiment to assess trends and temporal states. Behavioral researchers have further stated that cognitivists fail to make any distinction between rewards and reinforcers. They posit that these two words cannot be used synonymously. A reinforcer is an event that increases the frequency of the target behavior it follows, and a reward is a pleasant occurrence that has not been shown to necessarily strengthen behavior (Cameron & Pierce, 1994). Behaviorists' use of within-subject repeated-measures designs allows determination of whether a reward is actually a reinforcer for a particular subject. Compared with the large number of group studies examining this supposed event, few studies examine the effects of extrinsic reinforcement from a behavioral standpoint (Akin-Little & Little, 2004; Davidson & Bucher, 1978; Feingold & Mahoney, 1975; Mawhinney et al., 1989; Mintz, 2003; Vasta, Andrews, McLaughlin, Stirpe, & Comfort, 1978; Vasta & Stirpe, 1979).

Akin-Little and Little (2004) attempted to examine the possible overjustification effects of the implementation of token economy for appropriate behavior. Although exhibiting appropriate behavior in a classroom setting may not be seen as intrinsically motivated behavior, many reward contingency systems are used to increase compliant behavior. No previous study used appropriate classroom behavior as the dependent variable although classroom management, and student behavior is a major concern of many classroom teachers. The subjects in this study were elementary school students chosen by their teacher as high in compliant behavior to classroom rules. The token system was implemented in an actual classroom setting. Subjects' behavior was analyzed after a BI, reward procedure, BII, and follow-up period. No overjustification effect was found for any of the students (i.e., no student's behavior dropped below BI in either the BII or follow-up phase).

Mintz (2003) used a multielement, multiple-baseline-across-participant design with three children to test the overjustification effect on behaviors for which each child demonstrated a preference in the absence of external reinforcement. The purpose of the study was to examine the effect of expected and unexpected reinforcers on behavior that met the definition for intrinsically motivated behavior (i.e., one for which there exists no recognizable reward except the activity itself). Results provided no support for the overjustification effect. In fact, an additive effect was found. That is, after reinforcement was removed responding remained stable and at a higher level than was observed during baseline.

Flora and Flora (1999) evaluated the effects of extrinsic reinforcement for reading during childhood on reported reading habits of college students. Specifically, the effects of participation in a particular reading program and parental reinforcement for reading on reading habits of college students were investigated. Results indicated that being reinforced with neither money nor pizza increased or decreased the amount of reading, nor did it influence participant's self-reported intrinsic motivation for reading. These results provide no support for the hypothesis that extrinsic rewards for reading undermine intrinsic interest in reading. Rather, it appears that extrinsic rewards for reading set the conditions for continued interest in reading.

BEHAVIORAL CRITICISMS OF COGNITIVE RESEARCH

Neglect of the behavioral literature and principles has been too common in the majority of past studies on intrinsic motivation. This reality has served to encourage cognitive researchers to develop their own theories and explanations. Behavioral explanations for intrinsically motivated behavior such as anticipated future benefits (Bandura, 1977), intermittent reinforcement (Dickinson, 1989), competing response theory (Reiss & Sushinsky, 1975), behavioral contrast (Feingold & Mahoney, 1975; Killeen, 2014), and the presence of discriminative stimuli (Flora, 1990) have been ignored.

Reiss and Sushinsky (1975) were especially critical of the overjustification hypothesis, stating that the theory is too vague to be useful for scientific purposes and competing response theory more adequately accounts for any obtained decrements in intrinsic motivation. Competing response theory suggests that a student's intrinsic motivation may decrease because of other stimuli present in the environment. Students respond to these stimuli, and this results in a decrease of their response to the targeted activity before termination of contingencies occurs. Bates (1979) offered behavioral contrast as an additional explanation for decrements in intrinsic motivation.

In this paradigm, two behaviors are reinforced on different schedules. One behavior is then extinguished. This produces an increase in response of the other behavior. The classic example is of pigeons pecking at different colors. When the reinforcer for pecking at one color is withheld, the pecking at the remaining color increases in rate and intensity. Finally, Flora (1990) discussed the possibility of discriminative stimuli as an explanation. According to this account, behaviors occur in an environmental context. Instead of examining an unobservable construct such as intrinsic motivation, Flora suggested it is more useful to determine the discriminative stimulus and the reinforcers in the environment that maintain a functional relationship. These factors, Flora proposed, maintain behavior rate and occurrence.

Additionally, Dickinson (1989) proposed that decrements in intrinsic motivation may occur if the activity is one that subjects find boring or uninteresting, rewards are given for activities culturally praised as intrinsically motivated behaviors (e.g., artistic or creative activities), or rewards become aversive stimuli. In the first instance, motivation is decreased because satiation is reached through repeated exposure to sensory reinforcement. In the second illustration, decrement is explained through an examination of cultural norms. People are often praised if they engage in certain activities that supposedly offer specific intrinsic rewards (e.g., painting, dancing). If an individual is then extrinsically rewarded for this activity, the person may experience a decrease in praise. If praise is reinforcing for that person, he or she may engage in the activity less because the activity is now differentially correlated with the loss of praise. In the third example, subjects may not participate in the activity because they are angry with the experimenter for withholding the reward, they fail to meet the performance standards, or individuals are offered rewards for engaging in nonpreferred activities or threatened with punishment for noncompliance (Dickinson, 1989).

Eisenberger and Cameron (1996) also presented an interpretation of the specified conditions under which rewards may decrease intrinsic motivation. They stated that individuals who receive performance-independent rewards may perceive that they have no control over the reward. This perception may lead to a decrease in performance that may be misinterpreted as a decrease in intrinsic motivation. These authors suggested that the intrinsic interest decrement may be better explained by learned helplessness, which asserts that "uncontrollable aversive stimulation results in generalized motivational deficits" (p. 1156). The learned helplessness theory predicts a decrease in intrinsic motivation for performance-independent rewards. However, unlike cognitive evaluation theory, no prediction of a decrement is suggested following task-completion rewards.

Carton (1996) examined the social cognitivist assertion that praise appears to increase intrinsic motivation whereas the delivery of tangible rewards appears to decrease intrinsic motivation. These assumptions are based on cognitive evaluation theory (Deci & Ryan, 1985). However, as Carton further stated, operant psychologists' reviews of the literature on the effects of rewards on intrinsic motivation (e.g., Akin-Little et al., 2004; Dickinson, 1989; Flora, 1990) reach conclusions vastly different from those conducted by psychologists with decidedly cognitive viewpoints. Important points raised by operant psychologists include the finding that many social cognitivists have presumed that reinforcement decreases intrinsic motivation when in fact the rewards used in these particular studies often did not show a clear increase in response rate. Thus, by definition, these presumed rewards were not reinforcement. Furthermore, cognitive studies did not assess response rates for stability, behavioral observations included in most of these studies were often relatively brief, and these studies rarely included follow-up observations. Carton eloquently stated that a review of the literature finds little support for examples of a decrease in intrinsic motivation based on the cognitive evaluation theory and reveals three confounding effects: (a) temporal contiguity, (b) the number of reward administrations, and (c) discriminative stimuli associated with reward availability.

Carton (1996) also discussed the effects of temporal contiguity. *Temporal contiguity* refers to the amount of time between the occurrence of the target behavior and the delivery of the consequence. In an examination of the literature, Carton found time differences between the delivery of tangible rewards and verbal rewards (i.e., praise) in many studies. Most of the verbal rewards were delivered immediately after the target behavior occurred, thereby increasing the likelihood that behavior would be repeated. In contrast, tangible rewards were often delivered days or weeks after the treatment setting, virtually ensuring a decrease in the occurrence of the target behavior. Carton's finding that researchers in those studies have consistently found decreases in intrinsic motivation after the administration of tangible rewards and increases in intrinsic motivation after the administration of verbal rewards, then, is not surprising.

Meta-Analyses

Cameron and Pierce's (1994) meta-analytic findings that reinforcement did not harm intrinsic motivation have been criticized by researchers who stated that their methodology and, consequently, conclusions drawn were flawed (Kohn, 1996; Lepper et al., 1996). Kohn (1996) argued that Cameron and Pierce ignored important findings suggesting that the reception of tangible rewards is associated with less voluntary time on task as contrasted with the no-reward condition. Kohn further stated that Cameron and Pierce's methodology was flawed because results from studies in which informational praise was delivered (i.e., no detrimental effects on intrinsic motivation expected) with praise delivered that might be construed as manipulative (i.e., detrimental effects on intrinsic motivation expected) were combined to detect an overall effect. Further, Kohn pointed out that, in his view, the more common type of praise in a classroom is the latter, and therefore, studies that used manipulative praise should be examined separately. Lepper et al. (1996) labeled Cameron and Pierce's (1994) meta-analysis overly simplistic and of little theoretical value. Similar to Kohn, Lepper et al. wrote that the 1994 meta-analysis should not have focused on an overall effect because rewards have a variety of effects dependent on the nature of the activities, the manner in which the rewards are administered, and the situation surrounding administration. For example, the reception of a tangible reward would be expected to decrease intrinsic motivation, whereas the reception of a verbal reward (i.e., social reinforcement) would be expected to maintain or increase intrinsic motivation.

Cameron and Pierce (1996) responded to these criticisms by first stating that investigating the overall effect of extrinsic rewards is necessary for practical and theoretical reasons. From a practical standpoint, it is clear that many parents, educators, and administrators have embraced Kohn's (1993) view that overall, incentive systems are damaging. Many classroom teachers, however, still wish to adopt an incentive program. These teachers are, therefore, interested in whether, overall, rewards would disrupt intrinsic motivation for completing work or attaining a specified level of performance. The overall effect of reward, then, is critical (Cameron & Pierce, 1996). Theoretically, many academic journals and textbooks point to the overall detrimental effects of rewards or reinforcement. Consequently, many parents, teachers, and others are loath to use any reinforcement procedure under any conditions. It is necessary, then, according to Cameron and Pierce, to analyze the overall effect of rewards since many writers are criticizing the use of incentive programs in educational settings. These criticisms are based on research findings that some interpret as indicating an overall negative effect. Cameron and Pierce concluded their response by stating that their meta-analysis was the most thorough to date on this topic and compares favorably with Tang and Hall's (1995) analysis, which included 50 studies; Wiersma's (1992) analysis, which contained 20 studies; and Rummel and Feinberg's (1988) analysis, which comprised 45 studies. Each of these analyses discovered overall that extrinsic rewards had detrimental effects on intrinsic motivation. These findings were in direct contrast to the conclusions of Cameron and Pierce, who stated emphatically that their results, from an analysis of more than 100, illustrate that rewards can be used to maintain or even enhance intrinsic motivation. Further, and more important, the conditions under which detrimental effects to intrinsic motivation are exhibited occur under highly circumscribed conditions, situations that are easily eschewed by the proper use of token reinforcement programs.

In response to Cameron and Pierce's (1994) meta-analytic findings, Deci et al. (1999a) conducted a separate meta-analysis, in part to refute the previous findings. They included 128 studies and arranged the analysis to provide a test of CET. Deci and colleagues did find support for CET and substantial undermining effects after the use of external rewards. They specifically examined verbal rewards (termed *positive feedback*) separately from tangible rewards. They further divided tangible rewards into the categories of unexpected and expected. The expected reward category included the divisions of task noncontingent (rewards given not for engaging in the task specifically but for participation in the experiment), engagement contingent (rewards given for participation in the task), completion contingent (rewards given for completion of the task), and performance contingent (rewards given only for performing the task well or surpassing a previously set standard). A decrement in intrinsic motivation, measured by time on task for 101 of the studies and self-report of interest for 84 of the studies, was found in every category except in verbal rewards and unexpected rewards. Interestingly, Deci et al. divided the verbal reward studies into the categories of college-age and children. While verbal rewards enhanced the intrinsic motivation of college students (i.e., significant increase), the delivery of verbal rewards did not enhance children's intrinsic motivation. Deci also discussed the importance of the interpersonal context in the delivery of verbal reward (i.e., rewards delivered in a controlling manner will tend to decrease intrinsic motivation, whereas rewards delivered in a noncontrolling manner will tend to increase feelings of competence and, hence, intrinsic motivation).

On the basis of the finding that children exhibited less enhancement than college students from verbal rewards, Deci et al. (1999a) suggested that this finding has important implications for the use of verbal praise in the classroom writing "verbal rewards are less likely to have a positive effect for children ... [they] can even have a negative effect on intrinsic motivation" (p. 9). That is a misleading assumption. The importance (Maag & Katsiyannis, 1999) and effectiveness of teacher attention, particularly in the form of verbal praise, has been documented (e.g., Drevno et al., 1994). The assertion that verbal praise should not be used in a classroom setting is in direct opposition to the available data.

Cameron et al.'s (2001) meta-analysis found, in general, that rewards do not decrease intrinsic motivation. Cameron stated that this overall effect is important because educators and other school personnel often report that all rewards are harmful to motivation. Contrary to Deci et al. (1999a), Cameron et al. included the categories of high and low initial interest. Notably, they found that reward can enhance time on task intrinsic motivation. This is in accordance with Bandura's (1986) finding that most activities have little initial interest for people but that engagement in the activity may increase interest. This has important implications for schools because many children do not initially find academic tasks appealing. The use of reward then may be used to increase students' time on task and intrinsic motivation for a task. Cameron et al. did not find decremental effects with the use of verbal praise for either children or college students. Instead, they found a significant increase.

In terms of tangible reward, Cameron et al. (2001) found no detrimental effect for unexpected rewards or for rewards that are closely tied to specific standards of performance and to success. Detrimental effect was found when rewards were not explicitly connected to the task and signified failure (Cameron et al., 2001). This last finding is also important to educators who may be attempting to use reinforcement to increase either social or academic behavior. Oftentimes, teachers will set the goals for a student too high. Behavioral principles state that it is important to shape behavior, reinforcing the child's current competencies and giving him or her a chance for success.

The most recent meta-analysis examining 40 years of research on intrinsic motivation and extrinsic reward was conducted by Cerasoli, Nicklin, and Ford (2014). The meta-analysis encompassed 183 studies and 212,468 participants but failed to include single-case-design studies. The results generally supported the predictive validity of intrinsic motivation for performance, but the authors concluded that "incentives and intrinsic motivation are not of necessity antagonistic" (p. 1001). Further, they stated that both external incentives and intrinsic motivation are essential to performance.

It is also important to remember that these meta-analyses inconsistently examined the results of more behavioral studies (e.g., Feingold & Mahoney, 1975) and did not always include single-case-design studies. It is important to note that no study to date using single case design (e.g., Akin-Little & Little, 2004; Mintz, 2003) has found any detrimental effects with the use of reinforcement contingencies (Akin-Little et al., 2004). This is significant because those studies tend more typically to mimic the use of reward contingencies in classrooms. Perhaps if more behaviorally oriented studies were conducted, there would be more evidence to refute the notion of the supposed detrimental effects of the reward on any task or behavior.

BEST PRACTICES IN THE USE OF REINFORCEMENT PROCEDURES IN THE CLASSROOM

In 1991, the National Education Association published a document titled *How to Kill Creativity* (Tegano et al., 1991) that stated,

> The expectation of reward can actually undermine intrinsic motivation and creativity of performance. . . . A wide variety of rewards have now

been tested, and everything from good-player awards to marshmallows produces the expected decrements in intrinsic motivation and creativity of performance ... [making students] much less likely to take risks or to approach a task with a playful or experimental attitude. (p. 119)

However, a review of several educational psychology books (e.g., Slavin, 2012; Woolfolk, 2015) reveals a more balanced view of the effects of rewards. This is an encouraging sign given that many of the findings in this area support the effectiveness of reinforcement procedures in the classroom and many researchers have criticized the literature on supposed damaging effects (e.g., Bandura, 1986; Bates, 1979; Dickinson, 1989; Flora, 1990; Morgan, 1984).

Additionally, any detrimental effects of the use of extrinsic reinforcement can be easily avoided. Rewards should not be presented for mere participation in a task without regard for completion or quality. Decrements have also been found in the social cognitive literature when rewards are presented on a single occasion. This is not the most common method used in classrooms. In general, reward contingencies used in schools are presented repeatedly with appropriate thinning of schedules used when behavior change has occurred. Psychologists are advised to heed this advice when consulting and planning with teachers on the use of reinforcers in the school setting.

Teachers continually request training in behavior and classroom management (Maag, 1999). The irony is that techniques that aid teachers in improving their management skills have existed since Skinner's (1953) seminal work on the principles of operant conditioning. Techniques based on the use of extrinsic reinforcers (i.e., positive reinforcement) work in the classroom. These include verbal praise, token economies, group contingencies, contracts, and so on (Little & Akin-Little, 2003). The question, then, is why teacher education programs are not incorporating these principles into their curriculum. Why is there such resistance to the data? Axelrod (1996) suggested that some causes for the lack of both professional and popular acceptability may be that the use of positive reinforcement consumes too much time and attempts to eliminate human choice, and that there is little compensation for educational personnel to use these procedures. This is a somewhat discouraging view, and one can only hope that future and current teachers and educational personnel make evidence-based decisions when choosing interventions for children and youth. Perhaps with the increased use of the response to intervention (Gresham, Reschly, & Shinn, 2010) model and positive behavior supports (Simonsen & Sugai, 2009) in the schools, teachers may be opening up to the use of positive and proactive behavioral approaches in the classroom.

Bribery may be defined as an inducement to engage in illegal or inappropriate behavior. When education personnel, including school psychologists, extol the use of extrinsic reinforcement in the classroom, the motive is clearly not to "bribe" children and youth but to increase appropriate academic and social behavior. The goal is obviously not to decrease intrinsic motivation, although it is unclear that the construct exists or is useful in the science of psychology. It is apparent through an examination of the data that any decrease occurs only under specifically circumscribed conditions, conditions that are easily avoidable. Best practice would suggest that children and youth deserve interventions based on sound, empirical findings. The positive effect of the use of reinforcers in the classroom is one such conclusion.

REFERENCES

Akin-Little, K. A., Eckert, T. L., Lovett, B. J., & Little, S. G. (2004). Extrinsic reinforcement in the classroom: Bribery or best practice? *School Psychology Review, 33,* 344–362.

Akin-Little, K. A., & Little, S. G. (2004). Re-examining the overjustification effect: A case study. *Journal of Behavioral Education, 13,* 179–192. http://dx.doi.org/10.1023/B:JOBE.0000037628.81867.69

Alberto, P. A., & Troutman, A. C. (2013). *Applied behavior analysis for teachers* (9th ed.). Upper Saddle River, NJ: Pearson Prentice Hall.

Axelrod, S. (1996). What's wrong with behavior analysis? *Journal of Behavioral Education, 6,* 247–256. http://dx.doi.org/10.1007/BF02110126

Bandura, A. (1977). *Social learning theory.* Englewood Cliffs, NJ: Prentice Hall.

Bandura, A. (1986). *Social foundations of thought and action: A social cognitive theory.* Englewood Cliffs, NJ: Prentice Hall.

Barrish, H. H., Saunders, M., & Wolf, M. M. (1969). Good behavior game: Effects of individual contingencies for group consequences on disruptive behavior in a classroom. *Journal of Applied Behavior Analysis, 2,* 119–124.

Bates, J. A. (1979). Extrinsic reward and intrinsic motivation: A review with implications for the classroom. *Review of Educational Research, 49,* 557–576. http://dx.doi.org/10.3102/00346543049004557

Beavers, G. A., Iwata, B. A., & Lerman, D. C. (2013). Thirty years of research on the functional analysis of problem behavior. *Journal of Applied Behavior Analysis, 46,* 1–21. http://dx.doi.org/10.1002/jaba.30

Birnbrauer, J. S., Wolf, M. M., Kidder, J. D., & Tague, C. E. (1965). Classroom behavior of retarded pupils with token reinforcement. *Journal of Experimental Child Psychology, 2,* 219–235. http://dx.doi.org/10.1016/0022-0965(65)90045-7

Cameron, J., Banko, K. M., & Pierce, W. D. (2001). Pervasive negative effects of rewards on intrinsic motivation: The myth continues. *The Behavior Analyst, 24,* 1–44. http://dx.doi.org/10.1007/BF03392017

Cameron, J., & Pierce, W. D. (1994). Reinforcement, reward, and intrinsic motivation: A meta-analysis. *Review of Educational Research, 64,* 363–423. http://dx.doi.org/10.3102/00346543064003363

Cameron, J., & Pierce, W. D. (1996). The debate about rewards and intrinsic motivation: Protests and accusations do not alter the results. *Review of Educational Research, 66,* 39–51. http://dx.doi.org/10.3102/00346543066001039

Carton, J. S. (1996). The differential effects of tangible rewards and praise on intrinsic motivation: A comparison of cognitive evaluation theory and operant theory. *The Behavior Analyst, 19,* 237–255. http://dx.doi.org/10.1007/BF03393167

Cerasoli, C. P., Nicklin, J. M., & Ford, M. T. (2014). Intrinsic motivation and extrinsic incentives jointly predict performance: A 40-year meta-analysis. *Psychological Bulletin, 140,* 980–1008. http://dx.doi.org/10.1037/a0035661

Davidson, P., & Bucher, B. (1978). Intrinsic interest and extrinsic reward: The effects of a continuing token program on continuing nonconstrained preference. *Behavior Therapy, 9,* 222–234. http://dx.doi.org/10.1016/S0005-7894(78)80107-5

Deci, E. L., Koestner, R., & Ryan, R. M. (1999a). A meta-analytic review of experiments examining the effects of extrinsic rewards on intrinsic motivation. *Psychological Bulletin, 125,* 627–668. http://dx.doi.org/10.1037/0033-2909.125.6.627

Deci, E. L., Koestner, R., & Ryan, R. M. (1999b). The undermining effect is a reality after all—Extrinsic rewards, task interest, and self-determination: Reply to Eisenberger, Pierce, and Cameron (1999) and Lepper, Henderlong, and Gingras (1999). *Psychological Bulletin, 125,* 692–700. http://dx.doi.org/10.1037/0033-2909.125.6.692

Deci, E. L., Koestner, R., & Ryan, R. M. (2001). Extrinsic rewards and intrinsic motivation in education: Reconsidered once again. *Review of Educational Research, 71,* 1–27. http://dx.doi.org/10.3102/00346543071001001

Deci, E. L., & Ryan, R. (1985). *Intrinsic motivation and self-determination in human behavior.* New York, NY: Plenum. http://dx.doi.org/10.1007/978-1-4899-2271-7

Delaney, M. L., & Royal, M. A. (2017). Breaking engagement apart: The role of intrinsic and extrinsic motivation in engagement strategies. *Industrial and Organizational Psychology: Perspectives on Science and Practice, 10,* 127–140. http://dx.doi.org/10.1017/iop.2017.2

Dickinson, A. M. (1989). The detrimental effects of extrinsic reinforcement on "Intrinsic motivation." *The Behavior Analyst, 12,* 1–15. http://dx.doi.org/10.1007/BF03392473

Drevno, G. E., Kimball, J. W., Possi, M. K., Heward, W. L., Gardner, R., & Barbetta, P. M. (1994). Effects of active student response during error correction on the acquisition, maintenance, and generalization of science vocabulary by elementary students: A systematic replication. *Journal of Applied Behavior Analysis, 27,* 179–180.

Eisenberger, R., & Cameron, J. (1996). Detrimental effects of reward: Reality or myth? *American Psychologist, 51,* 1153–1166. http://dx.doi.org/10.1037/0003-066X.51.11.1153

Eisenberger, R., Pierce, W. D., & Cameron, J. (1999). Effects of reward on intrinsic motivation—Negative, neutral, and positive: Comment on Deci, Koestner, and Ryan (1999). *Psychological Bulletin, 125,* 677–691. http://dx.doi.org/10.1037/0033-2909.125.6.677

Fair, E. M., & Silvestri, L. (1992). Effects of reward, competition and outcome on intrinsic motivation. *Journal of Instructional Psychology, 19,* 3–8.

Feingold, B. D., & Mahoney, M. J. (1975). Reinforcement effects on intrinsic interest: Undermining the overjustification hypothesis. *Behavior Therapy, 6,* 367–377. http://dx.doi.org/10.1016/S0005-7894(75)80111-0

Flora, S. R. (1990). Undermining intrinsic interest from the standpoint of a behaviorist. *The Psychological Record, 40,* 323–346. http://dx.doi.org/10.1007/BF03399544

Flora, S. R., & Flora, D. B. (1999). Effects of *extrinsic reinforcement* for reading during childhood on reported reading habits of college students. *The Psychological Record, 49,* 3–14. http://dx.doi.org/10.1007/BF03395303

Gneezy, U., Meier, S., & Rey-Biel, P. (2011). When and why incentives (don't) work to modify behavior. *The Journal of Economic Perspectives, 25,* 191–210. http://dx.doi.org/10.1257/jep.25.4.191

Greene, D., & Lepper, M. R. (1974). Effects of extrinsic rewards on children's subsequent intrinsic interest. *Child Development, 45,* 1141–1145. http://dx.doi.org/10.2307/1128110

Gresham, F. M., Reschly, D., & Shinn, M. R. (2010). RTI as a driving force in educational improvement: Historical legal, research, and practice perspectives. In M. R. Shinn & H. M. Walker (Eds.), *Interventions for achievement and behavior problems in a three-tier model, including RTI* (pp. 47–77). Bethesda, MD: National Association of School Psychologists.

Halpern, S. D., French, B., Small, D. S., Saulsgiver, K., Harhay, M. O., Audrain-McGovern, J., . . . Volpp, K. G. (2015). Randomized trial of four financial-incentive programs for smoking cessation. *The New England Journal of Medicine, 372,* 2108–2117. http://dx.doi.org/10.1056/NEJMoa1414293

Hennessey, B. A. (2015). Reward, task motivation, creativity, and teaching: Towards a cross-cultural examination. *Teachers College Record, 117*(10), 1–28.

Horcones, C. L. (1987). The concept of consequences in the analysis of behavior. *The Behavior Analyst, 10,* 291–294. http://dx.doi.org/10.1007/BF03392441

Jackson, C. K. (2010). A little now for a lot later: A look at a Texas advanced placement incentive program. *The Journal of Human Resources, 45,* 591–639. http://dx.doi.org/10.3368/jhr.45.3.591

Killeen, P. R. (2014). A theory of behavioral contrast. *Journal of the Experimental Analysis of Behavior, 102,* 363–390. http://dx.doi.org/10.1002/jeab.107

Kohn, A. (1993). *Punished by rewards: The trouble with gold stars, incentive plans, A's, praise, and other bribes.* Boston, MA: Houghton Mifflin.

Kohn, A. (1996). By all available means: Cameron and Pierce's defense of extrinsic motivators. *Review of Educational Research, 66,* 1–4. http://dx.doi.org/10.3102/00346543066001001

Lepper, M. R. (1983). Extrinsic reward and intrinsic motivation: Implications for the classroom. In J. M. Levine & M. C. Wang (Eds.), *Teacher and student perceptions: Implications for learning* (pp. 281–317). Hillsdale, NJ: Erlbaum.

Lepper, M. R. (1998). A whole much less than the sum of its parts. *American Psychologist, 53,* 675–676. http://dx.doi.org/10.1037/0003-066X.53.6.675

Lepper, M. R., & Gilovich, T. (1981). The multiple functions of reward: A social developmental perspective. In S. S. Brehm, S. Kassin, & F. X. Gibbons (Eds.), *Developmental social psychology* (pp. 5–31). New York, NY: Oxford University Press.

Lepper, M. R., Greene, D., & Nisbett, R. E. (1973). Undermining children's intrinsic interest with extrinsic reward: A test of the "overjustification" hypothesis. *Journal of Personality and Social Psychology, 28,* 129–137. http://dx.doi.org/10.1037/h0035519

Lepper, M. R., Keavney, M., & Drake, M. (1996). Intrinsic motivation and extrinsic rewards: A commentary on Cameron and Pierce's meta-analysis. *Review of Educational Research, 66,* 5–32. http://dx.doi.org/10.3102/00346543066001005

Little, S. G., & Akin-Little, K. A. (2003). Classroom management. In W. O'Donohue, J. Fisher, & S. Hayes (Eds.), *Empirically supported techniques of cognitive behavioral therapy: A step-by-step guide for clinicians* (pp. 65–70). New York, NY: Wiley.

Maag, J. W. (1996). *Parenting without punishment.* Philadelphia, PA: The Charles Press.

Maag, J. W. (1999). *Behavior management: From the theoretical implications to practical applications.* San Diego, CA: Singular.

Maag, J. W., & Katsiyannis, A. (1999). Teacher preparation in E/BD: A national survey. *Behavioral Disorders, 24,* 189–196. http://dx.doi.org/10.1177/019874299902400305

Mann-Feder, V. R., & Varda, R. (1996). Adolescents in therapeutic communities. *Adolescence, 31,* 17–28.

Mawhinney, T. C., Dickinson, A. M., & Taylor, L. A., III. (1989). The use of concurrent schedules to evaluate the effects of extrinsic rewards on "intrinsic motivation." *Journal of Organizational Behavior Management, 10,* 109–129. http://dx.doi.org/10.1300/J075v10n01_07

Mintz, C. M. (2003). *A behavior analytic evaluation of the overjustification effect as it relates to education* (Unpublished doctoral dissertation). University of Nevada, Reno.

Morgan, M. (1984). Reward-induced decrements and increments in intrinsic motivation. *Review of Educational Research, 54,* 5–30. http://dx.doi.org/10.3102/00346543054001005

O'Leary, K. D., & Drabman, R. (1971). Token reinforcement programs in the classroom: A review. *Psychological Bulletin, 75*, 379–398. http://dx.doi.org/10.1037/h0031311

Pittman, T. S., Boggiano, A. K., & Ruble, D. N. (1983). Intrinsic and extrinsic motivational orientations: Limiting conditions on the undermining and enhancing effects of reward on intrinsic motivation. In J. M. Levine & M. C. Wang (Eds.), *Teacher and student perceptions: Implications for learning* (pp. 319–340). Hillsdale, NJ: Erlbaum.

Reiss, S., & Sushinsky, L. W. (1975). Overjustification, competing, responses, and the acquisition of intrinsic interest. *Journal of Personality and Social Psychology, 31*, 1116–1125. http://dx.doi.org/10.1037/h0076936

Rosenfield, D., Folger, R., & Adelman, H. F. (1980). When rewards reflect competence: A qualification of the overjustification effect. *Journal of Personality and Social Psychology, 39*, 368–376. http://dx.doi.org/10.1037/0022-3514.39.3.368

Ryan, R. M., & Deci, E. L. (1996). When paradigms clash: Comments on Cameron and Pierce's claim that rewards do not undermine intrinsic motivation. *Review of Educational Research, 66*, 33–38. http://dx.doi.org/10.3102/00346543066001033

Rummel, A., & Feinberg, R. (1988). Cognitive evaluation theory: A meta-analysis review of the literature. *Social Behavior and Personality, 16*, 147–164. http://dx.doi.org/10.2224/sbp.1988.16.2.147

Simonsen, B., & Sugai, G. (2009). School-wide positive behavior support: A systems-level application of behavioral principles. In A. Akin-Little, S. G. Little, M. A. Bray, & T. J. Kehle (Eds.), *Behavioral interventions in schools: Evidence-based positive strategies* (pp. 125–140). Washington, DC: American Psychological Association. http://dx.doi.org/10.1037/11886-008

Skinner, B. F. (1953). *Science and human behavior*. New York, NY: Macmillan.

Slavin, R. E. (2012). *Educational psychology: Theory and practice* (10th ed.). Upper Saddle River, NJ: Pearson Education.

Swiezy, N. B., Matson, J. L., & Box, P. (1992). The good behavior game: A token reinforcement system for preschoolers. *Child & Family Behavior Therapy, 14*, 21–32. http://dx.doi.org/10.1300/J019v14n03_02

Tang, S., & Hall, V. (1995). The overjustification effect: A meta-analysis. *Applied Cognitive Psychology, 9*, 365–404. http://dx.doi.org/10.1002/acp.2350090502

Tegano, D. W., Moran, D. J., III, & Sawyers, J. K. (1991). *Creativity in early childhood classrooms*. Washington, DC: National Education Association.

Vasta, R., Andrews, D. E., McLaughlin, A. M., Stirpe, L. A., & Comfort, C. (1978). Reinforcement effects on intrinsic interest: A classroom analog. *Journal of School Psychology, 16*, 161–166. http://dx.doi.org/10.1016/0022-4405(78)90055-9

Vasta, R., & Stirpe, L. A. (1979). Reinforcement effects on three measures of children's interest in math. *Behavior Modification, 3*, 223–244. http://dx.doi.org/10.1177/014544557932006

Wiersma, U. J. (1992). The effects of extrinsic rewards in intrinsic motivation: A meta-analysis. *Journal of Occupational and Organizational Psychology, 65,* 101–114. http://dx.doi.org/10.1111/j.2044-8325.1992.tb00488.x

Williams, B. W. (1980). Reinforcement, behavior constraint and the over-justification effect. *Journal of Personality and Social Psychology, 39,* 599–614. http://dx.doi.org/10.1037/0022-3514.39.4.599

Woolfolk, A. E. (2015). *Educational psychology* (13th ed.). Upper Saddle River, NJ: Pearson Education.

Zimmerman, B. J. (1985). The development of "intrinsic" motivation: A social learning analysis. *Annals of Child Development, 2,* 117–160.

7

APPLIED BEHAVIOR ANALYSIS IN EDUCATION: THE ROLE OF THE BOARD CERTIFIED BEHAVIOR ANALYST

MARK D. SHRIVER

More and more frequently, if you work in a school system, you are likely to come across another professional who works in the school system or is contracted with the school system and refers to him- or herself as a *behavior analyst*, an *applied behavior analyst*, or a *Board Certified Behavior Analyst®* (BCBA). You may have wondered who these professionals are, what is it that they are trained to do, and what role they play in the school system. You may have noticed that the applied behavior analyst likely is providing consulting services regarding educational programming and intervention for students with autism spectrum disorder (ASD). In fact, in the past 20 or more years, applied behavior analysis (ABA) has become widely known for its efficacy in the education and treatment of individuals with ASD (National Autism Center, 2009). It is also possible, however, that the behavior analyst is consulting with the educational team regarding educational programming and interventions for any student with a disability in the classroom, or even

---

http://dx.doi.org/10.1037/0000126-008
Behavioral Interventions in Schools: Evidence-Based Positive Strategies, Second Edition, S. G. Little and A. Akin-Little (Editors)
Copyright © 2019 by the American Psychological Association. All rights reserved.

for those students who are not identified for special education services but require intervention in the regular education classroom to be successful.

Many of the chapters in this book explicitly refer to the science and practice of behavior analysis as foundational to the evidence-based interventions presented in that particular chapter. Behavior analysis represents a philosophy, a science, and a practice applicable to any and all students in any and all educational contexts. In this chapter, I provide a brief introduction to behavior analysis, with particular emphasis on ABA. A brief overview of ABA in education also is presented, with particular attention to the applicability of ABA to all facets of the education of all students. The training currently required for minimal competency in the practice of ABA is described. Finally, I discuss the implications of this burgeoning discipline for interdisciplinary collaboration in the education of students.

BEHAVIOR ANALYSIS

When defining a field, it is probably best to look first to the organizations that are composed of members of that field. The primary organization for the science and practice of behavior analysis at this time is the Association for Behavior Analysis International (ABAI), which describes behavior analysis as follows:

> Behavior analysis is a natural science that seeks to understand the behavior of individuals. That is, behavior analysts study how biological, pharmacological, and experiential factors influence the behavior of humans and nonhuman animals. Recognizing that behavior is something that individuals do, behavior analysts place special emphasis on studying factors that reliably influence the behavior of individuals, an emphasis that works well when the goal is to acquire adaptive behavior or ameliorate problem behavior. The science of behavior analysis has made discoveries that have proven useful in addressing socially important behavior such as drug taking, healthy eating, workplace safety, education, and the treatment of pervasive developmental disabilities (e.g., autism). (ABAI, 2018)

The practice is termed *applied behavior analysis*. ABA is derived from the science of behavior analysis, which includes two scientific disciplines: (a) the experimental analysis of behavior and (b) the applied analysis of behavior. The experimental analysis of behavior is most consistent with basic or laboratory research and may include animal or human participants. The *Journal of the Experimental Analysis of Behavior* is a good example of this. The science of applied analysis of behavior is largely concerned with research demonstrating the application of behavior analysis and intervention to address socially relevant problems (Baer, Wolf, & Risley, 1968). The science of behavior analysis (experimental and applied) is grounded in a philosophy of science called *behaviorism*. *Radical behaviorism* is the particular philosophy of behaviorism currently most likely to be adhered to by behavior analysts as reflected in the Behavior Analyst Certification Board (BACB; 2012) Fourth Edition task list for minimal knowledge and skills needed for credentialing and is best exemplified by the works of B. F. Skinner (e.g., 1953, 1974; see also Baum, 2005, for a more recent perspective on behaviorism).

As a professional practice or discipline, ABA is used across a wide continuum of animal and human endeavors. It is widely used in animal training (e.g., Forthman & Ogden, 1992; Poling et al., 2011; Pryor, 2004). ABA is also the foundational science and practice for organizational behavior management, as illustrated by articles in the *Journal of Organizational Behavior Management* and multiple other books and articles (e.g., Daniels & Bailey, 2014). In addition, ABA is used in behavioral pediatrics and health psychology (e.g., Normand, 2016), sports psychology (Allison & Ayllon, 1980; Martin, Thompson, & Regehr, 2004), and community applications (e.g., Biglan, Brennan, Foster, & Holder, 2004; Fawcett, 1991). ABA is used in clinical psychology (e.g., Follette, Naugle, & Callaghan, 1996; Kanter, Baruch, & Gaynor, 2006; Vowles, 2015). Finally, most relevant for the present purposes, it has been used in education since the beginning of the science. Skinner wrote extensively about behavior analysis and education (e.g., Skinner, 1953, 1954, 1968, 1984). In fact, the first volume of the *Journal of Applied Behavior Analysis* (JABA) included 10 articles about the use of ABA in general education classrooms to improve student behavior and learning (JABA, Vol. 1, Nos. 1–4). More recently, a special online issue of *JABA* was published that included 12 research articles published in that journal between 2011 and 2015 specific to ABA in mainstream education (Austin, St. Peter, & Donaldson, 2016). This is but a small sample of ABA in education publications. There are literally hundreds, if not thousands, of research articles and related writings on ABA in education in many other journals and books that have been published since the mid-20th century.

APPLIED BEHAVIOR ANALYSIS IN EDUCATION

The empirical identification and application of principles of learning is an integral aspect of behavior analysis (e.g., Catania, 2013). In education, ABA has been the foundational science and practice for evidence-based practices such as direct instruction (Engelmann & Carnine, 1991; Kame'enui, Fien, & Korgesaar, 2013; Marchand-Martella, Slocum, & Martella, 2004); precision teaching (Merbitz, Vietez, Merbitz, & Pennypacker, 2004); personalized systems of instruction (Keller, 1968; Pear & Crone-Todd, 1999); behavioral consultation (Bergan & Kratochwill, 1990); positive behavior intervention support (Sugai, 2015); direct academic skills assessment (Shapiro, 2010); classroom management strategies, such as good behavior games (Barrish, Saunders, & Wolf, 1969; Kellam, Reid, & Balster, 2008) and token economies (Soares, Harrison, Vannest, & McClelland, 2016); and innumerable individualized behavior and educational interventions for students across the continuum of development and functional capabilities (e.g., Gardner et al., 1994; Moran & Malott, 2004; Walker, Ramsey, & Gresham, 2004). The functional behavior assessment and behavior intervention plans mandated in the Individuals With Disabilities Education Improvement Act of 1990 were derived largely from the science and practice of ABA (Gresham, Watson, & Skinner, 2001). As noted earlier, many of the interventions described in this book are founded on the science and practice of behavior analysis. This listing represents just the proverbial tip of the iceberg of ABA in education.

As is evident by the partial list of ABA in education practices described above, ABA is not only about intervening with students with ASD or related developmental disabilities; it is an evidence-based practice (Slocum et al., 2014) that is applicable to any and all students in special and general educational contexts and to any presenting problems (i.e., behavior, academic, social, cognitive, emotional). Unfortunately, few professionals within the field of education are adequately trained to use ABA effectively in school systems (e.g., Shriver & Watson, 1999). Those who try to implement ABA in schools without adequate training are likely to fail, and they may place blame for that failure on ABA when instead it should be placed on the implementation. In addition, many education professionals may not even be aware of ABA or of how it may be applied to facilitate school learning. There is a growing number of disciplined ABA providers, however, who are trained in educational contexts to facilitate learning for all students (Burning Glass Technologies, 2015). These practitioners are credentialed in behavior analysis and referred to as *Board Certified Behavior Analysts*.

COMPETENCY IN APPLIED BEHAVIOR ANALYSIS

The practice of ABA is largely defined by seven dimensions (Association of Professional Behavior Analysts [APBA], 2017) first described by Baer et al. (1968) and termed *applied, behavioral, analytic, technological, conceptual systems, effective,* and *generality*. Providing ABA services consistent with these defined dimensions requires specialized training. The current U.S. national standard for evidence of minimal competency in the practice of ABA is established by the BACB. Although there are some differences in licensing of ABA across the states, all states that do license practitioners of ABA rely on the BACB certification standards for licensing requirements. School systems are typically exempt from requiring certification or licensure of practitioners of ABA. However, it would seem to be highly problematic not to expect practitioners of ABA in schools to demonstrate the professional community's standard for minimal competency. Subsequently, the BACB standards should be attended to when evaluating a professional's qualifications for practicing ABA in the schools (for a summary of state requirements to be licensed/certified as a behavior analyst, see https://www.appliedbehavioranalysisedu.org/state-by-state-guide-to-aba-licensing/).

Board Certified Behavior Analyst Competencies

The minimal competencies required at this time for board certification as a behavior analyst are outlined explicitly in the BACB (2012) Fourth Edition Task List via three sections: (a) Basic Behavior-Analytic Skills, (b) Client-Centered Responsibilities, and (c) Foundational Knowledge. There are 163 skills and principles of behavior analysis listed in which every BCBA should have demonstrated mastery. In addition, BCBAs must be knowledgeable of and abide by the *Professional and Ethical Compliance Code for Behavior Analysts* (BACB, 2017). To acquire these basic competencies, students must complete at least 270 hours of behavior analytic coursework. This is typically taken as part of a master's or doctoral program in psychology, education, or behavior analysis. There are graduate training programs in school psychology and in special education with BACB-approved course sequences. The entry level for practice as a BCBA is at the master's level. In addition, all students must complete practicum or field work experiences supervised by a BCBA and focused on the practice of ABA. Practicum experiences are at least 750 hours or 1,000 hours, depending on the intensity of supervision. If a practicum is not taken for course credit through a university program, students may contract with a BCBA provider who has acquired BACB-approved supervision training to provide supervision for a 1,500-hour field work experience. In addition, many training programs have research requirements (i.e., a thesis or equivalent research project). After successfully completing approved ABA coursework, a practicum, and the master's or doctoral degree program, a student may apply to take the BCBA exam. Once the student has passed the exam, he or she may call him- or herself a BCBA. In addition, there are ongoing continuing education requirements for maintenance of the BCBA that professionals must complete yearly (see https://bacb.com/bcba).

Focus of Practice

The ethical guidelines of a BCBA require that the BCBA practice within his or her area of competency and training. Evidence-based treatment of autism and related developmental disabilities is currently driving the growth of much of the training of BCBAs, and many have demonstrable competency in ABA with these populations (Burning Glass Technologies, 2015). Thus, often BCBAs who are working in or with school systems are likely doing consultations regarding this population of students. However, BCBAs may also be more broadly trained to work with students in the general education classroom, with students who have other types of disabilities and diagnoses and with students presenting with problems that are not necessarily behavioral but that may be considered social, emotional, cognitive, or academic. BCBAs are typically trained to work at the individual student level, but many are also explicitly trained in systems or organization management. Unless the ABA course sequence for BCBA was a part of a school psychology or special education program, few other educational professionals in the school system have expertise in ABA. BCBAs have an expertise that is unrivaled by any other educational professional and therefore can have a positive effect on the education of all students. In sum, it is important that education teams use the expertise brought to the team by the BCBA to effectively educate and help students in need.

Board Certified Behavior Analysts in Schools

The role of a BCBA in the school likely will be that of a consultant or a teacher. Teachers who are BCBAs are most often work in special education classrooms; however, they may also teach in general education classrooms. Consultants who are BCBAs may be employed by the school or as part of a contracted service and likely work with the education team to develop educational programming and interventions for students. All BCBAs working in schools will have expertise in the functional assessment and analysis of behavior and the design of education programing and interventions to improve student performance at the individual or classroom level. Some BCBAs in the school may also have training and expertise in systems level change (e.g., positive behavior intervention and supports). BCBAs will likely have expertise relevant to helping students with ASD or related disabilities and students with significant behavior problems. However, as is ideally evident by the brief introduction of ABA presented at the beginning of this chapter and in other chapters in this book, they may also have expertise in ABA that is applicable to any student in the school (APBA, 2017).

Interdisciplinary Collaboration

On an interdisciplinary team in the school, the BCBA's expertise is most likely to be different from that of an occupational therapist, physical therapist, and administrator. The BCBA may have some overlap in expertise with the speech–language pathologist if the BCBA has had training in verbal behavior and instruction, in particular for younger children. Of course, a teacher who is also a BCBA will have the same expertise as any teacher in the school building but with an added specialization. A consultant who is a BCBA may have some overlap in expertise with a teacher, depending on the BCBA's experience with teaching and educational programming. Most likely, the consultant BCBA will have some overlap in expertise with other behavioral or mental health providers in the school system such as school psychologists, counselors, or social workers. School psychologists will likely have normative and other standardized assessment expertise. Counselors will have guidance and counseling expertise, and social workers likely will have case management and perhaps clinical counseling expertise. What a BCBA brings to the team that these other behavioral or mental health professionals typically do not are extensive training and expertise in behavior analysis (e.g., functional behavior assessment) and intervention. BCBAs can assist the team with identifying and defining student concerns and goals, assessing relevant functional environment–behavior relations, developing and implementing evidence-based educational programs and interventions, data collection and progress monitoring, and data-based decision making.

SUMMARY

ABA represents a philosophy—experimental and applied science—and practice that has a long history in education and psychology. Only recently, however, has the practice become more organized to include credentialing and licensing and to begin to define itself as a professional field of practice. Evidence-based practice in ASD treatment has been a substantial part of the growth of the professional practice of ABA. The advancement of evidence-based treatment for individuals with ASD has certainly been an inspiring and important development in education and psychology; however, ABA represents a field of practice much larger than ASD treatment. ABA represents a field of practice that touches on any and all aspects of human behavior. Professionals trained in ABA with evidence of competencies earned by the BCBA credential have unique and specialized knowledge and skills to bring to educational contexts and interdisciplinary teams to facilitate the success of all students.

REFERENCES

Allison, M. G., & Ayllon, T. (1980). Behavioral coaching in the development of skills in football, gymnastics, and tennis. *Journal of Applied Behavior Analysis, 13,* 297–314.

Austin, J., St. Peter, C., & Donaldson, J. (Eds.). (2016). Behavior analysis is mainstream education (2011–2015). *Journal of Applied Behavior Analysis* [Special online issue], *49*(3). http://ma6ek2jh6s.search.serialssolutions.com/?sid=sersol&SS_jc=JOUROFAPPBE&title=Journal%20of%20applied%20behavior%20analysis

Association for Behavior Analysis International. (2018). *What is behavior analysis?* Retrieved from https://www.abainternational.org/about-us/behavior-analysis.aspx

Association of Professional Behavior Analysts. (2017). *Identifying applied behavior analysis interventions.* San Diego, CA: Author.

Baer, D. M., Wolf, M. M., & Risley, T. R. (1968). Some current dimensions of applied behavior analysis. *Journal of Applied Behavior Analysis, 1,* 91–97.

Barrish, H. H., Saunders, M., & Wolf, M. M. (1969). Good behavior game: Effects of individual contingencies for group consequences on disruptive behavior in a classroom. *Journal of Applied Behavior Analysis, 2,* 119–124.

Baum, W. M. (2005). *Understanding Behaviorism: Behavior, culture, and evolution* (2nd ed.). Malden, MA: Blackwell.

Behavior Analyst Certification Board. (2012). *Fourth edition task list.* Retrieved from https://www.bacb.com/wp-content/uploads/2017/09/160101-BCBA-BCaBA-task-list-fourth-edition-english.pdf

Behavior Analyst Certification Board. (2017). *Professional and ethical compliance code for behavior analysts.* Retrieved from https://www.bacb.com/wp-content/uploads/170706r_compliance_code_english.pdf

Bergan, J. R., & Kratochwill, T. R. (1990). *Behavioral consultation and therapy.* New York, NY: Plenum Press.

Biglan, A., Brennan, P. A., Foster, S. L., & Holder, H. D. (2004). *Helping adolescents at risk: Prevention of multiple problem behaviors.* New York, NY: Guilford Press.

Burning Glass Technologies. (2015). *US behavior analyst workforce: Understanding the national demand for behavior analysts.* Retrieved from https://www.bacb.com/wp-content/uploads/2017/09/151009-burning-glass-report.pdf

Catania, A. C. (2013). *Learning* (5th ed.). Cornwall on Hudson, NY: Sloan.

Daniels, A. C., & Bailey, J. S. (2014). *Performance management: Changing behavior that drives organizational performance* (5th ed.). Atlanta, GA: Aubrey Daniels International.

Engelmann, S., & Carnine, D. W. (1991). *Theory of instruction: Principles and applications* (Rev. ed.). Eugene, OR: ADI Press.

Fawcett, S. B. (1991). Some values guiding community research and action. *Journal of Applied Behavior Analysis, 24,* 621–636. http://dx.doi.org/10.1901/jaba.1991.24-621

Follette, W. C., Naugle, A. E., & Callaghan, G. M. (1996). A radical behavioral understanding of the therapeutic relationship in effecting change. *Behavior Therapy, 27*, 623–641. http://dx.doi.org/10.1016/S0005-7894(96)80047-5

Forthman, D. L., & Ogden, J. (1992). The role of applied behavior analysis in zoo management: Today and tomorrow. *Journal of Applied Behavior Analysis, 25*, 647–652. http://dx.doi.org/10.1901/jaba.1992.25-647

Gardner, R., Sainato, D. M., Cooper, J. O., Heron, T. E., Heward, W. L., Eshleman, J., & Grossi, T. A. (1994). *Behavior analysis in education: Focus on measurably superior instruction*. Pacific Grove, CA: Brooks/Cole.

Gresham, F. M., Watson, T. S., & Skinner, C. H. (2001). Functional behavioral assessment: Principles, procedures, and future directions. *School Psychology Review, 30*, 156–172.

Individuals With Disabilities Education Improvement Act of 1990, 20 U.S.C. §§ 1400–1482.

Kame'enui, E. J., Fien, H., & Korgesaar, J. (2013). Direct instruction as *Eo nomine* and contronym: Why the right words and details matter. In H. L. Swanson, K. R. Harris, & S. Graham (Eds.), *Handbook of learning disabilities* (2nd ed., pp. 489–506). New York, NY: Guilford Press.

Kanter, J. W., Baruch, D. E., & Gaynor, S. T. (2006). Acceptance and commitment therapy and behavioral activation for the treatment of depression: Description and comparison. *The Behavior Analyst, 29*, 161–185. http://dx.doi.org/10.1007/BF03392129

Kellam, S. G., Reid, J., & Balster, R. L. (2008). Effects of a universal classroom behavior program in first and second grades on young adult problem outcomes. *Drug and Alcohol Dependence, 95*(Suppl. 1), S1–S4. http://dx.doi.org/10.1016/j.drugalcdep.2008.01.006

Keller, F. S. (1968). "Good-bye, teacher . . ." *Journal of Applied Behavior Analysis, 1*, 79–89. http://dx.doi.org/10.1901/jaba.1968.1-79

Marchand-Martella, N. E., Slocum, T. A., & Martella, R. C. (2004). *Introduction to direct instruction*. Boston, MA: Pearson.

Martin, G. L., Thompson, K., & Regehr, K. (2004). Studies using single-subject designs in sport psychology: 30 years of research. *The Behavior Analyst, 27*, 263–280. http://dx.doi.org/10.1007/BF03393185

Merbitz, C., Vietez, D., Merbitz, N. H., & Pennypacker, H. S. (2004). Precision teaching: Foundations and classroom applications. In D. J. Moran & R. W. Malott (Eds.), *Evidence-based educational methods* (pp. 47–62). San Diego, CA: Elsevier/Academic Press. http://dx.doi.org/10.1016/B978-012506041-7/50005-X

Moran, D. J., & Malott, R. W. (Eds.). (2004). *Evidence-based educational methods*. San Diego, CA: Elsevier/Academic Press. http://dx.doi.org/10.1016/B978-0-12-506041-7.X5000-1

National Autism Center. (2009). *National Standards Project: Findings and conclusions*. Randolph, MA: Author

Normand, M. (Associate Ed.). (2016). Health psychology and applied behavior analysis (2010–2014) [Special online issue]. *Journal of Applied Behavior Analysis, 49*(3). http://ma6ek2jh6s.search.serialssolutions.com/?sid=sersol&SS_jc=JOUROFAPPBE&title=Journal%20of%20applied%20behavior%20analysis

Pear, J. J., & Crone-Todd, D. E. (1999). Personalized system of instruction in cyberspace. *Journal of Applied Behavior Analysis, 32*, 205–209. http://dx.doi.org/10.1901/jaba.1999.32-205

Poling, A., Weetjens, B., Cox, C., Beyene, N. W., Bach, H., & Sully, A. (2011). Using trained pouched rats to detect land mines: Another victory for operant conditioning. *Journal of Applied Behavior Analysis, 44*, 351–355. http://dx.doi.org/10.1901/jaba.2011.44-351

Pryor, K. (2004). *Lads before the wind: Diary of a dolphin trainer*. MA: Sunshine Books.

Shapiro, E. S. (2010). *Academic skills problems: Direct assessment and intervention* (4th ed.). New York, NY: Guilford Press.

Shriver, M. D., & Watson, T. S. (1999). A survey of behavior analysis and behavioral consultation courses in school psychology: Implications for training school psychologists. *Journal of Behavioral Education, 9*, 211–221. http://dx.doi.org/10.1023/A:1022139615601

Skinner, B. F. (1953). *Science and human behavior*. New York, NY: Free Press.

Skinner, B. F. (1954). The science of learning and the art of teaching. *Harvard Educational Review, 24*, 86–97.

Skinner, B. F. (1968). *The technology of teaching*. Englewood Cliffs, NJ: Prentice-Hall.

Skinner, B. F. (1974). *About behaviorism*. New York, NY: Vintage Books.

Skinner, B. F. (1984). The shame of American education. *American Psychologist, 39*, 947–954. http://dx.doi.org/10.1037/0003-066X.39.9.947

Slocum, T. A., Detrich, R., Wilczynski, S. M., Spencer, T. D., Lewis, T., & Wolfe, K. (2014). The evidence-based practice of applied behavior analysis. *The Behavior Analyst, 37*, 41–56. http://dx.doi.org/10.1007/s40614-014-0005-2

Soares, D. A., Harrison, J. R., Vannest, K. J., & McClelland, S. S. (2016). Effect size for token economy use in contemporary classroom settings: A meta-analysis of single-case research. *School Psychology Review, 45*, 379–399. http://dx.doi.org/10.17105/SPR45-4.379-399

Sugai, G. (2015). *Positive behavioral interventions and supports: Application of a behavior analytic theory of action*. Oakland, CA: The Wings Institute. Retrieved from https://winginstitute.org/uploads/docs/2014WingSummitGS.pdf

Vowles, K. E. (2015). Editorial overview: Third wave behavior therapies. *Current Opinion in Psychology, 2*, v–viii. http://dx.doi.org/10.1016/j.copsyc.2015.03.008

Walker, H. M., Ramsey, E., & Gresham, F. M. (2004). *Antisocial behavior in school: Evidence-based practices* (2nd ed.). Belmont, CA: Wadsworth/Cengage Learning.

8

BEHAVIORAL INTERVENTIONS FOR ACADEMIC PERFORMANCE: A SUMMARY OF THE LITERATURE

ROBIN S. CODDING, KOURTNEY R. KROMMINGA, AND KRISTIN RUNNING

Children at risk for and with disabilities across grade levels require instructional supports in one or more of three central academic areas: (a) reading, (b) mathematics, and (c) writing. In order for teachers, instructional specialists, interventionists, consultants, and other support professionals to provide assistance to children struggling with core academic content, it is necessary for these professionals to have access to empirically supported practices. Evaluation of the special education and school psychology peer review literature indicates that intervention studies represent between 15.9% and 11.1% of all published articles, respectively (Mastropieri et al., 2009; Villarreal, Castro, Umaña, & Sullivan, 2017). Not surprisingly, more peer reviewed research has evaluated reading interventions or strategies than math or writing, with the least amount of empirical support available for writing interventions. Meta-analysis offers an important tool to bridge the research-to-practice gap by providing practitioners and researchers alike with

http://dx.doi.org/10.1037/0000126-009
Behavioral Interventions in Schools: Evidence-Based Positive Strategies, Second Edition, S. G. Little and A. Akin-Little (Editors)
Copyright © 2019 by the American Psychological Association. All rights reserved.

systematic syntheses of the literature that can be used to guide empirically supported practice (Kavale, 2001). Accordingly, when writing this chapter, we consulted 27 different meta-analytic reviews of the empirical intervention literature across reading, mathematics, and writing (see Table 8.1).

CONSIDERATIONS FOR EVIDENCE-BASED PRACTICE

Although it is necessary to identify research-supported academic interventions in an easily digestible manner, as we aim to do in this chapter, it not sufficient for promoting positive student outcomes (VanDerHeyden & Harvey, 2013). General ideas of what works, for whom, and under what conditions can serve as a useful and important starting point. However, it is imperative that practitioners use data-based decision making to appropriately match treatments to students' skill needs. One such data-based decision-making framework is the *Treatment × Skill interaction* (e.g., Burns, Codding, Boice, & Lukito, 2010). This interaction requires practitioners to use data, such as curriculum-based assessment, to specify not only the type of reading, mathematics, or writing problem that a student experiences but also to consider the stage of the student's skill development. A useful model for determining a student's stage of skill development is the *instructional hierarchy* (Daly, Hintze, & Hamler, 2000; Haring, Lovitt, Eaton, & Hansen, 1978). The instructional hierarchy consists of four stages of skill development: (a) acquisition, (b) fluency, (c) generalization, and (d) adaption. If a student is performing in the acquisition stage, his or her responding will be inaccurate as learning ensues. Within the fluency stage, a student displays accurate but slow responding. Once a student displays accuracy and fluency (accurate and fast responding), it will be more likely that he or she can maintain performance at expected levels over time and generalize that skill to other more complex tasks. Finally, adaption is observed when a student is able to use the skill in a novel way. These stages of skill development are aligned with recommended remediation practices. For example, a student who is in the acquisition stage of skill development likely will need explicit instruction, modeling, and guided practice, as well as frequent and immediate feedback on the accuracy of his or her responses (Haring et al., 1978). A student in the fluency stage will likely require many opportunities for productive and novel practice, with feedback directed toward the speed of responding (Daly, Hintze, & Hamler, 2000).

The second consideration is to recognize the barriers that interfere with accurate implementation of interventions and generate strategies to mitigate those barriers. One recent survey of teachers indicated that approximately 58% of barriers to intervention implementation was related to the

TABLE 8.1
Brief Descriptions of Academic Interventions According to Subject Area

Content area	Instruction or intervention	Brief description	Meta-analysis
Reading interventions			
Emergent skills	Alphabetic instruction	Letter naming, Letter sounds, Letter writing	Piasta & Wagner (2010)
	Phonemic awareness	Manipulation of the smallest units of language	Ehri, Nunes, Willows, et al. (2001); Ehri, Nunes, Stahl, & Willows (2001); Galuschka et al. (2014); Suggate (2016)
	Phonics instruction	Relationship between phonemes and graphemes	
Fluency	Repeated readings	Rereading the same passage multiple times	Burns & Wagner (2008); Morgan et al. (2012)
	Goal setting	Set a reading goal and receive verbal or graphic feedback on attainment	Burns & Wagner (2008); Morgan et al. (2012)
	Reinforcement	Providing a reward contingent on performance	Burns & Wagner (2008); Morgan et al. (2012)
Comprehension	Strategy instruction	Identification of key aspects of a passage or story combined with self-management	Berkeley et al. (2010); Suggate (2016)
	Text enhancements	Use of graphics, questions, or videos in text	Berkeley et al. (2010); Suggate (2016)
	Vocabulary preview	Review words and definitions in text or with flash cards	Wanzek et al. (2010)
Mathematics interventions			
Computation	Cover–copy–compare	5-step self-management procedure	Joseph et al. (2012)
	Explicit timing	Timed practice	Methe et al. (2012); Poncy et al. (2015)
	Incremental rehearsal	Flash card drill interspersing known and unknown facts	Codding et al. (2011)

(continues)

TABLE 8.1
Brief Descriptions of Academic Interventions According
to Subject Area   (*Continued*)

Content area	Instruction or intervention	Brief description	Meta-analysis
	Performance feedback	Verbal and graphic information on math performance	Gersten et al. (2009)
	Peer tutoring	Systematic paired or group work	Baker et al. (2002); Bowman-Perrott et al. (2013); Kunsch et al. (2007); Rohrbeck et al. (2003)
	Taped problems	Progressive time-delay procedure	Kleinert et al. (2018)
Word problems	Schema instruction	Explicit instruction of underlying structures using schematic visual representations	Xin & Jitendra (1999); Zhang & Xin (2012)
	Strategy instruction	Explicit instruction of the problem-solving process combined with self-management	Xin & Jitendra (1999); Zhang & Xin (2012)
Writing interventions			
General writing	Strategy instruction	Explicit instruction using graphic organizers and mnemonics/ heuristics with self-management	Gillespie & Graham (2014); Graham et al. (2012); Graham & Perin (2007); Rogers & Graham (2008)
General writing	Goal setting	Set objectives for students to enhance content, make edits, or increase productivity	Gillespie & Graham (2014); Graham et al. (2012); Graham & Perin (2007); Rogers & Graham (2008)
General writing	Peer assistance	Small groups that plan, draft, provide feedback on, or edit writing work	Gillespie & Graham (2014); Graham et al. (2012); Graham & Perin (2007); Rogers & Graham (2008)
General writing	Prewriting	Brainstorm ideas and plan writing	Graham & Perin (2007); Rogers & Graham (2008)

intervention itself (Long et al., 2016). These perceived barriers pertained to three factors: (a) compatibility of the intervention with the instructional environment, (b) time allocated to delivery of the intervention, and (c) materials and resources necessary for implementation. Fortunately, there are many parsimonious, low- or no-cost, instructional techniques and intervention strategies that require few materials available in the peer literature to guide practitioners.

EMPIRICALLY SUPPORTED INSTRUCTION AND INTERVENTION PRACTICES IN READING

Phonemic awareness, reading fluency, and comprehension are central aspects of reading (Morgan, Sideridis, & Hua, 2012; National Institute of Child Health and Human Development [NICHHD], 2000; Wanzek et al., 2016). A number of empirically supported reading intervention strategies that can inform practice have been evaluated in systematic reviews and meta-analyses. We highlight a few key instructional techniques or intervention strategies within each aspect of reading beginning with emergent reading skills. We then discuss empirically supported intervention strategies that promote reading fluency. Last, we review empirically supported strategies that improve comprehension.

Emergent Reading Skills

Early reading skills are often conceptualized as alphabet knowledge, phonemic awareness, and phonics (Ehri, Nunes, Stahl, & Willows, 2001; Ehri, Nunes, Willows, et al., 2001; Lovett, Warren-Chaplin, Ransby, & Borden, 1990; Piasta & Wagner, 2010). *Alphabet knowledge* is the ability to identify letters and their sounds (Scarborough, Shapiro, Accardo, & Capute, 1998). *Phonemic awareness* is the ability to alter the smallest sounds of language, as illustrated by activities such as phoneme isolation, blending, and segmentation (Ehri, Nunes, Willows, et al., 2001). *Phonics* instruction includes teaching students strategies such as letter–sound correspondence, as well as decoding and segmenting words in order to read and spell words (Ehri, Nunes, Stahl, & Willows, 2001). Below we provide a general description of strategies that are empirically supported to address each of these early reading areas.

Alphabet Knowledge

Strategies that address alphabet knowledge have yielded small to moderate mean effects across outcomes (i.e., letter naming, letter sounds, letter writing, spelling, phonological awareness, and reading; Piasta & Wagner, 2010). Not surprisingly, when intervention content was directly matched with intervention outcomes, larger effect sizes were found. For example, the largest mean effect sizes were found when letter naming instruction was used to improve letter naming outcomes and when letter naming or letter sound instruction was used to improve letter sound knowledge. Piasta and Wagner (2010) found that outcomes were enhanced when phonological awareness instruction (e.g., manipulating oral language through activities such as rhyming and sound matching, blending, or deletion) was combined with letter naming and letter sound instruction. Strategies that were used to address alphabet knowledge included asking students to: identify the names (i.e., letter naming) or produce the sounds of individual letters (e.g., letter sounds) and write letters of the alphabet when prompted (i.e., letter writing).

Phonemic Awareness

Interventions that target phonemic awareness often include skills such as comparing the first sounds of words, blending parts of words into a whole word, segmenting words into phonemes, and blending phonemes into words (NICHHD, 2000). The purpose is to focus students' attention on sounds in words and facilitate the manipulation of those sounds (Suggate, 2016). Phonemic awareness interventions include tasks such as asking students to identify the sounds that make up a word (e.g., phoneme segmentation), the sound that is the same within a list of words (i.e., phoneme identity), the smaller word within a large word if a particular phoneme is removed (e.g., phoneme deletion), or the word that does not sound like the others in a list (e.g., phoneme categorization; Ehri, Nunes, Willows, et al., 2001). Phonemic awareness instruction yields small to moderate mean effects on reading performance (Ehri, Nunes, Willows, et al., 2001; Suggate, 2016). For older school-age students and adolescents, phonemic awareness instructional alone has not demonstrated effectiveness, but the combination with phonics instruction has produced positive outcomes (Galuschka, Ise, Krick, & Schulte-Körne, 2014).

Phonics

Phonics interventions target the associations between phonemes and graphemes (written representation of sounds, such as a letter [s] or letters [sh]; Suggate, 2016). Mean effect sizes on reading performance have ranged from small to moderate across meta-analyses (Ehri, Nunes, Stahl, et al., 2001; Ehri, Nunes, Willows, et al., 2001; Galuschka et al., 2014; Suggate, 2016). Phonics instruction includes tasks that manipulate phonemes in language, such as word blending or word segmentation (Ehri, Nunes, Willows, et al.,

2001). Many types of systematic phonics instruction programs are available; these can include components such as converting graphemes to phonemes, word blending, identifying letter–sound relations, spelling, use of context or within-word clues, onset and rime blending, or combinations of these (Ehri, Nunes, Willows, et al., 2001).

Reading Fluency

Reading fluency is defined as reading connected text quickly with accuracy and prosody (i.e., using timing and emotion to read text fluidly; NICHHD, 2000). The seminal meta-analysis examining effective interventions to enhance reading fluency conducted by the National Reading Panel (see NICHHD, 2000) concluded that oral guided or repeated reading interventions produced a small to moderate effect size. More recently, Morgan et al. (2012) evaluated the impact of a comprehensive array of intervention strategies on reading fluency using multilevel modeling. Morgan and colleagues evaluated 44 single-case design and quasi-experimental (AB) studies that included 290 students in Grades 1 through 11 that included students identified with a disability (i.e., learning disabilities, cognitive delays, autism spectrum disorder, emotional, and behavioral disorders, visual impairments) and without a disability. They examined which intervention strategies impacted reading fluency most effectively as well as potential differences across disability type.

Morgan and colleagues (2012) found that immediate impacts (intercept or level) on reading fluency were largest with goal setting, followed by reinforcement, then previewing or repeated reading and, last, peer tutoring. This order of effectiveness differed when evaluating the impact of each intervention on growth over time. Goal setting produced the most significant growth, whereas reinforcement procedures did not yield growth over time. Although repeated readings and previewing exhibited some growth; the impact of these interventions waned over time. Peer tutoring did not produce substantial growth over time (Morgan et al., 2012). Word-level interventions (e.g., practicing saying and reading unknown words) and phonological instruction did not have an immediate effect on reading fluency. Although growth was observed, the impact of word-level and phonological instruction diminished over time and was less effective than the other strategies examined. Therefore, applying word-level or phonological instruction to improve reading fluency is not a recommended strategy. Below we provide details about each of the three most effective intervention strategies.

Students without disabilities exhibited better outcomes than those with disabilities. Students with learning disabilities or visual impairments made larger gains over their baseline fluency level than students within other disability categories, although all students made substantial fluency gains. It is likely that changes to the intensity of these interventions (e.g., increasing total treatment duration, the number of sessions per week, or the time per session; Barnett, Daly, Jones, & Lentz, 2004) or individualization of the approaches (e.g., use of brief experimental analysis; Burns & Wagner, 2008) will be necessary for students with cognitive delay, social-emotional and behavioral disorders, or autism spectrum disorder (Morgan et al., 2012).

Repeated Readings

Repeated readings is a procedure during which students reread a passage a preestablished number of times to a particular criterion of fluency and accuracy (Burns & Wagner, 2008). Recent meta-analyses have examined repeated readings and the combination of repeated readings with other intervention strategies (e.g., Burns & Wagner, 2008; Morgan, Sideridis, & Hua, 2012; Suggate, 2016; Wanzek, Wexler, Vaughn, & Ciullo, 2010). Used alone as an intervention, the impact of repeated reading on reading fluency has ranged from small (Galuschka et al., 2014; Mathes & Fuchs, 1993) to large (Burns & Wagner, 2008; O'Connor, White, & Swanson, 2007). Burns and Wagner (2008) found a number of treatment packages that combined repeated readings with listening passage preview, performance feedback with and without positive reinforcement, or key-word preview. The most effective combination was integrating repeated readings with listening passage preview and performance feedback (with or without positive reinforcement).

Goal Setting

During goal setting, students are asked to identify the length of time it will take them to read a passage aloud, the number of words read correctly per minute, or the number of errors he or she will make before engaging in passage reading (Eckert, Ardoin, Daisey, & Scarola, 2000). The goal may also be predetermined by using the student's past performance (e.g., multiplying the baseline score by 30%; Jones & Wickstrom, 2002). If reinforcement is included, then students will select a reward (usually from a preidentified set of potential reinforcers) before reading. The interventionist then will ask the student to read the preselected passage. After the passage has been read, students are provided with verbal or graphic (or a combination of verbal and graphic) feedback on number of errors, time, or accuracy of reading, and their progress is graphed (Eckert et al., 2000).

Reinforcement

Reinforcement has been used as an isolated strategy to improve fluency, but it also has been combined with repeated readings and goal setting. Morgan and colleagues (2012) found that reinforcement produced the second largest immediate impact on reading fluency. This outcome differs from that of Burns and Wagner (2008), whose meta-analysis did not yield positive effects for the use of reinforcement presented alone or with performance feedback or goal setting. This strategy typically provides a reinforcing tangible item or activity to a student when he or she meets a reading fluency goal that is set before the intervention is delivered by the interventionist. It is useful if a preference or reinforcer assessment is administered to a student before selection of the rewards to ensure that the reward menu is indeed reinforcing (e.g., Da Fonte et al., 2016).

Reading Comprehension

Reading comprehension can be defined as the ability to read text fluently while extracting meaning from text (Sideridis, Mouzaki, Simos, & Protopapas, 2006). Earlier meta-analyses of intervention strategies that improve reading comprehension found moderate to large mean effect sizes (Swanson, 1999; Talbott, Lloyd, & Tankersley, 1994). More recent meta-analyses have yielded a moderate mean effect sizes across criterion- and norm-referenced tests for a variety of comprehension strategies, and these effects were maintained or generalized (Berkeley, Scruggs, & Mastropieri, 2010; Suggate, 2016). These meta-analyses included reading comprehension strategies that were delivered to students at risk for and with reading disabilities across Grades 1 through 12. Below we review the most commonly researched types of reading comprehension strategies.

Strategy Instruction

Strategy instruction was broadly defined by Berkeley and colleagues (2010) as helping students identify key features of reading material by incorporating self-management strategies. Mean effects of this category of strategies was moderate for norm-referenced outcomes and large for criterion-referenced measures. Included in this definition were the following five strategies: (a) elaborative interrogation, (b) guided reading, (c) main idea strategy instruction with self-monitoring, (d) peer-assisted learning, and (e) text structure analysis. All of these strategies are used to provide students with the tools they need to comprehend written language. During elaborative interrogation, students learn to think critically about what they are reading by asking themselves why a fact may be true (Mastropieri et al., 1996). Main idea strategy instruction with self-monitoring applies explicit instruction for generating and interpreting main ideas within passages through the use of modeling, demonstration, prompt cards, and guided and independent practice (Jitendra, Hoppes, & Xin, 2000). A four-step self-monitoring process was used while students were engaging in main idea comprehension and required students to record completed steps. *Peer-assisted learning strategies* refers to the pairing of students during which one student acts as a tutor and the other as a tutoree. The tutoree reads the passage while the tutor listens and corrects errors in reading (e.g., Delquadri, Greenwood, Whorton, Carta, & Hall, 1986). Text structure analysis interventions include providing students with strategies to identify what the structure of a passage by locating, for example, the main idea or the order of events (e.g., notice words such as *first, then, finally*; Bakken, Mastropieri, & Scruggs, 1997). Another type of strategy instruction applies a specific heuristic referred to as *Think Before You Read, While Reading, and After Reading. Think Before You Read* asks students to think about the purpose of the passage or story, what is already known about the passage, and what they want to learn before reading. *During Reading* students are asked to think about the context within which they are reading, their reading speed, and whether they need to reread sections to understand them. Finally, *After Reading*, students develop a main idea and summarize the information from the passage (Wanzek et al., 2010).

Text Enhancements

Text enhancements use graphics, questions, or videos to encourage thought and comprehension while reading. Effect sizes on reading comprehension were moderate to large on norm- and criterion-referenced tests; for example, in-text questions could be placed within a reading passage for students to consider while reading, and students could also receive feedback on their responses (Berkeley et al., 2010). This can be accomplished by dividing reading passages into sections and inserting comprehension questions after each subsection. After reading and answering questions pertaining to each subsection, students are given a feedback sheet to self-evaluate their responses (Peverly & Wood, 2001). Graphic organizers that permit students to analyze a reading passage by making a diagram illustrating key information (e.g., lines, arrows, and schematic arrangements of information) can be used to facilitate reading comprehension (Darch & Eaves, 1986). *Hypermedia*, another form of text enhancement, is a form of computer-assisted instruction during which words or phrases that have links to supplemental material (e.g., vocabulary graphics or definitions, links to pronouns, and comprehension questions with assistance to find the answer) are embedded into reading passages (Higgins & Boone, 1991).

Vocabulary Preview

Interventions targeting reading comprehension with a vocabulary component have simply involved teaching students vocabulary words generated from a reading passage. Vocabulary words are practiced using flash cards or by simply having an interventionist preview the words in a passage before the student reads the material. Including vocabulary strategies has yielded moderate mean effects on reading comprehension (Wanzek et al., 2010). As an example, Hawkins, Hale, Sheeley, and Ling (2011) improved the reading comprehension of high school students when combining repeated reading with vocabulary preview. Vocabulary preview in this instance consisted of providing students with flash cards containing vocabulary words from the reading passage.

EMPIRICALLY SUPPORTED INSTRUCTION AND INTERVENTION PRACTICES IN MATHEMATICS

The National Governors' Association Center for Best Practices, Council of Chief State School Officers (2010) *Common Core State Standards for Mathematics* indicate that by the end of fifth grade, students should exhibit fluency with whole numbers. Students may exhibit a wide variety of mathematics difficulties; however, the five most frequently occurring mathematics problems include (a) solving word problems, (b) multistep procedural calculations, (c) mathematics language, (d) checking work and answers, and (e) automatic recall of basic facts (Bryant, Bryant, & Hammill, 2000). Given the importance of whole number fluency as a key foundation for algebra as well as the focus and the status of the extant literature, we now focus on a review of intervention strategies in the areas of computation and word problem solving.

Computation

Mathematics intervention research primarily has focused on investigating effective strategies for improving computational skills among students who have or are at risk for learning disabilities (e.g., Kroesbergen & Van Luit, 2003). As a consequence, numerous systematic reviews and meta-analyses have synthesized this empirical literature (e.g., Codding, Burns, & Lukito, 2011; Gersten et al., 2009; Kroesbergen & Van Luit, 2003; Swanson, 2009). The majority of these syntheses have emphasized instructional approaches as opposed to summarizing specific intervention strategies (e.g., Gersten et al., 2009; Kroesbergen & Van Luit, 2003; Swanson, 2009).

Findings from these meta-analyses are remarkably consistent, demonstrating that explicit instruction (i.e., modeling of concepts and principles; dividing skills into smaller, sequential subcomponents; promoting mastery learning; and controlling task difficulty) and strategy instruction (i.e., use of checklists for problem steps, heuristics, and student verbalizations) are fundamental for promoting mathematics performance. For example, mean effect sizes have ranged from moderate (Swanson, 2009) to large (Gersten et al., 2009) for explicit instruction alone. For strategy instruction, an overall small mean effect size was found (Swanson, 2009), with student verbalizations generating a large effect size (Gersten et al., 2009). Swanson (2009) illustrated that the combined mean effect size for explicit and strategy instruction was in the moderate range. Codding et al. (2011) took a different approach by analyzing the single-case design literature that used curriculum-based measurement outcomes. This synthesis indicated that practice with modeling, drill, and self-management procedures yielded moderate to large effect sizes. Below we briefly describe a few empirically supported intervention approaches that illustrate the use of these instructional principles for basic and multistep computation (readers should note that this is not a comprehensive list; for more information, see Codding, Volpe, & Poncy, 2017).

There are three considerations for using any of the following intervention strategies: (a) sequence targeted facts according to students' earliest unknown skill in the sequence, (b) introduce new facts in sets of no more than 10 (one study illustrated that students' exhibit greater retention when four new facts were introduced in a single session; Burns, Zaslofsky, Maki, & Kwong, 2016), and (c) identify a mastery performance criterion (Hasselbring, Lott, & Zydney, 2005; Stein, Kindler, Silbert, & Carnine, 2006; Woodward, 2006).

Cover–Copy–Compare

Cover–copy–compare (CCC) has been examined in more than 20 peer reviewed studies and applied to all four basic math operations as well as multidigit computation. A meta-analysis of 12 studies indicated that CCC yielded a moderate to large effect size (Joseph et al., 2012). CCC is a self-managed intervention that provides a series of learning trials with modeling within a short period of time through the use of five steps: (a) look at the problem with the answer, (b) cover the problem, (c) record the answer, (d) uncover the problem with the answer, and (e) compare the answer (Skinner, McLaughlin, & Logan, 1997). A specialized worksheet is generated that includes the problem with the answer recorded on the left and the problem without the answer on the right side of the page. Variations of this worksheet include several additional opportunities to use the CCC procedure by repeating the number of problems without the answer on the page.

Taped Problems

The taped problems technique has been examined in at least 11 peer reviewed studies and has been applied to all basic math operations as well as multidigit procedural calculations. A meta-analysis of these studies yielded a large effect size (Kleinert, Codding, Minami, & Gould, 2018). In this technique, students listen to an audio recording that presents math facts and the corresponding answer using a progressive-delay sequence (no delay to 4-s delay) between the presentation of the math fact and the answer (e.g., McCallum, Skinner, & Hutchins, 2004). Students are directed to record their answers on a corresponding worksheet before the answer is provided by the audio recording.

Incremental Rehearsal

Incremental rehearsal is a form of practice known as a *drill*, which provides students with opportunities to respond to basic facts in isolation (Burns, 2005; Codding, Archer, & Connell, 2010). Incremental rehearsal presents unknown facts while interspersing known facts, which may increase student engagement and preference for the activity (Skinner, Fletcher, Wildmon, & Belfiore, 1996). The ratio of known to unknown facts has varied by including 3 (*new facts*) to 7 (*known facts*) or 1 (*new fact*) to 9 (*known facts*; Burns, 2005; Codding et al., 2010; Cooke, Guzaukas, Pressley, & Kerr, 1993; Schnorr, 1989).

Explicit Timing

Explicit timing (ET) has been shown to be an effective intervention across recent meta-analyses (Methe, Kilgus, Neiman, & Riley-Tillman, 2012; Poncy et al., 2015). The procedures associated with ET are very simple: Only a worksheet encompassing math facts or multidigit problems that are within a student's appropriate instructional level and a timer are required. There are two different approaches to ET. The first is to allocate a set amount of time within which students are to work on the math worksheet (Miller & Hudson, 2007). Typically, 1-, 2-, or 4-minute intervals are used, and ET delivered in this way is most effective when students are provided with these opportunities multiple times per day (two to four; Schutte et al., 2015). The second approach is to ask students to mark their progress at 30-second or 1-minute intervals until an assignment is complete or the designated time allocated to practice has ended (e.g., 5–10 minutes of total practice; Codding, Eckert, Fanning, Shiyko, & Solomon, 2007). Requiring students to briefly stop and circle or underline a problem that was completed within these shorter intervals provides immediate feedback on fluency-related outcomes (e.g., how many problems completed in 30 seconds) and makes progress more salient (Rhymer et al., 2002; Van Houten & Thompson, 1976).

Performance Feedback

Performance feedback is the provision of verbal or graphic information to students regarding their specific performance on an activity (Codding,

Chan-Iannetta, Palmer, & Lukito, 2009; Shapiro, 2011). One meta-analysis indicated that providing information to students on their progress in graphic form yielded a small effect size (Gersten et al., 2009). Performance feedback can be provided by teachers as well as by computers and often includes student- or teacher-directed goal setting or information about goal attainment (e.g., Codding et al., 2009). For example, students might be provided with the number of correct problems they previously performed as well as the number they should try to complete in a specified amount of time (Codding et al., 2009, 2007). Including the time required, or rate at which, students accurately complete problems is important if fluency is the instructional objective (Codding et al., 2009).

Peer Tutoring

Peer tutoring refers to a process whereby students work together in pairs or, more broadly, in small groups (e.g., cooperative learning). Effect sizes have ranged from small to large across various meta-analyses (Baker, Gersten, & Lee, 2002; Bowman-Perrott et al., 2013; Gersten et al., 2009; Kroesbergen & Van Luit, 2003; Kunsch, Jitendra, & Sood, 2007; Rohrbeck, Ginsburg-Block, Fantuzzo, & Miller, 2003). Peer tutoring tends to be more effective when provided in general education than special education settings (Kunsch et al., 2007), and it improves outcomes for students at risk for learning disabilities more so than for students with learning disabilities (Baker et al., 2002; Gersten et al., 2009; Kroesbergen & Van Luit, 2003). Peer-assisted learning appears to be more effective when it includes the following four components: (a) interdependent group contingencies, (b) student-directed goal setting, (c) self-monitoring, and (d) performance feedback (Bowman-Perrott et al., 2013; Rohrbeck et al., 2003). A specific review of the same- and cross-age tutoring literature found that both types are useful for increasing mathematics achievement and students serving as both a tutor and tutoree may yield larger academic gains than students who serve in either role in isolation (Robinson, Schofield, & Steers-Wentzell, 2005).

Word Problem Solving

Word problem solving is one of the most complex forms of mathematical problem solving (Bryant et al., 2000; Jonassen, 2003). Common problems students experience include understanding the language embedded in the story problem, selecting an appropriate strategy to solve the problem, following a sequential plan to solve the problem, self-monitoring and evaluating the problem-solving process, and generalizing learned strategies to novel word problems (Bryant et al., 2000; Gersten et al., 2009; Shin & Bryant, 2015).

The current literature supports the use of schema instruction, strategy instruction, and computer-assisted instruction (Xin & Jitendra, 1999; Zhang & Xin, 2012). Meta-analyses have yielded strong effects for all three types of instruction, but the impact of these techniques was strongest with the simplest word problems (i.e., one-step word problems; Xin & Jitendra, 1999; Zhang & Xin, 2012). Evidence of maintenance and generalization to other tasks and settings was found for strategy instruction (i.e., moderate to large effect sizes). Below we review schema and strategy instruction. Unfortunately, many of the computer-assisted instruction programs that formed the basis of previous reviews are no longer available, so we do not describe this category.

Schema Instruction

Representation techniques refer to the use of visual representations to illustrate a math concept, idea, or word problem, such as pictures, drawings, diagrams, maps, or schemas (Jitendra, Nelson, Pulles, Kiss, & Houseworth, 2016). *Diagramming* refers to the use of a spatial layout that illustrates the parts of a word problem and the relations between those parts (van Garderen, 2007). Word problems can be represented through a number of different types of diagrams (e.g., line, tree, circle, bar) that align with different types of problems (e.g., change, group, compare, equal groups, multiplicative comparison; Jitendra, DiPipi, & Perron-Jones, 2002; Xin, 2008). Diagrams are used to directly teach the underlying structure of word problems. Teaching students the underlying structures of word problems provides students with a mechanism for generalization; that is, students should be able to solve novel word problems (Powell, 2011). *Schema instruction* is a specific technique that uses explicit instruction and diagramming to help students recognize different problem types as well as generate and solve a corresponding number sentence.

Strategy Instruction

Strategy instruction integrates explicit instruction of the problem-solving process with self-management strategies (e.g., self-questioning, self-instruction, self-monitoring, and self-evaluation; Montague, 2008). For example, students might be taught a five-part sequential strategy for approaching a word problem, such as (a) read the problem, (b) underline key words, (c) draw the problem, (d) write the number sentence, and (e) write the solution (Case, Harris, & Graham, 1992). In addition, students may be taught a heuristic such as SAY (e.g., self-instruction: say the steps), ASK (e.g., self-question: ask a relevant question about the step), or CHECK (e.g., self-monitor: indicate whether the step was completed), which reminds students to apply self-management strategies while engaging in the problem-solving steps (Cassel & Reid, 1996; Montague, 2008).

EMPIRICALLY SUPPORTED INSTRUCTION AND INTERVENTION PRACTICES IN WRITING

Developing strong writing skills is crucial for precise and successful communication. All students in the classroom, regardless if they are at risk for low writing achievement, have a learning disability, or write with grade-level proficiency, could benefit from improved writing instruction or intervention. Although fewer studies have examined writing intervention effects compared with those that have focused on math or reading, the research consistently shows that specific classroom supports improve the quality of students' writing (Villarreal et al., 2017). Four different meta-analyses have identified effective techniques to improve writing in the classroom (Gillespie & Graham, 2014; Graham, McKeown, Kiuhara, & Harris, 2012; Graham & Perin, 2007; Rogers & Graham, 2008). Across these meta-analyses, four instruction techniques were most commonly cited: (a) strategy instruction (including self-regulated strategy development), (b) goal setting, (c) peer assistance, and (d) prewriting. Using these empirically supported writing interventions and instruction techniques may help students write more clearly, concisely, and compellingly.

Strategy Instruction

Strategy instruction has yielded large effect sizes (Gillespie & Graham, 2014; Graham et al., 2012; Graham & Perin, 2007; Rogers & Graham, 2008). It has generated positive outcomes for whole classrooms (students mostly writing at grade-level proficiency), students at risk of low writing achievement (students in need of targeted intervention supports), and students with learning disabilities. Research has shown that strategy instruction is effective for both elementary and secondary students, so long as grade-level writing strategies are taught.

Strategy instruction involves modeling predetermined writing strategies for students. These strategies may pertain to universal aspects of the writing process through the explicit teaching of planning, drafting, and revising texts. Strategies may also focus on ways to improve different types of writing; for instance, different strategies may be more effective for teaching expository, persuasive, or narrative essay writing. Strategy instruction uses organizers to structure the writing process and mnemonic devices to help students remember every step in the writing strategy. There are different writing strategies for different writing skills, details for which can be found in the Institute of

Education Sciences' *Educator's Practice Guides for Writing* (Graham et al., 2012, 2016). One example of strategy instruction that can be used for the writing process is P.L.A.N.: Pay attention to the prompt, List main ideas, Add supporting information, and Number major points. This strategy helps scaffold the writing process, breaking it down into more manageable tasks for novice writers. An example of a drafting strategy is W.R.I.T.E.: Work from a plan to develop a thesis, Remember writing goals, Include transition words, Try to use different types of sentences, and use Exciting words. This drafting strategy challenges students to critically examine their own work to improve word choice and argument or essay structure. The ultimate goal of these writing strategies is to provide a foundational resource for students to write independently. Although planning, drafting, and revising strategies are most commonly taught, there are other instruction strategies teachers or interventionists may find useful. For example, a meta-analysis by Graham and Perin (2007) yielded a large mean effect size for use of summarization strategies to improve writing outcomes. Summarization involves teaching students to summarize texts succinctly by identifying main ideas and arguments.

Modeling and guiding practice are key aspects of strategy instruction. In modeling, the teacher or interventionist demonstrates how to use the writing strategies. During this initial example, the teacher breaks down the strategy by explicitly explaining each procedural step and how that step ultimately improves the written product. After the teacher has fully modeled the strategy, students should start to practice it themselves. Students may practice the strategy in small groups as the teacher prompts them with each strategy step. Guided practice should progress to let students work more independently. This helps build up and reinforce the students' individual writing skills. During guided practice, the teacher should provide immediate and corrective performance feedback.

The self-regulated strategy development (SRSD) model, developed by Harris and Graham (1996), is one of the most widely researched and successful forms of strategy instruction and has yielded large mean effect sizes (Graham et al., 2012; Graham & Perin, 2007, Rogers & Graham, 2008). The SRSD model has been shown to yield a larger effect size than all other methods of strategy instruction combined (Graham & Perin, 2007). SRSD also has yielded large effect sizes for students with learning disabilities (Gillespie & Graham, 2014).

SRSD involves students setting personal writing goals, self-assessing their work, and self-monitoring writing behaviors. Self-monitoring requires students to reflect on their writing process to ensure they complete all necessary stages of writing. Other forms of strategy instruction, such as using writing strategy mnemonics, can assist self-monitoring practices. A student could refer back to a writing strategy chart to make sure that he or she has completed all of the writing steps. Self-monitoring is a good way to help students become aware of how much time they spend on and off task. SRSD also addresses negative perceptions of writing; students may be exposed to positive statements about writing or given positive self-instructions if they become overwhelmed during the writing process (Harris, Graham, Mason, & Saddler, 2002). This is meant to help increase students' motivation to write. Like other forms of strategy instruction, SRSD begins with teacher instruction and guided practice, but it ultimately prepares students to apply self-management strategies and write independently.

Goal Setting

All four meta-analyses (Gillespie & Graham, 2014; Graham et al., 2012; Graham & Perin, 2007; Rogers & Graham, 2008) have illustrated that setting product goals alone is an effective (i.e., yielding moderate mean effect sizes) way to improve writing quality. Goal setting has been shown to benefit general education students across elementary and secondary schools as well as struggling writers and students with learning disabilities. Not only does students' writing productivity improve with goal setting, but also the quality of their writing improves (Rogers & Graham, 2008).

Teachers or interventionists should outline specific, clear objectives for the format and content of writing products. This includes explaining the purposes of different types of writing; for example, teachers may differentiate the purposes of persuasive versus narrative writing. Specific revision or drafting goals can also be generated to help students during the writing process. This means a teacher may assign a specific number of student revisions to encourage students to think critically about how to improve their written work. Productivity goals that ask students to write a certain number of pages or increase the percentage of writing assignments completed, or that encourage students to write more words than they have previously, can also be established for or with students (Rogers & Graham, 2008).

Peer Assistance

Moderate to large mean effect sizes were found for peer assistance when used in the general education classroom with typical learners as well as students at risk for writing difficulties (Graham et al., 2012; Graham & Perin, 2007). More evidence is needed to determine whether peer assistance improves the writing of students with learning disabilities. Peer assistance can involve small groups of students working together to plan, draft, or revise written texts. It could also require students to edit or provide feedback on each other's work. By adding different perspectives to a paper, peers help challenge a paper's ideas, and this process may ultimately improve its argument, structure, or word choice (Graham & Perin, 2007). Peer assistance may also be effective because it can improve engagement and motivation during writing tasks.

Prewriting

According to two meta-analyses, prewriting activities yield small effect sizes across group (Graham & Perin, 2007) and single-case design studies (Rogers & Graham, 2008) on the quality of typical and struggling students' writing. Prewriting activities help students generate and organize writing ideas before the drafting process begins. Students can plan their writing by researching background information about their topic, creating webs of topic ideas, or even brainstorming aloud with a small group (Graham & Perin, 2007).

CONCLUSION

Practitioners can draw on numerous meta-analyses to identify and implement instructional procedures and intervention strategies that will improve the reading, mathematics, and writing performance of students at risk for and with learning and other disabilities. We have offered a brief summary of some of the instruction and intervention strategies with the most robust effects as a guide for practitioners. There were several commonalities within the empirically supported practices identified by these research syntheses across subject areas, including the benefits of explicit and strategy instructional techniques, goal setting and feedback, and peer tutoring or assistance. A summary of this literature also suggests that for some academic areas, such as reading fluency, computation, and writing, specific, simple, and brief strategies have been detailed. For other areas, however, such as emergent reading and comprehension, active treatment ingredients remain relatively unclear and warrant further analysis.

REFERENCES

Baker, S., Gersten, R., & Lee, D. (2002). A synthesis of empirical research on teaching mathematics to low-achieving students. *The Elementary School Journal, 103*, 51–73. http://dx.doi.org/10.1086/499715

Bakken, J. P., Mastropieri, M. A., & Scruggs, T. E. (1997). Reading comprehension of expository science material and students with learning disabilities:

A comparison of strategies. *The Journal of Special Education, 31,* 300–324. http://dx.doi.org/10.1177/002246699703100302

Barnett, D. W., Daly, E. J., III, Jones, K. M., & Lentz, E., Jr. (2004). Response to intervention: Empirically based special service divisions from single-case designs of increasing and decreasing intensity. *The Journal of Special Education, 38,* 66–79. http://dx.doi.org/10.1177/00224669040380020101

Berkeley, S., Scruggs, T. E., & Mastropieri, M. (2010). Reading comprehension instruction for students with learning disabilities, 1995–2006: A meta-analysis. *Remedial and Special Education, 31,* 423–436. http://dx.doi.org/10.1177/0741932509355988

Bowman-Perrott, L., Davis, H., Vannest, K., Williams, L., Greenwood, C., & Parker, R. (2013). Academic benefits of peer tutoring: A meta-analytic review of single-case research. *School Psychology Review, 42,* 39–55.

Bryant, D. P., Bryant, B. R., & Hammill, D. D. (2000). Characteristic behaviors of students with LD who have teacher-identified math weaknesses. *Journal of Learning Disabilities, 33,* 168–177, 199. http://dx.doi.org/10.1177/002221940003300205

Burns, M. K. (2005). Using incremental rehearsal to increase fluency of single-digit multiplication facts with children identified as learning disabled in mathematics computation. *Education and Treatment of Children, 28,* 237–249.

Burns, M. K., Codding, R. S., Boice, C. H., & Lukito, G. (2010). Meta-analysis of acquisition and fluency math interventions with instructional and frustration level skills: Evidence for a skill by treatment interaction. *School Psychology Review, 39,* 69–83.

Burns, M. K., & Wagner, D. (2008). Determining an effective intervention within a brief experimental analysis for reading. *School Psychology Review, 37,* 126–136.

Burns, M. K., Zaslofsky, A. F., Maki, K. E., & Kwong, E. (2016). Effect of modifying intervention set size with acquisition rate data while practicing single-digit multiplication facts. *Assessment for Effective Intervention, 41,* 131–140. http://dx.doi.org/10.1177/1534508415593529

Case, L., Harris, K. R., & Graham, S. (1992). Improving the mathematical problem-solving skills of students with learning disabilities: Self-regulated strategy development. *The Journal of Special Education, 26,* 1–19. http://dx.doi.org/10.1177/002246699202600101

Cassel, J., & Reid, R. (1996). Use of a self-regulated strategy intervention to improve word problem-solving skills of students with mild disabilities. *Journal of Behavioral Education, 6,* 153–172. http://dx.doi.org/10.1007/BF02110230

Codding, R. S., Archer, J., & Connell, J. (2010). A systematic replication and extension using incremental rehearsal to improve multiplication skills: An investigation of generalization. *Journal of Behavioral Education, 19,* 93–105. http://dx.doi.org/10.1007/s10864-010-9102-9

Codding, R. S., Burns, M. K., & Lukito, G. (2011). Meta-analysis of basic-fact fluency interventions: A component analysis. *Learning Disabilities Research & Practice, 26*, 36–47. http://dx.doi.org/10.1111/j.1540-5826.2010.00323.x

Codding, R. S., Chan-Iannetta, L., Palmer, M., & Lukito, G. (2009). Examining a class-wide application of cover–copy–compare with and without goal setting to enhance mathematics fluency. *School Psychology Quarterly, 24*, 173–185. http://dx.doi.org/10.1037/a0017192

Codding, R. S., Eckert, T. L., Fanning, E., Shiyko, M., & Solomon, E. (2007). Comparing mathematics interventions: The effects of cover–copy–compare alone and combined with performance feedback on digits correct and incorrect. *Journal of Behavioral Education, 16*, 125–141. http://dx.doi.org/10.1007/s10864-006-9006-x

Codding, R. S., Volpe, R. J., & Poncy, B. C. (2017). *Effective math interventions: A guide to improving whole-number knowledge*. New York, NY: Guilford Press.

Cooke, N. L., Guzaukas, R., Pressley, J. S., & Kerr, K. (1993). Effects of using a ratio of new items to review items during drill and practice: Three experiments. *Education and Treatment of Children, 16*, 213–234.

Da Fonte, M. A., Boesch, M. C., Edwards-Bowyer, M. E., Restrepo, M. W., Bennett, B. P., & Diamond, G. P. (2016). A three-step reinforcer identification framework: A step-by-step process. *Education and Treatment of Children, 39*, 389–409. http://dx.doi.org/10.1353/etc.2016.0017

Daly, E. J., III, Hintze, J. M., & Hamler, K. R. (2000). Improving practice by taking steps toward technological improvements in academic intervention in the new millennium. *Psychology in the Schools, 37*, 61–72.

Darch, C., & Eaves, R. C. (1986). Visual displays to increase comprehension of high school learning-disabled students. *The Journal of Special Education, 20*, 309–318. http://dx.doi.org/10.1177/002246698602000305

Delquadri, J., Greenwood, C. R., Whorton, D., Carta, J. J., & Hall, R. V. (1986). Classwide peer tutoring. *Exceptional Children, 52*, 535–542. http://dx.doi.org/10.1177/001440298605200606

Eckert, T. L., Ardoin, S. P., Daisey, D. M., & Scarola, M. D. (2000). Empirically evaluating the effectiveness of reading interventions: The use of brief experimental analysis and single case designs. *Psychology in the Schools, 37*, 463–473. http://dx.doi.org/10.1002/1520-6807(200009)37:5<463::AID-PITS6>3.0.CO;2-X

Ehri, L. C., Nunes, S. R., Stahl, S. A., & Willows, D. M. (2001). Systematic phonics instruction helps students learn to read: Evidence from the National Reading Panel's meta-analysis. *Review of Educational Research, 71*, 393–447. http://dx.doi.org/10.3102/00346543071003393

Ehri, L. C., Nunes, S. R., Willows, D. M., Schuster, B., Yaghoub-Zadeh, Z., & Shanahan, T. (2001). Phonemic awareness instruction helps children learn to read: Evidence from the National Reading Panel's meta-analysis. *Reading Research Quarterly, 36*, 250–287. http://dx.doi.org/10.1598/RRQ.36.3.2

Galuschka, K., Ise, E., Krick, K., & Schulte-Körne, G. (2014). Effectiveness of treatment approaches for children and adolescents with reading disabilities: A meta-analysis of randomized controlled trials. *PLoS One, 9*(2), e89900. Advance online publication. http://dx.doi.org/10.1371/journal.pone.0089900

Gersten, R., Chard, D. J., Jayanthi, M., Baker, S. K., Morphy, P., & Flojo, J. (2009). Mathematics instruction for students with learning disabilities: A meta-analysis of instructional components. *Review of Educational Research, 79,* 1202–1242. http://dx.doi.org/10.3102/0034654309334431

Gillespie, A., & Graham, S. (2014). A meta-analysis of writing interventions for students with learning disabilities. *Exceptional Children, 80,* 454–473. http://dx.doi.org/10.1177/0014402914527238

Graham, S., Bruch, J., Fitzgerald, J., Friedrich, L., Furgeson, J., Greene, K., . . . Smither Wulsin, C. (2016). *Teaching secondary students to write effectively* (Publication No. NCEE 2017-4002). Washington, DC: National Center for Education Evaluation and Regional Assistance, Institute of Education Sciences, U.S. Department of Education.

Graham, S., McKeown, D., Kiuhara, S., & Harris, K. R. (2012). A meta-analysis of writing instruction for students in the elementary grades. *Journal of Educational Psychology, 104,* 879–896. http://dx.doi.org/10.1037/a0029185

Graham, S., & Perin, D. (2007). A meta-analysis of writing instruction for adolescent students. *Journal of Educational Psychology, 99,* 445–476. http://dx.doi.org/10.1037/0022-0663.99.3.445

Haring, N. G., Lovitt, T. C., Eaton, M. D., & Hansen, C. L. (1978). *The fourth R: Research in the classroom.* Columbus, OH: Merrill.

Harris, K. R., & Graham, S. (1996). *Making the writing process work: Strategies for composition and self-regulation* (2nd ed.). Cambridge, MA: Brookline Books.

Harris, K. R., Graham, S., Mason, L. H., & Saddler, B. (2002). Developing self-regulated writers. *Theory into Practice, 41,* 110–115. http://dx.doi.org/10.1207/s15430421tip4102_7

Hasselbring, T. S., Lott, A. C., & Zydney, J. M. (2005). Technology-supported math instruction for students with disabilities: Two decades of research and development. *LDonline,* Article 6291. Retrieved from http://www.ldonline.org/article/6291/

Hawkins, R. O., Hale, A., Sheeley, W., & Ling, S. (2011). Repeated reading and vocabulary-previewing interventions to improve fluency and comprehension for struggling high-school readers. *Psychology in the Schools, 48,* 59–77. http://dx.doi.org/10.1002/pits.20545

Higgins, K., & Boone, R. (1991). Hypermedia CAI: A supplement to an elementary school basal reader program. *Journal of Special Education Technology, 11,* 1–15. http://dx.doi.org/10.1177/016264349101100101

Jitendra, A., DiPipi, C. M., & Perron-Jones, N. (2002). An exploratory study of schema-based word-problem-solving instruction for middle school students with learning disabilities: An emphasis on conceptual and procedural understanding. *Journal of Special Education, 36,* 23–38.

Jitendra, A. K., Hoppes, M. K., & Xin, Y. P. (2000). Enhancing main idea comprehension for students with learning problems: The role of a summarization strategy and self-monitoring instruction. *The Journal of Special Education, 34,* 127–139. http://dx.doi.org/10.1177/002246690003400302

Jitendra, A. K., Nelson, G., Pulles, S. M., Kiss, A. J., & Houseworth, J. (2016). Is mathematical representation of problems an evidence-based strategy for students with mathematics difficulties. *Exceptional Children, 83,* 8–25. http://dx.doi.org/10.1177/0014402915625062

Jonassen, D. H. (2003). Designing research-based instruction for story problems. *Educational Psychology Review, 15,* 267–296. http://dx.doi.org/10.1023/A:1024648217919

Jones, K. M., & Wickstrom, K. F. (2002). Done in sixty seconds: Further analysis of the brief assessment model for academic problems. *School Psychology Review, 31,* 554–568.

Joseph, L. M., Konrad, M., Cates, G., Vajcner, T., Eveleigh, E., & Fishley, K. M. (2012). A meta-analytic review of the cover–copy–compare and variations of this self-management procedure. *Psychology in the Schools, 49,* 122–136. http://dx.doi.org/10.1002/pits.20622

Kavale, K. A. (2001). Decision making in special education: The function of meta-analysis. *Exceptionality, 9,* 245–268. http://dx.doi.org/10.1207/S15327035EX0904_6

Kleinert, W. L., Codding, R. S., Minami, T., & Gould, K. (2018). A meta-analysis of the taped problems intervention. *Journal of Behavioral Education, 27,* 53–80. http://dx.doi.org/.10.1007/s10864-017-9284-5

Kroesbergen, E. H., & Van Luit, J. E. H. (2003). Mathematics interventions for children with special education needs: A meta-analysis. *Remedial and Special Education, 24,* 97–114. http://dx.doi.org/10.1177/07419325030240020501

Kunsch, C. A., Jitendra, A. K., & Sood, S. (2007). The effects of peer-mediated instruction in mathematics for students with learning problems: A research synthesis. *Learning Disabilities Research & Practice, 22,* 1–12.

Long, A. C. J., Hagermoser Sanetti, L. M., Collier-Meek, M. A., Gallucci, J., Altschaefl, M., & Kratochwill, T. R. (2016). An exploratory investigation of teachers' intervention planning and perceived implementation barriers. *Journal of School Psychology, 55,* 1–26. http://dx.doi.org/10.1016/j.jsp.2015.12.002

Lovett, M. W., Warren-Chaplin, P. M., Ransby, M. J., & Borden, S. L. (1990). Training the word recognition skills of reading disabled children: Treatment and transfer effects. *Journal of Educational Psychology, 82,* 769–780. http://dx.doi.org/10.1037/0022-0663.82.4.769

Mastropieri, M. A., Berkeley, S., McDuffie, K. A., Graff, H., Marshak, L., Conners, N. A., . . . Cuenca-Sanchez, Y. (2009). What is published in the field of special education? An analysis of 11 prominent journals. *Exceptional Children, 76,* 95–109. http://dx.doi.org/10.1177/001440290907600105

Mastropieri, M. A., Scruggs, T. E., Hamilton, S. L., Wolfe, S., Whedon, C., & Canevaro, A. (1996). Promoting thinking skills of students with learning disabilities: Effects on recall and comprehension of expository prose. *Exceptionality, 6,* 1–11. http://dx.doi.org/10.1207/s15327035ex0601_1

Mathes, P. G., & Fuchs, L. S. (1993). Peer-mediated reading instruction in special education resource rooms. *Learning Disabilities Research & Practice, 8,* 233–243.

McCallum, E., Skinner, C. H., & Hutchins, H. (2004). The taped-problems intervention: Increasing division fact fluency using a low-tech self-managed time-delay intervention. *Journal of Applied School Psychology, 20,* 129–147. http://dx.doi.org/10.1300/J370v20n02_08

Methe, S. A., Kilgus, S. P., Neiman, C., & Riley-Tillman, T. C. (2012). Meta-analysis of interventions for basic mathematics computation in single-case research. *Journal of Behavioral Education, 21,* 230–253. http://dx.doi.org/10.1007/s10864-012-9161-1

Miller, S. P., & Hudson, P. J. (2007). Using evidence-based practices to build mathematics competence related to conceptual, procedural, and declarative knowledge. *Learning Disabilities Research & Practice, 22,* 47–57. http://dx.doi.org/10.1111/j.1540-5826.2007.00230.x

Montague, M. (2008). Self-regulation strategies to improve mathematical problem solving for students with learning disabilities. *Learning Disability Quarterly, 31,* 37–44.

Morgan, P. L., Sideridis, G., & Hua, Y. (2012). Initial and over-time effects of fluency interventions for students with or at risk for disabilities. *The Journal of Special Education, 46,* 94–116. http://dx.doi.org/10.1177/0022466910398016

National Governors' Association Center for Best Practices, Council of Chief State School Officers. (2010). *Common Core State Standards for Mathematics.* Washington, DC: Author.

National Institute of Child Health and Human Development. (2000). *Report of the National Reading Panel: Teaching children to read. An evidence-based assessment of the scientific literature on reading and its implications for reading instruction: Reports of the subgroups* (NIH Publication No. 00-4754). Washington, DC: U.S. Government Printing Office.

O'Connor, R. E., White, A., & Swanson, H. L. (2007). Repeated reading versus continuous reading: Influences on reading fluency and comprehension. *Exceptional Children, 74,* 31–46. http://dx.doi.org/10.1177/001440290707400102

Peverly, S. T., & Wood, R. (2001). The effects of adjunct questions and feedback on improving the reading comprehension skills of learning-disabled adolescents. *Contemporary Educational Psychology, 26,* 25–43. http://dx.doi.org/10.1006/ceps.1999.1025

Piasta, S. B., & Wagner, R. K. (2010). Developing early literacy skills: A meta-analysis of alphabet learning and instruction. *Reading Research Quarterly, 45,* 8–38. http://dx.doi.org/10.1598/RRQ.45.1.2

Poncy, B. C., Solomon, B., Duhon, G., Skinner, C., Moore, K., & Simons, S. (2015). An analysis of learning rate and curricular scope: Caution when choosing academic interventions based on aggregated outcomes. *School Psychology Review, 44,* 289–305. http://dx.doi.org/10.17105/spr-14-0044.1

Powell, S. R. (2011). Solving word problems using schemas: A review of the literature. *Learning Disabilities Research & Practice, 26,* 94–108. http://dx.doi.org/10.1111/j.1540-5826.2011.00329.x

Rhymer, K. N., Skinner, C. H., Jackson, S., McNeill, S., Smith, T., & Jackson, B. (2002). The 1-minute explicit timing intervention: The influence of mathematics problem difficulty. *Journal of Instructional Psychology, 29,* 305–311.

Robinson, D. R., Schofield, J. W., & Steers-Wentzell, K. L. (2005). Peer and cross-age tutoring in math: Outcomes and their design implications. *Educational Psychology Review, 17,* 327–362. http://dx.doi.org/10.1007/s10648-005-8137-2

Rogers, L. A., & Graham, S. (2008). A meta-analysis of single subject design writing intervention research. *Journal of Educational Psychology, 100,* 879–906. http://dx.doi.org/10.1037/0022-0663.100.4.879

Rohrbeck, C. A., Ginsburg-Block, M. D., Fantuzzo, J. W., & Miller, T. R. (2003). Peer-assisted learning intervention with elementary school students. A meta-analytic review. *Journal of Educational Psychology, 95,* 240–257. http://dx.doi.org/10.1037/0022-0663.95.2.240

Scarborough, H. S., Shapiro, B. K., Accardo, P. J., & Capute, A. J. (1998). Early identification of children at risk for reading disabilities: Phonological awareness and some other promising predictors. In B. K. Shapiro, P. J. Accardo, & A. J. Capute (Eds.), *Specific reading disability: A view of the spectrum* (pp. 75–119). San Antonio, TX: Pro-Ed.

Schnorr, J. M. (1989). Practicing math facts on the computer. *Teacher Education and Special Education, 12,* 65–69. http://dx.doi.org/10.1177/088840648901200112

Schutte, G. M., Duhon, G. J., Solomon, B. G., Poncy, B. C., Moore, K., & Story, B. (2015). A comparative analysis of massed vs. distributed practice on basic math fact fluency growth rates. *Journal of School Psychology, 53,* 149–159. http://dx.doi.org/10.1016/j.jsp.2014.12.003

Shapiro, E. S. (2011). *Academic skills problems: Direct assessment and intervention.* New York, NY: Guilford Press.

Shin, M., & Bryant, D. P. (2015). A synthesis of mathematical and cognitive performances of students with mathematics learning disabilities. *Journal of Learning Disabilities, 48,* 96–112. http://dx.doi.org/10.1177/0022219413508324

Sideridis, G. D., Mouzaki, A., Simos, P., & Protopapas, A. (2006). Classification of students with reading comprehension difficulties: The roles of motivation, affect, and psychopathology. *Learning Disability Quarterly, 29,* 159–180. http://dx.doi.org/10.2307/30035505

Skinner, C. H., Fletcher, P. A., Wildmon, M., & Belfiore, P. J. (1996). Improving assignment preference through interspersing additional problems: Brief versus easy problems. *Journal of Behavioral Education, 6,* 427–436. http://dx.doi.org/10.1007/BF02110515

Skinner, C. H., McLaughlin, T. F., & Logan, P. (1997). Cover, copy, and compare: A self-managed academic intervention effective across skills, students, and settings. *Journal of Behavioral Education, 7,* 295–306. http://dx.doi.org/10.1023/A:1022823522040

Stein, M., Kindler, D., Silbert, J., & Carnine, D. W. (2006). *Designing effective mathematics instruction: A direct instruction approach* (4th ed.). Columbus, OH: Merrill/Prentice Hall.

Suggate, S. P. (2016). A meta-analysis of the long-term effects of phonemic awareness, phonics, fluency, and reading comprehension interventions. *Journal of Learning Disabilities, 49,* 77–96. http://dx.doi.org/10.1177/0022219414528540

Swanson, H. L. (1999). Reading research for students with LD: A meta-analysis of intervention outcomes. *Journal of Learning Disabilities, 32,* 504–532. http://dx.doi.org/10.1177/002221949903200605

Swanson, H. L. (2009). Science-supported math instruction for children with math difficulties: Converting a meta-analysis to practice. In S. Rosenfield & V. Berninger (Eds.), *Translating science-supported instruction into evidence-based practices: Understanding and applying implementation processes* (pp. 85–106). New York, NY: Oxford University Press. http://dx.doi.org/10.1093/med:psych/9780195325355.003.0003

Talbott, E., Lloyd, J. W., & Tankersley, M. (1994). Effects of reading comprehension interventions for students with learning disabilities. *Learning Disability Quarterly, 17,* 223–232. http://dx.doi.org/10.2307/1511075

VanDerHeyden, A., & Harvey, M. (2013). Using data to advance learning outcomes in schools. *Journal of Positive Behavior Interventions, 15,* 205–213. http://dx.doi.org/10.1177/1098300712442387

van Garderen, D. (2007). Teaching students with LD to use diagrams to solve mathematical word problems. *Journal of Learning Disabilities, 40,* 540–553. http://dx.doi.org/10.1177/00222194070400060501

Van Houten, R., & Thompson, C. (1976). The effects of explicit timing on math performance. *Journal of Applied Behavior Analysis, 9,* 227–230.

Villarreal, V., Castro, M. J., Umaña, I., & Sullivan, J. R. (2017). Characteristics of Intervention Research in School Psychology Journals: 2010–2014. *Psychology in the Schools, 54,* 548–559. http://dx.doi.org/10.1002/pits.22012

Wanzek, J., Vaughn, S., Scammacca, N., Gatlin, B., Walker, M. A., & Capin, P. (2016). Meta-analyses of the effects of Tier 2 type reading interventions in grades K–3. *Educational Psychology Review, 28,* 551–576. http://dx.doi.org/10.1007/s10648-015-9321-7

Wanzek, J., Wexler, J., Vaughn, S., & Ciullo, S. (2010). Reading interventions for struggling readers in the upper elementary grades: A synthesis of 20 years of research. *Reading and Writing, 23*, 889–912. http://dx.doi.org/10.1007/s11145-009-9179-5

Woodward, J. (2006). Developing automaticity in multiplication facts: Integrating strategy instruction with timed practice drills. *Learning Disability Quarterly, 29*, 269–289. http://dx.doi.org/10.2307/30035554

Xin, Y. P. (2008). The effect of schema-based instruction in solving mathematics word problems: An emphasis on pre-algebraic conceptualization of multiplicative relations. *Journal for Research in Mathematics Education, 39*, 526–551.

Xin, Y. P., & Jitendra, A. K. (1999). The effects of instruction in solving mathematical word problems for students with learning problems: A meta-analysis. *The Journal of Special Education, 32*, 207–225. http://dx.doi.org/10.1177/002246699903200402

Zhang, D., & Xin, Y. P. (2012). A follow-up meta-analysis for word-problem–solving interventions for students with mathematics difficulties. *The Journal of Educational Research, 105*, 303–318. http://dx.doi.org/10.1080/00220671.2011.627397

9

ADULTS AS CHANGE AGENTS: APPLICATIONS OF BEHAVIORAL CONSULTATION

WILLIAM P. ERCHUL, ANN C. SCHULTE, AUSTIN H. JOHNSON, AND CATHLEEN A. GERAGHTY

Suppose you are a beginning second-grade teacher who is experiencing great difficulty with a student named Jerry. It seems Jerry is out of control—disrupting children around him and interfering with your attempts to teach the class. To deal with this situation, you decide to meet with the school psychologist, Dr. Smith. In the first session, Dr. Smith asks you to describe in observable terms what you mean by Jerry being "disruptive" and "interfering." In reply to her series of questions, you inform Dr. Smith that Jerry (a) is generally a capable student but often leaves his seat for several minutes at a time while you are busy working with a small group, and he is among the students who are supposed to be doing independent math work, and (b) repeatedly calls out answers without raising his hand when you are teaching phonics. Dr. Smith then asks you to describe what is going on in the classroom before, during, and after Jerry leaves his seat and blurts out answers. This meeting ends with Dr. Smith's request that you keep track of how often these two problem

---

http://dx.doi.org/10.1037/0000126-010
Behavioral Interventions in Schools: Evidence-Based Positive Strategies, Second Edition, S. G. Little and A. Akin-Little (Editors)
Copyright © 2019 by the American Psychological Association. All rights reserved.

behaviors occur each day. She also asks to visit your classroom tomorrow to see Jerry "in action."

The following week, a second meeting is held, and, through sharing insights gained from the more systematic analysis of Jerry's behavior, you and Dr. Smith note several patterns: Jerry often leaves his seat because Jimmy motions for him to go to the pencil sharpener (i.e., work avoidance, peer attention); you do not have a clear line of sight to the class members doing independent work while you are teaching small-group math; Jerry frequently does not finish his math work as a result of leaving his seat; and when Jerry calls out answers in phonics, you often acknowledge his answer (i.e., give him teacher attention) in order not to interrupt the flow of instruction. Armed with this information, you and Dr. Smith decide on an intervention. You both discuss and agree that you will aim for four objectives: (a) reposition Jimmy so that he is not in Jerry's line of sight, and change your position during math small-group work, thereby modifying some of antecedents to the problem behavior; (b) allow Jerry extra screen time at the end of the day if he completes his math seatwork, thereby reinforcing a desirable behavior that competes with leaving his seat during math; (c) reemphasize the existing rules of classroom etiquette, then ignore Jerry's calls in order to extinguish this inappropriate behavior during phonics; and (d) positively reinforce Jerry's appropriate behavior by calling on him only when his hand is raised. Before the meeting ends, Dr. Smith and you role-play what you will say to Jerry in particular as you begin to implement this intervention plan and how to respond to peers who ask why Jerry gets extra screen time. She also asks that you continue to keep track of the daily occurrence of the two problem behaviors.

With Dr. Smith's support, you carry out this plan for 2 weeks, and in the next session you meet to assess the plan's impact on the target behaviors. Although far from perfect, it seems that the intervention has succeeded in lowering Jerry's out-of-seat behavior by an average of 50% (i.e., from four to two times each day) and blurting out answers by an average of 67% (i.e., from three times a day to one time per day). You are fairly satisfied with this progress and decide to keep the plan in place awhile longer. Dr. Smith then encourages you to start keeping track of the number of times Jerry appropriately raises his hand during phonics instruction, and you agree to do this. You both compare calendars and schedule a final meeting for 2 weeks from today.

This case study is an example of *human services consultation*, a helping process in which an intervention is provided to a *client* (e.g., student) directly by a *consultee* (e.g., teacher, parent) but indirectly by a *consultant* (e.g., school psychologist). The consultant's primary role historically has been to support and assist the consultee, and it is possible a consultant may never meet face to face with a particular client. Along these lines, because the ultimate responsibility for the client's welfare rests with the consultee it is usually the consultee who carries out the intervention with the client. Consultation has a dual purpose: (a) to help the consultee with a current work problem and (b) to give him or her added skills and insights that will enhance future professional functioning. It is the latter purpose that promotes consultation as a means to prevent educational and psychological problems. Note that, unlike other interventions described in this book, consultation involves a *triadic relationship* (i.e., consultant/behavioral specialist–consultee–client) instead of a dyadic relationship (i.e., behavioral specialist–client; Brown, Pryzwansky, & Schulte, 2011; Erchul & Martens, 2010).

More specifically, our opening scenario is an example of *behavioral consultation* (Bergan, 1977; Bergan & Kratochwill, 1990; Kratochwill, 2008; Martens, DiGennaro Reed, & Magnuson, 2014). Behavioral consultation is built on a strong foundation of behavioral psychology, emphasizing concepts such as quantification, current environmental causality, and a close association between assessment and intervention (Haynes, 1978). Obviously, many interventions selected and implemented within behavioral consultation are those that are described in previous chapters of this volume.

Particularly within a behavioral framework, consultation is an established means to change adult behavior (Bergan & Kratochwill, 1990; Erchul & Martens, 2010; Martens et al., 2014). Similar to the chapter appearing in the first edition of this book (i.e., Erchul & Schulte, 2009), the primary goal of the current chapter is to provide basic information about behavioral consultation. In addition, we consider two other perspectives relevant to adults serving as change agents: (a) Raven's (1992) power/interaction model of interpersonal influence and (b) findings from the performance feedback literature. Of the many possible perspectives to consider, we chose these two because they are complementary: Raven's model offers a broad, comprehensive lens through which to view how adults' behaviors can be changed through the application of a well-established typology of social power bases, and the performance feedback literature provides specific guidance about how to change adults' behavior within the critical intervention implementation phase of behavioral consultation. Throughout the chapter, key references are cited that we strongly encourage readers to consult for more detailed information.

BEHAVIORAL CONSULTATION

Influenced by behavioral and cognitive psychology, and extending ideas advanced by D'Zurilla and Goldfried (1971) and Tharp and Wetzel (1969), John Bergan (1977, 1995) proposed his model of behavioral consultation.

Although there are many variations, today when one hears the term *behavioral consultation* the chances are very good that the speaker is referring to Bergan's specific model. Relative to other topics presented in this volume, Bergan's model combines the strategies and tactics of behavior analysis with a step-by-step problem-solving approach, uses behavioral technology to develop interventions, and applies the technology of behavior analysis to evaluate intervention outcomes (Erchul & Martens, 2010). Although his initial articulation of the model (Bergan, 1977) is still a useful source for information about it, the model also has been thoroughly described in more recent sources (e.g., Kratochwill, 2008; Kratochwill & Bergan, 1990; Sheridan & Kratochwill, 2008).

Key Assumptions

Bergan (1977) identified a number of key assumptions of behavioral consultation. Central to our discussion are the following assumptions about it:

- assumes the consultee (e.g., teacher) is an active participant throughout consultation;
- offers a means through which the consultant can link knowledge producers (e.g., education researchers) with knowledge consumers (e.g., teachers);
- attempts to connect decision making to empirical evidence by using, for example, direct observations of client behavior and scientific findings about changing behavior;
- defines problems presented in consultation as being outside the character of the client, so common diagnostic labels applied to clients (e.g., *learning disabled, emotionally disturbed*) are not viewed as helpful and generally are not used;
- emphasizes the role of environmental factors in maintaining and changing behavior, such that respondent, operant, and modeling procedures are generally employed; and
- centers its evaluation on goal attainment and plan effectiveness (i.e., accomplishments) rather than on client characteristics, which often suggest deficiencies.

Stages, Interviews, and Objectives

Bergan's (1977) model of behavioral consultation is essentially a four-stage problem-solving process, and the model's stages include three separate interviews, each of which contains specific objectives that the consultant is expected to address. The four stages are (a) problem identification, (b) problem analysis, (c) plan implementation, and (d) problem evaluation. More recently, plan implementation has been called *treatment implementation* and problem evaluation has been called *treatment evaluation* (Sheridan & Kratochwill, 2008) or *plan evaluation* (Kratochwill, 2008). The term *behavioral consultation* itself seems to have changed in some contexts to *problem-solving consultation* to acknowledge influences in the contemporary model that extend beyond behavioral psychology (cf. Kratochwill, 2008). These slight name changes notwithstanding, behavioral consultation and its stages have remained essentially the same for over 40 years. Next, we describe the stages and their corresponding interviews and objectives.

Problem Identification

The first stage involves specifying the problem to be solved as a result of consultation. Problem identification is accomplished through a *problem identification interview* (PII), which the consultant conducts with the consultee. The PII is a critical point within behavioral consultation because it creates expectations for the use of a behavioral, rather than a medical model, perspective on the client's problems, and it stresses the role of current environmental events as being primarily responsible for the problem. The specific objectives associated with the PII are to

- assess the range of consultee concerns;
- identify a problem area to target and prioritize components of the problem;
- define the problem in observable, behavioral terms;
- estimate the frequency, intensity, and duration of the problem behavior;
- inquire about client strengths;
- identify tentative goals for behavior change;
- begin to identify environmental conditions surrounding the problem behavior (i.e., antecedent, sequential, and consequent behaviors);
- establish and agree on data collection procedures and responsibilities; and
- schedule the next interview.

Before the next interview, typically observations of the client are conducted and baseline (i.e., preintervention) data are collected on the problem behavior in order to offer a starting point for evaluating the effectiveness of the intervention plan that is to be implemented.

Problem Analysis

During the second stage of behavioral consultation, the problem behavior is examined further and an intervention is designed to solve it. The *problem analysis interview* has six objectives:

1. determine whether the baseline data are sufficient to document the existence of a problem,
2. establish goals for behavior change,
3. continue the analysis of environmental conditions surrounding the problem behavior (i.e., antecedent, sequential, and consequent behaviors),
4. design and prepare to implement an intervention plan,
5. reaffirm data collection procedures, and
6. schedule the next interview.

Plan Implementation

Although the third stage of the model does not involve a formal interview, it assumes that the consultant and consultee will continue to exchange information through brief contacts. During plan implementation, the consultant monitors and assists the consultee in implementing the intervention as agreed to by both parties. There are three specific objectives associated with plan implementation: (a) determine whether the consultee has the necessary skills to implement the intervention; (b) monitor data collection and overall plan operations; and (c) determine the need for plan revisions, if necessary.

Problem Evaluation

The final stage of behavior consultation is problem evaluation, which occurs after the intervention has been in place long enough to have a chance to produce a change in behavior (e.g., 1 week or longer). Problem evaluation involves determining the extent to which the problem has been solved and the plan was effective. Problem evaluation is carried out through the *problem evaluation interview*, which has four objectives: (a) determine whether intervention goals were met; (b) assess plan effectiveness; (c) discuss continuation, modification, or termination of the plan; and (d) terminate consultation or schedule additional meetings to recycle through the problem-solving process (Bergan, 1977; Bergan & Kratochwill, 1990; Erchul & Martens, 2010; Kratochwill & Bergan, 1990).

Although the foregoing presentation lists the widely recognized steps and consultant tasks found in behavioral consultation, it is worth noting that others have introduced additional stages and consultant tasks to the model. For example, realizing the significance of the working relationship between consultant and consultee to promote cooperation and decrease resistance, Kratochwill (2008) advanced an initial stage, termed *Establishing Relationships*. Similarly, acknowledging that few interventions developed in consultation will succeed unless implemented with integrity (Noell & Gansle, 2014), Wilkinson (2006) proposed the Treatment Monitoring Interview, which occurs between plan implementation and the problem evaluation interview.

Relevant Outcome Research on Behavioral Consultation

Although space limitations preclude a detailed summary, it is useful to highlight some important findings generated from studies of school-based behavioral consultation. Relative to outcomes (i.e., does behavior consultation "work"?), there is considerable evidence indicating that behavioral consultation is effective (Erchul & Sheridan, 2014). Much of this evidence is based on *meta-analysis*, a statistical means of summarizing the impact of an intervention across many research studies that used that specific intervention. In an early meta-analysis, Medway and Updyke (1985) presented the results of 18 studies of behavioral consultation published from 1972 to 1982 that together reported 64 consultee and client outcome measures (i.e., changes in attitudes, behavior, and achievement). They found the average effect size (ES) for behavioral consultation to be .44 for consultee effects and .43 for client effects, meaning that the average consultee and client participating in consultation each fell at the 67th percentile relative to the participants in the control group on the same outcome measure. Adapting meta-analytic procedures to single cases, Busse, Kratochwill, and Elliott (1995) reported an average between-phase ES of .95 for 23 cases of behavioral consultation with teachers. Finally, Sheridan, Welch, and Orme (1996) completed a comprehensive review of school consultation outcome studies published from 1985 to 1995 and concluded that 89% of the behavioral consultation studies reported positive results, 11% were neutral, and none were negative. Results from more recent randomized control trials of behavioral consultation (e.g., Sheridan et al., 2012) further strengthen the conclusion that outcome research on behavioral consultation conducted over the past 45 years has consistently illustrated its effectiveness.

Psychologists and other specialists in schools have the potential to influence and therefore change teacher behavior. However, not all accept this concept or perhaps are unaware of effective strategies for achieving behavior change in teachers (i.e., the second paradox of school psychology; Erchul, Grissom, Getty, & Bennett, 2014). As school systems establish and maintain multitiered systems of supports and response-to-intervention programming (e.g., Jimerson, Burns, & VanDerHeyden, 2016), increased attention is paid to federal mandates to implement evidence-based interventions in schools. This context strengthens the importance of the consultant role and further legitimizes consultants' attempts to influence teachers' adoption and implementation of classroom interventions (Erchul, 2013). Along these lines, we next present French and Raven's (1959) and Raven's (1992) bases of power model as a useful framework to augment the practice of behavioral consultation.

SOCIAL INFLUENCE: BASES OF POWER MODEL

Social influence refers to a demonstrated change in beliefs, attitudes, or behaviors in a target of influence resulting from the action or presence of an influencing agent (French & Raven, 1959). Social power is the potential for such influence to occur and is the basis for one of the best-known frameworks for examining social influence, namely, that of Raven and colleagues (French & Raven, 1959; Raven, 1965, 1992).

French and Raven's (1959) original framework presents five bases of power that an agent can use to change the beliefs, attitudes, or behaviors of a target. The original five power bases, as well as a sixth base (i.e., informational power; Raven, 1965) are listed below, along with an example of how each base looks within the context of school consultation:

1. *Coercive power:* The teacher's perception that the consultant can punish her for noncompliance. The strength of coercive power depends on how aversive the teacher perceives the punishment as well as the teacher's perception that she can avoid the punishment by following the recommendation made by the consultant.
2. *Reward power:* The teacher's view that the consultant is ready and able to reward her if she follows the consultant's recommendations.
3. *Legitimate power:* The teacher's perception that she is obliged to accept the consultant's influence attempt because the consultant has a legitimate right to influence because of the consultant's professional role, status, or position.
4. *Expert power:* The teacher's perception that the consultant has knowledge or expertise relevant to her current situation.
5. *Referent power:* The consultant's potential to influence the teacher based on the teacher's identification with the consultant and the desire for such identification.
6. *Informational power:* The consultant's potential to influence the teacher because of the judged relevance of the information

contained in the consultant's message (e.g., logical explanations or new information that might produce change).

The utility of French and Raven's (1959) model has been demonstrated convincingly within organizational psychology. For example, a major review concluded that managers' and superiors' use of expert and referent power correlate positively with employees' and subordinates' satisfaction with supervision and related outcomes, whereas reward, coercive, and legitimate power generally correlate negatively with these outcomes (Podsakoff & Schriesheim, 1985).

This original framework was later updated and termed the *power/ interaction model of interpersonal influence* (Raven, 1992). It includes 14 power bases, each of which stems from the original six; specifically, reward and coercive power are now differentiated into personal and impersonal forms, and expert and referent power have positive and negative forms. Informational power is now composed of direct and indirect forms, and legitimate power has four forms: (a) formal legitimate, (b) legitimate reciprocity, (c) legitimate equity, and (d) legitimate dependence. Furthermore, these bases of power have been subdivided empirically into two groups (i.e., soft and harsh). *Soft bases* are subtle, indirect, and noncoercive in nature; *harsh bases* are more coercive, overt, restricting of autonomy, use hierarchical forms of power, or some combination of these (Erchul, Raven, & Whichard, 2001).

To date, seven published or in-press studies (see Table 14.3 in Erchul et al., 2014) have used the power/interaction model of interpersonal influence to assess social influence in school consultation. In studies conducted by Erchul, Raven, and Ray (2001) and Erchul, Raven, and Whichard (2001), respondents indicated that soft bases (e.g., direct informational, positive expert, and positive referent power) would be more effective (i.e., influential) than harsh bases when consulting with an initially resistant teacher. Looking at the soft–harsh distinction relative to gender differences, Erchul, Raven, and Wilson (2004) found that female consultants perceived soft bases to be more effective than did male consultants. However, there were no gender differences regarding the effectiveness of individual bases in Raven's (1992) model.

Because of practical as well as ethical reasons, a particular power base judged as effective may not be used often. As a consequence, follow-up research has asked, "Which power bases do consultants indicate they would be *most likely to use* to influence an initially resistant teacher?" Two studies have examined the likelihood of using specific power bases in consultation. Wilson, Erchul, and Raven (2008) surveyed a national sample of school psychologists and found three things: (a) consultants overall were more likely to use soft power bases than harsh bases; (b) female consultants were no more likely to use soft power bases than were male consultants; and (c) when considering all the bases in Raven's (1992) model, consultants indicated they were likely to use positive expert power only slightly less than direct informational power and both more than the other bases in the model. Getty and Erchul (2009) then examined consultants' likelihood of using soft bases (which they defined as positive expert, positive referent, legitimate dependence, direct informational, and legitimate position power). When considering consultation with a female teacher, male consultants were more likely to use positive expert power than the other four soft bases combined, and female consultants were less likely to use positive referent power than the other four soft bases combined.

Finally, in a study that applied Raven's (1992) model to actual, ongoing consultation cases, Owens et al. (2017) found that teachers who reported being influenced by soft bases experienced a greater positive change in their behaviors and their students' behaviors than those who reported not being influenced by such bases. Further refinements in the application of Raven's power/interaction model of interpersonal influence no doubt will produce noticeable gains in teacher evidence–based intervention endorsement and intervention integrity.

When considering incorporating Raven's (1992) model into behavioral consultation, consultants should be more aware of the role that social influence plays in their attempts to change adult behavior. Research has shown that influence strategies drawn from soft bases may be especially effective in this context. Choosing to use soft bases over harsh bases has the potential to increase intervention implementation efforts and improve student outcomes, especially when teachers report being influenced by soft bases.

Next, we consider the topic of performance feedback. Although having no formal ties to Raven's (1992) model, the performance feedback literature illustrates how influence strategies drawn primarily from positive expert and direct informational power may be used to change consultee behavior with regard to plan implementation.

PERFORMANCE FEEDBACK: IMPROVING PLAN IMPLEMENTATION

A goal of behavioral consultation is to improve client outcomes through an indirect service delivery model (Kratochwill & Bergan, 1990). Achieving this goal requires some level of adult behavior change, primarily during the treatment implementation stage. Although Raven's (1992) power/interaction model may be used to change the beliefs, attitudes, and behaviors of the consultee, this is not always enough to result in acceptable levels of implementation. At some point, any consultant will be faced with the challenge of what to do when a consultee is not implementing the agreed-on intervention.

Treatment Integrity

This dilemma is often characterized in the literature as *treatment integrity*, which has been defined as "the extent to which essential intervention components are delivered in a comprehensive and consistent manner" (Sanetti & Kratochwill, 2009, p. 448). Research that has examined treatment integrity within academic and behavioral interventions has consistently documented low and declining levels of implementation in the absence of support (Solomon, Klein, & Polityo, 2012; Noell et al., 2014), with some research suggesting that this decline typically occurs within approximately 2 weeks of implementation (e.g., Noell, Witt, Gilbertson, Ranier, & Freeland, 1997). Thus, from a behavioral and health sciences perspective, prevention of implementation drift should serve as a core component of any intervention or consultation plan, as has been explored in work on direct training (Sterling-Turner, Watson, & Moore, 2002) and implementation planning (Sanetti, Collier-Meek, Long, Byron, & Kratochwill, 2015). However, when responsive interventions are needed to increase treatment integrity during consultation, performance feedback may act as one critical, evidence-based tool to support implementation.

Performance Feedback

Performance feedback may be defined as a process of systematically providing a treatment implementer (consultee) with objective data regarding plan implementation (DiGennaro, Martens, & Kleinmann, 2007; Dufrene, Zoder-Martell, Dieringer, & LaBrot, 2016; Jones, Wickstrom, & Friman, 1997). This feedback typically involves a review of treatment integrity data and student outcome data, reinforcement for intervention steps consistently implemented, discussion and practice of missed intervention steps, and commitment from the implementer to improve implementation (Fallon, Collier-Meek, Maggin, Sanetti, & Johnson, 2015). Many applications of performance feedback also include graphic feedback (e.g., Myers, Simonsen, & Sugai, 2011) as a main component of the intervention alongside verbal feedback, with additional applications using strategies such as written feedback (Thier, 2003), video self-modeling (Hawkins & Heflin, 2011), and motivational interviewing techniques (Gueldner & Merrell, 2011). In addition, although many studies focus on face-to-face meetings as the main vehicle for the delivery of performance feedback, some researchers have begun leveraging the internet for their consultative work through modes such as video teleconferencing (Machalicek et al., 2010) and email (Hemmeter, Snyder, Kinder, & Artman, 2011).

Key Research

Early Work

In 1997, two of the first studies to explicitly examine the application of performance feedback to educational interventions were published (Noell et al., 1997; Witt, Noell, LaFleur, & Mortenson, 1997). In the first, four general-education elementary school teachers were trained to implement a reinforcement-focused intervention to improve academic performance (Witt et al., 1997). After intensive training took place and intervention implementation began, data on implementation were graphically and verbally presented to teachers, with specific recommendations provided on how to improve implementation. The results suggested that implementation was initially very high for all teachers, with posttraining implementation (in the form of percentage of intervention steps completed) following a decreasing trend for all teachers. Data gathered during the provision of performance feedback demonstrated immediate effects for two teachers, with positive trends observed for all. Noell and colleagues (1997) extended this initial study with less intensive training in order to more closely approximate consultation in school settings and obtained similar results: Initially high levels of implementation decreased over time, with immediate and positive results observed upon the application of performance feedback. Since the publication of these two articles, more than 50 studies have examined the application of performance feedback in educational contexts for academically and behaviorally based interventions (Collier-Meek, Fallon, Gould, Morizio, & Kleinert, 2018), including studies that have used a group design (e.g., Noell, Witt, Slider, & Connell, 2005).

Systematic Reviews and Syntheses

Given the depth and breadth of the performance feedback literature to this point, it is unsurprising that systematic reviews, syntheses, and meta-analyses have been conducted to provide a holistic understanding of the performance feedback literature. Findings across these broad examinations have supported the use of performance feedback as an effective method for promoting high levels of treatment integrity. Solomon et al. (2012) conducted a meta-analysis that incorporated 36 studies with 127 participants and examined both teacher implementation and student behavioral outcomes. Declining patterns of implementation were generally observed before the application of performance feedback, and moderate effects were found for both teacher and student outcomes. In their meta-analysis of interventions used to support fidelity of implementation, Noell and colleagues (2014) included 29 studies and 113 teachers. These authors similarly found low initial levels and a decreasing trend in treatment integrity levels prior to initiation of performance feedback. The results of their meta-analysis suggested that performance feedback, self-monitoring, and interventions that combined performance feedback with other strategies all resulted in significant gains in treatment integrity, with "performance feedback only" demonstrating the largest overall effect size of the studies intervention types. Most recently, Fallon and colleagues (2015) applied What Works Clearinghouse standards for single-case design studies (Kratochwill et al., 2010) to the performance feedback literature, with results suggesting that performance feedback interventions result in large, positive effects on implementation and that this body of work meets criteria for designation as an evidence-based practice.

Application to Behavioral Interventions in Schools

Evidence generally supports the use of performance feedback to improve treatment fidelity among educators in school settings, with applications of this strategy appearing in the literature for both academic and behavioral intervention. Indeed, the meta-analysis conducted by Noell and colleagues (2014) included more than twice as many data points for behavioral concerns as were included for academic concerns. Specific behavioral strategies that have been examined alongside performance feedback include differential reinforcement (Auld, Belfiore, & Scheeler, 2010; DiGennaro et al., 2007), the provision of praise (Duchaine, Jolivette, & Fredrick, 2011; Hemmeter et al., 2011) or praise and tokens (Jones et al., 1997), as well as more complex class-wide behavior plans (Codding, Livanis, Pace, & Vaca, 2008). The breadth of performance feedback literature supports its use within a behavior consultation model to positively change adult behavior during plan implementation. Performance feedback also has been applied to procedural components of consultation, such as collecting data on student behavior (Pellecchia et al., 2011), conducting functional analyses (Machalicek et al., 2010), and clinical directors providing supervision to educators (Luiselli, 2008).

CONCLUSION

We end this chapter by reinforcing the idea that all interventions described in this volume will be enhanced to the extent that adults understand how to be effective change agents with regard to child, youth, and adult behavior. With regard to changing adult behavior, a concerted focus on behavioral consultation, social influence, and performance feedback may prove especially beneficial when implementing evidence-based positive strategies in the schools.

REFERENCES

Auld, R. G., Belfiore, P. J., & Scheeler, M. C. (2010). Increasing pre-service teachers' use of differential reinforcement: Effects of performance feedback on consequences for student behavior. *Journal of Behavioral Education, 19,* 169–183. http://dx.doi.org/10.1007/s10864-010-9107-4

Bergan, J. R. (1977). *Behavioral consultation.* Columbus, OH: Merrill.

Bergan, J. R. (1995). Evolution of a problem-solving model of consultation. *Journal of Educational & Psychological Consultation, 6,* 111–123. http://dx.doi.org/10.1207/s1532768xjepc0602_2

Bergan, J. R., & Kratochwill, T. R. (1990). *Behavioral consultation and therapy.* New York, NY: Plenum Press.

Brown, D., Pryzwansky, W. B., & Schulte, A. C. (2011). *Psychological consultation and collaboration: Introduction to theory and practice* (7th ed.). Boston, MA: Pearson.

Busse, R. T., Kratochwill, T. R., & Elliott, S. N. (1995). Meta-analysis for single-case consultation outcomes: Applications to research and practice. *Journal of School Psychology, 33,* 269–285. http://dx.doi.org/10.1016/0022-4405(95)00014-D

Codding, R. S., Livanis, A., Pace, G. M., & Vaca, L. (2008). Using performance feedback to improve treatment integrity of classwide behavior plans: An investigation of observer reactivity. *Journal of Applied Behavior Analysis, 41,* 417–422. http://dx.doi.org/10.1901/jaba.2008.41-417

Collier-Meek, M. A., Fallon, L. M., Gould, K., Morizio, L., & Kleinert, W. (2018). How are treatment integrity data assessed? Reviewing the performance feedback literature. *School Psychology Quarterly.* Advance online publication. http://dx.doi.org/10.1037/spq0000239

DiGennaro, F. D., Martens, B. K., & Kleinmann, A. E. (2007). A comparison of performance feedback procedures on teachers' treatment implementation integrity and students' inappropriate behavior in special education classrooms. *Journal of Applied Behavior Analysis, 40,* 447–461. http://dx.doi.org/10.1901/jaba.2007.40-447

Duchaine, E. L., Jolivette, K., & Fredrick, L. D. (2011). The effect of teacher coaching with performance feedback on behavior-specific praise in inclusion classrooms. *Education & Treatment of Children, 34,* 209–227. http://dx.doi.org/10.1353/etc.2011.0009

Dufrene, B., Zoder-Martell, K., Dieringer, S. T., & LaBrot, Z. C. (2016). Behavior analytic consultation for academic referral concerns. *Psychology in the Schools, 53*, 8–23. http://dx.doi.org/10.1002/pits.21885

D'Zurilla, T. J., & Goldfried, M. R. (1971). Problem solving and behavior modification. *Journal of Abnormal Psychology, 78*, 107–126. http://dx.doi.org/10.1037/h0031360

Erchul, W. P. (2013). Treatment integrity enhancement via performance feedback conceptualized as an exercise in social influence. *Journal of Educational and Psychological Consultation, 23*, 300–306. http://dx.doi.org/10.1080/10474412.2013.845497

Erchul, W. P., Grissom, P. F., Getty, K. C., & Bennett, M. S. (2014). Researching interpersonal influence within school consultation: Social power base and relational communication perspectives. In W. P. Erchul & S. M. Sheridan (Eds.), *Handbook of research in school consultation* (2nd ed., pp. 349–385). New York, NY: Routledge.

Erchul, W. P., & Martens, B. K. (2010). *School consultation: Conceptual and empirical bases of practice* (3rd ed.). New York, NY: Springer. http://dx.doi.org/10.1007/978-1-4419-5747-4

Erchul, W. P., Raven, B. H., & Ray, A. G. (2001). School psychologists' perceptions of social power bases in teacher consultation. *Journal of Educational and Psychological Consultation, 12*, 1–23. http://dx.doi.org/10.1207/S1532768XJEPC1201_01

Erchul, W. P., Raven, B. H., & Whichard, S. M. (2001). School psychologist and teacher perceptions of social power in consultation. *Journal of School Psychology, 39*, 483–497. http://dx.doi.org/10.1016/S0022-4405(01)00085-1

Erchul, W. P., Raven, B. H., & Wilson, K. E. (2004). The relationship between gender of consultant and social power in consultation. *School Psychology Review, 33*, 582–590.

Erchul, W. P., & Schulte, A. C. (2009). Behavioral consultation. In A. Akin-Little, S. G. Little, M. Bray, & T. Kehle (Eds.), *Behavioral interventions in schools: Evidence-based positive strategies* (pp. 13–25). Washington, DC: American Psychological Association. http://dx.doi.org/10.1037/11886-001

Erchul, W. P., & Sheridan, S. M. (2014). Overview: The state of scientific research in school consultation. In W. P. Erchul & S. M. Sheridan (Eds.), *Handbook of research in school consultation* (2nd ed., pp. 3–17). New York, NY: Routledge.

Fallon, L. M., Collier-Meek, M. A., Maggin, D. M., Sanetti, L. M., & Johnson, A. H. (2015). Is performance feedback for educators an evidence-based practice? A systematic review and evaluation based on single-case research. *Exceptional Children, 81*, 227–246. http://dx.doi.org/10.1177/0014402914551738

French, J. R. P., & Raven, B. H. (1959). The bases of social power. In D. Cartwright (Ed.), *Studies in social power* (pp. 150–167). Ann Arbor, MI: Institute for Social Research.

Getty, K. C., & Erchul, W. P. (2009). The influence of gender on the likelihood of using soft social power strategies in school consultation. *Psychology in the Schools, 46*, 447–458. http://dx.doi.org/10.1002/pits.20389

Gueldner, B., & Merrell, K. (2011). Evaluation of a social-emotional learning program in conjunction with the exploratory application of performance feedback incorporating motivational interviewing techniques. *Journal of Educational and Psychological Consultation, 21,* 1–27. http://dx.doi.org/10.1080/10474412.2010.522876

Hawkins, S. M., & Heflin, L. J. (2011). Increasing secondary teachers' behavior-specific praise using a video self-modeling and visual performance feedback intervention. *Journal of Positive Behavior Interventions, 13,* 97–108. http://dx.doi.org/10.1177/1098300709358110

Haynes, S. N. (1978). *Principles of behavioral assessment.* New York, NY: Gardner Press.

Hemmeter, M. L., Snyder, P., Kinder, K., & Artman, K. (2011). Impact of performance feedback delivered via electronic mail on preschool teachers' use of descriptive praise. *Early Childhood Research Quarterly, 26,* 96–109. http://dx.doi.org/10.1016 j.ecresq.2010.05.004

Jimerson, S. R., Burns, M. K., & VanDerHeyden, A. M. (Eds.). (2016). *Handbook of response to intervention: The science and practice of multi-tiered systems of support* (2nd ed.). New York, NY: Springer.

Jones, K. M., Wickstrom, K. F., & Friman, P. C. (1997). The effects of observational feedback on treatment integrity in school-based behavioral consultation. *School Psychology Quarterly, 12,* 316–326. http://dx.doi.org/10.1037/h0088965

Kratochwill, T. R. (2008). Best practices in problem-solving consultation: Applications in prevention and intervention systems. In A. Thomas & J. Grimes (Eds.), *Best practices in school psychology* (Vol. 5, pp. 1673–1688). Bethesda, MD: National Association of School Psychologists.

Kratochwill, T. R., & Bergan, J. R. (1990). *Behavioral consultation in applied settings: An individual guide.* New York, NY: Springer.

Kratochwill, T. R., Hitchcock, J., Horner, R. H., Levin, J. R., Odom, S. L., Rindskopf, D. M., & Shadish, W. R. (2010). *Single-case designs technical documentation, Version 1 (pilot).* Retrieved from https://ies.ed.gov/ncee/wwc/Docs/ReferenceResources/wwc_scd.pdf

Luiselli, J. K. (2008). Effects of a performance management intervention on frequency of behavioral supervision at a specialized school for students with developmental disabilities. *Journal of Developmental and Physical Disabilities, 20,* 53–61. http://dx.doi.org/10.1007/s10882-007-9079-z

Machalicek, W., O'Reilly, M. F., Rispoli, M., Davis, T., Lang, R., Franco, J. H., & Chan, J. M. (2010). Training teachers to assess the challenging behaviors of students with autism using video tele-conferencing. *Education and Training in Autism and Developmental Disabilities, 45,* 203–215.

Martens, B. K., DiGennaro Reed, F. D., & Magnuson, J. D. (2014). Behavioral consultation: Contemporary research and emerging challenges. In W. P. Erchul & S. M. Sheridan (Eds.), *Handbook of research in school consultation* (2nd ed., pp. 180–209). New York, NY: Routledge.

Medway, F. J., & Updyke, J. F. (1985). Meta-analysis of consultation outcome studies. *American Journal of Community Psychology, 13*, 489–505.

Myers, D. M., Simonsen, B., & Sugai, G. (2011). Increasing teachers' use of praise with a response-to-intervention approach. *Education and Treatment of Children, 34*, 35–59. http://dx.doi.org/10.1353/etc.2011.0004

Noell, G. H., & Gansle, K. A. (2014). Research examining the relationships between consultation procedures, treatment integrity, and outcomes. In W. P. Erchul & S. M. Sheridan (Eds.), *Handbook of research in school consultation* (2nd ed., pp. 386–408). New York, NY: Routledge.

Noell, G. H., Gansle, K. A., Mevers, J. L., Knox, R. M., Mintz, J. C., & Dahir, A. (2014). Improving treatment plan implementation in schools: A meta-analysis of single subject design studies. *Journal of Behavioral Education, 23*, 168–191. http://dx.doi.org/10.1007/s10864-013-9177-1

Noell, G. H., Witt, J. C., Gilbertson, D. N., Ranier, D. D., & Freeland, J. T. (1997). Increasing teacher intervention implementation in general education settings through consultation and performance feedback. *School Psychology Quarterly, 12*, 77–88. http://dx.doi.org/10.1037/h0088949

Noell, G. H., Witt, J. C., Slider, N. J., & Connell, J. E. (2005). Treatment implementation following behavioral consultation in schools: A comparison of three follow-up strategies. *School Psychology Review, 34*, 87–106.

Owens, J. S., Schwartz, M. E., Erchul, W. P., Himawan, L. K., Evans, S. W., Coles, E. K., & Schulte, A. C. (2017). Teacher perceptions of school consultant social influence strategies: Replication and expansion. *Journal of Educational and Psychological Consultation, 27*, 411–436. http://dx.doi.org/10.1080/10474412.2016.1275649

Pellecchia, M., Connell, J. E., Eisenhart, D., Kane, M., Schoener, C., Turkel, K., . . . Mandell, D. S. (2011). We're all in this together now: Group performance feedback to increase classroom team data collection. *Journal of School Psychology, 49*, 411–431. http://dx.doi.org/10.1016/j.jsp.2011.04.003

Podsakoff, P. M., & Schriescheim, C. A. (1985). Field studies of French and Raven's bases of power: Critique, reanalysis, and suggestions for future research. *Psychological Bulletin, 97*, 387–411. http://dx.doi.org/10.1037/0033-2909.97.3.387

Raven, B. H. (1965). Social influence and power. In I. D. Steiner & M. Fishbein (Eds.), *Current studies in social psychology* (pp. 371–381). New York, NY: Holt, Rinehart & Winston.

Raven, B. H. (1992). A power/interaction model of interpersonal influence: French and Raven thirty years later. *Journal of Social Behavior and Personality, 7*, 217–244.

Sanetti, L. M. H., Collier-Meek, M. A., Long, A. C. J., Byron, J., & Kratochwill, T. R. (2015). Increasing teacher treatment integrity of behavior support plans through consultation and implementation planning. *Journal of School Psychology, 53*, 209–229. http://dx.doi.org/10.1016/j.jsp.2015.03.002

Sanetti, L. M. H., & Kratochwill, T. R. (2009). Toward developing a science of treatment integrity: Introduction to the special series. *School Psychology Review, 38,* 445–459.

Sheridan, S. M., Bovaird, J. A., Glover, T. A., Garbacz, S. A., Witte, A., & Kwon, K. (2012). A randomized trial examining the effects of conjoint behavioral consultation and the mediating role of the parent–teacher relationship. *School Psychology Review, 41,* 23–46.

Sheridan, S. M., & Kratochwill, T. R. (2008). *Conjoint behavioral consultation: Promoting family-school connections and interventions.* New York, NY: Springer.

Sheridan, S. M., Welch, M., & Orme, S. F. (1996). Is consultation effective? A review of outcome research. *Remedial and Special Education, 17,* 341–354. http://dx.doi.org/10.1177/074193259601700605

Solomon, B. G., Klein, S. A., & Politylo, B. C. (2012). The effect of performance feedback on teachers' treatment integrity: A meta-analysis of the single-case literature. *School Psychology Review, 41,* 160–175.

Sterling-Turner, H. E., Watson, T. S., & Moore, J. W. (2002). The effects of direct training and treatment integrity on treatment outcomes in school consultation. *School Psychology Quarterly, 17,* 47–77. http://dx.doi.org/10.1521/scpq.17.1.47.19906

Tharp, R. G., & Wetzel, R. J. (1969). *Behavior modification in the natural environment.* New York, NY: Academic Press.

Thier, K. S. (2003). *Effects of preferred components of performance feedback interventions on treatment integrity scores of teacher implemented function-based student behavior support plans* (Doctoral dissertation). Available from ProQuest Dissertations and Theses database. (UMI No. 3102192)

Wilkinson, L. A. (2006). Monitoring treatment integrity: An alternative to the "consult and hope" strategy in school-based behavioural consultation. *School Psychology International, 27,* 426–438. http://dx.doi.org/10.1177/0143034306070428

Wilson, K. E., Erchul, W. P., & Raven, B. H. (2008). The likelihood of use of social power strategies by school psychologists when consulting with teachers. *Journal of Educational and Psychological Consultation, 18,* 101–123. http://dx.doi.org/10.1080/10474410701864321

Witt, J. C., Noell, G. H., LaFleur, L. H., & Mortenson, B. P. (1997). Teacher use of interventions in general education settings: Measurement and analysis of the independent variable. *Journal of Applied Behavior Analysis, 30,* 693–696. http://dx.doi.org/10.1901/jaba.1997.30-693

II
WORKING WITH CHILDREN WITH AUTISM SPECTRUM DISORDER

10

AUTISM SPECTRUM DISORDER: SCREENING AND DIAGNOSIS

STEVEN G. LITTLE, ANGELEQUE AKIN-LITTLE,
AND GERI M. HARRIS

As the prevalence of autism spectrum disorder (ASD) has increased markedly over the past 2 decades, rising from two per 10,000 in 1990 to one in 68 children and one in 42 boys by age 8 today (Blumberg et al., 2013; Centers for Disease Control and Prevention [CDC], 2014), screening, evaluating, and diagnosing children with ASD as early as possible is important for ensuring that these children have access to the services and supports they need (CDC, 2014; Eikeseth, Smith, Jahr, & Eldevik, 2007). Diagnosis occurs when a psychologist or other professional conducts a comprehensive evaluation to determine if a child has ASD based on the criteria in the *Diagnostic and Statistical Manual of Mental Disorders* (fifth ed. *[DSM–5]*; American Psychiatric Association, 2013) or the 1997 amendments to the Individuals With Disabilities Education Act (https://sites.ed.gov/idea/regs/b/a/300.8/c/1). According to the *DSM–5*, ASD diagnosis requires (a) persistent deficits in social communication and social interaction across multiple contexts and (b) restricted, repetitive patterns of behavior, interests, or activities. Therefore, the focus of assessment is on identifying language delays; social skills deficits; and restricted, repetitive, and stereotyped patterns of behavior. In addition, as there is a great deal of heterogeneity of features in individual children with ASD (Johnson, Myers, & the Council on Children With Disabilities, 2007), observation and functional assessment of behavior is essential to link assessment and subsequent intervention. Diagnosis of ASD is possible in children as young as 14 months of age (Johnston et al., 2009); however, because of factors such as autistic regression and difficulty in identifying symptoms of ASD in very young children, most children with ASD are not diagnosed until after age 3. This is especially true for individuals with average or above average language and cognitive abilities (Mandell, Novak, & Zubritsky, 2005: Mandell et al., 2010; Manning et al., 2011; Pinto-Martin & Levy, 2004). Therefore, this chapter focuses on children from 3 to 18 years of age.

DIAGNOSING AUTISM

Within the latest edition of the *DSM* (*DSM–5*; American Psychiatric Association, 2013), several previously separate disorders (autistic disorder, Asperger's disorder, pervasive developmental disorder not otherwise specified [PDD-NOS], Retts syndrome, and childhood disintegrative disorder) have been placed under one umbrella. To be classified ASD in the *DSM–5*, a child must present with symptoms in early childhood, which cause impaired ability for the child to function in daily life activities. These symptoms may not fully manifest until social demands exceed capacity, for instance in middle school, later adolescent, and young adulthood (Casey et al., 2013). ASD is characterized by two core domains dealing with significant difficulties in practical verbal and nonverbal social communication and repetitive patterns of behavior, interests, and activities. The child must present in all three deficit categories in the social communication domain (American Psychiatric Association, 2013, p. 50): (a) deficits in social-emotion reciprocity, ranging, for example, from abnormal social approach and failure of normal back-and-forth conversation; to reduced sharing of interests, emotions, or affect; to failure to initiate or respond to social interactions; (b) deficits in nonverbal communicative behaviors used for social interaction, ranging, for example, from poorly integrated verbal and nonverbal communication; to abnormalities in eye contact and body language or deficits in understanding and use of gestures; to a total lack of facial expressions and nonverbal communication; and (c) deficits in developing, maintaining, and understanding relationships, ranging, for example, from difficulties adjusting behavior to suit various social contexts; to difficulties in sharing imaginative play or in making friends; to absence of interest in peers.

In addition, a minimum of two of the four criteria in the restricted and repetitive patterns of behaviors domain are required for an ASD diagnosis (American Psychiatric Association, 2013, p. 50): (a) stereotyped or repetitive motor movements, use of objects, or speech (e.g., stereotypies, lining up toys or flipping objects, echolalia, idiosyncratic phrases); (b) insistence on sameness, inflexible adherence to routines, or ritualized patterns of verbal or nonverbal behavior (e.g., extreme distress at small changes, difficulties with transitions, rigid thinking patterns, greeting rituals, need to take same route or eat same food every day); (c) highly restricted, fixated interests that are abnormal in intensity or focus (e.g., strong attachment to or preoccupation with unusual objects, excessively circumscribed or perseverative interests); and (d) hyper- or hypo-reactivity to sensory input or unusual interest in sensory aspects of environment (e.g., apparent indifference to pain, temperature, adverse response to specific sounds or textures, excessive smelling or touching of objects, visual fascination with lights or movement).

Symptoms must also be present in early development, cause clinically significant impairment in current functioning, and are not better explained by intellectual disability or global developmental delay. The *DSM–5* identifies three severity levels, based on support needed within two domains: (a) social communication and (b) restricted repetitive patterns of behavior. Symptom severity is classified as Level 1 (requiring very substantial support), Level 2 (requiring substantial support), or Level 3 (requiring support).

The behaviors associated with ASD vary in range. Some individuals may have verbal capabilities and still be unable to use language in a socially meaningful manner, whereas others may have no verbal ability whatsoever. Some may engage in self-stimulatory behaviors such as rocking or twirling their bodies, flapping their hands, whereas others diagnosed with an ASD may not. Individuals diagnosed with an ASD typically do not engage in pretend play, although some may engage in various pretend play activities but usually at a level less than that of same-aged typically developing peers (Strock, 2004). In addition, Andersen, Skogli, Hovik, Egeland, and Øie (2015) noted that ASD is associated with an impairment in executive functioning that involves planning ahead and organizational abilities. This executive functioning deficit may contribute to the lack of flexibility and inability to shift behavior easily that is often associated with the disorder.

AUTISM ASSESSMENT: SCREENING AND COMPREHENSIVE EVALUATION

As previously mentioned, early identification of autism is crucial as it enables early intervention. Early identification and intervention of autism in children as young as age 2 has been found not only to be reliable, valid, and stable, but also to promote positive long-term outcomes (Coonrod & Stone, 2005). Nevertheless, many children do not receive a definitive diagnosis until much later, which means they miss out on the long-term benefits of early intervention (Coonrod & Stone, 2005).

Although autism cannot be detected with any one medical test, Volker and Lopata (2008) discussed various medical evaluations that are components of the overall ASD assessment process. There are tests used to rule out speech and hearing problems, which may account for the symptoms of language problems common in ASD. Neurological tests are used to assess for seizure activity or other brain abnormalities that may occur either in the presence of ASD or as an exclusion. Genetic testing identifies chromosomal abnormalities, and other tests assess for allergies and additional medical conditions that may be comorbid with an ASD. However, none of these medical procedures can ascertain whether an individual has an ASD. Rather, assessment relies on behavioral observations and comparison to criteria set forth by diagnostic systems such as the *DSM–5* (American Psychiatric Association, 2013).

ASD assessment consists of two stages; the first is screening and the second is a comprehensive diagnostic evaluation (Strock, 2004). Screening is a brief assessment that is conducted to identify children with developmental difficulties who exhibit symptoms typical of ASD and are therefore in need of a more comprehensive evaluation. Screening, which requires less time and expertise than a full evaluation, often begins with the pediatrician or family physician during the child's routine visits; however, schools, child-find agencies, and early intervention programs also screen for ASD (Coonrod & Stone, 2005). Screening involves behavioral observations and may also include screening instruments such as checklists and parent and/or teacher questionnaires. Screening tools help provide information regarding developmental delays in cognitive development, language, and motor movements/skills; however, they should not be used in isolation to make a diagnosis. On the contrary, screening paves the way for referrals, which may then lead to a formal diagnosis from which intervention can be planned and financed.

Coonrod and Stone (2005) described several commonly used instruments that are used for varying purposes in the screening process. Level 1 screening measures are offered to all children, typically at pediatrician offices. Some of these are specifically designed to identify ASD; however, most are used to identify nonspecific developmental problems, such as cognitive, motor, or language problems. Level 2 consists of autism-specific measures that are designed to differentiate children who are more likely to have ASD than other developmental problems.

Although several individuals may be involved in the screening process, a formal diagnosis can only be rendered by a medical doctor, psychologist, or multidisciplinary team that includes one or both of the aforementioned professionals. School counselors, teachers, speech therapists, occupational therapists, parents, and others who are not psychologists or physicians cannot diagnose autism even though they may indeed recognize the presence of autistic symptoms (Waltz, 2002) and may play an important role in the assessment process. A formal diagnosis is typically rendered by way of a comprehensive diagnostic evaluation (Strock, 2004).

A comprehensive diagnostic evaluation is the second step in the process toward diagnosis. This thorough evaluation includes the use of parent/caregiver questionnaires; however, it also involves clinical observations, including a functional behavior assessment (FBA) and parent/caregiver interviews. The CDC (2015) has advised that no single source of information should serve alone for diagnostic purposes, and one or more diagnostic scales may be used. The CDC identified the following as examples of screening tools for children ages 3 and older: Ages and Stages Questionnaire (ASQ), Communication and Symbolic Behavior Scales (CSBS), and Parents' Evaluation of Developmental Status (PEDS). The CDC identified the following as examples of ASD diagnostic tools: Autism Diagnostic Interview—Revised (ADI–R), Autism Diagnostic Observation Schedule (ADOS), Childhood Autism Rating Scale (CARS), and the Gilliam Autism Rating Scale, Second Edition (GARS–2).

Autistic Regression

Most children who receive an ASD diagnosis demonstrate a gradually unfolding pattern of symptoms during their first 2 years of life (Stefanatos, 2008; Zwaigenbaum et al., 2005). Not all children with ASD demonstrate this pattern of symptoms, however. Various sources report from 15% to 56% of children with ASD display a pattern characterized by regression in one or more domains of behavior (Lord, Shulman, & DiLavore, 2004; S. J. Rogers, 2004) or the worsening of previously reported ASD features (Ekinci, Arman, Melek, Bez, & Berkem, 2012). Stefanatos (2008) identified three types of autistic regression. The most common type involves symptoms of ASD emerging during the first year of life, but the saliency of these delays or increases in deviations in behavior do not trigger parental concern until later in the developmental period (Dawson et al., 2007). In the second type, children demonstrate normal or near-normal early development but then exhibit an unexpected arrest or expansion in development, usually in their second year of life (Landa & Garrett-Mayer, 2006; Landa, Holman, & Garrett-Mayer, 2007). The third type is illustrated by developmental regression or reversal of behavioral functioning in one or more domains (Lord et al., 2004). In this type, there is not only a cessation of skill acquisition, but also a loss of previously acquired skills. This usually occurs between 15 and 30 months of age (Hoshino et al., 1987). Ekinci et al. (2012) reported that 56% of children with ASD in their clinically referred sample demonstrated some indicators of autistic regression, whereas Davidovitch, Glick, Holtzman, Tirosh, and Safir (2000) reported a rate of 47.5% in a similar sample. Overall, most studies reported rates between 20% and 49% (Bernabei, Cerquiglini, Cortesi, & D'Ardia, 2007), illustrating the importance of ASD assessment in children ages 3 and older.

Other Assessment

Although ASD-specific measures are an essential element in the assessment and diagnosis of an ASD, they are by no means comprehensive if used as the sole measure. It is important that assessment lead not just to diagnosis, but also to efficacious intervention, and a variety of other measures may be needed on a case-by-case basis.

Functional Behavior Assessment

An FBA is essential to the link between assessment and intervention. It attempts to identify the relationship between events in a person's environment and the occurrence of challenging behaviors to develop an effective intervention (Cooper, Heron, & Heward, 2007). The main outcomes of an FBA are a clear definition or description of the behavior(s); predictions as to the times and situations in which the behavior might or might not occur; and identification of what function the behavior(s) may serve (E. L. Rogers, 2001). The logic behind an FBA is that behavior occurs within a particular context and serves a specific purpose (i.e., positive reinforcement, negative reinforcement, self-stimulation). Individuals engage in behaviors that maximize the likelihood that a desired outcome will result. Identifying the function of specific behaviors provides information that is essential to developing instructional strategies and supports to reduce or eliminate maladaptive behaviors and increasing the frequency of adaptive behaviors.

Functional assessment has been classified into three categories: indirect, descriptive, and experimental. Indirect FBA involves conducting an interview with parents/caregivers and/or the client to hypothesize the function of a behavior. The Questions About Behavioral Function (QABF; Matson & Vollmer, 1995) is an indirect assessment tool with a significant amount of research supporting its use (Tarbox et al., 2009). Descriptive FBAs involve direct observation and measurement of the target behavior and environmental variables that are presumed to be functionally relevant (Cooper et al., 2007). The most common descriptive measure is an ABC (antecedent-behavior-consequence) observation. After data collection, antecedents and consequences are analyzed and summarized to hypothesize the potential function of the behavior. Experimental functional assessments, also referred to as "functional analyses," involve direct manipulation of antecedents and consequences to the target behavior to experimentally demonstrate a functional relationship between behavior and the environment. Tarbox and colleagues (2009) compared indirect, descriptive, and experimental functional assessments using seven children with autism. Results suggested that descriptive assessment did not produce conclusive results, whereas the indirect and experimental assessments generally did.

Cognitive Functioning

A significant subset of children with ASD also have an intellectual disability (ID; Saunders et al., 2015). In addition, ASD and ID can present similarly, as children with either disorder may demonstrate difficulty with communication, social skills, and behavior (Johnson & Walker, 2006). Therefore, it is frequently important to get a measure of cognitive ability as part of a comprehensive ASD assessment. The Wechsler Intelligence Scale for Children—Fifth Edition (WISC–V) and other Wechsler tests (e.g., Wechsler Preschool and Primary Scales of Intelligence—Fourth Edition [WPPSI–IV]) have been used in the ASD assessment process for many years, particularly for higher functioning individuals (Campbell, Ruble, & Hammond, 2014). Other commonly used cognitive assessment measures include the Woodcock–Johnson III Tests of Cognitive Ability (WJ–III) and the Stanford–Binet Intelligence Scales—Fifth Edition (SB–5). Because of communication deficits fundamental to an ASD diagnosis, language-related subtests on these scales may be depressed. Therefore, caution should be used in interpreting any global measure of cognitive ability generated by these instruments. Cognitive measures that are less reliant on language, such as the Leiter International Performance Scale—Revised (Leiter–R) or the Universal Nonverbal Intelligence Test (UNIT–2) should be considered when individuals with ASD present with significant language deficits (Campbell et al., 2014).

Adaptive Behavior

In addition to deficits in intellectual functioning, an ID diagnosis also requires deficits in adaptive functioning (American Psychiatric Association,

2013). The DSM–5 defines *adaptive functioning* as "how well a person meets community standards of personal independence and social responsibility" and "involves adaptive reasoning in three domains: conceptual, social, and practical" (p. 37). Measures such as the Vineland Adaptive Behavior Scales—Second Edition (Vineland–II), or the Adaptive Behavior Assessment System—Second Edition (ABAS–2), should also be considered. Tomanik, Pearson, Loveland, Lane, and Bryant Shaw (2007) found that, even in the absence of ID and a cognitive measure, including a measure of adaptive behavior (e.g., Vineland) improved diagnostic accuracy from 75% to 84% from using the ADI–R and ADOS alone. A measure of adaptive behavior may also prove useful in program planning.

Communication

Evaluation of communication skills is a fundamental component of any ASD assessment. The scales discussed previously under both screening and diagnostic assessment all contain a language/communication component as do measures of adaptive behavior (e.g., Vineland). As the goal of any assessment should be to not only diagnose but also direct subsequent interventions, a more detailed language assessment is recommended. In most cases this will be conducted by a speech–language pathologist (SLP) and include an assessment of receptive, expressive, and pragmatic language skills. An example of a standardized test that may be administered by an SLP is the Clinical Evaluation of Language Fundamentals—Fifth Edition (CELF–5; Wiig, Semel, & Secord, 2013). This instrument provides a comprehensive evaluation of language, is helpful in determining eligibility for language services in schools, and provides information that is useful in developing language-based interventions.

Social Skills

Another common area in which additional assessment may be needed for diagnostic and intervention planning purposes is social skills. As with communication deficits, social skills deficits are a core feature of autism and assessed on the screening and diagnostic measures discussed earlier. A more detailed assessment of social skills may be warranted to get a more in-depth understanding of the social functioning of the individual and as an aid to intervention development. Two common measures of social skills are the Social Skills Rating Scale (SSRS), now part of the Social Skills Improvement System (SSIS), and the Preschool and Kindergarten Behavior Scale (PKBS). Wang, Sandall, Davis, and Thomas (2011) examined the usefulness of these scales with children with ASD. Results indicated that both measures were predictive of observations of behavior in the natural setting. However, their usefulness in detecting social skills progress over time or intervention outcomes was not satisfactory.

CONCLUSION

The assessment of ASD serves multiple purposes in preschool, early childhood, and adolescence (ages 3–18). First and foremost is diagnosis. Although it is ideal for ASD to be diagnosed as early as possible, diagnosis prior to the age of 3 years is not always possible. Factors such as autistic regression, cognitive development, and social–emotional development may limit the manifestation of ASD symptomatology until the child is into the preschool and elementary school years. This is particularly evident with those children higher on the spectrum (ASD—Level 3). In addition to diagnosis, ASD assessment plays an important role in selecting intervention methodology and monitoring intervention effectiveness. The focus of diagnostic assessment is on identifying language delays; social skills deficits; and restricted, repetitive, and stereotyped patterns of behavior as these are the areas of functioning specified in the *DSM–5*.

Assessment relies on behavioral observations by psychologists or reports on behavior by parents, teachers, or other caregivers. ASD diagnosis involves a comparison of these behaviors to criteria set forth by diagnostic systems such as the *DSM–5* (American Psychiatric Association, 2013) and consists of two stages: screening and comprehensive evaluation (Strock, 2004). Screening is a brief assessment that is conducted to identify children with developmental difficulties who exhibit symptoms typical of ASD and are therefore in need of a more comprehensive evaluation. Screening frequently involves behavioral observations and the use of screening instruments such as checklists and parent and/or teacher questionnaires. In addition to screening for diagnosis, each of these screening instruments can also be used to track an individual's response to intervention, although these measures may not be sensitive enough to evaluate small increments of progress. Identifying and operationally defining specific target behaviors and conducting systematic behavioral observations would generally be considered a more sensitive response to intervention monitoring procedures.

Although ASD-specific measures are an important element of ASD assessment, they should not be considered sufficient as the sole measure of ASD diagnosis. It is also important that assessment lead not just to diagnosis but also to efficacious intervention. Therefore, other instruments and procedures, as well as input from other professionals, are an important component of ASD assessment and diagnosis. It is also recommended that ASD diagnosis and program planning not be made by a sole professional but by a multidisciplinary team that may include professionals such as a pediatrician, a psychologist, a speech pathologist, and an occupational therapist on the basis of the specific needs of the individual being assessed (Robertson, Stafford, Benedicto, & Hocking, 2013). Information gathered from an FBA and assessment of cognitive, communicative, adaptive, and social/emotional functioning can all add to both diagnosis and program planning.

REFERENCES

American Psychiatric Association. (2013). *Diagnostic and statistical manual of mental disorders* (5th ed.). Washington, DC: Author.

Andersen, P. N., Skogli, E. W., Hovik, K. T., Egeland, J., & Øie, M. (2015). Associations among symptoms of autism, symptoms of depression and executive functions in children with high-functioning autism: A 2 year follow-up study. *Journal of Autism and Developmental Disorders, 45*, 2497–2507. http://dx.doi.org/10.1007/s10803-015-2415-8

Bernabei, P., Cerquiglini, A., Cortesi, F., & D'Ardia, C. (2007). Regression versus no regression in the autistic disorder: Developmental trajectories. *Journal of Autism and Developmental Disorders, 37*, 580–588. http://dx.doi.org/10.1007/s10803-006-0201-3

Blumberg, S. J., Bramlett, M. D., Kogan, M. D., Schieve, L. A., Jones, J. R., & Lu, M. C. (2013). Changes in prevalence of parent-reported autism spectrum disorders in school-aged U.S. children: 2007 to 2011–12. *National Health Statistics Reports, 64*, 1–12.

Campbell, J. M., Ruble, L. A., & Hammond, R. K. (2014). Comprehensive developmental approach assessment model. In L. A. Wilkinson (Ed.), *Autism spectrum disorder in children and adolescents: Evidence-based assessment and intervention* (pp. 51–73). Washington, DC: American Psychological Association.

Casey, B. J., Craddock, N., Cuthbert, B. N., Hyman, S. E., Lee, F. S., & Ressler, K. J. (2013). DSM–5 and RDoC: Progress in psychiatry research? *Nature Reviews Neuroscience, 14*, 810–814. http://dx.doi.org/10.1038/nrn3621

Centers for Disease Control and Prevention. (2014). Prevalence of autism spectrum disorder among children aged 8 years—Autism and Developmental Disabilities Monitoring Network, 11 sites, United States, 2010. *MMWR, 63*(SS02), 1–21.

Centers for Disease Control and Prevention. (2015). *Autism spectrum disorder (ASD): Screening and diagnosis for healthcare providers.* Retrieved from http://www.cdc.gov/ncbddd/autism/hcp-screening.html

Coonrod, E. E., & Stone, W. L. (2005). Screening for autism in young children. In F. R. Volkmar, R. Paul, A. Klin, & D. Cohen (Eds.), *Handbook of autism and pervasive developmental disorders: Assessment, interventions, and policy* (Vol. 2, 3rd ed., pp. 707–720). Hoboken, NJ: Wiley.

Cooper, J. O., Heron, T. E., & Heward, W. L. (2007). *Applied behavior analysis* (2nd ed.). Upper Saddle River, NJ: Pearson Education.

Davidovitch, M., Glick, L., Holtzman, G., Tirosh, E., & Safir, M. P. (2000). Developmental regression in autism: Maternal perception. *Journal of Autism and Developmental Disorders, 30,* 113–119. http://dx.doi.org/10.1023/A:1005403421141

Dawson, G., Munson, J., Webb, S. J., Nalty, T., Abbott, R., & Toth, K. (2007). Rate of head growth decelerates and symptoms worsen in the second year of life in autism. *Biological Psychiatry, 61,* 458–464. http://dx.doi.org/10.1016/j.biopsych.2006.07.016

Eikeseth, S., Smith, T., Jahr, E., & Eldevik, S. (2007). Outcome for children with autism who began intensive behavioral treatment between ages 4 and 7: A comparison controlled study. *Behavior Modification, 31,* 264–278. http://dx.doi.org/10.1177/0145445506291396

Ekinci, O., Arman, A. R., Melek, I., Bez, Y., & Berkem, M. (2012). The phenomenology of autistic regression: Subtypes and associated factors. *European Child & Adolescent Psychiatry, 21,* 23–29. http://dx.doi.org/10.1007/s00787-011-0228-7

Hoshino, Y., Kaneko, M., Yashima, Y., Kumashiro, H., Volkmar, F. R., & Cohen, D. J. (1987). Clinical features of autistic children with setback course in their infancy. *The Japanese Journal of Psychiatry and Neurology, 41,* 237–245.

Individuals With Disabilities Education Act of 1997, 20 U.S.C. 1400 et seq. (1997).

Johnson, C. P., Myers, S. M., & the Council on Children With Disabilities. (2007). Identification and evaluation of children with autism spectrum disorders. *Pediatrics, 120,* 1183–1215. http://dx.doi.org/10.1542/peds.2007-2361

Johnson, C. P., & Walker, W. O., Jr. (2006). Mental retardation: Management and prognosis. *Pediatrics in Review, 27,* 249–256. http://dx.doi.org/10.1542/pir.27-7-249

Johnston, M. V., Ishida, A., Ishida, W. N., Matsushita, H. B., Nishimura, A., & Tsuji, M. (2009). Plasticity and injury in the developing brain. *Brain & Development, 31,* 1–10. http://dx.doi.org/10.1016/j.braindev.2008.03.014

Landa, R., & Garrett-Mayer, E. (2006). Development in infants with autism spectrum disorders: A prospective study. *Journal of Child Psychology and Psychiatry, 47,* 629–638. http://dx.doi.org/10.1111/j.1469-7610.2006.01531.x

Landa, R. J., Holman, K. C., & Garrett-Mayer, E. (2007). Social and communication development in toddlers with early and later diagnosis of autism spectrum disorders. *Archives of General Psychiatry, 64,* 853–864. http://dx.doi.org/10.1001/archpsyc.64.7.853

Lord, C., Shulman, C., & DiLavore, P. (2004). Regression and word loss in autistic spectrum disorders. *Journal of Child Psychology and Psychiatry, 45,* 936–955. http://dx.doi.org/10.1111/j.1469-7610.2004.t01-1-00287.x

Mandell, D. S., Morales, K. H., Xie, M., Lawer, L. J., Stahmer, A. C., & Marcus, S. C. (2010). Age of diagnosis among Medicaid-enrolled children with autism,

2001–2004. *Psychiatric Services, 61,* 822–829. http://dx.doi.org/10.1176/ps.2010.61.8.822

Mandell, D. S., Novak, M. M., & Zubritsky, C. D. (2005). Factors associated with age of diagnosis among children with autism spectrum disorders. *Pediatrics, 116,* 1480–1486. http://dx.doi.org/10.1542/peds.2005-0185

Manning, S. E., Davin, C. A., Barfield, W. D., Kotelchuck, M., Clements, K., Diop, H., . . . Smith, L. A. (2011). Early diagnoses of autism spectrum disorders in Massachusetts birth cohorts, 2001–2005. *Pediatrics, 127,* 1043–1051. http://dx.doi.org/10.1542/peds.2010-2943

Matson, J. L., & Vollmer, T. (1995). *Questions about behavioral function (QABF).* Baton Rouge, LA: Scientific.

Pinto-Martin, J., & Levy, S. E. (2004). Early diagnosis of autism spectrum disorders. *Current Treatment Options in Neurology, 6,* 391–400. http://dx.doi.org/10.1007/s11940-996-0030-x

Robertson, K., Stafford, T., Benedicto, J., & Hocking, N. (2013). Autism assessment: The Melton Health model. *Journal of Paediatrics and Child Health, 49,* 1057–1062. http://dx.doi.org/10.1111/jpc.12303

Rogers, E. L. (2001). Functional behavioral assessment and children with autism: Working as a team. *Focus on Autism and Other Developmental Disabilities, 16,* 228–231. http://dx.doi.org/10.1177/108835760101600405

Rogers, S. J. (2004). Developmental regression in autism spectrum disorders. *Mental Retardation and Developmental Disabilities Research Reviews, 10,* 139–143. http://dx.doi.org/10.1002/mrdd.20027

Saunders, B. S., Tilford, J. M., Fussell, J. J., Schulz, E. G., Casey, P. H., & Kuo, D. Z. (2015). Financial and employment impact of intellectual disability on families of children with autism. *Families, Systems, & Health, 33,* 36–45. http://dx.doi.org/10.1037/fsh0000102

Stefanatos, G. A. (2008). Regression in autistic spectrum disorders. *Neuropsychology Review, 18,* 305–319. http://dx.doi.org/10.1007/s11065-008-9073-y

Strock, M. (2004). *Autism spectrum disorders (pervasive developmental disorders).* (NIMH Publication No. NIH-04-5511). Bethesda, MD: National Institute of Mental Health, National Institutes of Health, U.S. Department of Health and Human Services.

Tarbox, J., Wilke, A. E., Najdowski, A. C., Findel-Pyles, R. S., Balasanyan, S., Caveney, A. C., . . . Tia, B. (2009). Comparing indirect, descriptive, and experimental functional assessments of challenging behavior in children with autism. *Journal of Developmental and Physical Disabilities, 21,* 493–514. http://dx.doi.org/10.1007/s10882-009-9154-8

Tomanik, S. S., Pearson, D. A., Loveland, K. A., Lane, D. M., & Bryant Shaw, J. (2007). Improving the reliability of autism diagnoses: Examining the utility of adaptive behavior. *Journal of Autism and Developmental Disorders, 37,* 921–928. http://dx.doi.org/10.1007/s10803-006-0227-6

Volker, M. A., & Lopata, C. (2008). Autism: A review of biological bases, assessment, and intervention. *School Psychology Quarterly, 23*, 258–270. http://dx.doi.org/10.1037/1045-3830.23.2.258

Waltz, M. (2002). *Autistic spectrum disorders: Finding a diagnosis and getting help.* Sebastopol, CA: O'Reilly & Associates.

Wang, H. T., Sandall, S. R., Davis, C. A., & Thomas, C. J. (2011). Social skills assessment in young children with autism: A comparison evaluation of the SSRS and PKBS. *Journal of Autism and Developmental Disorders, 41*, 1487–1495. http://dx.doi.org/10.1007/s10803-010-1175-8

Wiig, E. H., Semel, E., & Secord, W. A. (2013). *Clinical evaluation of language fundamentals* (5th ed.). San Antonio, TX: Pearson Assessment.

Zwaigenbaum, L., Bryson, S., Rogers, T., Roberts, W., Brian, J., & Szatmari, P. (2005). Behavioral manifestations of autism in the first year of life. *International Journal of Developmental Neuroscience, 23*, 143–152. http://dx.doi.org/10.1016/j.ijdevneu.2004.05.001

11

OVERVIEW OF APPLIED BEHAVIOR ANALYSIS AND EARLY INTERVENTION FOR AUTISM SPECTRUM DISORDER

CAITLIN IRWIN AND JUDAH B. AXE

As the prevalence of autism spectrum disorder (ASD) has continued to rise, so too has the need for specialized behavioral and educational interventions to address the unique learning needs of children with this condition. The practices and procedures with the most empirical support have been derived from the science and practice of applied behavior analysis (ABA; Wong et al., 2015). ABA is a data-driven approach that emphasizes behaviorally based assessment and treatment methods that produce meaningful changes in behaviors important to the learner, his family, and his community. Specifically, ABA is used to increase social, communicative, and self-help skills, as well as decrease stereotypic and problem behaviors. This chapter describes the history and basic principles of ABA; the defining features of ABA; the foundational research on ABA; methods of assessment, intervention, and data collection for increasing prosocial and decreasing problem behavior with learners with ASD in schools; and future directions for the field of ABA.

http://dx.doi.org/10.1037/0000126-012
Behavioral Interventions in Schools: Evidence-Based Positive Strategies, Second Edition, S. G. Little and A. Akin-Little (Editors)
Copyright © 2019 by the American Psychological Association. All rights reserved.

HISTORY AND BASIC PRINCIPLES OF ABA

Understanding and appreciating current applications of ABA with children with ASD requires acknowledging the basic research foundation of ABA, the behavioral principles that underlie the practice, and the applied research evidence.

Basic Principles

Research and practice in ABA can be traced back to the work of B. F. Skinner, whose 1938 book, *The Behavior of Organisms*, introduced the science of behavior analysis by describing the results of his laboratory experiments with rats. These animals were placed in an operant chamber that contained a lever for responding, a method for delivering bits of food and water, and the means of presenting various stimuli such as colored lights and audible tones. Thousands of hours of experimentation with precise, automated data collection allowed for the elucidation of the basic principles of behavior analysis, including reinforcement, extinction, differential reinforcement, shaping, stimulus control, motivating operations, and punishment.

Positive reinforcement is the most significant concept in behavior analysis and occurs when a stimulus is presented immediately following a behavior and increases the future probability of that behavior being repeated. This can be shown in the operant chamber when a rat presses a lever, food is delivered, and the rat presses the lever more often. We observe positive reinforcement in our own behavior when the presentation of a steaming cup of coffee results in more coffee ordering at the cafe. Similarly, we use positive reinforcement by providing a high-five to a learner with ASD when he approaches a peer; we know this was in fact positive reinforcement when we observe the child approach peers more often. *Negative reinforcement* describes the strengthening of behavior through the immediate removal of an aversive stimulus. When an electric shock is terminated by pressing the lever, the response of pressing the lever in the future increases. When our alarm clock stops blaring when we press the snooze button, we are more likely to press snooze in the future. When a therapist stops asking questions when the learner asks for a break, the learner is more likely to ask for a break in the future.

Behavior can be weakened by discontinuing a previous response–reinforcer relationship in a process known as *extinction*. If food has historically followed pressing the lever, but the food delivery mechanism is jammed, the frequency of pressing the lever will gradually diminish to the point of near elimination. When a friend stops returning our calls, we ultimately stop leaving messages. If a learner no longer receives the cookies he asks for, he will eventually stop requesting cookies. Extinction can be combined with reinforcement in the principle known as *differential reinforcement*, in which one behavior is reinforced and another behavior is not reinforced. A rat may turn in circles more often than pushing a lever because of reinforcement for the former and not the latter. On Mondays, we tend to go to work rather than sit on the couch as only the former is reinforced with money and other types of fulfillment. A learner may request toys rather than hit when toys are delivered only for requesting. A particular type of differential reinforcement is *shaping*, defined as differentially reinforcing successive approximations to a target behavior. Shaping has been used to teach rats to play basketball, humans to perform complex gymnastics moves, and learners with ASD to approach items they previously feared.

The combination of reinforcement and extinction also allows behavior to come under *stimulus control*, or to become more likely in the presence of one aspect of the environment than another. If food is presented when the lever is pressed only when a light is on, and is never presented when the chamber is dark, lever pressing will become restricted to times when the chamber is illuminated. If our favorite TV show only plays at 8 p.m., we are more likely to turn on the TV in the evening than in the afternoon. If our learner is tickled by his therapist but not by his peers, he will increase requesting for tickles from his therapist, but will stop asking his peers.

Motivating operations are environmental changes that have a temporary effect on the value of a stimulus as a reinforcer and thereby change the frequency of behaviors that have previously produced that reinforcer. For example, having recently eaten lunch will reduce the value of food as a reinforcer, and a learner is less likely to ask for food or complete academic activities that are typically reinforced by food. On the other hand, fasting for blood work will greatly increase the value of food as a reinforcer, and we would expect academic behaviors to increase in frequency. For many learners, the presence of work increases the value of escape from work, and the learner is more likely to exhibit challenging behaviors as a session progresses and the value of escape increases above the value of the reinforcers the child is earning.

Punishment is a technical term in behavior analysis and does not connote spanking or detention. Punishment is defined as adding or removing a stimulus immediately following a behavior and observing a future decrease in that behavior. *Positive punishment* describes the decrease in a behavior's future frequency following the presentation of a stimulus. When an electric shock is introduced when the rat turns toward the back of the cage, the rat is less likely to turn toward the back of the cage in the future. We quickly learn to stop asking questions of the boss who loudly criticizes our every mistake. A learner will stop climbing on the furniture when doing so is always followed by a sharp "no." *Negative punishment* describes the weakening of a behavior through the immediate removal of a stimulus. When the food container closes each time the rat rises onto its back paws, rising onto the back paws becomes less likely in the future. When our favorite app closes each time we swipe in a certain direction, we are less likely to repeat that swiping motion in the future. A trip to time-out following hitting a peer will reduce the future likelihood of aggression. These basic principles of behavior resulted from basic research and form the basis for applied research and practice in ABA.

Defining Characteristics

Distinct from the experimental analysis of behavior responsible for refining the above principles, ABA is an applied science focused on discovering environmental variables responsible for improving socially significant behaviors (Cooper, Heron, & Heward, 2007). The science has produced methods of analysis and procedures that comprise the practice of ABA. In the inaugural issue of the premier journal on ABA, the *Journal of Applied Behavior Analysis* (JABA), Baer, Wolf, and Risley (1968) published "Some Current Dimensions of Applied Behavior Analysis" in which they described seven core attributes of the science of ABA. These seven dimensions of ABA remain the criteria used to assess the appropriateness of interventions used by ABA researchers and practitioners. The dimensions are applied, behavioral, analytic, technological, effective, generality, and conceptually systematic.

The *applied* nature of ABA means that the goals addressed have social validity—they matter to the learner and are useful in her environment. An example of an applied goal for an early learner with ASD would be to request help when she could not open her lunchbox. ABA is *behavioral* as it focuses on observing, analyzing, and changing observable and measurable behaviors, or motor movements, of an individual. This is contrasted with targeting verbal reports about behavior; cognitive constructs, such as memory or intent; and emotional states, such as feelings or moods. Having a precise description of the behavior of interest is necessary because ABA is *analytic*, meaning that researchers and practitioners seek to demonstrate clear cause-and-effect relationships between the interventions introduced and the behaviors that are changed. These associations, called functional relations, are identified by examining behaviors when interventions are both present and absent in carefully controlled arrangements that attempt to rule out the influence of variables other than the intervention.

A fourth attribute of ABA is that it is *technological*, meaning that the procedures are described in specific detail so that they can be replicated by others. A technological description of a common procedure in ABA, social praise, might be, "Each time the learner correctly names the picture printed on the flashcard, the therapist immediately says, 'That's right,' smiles, and waits 5 seconds before presenting the next flashcard." A nontechnological description of that same procedure may be, "Say something encouraging following each correct response." The specific descriptions and careful measurement allow behavior analysts to determine whether interventions are effective. *Effective* strategies produce a measurable change in the behavior of interest. If a learner initially ignored his peers, and following intervention greeted three peers each time he entered his classroom, his intervention could be described as effective.

Once we have a technological description of the intervention that has been effective in changing an applied behavior, we turn our attention to *generality*, or a change that is demonstrated across environments, stimuli, and people and that endures across time. If a learner is initially taught to count buttons at his desk by his one-to-one therapist, generality could be demonstrated when he counts building blocks with a peer when playing on the rug 2 weeks later. Finally, ABA is *conceptually systematic*, meaning that any technique used in the practice of ABA can be connected to a basic principle of behavior, such as positive reinforcement. In other words, rather than being simply a collection of strategies or tips, the practice of ABA is rooted in the basic science of behavior. The seven dimensions of ABA provide a framework for implementing and evaluating ABA-based treatments for children with ASD.

Foundational Research

Ivar Lovaas and his team at the Young Autism Project of the University of California Los Angeles (UCLA) were the first to demonstrate the effectiveness of applying behavioral principles to the treatment of young children with ASD and related disorders. Although their work began in the 1960s, the first publication to draw attention to this model was Lovaas's (1987) "Behavioral Treatment and Normal Educational and Intellectual Functioning in Young Autistic Children." This article reported on 15 years of research comparing the educational and behavioral outcomes for children with ASD who had received either intensive behavioral programming (more than 40 hours per week) or minimal treatment (fewer than 10 hours per week) delivered for a period of 2 years or longer.

Lovaas (1987) found that the children receiving the intensive treatment made significant gains in intellectual functioning, and 47% were successfully included in a general education first-grade classroom. In comparison, those children in the control group demonstrated no significant gains in intellectual functioning, and only one child was successfully included in a general education classroom. Although this study has since received criticism because of the nonrandom assignment of children to conditions and the use of the term *recovered* to describe the mainstreamed children (Gresham &

MacMillan, 1998; Schopler, Short, & Mesibov, 1989), it was the first piece of evidence to suggest that with early intensive behavioral intervention (EIBI), children with ASD could make meaningful gains in intellectual and adaptive functioning.

More recent studies have continued to demonstrate the effectiveness of the EIBI model. For example, Smith, Groen, and Wynn (2000) conducted a randomized controlled clinical trial to compare the outcomes for children with ASD or pervasive developmental disorder receiving either 30 hours per week of EIBI or a combination of services including parent training, parent-led therapy, and traditional special education. Children in the EIBI group demonstrated significantly improved IQ and language in comparison to the control group and made equivalent gains in adaptive functioning and behavioral problems. Meta-analyses of the peer-reviewed literature found moderate-to-large effect sizes for improvements in language, IQ, and adaptive behavior in the EIBI groups relative to the control groups (Makrygianni & Reed, 2010; Peters-Scheffer, Didden, Korzilius, & Sturmey, 2011). The accumulating evidence has resulted in the conclusion that EIBI is the only treatment that can currently be classified as "well-established" for the treatment of young children with ASD (Rogers & Vismara, 2008).

Although between-group comparison studies continue to serve as the gold standard for establishing evidence in behavioral interventions for children with ASD, behavior analysts use the research methodology of single-subject design to discover environment–behavior relationships, including effective interventions (Heyvaert, Saenen, Campbell, Maes, & Onghena, 2014; Horner et al., 2005; Mayton, Wheeler, Menendez, & Zhang, 2010; Odom et al., 2003; Odom & Strain, 2002). Single-subject design studies allow behavior analysts to continually identify effective ways to use ABA to improve the lives of learners with ASD.

APPLICATION OF ABA TO YOUNG LEARNERS WITH ASD

As defined in the preceding chapter, learners with ASD demonstrate challenges in the areas of communication, social interaction, and repetitive behavior. These core deficits can produce behavioral difficulties that manifest in the classroom setting. Compared with their neurotypical peers, learners with ASD are more likely to exhibit aggression, noncompliance, and inattention and less likely to perform at the academic level predicted by their IQ (Ashburner, Ziviani, & Rodger, 2010). As a result, many of these students require either behavioral support within a general education classroom or specially designed instruction delivered in an alternative setting to reach their academic potential. First in terms of increasing social, academic, and self-help behaviors, and then in terms of decreasing problem behaviors, this section describes behavior analytic assessment tools, intervention procedures, and data collection strategies. It is important that those delivering these intensive services are board-certified behavior analysts (BCBAs) or working under the supervision of a BCBA.

Increasing Communication, Social, Academic, and Self-Help Skills

The most common deficits, and therefore the most common assessment and intervention targets, for learners with ASD are in the areas of communication, social, academic, and self-help skills. This section will describe assessments, interventions, and data collection strategies focused on increasing these repertoires.

Preference Assessment

As stated previously, the most significant principle in ABA is positive reinforcement. Because praise and attention may not function as positive reinforcers for the behavior of children with ASD (Axe & Laprime, 2017), it is critical that behavior analysts identify positive reinforcers to strengthen social, academic, and self-help skills. Common positive reinforcers used in ABA programs are toys, foods, drinks, and physical interactions (e.g., tickles). The simplest method for conducting a preference assessment is asking familiar individuals about items the learner enjoys. However, because this method has limitations, another method is conducting direct observations of students within natural choice-making opportunities, such as during a free-play period (Reid, DiCarlo, Schepis, Hawkins, & Stricklin, 2003). Observations as short as 5 minutes conducted daily over the course of a week may be sufficient to develop a relative toy-preference ranking for learners with ASD in inclusive preschool and early intervention classrooms. For learners who lack the prerequisite skills to independently select toys during free time (e.g., scanning the environment, choosing one item, engaging with the item for an extended duration), alternative approaches include recording whether the child engages with materials presented one at a time (Pace, Ivancic, Edwards, Iwata, & Page, 1985), systematically offering the child pairs of items and observing which he or she selects (Fisher et al., 1992), or arranging a large array of stimuli and identifying the order in which a child engages with each item (DeLeon & Iwata, 1996).

Preference assessments should be conducted frequently because the motivating operation for certain items functioning as reinforcers can change from moment to moment. For example, Toussaint, Kodak, and Vladescu (2016) demonstrated that preschoolers with ASD acquired academic skills faster when allowed to select a reinforcer from an array of three preferred options after each response than when the same reinforcer was preselected by the experimenter. Outcomes from a preference assessment can be verified by conducting a reinforcement assessment in which a behavior analyst measures the frequency of behavior when the identified items are presented after each behavior.

Language Assessment

In addition to identifying positive reinforcers, a successful early intervention program based on ABA is dependent on effectively determining gaps in a child's repertoire and consequently targeting those skills for intervention. To conduct such assessments, behavior analysts rely on two key tools: (a) the Verbal Behavior Milestones Assessment and Placement Program (VB-MAPP; Sundberg, 2008) and (b) the Assessment of Basic Language and Learning Skills—Revised (ABLLS-R; Partington, 2008). These assessments both contain operationally defined target behaviors, a sequence of skills based on prerequisites and increasingly complex behaviors, and specific guidelines for directly measuring skill acquisition. Both tools are criterion referenced, meaning that the learner's specific behaviors are measured with respect to a target criterion (e.g., labeling at least 10 body parts on request) rather than in comparison to peer performance. Both tools emphasize a functional approach to language based on Skinner's (1957) book *Verbal Behavior*. Using these guidelines, communication is classified on the basis of the purpose it serves (e.g., to request, to label, to respond to another's communication) rather than its form (e.g., noun, adjective, preposition). For example, a child would not be assessed on whether he or she "knows" the word *candy*, but whether he or she requests candy when hungry, labels candy when it is placed on the table, responds "candy" when asked to identify something sweet, and repeats "candy" when an adult asks him or her to say "candy." This careful analysis allows for a clear identification of deficits in the learner's repertoire and can be easily converted into measurable intervention goals.

Despite their similarities, the ABLLS-R and VB-MAPP possess unique qualities. The ABLLS-R assesses 544 skills across a broad range, including motor development, adaptive behavior, social interactions, adherence to classroom routines, early academics, and language. In contrast, the VB-MAPP assesses 170 skills and focuses more specifically on language development, with some analysis of classroom participation, early academics, and social skills. Although the ABLLS-R does not attempt to make norm-based classifications, the skills in the VB-MAPP are divided into three tiers corresponding to typical child development at 0–18 months, 18–30 months, and 30–48 months. This categorization system can be useful for ensuring the developmental appropriateness of goals when intervening with young children but may be less valuable when assessing older learners. The Milestones Assessment of the VB-MAPP is accompanied by several other assessment tools aimed to assist in the decision-making process when designing interventions for young learners. The Barriers Assessment examines skill deficits and maladaptive behaviors that may interfere with the acquisition of new skills or with participation in classroom routines, and the Transition Assessment incorporates the outcomes from the Milestones and Barriers Assessments to make recommendations regarding placement in the least restrictive environment. Finally, there is research to support training practitioners to conduct the VB-MAPP (Barnes, Mellor, & Rehfeldt, 2014).

In addition to assessments of language and problem behavior, children with ASD benefit from an analysis of social skills and adaptive behaviors. Gould, Dixon, Najdowski, Smith, and Tarbox (2011) reviewed the assessments currently in use in EIBI programs and identified poor consistency between treatment centers when choosing assessments to administer. To guide the assessment selection process, Gould and colleagues identified five criteria: (a) assessment across all domains affected in ASD, including social and language skills and adaptive and maladaptive behaviors; (b) an emphasis on the behavior and skills expected of young children, allowing assessment and intervention to begin as early as possible; (c) a focus on the role the behavior serves in the child's repertoire (i.e., the behavior's function) as opposed to just its form; (d) clear and specific behavioral definitions that can be easily translated from assessment score to intervention development; and (e) simple and time-limited assessment procedures that allow for repetition to track progress. On the basis of these criteria, Gould and colleagues recommended the VB-MAPP (Sundberg, 2008) for the analysis of language, the Brigance Diagnostic Inventory of Early Development II (Brigance, 2004) for the assessment of motor and academic behaviors, and the Vineland Adaptive Behavior Scales—Second Edition (Sparrow, Cicchetti, & Balla, 2005) for the measurement of daily living skills.

Intervention

Once reinforcers and instructional targets have been identified, intervention begins. ABA approaches to teaching children with ASD center on three primary teaching methods: discrete trial training, natural environment teaching, and task analysis. This section provides an overview of these three strategies.

Discrete trial training (DTT; see Chapter 12) is the teaching methodology most commonly associated with ABA (Lovaas, 1987, 2003). This approach is unique in that complex skills are broken down into smaller teachable units, which are then taught in a carefully organized sequence in a highly controlled environment. Typically, the behavior analyst sits across from the child at a table and delivers a series of trials, each containing an instruction, prompts, a response, and a consequence. For example, to teach a child to name classroom supplies, a trial would consist of the behavior analyst presenting the child with a crayon while saying "What is it?" and waiting for the child to respond, then providing either praise and brief tickling for saying "Crayon," or saying "Crayon. Try again—What is it?" if the child responds in any other way. The behavior analyst would then wait 2 to 3 seconds before presenting a different object, and the cycle would repeat for 10 trials at which point the child would be offered a break while the behavior analyst gathers materials to teach the next skill (Delfs, Conine, Frampton, Shillingsburg, & Robinson, 2014). More information about the components and variations of DTT can be found in Chapter 12.

Natural environment teaching (NET), also referred to as incidental teaching, occurs in a less rigidly structured context. Opportunities to practice a specific skill are arranged within the learner's everyday environment, such as during meal times, on the rug, and at the arts table. The behavior analyst observes the learner's current motivation and contrives an opportunity for the learner to respond. For example, in a play area in a classroom, a behavior analyst may place a preferred toy truck out of reach; when the child looks at and reaches for the truck, the behavior analyst prompts the child to say, "I want blue truck" and then delivers the truck (Hart & Risley, 1968). This approach provides opportunities to practice communication and social skills across the day, in various environments, and with several possible listeners, thus increasing the probability of successful generalization to novel environments. NET has been used to teach students with a variety of disabilities academic, social, and adaptive skills in both inclusion and self-contained preschool classrooms (Snyder et al., 2015). Sundberg and Partington (1999) provided guidelines regarding the optimal combination of DTT and NET arrangements at various stages of ABA intervention.

As prompting is a hallmark of DTT and NET, there are specific methods of *prompt fading*. With most-to-least prompting, the most helpful and necessary prompts (e.g., physical prompts) are provided at first and then gradually faded until a child is independent (Libby, Weiss, Bancroft, & Ahearn, 2008). A behavior analyst uses the quick-transfer-of-stimulus-control procedure when she presents an instruction with a prompt, reinforces a response, immediately repeats the instruction without a prompt, and reinforces the subsequent response (Barbera & Kubina, 2005). With least-to-most prompting, the behavior analyst starts with the least helpful prompts (e.g., verbal prompts) and, as needed, gradually adds more helpful prompts (Davis-Temple, Jung, & Sainato, 2014). Finally, time delay is presenting an instruction and waiting a specified period of time (e.g., 3 seconds) until providing a prompt to ultimately fade prompts and provide opportunities for independence (Liber, Frea, & Symon, 2008).

Task analysis is commonly used to teach self-help skills, such as hand washing, tooth brushing, and dressing, as those skills often contain multiple steps. The behavior analyst first makes a list of each behavior in the chain of the complex skill and then teaches the learner each behavior one at a time. For example, Garcia, Dukes, Brady, Scott, and Wilson (2016) were interested in teaching three preschoolers with ASD to respond to a fire alarm by leaving the building and informing an adult. The researcher first observed the responses of typical peers and broke down the skill into six steps. Training began by the instructor modeling the steps in the correct sequence, performing the sequence while the learner labeled each step, and then providing the learner an opportunity for independent practice with vocal or physical prompts to correct errors. All participants acquired the evacuation routine and maintained 100% accuracy at a 5-week follow-up and in novel settings where they had not previously encountered a fire alarm. Recent research has demonstrated the successful incorporation of technology into these teaching procedures, including the use of video models rather than live models (e.g., Shrestha, Anderson, & Moore, 2013). Further information about this strategy can be found in Chapter 15.

Data Collection

Data-based decision making is a core tenet of any behavior analytic intervention. Although repeated administrations of assessments such as the VB-MAPP, ABLLS-R, and Vineland can be used to identify large-scale changes in behavioral repertoires that may affect placement, staffing, and related service provision, they do not allow for the detection of session-to-session behavioral changes that inform adjustments to programming and allow for true individualization of the educational interventions.

During academic instruction, the behavior analyst collects data on correct and incorrect responses, as well as responses that required prompting versus those that were independent. Following a 10-trial session, the behavior analyst calculates the percentage of correct responses by dividing the number of accurate responses by the total number of trials. Similarly, when teaching with a task analysis, each step is scored as independent or prompted, and the results are summarized by dividing the number of independent responses by the total number of steps in the chain. In both cases, these percentages are then used to determine the amount of prompting necessary on the next occasion the skill is taught, as well as when a skill is mastered.

Data collected across several days or weeks of programming may be used to identify trends that require adjustments to the teaching procedure.

For example, if a student continues to wait for prompting when responding to questions, the consequences of responding may need to be changed such that independent responses result in either more or stronger reinforcers than prompted responses (Cividini-Motta & Ahearn, 2013). On the other hand, a student who responds to novel questions with errors may need to be taught to say, "I don't know" and wait for an instruction rather than guessing (Ingvarsson, Tiger, Hanley, & Stephenson, 2007). Finally, a student who demonstrates maladaptive responses when corrected or given certain prompts may require teaching interventions specifically designed to reduce errors (see Mueller, Palkovic, & Maynard, 2007, for a review). Combining careful assessment, the implementation of effective intervention strategies, and frequent data collection allow behavior analysts to increase desired behaviors, as well as decrease undesired behaviors.

Decreasing Problem Behaviors

Learners with ASD commonly exhibit problems behaviors, such as aggression, property destruction, self-injurious behavior, and other disruptive behavior. Effective reduction of problem behaviors requires a complete assessment of the function of the problem behaviors and implementation of an intervention based on that function using the basic principles of behavior.

Functional Behavior Assessment

Since the 1997 amendment of the Individuals With Disabilities Education Act, conducting a *functional behavior assessment* (FBA) of problem behavior has been mandated prior to recommending a student to a more restrictive placement. An FBA commonly contains a number of steps (O'Neill et al., 1997). First, the behavior analyst interviews teachers, parents, and other individuals who frequently interact with the target student to gather information about the nature of the problem behavior and the circumstances under which it occurs. Second, the behavior analyst may have a teacher or parent fill out a systematic questionnaire designed to provide information about the function of the problem behavior, such as the Motivation Assessment Scale (Durand & Crimmins, 1988) or the Functional Analysis Screening Tool (Iwata, DeLeon, & Roscoe, 2013). Because it is always more advantageous to directly observe behavior than solely rely on verbal reports about it, the third method is directly observing and recording what occurs immediately before and after each instance of the problem behavior. This allows the practitioner to hypothesize about the motivating operations evoking the problem behavior and the reinforcers maintaining the problem behavior. Finally, a behavior analyst may conduct an experimental analysis by systematically presenting and withdrawing possible reinforcers for problem behavior in a series of carefully designed and sequenced sessions (Hanley, Jin, Vanselow, & Hanratty, 2014; Iwata, Dorsey, Slifer, Bauman, & Richman, 1994).

Functions of problem behavior commonly fall into four broad categories: attention, escape, tangible, and automatic reinforcement. An *attention function* is hypothesized when the antecedent is diverted attention and the consequence is delivery of attention. For example, a learner may make unusual noises until a peer turns around and stares at him, which will demonstrate that making noises is an effective way to secure peer attention. During instruction, the learner might call out because this has been historically followed by the teacher reminding him to raise his hand. An *escape function* is hypothesized when the antecedent is demands or other aversive events and the consequence is the reduction or termination of the aversive events. A learner may slap a peer who approaches her desk as this has previously resulted in the peer walking away. She may bang her head when presented with requests to clean up because the teacher has paused the requests to ensure safety. A *tangible function* is identified when a behavior has been followed by access to a preferred item or event. For example, a learner who is noncompliant with requests to leave the computer may receive extended access to computer time. A learner who steals his peer's snacks enjoys the consumption of the pilfered item. Finally, an *automatic function* is identified when the occurrence of the behavior is not related to the actions of others, and the behavior is instead followed by a sensory outcome. For example, a learner may repeat nonsense syllables because of the pleasing vibration feeling produced in his throat or may flap his hands in front of his eyes to access the resulting visual distortion.

Intervention

Once the behavior analyst has identified the probable motivating operations and reinforcers for the problem behavior, he can develop a function-based intervention in which the hypothesized reinforcer is delivered contingent on appropriate behaviors and withheld for instances of the problem behavior. One common function-based intervention is *functional communication training* (FCT) in which a reinforcer is withheld for problem behavior and delivered contingent on requests for the reinforcer (Carr & Durand, 1985). For example, Braithwaite and Richdale (2000) determined that the hitting of peers and head banging of a 7-year-old boy with autism were reinforced with escape from demands and access to preferred items, such as a slinky. In his classroom, the boy was taught to make requests for help with work and for access to his slinky, which reduced his problem behaviors and increased his requests. It is critical to match the intervention to the function of the problem behavior. A learner whose self-injury is maintained by escape might be taught to ask for a break, while a learner whose self-injury is maintained by attention might be taught to raise his hand or tap a teacher on the shoulder. When an individual can engage in the adaptive response to receive the desired consequence, the likelihood of problem behavior is reduced. Previous research with young children with disabilities has demonstrated the value of function-based interventions in reducing problem behavior (Larkin, Hawkins, & Collins, 2016; Perrin, Perrin, Hill, & DiNovi, 2008; Reeves, Umbreit, Ferro, & Liaupsin, 2013).

A second type of function-based intervention is *antecedent modifications* to a child's environment that will reduce the likelihood of the problem behavior being emitted (Carbone, Morgenstern, Zecchin-Tirri, & Kolberg, 2010). For example, Ducharme and Ng (2012) identified demands likely to evoke compliance (e.g., "Color this picture") and demands likely to evoke problem behavior (e.g., "Write your name"). By initially presenting only the demands that occasioned compliance and gradually fading in the less preferred demands, the authors increased the on-task behavior and reduced the problem behaviors of three young students with ASD. Rispoli and colleagues (2013) addressed less preferred demands by incorporating choice-making opportunities. Learners who were asked to complete a worksheet were given a choice of writing utensils, whereas learners given independent work tasks were allowed to select the order in which activities would be completed. All four school-aged children with ASD demonstrated fewer problem behaviors when offered choices. Finally, Kelly, Axe, Allen, and Maguire (2015) demonstrated that presession pairing, or engaging in reinforcing activities prior to presenting demands, reduced the challenging behavior of three children with ASD during instruction.

Data Collection

As with behaviors targeted for increase, data collection on problem behaviors is crucial for making data-based decisions. When assessing problem behavior, a variety of characteristics may be examined, depending on the topography, or form, of the behavior. For example, for a temper tantrum, it may be most useful to identify how long the tantrum lasted (i.e., duration) or how much time passed between the academic demand and the start of the tantrum (i.e., latency). If a tantrum includes aggression, it may be significant to know either the number of hits (i.e., frequency) or the forcefulness of the punches (i.e., magnitude). Different tools, including timers, counters, and rating scales, may be used to collect data, which can then be graphed and interpreted. In addition, behavior analysts may use *event recording* to count each instance of a behavior, or they may use an *interval recording* method to yield a percentage of intervals during which a problem behavior occurred

(Meany-Daboul, Roscoe, Bourret, & Ahearn, 2007; these methods are also used to measure prosocial behaviors). The analysis of daily behavior data and the resulting programming adjustments allow the behavioral interventions to be continuously customized to meet the needs of each learner.

FUTURE DIRECTIONS

In addition to a wealth of research evidence supporting the use of ABA to improve the lives of children with ASD, there are numerous future directions for the field. For example, the optimal parameters for administering ABA and how to standardize treatments and evaluations across settings are not yet clear. In their survey of 211 EIBI programs, Love, Carr, Almason, and Petursdottir (2009) found differences in the amount of therapy provided per week (10 vs. 40 hours), the amount of training for therapists, and the type of data collection used. The inconsistent outcomes may be attributable to the lack of a standard tool for assessing progress in EIBI (Matson & Goldin, 2014). Only once standardization has been achieved in participant variables, treatment variables, and outcome measures can reliable conclusions be drawn regarding the effects of EIBI. A second concern is how to disseminate ABA services, particularly in environments with few trained staff and limited resources. It is critical that those overseeing ABA interventions with children with ASD in schools are BCBAs or supervised by BCBAs. Behavior analysts must use evidence-based practices, such as behavioral skills training, which is comprised of instructions, modeling, role-playing, and feedback, to teach behavioral therapists to implement ABA procedures (Gianoumis, Seiverling, & Sturmey, 2012; Hogan, Knez, & Kahng, 2015; Lerman, Hawkins, Hillman, Shireman, & Nissen, 2015; Sarokoff & Sturmey, 2008). Emerging studies have demonstrated effective online and telehealth parent training (Meadan et al., 2016; Wacker et al., 2013; Wainer & Ingersoll, 2015), as well as computer-based staff training (Machalicek et al., 2009; Pollard, Higbee, Akers, & Brodhead, 2014). Future researchers should continue evaluating efficient ways of training school staff to implement ABA procedures with children with ASD.

A final direction for future research is the generalization of behavioral strategies to assist learners with autism in participating successfully in inclusive environments alongside their typical peers (Stokes & Baer, 1977). Fleury, Thompson, and Wong (2015) identified 18 evidence-based strategies for increasing the school-readiness skills of preschoolers with autism, such as functional behavior assessments, functional communication training, antecedent interventions, prompting, modeling, and reinforcement. To promote successful inclusion, behavior analysts must program for the improvement of social skills (Koegel, Koegel, Frea, & Fredeen, 2001). Script fading is a promising procedure in which a child is taught to read a script for engaging in a social behavior, such as initiating to peers, and text from the script is gradually faded (Garcia-Albea, Reeve, Brothers, & Reeve, 2014; Groskreutz, Peters, Groskreutz, & Higbee, 2015). Given the high student–teacher ratios in general education classrooms, additional research on interventions that promote interactions in the absence of an adult to prompt responding is a necessary future direction.

CONCLUSION

As the prevalence of children with ASD included in public schools continues to increase, educators must use ABA as the primary method of assessment and intervention as it has the most research evidence compared with other approaches. ABA is used as a framework for assessment, intervention, and ongoing data collection for increasing communication, social, academic, and self-help skills, as well as decreasing problem behaviors. All ABA procedures, such as token reinforcement, prompt fading, and functional communication training, are based on the basic principles of behavior discovered in a laboratory, making the practice conceptually systematic. Although there is a substantial evidence base for ABA interventions for young children with ASD, future researchers should continue evaluating methods of standardizing evaluations, disseminating services, and promoting the generalization of learned skills.

REFERENCES

Ashburner, J., Ziviani, J., & Rodger, S. (2010). Surviving in the mainstream: Capacity of children with autism spectrum disorders to perform academically and regulate their emotions and behavior at school. *Research in Autism Spectrum Disorders, 4,* 18–27. http://dx.doi.org/10.1016/j.rasd.2009.07.002

Axe, J. B., & Laprime, A. P. (2017). The effects of contingent pairing on establishing praise as a reinforcer with children with autism. *Journal of Developmental and Physical Disabilities, 29,* 325–340.

Baer, D. M., Wolf, M. M., & Risley, T. R. (1968). Some current dimensions of applied behavior analysis. *Journal of Applied Behavior Analysis, 1,* 91–97. http://dx.doi.org/10.1901/jaba.1968.1-91

Barbera, M. L., & Kubina, R. M., Jr. (2005). Using transfer procedures to teach tacts to a child with autism. *Analysis of Verbal Behavior, 21,* 155–161. http://dx.doi.org/10.1007/BF03393017

Barnes, C. S., Mellor, J. R., & Rehfeldt, R. A. (2014). Implementing the Verbal Behavior Milestones Assessment and Placement Program (VB-MAPP): Teaching assessment techniques. *Analysis of Verbal Behavior, 30,* 36–47. http://dx.doi.org/10.1007/s40616-013-0004-5

Braithwaite, K. L., & Richdale, A. L. (2000). Functional communication training to replace challenging behaviors across two behavioral outcomes. *Behavioral Interventions, 15,* 21–36. http://dx.doi.org/10.1002/(SICI)1099-078X(200001/03)15:1<21::AID-BIN45>3.0.CO;2-#

Brigance, A. H. (2004). *Brigance Diagnostic Inventory of Early Development II.* North Billerica, MA: Curriculum Associates.

Carbone, V. J., Morgenstern, B., Zecchin-Tirri, G., & Kolberg, L. (2010). The role of the reflexive conditioned motivating operation (CMO-R) during discrete trial instruction of children with autism. *Focus on Autism and Other Developmental Disabilities, 25,* 110–124. http://dx.doi.org/10.1177/1088357610364393

Carr, E. G., & Durand, V. M. (1985). Reducing behavior problems through functional communication training. *Journal of Applied Behavior Analysis, 18,* 111–126.

Cividini-Motta, C., & Ahearn, W. H. (2013). Effects of two variations of differential reinforcement on prompt dependency. *Journal of Applied Behavior Analysis, 46,* 640–650. http://dx.doi.org/10.1002/jaba.67

Cooper, J. O., Heron, T. E., & Heward, W. L. (2007). *Applied behavior analysis* (2nd ed.). Upper Saddle River, NJ: Pearson.

Davis-Temple, J., Jung, S., & Sainato, D. M. (2014). Teaching young children with special needs and their peers to play board games: Effects of a least to most prompting procedure to increase independent performance. *Behavior Analysis in Practice, 7,* 21–30. http://dx.doi.org/10.1007/s40617-014-0001-8

DeLeon, I. G., & Iwata, B. A. (1996). Evaluation of a multiple-stimulus presentation format for assessing reinforcer preferences. *Journal of Applied Behavior Analysis, 29,* 519–533. http://dx.doi.org/10.1901/jaba.1996.29-519

Delfs, C. H., Conine, D. E., Frampton, S. E., Shillingsburg, M. A., & Robinson, H. C. (2014). Evaluation of the efficiency of listener and tact instruction for children with autism. *Journal of Applied Behavior Analysis, 47,* 793–809. http://dx.doi.org/10.1002/jaba.166

Ducharme, J. M., & Ng, O. (2012). Errorless academic compliance training: A school-based application for young students with autism. *Behavior Modification, 36,* 650–669. http://dx.doi.org/10.1177/0145445511436006

Durand, V. M., & Crimmins, D. B. (1988). Identifying the variables maintaining self-injurious behavior. *Journal of Autism and Developmental Disorders, 18,* 99–117. http://dx.doi.org/10.1007/BF02211821

Fisher, W., Piazza, C. C., Bowman, L. G., Hagopian, L. P., Owens, J. C., & Slevin, I. (1992). A comparison of two approaches for identifying reinforcers for persons with severe and profound disabilities. *Journal of Applied Behavior Analysis, 25,* 491–498. http://dx.doi.org/10.1901/jaba.1992.25-491

Fleury, V. P., Thompson, J. L., & Wong, C. (2015). Learning how to be a student: An overview of instructional practices targeting school readiness skills for preschoolers with autism spectrum disorder. *Behavior Modification, 39*, 69–97. http://dx.doi.org/10.1177/0145445514551384

Garcia, D., Dukes, C., Brady, M. P., Scott, J., & Wilson, C. L. (2016). Using modeling and rehearsal to teach fire safety to children with autism. *Journal of Applied Behavior Analysis, 49*, 699–704. http://dx.doi.org/10.1002/jaba.331

Garcia-Albea, E., Reeve, S. A., Brothers, K. J., & Reeve, K. F. (2014). Using audio script fading and multiple-exemplar training to increase vocal interactions in children with autism. *Journal of Applied Behavior Analysis, 47*, 325–343. http://dx.doi.org/10.1002/jaba.125

Gianoumis, S., Seiverling, L., & Sturmey, P. (2012). The effects of behavior skills training on correct teacher implementation of natural language paradigm teaching skills and child behavior. *Behavioral Interventions, 27*, 57–74. http://dx.doi.org/10.1002/bin.1334

Gould, E., Dixon, D. R., Najdowski, A. C., Smith, M. N., & Tarbox, J. (2011). A review of assessments for determining the content of early intensive behavioral intervention programs for autism spectrum disorders. *Research in Autism Spectrum Disorders, 5*, 990–1002. http://dx.doi.org/10.1016/j.rasd.2011.01.012

Gresham, F. M., & MacMillan, D. L. (1998). Early Intervention Project: Can its claims be substantiated and its effects replicated? *Journal of Autism and Developmental Disorders, 28*, 5–13. http://dx.doi.org/10.1023/A:1026002717402

Groskreutz, M. P., Peters, A., Groskreutz, N. C., & Higbee, T. S. (2015). Increasing play-based commenting in children with autism spectrum disorder using a novel script-frame procedure. *Journal of Applied Behavior Analysis, 48*, 442–447. http://dx.doi.org/10.1002/jaba.194

Hanley, G. P., Jin, C. S., Vanselow, N. R., & Hanratty, L. A. (2014). Producing meaningful improvements in problem behavior of children with autism via synthesized analyses and treatments. *Journal of Applied Behavior Analysis, 47*, 16–36. http://dx.doi.org/10.1002/jaba.106

Hart, B. M., & Risley, T. R. (1968). Establishing use of descriptive adjectives in the spontaneous speech of disadvantaged preschool children. *Journal of Applied Behavior Analysis, 1*, 109–120.

Heyvaert, M., Saenen, L., Campbell, J. M., Maes, B., & Onghena, P. (2014). Efficacy of behavioral interventions for reducing problem behavior in persons with autism: An updated quantitative synthesis of single-subject research. *Research in Developmental Disabilities, 35*, 2463–2476. http://dx.doi.org/10.1016/j.ridd.2014.06.017

Hogan, A., Knez, N., & Kahng, S. (2015). Evaluating the use of behavioral skills training to improve school staffs' implementation of behavior intervention plans. *Journal of Behavioral Education, 24*, 242–254. http://dx.doi.org/10.1007/s10864-014-9213-9

Horner, R. H., Carr, E. G., Halle, J., McGee, G., Odom, S., & Wolery, M. (2005). The use of single-subject research to identify evidence-based practice in special education. *Exceptional Children, 71,* 165–179. http://dx.doi.org/10.1177/001440290507100203

Individuals With Disabilities Education Act of 1997, 20 U.S.C. 1400 et seq. (1997).

Ingvarsson, E. T., Tiger, J. H., Hanley, G. P., & Stephenson, K. M. (2007). An evaluation of intraverbal training to generate socially appropriate responses to novel questions. *Journal of Applied Behavior Analysis, 40,* 411–429. http://dx.doi.org/10.1901/jaba.2007.40-411

Iwata, B. A., DeLeon, I. G., & Roscoe, E. M. (2013). Reliability and validity of the functional analysis screening tool. *Journal of Applied Behavior Analysis, 46,* 271–284. http://dx.doi.org/10.1002/jaba.31

Iwata, B. A., Dorsey, M. F., Slifer, K. J., Bauman, K. E., & Richman, G. S. (1994). Toward a functional analysis of self-injury. *Journal of Applied Behavior Analysis, 27,* 197–209.

Kelly, A. N., Axe, J. B., Allen, R. F., & Maguire, R. W. (2015). Effects of presession pairing on the challenging behavior and academic responding of children with autism. *Behavioral Interventions, 30,* 135–156. http://dx.doi.org/10.1002/bin.1408

Koegel, L. K., Koegel, R. L., Frea, W. D., & Fredeen, R. M. (2001). Identifying early intervention targets for children with autism in inclusive school settings. *Behavior Modification, 25,* 745–761. http://dx.doi.org/10.1177/0145445501255005

Larkin, W., Hawkins, R. O., & Collins, T. (2016). Using trial-based functional analysis to design effective interventions for students diagnosed with autism spectrum disorder. *School Psychology Quarterly, 31,* 534–547. http://dx.doi.org/10.1037/spq0000158

Lerman, D. C., Hawkins, L., Hillman, C., Shireman, M., & Nissen, M. A. (2015). Adults with autism spectrum disorder as behavior technicians for young children with autism: Outcomes of a behavioral skills training program. *Journal of Applied Behavior Analysis, 48,* 233–256. http://dx.doi.org/10.1002/jaba.196

Libby, M. E., Weiss, J. S., Bancroft, S., & Ahearn, W. H. (2008). A comparison of most-to-least and least-to-most prompting on the acquisition of solitary play skills. *Behavior Analysis in Practice, 1,* 37–43. http://dx.doi.org/10.1007/BF03391719

Liber, D. B., Frea, W. D., & Symon, J. B. (2008). Using time-delay to improve social play skills with peers for children with autism. *Journal of Autism and Developmental Disorders, 38,* 312–323. http://dx.doi.org/10.1007/s10803-007-0395-z

Lovaas, O. I. (1987). Behavioral treatment and normal educational and intellectual functioning in young autistic children. *Journal of Consulting and Clinical Psychology, 55,* 3–9. http://dx.doi.org/10.1037/0022-006X.55.1.3

Lovaas, O. I. (2003). *Teaching individuals with developmental delays: Basic intervention techniques.* Austin, TX: PRO-ED Books.

Love, J. R., Carr, J. E., Almason, S. M., & Petursdottir, A. I. (2009). Early and intensive behavioral intervention for autism: A survey of clinical practices. *Research in Autism Spectrum Disorders, 3,* 421–428. http://dx.doi.org/10.1016/j.rasd.2008.08.008

Machalicek, W., O'Reilly, M., Chan, J. M., Rispoli, M., Lang, R., Davis, T., . . . Langthorne, P. (2009). Using videoconferencing to support teachers to conduct preference assessments with students with autism and developmental disabilities. *Research in Autism Spectrum Disorders, 3,* 32–41. http://dx.doi.org/10.1016/j.rasd.2008.03.004

Makrygianni, M. K., & Reed, P. (2010). A meta-analytic review of the effectiveness of behavioural early intervention programs for children with autistic spectrum disorders. *Research in Autism Spectrum Disorders, 4,* 577–593. http://dx.doi.org/10.1016/j.rasd.2010.01.014

Matson, J. L., & Goldin, R. L. (2014). Early intensive behavioral interventions: Selecting behaviors for treatment and assessing treatment effectiveness. *Research in Autism Spectrum Disorders, 8,* 138–142. http://dx.doi.org/10.1016/j.rasd.2013.11.005

Mayton, M. R., Wheeler, J. J., Menendez, A. L., & Zhang, J. (2010). An analysis of evidence-based practices in the education and treatment of learners with autism spectrum disorders. *Education and Training in Autism and Developmental Disabilities, 45,* 539–551.

Meadan, H., Snodgrass, M. R., Meyer, L. E., Fisher, K. W., Chung, M. Y., & Halle, J. W. (2016). Internet-based parent-implemented intervention for young children with autism: A pilot study. *Journal of Early Intervention, 38,* 3–23. http://dx.doi.org/10.1177/1053815116630327

Meany-Daboul, M. G., Roscoe, E. M., Bourret, J. C., & Ahearn, W. H. (2007). A comparison of momentary time sampling and partial-interval recording for evaluating functional relations. *Journal of Applied Behavior Analysis, 40,* 501–514. http://dx.doi.org/10.1901/jaba.2007.40-501

Mueller, M. M., Palkovic, C. M., & Maynard, C. S. (2007). Errorless learning: Review and practical application for teaching children with pervasive developmental disorders. *Psychology in the Schools, 44,* 691–700. http://dx.doi.org/10.1002/pits.20258

Odom, S. L., Brown, W. H., Frey, T., Karasu, N., Smith-Canter, L. L., & Strain, P. S. (2003). Evidence-based practices for young children with autism: Contributions for single-subject design research. *Focus on Autism and Other Developmental Disabilities, 18,* 166–175. http://dx.doi.org/10.1177/10883576030180030401

Odom, S. L., & Strain, P. S. (2002). Evidence-based practice in early intervention/early childhood special education: Single-subject design research. *Journal of Early Intervention, 25,* 151–160. http://dx.doi.org/10.1177/105381510202500212

O'Neill, R. E., Horner, R. H., Albin, R. W., Sprague, J. R., Storey, K., & Newton, J. S. (1997). *Functional assessment and program development for problem behavior: A practical handbook* (2nd ed.). Belmont, CA: Wadsworth.

Pace, G. M., Ivancic, M. T., Edwards, G. L., Iwata, B. A., & Page, T. J. (1985). Assessment of stimulus preference and reinforcer value with profoundly retarded individuals. *Journal of Applied Behavior Analysis, 18,* 249–255.

Partington, J. W. (2008). *The Assessment of Basics Language and Learning Skills—Revised: Scoring instructions and IEP development guide.* Pleasant Hill, CA: Behavior Analysts.

Perrin, C. J., Perrin, S. H., Hill, E. A., & DiNovi, K. (2008). Brief functional analysis and treatment of elopement in preschoolers with autism. *Behavioral Interventions, 23,* 87–98. http://dx.doi.org/10.1002/bin.256

Peters-Scheffer, N., Didden, R., Korzilius, H., & Sturmey, P. (2011). A meta-analytic study on the effectiveness of comprehensive ABA-based early intervention programs for children with autism spectrum disorders. *Research in Autism Spectrum Disorders, 5,* 60–69. http://dx.doi.org/10.1016/j.rasd.2010.03.011

Pollard, J. S., Higbee, T. S., Akers, J. S., & Brodhead, M. T. (2014). An evaluation of interactive computer training to teach instructors to implement discrete trials with children with autism. *Journal of Applied Behavior Analysis, 47,* 765–776. http://dx.doi.org/10.1002/jaba.152

Reeves, L. M., Umbreit, J., Ferro, J. B., & Liaupsin, C. J. (2013). Function-based intervention to support the inclusion of students with autism. *Education and Training in Autism and Developmental Disabilities, 48,* 379–391.

Reid, D. H., DiCarlo, C. F., Schepis, M. M., Hawkins, J., & Stricklin, S. B. (2003). Observational assessment of toy preferences among young children with disabilities in inclusive settings: Efficiency analysis and comparison with staff opinion. *Behavior Modification, 27,* 233–250. http://dx.doi.org/10.1177/0145445503251588

Rispoli, M., Lang, R., Neely, L., Camargo, S., Hutchins, N., Davenport, K., & Goodwyn, F. (2013). A comparison of within- and across-activity choices for reducing challenging behavior in children with autism spectrum disorders. *Journal of Behavioral Education, 22,* 66–83. http://dx.doi.org/10.1007/s10864-012-9164-y

Rogers, S. J., & Vismara, L. A. (2008). Evidence-based comprehensive treatments for early autism. *Journal of Clinical Child and Adolescent Psychology, 37,* 8–38. http://dx.doi.org/10.1080/15374410701817808

Sarokoff, R. A., & Sturmey, P. (2008). The effects of instructions, rehearsal, modeling, and feedback on acquisition and generalization of staff use of discrete trial teaching and student correct responses. *Research in Autism Spectrum Disorders, 2,* 125–136. http://dx.doi.org/10.1016/j.rasd.2007.04.002

Schopler, E., Short, A., & Mesibov, G. (1989). Relation of behavioral treatment to "normal functioning": Comment on Lovaas. *Journal of Consulting and Clinical Psychology, 57,* 162–164. http://dx.doi.org/10.1037/0022-006X.57.1.162

Shrestha, A., Anderson, A., & Moore, D. W. (2013). Using point-of-view video modeling and forward chaining to teach a functional self-help skill to a child with autism. *Journal of Behavioral Education, 22,* 157–167. http://dx.doi.org/10.1007/s10864-012-9165-x

Skinner, B. F. (1938). *The behavior of organisms: An experimental analysis.* New York, NY: Appleton-Century-Crofts.

Skinner, B. F. (1957). *Verbal behavior.* Acton, MA: Copley. http://dx.doi.org/10.1037/11256-000

Smith, T., Groen, A. D., & Wynn, J. W. (2000). Randomized trial of intensive early intervention for children with pervasive developmental disorder. *American Journal on Mental Retardation, 105,* 269–285. http://dx.doi.org/10.1352/0895-8017(2000)105<0269:RTOIEI>2.0.CO;2

Snyder, P. A., Rakap, S., Hemmeter, M. L., McLaughlin, T. W., Sandall, S., & McLean, M. E. (2015). Naturalistic instructional approaches in early learning: A systematic review. *Journal of Early Intervention, 37,* 69–97. http://dx.doi.org/10.1177/1053815115595461

Sparrow, S. S., Cicchetti, D. V., & Balla, D. A. (2005). *Vineland–II: Vineland Adaptive Behavior Scales.* Circle Pines, MN: American Guidance Service.

Stokes, T. F., & Baer, D. M. (1977). An implicit technology of generalization. *Journal of Applied Behavior Analysis, 10,* 349–367.

Sundberg, M. L. (2008). *Verbal Behavior Milestones Assessment and Placement Program (VB-MAPP).* Concord, CA: AVB Press.

Sundberg, M. L., & Partington, J. W. (1999). The need for both discrete trial and natural environment language training for children with autism. In P. M. Ghezzi, W. L. Williams, & J. E. Carr (Eds.), *Autism: Behavior analytic perspectives* (pp. 139–156). Reno, NV: Context Press.

Toussaint, K. A., Kodak, T., & Vladescu, J. C. (2016). An evaluation of choice on instructional efficacy and individual preferences among children with autism. *Journal of Applied Behavior Analysis, 49,* 170–175. http://dx.doi.org/10.1002/jaba.263

Wacker, D. P., Lee, J. F., Padilla Dalmau, Y. C., Kopelman, T. G., Lindgren, S. D., Kuhle, J., . . . Waldron, D. B. (2013). Conducting functional communication training via telehealth to reduce the problem behavior of young children with autism. *Journal of Developmental and Physical Disabilities, 25,* 35–48. http://dx.doi.org/10.1007/s10882-012-9314-0

Wainer, A. L., & Ingersoll, B. R. (2015). Increasing access to an ASD imitation intervention via a telehealth parent training program. *Journal of Autism and Developmental Disorders, 45,* 3877–3890. http://dx.doi.org/10.1007/s10803-014-2186-7

Wong, C., Odom, S. L., Hume, K. A., Cox, A. W., Fettig, A., Kucharczyk, S., . . . Schultz, T. R. (2015). Evidence-based practices for children, youth, and young adults with autism spectrum disorder: A comprehensive review. *Journal of Autism and Developmental Disorders, 45,* 1951–1966. http://dx.doi.org/10.1007/s10803-014-2351-z

12

DISCRETE TRIAL TRAINING: A STRUCTURED LEARNING APPROACH FOR CHILDREN WITH ASD

JEFF SIGAFOOS, AMARIE CARNETT, MARK F. O'REILLY, AND GIULIO E. LANCIONI

A considerable amount of research has focused on developing effective[1] instructional approaches for students with autism spectrum disorder (ASD). A recent review of contemporary research in this area suggested that students with ASD will generally respond fairly positively to a highly structured and systematic instructional approach (Wong et al., 2015). This conclusion is consistent with evidence emerging since the 1960s that has repeatedly demonstrated the effectiveness of systematic and structured behavioral interventions for teaching children with ASD (Lovaas, 1987; Lovaas, Berberich, Perloff, & Schaeffer, 1966; Lovaas, Koegel, Simmons, & Long, 1973). Indeed, structured and systematic teaching approaches, based on behavior analytic principles and procedures (e.g., shaping, prompting, fading, discrimination training, reinforcement), have proven to be consistently effective

---

[1]Except where noted, the terms *effective* and *effectiveness* refer to interventions that produced positive outcomes regardless of whether that intervention was undertaken in highly controlled settings or more real-world contexts.

http://dx.doi.org/10.1037/0000126-013
Behavioral Interventions in Schools: Evidence-Based Positive Strategies, Second Edition, S. G. Little and A. Akin-Little (Editors)
Copyright © 2019 by the American Psychological Association. All rights reserved.

for ameliorating the behavioral deficits and excesses associated with ASD (Ahearn, MacDonald, Graff, & Dube, 2007; Lovaas, 2003; Snell & Brown, 2006). A good educational program for a student with ASD might therefore depend on the extent to which teachers effectively create structured learning opportunities and incorporate systematic, behaviorally based instructional procedures into those opportunities.

Unlike their typically developing peers, children with ASD often fail to acquire appropriate adaptive behavior (e.g., self-care, communication, social, play/recreation skills) through the normal course of development (Sturmey, 2014). Rodrigue, Morgan, and Geffken (1991), for example, found that school-aged children with ASD had significantly greater communication, socialization, and daily living skill deficits than similarly aged children with Down syndrome and younger typically developing children. Children with ASD are also more likely to develop emotional and behavioral problems, such as anxiety, aggressive behavior, self-injury, stereotypic mannerisms, disruptive acts, and extreme tantrums (Sturmey & Didden, 2014). Brereton, Tonge, and Einfeld (2006), for example, documented high levels of emotional and behavioral problems in children with ASD.

The nature and magnitude of the behavioral deficits and excesses associated with ASD suggest that such children may have considerable difficulty learning in the usual way. Fortunately, as mentioned before, learning outcomes for children with ASD can be enhanced by adopting a more structured and systematic instructional approach (Lovaas, 1987, 2003; Smith, McAdam, & Napolitano, 2007). In addition to the potential benefits of adopting a structured and systematic instructional approach, children with ASD might also benefit from receiving an increased number of structured learning opportunities (Lerman, Valentino, & LeBlanc, 2016). Frequent, repeated, and highly structured learning opportunities may enable the child to more quickly reach proficiency in skill areas where he or she is deficient. Indeed, the number and type of structured learning opportunities that a student receives appears to be one of the strongest predictors of teaching effectiveness (Greer & McDonough, 1999).

Many children with ASD have comorbid intellectual impairment (Matson & Shoemaker, 2009), which could help to explain why they tend to acquire skills more slowly than their typically developing peers (Rodrigue et al., 1991). Lack of social initiative might also account for delayed learning in some children with ASD. Lerman et al. (2016), for example, noted that children with ASD often appear to lack the motivation to initiate learning opportunities. More specifically, while a typically developing 3-or 4-year-old might ask a parent for the name of an unfamiliar object and thereafter use that name to label and request the object, children with ASD appear less likely to engage in this sort of information seeking (Young, Hudry, Trembath,

& Vivanti, 2016). Limited initiation of social interaction could result in a child receiving fewer learning opportunities. This, in turn, might result in delayed acquisition of important developmental milestones and skills. To compensate, it may be helpful for parents and teachers to create more frequent and more structured learning opportunities. In line with this logic, researchers have developed and evaluated several different ways of creating structured learning opportunities for children with ASD and other developmental disabilities (Mulligan, Guess, Holvoet, & Brown, 1980; Schreibman et al., 2015).

Discrete trial training (DTT) is one approach for creating structured learning opportunities. It is an approach that has been widely adopted in instructional programs and related behavioral interventions for children with ASD (Lerman et al., 2016; Lovaas, 2003; Smith, 2001; Sturmey, 2011). Sturmey (2011) noted that DTT is "probably the most commonly used method . . . to teach skills to students who have autism spectrum disorders" (p. 168).

This chapter focuses on the application of DTT in the education of students with ASD. We begin by delineating the components and characteristics of DTT. Next, we compare DTT with other approaches that have been used to create and structure learning opportunities for students with ASD. After this comparison, we provide an overview of how DTT has been applied and evaluated in educational programs for students with ASD and other developmental disabilities. The penultimate section reviews studies that aimed to evaluate procedures for training instructors to implement DTT with students with ASD. The chapter ends with a summary and conclusion.

COMPONENTS OF DTT

A basic principle underpinning behavior analysis and behavioral intervention is the concept of the three-term (reinforcement) contingency (Skinner, 1968). A *reinforcement contingency* refers to the relation between responses and environmental stimuli. At its most basic expression, a contingency of reinforcement is a relational unit that comprises three components: (a) the antecedent conditions or discriminative stimuli that set the occasion for a response, (b) the [operant] response(s) evoked by the antecedent conditions, and (c) the reinforcing consequence(s) produced by the response(s).

Contingencies of reinforcement comprising these three components are found naturally in daily life and are also often contrived or created by teachers for educational purposes (Skinner, 1982). A natural contingency of reinforcement can be illustrated by considering the relation between bright sunshine and moving into the shade. Specifically, when it's sunny outside (antecedent), moving into the shade or wearing sunglasses (responses) reduces the irritating glare and enables one to see better without squinting (reinforcing consequences). A contrived reinforcement contingency can be illustrated by considering a vocabulary-building activity that might occur in a classroom setting. To teach a child to label or name objects, for example, a teacher could present various objects (e.g., a watch, fork, stapler) and ask, *What's this?* (antecedent). Under these antecedent conditions, the child would be reinforced (e.g., with praise, attention, and/or access to preferred stimuli) for correctly naming each object. If the consequences are in fact reinforcing, then learning (i.e., an increase in correct object naming) should occur.

DTT is a behaviorally based teaching approach relying on the basic structure of the three-term contingency (Schreibman et al., 2015). In applying DTT, the teacher's role includes presenting discrete learning opportunities or trials, each of which consists of at least one antecedent, at least one response, and at least one response-contingent consequence. Presenting clear antecedents can "help the child understand when to respond" (Schreibman et al., 2015, p. 2417), and presenting reinforcing consequences increases the probability that similar responses will recur under similar antecedent conditions. Any such increase in responding provides evidence that learning has occurred (Schlinger, Blakely, Fillhard, & Poling, 1991). Table 12.1 provides examples of discrete trials that might arise naturally or be created by a teacher in school and classroom settings. The three-term contingencies outlined in Table 12.1 could become the context for teaching adaptive skills to children with ASD using a DTT approach.

However, merely creating discrete trials of the type illustrated in Table 12.1 will not necessarily ensure learning. Presenting a clear antecedent (i.e., showing the child an object and asking, *What's this?*) provides no guarantee that the correct response will be evoked. And if the desired response does not occur, then it obviously cannot be reinforced. To ensure learning within a DTT approach, teachers often need to add additional components to the three-term contingency, such as using an instructional cue and/or response prompt to ensure the correct response does in fact occur in the presence of the antecedent. For example, in teaching a child to wash the dishes after eating, it might not be enough to simply wait for the response to occur. Instead it might be necessary to provide an instructional cue (e.g., *Wash dishes*). In addition to instructional cues, the child may require prompting, such as modeling the desired responses and/or physically guiding the child to complete the task. Cueing and prompting might have to be used several times before the child would be expected to begin showing some independent proficiency in the task. In addition, the teacher would eventually want the child to initiate dish washing after finishing his or her meal, rather than only when instructed

TABLE 12.1
Examples of Discrete Trials for Teaching Adaptive Skills to Children With Autism Spectrum Disorder

Skill domain	Antecedent	Response	Consequence
Self-care	After the child uses the toilet, the teacher provides the instructional cue, *Wash hands*.	The child washes and dries his/her hands.	Child receives praise from the teacher and has clean hands.
Daily living	After lunch, the teacher points to the sink and says *Wash dishes*.	The child takes his/her plate and utensils to the sink and washes and dries the dishes.	Child receives praise from the teacher.
Communication	At lunchtime, the child is unable to open a package of his/her preferred snack. The teacher asks *What do you need?*	The child uses a communication device to ask for help.	Teacher provides the needed assistance, allowing the child to access the snack.
Social	Teacher approaches and looks at the child.	Child says *Hello*.	Teacher replies *Hello, nice to see you*.
Academic	Child shown two photos and asked to *Point to X*.	Child points to correct photograph.	Teacher praises the child (*Right, good job*).
Play	Child and peer on playground with soccer ball. Peer shows the child how to kick the ball and says *Now kick it to me*.	Child kicks ball to peer.	Peer gives praise (*Great kick*) and kicks the ball back to the child.

and/or prompted to do so. Thus, effective use of DTT not only occurs in the context of discrete trials but also often requires some degree of instructional cueing and prompting behavior.

To this end, there are many different types of instructional cues and prompts that a teacher could use. To prompt an object-labeling response, for example, a teacher might find it sufficient to model the correct form for the child to imitate (e.g., *Say watch* or *Say fork*). To prompt other responses (e.g., producing a manual sign, sorting objects by shape or color, kicking a soccer ball, playing with toys, washing one's hands, reading a poem, drawing an object), teachers have a menu of other types of cues and prompts that they could draw on, such as telling the child what to do or even physically assisting the child to make the response. Whatever type of cue or prompt is used, it is important that the prompt is effective in ensuring the response occurs so that it can then be reinforced in the presence of the (natural) antecedent.

Although cueing and prompting might be necessary during the initial stages of DTT, it is important for the teacher to work toward fading out the need for any instructional cueing and prompting. The aim of fading is to transfer control of the child's responses from the cue and/or prompt (e.g., *Wash dishes*) to the natural antecedent (i.e., having finished the meal). Fortunately, research in applied behavior analysis has led to the development of a number of systematic instructional procedures (e.g., most-to-least prompting, least-to-most prompting, graduated guidance, stimulus fading, time delay) that have been successfully used to both cue/prompt behavior as well as fade out the need for cueing and prompting (Lovaas, 2003; Snell & Brown, 2006). These procedures have been used successfully to transfer control of responding from cue and prompts to more natural antecedents (Ahearn et al., 2007; Duker, Didden, & Sigafoos, 2004). Incorporating these types of systematic instructional procedures into the basic three-term contingency is often essential to the effectiveness of DTT.

In summary, a discrete trial is a sequence that consists of an environmental antecedent, a response, and a consequence. DTT involves presenting discrete trials in ways that are intended to maximize the probability of learning. Learning is maximized by presenting frequent and repeated learning trials or opportunities and incorporating systematic instructional procedures into those trials. Systematic instructional procedures are used to ensure the desired response or responses occur in the presence of the antecedent and are followed by reinforcing consequences.

CHARACTERISTICS OF DTT

In addition to the integration of systematic instructional procedures with discrete trials based on the three-term contingency (i.e., antecedent–response–consequence), DTT is characterized by a number of other distinct features. Koegel, Koegel, Koegel, and Vernon (2014) classified the distinguishing features or characteristics of DTT in terms of the types of (a) stimulus items, (b) interactions, (c) environments, (d) responses, and (e) reinforcements that are generally associated with DTT. In terms of stimulus items, DTT typically focuses on teaching the child to respond to a specific/precise antecedent/discriminative stimulus. For example, the teacher might identify a number of motor actions that he or she wants the child to imitate (e.g., raise arm, clap hands, touch nose) and then begin intervention by focusing on training only one response at a time (e.g., raise arm). That is, training is generally restricted to one response or stimulus at a time. Training begins with this first response or stimulus and new responses or stimuli are taught only after the child has achieved mastery on the initial target. With respect to interaction, the discrete trials created in a DTT approach are generally always teacher initiated. For example, the teacher might initiate an imitation training trial by first gaining the child's attention (e.g., saying *Look at me*) and then modeling a motor action (e.g., raising an arm) while instructing the child, *Do this?* In terms of the environment, DTT is generally conducted in structured, distraction-free settings and also usually in a one-to-one (teacher–student) grouping. For example, imitation training might be conducted with the teacher and child seated at a table in a quiet corner of the classroom. With respect to response features, Koegel et al. (2014) pointed out that in DTT, it is usually the teacher who determines what responses will be considered correct, and only those responses would be reinforced. Finally, the reinforcers used in DTT are selected for their potency and often have no functional relation to the child's response. Correct imitative responses might be reinforced by giving the child a preferred edible, for example.

Although the features Koegel et al. (2014) delineated do seem to reflect how DTT is most typically implemented (Lovaas, 2003; Schreibman et al., 2015), effective use of this teaching approach does not necessarily require strict adherence to all of the characteristics they described. Lerman et al. (2016), for example, reviewed evidence related to the issue of focusing on a single instructional target versus focusing on training several targets concurrently. With the former (i.e., sequential task) approach, the teacher might first aim to teach the child to imitate a single motor action (e.g., raising an arm). With the latter (task interspersal) approach, training focuses on concurrently teaching several responses (e.g., raise arm, clap hands, touch nose). Evidence has suggested that learning is often more rapid when tasks are interspersed. One possible reason for the superiority of task interspersal is that it requires the child to discriminate among antecedents and response forms from the beginning of intervention. With a sequential approach, in contrast, the child will likely acquire a history of reinforcement for making a single response form. It is therefore not surprising that this previously reinforced form is likely to persist even when a new, yet similar antecedent is later presented. As we point out in the next two sections, the frequency or density of training trials and the types and degree of structure imposed by the teacher are other features that might also be varied without diminishing the effectiveness of DTT.

MASSED, DISTRIBUTED, AND SPACED TRIAL TRAINING

Mulligan et al. (1980) distinguished between three different configurations or schedules for sequencing the delivery of discrete training trials; that is, massed, distributed, and spaced trial sequencing. Massed trial sequencing involves training sessions that consist of presenting a block of discrete trials, all of which focus on training the same single response form or skill. For example, the teacher might present 10 opportunities for the child to learn a receptive language skill, such as pointing to the photograph named by the teacher from an array of two photographs. Each trial or opportunity would involve the teacher presenting two photographs and instructing the student to *Point to X*. After this antecedent, the child would have a set amount of time (e.g., 5 seconds) to respond by pointing to the correct photograph. If the child did not point to the correct photograph within 5 seconds, then the teacher would prompt a correct response. Reinforcement of the correct response completes each trial. Then, after a brief intertrial interval of perhaps 5 to 10 seconds, the next trial is presented until the entire block of 10 trials has been completed.

With a distributed trial format, in contrast, instruction occurs on two or more skills within a single teaching session. For example, the teacher might alternate between receptive language training trials (i.e., pointing to the object named by the teacher) and expressive language training trials (e.g., naming the object that the teacher points to). A teaching session using this format might thus consist of alternating between receptive and expressive language training trials until 10 trials of each type had been conducted.

In a spaced trial format, the teacher builds in longer intervals (i.e., pauses) between trials. For example, the child might be taught to request access to preferred toys using manual signs during a 30-minute play session. After each correct request, the child would be allowed to play with the requested toy for a reasonable period of time (e.g., 5 minutes) before the next training trial is conducted. With this format, the teacher could provide 10 discrete training trials on the requesting skill within a 45-minute session.

DTT is often associated with the massed trial training format (Koegel et al., 2014; Lovaas, 1977, 2003; Schreibman et al., 2015). This format is often considered to be the most efficient configuration for promoting rapid skill acquisition (Reichle & Sigafoos, 1991). A massed trial format might thus be indicated for use at the beginning stages of intervention and perhaps especially for children with more significant cognitive impairment and adaptive behavior deficits (Reichle & Sigafoos, 1991). Distributed trial formats, in contrast, might be indicated when teaching skills are functionally related, such as receptively identifying and expressively naming the same set of objects. Acquisition of functionally related skills might be facilitated by a distributed trial format because of the possibility that this format would perhaps allow for desirable carryover effects to have a greater influence than massed trial formats (Hains & Baer, 1989). That is, the teaching that occurs on one of the targeted skills in a distributed trial format might facilitate acquisition of the other skills that are also being taught in the training sequence. Spaced trial formats might also be considered of potential value when the natural consequence requires some time to "consume" and/or is likely to produce satiation. Spaced trial formats might also be indicated for children with attention or compliance issues.

Each of these three trial configurations has potential indications (Mulligan et al., 1980), and comparison studies have suggested they may be equally effective for teaching new skills. Mulligan, Lacy, and Guess (1982), for example, compared massed, distributed, and spaced trial sequencing for teaching 11 students with severe disabilities. The authors found no major differences across the three conditions in terms of acquisition curves, although the mean level of performance was higher under the distributed versus the massed trial format.

DTT AND MORE NATURALISTIC TRAINING APPROACHES

Schreibman et al. (2015) distinguished between two general approaches for providing systematic instruction to children with ASD—that is, DTT versus naturalistic developmental behavioral interventions. In line with the distinguishing features of DTT outlined by Koegel et al. (2014), Schreibman et al. (2015) also pointed out that DTT has historically focused on using a massed-trial format to teaching isolated skills (e.g., imitating a word or sound) until that skill was mastered and only then teaching the child to use that skill functionally (e.g., using the acquired words to make requests; Lovaas, 1977). Schreibman et al. (2015) argued that although the more highly structured DTT approach has demonstrated effectiveness for promoting skill acquisition, concerns have emerged regarding the extent to which skills acquired under DTT were likely to generalize across settings, people, and materials. An additional concern was the possibility that highly structured training would inadvertently lead to a lack of spontaneity due to establishing overly precise stimulus control and prompt dependency (Halle, 1987). For example, instruction in a highly structured setting using very precise antecedent cues may lead to a situation in which the child learns to respond only in that setting and only to those same cues.

A further concern is that the instructional demands associated with DTT might evoke problem behavior, such as tantrums and aggression (Koegel,

Koegel, & Surratt, 1992). For example, Sigafoos et al. (2006) reported some preliminary evidence to support this concern. Specifically, they compared the effects of using a DTT approach versus a more naturalistic instruction arrangement on the frequency of self-injury, correct responding, and mood (i.e., happy, sad) in a 12-year-old boy with ASD. The results showed that DTT evoked more self-injury and was associated with less positive mood ratings. Correct responding was also lower in the DTT condition. The authors tentatively suggested that these results might have stemmed from the more demanding instructional context associated with DTT. This suggestion was based on a hypothesis that escape from task demands appeared to be maintaining the child's self-injury.

Compared with DTT, naturalistic behavioral interventions rely more heavily on child-initiated learning opportunities (Koegel et al., 2014; Schreibman et al., 2015). In addition, instruction occurs in the context of naturally arising opportunities within typical routines, rather than repeatedly presenting highly structured trials during designated teaching sessions. For example, a teacher might wait for a child to reach for a toy and then use this opportunity to enhance the child's requesting skills, such as by shaping the reach into a more sophisticated communicative gesture. Once the request had been made, access to the toy constituted natural reinforcement.

Delprato (2001) reviewed 10 studies comparing DTT with more naturalistic interventions for teaching language skills to children with ASD. The results of this review suggested that naturalistic interventions might be a more effective approach than DTT "for developing a significant range of language responses in young children with autism" (Delprato, 2001, p. 323). However, the effectiveness of naturalistic approaches may depend to some extent on the frequency with which a child initiates and the extent to which natural consequences function as effective types of reinforcement.

Naturalistic behavioral interventions and DTT differ in terms of the amount of structure and reliance on child-initiated versus teacher-initiated opportunities, but they are both based on the three-term contingency (Schreibman et al., 2015). In addition, both also make use of systematic instructional procedures based on behavior analytic principles. In light of these shared characteristics, DTT and more naturalistic applications of behaviorally based teaching could be viewed in terms of a continuum of structure and teacher directedness. Viewed in this way, DTT and more naturalistic approaches are neither incompatible nor mutually exclusive. Delprato (2001) noted that DTT and naturalistic interventions are complimentary, with DTT used to promote acquisition and naturalistic approaches used to program for generalization and maintenance. As with massed, distributed, and spaced trial sequencing, it is possible that the degree of structure needed to ensure acquisition and promote generalization and maintenance might depend on the characteristics of the child, the nature of the target skills, and the context(s) of instruction. In addition, some combination of DTT and more naturalistic approaches might be configured that would complement these two related approaches. Along these lines, Geiger et al. (2012) found that DTT could be effectively implemented in a more naturalistic play activity. In fact, DTT conducted in a more naturalistic context proved equally effective to DTT used in a more traditional one-to-one and distraction-free context.

APPLICATION AND EVALUATION OF DTT IN EDUCATIONAL SETTINGS

DTT has been used in educational settings to (a) teach new skills, (b) increase the fluency/accuracy of responding, and (c) establish stimulus control over responding (Nopprapun & Holloway, 2014; Smith, 2001). Skills taught using DTT include (a) motor and vocal imitation, (b) receptive and expressive language, (c) self-care, (d) socialization, (e) academic, and (f) play/recreation skills (Duker et al., 2004; Geiger et al., 2012; Lerman et al., 2016; Lovaas, 2003; Schreibman et al., 2015; Smith, 2001). Although DTT has demonstrated efficacy for teaching students with ASD (Lerman et al., 2016; Lovaas, 1987; Smith, 2001), most of this research has occurred under highly structured, one-to-one teaching arrangements. Such structured conditions might be optimal for implementing DTT but may be difficult to implement in some classroom settings.

Researchers have distinguished between efficacy and effectiveness research (Singal, Higgins, & Waljee, 2014). *Efficacy* refers to the extent to which an intervention produces positive outcomes when it is applied and evaluated under ideal and controlled circumstances, such as in a research study. *Effectiveness*, in contrast, refers to the extent to which an intervention produces positive outcomes when it is applied and evaluated under real-world conditions, such as when implemented by teachers in the classroom.

As noted before, there is considerable evidence supporting the efficacy of DTT (Lerman et al., 2016; Lovaas, 1987; Smith, 2001). There is also evidence suggesting its effectiveness. Downs, Downs, Johansen, and Fossum (2007), for example, evaluated the effectiveness of DTT when applied under the real-world conditions of public preschool programs. The researchers recruited 12 (32–63-month-old) children with developmental disabilities from a preschool program in a rural area of Washington state.

The children were randomly assigned to an experimental or control group. The experimental group received one-to-one DTT in a quiet, distraction-free setting. DTT was delivered by preschool staff, caregivers, and university students, and it focused on teaching a range of academic and adaptive behaviors (e.g., receptive and expressive language, social skills, identifying letters and numbers, counting, imitation, following directions, drawing and cutting). The children received from 30 to 42 hours of DTT over a 27-week period. In contrast, children in the control group received the usual preschool program, which relied on modeling and incidental teaching procedures. The usual preschool program was described as child centered and focused on enhancing the children's social and emotional development. To evaluate the effects of DTT compared with treatment-as-usual, a variety of standardized measures were collected pre- and postintervention, including measures of cognitive and language functioning, adaptive behavior, and emotional understanding. The results indicated that children receiving DTT showed significantly greater gains in several areas of adaptive behavior functioning (i.e., communication, daily living skills, and socialization) compared with children in the control group. However, no differences between groups were noted with respect to cognitive functioning (i.e., IQ scores). Overall, the results of this study demonstrate the feasibility of implementing DTT in the real-world preschool context, although outside (i.e., university students) trainers were added to this context. Still, the positive outcomes from this study suggest that with some additional personnel and some structured one-to-one time (about 90 minutes per week of one-to-one time for each child), it may be feasible and practical to apply DTT as part of an early intervention program for preschool children with ASD.

With respect to the need for one-to-one training, Leaf et al. (2013) compared the effectiveness of DTT when used in a group versus a one-to-one format. The study involved six 4-year-old children with ASD. The children received DTT in a clinical setting with sessions conducted by research personnel. Training focused on teaching 12 different skills, with half the skills assigned to the group format and the other half assigned to the one-to-one format. Group training involved the researcher teaching three children at a time, with each child receiving 10 to 20 discrete trials during 30- to 45-minute sessions. One-to-one training involved the researcher teaching just one child, who received 10 to 20 teaching trials per session. The results revealed that the group and one-to-one formats were equally effective in promoting learning. An interesting potential benefit of group instruction was that this format appeared to have resulted in some incidental observational learning. Overall, the results of this study suggest that DTT can be effective when applied in a group-based teaching format.

TRAINING INSTRUCTORS TO USE DTT

Teachers and other instructional personnel may require explicit training to be able to successfully implement DTT. Downs et al.'s (2007) results suggested that preschool personnel could be trained to implement DTT effectively after receiving 15 to 20 hours of didactic instruction on five specific steps: (a) presenting the cue, (b) observing the child's response, (c) prompting correct responses, (d) reinforcing correct responses, and (e) pausing before implementing the next trial. Their training program included modeling these steps and giving trainees the opportunity to practice implementing the steps while receiving feedback.

Downs and Downs (2013) used similar procedures in teaching eight undergraduate students to implement DTT. The 8-hour training program included didactic instruction, modeling, and practice with corrective feedback. Results showed that knowledge and competency increased after training, although not always to mastery levels. A major strength of the study was that the trained undergraduates were able to implement DTT with acceptable fidelity with 3- to 5-year-old children with ASD. The results of this study are encouraging in suggesting that a relatively brief training program may be sufficient for training personnel to implement DTT.

Another resource that schools might be able to draw on to implement DTT are peers. Radley, Dart, Furlow, and Ness (2015), for example, investigated the feasibility of having typically developing students implement DTT with their peers with ASD. The study involved two children with ASD and six typically developing peers. The children with ASD were ages 6 and 7, and the peers were 10 to 11 years old. All of these students attended the same public school. The children with ASD were placed in self-contained classrooms in the school, and this is also where the peers implemented DTT sessions with the children with ASD. DTT focused on teaching matching and receptive language skills to the two children with ASD. To achieve these objectives, peers were taught to implement an eight-step protocol (e.g., gaining child's attention, presenting a clear cue to initiate a trial, reinforcing correct responses). Training peers to implement this protocol involved providing them with written instructions, reviewing and discussing the instructions, watching how the protocol was to be implemented (i.e., modeling), and practice implementing the protocol. Results suggested that this training program was effective in teaching the peers how to implement the DTT protocol with fidelity. In addition, their use of DTT resulted in mastery of the targeted skills by the children with ASD. The peers also appeared to enjoy serving as DTT instructors. The authors noted that enlisting peers as instructors may eliminate one potential barrier (i.e., lack of personnel) to the use of DTT in schools.

SUMMARY AND CONCLUSION

DTT is a widely used instructional approach for students with ASD. It is an approach grounded in behavior analytic principles and procedures. DTT has been successfully used to teach a range of adaptive behaviors and academic skills to children with ASD. It is characterized by repeated presentation of structured learning trials based on the basic three-term contingency (i.e., antecedent-response-consequence). DTT sessions are often focused on teaching a single, specific skill to mastery with repeated learning trials conducted at a fast pace in a one-to-one, distraction-free context. However, DTT has also been successfully applied in more natural contexts, with interspersed skills targets, and in a small-group rather than one-to-one format. There is sufficient evidence to support the efficacy of DTT as an instructional approach for students with ASD. Emerging evidence suggests that DTT is practical and feasible for use in typical classroom environments, although school personnel may need explicit training to implement DTT with fidelity. Overall, DTT can be classified as a well-established, evidence-based approach for teaching students with ASD.

REFERENCES

Ahearn, W. H., MacDonald, R., Graff, R. B., & Dube, W. V. (2007). Behavior analytic teaching procedures: Basic principles, empirically derived practices. In P. Sturmey & A. Fitzer (Eds.), *Autism spectrum disorders: Applied behavior analysis, evidence, and practice* (pp. 31–83). Austin, TX: PRO-ED.

Brereton, A. V., Tonge, B. J., & Einfeld, S. L. (2006). Psychopathology in children and adolescents with autism compared to young people with intellectual disability. *Journal of Autism and Developmental Disorders, 36*, 863–870. http://dx.doi.org/10.1007/s10803-006-0125-y

Delprato, D. J. (2001). Comparisons of discrete-trial and normalized behavioral language intervention for young children with autism. *Journal of Autism and Developmental Disorders, 31*, 315–325. http://dx.doi.org/10.1023/A:1010747303957

Downs, A., & Downs, R. C. (2013). Training new instructors to implement discrete trial teaching strategies with children with autism in a community-based intervention program. *Focus on Autism and Other Developmental Disabilities, 28*, 212–221. http://dx.doi.org/10.1177/1088357612465120

Downs, A., Downs, R. C., Johansen, M., & Fossum, M. (2007). Using discrete trial teaching within a public preschool program to facilitate skill development in students with developmental disabilities. *Education & Treatment of Children, 30*, 1–27. http://dx.doi.org/10.1353/etc.2007.0015

Duker, P., Didden, R., & Sigafoos, J. (2004). *One-to-one training: Instructional procedures for learners with developmental disabilities.* Austin, TX: PRO-ED.

Geiger, K. B., Carr, J. E., Leblanc, L. A., Hanney, N. M., Polick, A. S., & Heinicke, M. R. (2012). Teaching receptive discriminations to children with autism: A comparison of traditional and embedded discrete trial teaching. *Behavior Analysis in Practice, 5,* 49–59. http://dx.doi.org/10.1007/BF03391823

Greer, R. D., & McDonough, S. H. (1999). Is the learn unit a fundamental measure of pedagogy? *The Behavior Analyst, 22,* 5–16. http://dx.doi.org/10.1007/BF03391973

Hains, A. H., & Baer, D. M. (1989). Interaction effects in multielement designs: Inevitable, desirable, and ignorable. *Journal of Applied Behavior Analysis, 22,* 57–69. http://dx.doi.org/10.1901/jaba.1989.22-57

Halle, J. W. (1987). Teaching language in the natural environment: An analysis of spontaneity. *Journal of the Association for Persons with Severe Handicaps, 12,* 28–37. http://dx.doi.org/10.1177/154079698701200105

Koegel, L. K., Koegel, B. L., Koegel, R. L., & Vernon, T. W. (2014). Pivotal response treatment. In J. K. Luiselli (Ed.), *Children and youth with autism spectrum disorder (ASD): Recent advances and innovations in assessment, education, and intervention* (pp. 134–144). New York, NY: Oxford University Press. http://dx.doi.org/10.1093/med:psych/9780199941575.003.0009

Koegel, R. L., Koegel, L. K., & Surratt, A. (1992). Language intervention and disruptive behavior in preschool children with autism. *Journal of Autism and Developmental Disorders, 22,* 141–153. http://dx.doi.org/10.1007/BF01058147

Leaf, J. B., Tsuji, K. H., Lentell, A. E., Dale, S. E., Kassardjian, A., Taubman, M., . . . Oppenheim-Leaf, M. L. (2013). A comparison of discrete-trial teaching implemented in a one-to-one instructional format and in a group instructional format. *Behavioral Interventions, 28,* 82–106. http://dx.doi.org/10.1002/bin.1357

Lerman, D. C., Valentino, A. L., & LeBlanc, L. A. (2016). Discrete trial training. In R. Lang, T. B. Hancock, & N. N. Singh (Eds.), *Early intervention for young children with autism spectrum disorder* (pp. 47–83). New York, NY: Springer.

Lovaas, O. I. (1977). *The autistic child: Language development through behavior modification.* New York, NY: Irvington.

Lovaas, O. I. (1987). Behavioral treatment and normal educational and intellectual functioning in young autistic children. *Journal of Consulting and Clinical Psychology, 55,* 3–9. http://dx.doi.org/10.1037/0022-006X.55.1.3

Lovaas, O. I. (2003). *Teaching individuals with developmental delay: Basic intervention techniques.* Austin, TX: PRO-ED.

Lovaas, O. I., Berberich, J. P., Perloff, B. F., & Schaeffer, B. (1966). Acquisition of imitative speech by schizophrenic children. *Science, 151,* 705–707. http://dx.doi.org/10.1126/science.151.3711.705

Lovaas, O. I., Koegel, R., Simmons, J. Q., & Long, J. S. (1973). Some generalization and follow-up measures on autistic children in behavior therapy. *Journal of Applied Behavior Analysis, 6,* 131–165.

Matson, J. L., & Shoemaker, M. (2009). Intellectual disability and its relationship to autism spectrum disorders. *Research in Developmental Disabilities, 30*, 1107–1114. http://dx.doi.org/10.1016/j.ridd.2009.06.003

Mulligan, M., Guess, D., Holvoet, J., & Brown, F. (1980). The individualized curriculum sequencing model (I): Implications for research on massed, distributed, or spaced trial training. *The Journal of the Association for Persons with Severe Handicaps, 5*, 325–336.

Mulligan, M., Lacy, L., & Guess, D. (1982). Effects of massed, distributed, and spaced trial sequencing on severe handicapped students' performance. *The Journal of the Association for Persons with Severe Handicaps, 7*, 48–61.

Nopprapun, M., & Holloway, J. (2014). A comparison of fluency training and discrete trial instruction to teach letter sounds to children with ASD: Acquisition and learning outcomes. *Research in Autism Spectrum Disorders, 8*, 788–802. http://dx.doi.org/10.1016/j.rasd.2014.03.015

Radley, K. C., Dart, E. H., Furlow, C. M., & Ness, E. J. (2015). Peer-mediated discrete trial training within a school setting. *Research in Autism Spectrum Disorders, 9*, 53–67. http://dx.doi.org/10.1016/j.rasd.2014.10.001

Reichle, J., & Sigafoos, J. (1991). Bringing communicative behavior under the control of appropriate stimuli. In J. Reichle, J. York, & J. Sigafoos (Eds.), *Implementing augmentative and alternative communication: Strategies for learners with severe disabilities* (pp. 193–213). Baltimore, MD: Paul H. Brookes.

Rodrigue, J. R., Morgan, S. B., & Geffken, G. R. (1991). A comparative evaluation of adaptive behavior in children and adolescents with autism, Down syndrome, and normal development. *Journal of Autism and Developmental Disorders, 21*, 187–196. http://dx.doi.org/10.1007/BF02284759

Schlinger, H. D., Jr., Blakely, E., Fillhard, J., & Poling, A. (1991). Defining terms in behavior analysis: Reinforcer and discriminative stimulus. *Analysis of Verbal Behavior, 9*, 153–161. http://dx.doi.org/10.1007/BF03392869

Schreibman, L., Dawson, G., Stahmer, A. C., Landa, R., Rogers, S. J., McGee, G. G., . . . Halladay, A. (2015). Naturalistic developmental behavioral interventions: Empirically validated treatments for autism spectrum disorder. *Journal of Autism and Developmental Disorders, 45*, 2411–2428. http://dx.doi.org/10.1007/s10803-015-2407-8

Sigafoos, J., O'Reilly, M., Ma, C. H., Edrisinha, C., Cannella, H., & Lancioni, G. E. (2006). Effects of embedded instruction versus discrete-trial training on self-injury, correct responding, and mood in a child with autism. *Journal of Intellectual & Developmental Disability, 31*, 196–203. http://dx.doi.org/10.1080/13668250600999160

Singal, A. G., Higgins, P. D. R., & Waljee, A. K. (2014). A primer on effectiveness and efficacy trials. *Clinical and Translational Gastroenterology, 5*, e45. http://dx.doi.org/10.1038/ctg.2013.13

Skinner, B. F. (1968). *The technology of teaching*. New York, NY: Appleton-Century-Crofts.

Skinner, B. F. (1982). Contrived reinforcement. *The Behavior Analyst, 5*, 3–8. http://dx.doi.org/10.1007/BF03393135

Smith, T. (2001). Discrete trial training in the treatment of autism. *Focus on Autism and Other Developmental Disabilities, 16*, 86–92. http://dx.doi.org/10.1177/108835760101600204

Smith, T., McAdam, D., & Napolitano, D. (2007). Autism and applied behavior analysis. In P. Sturmey & A. Fitzer (Eds.), *Autism spectrum disorders: Applied behavior analysis, evidence, and practice* (pp. 1–29). Austin, TX: PRO-ED.

Snell, M. E., & Brown, F. (2006). *Instruction of students with severe disabilities* (6th ed.). Upper Saddle River, NJ: Pearson.

Sturmey, P. (2011). Discrete trial teaching. In J. K. Luiselli (Ed.), *Teaching and behavior support for children and adults with autism spectrum disorder* (pp. 167–172). New York, NY: Oxford University Press.

Sturmey, P. (2014). Adaptive behavior. In P. Sturmey & R. Didden (Eds.), *Evidence-based practice and intellectual disability* (pp. 29–61). Chichester, England: Wiley. http://dx.doi.org/10.1002/9781118326077.ch2

Sturmey, P., & Didden, R. (Eds.). (2014). *Evidence-based practice and intellectual disability*. Chichester, England: Wiley. http://dx.doi.org/10.1002/9781118326077

Wong, C., Odom, S. L., Hume, K. A., Cox, A. W., Fettig, A., Kucharczyk, S., . . . Schultz, T. R. (2015). Evidence-based practices for children, youth, and young adults with autism spectrum disorder: A comprehensive review. *Journal of Autism and Developmental Disorders, 45*, 1951–1966. http://dx.doi.org/10.1007/s10803-014-2351-z

Young, N., Hudry, K., Trembath, D., & Vivanti, G. (2016). Children with autism show reduced information seeking when learning new tasks. *American Journal on Intellectual and Developmental Disabilities, 121*, 65–73. http://dx.doi.org/10.1352/1944-7558-121.1.65

13

CLASSROOM PIVOTAL RESPONSE TEACHING

RIANNE VERSCHUUR, BIBI HUSKENS, AND LAURIE McLAY

Providing educational services to children with autism spectrum disorder (ASD) poses a challenge to educators. Although an increasing number of evidence-based practices (EBPs) have been developed for this population (e.g., Odom, Collet-Klingenberg, Rogers, & Hatton, 2010; Wong et al., 2015), few have been systematically implemented in school settings (Kasari & Smith, 2013; Stahmer, Rieth, et al., 2015; Stahmer, Suhrheinrich, Reed, & Schreibman, 2012). Barriers to the implementation of EBPs in school settings include the complexity of the intervention procedures, a poor fit between intervention procedures and the classroom context, and limited evidence of the effectiveness of EBPs in school settings (Kasari & Smith, 2013; Stahmer, Rieth, et al., 2015; Stahmer, Suhrheinrich, et al., 2012; Suhrheinrich et al., 2013).

For example, several EBIs for children with ASD are typically designed for implementation during one-to-one training. This contrasts with group instructional methods commonly used in classrooms. To implement EBIs in

---

http://dx.doi.org/10.1037/0000126-014
Behavioral Interventions in Schools: Evidence-Based Positive Strategies, Second Edition, S. G. Little and A. Akin-Little (Editors)
Copyright © 2019 by the American Psychological Association. All rights reserved.

the classroom setting, teachers are often required to adapt and combine EBPs to meet the specific needs of the children. It is unclear whether adapted interventions are as effective as the traditional method of delivering these interventions (Stahmer et al., 2012). Pivotal response treatment (PRT) provides an example of an intervention that has been adapted for classroom settings. During the last decade, collaboration between researchers and special education has resulted in the development of classroom pivotal response teaching (CPRT; Stahmer, Suhrheinrich, Reed, Schreibman, & Bolduc, 2011; Stahmer, Suhrheinrich, & Rieth, 2016). This chapter provides readers with information regarding the theoretical underpinnings and historical background of CPRT, the components of CPRT, and the implementation of this approach in schools. One case vignette is presented to illustrate how teachers can use CPRT to target communication, play, social, and academic skills in children with ASD.

FOUNDATIONS OF CPRT

CPRT is a form of PRT that has been adapted for classroom settings. PRT is an evidence-based, naturalistic behavioral intervention model that uses motivational techniques to teach pivotal behaviors to children with ASD to achieve collateral improvements in their functioning (Koegel, Ashbaugh, & Koegel, 2016). PRT is designed to be implemented in natural environments, during everyday activities. Family involvement is therefore essential. PRT is derived from the principles of applied behavior analysis (ABA). ABA is the science that systematically applies the principles of learning to produce socially significant changes in behavior (Cooper, Heron, & Heward, 2013). ABA is based on the assumption that behavior is determined by antecedent stimuli (i.e., events that precede a behavior, including setting events) and consequent stimuli (i.e., events that follow a behavior). A *stimulus* is an object, event, or condition that affects an organism. Systematic analysis and manipulation of antecedent and consequent stimuli can result in behavior change. By presenting specific consequences after a behavior, the likelihood of the behavior occurring again in the future increases or decreases depending on the type of consequence that follows the behavior (Cooper et al., 2013). This is called *operant conditioning*. Consequences that lead to an increase in behavior are referred to as *reinforcement*, and consequences that result in a decrease in behavior are referred to as *punishment*. The antecedent-behavior-consequence sequence is referred to as the *three-term contingency* or *ABC pattern of behavior* (Cooper et al., 2013).

Since the 1960s, a wide range of interventions have been developed on the basis of the principles of ABA to teach adaptive skills to children with

ASD and to reduce maladaptive behaviors, for example, discrete trial teaching (DTT), functional communication training, incidental teaching, picture exchange communication system (PECS), and PRT (Vismara & Rogers, 2010). A large body of research has demonstrated the effectiveness of these interventions (e.g., Reichow, 2012; Smith & Iadarola, 2015; Virués-Ortega, 2010). Early behavioral interventions generally involved teaching of target behaviors in a structured and controlled one-to-one setting to minimize distractions (Duker, Didden, & Sigafoos, 2004). Therapists selected teaching materials and initiated teaching opportunities. For example, the therapist asks the child, "What is it?" while showing a picture of a dog (i.e., stimulus). If the child answers "dog" (i.e., response), the teacher says, "Good job, that's a dog" and gives the child access to a favorite toy (i.e., reinforcement). These practice opportunities were frequently repeated. These early interventions, sometimes referred to as DTT, often resulted in substantial improvements in the language, social, and cognitive skills of children with ASD as well as reductions in their maladaptive behavior (e.g., Lovaas, 1987); however, these approaches also had potential disadvantages. First, these interventions were time-consuming to implement and thus costly (Vismara & Rogers, 2010). Second, as teaching did not take place in the natural environment, generalized use of target behaviors often did not occur without additional training (Stokes & Baer, 1977). Finally, because learning opportunities were teacher initiated, at times teaching took place without the child being motivated to engage in these interactions (Koegel et al., 2016). To address these limitations, naturalistic interventions have been developed. Naturalistic interventions are more loosely structured and conducted in a variety of natural settings (e.g., home, classroom, playground). Opportunities are child initiated, and reinforcement is natural (i.e., reinforcement is naturally related to the target response; Delprato, 2001). For example, the therapist is holding a ball that is desired by the child (i.e., stimulus). If the child asks for the ball (i.e., response), the teacher gives the ball to child (i.e., reinforcement). PRT is an example of a naturalistic intervention model.

The main purpose of PRT is to teach pivotal behaviors to children with ASD to achieve collateral improvements in their functioning (Koegel et al., 2016). *Pivotal* behaviors are behaviors that, when targeted, lead to improvements in untargeted behaviors. Research has indicated that motivation to respond, initiations, responding to multiple cues (i.e., the ability to pay attention and respond appropriately to several features of objects or situations), and self-management are pivotal behaviors. There is preliminary evidence to suggest that empathy might also be a pivotal behavior (e.g., Koegel et al., 2016). Motivation appears to be the most important pivotal behavior (Koegel & Koegel, 2012). Many children with ASD demonstrate a lack of motivation to respond and have difficulties completing tasks or learning new skills. Parents, siblings, teachers, and peers often automatically help the struggling child or do not reinforce the child after a reasonable attempt. As a result, children with ASD do not learn that there is a relationship between their response and the reinforcement that follows their response. This can lead children to develop learned helplessness, which further weakens their motivation to respond and thus reduces the likelihood that they will try to demonstrate the skill in a future situation (Koegel et al., 2016). To overcome learned helplessness, it is important to increase children's motivation to respond and strengthen the relationship between a response and reinforcement (e.g., Koegel & Koegel, 2006). In the 1980s, research focused on techniques to increase the motivation of children with ASD. These techniques included (a) incorporating child choice, (b) presenting clear opportunities, (c) varying tasks, (d) interspersing maintenance and acquisition tasks, (e) using natural reinforcement, and (f) reinforcing attempts at target behaviors (Koegel et al., 2016). Table 13.1 presents an example of each motivational technique as used by therapists during one-to-one sessions. Research has indicated that each motivational

TABLE 13.1
Examples of Motivational Techniques

Technique	Example
Incorporating child choice	One of the child's favorite activities is drawing. To practice requesting objects, the therapist and child are going to draw. The child may choose the color of the page. The therapist then holds up two boxes and states, "I have pencils and crayons" to provide the child with a choice and an opportunity to request.
Presenting clear opportunities	During a board game the therapist holds the dice when it is the child's turn. If the child does not ask for the dice, the therapist helps the child by asking, "What could you ask me?"
Varying tasks	The child is learning to name colors. While playing with his favorite trains, the therapist varies opportunities for requesting different colored trains with other opportunities for communication.
Interspersing maintenance and acquisition tasks	A child is good at requesting objects but finds it difficult to ask for help. During a baking activity the therapist presents her with many opportunities to request materials and with a few opportunities to request help.
Natural reinforcement	The therapist helps the child to open his lunchbox immediately after he asks, "Can you help?"
Reinforcement of attempts	The child says, "tick-oh," and the therapist tickles the child, in spite of the fact that his pronunciation of *tickle* was not perfect.

technique resulted in increased responsiveness to social and environmental stimuli (Dunlap & Koegel, 1980; Koegel, Dyer, & Bell, 1987; Koegel, O'Dell, & Dunlap, 1988; Koegel & Williams, 1980). Since the 1990s, the combination of these motivational techniques is referred to as PRT.

A large number of studies have investigated the effectiveness of PRT. For example, a systematic review analyzed intervention studies to evaluate the evidence base of PRT for improving the skills of children with ASD (Verschuur, Didden, Lang, Sigafoos, & Huskens, 2014). A systematic search identified 43 intervention studies published between 1987 and 2013. On the basis of these studies, it was concluded that PRT resulted in increases in initiations and generalized improvements in language, communication, play, affect, and maladaptive behaviors (Verschuur et al., 2014). A recent randomized controlled trial also showed that PRT led to greater improvements in mean length of utterance and pragmatic language skills than a more structured ABA intervention (Mohammadzaheri, Koegel, Rezaee, & Rafiee, 2014), and another study suggested a reduction in the severity of ASD symptoms as a result of PRT (Duifhuis et al., 2017).

A key characteristic of PRT is that it is implemented in natural environments—for example, the home or classroom. Because the classroom setting is a natural environment and children with ASD are in school for several hours a day, PRT is an appropriate intervention to be translated into school settings. To translate PRT to school settings, Stahmer and colleagues conducted a series of studies in collaboration with special education teachers. First, they conducted focus groups were conducted to gather information about the feasibility of PRT techniques in classrooms (Stahmer et al., 2012). Teachers had positive attitudes toward PRT, but reported difficulties using PRT with multiple children and in using some of the PRT techniques in their classrooms (e.g., incorporating child choice, interspersing maintenance and acquisition tasks, using contingent and natural reinforcement). For example, teachers indicated that it was often unrealistic to allow children to choose activities because in the classroom context certain activities are mandatory. Some teachers also reported that PRT lacked structure, which made it difficult to understand the sequence in which PRT techniques should be used. Finally, teachers found it difficult to integrate PRT into their teaching and to determine goals, because PRT was not tied to a specific curriculum (e.g., mathematics, reading) and could be integrated into almost any classroom activity. In a second study, teachers' use of PRT was examined by assessing the fidelity of implementation (Suhrheinrich et al., 2013). *Fidelity of implementation* refers to the degree to which an intervention is implemented as designed. The results of this study confirmed those of the focus groups. Some PRT techniques were indeed implemented with low fidelity and thus were difficult to use in classrooms. On the basis of these two studies, the original manual of PRT was adapted for implementation in classrooms (Stahmer et al., 2011). The adapted intervention is called CPRT.

COMPONENTS OF CPRT

CPRT can be used to target communication, play, and social and academic skills in children with ASD (Stahmer et al., 2011) and consists of antecedent and consequent components. The *antecedent* components are used to elicit behavior from the child and include (a) child attention, (b) clear and appropriate cues, (c) interspersion of maintenance and acquisition tasks, (d) shared control, and (e) multiple cues. The *consequent* components are used to respond to the child's behavior and consist of (f) direct reinforcement, (g) contingent reinforcement, and (h) reinforcement of attempts. The successive implementation of the components of CPRT forms a learning opportunity for the child. Following is a description of the components of CPRT, including examples of how to use CPRT in naturally occurring one-to-one and group situations. Figure 13.1 presents a schematic representation of a learning opportunity and the CPRT components.

Child Attention

Children with ASD often have difficulties directing, sustaining, and shifting their attention toward relevant stimuli (e.g., Patten & Watson, 2011). However, it is important that teachers provide opportunities to respond only when children are paying attention. If a child is not paying attention, he or she is less likely to respond (correctly). To gain the child's attention, it is important to incorporate motivating materials, activities, and topics (Koegel et al., 1987); to maintain close proximity to and visibility for the target child; and to gradually increase the length of time that individual children are expected to pay attention. Preference assessments can be conducted to identify materials, activities, and topics that are motivating for each individual child.

Clear and Appropriate Cues

After gaining the child's attention, the second step in creating a learning opportunity involves presenting a cue. A *cue* is the first signal for a child to respond or engage in a behavior (Stahmer et al., 2011). There are several types of cues, such as instructions, questions, leading comments, facial expressions, and situational arrangements. These cues differ with regard to their level of intrusiveness (Stahmer et al., 2011). For example, a child may

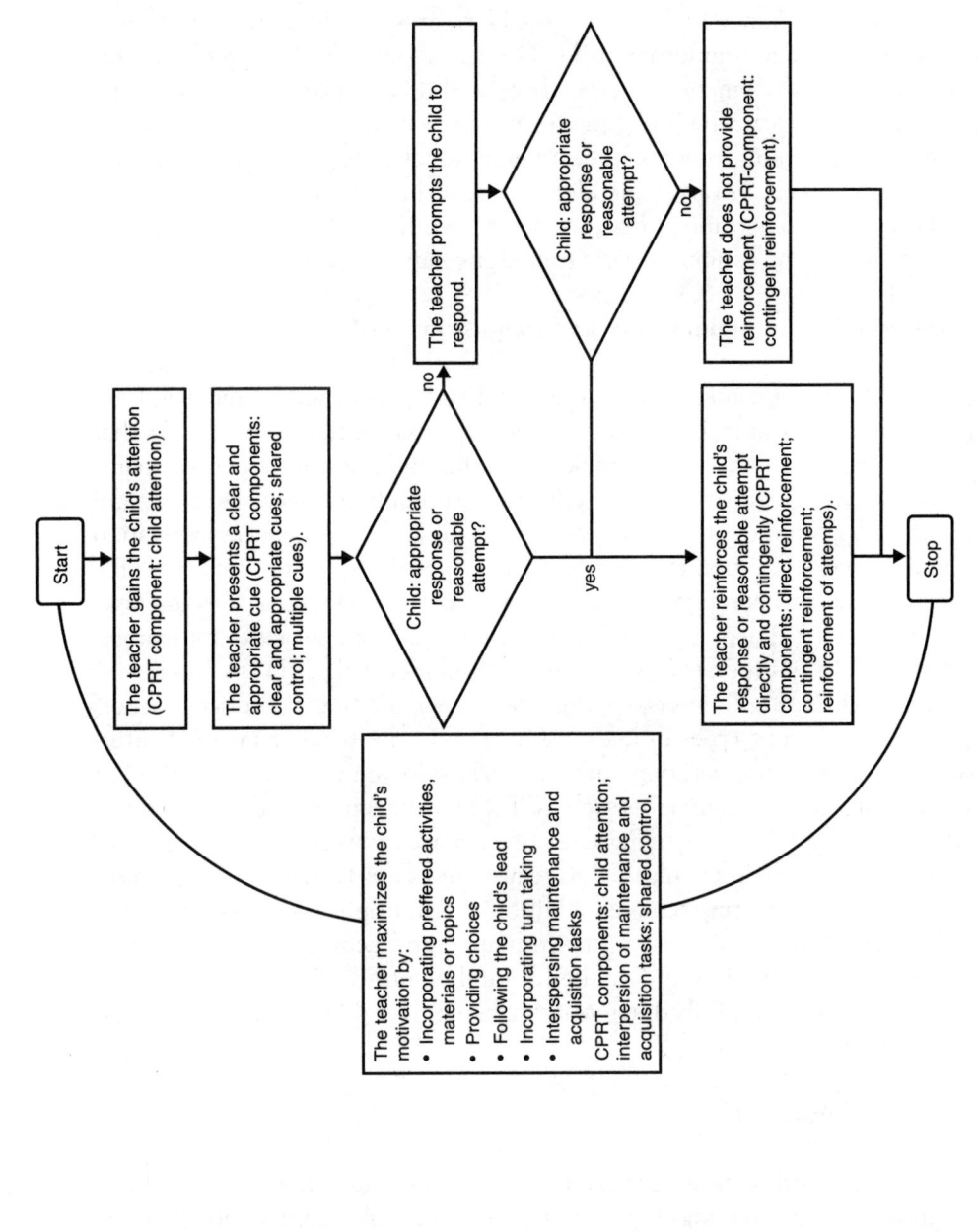

Figure 13.1. Schematic representation of an opportunity to respond. CPRT = classroom pivotal response teaching.

be more likely to respond to a direct instruction (e.g., "Throw the ball to me") than a facial expression (e.g., the teacher gives the child an expectant look with her arms outstretched). When providing an opportunity to respond, the cue should be clear, which means that the cue is unambiguous and uninterrupted. For example, if the teacher asks the child a question (e.g., "What is the capital of France?"), he or she should wait for the child's response before presenting a cue to another child. The cue should also be appropriate for the child's developmental level, so that the child can learn to understand the cue and can learn which response or behavior is expected from him or her. In group situations, cues might be different for children with different developmental levels. For example, during circle time one child may be asked, "Did you do something fun last weekend?" while another child is presented with the leading comment "I did something very fun yesterday."

Interspersion of Maintenance and Acquisition Tasks

Maintenance tasks are tasks that children have already mastered and can complete easily and consistently. *Acquisition tasks* are new tasks or tasks that continue to be difficult to complete. Varying tasks and interspersing maintenance and acquisition tasks helps to ensure a high level of success and regular opportunities to provide reinforcement, and thus enhances motivation and reduces frustration (Dunlap & Koegel, 1980). This component of CPRT ensures that an appropriate proportion of maintenance versus acquisition tasks is maintained. There is no set rule for this proportion, but ratios for maintenance and acquisition tasks vary from 2:1 (Stahmer et al., 2011) to 7:1 (Koegel & Koegel, 2012). To intersperse maintenance and acquisition tasks, teachers can use different types of cues. For example, the teacher may (a) intersperse open-ended questions such as "What do you need to solve the last sum?" and leading comments such as "I see you haven't solved the last sum," (b) ask the child to use varying levels of language complexity (e.g., "Help me" or "Could you help me please?" to request help), or (c) vary the content of tasks (e.g., alternating between addition and multiplication problems). For each child in the classroom, maintenance and acquisition tasks will be different. Nonetheless, all children should be provided both maintenance and acquisition tasks. By differentiating between children, peers can serve as a model for each other.

Shared Control

The fourth antecedent CPRT component serves to maximize children's motivation by providing choices, following the child's lead, and incorporating turn taking (Stahmer et al., 2011). Teachers can provide choices by allowing children to choose between activities (e.g., reading or mathematics), the nature of activities (e.g., independent reading or buddy reading), or materials (e.g., pencil or marker). Teachers can also embed children's preferred topics or materials in activities. For example, if a child likes racing cars, the teacher could use racing cars and a race circuit to teach multiplication. Because children's preferences often change, ongoing preference assessments are recommended (see Cooper et al., 2013, and Stahmer et al., 2011, for examples). Following the child's lead implies that the teacher allows the child to switch to another preferred activity or material at any time. For example, if a child initially chooses to draw, drawing is continued until the child indicates he or she wants to do another activity. It is important to note that shared control does not mean that children have complete control over teaching interactions; teachers should ultimately control a learning situation. Turn taking is a third strategy to share control and involves a back-and-forth interaction between the child and the teacher or a peer (Stahmer et al., 2011). Turn taking allows the teacher or peer to model adequate or more advanced responses and allows the child to become accustomed to the give-and-take nature of social and play interactions. Turn taking is also a strategy to regain control over teaching materials, allowing the teacher to create opportunities for requesting materials (Rieth et al., 2014). Shared control could thus be implemented when presenting a cue (e.g., the teacher asks, "Do you want to use a pencil or a marker?" or holds up the toy car after her turn) but could also be implemented between learning opportunities as provided by the teacher. In a classroom with multiple children, it requires preparation to incorporate preferred activities or materials for each child, but turn taking often occurs naturally (Stahmer et al., 2011).

Multiple Cues

Research has indicated that some children with ASD have difficulties responding to multiple cues (e.g., Rieth, Stahmer, Suhrheinrich, & Schreibman, 2015). *Responding to multiple cues* refers to the ability to pay attention and respond appropriately to several features of objects or situations—for example, shape, color, and size (Stahmer et al., 2011). To enhance children's responsivity to multiple cues, teachers could use various examples of materials and concepts in their teaching, in both one-to-one and group instructions. For example, when teaching fractions, a teacher could use chocolate bars or pies to broaden the child's idea of what fractions mean. Teachers could also use conditional discrimination tasks to teach responding to multiple cues. An example of a conditional discrimination is asking the child to find a green pyramid in a box with blocks with different colors and shapes. The child has to attend to both color (green and not another color) and shape (pyramid and not another shape). It is important to note that typically developing children acquire the skill to respond to multiple cues at approximately 36 months of age (Reed, Stahmer, Suhrheinrich, & Schreibman, 2013). Before this developmental age, it might not be appropriate to teach responding to multiple cues.

Direct Reinforcement

If a child responds appropriately or adequately to a cue, the teacher provides direct reinforcement (Stahmer et al., 2011). *Direct reinforcement* means that the consequence that follows the child's response is logically or naturally related to this response. For example, if a child requests a toy car by saying the word "car," providing access to the toy car would be an example of direct and natural reinforcement. If the teacher had given the child food or a token, reinforcement would have been indirect, because these reinforcers are unrelated to the child's response. Research has indicated that direct reinforcement strengthens the relation between responses and reinforcement, and promotes generalization and maintenance of the targeted responses (Koegel & Williams, 1980). Whether a teacher is working individually with a child or with a group, appropriate or adequate responses should be reinforced in a natural way (Stahmer et al., 2011).

Contingent Reinforcement

Reinforcement should also be contingent on the child's response, both in one-to-one and group situations. *Contingent reinforcement* means that the teacher provides a consequence immediately after the child demonstrates an appropriate or adequate response, and that the delivery of a consequence is dependent on the child's response (i.e., reinforcement would only be provided if the child demonstrated the target behavior; Stahmer et al., 2011). Consequences that are delivered contingently are stronger and more effective than delayed consequences, particularly in the initial stage of teaching a response, because contingent consequences strengthen the relation between a response and its reinforcement (Cooper et al., 2013).

Reinforcement of Attempts

CPRT recommends that reinforcement is provided not only contingently but also for reasonable attempts at the target response. Reinforcing approximations of the target behavior ensures that children's motivation is maintained, and frustration is reduced, when they are presented with new and challenging tasks (Koegel et al., 1988). Reinforcement of attempts often also results in more rapid acquisition of new skills because the child is motivated to try again in the future (Koegel et al., 1988). For example, if a child is learning how to say his first words and says "Ba" to request a ball, the teacher gives the child access to the ball, because "ba" is a reasonable attempt at what the child has shown to be able to say. It is important to note that reinforcing attempts does not guarantee that the child's future responses will be correct; however, these responses can be shaped over time.

IMPLEMENTATION OF CPRT

It is important that an intervention is implemented with high levels of treatment fidelity because intervention outcomes can depend on adherence to specific intervention procedures (Allen & Warzak, 2000). Treatment fidelity, or the degree to which an intervention is implemented as designed, is often associated with the quality of teacher and paraprofessional training (Reid & Fitch, 2011), yet teachers often receive no or insufficient training in implementing EBIs for children with ASD (e.g., Lang et al., 2010; Morrier, Hess, & Heflin, 2011). In the past decade, the number of studies focusing on training teachers and paraprofessionals has increased, including studies on the effectiveness of CPRT training (e.g., Robinson, 2011; Stahmer, Rieth, et al., 2015; Stahmer, Suhrheinrich, & Rieth, 2016; Suhrheinrich, 2011, 2015; Suhrheinrich, Stahmer, Reed, et al., 2013; Suhrheinrich, Stahmer, & Schreibman, 2007). These studies indicate that a combination of training components is effective in teaching teachers and paraprofessionals to implement CPRT with fidelity.

Training Teachers to Implement CPRT

Training in CPRT often starts with group instruction sessions, conducted by a trainer in CPRT (e.g., Stahmer et al., 2016; Suhrheinrich, 2011). During these sessions teachers are first introduced to ABA and CPRT. Subsequently, they receive didactic instruction in the CPRT components and watch video examples of the components or receive in vivo modeling. Teachers also practice the CPRT components during these sessions, (e.g., during role-plays) and receive feedback on their implementation of CPRT. Finally, teachers are given an introduction to how the fidelity of CPRT implementation is assessed. Teachers are asked to practice the CPRT components in their classrooms between group instruction sessions. After group instruction, teachers usually participate in individual coaching sessions (e.g., Stahmer et al., 2016; Suhrheinrich, 2011). During coaching sessions, teachers first work with one or more children in their classroom while using CPRT. The trainer records the CPRT session with a video camera to assess the fidelity of implementation and provide video feedback. Next, the trainer assesses fidelity of implementation and then provides video feedback. Although several studies have indicated that video feedback might not be as effective as live feedback because of the delay in feedback (e.g., O'Reilly, Renzaglia, & Lee, 1994), an advantage of video feedback is that it allows the trainer to observe and discuss the teacher's skills in great detail while replaying the video (Robinson, 2011). During video feedback the trainer provides praise if the teacher implements CPRT components correctly; corrective feedback as well as suggestions for improvement are provided if CPRT components are not implemented or are incorrectly implemented (e.g., Robinson, 2011; Suhrheinrich, 2011). Coaching sessions typically continue until teachers meet fidelity of implementation criteria (e.g., 80% correct implementation of all CPRT components across two consecutive CPRT sessions; Robinson, 2011). To maintain high levels of fidelity of implementation, it is important that ongoing support and feedback are provided (e.g., Reid & Fitch, 2011). A pyramidal training or train-the-trainer model might be effective for this purpose (Suhrheinrich, 2015). In addition to training teachers and paraprofessionals to implement the CPRT components, it is important that they receive adequate training in goal setting, monitoring, and review (Koegel, Matos-Freden, Lang, & Koegel, 2012; Pinkelman & Horner, 2017). These skills can be taught using the combination of components that is also used to teach the CPRT components (i.e., didactic instruction, modeling, guided practice, and performance feedback; Pinkelman & Horner, 2017). In the next section, a case vignette is presented to illustrate how a teacher might target a child's individual goals using CPRT components.

Case Vignette

Kevin is a 6-year-old boy with a diagnosis of ASD. Kevin likes to play with LEGO blocks. In the classroom, he often yells "No" in response to instructions from his teacher or refuses to do the task. It is difficult for him to ask questions, for example, to request help. The teacher discovers that his refusal behavior always follows instructions to complete new and unfamiliar tasks. If Kevin is more familiar with tasks, he cooperates and follows instructions. Because Kevin likes to play with LEGO blocks, the teacher decides to use these materials to motivate him to cooperate during a new math activity. She starts the lesson by making a remark: "We are going to do something fun" and waits for the children to react. Kevin is curious and asks the teacher, "What are we going to do?" The teacher reinforces his question by saying that they are going to do something with the LEGO blocks and gives him a compliment for his response. Then she asks Kevin,

"Can you get seven red LEGO blocks and five yellow LEGO blocks?" Kevin walks over to the box of LEGO and returns with the requested blocks. The teacher says, "Great listening, Kevin, now you have got seven red LEGO blocks and five yellow." Next, she instructs Kevin to give three red blocks to the boy next to him. Reluctantly Kevin hands over the three blocks. "Well done, Kevin" the teacher says. Then, she says to him, "You had seven red blocks and gave three red blocks away, how many blocks you have got left?" Kevin answers, "Four." The teacher provides Kevin with verbal reinforcement: "That's right, seven minus three is four." This was an example of an easy or maintenance task for Kevin. "Who can write this calculation?" she asks. A couple of children raise their hand. The teacher hands over paper and pencil to one of the children and asks this child to write down the calculation. Then, she provides another calculation using Kevin's LEGO blocks. This time she instructs him to write down the calculation. Kevin does not have paper or a pencil. The teacher waits and looks at him. Kevin looks around and wants to get out of his seat. Asking questions is a difficult or acquisition task for Kevin. The teacher provides additional support (i.e., a prompt) using an open question: "What question can you ask me?" Kevin responds by asking, "Can I have a paper and pencil?" The teacher reinforces him by handing him the requested items and saying, "Of course, here you go, good asking!" The teacher takes a yellow LEGO block, a red LEGO block, and a yellow wooden block in her hand. She says to Kevin, "Kevin, you have five yellow LEGO blocks. I have 3 blocks in my hand. What block do you need to have six yellow LEGO blocks?" Kevin responds, "The yellow LEGO block." "Splendid!" the teacher says, and she continues, "Take it." Kevin takes the yellow LEGO block. Next, the teacher asks Kevin to add a red LEGO block to his stack. The teacher still has the red block. Kevin asks, "Red block?" The teacher reinforces his attempt to ask for the red block by giving it to him and saying, "Sure, you can have the red block!"

In this example the teacher uses several cues, such as instructions, questions, remarks, and wait and see. She also prompts Kevin to ask a question. The teacher uses interspersion of maintenance and acquisition tasks. Kevin cooperates in this math lesson and asks questions. Because she draws on Kevin's motivation and reinforces his appropriate behavior and attempts, Kevin refrains from yelling and cooperates with the task. By asking Kevin to take a block out of her hand, she is providing multiple cues. The teacher has a yellow and red LEGO block and a yellow wooden block. This means she has two types of blocks (LEGO and wooden) and two colors (yellow and red). Kevin has to take the yellow LEGO block. At the end of the lesson Kevin was making math calculations using paper and pencil.

CONCLUSION

There are a large number of EBIs for children with ASD. Many of these approaches are based on the principles of ABA, for example, DTT, PECS, and functional communication training. Although there is a strong evidence base to support the use of these approaches, they have traditionally been implemented in highly structured and controlled environments in which teaching interactions are led by the teacher. Critics argue that this results in a lack of generalization of target behaviors and a reduction in children's motivation to engage in learning opportunities. Furthermore, given the intensity of these approaches, they are often time-consuming and costly to implement. PRT is an evidence-based approach to intervention, based on the principles of ABA, that is implemented in naturalistic contexts and that applies motivational techniques to teach pivotal behaviors to children with ASD. CPRT is a program that has been derived from the principles of PRT, for use in classroom contexts. It consists of several antecedent and consequent components—for example, providing the child with clear and appropriate cues, interspersing maintenance and acquisition tasks, and using direct and contingent reinforcement. Because of the complexity of implementing CPRT in the classroom, research has suggested that it is important that teachers receive the training necessary to enable them to implement these techniques with fidelity. Furthermore, although PRT has a strong evidence base, further research is required to establish the efficacy of CPRT as a classroom-based intervention.

REFERENCES

Allen, K. D., & Warzak, W. J. (2000). The problem of parental nonadherence in clinical behavior analysis: Effective treatment is not enough. *Journal of Applied Behavior Analysis, 33*, 373–391. http://dx.doi.org/10.1901/jaba.2000.33-373

Cooper, J. O., Heron, T. E., & Heward, W. L. (2013). *Applied behavior analysis.* Harlow, England: Pearson Education.

Delprato, D. J. (2001). Comparisons of discrete-trial and normalized behavioral language intervention for young children with autism. *Journal of Autism and Developmental Disorders, 31*, 315–325. http://dx.doi.org/10.1023/A:1010747303957

Duifhuis, E. A., den Boer, J. C., Doornbos, A., Buitelaar, J. K., Oosterling, I. J., & Klip, H. (2017). The effect of pivotal response treatment in children with autism spectrum disorders: A non-randomized study with a blinded outcome measure. *Journal of Autism and Developmental Disorders, 47*, 231–242.

Duker, P., Didden, R., & Sigafoos, J. (2004). *One-to-one training: Instructional procedures for learners with developmental disabilities.* Austin, TX: PRO-ED.

Dunlap, G., & Koegel, R. L. (1980). Motivating autistic children through stimulus variation. *Journal of Applied Behavior Analysis, 13*, 619–627.

Kasari, C., & Smith, T. (2013). Interventions in schools for children with autism spectrum disorder: Methods and recommendations. *Autism, 17*, 254–267. http://dx.doi.org/10.1177/1362361312470496

Koegel, L. K., Ashbaugh, K., & Koegel, R. L. (2016). Pivotal response treatment. In R. Lang, T. B. Hancock, & N. N. Singh (Eds.), *Early intervention for young children with autism spectrum disorder* (pp. 85–112). Cham, Switzerland: Springer.

Koegel, L. K., Matos-Freden, R., Lang, R., & Koegel, R. L. (2012). Interventions for children with autism spectrum disorders in inclusive school settings. *Cognitive and Behavioral Practice, 19*, 401–412. http://dx.doi.org/10.1016/j.cbpra.2010.11.003

Koegel, R. L., Dyer, K., & Bell, L. K. (1987). The influence of child-preferred activities on autistic children's social behavior. *Journal of Applied Behavior Analysis, 20*, 243–252. http://dx.doi.org/10.1901/jaba.1987.20-243

Koegel, R. L., & Koegel, L. K. (2006). *Pivotal response treatments for autism: Communication, social, & academic development.* Baltimore, MD: Paul H. Brookes.

Koegel, R. L., & Koegel, L. K. (2012). *The PRT pocket guide.* Baltimore, MD: Paul H. Brookes.

Koegel, R. L., O'Dell, M., & Dunlap, G. (1988). Producing speech use in nonverbal autistic children by reinforcing attempts. *Journal of Autism and Developmental Disorders, 18*, 525–538. http://dx.doi.org/10.1007/BF02211871

Koegel, R. L., & Williams, J. A. (1980). Direct versus indirect response-reinforcer relationships in teaching autistic children. *Journal of Abnormal Child Psychology, 8*, 537–547. http://dx.doi.org/10.1007/BF00916505

Lang, R., O'Reilly, M. F., Sigafoos, J., Machalicek, W., Rispoli, M., Shogren, K., . . . Hopkins, S. (2010). Review of teacher involvement in the applied intervention research for children with autism spectrum disorders. *Education and Training in Autism and Developmental Disabilities, 45*, 268–283.

Lovaas, O. I. (1987). Behavioral treatment and normal educational and intellectual functioning in young autistic children. *Journal of Consulting and Clinical Psychology, 55*, 3–9. http://dx.doi.org/10.1037/0022-006X.55.1.3

Mohammadzaheri, F., Koegel, L. K., Rezaee, M., & Rafiee, S. M. (2014). A randomized clinical trial comparison between pivotal response treatment (PRT) and structured applied behavior analysis (ABA) intervention for children with autism. *Journal of Autism and Developmental Disorders, 44*, 2769–2777. http://dx.doi.org/10.1007/s10803-014-2137-3

Morrier, M. J., Hess, K. L., & Heflin, L. J. (2011). Teacher training for implementation of teaching strategies for students with autism spectrum disorders. *Teacher Education and Special Education, 34*, 119–132. http://dx.doi.org/10.1177/0888406410376660

Odom, S. L., Collet-Klingenberg, L., Rogers, S. J., & Hatton, D. D. (2010). Evidence-based practices in interventions for children and youth with autism spectrum disorders. *Preventing School Failure, 54*, 275–282. http://dx.doi.org/10.1080/10459881003785506

O'Reilly, M. F., Renzaglia, A., & Lee, S. (1994). An analysis of acquisition, generalization and maintenance of systematic instruction competencies by preservice teachers using behavioural supervision techniques. *Education and Training in Mental Retardation and Developmental Disabilities, 29*, 22–33. Retrieved from http://www.jstor.org/stable/23879183

Patten, E., & Watson, L. R. (2011). Interventions targeting attention in young children with autism. *American Journal of Speech-Language Pathology, 20*, 60–69. http://dx.doi.org/10.1044/1058-0360(2010/09-0081)

Pinkelman, S. E., & Horner, R. H. (2017). Improving implementation of function-based interventions: Self-monitoring, data collection, and data review. *Journal of Positive Behavior Interventions, 19*, 228–238.

Reed, S. R., Stahmer, A. C., Suhrheinrich, J., & Schreibman, L. (2013). Stimulus overselectivity in typical development: Implications for teaching children with autism. *Journal of Autism and Developmental Disorders, 43*, 1249–1257. http://dx.doi.org/10.1007/s10803-012-1658-x

Reichow, B. (2012). Overview of meta-analyses on early intensive behavioral intervention for young children with autism spectrum disorders. *Journal of Autism and Developmental Disorders, 42*, 512–520. http://dx.doi.org/10.1007/s10803-011-1218-9

Reid, D. H., & Fitch, W. H. (2011). Training staff and parents: Evidence-based approaches. In J. L. Matson & P. Sturmey (Eds.), *International handbook of autism and pervasive developmental disorders* (pp. 509–519). New York, NY: Springer-Verlag. http://dx.doi.org/10.1007/978-1-4419-8065-6_32

Rieth, S. R., Stahmer, A. C., Suhrheinrich, J., & Schreibman, L. (2015). Examination of the prevalence of stimulus overselectivity in children with ASD. *Journal of Applied Behavior Analysis, 48*, 71–84. http://dx.doi.org/10.1002/jaba.165

Rieth, S. R., Stahmer, A. C., Suhrheinrich, J., Schreibman, L., Kennedy, J., & Ross, B. (2014). Identifying critical elements of treatment: Examining the use of turn taking in autism intervention. *Focus on Autism and Other Developmental Disabilities, 29*, 168–179. http://dx.doi.org/10.1177/1088357613513792

Robinson, S. E. (2011). Teaching paraprofessional of students with autism to implement pivotal response treatment in inclusive school settings using a brief video feedback training package. *Focus on Autism and Other Developmental Disabilities, 26*, 105–118. http://dx.doi.org/10.1177/1088357611407063

Smith, T., & Iadarola, S. (2015). Evidence base update for autism spectrum disorder. *Journal of Clinical Child and Adolescent Psychology, 44*, 897–922. http://dx.doi.org/10.1080/15374416.2015.1077448

Stahmer, A. C., Rieth, S., Lee, E., Reisinger, E. M., Mandell, D. S., & Connell, J. E. (2015). Training teachers to use evidence-based practices for autism: Examining procedural fidelity. *Psychology in the Schools, 52*, 181–195. http://dx.doi.org/10.1002/pits.21815

Stahmer, A. C., Suhrheinrich, J., Reed, S., & Schreibman, L. (2012). What works for you? Using teacher feedback to inform adaptations of pivotal response training for classroom use. *Autism Research and Treatment, 2012,* 709861. Advance online publication. http://dx.doi.org/10.1155/2012/709861

Stahmer, A. C., Suhrheinrich, J., Reed, S., Schreibman, L., & Bolduc, C. (2011). *Classroom pivotal response teaching for children with autism.* New York, NY: Guilford Press.

Stahmer, A. C., Suhrheinrich, J., & Rieth, S. (2016). A pilot examination of the adapted protocol for classroom pivotal response teaching. *Journal of the American Academy of Special Education Professionals, 2016*(Winter), 119–139.

Stokes, T. F., & Baer, D. M. (1977). An implicit technology of generalization. *Journal of Applied Behavior Analysis, 10,* 349–367.

Suhrheinrich, J. (2011). Training teachers to use pivotal response training with children with autism: Coaching as a critical component. *Teacher Education and Special Education, 34,* 339–349. http://dx.doi.org/10.1177/0888406411406553

Suhrheinrich, J. (2015). A sustainable model for training teachers to use pivotal response training. *Autism, 19,* 713–723. http://dx.doi.org/10.1177/1362361314552200

Suhrheinrich, J., Stahmer, A. C., Reed, S., Schreibman, L., Reisinger, E., & Mandell, D. (2013). Implementation challenges in translating pivotal response training into community settings. *Journal of Autism and Developmental Disorders, 43,* 2970–2976. http://dx.doi.org/10.1007/s10803-013-1826-7

Suhrheinrich, J., Stahmer, A. C., & Schreibman, L. (2007). A preliminary assessment of teachers' implementation of pivotal response training. *The Journal of Speech and Language Pathology—Applied Behavior Analysis, 2,* 1–13. http://dx.doi.org/10.1037/h0100202

Verschuur, R., Didden, R., Lang, R., Sigafoos, J., & Huskens, B. (2014). Pivotal response treatment for children with autism spectrum disorders: A systematic review. *Review Journal of Autism and Developmental Disorders, 1,* 34–61. http://dx.doi.org/10.1007/s40489-013-0008-z

Virués-Ortega, J. (2010). Applied behavior analytic intervention for autism in early childhood: Meta-analysis, meta-regression and dose-response meta-analysis of multiple outcomes. *Clinical Psychology Review, 30,* 387–399. http://dx.doi.org/10.1016/j.cpr.2010.01.008

Vismara, L. A., & Rogers, S. J. (2010). Behavioral treatments in autism spectrum disorder: What do we know? *Annual Review of Clinical Psychology, 6,* 447–468. http://dx.doi.org/10.1146/annurev.clinpsy.121208.131151

Wong, C., Odom, S. L., Hume, K. A., Cox, A. W., Fettig, A., Kucharczyk, S., . . . Schultz, T. R. (2015). Evidence-based practices for children, youth, and young adults with autism spectrum disorder: A comprehensive review. *Journal of Autism and Developmental Disorders, 45,* 1951–1966. http://dx.doi.org/10.1007/s10803-014-2351-z

14

VERBAL BEHAVIOR INTERVENTION IN AUTISM SPECTRUM DISORDERS

ELIZABETH R. LORAH, MATT TINCANI, AND ASHLEY PARNELL

Autism spectrum disorder (ASD) is a neurodevelopmental disorder characterized by persistent impairments in social communication and social interaction and by restricted, repetitive patterns of behavior, interests, or activities. Deficits in social communication and interaction manifest in problems with social reciprocity (i.e., joint attention), nonvocal communicative behaviors (i.e., gestures), and acquisition of relationships (American Psychiatric Association, 2013). With the publication of the fifth edition of the *Diagnostic and Statistical Manual of Mental Disorders* (DSM–5), the American Psychiatric Association (2013) developed three levels across which an individual with a diagnosis of ASD may present in terms of social communication impairments. These characteristics are presented in Table 14.1.

The intervention approach most thoroughly researched in terms of the treatment of ASD is that of applied behavior analysis (ABA; Cooper, Heron, & Heward, 2007; Virués-Ortega, 2010). As communication is the

http://dx.doi.org/10.1037/0000126-015
Behavioral Interventions in Schools: Evidence-Based Positive Strategies, Second Edition, S. G. Little and A. Akin-Little (Editors)
Copyright © 2019 by the American Psychological Association. All rights reserved.

TABLE 14.1
Communication Characteristics of Individuals
With Autism Spectrum Disorder

Communication deficit	Example
Social–emotional reciprocity	Failure to initiate and sustain conversation
	Failure to initiate or respond to social interactions
Nonvocal communicative behaviors	Abnormal eye contact and body language
	Lack of facial expressions and use of gestures
Developing, maintaining, and understanding relationships	Failure or difficulty to adjust behavior on the basis of context
	Limited or no interest in peers

basis for most learning and is a core deficit for an individual with ASD, the development of communication skills or language is seen as a primary goal in any intervention based on the methodology of ABA. The ABA approach has generally been more effective than approaches rooted in psychoanalysis, sensory integration, facilitated communication, and others (Lang et al., 2012; Sundberg & Michael, 2001; Travers, Tincani, & Lang, 2014). In some cases, individuals receiving intervention based on the methodology of ABA enter regular education classrooms (e.g., Lovaas, 1987; McEachin, Smith, & Lovaas, 1993). Although such outcomes are not a guarantee, at the very least, the vast majority of individuals receiving ABA-based interventions acquire more effective social communication (Tincani & Devis, 2011; van der Meer & Rispoli, 2010; Virués-Ortega, 2010).

VERBAL BEHAVIOR

Traditional language theories often attribute the development of language to internal processing systems and innate physiological functions, such as Chomsky's (1959) generative grammar. In effect, language is said to be a manifestation of biological and cognitive variables. Traditional linguistic analysis tends to focus on the topographical or structural forms of language, such as written or vocal responding, as classified in terms of syntax, grammar, and semantics. Language commonly refers to a possession, or an abstraction acquired and used, rather than a behavior learned from the environment. B. F. Skinner's (1957) environmental approach to language differs substantially from these traditional views of language.

Skinner (1957) defined *verbal behavior* as behavior that is mediated by another person's behavior (i.e., the listener). Thus, by the very nature of the definition, all verbal behavior or communication is social in nature. Rather than placing focus on the structure of verbal behavior (i.e., vocal communication) and the practices of the verbal community (i.e., grammar and syntax), Skinner places emphasis on the *functional relationship* between the responding and the environmental conditions that occasion (i.e., discriminative stimulus) and maintain (i.e., reinforcement) the behavior. Further, Skinner categorized these responses into classes of behaviors or *verbal operants*.

Like other operant behavior, verbal behavior may be investigated in terms of environmental contingencies: (a) antecedent conditions (discriminative stimuli and establishing operations), (b) the response or operant, and (c) the reinforcer (i.e., consequence) that follows or has followed that type of responding (Moore, 2008; Sundberg & Michael, 2001). The events that surround and maintain one's behavior become the focus, rather than internal causes or the structure of verbal behavior.

Traditionally, communication is divided into two categories: receptive and expressive, with little attention given to the function of the communication, thereby placing focus on the structure of the behavior rather than on the outcome of the behavior (Sundberg & Michael, 2001). A secondary distinction between Skinner's verbal behavior and traditional language theory is the emphasis on the distinction between the behavior of the speaker and that of the listener. Skinner avoided the use of the terms *receptive* and *expressive language* because they tell us little about the function of behavior in terms of speaker and listener contingencies. Rather, classifying responding as that of a listener or a speaker provides more information as to the function of the behavior. For example, telling an individual to "touch the color red" would in a traditional language paradigm be classified as *receptive language*. Conversely, holding up a picture of the color red and asking an individual "What color is this?" would be classified as *expressive language*. In a behavior analytic account, both responses would be classified as *listener behavior*, as in both examples the behavior of the individual was occasioned by the behavior of another, and responding accurately to both scenarios would produce the outcome of social praise (i.e., "Well done!").

Speaker Versus Listener

The distinction between the speaker and listener is an important one in terms of verbal operants. In a behavioral account of verbal behavior, initial emphasis is placed on the occasioning antecedent variables. These variables can be broken into two different and distinct units, the *motivating operation or establishing operation* (MO/EO) and the *discriminative stimulus* (S^D). Simply put, the MO/EO is a condition of deprivation (i.e., not eating for a period of time) or aversive stimulation (i.e., cold), which increases the likelihood of an S^D (i.e., food or a jacket) to occasion a specific response (i.e., eating or putting on a jacket), while increasing the value of reinforcement for that response.

The S^D is the stimulus that occasions the response when reinforcement is more probable. In terms of verbal behavior, the behavior of the speaker is categorized as occasioned by environmental variables, whereas the behavior of the listener is categorized as occasioned by the behavior of a speaker (Skinner, 1957).

Verbal Operants: Speaker

As previously mentioned, Skinner (1957) described several different classifications of verbal behavior or verbal operants (see Table 14.2). Further emphasizing the distinction between the speaker and listener, the following elementary speaker verbal operants are described. The *mand* is a verbal operant that is controlled by the MO/EO and is the only verbal operant that directly benefits the speaker through specific reinforcement specified by the speaker. The mand is loosely derived from the term com*mand*. The *tact* is a verbal operant that is controlled by a nonverbal stimulus and allows the speaker and listener to make con*tact* with a shared environmental variable. The *echoic*, *intraverbal*, *textual*, and *transcriptive* are all verbal operants that are occasioned by a verbal stimulus, differing with regard to the response form.

Verbal Operants: Listener

Zettle and Hayes (1982) furthered Skinner's 1957 work by conducting an analysis of functional relations of listener behavior (i.e., listener verbal operants). Coining the terms *pliance*, taken from com*pliance* (which parallels the mand), *tracking* (which parallels the tact), and *augmenting* (which may parallel various speaker verbal operants such as intraverbal, tact, mand), Zettle and Hayes delineated and elaborated on primary types of listener operants (see Table 14.2).

Pliance can be described as rule following that occurs because of a history of correspondence between instruction/rule following and social consequences (Catania, 1992; Moore, 2008; Zettle & Hayes, 1982). When the listener responds to a speaker's mand, by compiling to that mand, he or she is demonstrating pliance. Tracking occurs when a listener responds according to specified rules because of correspondence between that behavior and environmental stimuli (Catania, 1992; Moore, 2008; Zettle & Hayes, 1982). For example, if the speaker tacts an environmental event and the listener provides a social comment acknowledging the same environmental event, he or she is demonstrating tracking. Augmenting, a third type of listener behavior, oftentimes occurs in conjunction with tracking or pliance (Zettle & Hayes, 1982). Associated more with a change in establishing operation than a discriminative stimulus, augmenting describes rule-governed behavior

TABLE 14.2
Verbal Operants

Operant	Controlling variable or antecedent	Listener response (consequence)	Example
Mand	Motivating operation—state of deprivation or aversive stimulation	Pliance—specific reinforcement, with 1:1 correspondence	Student is completing a math assignment and has a dull pencil. Student states to teacher "I need a pencil." Teacher hands student pencil.
Echoic	Discriminative stimulus—verbal stimulus, with 1:1 correspondence and topographic similarity	Nonspecific generalized reinforcement	Teacher says "Cat," student responds "Cat," teacher provides social praise such as "Nice job!"
Tact	Discriminative stimulus—nonverbal environmental stimulus	Tracking—nonspecific generalized reinforcement	While walking through a toy store a child points out a doll and states, "Doll!" The parent responds, "Yes, that is a doll."
Intraverbal	Discriminative stimulus—verbal stimulus, without 1:1 correspondence and topographic similarity	Augmenting—nonspecific reinforcement	Teacher says "I pledge allegiance to the . . ." Student responds, "Flag."
Pliance-Tact (multiply controlled operant)	Example: Teacher holds up a site word card and asks student "What word?" Student responds, "Stop."	Example—Student responds, "Stop."	

that modifies the seeming reinforcing value of a consequence (Moore, 2008; Zettle & Hayes, 1982). When considering listener verbal operants, one should note that rules might be in the form of text, speech, sign, or other modalities (Zettle & Hayes, 1982). For example, a driver who stops at a stop sign while driving is demonstrating pliance.

Multiply Controlled Operants

The elementary verbal operants form the foundation of a verbal behavior analysis and more complex verbal relations. As such, naturally occurring verbal behavior is almost always multiply controlled, or controlled by more than one variable. Pure forms of verbal operants rarely exist (Skinner, 1957; Sundberg & Michael, 2001). For instance, a "yes" or "no" response may be simultaneously strengthened by a nonverbal stimuli (e.g., a cookie), establishing operation (e.g., food deprivation), and a verbal stimulus (e.g., "Do you want a cookie?"), thereby resulting in what one may term a *mand-tact-intraverbal*. Multiply controlled operants are an important consideration for verbal behavior intervention. For example, if we hold up a picture of a red color card and ask a child "What color is it?" his or her behavior is under the control of two conditions: the question "What color is it?" and the environmental stimuli of the red color card. Thus, within this scenario, the child is exhibiting speaker and listener behavior, and the behavior would be classified as a pliance-tact.

The Importance of Skinner's Analysis of Verbal Behavior

A behavioral approach to the development of social communication for an individual with a diagnosis of ASD is methodologically and conceptually relevant. By placing emphasis on the environmental variables that occasion and maintain behavior, rather than on the individual and his or her diagnosis, a verbal behavior approach works to engineer an environment that will effectively occasion and maintain verbal operants. These operants can be seen as the building blocks for the acquisition of a more advanced social communicative repertoire (Sundberg & Michael, 2001). A verbal behavior approach breaks down complex social communicative responding into discrete units, using evidence-based practices for instruction (see Table 14.3). Within the verbal behavior approach, there is a heavy emphasis on natural environment teaching (NET) for mand and intraverbal training, whereas an emphasis is placed on more direct instructional methodologies such as discrete trial training (DTT; see Chapter 12) for tact, intraverbal, and listener responding training. Thus, a comprehensive social communication repertoire would be acquired from a combination of instructional behaviorally based methodologies (Sundberg & Michael, 2001).

ASSESSING VERBAL BEHAVIOR

As is the case with any behavior analytic intervention, an assessment of *baseline* or pretreatment behavior is necessary. Within the verbal behavior approach, there are two commonly used assessments: The Assessment of Basic Language and Learning Skills—Revised (ABLLS-R; Partington, 2010)

TABLE 14.3
Evidence-Based Practice for Teaching Verbal Behavior

Intervention	Description	Example
Antecedent-based intervention (ABI)	An instructional strategy that manipulates the motivating operation and discriminative stimuli to occasion a specific response	The use of a video model of a student engaging in appropriate peer interactions on the playground, prior to the student going to recess
Behavioral interventions	The use of applied behavior analysis as a comprehensive program for skill acquisition and behavior reduction	The use of an early intensive behavior intervention curriculum to systematically teach verbal operants and other learner skills
Differential reinforcement (DR)	Providing reinforcement to a response other than the target response, or a response that is an alternative to the target response, or a response that is incompatible to the target response	Reinforcing the behavior of manding for access to preferred items, as an alternative to the engagement of problem behavior to access preferred items
Discrete trial training (DTT)	The explicit and systematic arrangement of antecedent stimuli to occasion a response, while providing contingency reinforcement for the demonstration of a response	In a 1:1 teacher: student ratio, instructing a child to "clap"; if the child claps independently, providing access to tangible reinforcement; if the child does not clap, providing a prompt to occasion clapping
Functional communication training (FCT)	An ABI and DR procedure where a problem behavior is placed on extinction and a functional communicative equivalent to the target behavior is taught and reinforced	Following the conduction of a behavior assessment, a problem behavior is found to function for access to a tangible item, then instruction is provided to teach student to mand for access to the item, rather than engage in the problem behavior
Modeling and video modeling	The demonstration of a target behavior, either live or via a video, which is subsequently imitated, either independently or with prompting, and reinforced	While holding up a picture of a car you state "car," the child models your response, thereby engaging in an echoic-tact response

(*continues*)

TABLE 14.3
Evidence-Based Practice for Teaching Verbal Behavior (*Continued*)

Intervention	Description	Example
Naturalistic interventions	Instruction that occurs in the environment in which the behavior would naturally occur, uses the learner's motivation and prompts, which are systematically faded	While playing with a child, providing mand instruction for access to preferred play items
Peer-mediated intervention	An instructional strategy where a neurotypical peer provides prompting and reinforcement for the child with autism spectrum disorder (ASD)	A trained neurotypical peer asks the child with ASD, "What is your name?" and then provides a prompt to the child to respond "Bill"
Picture exchange communication system (PECS)	An augmentative and alternative communication system that uses a six-phased instructional sequence	The speaker exchanges a picture with the listener and instruction involves the following sequence: (1) how to communicate, (2) distance and persistence, (3) discrimination, (4) sentence structure, (5) responsive requesting, (6) commenting
Pivotal response training (PRT)	An instructional strategy that targets specific pivotal behaviors, using child interests and initiative	While targeting the pivotal area of motivation during a play scenario, the child begins to mand for access to an item for play
Prompting	The use of verbal or physical guidance to occasion a target response, in the presence of a specific stimulus, prompts are systematically faded producing independent responding	During mand training with a speech-generating device, the child is presented with a preferred item and the teacher provides a gestural prompt to the picture representing the item on the screen of the device, the child mands for the item and is granted access to the item
Positive reinforcement	The contingent presentation of a preferred item or activity, following the demonstration of a target behavior	When a child independently mands for a cookie, he or she is provided access to a cookie (positive reinforcement)

TABLE 14.3
Evidence-Based Practice for Teaching Verbal Behavior *(Continued)*

Intervention	Description	Example
Scripting	An instructional strategy that uses a written or spoken narrative about a target skill, which is then produced by the learner, following acquisition of the target behavior, the scripts become an ABI	Before the child goes to lunch, a narrative describing the steps to order lunch are reviewed with the child; during lunch the child repeats the script to place lunch order
Social narratives	An ABI where a narrative or picture story describes in detail a target response	See above (ABI)
Technology-aided Instruction	Interventions or instruction that uses technology as the central feature to augment acquisition of a skill or the reduction of a behavior	The use of a speech-generating device as an augmentative and alternative communication system
Time delay	In the presence of an occasioning stimulus, a specified delay occurs behavior prompting is used to occasion a target response	A child is instructed to "stand up"; following a five-second latency, the child is physically prompted to stand up

and the Verbal Behavior Milestones Assessment and Placement Program (VB-MAPP; Sundberg, 2008). Both assessments apply Skinner's functional analysis of verbal behavior to assess the current language and related skills of children with autism or other developmental disabilities. Unlike traditional assessments that measure language in terms of formal properties (i.e., words, phrases, sentences) alone, behaviorally based language assessments examine both the formal and functional (i.e., causal) properties of language, meaning both the behavior of the speaker and the environmental conditions that shape and maintain those behaviors (Sundberg, 2008).

Within these assessments, verbal responses are defined and measured in terms of verbal operants. Practitioners examine the effectiveness of each speaker and listener verbal operant repertoires (mand, tact, intraverbal, echoic, listener responding), investigating each verbal relation under the relevant antecedent conditions and corresponding consequences (Rehfeldt & Barnes-Holmes, 2009). The topography of the response is useful only in the context of the functional unit or verbal operant, as similar response forms may be controlled by various environmental variables (Esch, LaLonde, &

Esch, 2010). Although this function-based approach to assessing language is consistent across both the ABLLS-R and VP-MAPP, additional similarities and differences between the assessments exist.

The ABLLS-R (Partington, 2010) is a criterion-referenced assessment tool designed to identify language and other critical skills necessary for individuals to communicate successfully and to learn from their everyday experiences. The ABLLS-R presents a task analysis of 544 skills categorized with 25 curricular domains that most children acquire before age 5. Domains are further organized into sections including (a) basic learner skills (first 15 domains), (b) academic skills, (c) self-help skills, and (d) fine and gross motor skills. Instructional priority is placed on the basic learning skill domains (cooperation, verbal operants, social and play skills, group instruction), as these skills are considered most critical, although skills are not developmentally sequenced within or across domains. Skills are arranged sequentially, progressing from simple to more complex. The ABLLS-R also contains a skills tracking system, a visual display grid used to chart and track learners' progress through the domains and skills.

An alternative to the ABLLS-R is the VB-MAPP (Sundberg, 2008). The VB-MAPP offers a developmentally based criterion-referenced assessment that has been field tested with typically development children and children with ASD. The VB-MAPP includes three main components: (a) the Milestone Assessment, (b) the Barriers Assessment, and (c) the Transition Assessment. Based on typical development language milestones, the Milestone Assessment contains 170 verbal behavior milestones across three developmental levels (0–18 months, 18–30 months, and 30–48 months) and 16 different verbal and related skills. Skills are approximately balanced across skill levels and areas in terms of typical age of acquisition. Skills assessed include verbal operant repertoires, imitation, independent play, social play, group/classroom instruction, linguistic structure, visual perception/matching to sample, and early academics. A color-coded, master-scoring grid allows for skill tracking and progress monitoring. The Barriers Assessment examines 24 common learning and language barriers that often impede learning efficacy and efficiency. Also included is the VB-MAPP Transition Assessment that measures 18 areas that aid educators and parents in making informed individualized decisions in regard to education placement and instructional format.

Although the ABLLS-R and VB-MAPP allow practitioners to identify current skills levels across domains, select appropriate targets for intervention, and track progress, both tools provide little information as to how to teach those skills or targets. Hence, the next step for practitioners involves selecting effective and efficient teaching procedures for targeting the skills selected for intervention.

VERBAL BEHAVIOR INTERVENTION: EVIDENCE-BASED PRACTICES

Two comprehensive, systematic reviews of the literature on interventions for children and youth with ASD have been conducted by the National Standards Project (NSP) at the National Autism Center (NAC; 2009, 2015) and the National Professional Development Center on ASD (NPDC). Although notably similar in results and intent, some degree of variance exists between the two reviews. First, NPDC concentrated on focused interventions, defined as interventions designed to target a single skill or goal of a student diagnosed with ASD (e.g., discrete trial instruction [DTI], functional communication training [FCT]; Odom, Collet-Klingenberg, Rogers, & Hatton, 2010). In slight contrast, NSP evaluated, categorized, and delineated interventions used in isolation (e.g., scripting, modeling) and intervention packages/models that incorporated a number of elements or strategies (NAC, 2015; e.g., behavioral interventions, comprehensive behavioral treatment for young children). In effect, a number of the established interventions identified by the NSP are derived from behavioral analytic research and could be identified as behavioral interventions, but were not categorized as ABA interventions because they were packed and evaluated with nonbehavioral interventions (e.g., peer training).

Ultimately, significant findings across systematic reviews align. As depicted in Table 14.3, interventions based on ABA consistently document the strongest evidence-base for teaching communication skills to individuals with autism (NAC, 2015). In particular, behaviorally based interventions that enhance communication include DTT, naturalistic teaching strategies (NTS), pivotal response training (PRT), FCT, and antecedent-based interventions (ABI). Further, behaviorally based comprehensive treatment models (ABA or early intensive behavior intervention [EIBI] programs) that incorporate a combination of focused intervention strategies have been identified as having a high degree of empirical support in terms of broad learning and developmental impact on core deficit areas of ASD (NAC, 2015; National Research Council, 2001; Odom et al., 2010). It should also be noted that many of the specific behavioral techniques (e.g., modeling, extinction, differential reinforcement) are incorporated into the communication teaching procedures discussed in the following sections.

Within the behavioral literature, two common approaches to communication instruction include DTT and NET. Although quite different, both teaching procedures have been shown to be highly effective, and both have characteristic strengths detailed next. As a result, a verbal behavior approach generally incorporates a mix of NTS and DTT, with the ratio based on child-specific skills repertoires and instructional targets (Sundberg & Partington, 2010).

Discrete Trial Instruction

DTI is a primary instructional strategy for teaching new behaviors and new discriminations to children with autism. DTI consists of a series of discrete learning units implemented in a highly specified and structured manner using a stimulus-response-consequence teaching format (Ghezzi, 2007). In this teaching sequence, a stimulus is presented (i.e., instruction, cue, and/or object/item), the child responds or the response is prompted, and a consequence to reinforce the response (i.e., tangible reinforcement paired with social praise/attention) occurs. Prompts are systematically faded until the child responds independently in the presence of the relevant discriminative stimulus. Targeted skills are broken into small, attainable tasks so that the child can obtain success and receive reinforcement often. Using a clear, explicit method of teaching simplifies instruction, enhances motivation, and increases learning opportunities for children with autism. DTI can be used to establish and expand speaker and listener verbal operants; however, DTI has shown to be particularly effective in establishing early echoic, tacting, intraverbal, and listener responding skills.

Naturalistic Teaching Strategies

Although NTS or naturalistic interventions (NI) follow the same stimulus-response-consequence teaching pattern as DTI, instruction is embedded into natural occurring contexts, settings, or activities (Sundberg & Partington, 2010). Teaching sessions can be conducted in the child's home, school, or community. A child's immediate interests and activities are used as natural MOs/EOs and serve as a guide for language instruction, thus creating a more natural and less structured teaching environment than that of more formal teaching approaches such as DTI (Sundberg & Partington, 2010). For example, during play time, a variety of preferred items and activities can be used as MOs/EOs to teach manding. Specifically, preferred items could be placed in sight, but out of child's reach so that the child must mand to obtain a desired item. In addition, instructional tools or targets may be selected based on the learner's area of interest. For example, if the child enjoys Disney characters, a book containing the characters can be used to teach tacting of animals, colors, shapes, sizes, and so on. To promote stimulus and response generalization, NTS incorporate natural change agents (i.e., parents, siblings, and teachers); implement multiple exemplar training; and use natural, relevant reinforcers (LeBlanc, Esch, Sidener, & Firth, 2006). NTS have proved effective for acquisition, generalization, and maintenance of all speaker and listener verbal operants (McGee & Daly, 2007; Olive et al., 2007). In particular, the emphasis placed on the use of child-specific

EOs/MOs and specific, natural reinforcement make naturalistic teaching approaches ideal for mand training, which requires (a) contriving of an MO/EO, (b) using supplemental antecedent stimuli (i.e., prompts) to evoke a target mand, and (c) listener delivery of a corresponding reinforcer (Hall & Sundberg, 1987).

A number of naturalistic interventions/teaching approaches exist, including NET, enhanced mileau teaching (EMT), mand-model procedures, and PRT. Some degree of conceptual and procedural differences between treatments should be noted, but it is beyond the scope of this chapter. For further analysis of these differences, see LeBlanc et al. (2006).

Pivotal Response Training

PRT is a naturalistic intervention that focuses on core deficit areas of ASD, resulting in broad, generalized behavioral gains instead of isolated skill development (Koegel & Koegel, 2006). The pivotal areas or behaviors include motivation, initiation, responsivity to multiple cues, and self-management. Targeting these pivotal behaviors, it is argued, produces collateral changes in other untargeted areas of functioning and responding, thus increasing the efficiency and scale of intervention outcomes (Koegel & Koegel, 2006). In particular, research supports the effectiveness of PRT for increasing communication skills for children with ASD, including early and advanced manding, vocal imitation (i.e., echoics), conversation initiation, and tacting during play (Koegel, Camarata, Koegel, Ben-Tall, & Smith, 1998; Koegel, Carter, & Koegel, 2003; Pierce & Schreibman, 1995).

Functional Communication Training

FCT is an application of differential reinforcement procedures to treat problem behavior (Carr & Durand, 1985). The purpose of FCT is to teach an individual a more appropriate communicative and effective response (i.e., mand) to access the same class of reinforcement that maintained the problem behavior (Mayer, Sulzer-Azaroff, & Wallace, 2014). FCT typically begins with a functional behavior assessment used to determine the maintaining reinforcer (i.e., function) of the problem behavior (NAC, 2015). Once the function is determined, a more effective and efficient replacement behavior and form that serves the same function should be identified and then explicitly taught to the learner in the natural context. At the same time, problem behavior is placed on extinction and the replacement behavior is reinforced. Replacement behaviors may include the use of a break card, raising hand to ask for help, or use of picture exchange systems to request preferred items/activities.

Antecedent-Based Interventions

ABIs comprise a collection of strategies that involve modification of antecedent events that typically precede interfering behavior. Antecedents may include physical, social, verbal, gestural, or other classes of stimuli. By altering or changing these environmental stimuli, practitioners can increase the likelihood of a wanted response or reduce the likelihood of interfering behavior. A large number of behavioral procedures fall into the ABI category, many of which are fundamental to the aforementioned evidence-based practices for teaching communication to children with autism (i.e., DTI, NI, FCT). Specific examples include capturing, contriving, and manipulating a learner-specific EO/MO (e.g., deprivation of preferred snack, child choice of board games, interrupted chain procedure), which document positive effects on early and advanced manding skills, tacting ongoing actions, social initiations toward peers, and listener responding (Baker, 2000; Carter, 2001; Endicott & Higbee, 2007; Matson, Sevin, Box, Francis, & Sevin, 1993; Roberts-Pennell & Sigafoos, 1999; Taylor et al., 2005; Taylor & Harris, 1995). Also, errorless learning and prompting/prompt fading procedures (i.e., simultaneous prompting, time-delay procedures) have been used to successfully teach and increase the frequency of independent speaker and listener verbal behavior (Akmanoglu-Uludag & Batu, 2005; Finkel & Williams, 2001; Ingenmey & Van Houten, 1991; Miller, Collins, & Hemmeter, 2002). Instructional sequence modifications such as behavioral momentum and other forms of task interspersal have also proven effective strategies for training both listener and speaker verbal operants (Davis, Brady, Hamilton, McEvoy, & Williams, 1994; Dunlap, 1984). ABIs used to teach verbal behavior are not limited to these examples or these skills.

AUGMENTATIVE AND ALTERNATIVE COMMUNICATION

Given the rates of individuals diagnosed with ASD who fail to develop adequate vocal speech, it is often useful to incorporate an augmentative and alternative communication (AAC) system when establishing a functional communication or mand repertoire (Ganz, Earles-Vollrath, et al., 2012; Lorah, Parnell, Whitby, & Hantula, 2015). AAC systems can be used to either supplement (i.e., augment) limited speech or act as the primary (i.e., alternative) method of communication (Ganz, Earles-Vollrath, et al., 2012). The overarching goal of AAC is the development of generalized and functional communication within the natural environment throughout the lifetime of the individual (Mirenda, 2003). The use of AAC to establish a verbal behavior repertoire for individuals diagnosed with ASD has been noted in the literature since the 1970s (Ogletree & Harn, 2001). Furthermore, the benefits of AAC in the enhancement of a communicative repertoire are generally well recognized within the literature (Millar, Light, & Schlosser, 2006; Mirenda, 2003, 2001; Schlosser & Wendt, 2008).

Within the domain of AAC, two broad categories exist: *aided* and *unaided* (Mirenda, 2003). Unaided communication is categorized as such because it does not require any equipment and includes manual sign and gestures (Mirenda, 2003). Aided AAC includes the picture exchange communication system (PECS; Frost & Bondy, 2002), other forms of picture exchange (PE) communication (Mirenda, 2003), and voice output communication aids (VOCAs) or speech-generating devices (SGDs). PECS and PE rely on the selection and exchange of a picture, depicting the requested item or activity as the mode of communication (Michael, 1985). VOCAs or SGDs are electronic devices that rely on the speaker pressing a picture depicting the requested item or activity on an electronic screen with enough force to evoke a digitized vocal message (Lancioni et al., 2007). For example, if an individual desires a cookie, he or she would press a picture of a cookie on the touch screen of the electronic device that would produce the digitized output "I want cookie."

Unaided Systems

Although the use of sign language has been used to teach individuals with ASD to communicate, there are several limitations to its use when compared with aided AAC. One limitation is a reliance on the listener's knowledge within the natural environment. For example, a clerk at a store and a server at a restaurant may not possess knowledge of sign language (Bondy & Frost, 1994; Mirenda, 2003). An additional limitation of the use of unaided AAC is that individuals with ASD often demonstrate motor impairments and difficulty with imitative skills, which can limit their ability to acquire unaided AAC (Bondy & Frost, 1994; Mirenda, 2003; Seal & Bonvillian, 1997). Finally, unaided AAC requires that the learner acquire many responses that are topographically dissimilar, whereas aided AAC require that the learner acquire one response, such as pointing or exchanging a picture symbol (Bondy, Tincani, & Frost, 2004).

Picture Exchange Communication System and Picture Exchange

The PECS was developed by Bondy and Frost (1994) and entails what is currently a six-phase training sequence (Frost & Bondy, 2002). As such, if the training protocol does not follow their outlined six-phase sequence, the communication strategy should be classified as PE (Lancioni et al., 2007). Phase I of the training protocol focuses on *the physical exchange*. During this phase the speaker acquires the ability to exchange a picture depicting an item or activity with the listener who in exchange provides the speaker with the item or activity depicted in the picture. This phase requires two trainers to be present, one assuming the role of the listener and the other the role of the trainer who facilitates this acquisition through the prompting of responding. Phase II, called *expanding spontaneity*, requires the speaker to travel a progressively increasing distance from the communication book to their listener. Placement of the picture of the desired item is varied, and generalization across speakers and contexts is targeted (Flippin, Reszka, & Watson, 2010). During Phase III, *picture discrimination*, the speaker acquires the ability to discriminate between pictures, which vary in location within and on the cover of the communication book. Phase IV, referred to as *sentence structure*, requires the speaker to request desired items and activities using the sentence frame "I want." During this phase of training, a time-delay procedure is introduced. During Phase V, described as *responding to "What do you want?"* the communication partner asks, "What do you want?" and the speaker acquires the ability to answer the question independently. Finally in Phase VI, *responsive and spontaneous commenting*, the speaker acquires the ability to comment on environmental stimuli, through the use of carrier phrases such as "I see" and "I have" and by providing responses to questions such as "What do you see?" and "What do you have?" and so forth. The effectiveness of PECS has been demonstrated in several studies including single-subject research designs, quasi-experimental group research designs, and randomized control studies (Flippin et al., 2010; Ganz, Davis, Lund, Goodwyn, & Simpson, 2012; Tincani & Devis, 2011).

Speech-Generating Devices

The second category of aided augmentative and alternative communication systems is referred to as either VOCAs or SGDs. SGDs are electronic devices that rely on the speaker's pressing of a picture depicting the desired item or activity on an electronic screen with enough force to evoke a digitized vocal message (Lancioni et al., 2007). SGDs differ from PECS or PE in that the speaker is not required to first gain the attention of their listener, prior to requesting an item or activity; therefore, the listener is able to interpret the request even if he or she is not looking at or attending to the speaker (Lancioni et al., 2007). Dozens of SGDs exist and range greatly in cost and technological capabilities (Lancioni et al., 2007). Costs not withstanding, the use of SGDs has proven beneficial for individuals who do not demonstrate speech capabilities (Lancioni et al., 2007).

Handheld Computing Technology as an SGD

Recent technological advances in the development of powerful, portable, off-the-shelf handheld devices such as tablet computers (i.e., the iPad, Galaxy), portable media players (i.e., the iPod), and applications such as Proloqu2Go, which can be adopted to function as an SGD, has changed the way many use AAC. For example, in their review of the literature, Lorah et al. (2015) found that 93% of participants in the studies demonstrated an increased ability to communicate with portable devices. Additionally, they found that iPad-based SGDs were as effective as picture-based communication methods in establishing mands and were often more effective than manual sign language training in establishing mands. Furthermore, 84% of participants preferred the use of the iPad SGD when compared with manual sign or picture-based communication systems (Lorah et al., 2015).

To support these promising results, several specific advantages can be identified for the use of handheld computing technology as an SGD. The first advantage is availability and durability. Because portable technology devices are available at most electronic and department retail stores, they are widely available. Additionally, the devices can be serviced where they are sold, which enhances their durability. Additionally, given the widespread popularity of such devices, the use of tablet computers and/or portable multimedia players may be less stigmatizing than traditional SGDs or picture-based communication systems. Finally, these devices are multifunctional and can be used for academic (i.e., Lorah, Parnell, & Speight, 2014) and/or leisure activities (Lorah et al., 2014).

CONCLUSION

By placing emphasis on the context rather than the form of behavior, verbal behavior intervention for ASD works to structure an environment that will effectively occasion and maintain the demonstration of verbal operants. As with any quality instructional program, verbal behavior intervention first begins with an assessment of baseline skills (i.e., the VB-MAPP) and the systematic identification of those skills necessary (e.g., the mand) for an individual with ASD to develop a verbal behavior repertoire. Should an individual with ASD fail to present with functional vocal output capabilities, various methods of AAC exist to supplement his or her verbal behavior acquisition. Verbal behavior intervention relies on evidence-based practices for instructional purposes, such as time delay, prompting, and reinforcement.

REFERENCES

Akmanoglu-Uludag, N., & Batu, S. (2005). Teaching naming relatives to individuals with autism using simultaneous prompting. *Education and Training in Developmental Disabilities, 40,* 401–410.

American Psychiatric Association. (2013). *Diagnostic and statistical manual of mental disorders* (5th ed.). Washington, DC: Author.

Baker, M. J. (2000). Incorporating the thematic ritualistic behaviors of children with autism into games: Increasing social play interactions with siblings. *Journal of Positive Behavior Interventions, 2,* 66–84. http://dx.doi.org/10.1177/109830070000200201

Bondy, A. S., & Frost, L. A. (1994). The picture exchange communication system. *Focus on Autism and Other Developmental Disabilities, 9,* 1–19.

Bondy, A., Tincani, M., & Frost, L. (2004). Multiply controlled verbal operants: An analysis and extension to the picture exchange communication system. *The Behavior Analyst, 27,* 247–261. http://dx.doi.org/10.1007/BF03393184

Carr, E. G., & Durand, V. M. (1985). Reducing behavior problems through functional communication training. *Journal of Applied Behavior Analysis, 18,* 111–126. http://dx.doi.org/10.1901/jaba.1985.18-111

Carter, C. M. (2001). Using choice with game play to increase language skills and interactive behaviors in children with autism. *Journal of Positive Behavior Interventions, 3,* 131–151. http://dx.doi.org/10.1177/109830070100300302

Catania, A. C. (1992). *Learning.* Englewood Cliffs, NJ: Prentice Hall.

Chomsky, N. (1959). *On certain formal properties of grammars.* Oxford, England: Elsevier.

Cooper, J. O., Heron, T. E., & Heward, W. L. (2007). *Applied behavior analysis.* Upper Saddle River, NJ: Pearson Prentice Hall.

Davis, C. A., Brady, M. P., Hamilton, R., McEvoy, M. A., & Williams, R. E. (1994). Effects of high-probability requests on the social interactions of young children with severe disabilities. *Journal of Applied Behavior Analysis, 27,* 619–637. http://dx.doi.org/10.1901/jaba.1994.27-619

Dunlap, G. (1984). The influence of task variation and maintenance tasks on the learning and affect of autistic children. *Journal of Experimental Child Psychology, 37,* 41–64. http://dx.doi.org/10.1016/0022-0965(84)90057-2

Endicott, K., & Higbee, T. S. (2007). Contriving motivating operations to evoke mands for information in preschoolers with autism. *Research in Autism Spectrum Disorders, 1,* 210–217. http://dx.doi.org/10.1016/j.rasd.2006.10.003

Esch, B. E., LaLonde, K. B., & Esch, J. W. (2010). Speech and language assessment: A verbal behavior analysis. *The Journal of Speech and Language Pathology—Applied Behavior Analysis, 5,* 166–191. http://dx.doi.org/10.1037/h0100270

Finkel, A. S., & Williams, R. L. (2001). A comparison of textual and echoic prompts on the acquisition of intraverbal behavior in a six-year-old boy with autism. *Analysis of Verbal Behavior, 18,* 61–70. http://dx.doi.org/10.1007/BF03392971

Flippin, M., Reszka, S., & Watson, L. R. (2010). Effectiveness of the Picture Exchange Communication System (PECS) on communication and speech for children with autism spectrum disorders: A meta-analysis. *American Journal of Speech-Language Pathology, 19*, 178–195. http://dx.doi.org/10.1044/1058-0360(2010/09-0022)

Frost, L., & Bondy, A. (2002). *The Picture Exchange Communication System training manual*. Newark, DE: Pyramid Educational Products.

Ganz, J. B., Davis, J. L., Lund, E. M., Goodwyn, F. D., & Simpson, R. L. (2012). Meta-analysis of PECS with individuals with ASD: Investigation of targeted versus non-targeted outcomes, participant characteristics, and implementation phase. *Research in Developmental Disabilities, 33*, 406–418. http://dx.doi.org/10.1016/j.ridd.2011.09.023

Ganz, J. B., Earles-Vollrath, T. L., Heath, A. K., Parker, R. I., Rispoli, M. J., & Duran, J. B. (2012). A meta-analysis of single case research studies on aided augmentative and alternative communication systems with individuals with autism spectrum disorders. *Journal of Autism and Developmental Disorders, 42*, 60–74. http://dx.doi.org/10.1007/s10803-011-1212-2

Ghezzi, P. M. (2007). Discrete trials teaching. *Psychology in the Schools, 44*, 667–679. http://dx.doi.org/10.1002/pits.20256

Hall, G., & Sundberg, M. L. (1987). Teaching mands by manipulating conditioned establishing operations. *Analysis of Verbal Behavior, 5*, 41–53. http://dx.doi.org/10.1007/BF03392819

Ingenmey, R., & Van Houten, R. (1991). Using time delay to promote spontaneous speech in an autistic child. *Journal of Applied Behavior Analysis, 24*, 591–596. http://dx.doi.org/10.1901/jaba.1991.24-591

Koegel, L. K., Carter, C. M., & Koegel, R. L. (2003). Teaching children with autism self-initiations as a pivotal response. *Topics in Language Disorders, 23*, 134–145. http://dx.doi.org/10.1097/00011363-200304000-00006

Koegel, R. L., Camarata, S., Koegel, L. K., Ben-Tall, A., & Smith, A. E. (1998). Increasing speech intelligibility in children with autism. *Journal of Autism and Developmental Disorders, 28*, 241–251. http://dx.doi.org/10.1023/A:1026073522897

Koegel, R. L., & Koegel, L. K. (2006). *Pivotal response treatments for autism: Communication, social, and academic development*. Baltimore, MD: Paul H. Brookes.

Lancioni, G. E., O'Reilly, M. F., Cuvo, A. J., Singh, N. N., Sigafoos, J., & Didden, R. (2007). PECS and VOCAs to enable students with developmental disabilities to make requests: An overview of the literature. *Research in Developmental Disabilities, 28*, 468–488. http://dx.doi.org/10.1016/j.ridd.2006.06.003

Lang, R., O'Reilly, M., Healy, O., Rispoli, M., Lydon, H., Streusand, W., . . . Giesbers, S. (2012). Sensory integration therapy for autism spectrum disorders: A systematic review. *Research in Autism Spectrum Disorders, 6*, 1004–1018. http://dx.doi.org/10.1016/j.rasd.2012.01.006

LeBlanc, L. A., Esch, J., Sidener, T. M., & Firth, A. M. (2006). Behavioral language interventions for children with autism: Comparing applied verbal behavior and naturalistic teaching approaches. *Analysis of Verbal Behavior, 22*, 49–60. http://dx.doi.org/10.1007/BF03393026

Lorah, E. R., Parnell, A., & Speight, D. R. (2014). Acquisition of sentence frame discrimination using the iPad™ as a speech generating device in young children with developmental disabilities. *Research in Autism Spectrum Disorders, 8*, 1734–1740. http://dx.doi.org/10.1016/j.rasd.2014.09.004

Lorah, E. R., Parnell, A., Whitby, P. S., & Hantula, D. (2015). A systematic review of tablet computers and portable media players as speech generating devices for individuals with autism spectrum disorder. *Journal of Autism and Developmental Disorders, 45*, 3792–3804. http://dx.doi.org/10.1007/s10803-014-2314-4

Lovaas, O. I. (1987). Behavioral treatment and normal educational and intellectual functioning in young autistic children. *Journal of Consulting and Clinical Psychology, 55*, 3–9. http://dx.doi.org/10.1037/0022-006X.55.1.3

Matson, J. L., Sevin, J. A., Box, M. L., Francis, K. L., & Sevin, B. M. (1993). An evaluation of two methods for increasing self-initiated verbalizations in autistic children. *Journal of Applied Behavior Analysis, 26*, 389–398. http://dx.doi.org/10.1901/jaba.1993.26-389

Mayer, G. R., Sulzer-Azaroff, B., & Wallace, M. (2014). *Behavior analysis for lasting change*. Cornwall-on-Hudson, NY: Sloan.

McEachin, J. J., Smith, T., & Lovaas, O. I. (1993). Long-term outcome for children with autism who received early intensive behavioral treatment. *American Journal on Mental Retardation, 97*, 359–372.

McGee, G. G., & Daly, T. (2007). Incidental teaching of age-appropriate social phrases to children with autism. *Research and Practice for Persons with Severe Disabilities, 32*, 112–123. http://dx.doi.org/10.2511/rpsd.32.2.112

Michael, J. (1985). Two kinds of verbal behavior plus a possible third. *Analysis of Verbal Behavior, 3*, 1–4. http://dx.doi.org/10.1007/BF03392802

Millar, D. C., Light, J. C., & Schlosser, R. W. (2006). The impact of augmentative and alternative communication intervention on the speech production of individuals with developmental disabilities: A research review. *Journal of Speech, Language, and Hearing Research, 49*, 248–264. http://dx.doi.org/10.1044/1092-4388(2006/021)

Miller, C., Collins, B. C., & Hemmeter, M. L. (2002). Using a naturalistic time delay procedure to teach nonverbal adolescents with moderate-to-severe mental disabilities to initiate manual signs. *Journal of Developmental and Physical Disabilities, 14*, 247–261. http://dx.doi.org/10.1023/A:1016072321661

Mirenda, P. (2001). Autism, augmentative communication, and assistive technology: What do we really know? *Focus on Autism and Other Developmental Disabilities, 16*, 141–151. http://dx.doi.org/10.1177/108835760101600302

Mirenda, P. (2003). Toward functional augmentative and alternative communication for students with autism. *Language, Speech, and Hearing Services in Schools, 34*, 203–216. http://dx.doi.org/10.1044/0161-1461(2003/017)

Moore, J. (2008). *Conceptual foundations of radical behaviorism*. Cornwall-on-Hudson, NY: Sloan.

National Autism Center. (2009). *Findings and conclusions: National standards project*. Randolph, MA: Author.

National Autism Center. (2015). *Findings and conclusions: National standards project, phase 2*. Randolph, MA: Author.

National Research Council. (2001). *Educating children with autism*. Washington, DC: National Academies Press.

Odom, S. L., Collet-Klingenberg, L., Rogers, S. J., & Hatton, D. D. (2010). Evidence-based practices in interventions for children and youth with autism spectrum disorders. *Preventing School Failure, 54*, 275–282. http://dx.doi.org/10.1080/10459881003785506

Ogletree, B. T., & Harn, W. E. (2001). Augmentative and alternative communication for persons with autism: History, issues, and unanswered questions. *Focus on Autism and Other Developmental Disabilities, 16*, 138–140. http://dx.doi.org/10.1177/108835760101600301

Olive, M. L., de la Cruz, B., Davis, T. N., Chan, J. M., Lang, R. B., O'Reilly, M. F., & Dickson, S. M. (2007). The effects of enhanced milieu teaching and a voice output communication aid on the requesting of three children with autism. *Journal of Autism and Developmental Disorders, 37*, 1505–1513. http://dx.doi.org/10.1007/s10803-006-0243-6

Partington, J. W. (2010). *The Assessment of Basic Language and Learning Skills—Revised (ABLLS-R)*. Pleasant Hill, CA: Behavior Analysts.

Pierce, K., & Schreibman, L. (1995). Increasing complex social behaviors in children with autism: Effects of peer-implemented pivotal response training. *Journal of Applied Behavior Analysis, 28*, 285–295. http://dx.doi.org/10.1901/jaba.1995.28-285

Rehfeldt, R. A., & Barnes-Holmes, Y. (2009). *Derived relational responding: Applications for learners with autism and other developmental disabilities*. Reno, NV: Context Press.

Roberts-Pennell, D., & Sigafoos, J. (1999). Teaching young children with developmental disabilities to request more play using the behavior chain interruption strategy. *Journal of Applied Research in Intellectual Disabilities, 12*, 100–112. http://dx.doi.org/10.1111/j.1468-3148.1999.tb00069.x

Schlosser, R. W., & Wendt, O. (2008). Effects of augmentative and alternative communication intervention on speech production in children with autism: A systematic review. *American Journal of Speech-Language Pathology, 17*, 212–230. http://dx.doi.org/10.1044/1058-0360(2008/021)

Seal, B. C., & Bonvillian, J. D. (1997). Sign language and motor functioning in students with autistic disorder. *Journal of Autism and Developmental Disorders, 27*, 437–466. http://dx.doi.org/10.1023/A:1025809506097

Skinner, B. F. (1957). *Verbal behavior*. New York, NY: Appleton-Century-Crofts. http://dx.doi.org/10.1037/11256-000

Sundberg, M. L. (2008). *Verbal behavior milestones assessment and placement program: A language and social skills assessment program for children with autism or other developmental disabilities: Guide.* Concord, CA: AVB Press.

Sundberg, M. L., & Michael, J. (2001). The benefits of Skinner's analysis of verbal behavior for children with autism. *Behavior Modification, 25,* 698–724. http://dx.doi.org/10.1177/0145445501255003

Sundberg, M. L., & Partington, J. W. (2010). *Teaching language to children with autism or other developmental disabilities.* Concord, CA: AVB Press.

Taylor, B. A., & Harris, S. L. (1995). Teaching children with autism to seek information: Acquisition of novel information and generalization of responding. *Journal of Applied Behavior Analysis, 28,* 3–14. http://dx.doi.org/10.1901/jaba.1995.28-3

Taylor, B. A., Hoch, H., Potter, B., Rodriguez, A., Spinnato, D., & Kalaigian, M. (2005). Manipulating establishing operations to promote initiations toward peers in children with autism. *Research in Developmental Disabilities, 26,* 385–392. http://dx.doi.org/10.1016/j.ridd.2004.11.003

Tincani, M., & Devis, K. (2011). Quantitative synthesis and component analysis of single-participant studies on the picture exchange communication system. *Remedial and Special Education, 32,* 458–470. http://dx.doi.org/10.1177/0741932510362494

Travers, J. C., Tincani, M. J., & Lang, R. (2014). Facilitated communication denies people with disabilities their voice. *Research and Practice for Persons with Severe Disabilities, 39,* 195–202. http://dx.doi.org/10.1177/1540796914556778

van der Meer, L. A., & Rispoli, M. (2010). Communication interventions involving speech-generating devices for children with autism: A review of the literature. *Developmental Neurorehabilitation, 13,* 294–306. http://dx.doi.org/10.3109/17518421003671494

Virués-Ortega, J. (2010). Applied behavior analytic intervention for autism in early childhood: Meta-analysis, meta-regression and dose-response meta-analysis of multiple outcomes. *Clinical Psychology Review, 30,* 387–399. http://dx.doi.org/10.1016/j.cpr.2010.01.008

Zettle, R. D., & Hayes, S. C. (1982). Rule-governed behavior: A potential theoretical framework for cognitive–behavioral therapy. In P. C. Kendall (Eds.), *Advances in cognitive–behavioral research and therapy* (pp. 73–118). New York, NY: Academic Press.

15

VIDEO-BASED INTERVENTIONS FOR CHILDREN WITH AUTISM SPECTRUM DISORDER

STEVEN G. LITTLE, LAURETTA K. MONTES, JOHN SPANGLER, AND ANGELEQUE AKIN-LITTLE

Video-based interventions (VBIs) have become increasingly used in a wide variety of mental health treatment applications in recent years. VBI, as a class of interventions, is comprised of several different but related uses of video during a therapeutic encounter. *Video modeling* (VM) consists of a video of a model performing a desired behavior that the client is then asked to imitate. In *video self-modeling* (VSM), the therapist uses carefully edited video of clients themselves performing a behavior proficiently. Seeing themselves being successful provides not only instruction in the quality of the behavior but is also thought to effect change because it increases motivation and a sense self-efficacy. *Video feedback* (VF) is used in applications where the therapist's goal is to highlight areas of competence as well as provide specific information about behaviors that require further development. Finally, psychoeducational videos have been used in preparing clients for the therapy process and for developing coping skills, for example, to deal with severe or chronic physical ailments.

---

http://dx.doi.org/10.1037/0000126-016
Behavioral Interventions in Schools: Evidence-Based Positive Strategies, Second Edition, S. G. Little and A. Akin-Little (Editors)
Copyright © 2019 by the American Psychological Association. All rights reserved.

Examples of VBI for intervention and treatment include treatment of anxiety and depression in youth (Farrer et al., 2013), improving parent–child interactions by using VF (Steele et al., 2014), improving sleep in patients with breast cancer (Savard, Ivers, Savard, & Morin, 2014), and increasing coping skills for family members dealing with Alzheimer's disease (Williams et al., 2010). One of the most promising applications, however, is the use of VSM with children with autism spectrum disorder (ASD; Williamson, Casey, Robertson, & Buggey, 2013). Because of the increasing availability of digital video producing equipment, and the greater possibilities for disseminating videos via web-based applications, VBI holds promise as an evidence-based practice with wide applications not only for children with ASD but also in mental health in general.

ASD is characterized by deficits in language, behavior, and social skills. The most empirically supported approach to the treatment of ASD involves applications of applied behavior analysis (ABA; Peters-Scheffer, Didden, Korzilius, & Sturmey, 2011). ABA, however, involves intensive, long-duration, direct behavioral interventions (Howard, Sparkman, Cohen, Green, & Stanislaw, 2005; Sallows & Graupner, 2005). Although empirically supported, these interventions are often not practical for wide-spread implementation. On the other hand, VSM can be effectively used in school or home settings to increase social and academic behaviors in children with ASD in a time-efficient, cost-effective, and user-friendly manner. Therefore, at least with higher functioning individuals with ASD, it may be an alternative to lengthy behavioral treatments.

Learning through the use of video has been incorporated into our everyday lives since the advent of television and subsequent availability of videotape, and later, digital recordings and playback systems. Public television in the United States has made educational programming widespread for many decades. Public schools incorporated video lessons in classrooms as part of instruction early on, whether through use of filmstrips, movie reels, or video recordings. Currently, online education makes use of video to teach a variety of academic topics, vocational skills, and personal improvement programs. Because video is now so accessible and so widely accepted in many areas of our lives, it may seem obvious that we believe people can learn new ways of behaving through the use of video.

THEORETICAL FOUNDATION FOR VBI

Bandura's social learning theory explains how behavior change can be based in cognitive processes that are not explained solely in terms of direct experience, associated experience, or rewarding consequences and serves as the foundation of VBI. In fact, direct contact with a stimulus is not necessarily required. Bandura (1971) proposed a different explanation; people could develop new behaviors through a process of *vicarious learning*—watching a model behave in a certain way, identifying with the model, and deciding that performing as the model performed would be efficacious (Bandura, 1971). The core components of social learning theory are that learning occurs not only through direct problem solving, which requires a high degree of effort with the opportunity for failure, but also through observational learning and imitation of a successful model. Social learning requires several steps, including attending to the model, retaining the observation in memory, reproducing the behavior at a later time under suitable conditions, and having the motivation to reproduce the behavior (Bandura, 1971). VM and VSM interventions, in particular, incorporate all of these steps into the training process. By making videos of the self, making them brief and salient to the learning context, and editing them to show the person performing at mastery level, it is expected that people will attend, remember, and be motivated to perform similarly in the future.

In addition, by using the individual herself or himself as the model, as is the case with VSM, the similarity between the observer and the model is maximized. Self-efficacy, according to Bandura (1977), indicates the belief in one's own abilities to organize and carry out the courses of action required to manage prospective situations. In other words, it is a person's belief in her or his ability to succeed in a certain situation. According to Bandura, these beliefs are determinants of the way people feel, behave, and think. The notion of self-efficacy is key to Bandura's theory, which underscores the role of reciprocal determinism, observational learning, as well as social experience. An individual's abilities, attitudes, and cognitive skills make up what is referred to as the self-system, which actually plays a key role in the way a person perceives situations and the way a person behaves in response to various situations (Bandura, 1977). Self-efficacy plays a critical part in this self-system. Furthermore, Bandura maintained that self-efficacy could be a significant factor in behavior change. Self-modeling, as Bandura pointed out, provides the vital constituents of self-efficacy (Buggey & Ogle, 2012). When an observer sees a self-image, he or she pays more attention, and if the behavior being demonstrated is valued, it will provide a clear source of self-belief. On the contrary, an image of another person will produce less attention and is in fact a weaker source of self-efficacy (Manz & Sims, 1981).

TYPES OF VIDEO-BASED INTERVENTIONS

Video Modeling

Psychologists, educators, and speech-language pathologists have had great success using VM with children diagnosed with ASD. Considered an evidence-based strategy, VM can effectively improve behavior and increase socialization skills. According to Charlop-Christy, Le, and Freeman (2000), VM accelerates task acquisition and generalization. Banda, Copple, Koul, Sancibrian, and Bogschutz (2010) maintained that VM is an effective therapy technique to improve life skills including, but not limited to, social initiation. To clarify, in VM, the subject who views the video is not in the video. VM requires individuals (adults, peers, family, friends) other than the intentional observer as models (Charlop-Christy et al., 2000). Children who find media outlets reinforcing are ideal candidates for successful VM therapy (Mazurek & Wenstrup, 2013). VSM has shown significant advancements in teaching children with ASD. Children with autism are historically visual learners, rendering the standard learning process ineffective (Nemeth & Janacsek, 2011). Educators find VM effective because of the ability to remove the unwanted behavior from the video and present only the acceptable behavior. According to Banda et al. (2010), using VM with multiple targeted behaviors is appropriate for children with ASD.

Video Self-Modeling

According to Bellini and McConnell (2010), VSM is an effective modeling technique for children diagnosed with ASD. VSM requires the child to model the targeted behavior. The child watches the video of himself/herself performing the targeted behavior successfully. VSM is more likely to motivate individuals to engage in desired behavior, as they pay greater attention to watching themselves perform the behavior. Especially children diagnosed with ASD enjoy viewing themselves on a monitor (Cihak, Fahrenkrog, Ayres, & Smith, 2010). Montgomerie, Little, and Akin-Little (2014) reported that individuals pay more attention to self-imaging video if there is a fundamental value in the demonstrated behavior. The key success of VSM is in the individual viewing themselves executing the targeted behavior.

Two types of modeling, *positive self-review* and *feedforward* modeling have been found to promote positive outcomes. Positive self-review requires carefully constructed video depicting stellar examples of desired adaptive behavior. Positive self-review VSM increases the response rate of specific behavior and significantly improves students' on-task behaviors (Schmidt & Bonds-Raacke, 2013).

Unlike the subjects of positive self-review video, the individuals in feedforward self-modeling may not have fully acquired a specific desired skill or behavior. The final cut of a feedforward VSM video illustrates a positive skill to be acquired or a negative skill to be avoided in a particular setting (Boudreau & Harvey, 2013). Although both self-review and feedforward modeling have similar characteristics, a detailed description of their processes is provided next for calcification.

Self-Review VSM

With self-review, a person who has a moderately well-developed skill watches examples of his or her most excellent performances. This method is used to increase the frequency of adaptive behaviors, which occur at low frequency. It is also used to increase adaptive behavior, which is combined together with unwanted behavior. It helps improve a behavior that is already in the behavioral repertoire of the individual (Dowrick, 1999). In VSM, the child acts as her own or his own model. Making use of a self-model maximizes similarity between the model and the subject, which would be helpful in increasing the child's self-efficacy for performing the targeted behavior. When the child views his or her own success in the video, the child might have more confidence in his or her capability to perform the required behavior (Montgomerie et al., 2014). VSM has been found to be very motivating for children, as they take center stage on TV and become stars (Buggey, 2007). Because VSM interventions are typically engaging, the child is likely to be attentive throughout the intervention.

Feedforward VSM

This method is used when a new skill is emerging or with individuals who have not demonstrated the skill at all, although they possess the prerequisite skills to perform the behavior. Feedforward, therefore, is commonly used in clinical or instructional settings. Because this method entails new behaviors or skills, which the viewer performs, it normally requires some level of video editing to make it look like the viewer is actually performing very well (Ortiz, Burlingame, Onuegbulem, Yoshikawa, & Rojas, 2012). The phrase *feedforward* could be contrasted with the phrase *feedback*, which implies being given information regarding performance. In essence, feedback allows a person to see how he or she is doing. On the other hand, feedforward enables a person to see how he or she could be performing, that is, to see a future self (Buggey, 2007). Feedforward is largely used in therapy and education circles and mostly with children who have disabilities. Researchers have found this technique to be particularly effective with children with autism who are inclined to be visual learners and who attend better to monitors than they do to models.

Implementation of VSM

VSM involves using oneself as the model. The person of interest sees himself or herself performing the targeted skill (Bellini & Akullian, 2007) from a prerecorded video. The VSM feedforward process shows the subject successfully and accurately performing the targeted skill. It follows several steps, as outlined next.

1. *Determine the target behavior.* Consideration must be given to clearly identify and define the skill. The defining skill must include a task analysis, which is a systematic instruction.
2. *Acquire the appropriate equipment.* With the advancement of technology, any video recording equipment would be suitable. The equipment must be user friendly and include editing capabilities. A laptop, iPhone, or iPad would suffice. Considerations in terms of security and privacy of the video must be addressed. Who gets the video? Who has access to the video? Where will the video be stored, and if deleted, who deletes the video?
3. *Establish baseline.* Prior to the intervention of viewing the completed video, the rate of the target behavior must be documented and recorded via baseline measurement. A minimum of three baseline data points has to be collected to determine any trends in the frequency of the target behavior (Watson & Watson, 2009).
4. *Script the recording.* A well-written script follows the task analysis of the behavior and promotes consistency among subjects. Environmental factors must be addressed to limit distractions and audio interference. Additionally, timing is critical to acquire an unscripted baseline of expected behavior.
5. *Record.* Record the child's successful completion of each step in the sequence of the targeted behavior. Real-time editing may be required to produce a seamless video displaying model behavior.
6. *Consider other factors.* Consider the environment, time of day, frequency of viewing the video, and rewards for on-task behavior.
7. *Showing.* Consistency should be maintained with all subjects. If multiple subjects were to view the video, consistency and equal accessibility must be considered. If reviewed on a daily basis, then all subjects should have equal time.
8. *Collect data.* Collect the data within the guidelines of the task analysis. The task analysis guidelines will provide a preliminary determination of the subject's ability to perform the targeted behavior.
9. *Thin schedule of video use.* Once the targeted behavior has been successfully exhibited, reduce the video reviewing process until the target behavior is being maintained at a predetermined rate in the natural environment.

Video Feedback

In VF, the actions of the client (and sometimes those of other individuals and/or the therapist) are recorded during a therapy session. The purpose is to use it later as part of a therapist-guided review with the client to increase awareness of helpful or unhelpful behaviors, or to challenge cognitive distortion by the depiction of evidence contrary to the person's negative self-evaluation. For example, VF may be used with people who have social anxiety who (incorrectly) believe that they have done very poorly delivering a speech, when in fact they did a very good job presenting ideas to others (Aderka, 2009; Laposa & Rector, 2014). VF can also be used with parents of infants to teach specific behaviors to help both parent and child mental health outcomes (Lawrence, Davies, & Ramchandani, 2013; Reddy et al., 2014).

EMPIRICAL SUPPORT FOR VBI

There is a well-established and growing literature supporting the use of VBI in treatment of ASD in home, school, and community settings (Bellini & Akullian, 2007; Bellini & McConnell, 2010). Children and youth with autism are the major population associated with VBI interventions such as VSM (especially video feedforward techniques) to improve social functioning and independent living skills (Dowrick, 2012). The focus in the rest of this section is VSM, as it is the most frequently used technique with children with ASD.

VSM has been used to teach and strengthen various behaviors such as increasing verbal communications (Buggey, 2005; Buggey, Toombs, Gardener, & Cervetti, 1999; Hartley, Kehle, & Bray, 2002; Stone, 2000; Victor, Little, & Akin-Little, 2011), promoting social skills (Boudreau & Harvey, 2013; Gelbar, Anderson, McCarthy, & Buggey, 2012), reducing aggressive behaviors (Buggey, 2005), teaching cooking skills (McGraw-Hunter, Faw, & Davis, 2006), and reducing fidgeting and distractibility (Woltersdorf, 1992).

An area that is less researched but very promising is the use of VSM for treating academic deficits. Ayala and O'Connor (2013) effectively used a VSM treatment plan for children with ASD in the treatment of reading disabilities. Montgomerie and colleagues (2014) demonstrated the success of VSM for improving oral reading fluency in typically developing children in New Zealand. Additionally, Miller (2013) demonstrated how VSM could be used to improve the writing skills of children with learning disabilities. The greatest amount of research has demonstrated the applicability of VSM with social initiation/communication in individuals with ASD.

Buggey et al. (1999) used VSM across a variety of behaviors, including aggression, tantrums, social initiations, and use of language with students with autism. Analyses of multiple-baseline designs showed that all participants showed immediate gains. Additionally, all participants showed considerable increases in positive behaviors that were maintained even after the intervention was terminated. Wert and Neisworth (2003) also used VSM to increase the frequency of spontaneous request behaviors for young children with autism. In their study, parents were asked to show the video interventions at home no less than 60 minutes prior to their child's arrival at school. Results of this study indicated that VSM was effective in increasing the frequency of spontaneous requesting. They also found that the skill was generalized from home to school even though generalization was not programmed into the videos. Buggey (2005) demonstrated that VSM was successful in increasing the frequency of social initiation as well as in the reduction in the rate and duration of tantrums for their two participants. He also found that results were immediate and that the procedures were relatively unobtrusive, meaning those children missed little to no instructional time while participating in the study. Delano (2007) found that the use of VSM increased the number of words written with adolescents with Aspergers. Additionally, Bellini, Akullian, and Hopf (2007) saw increases in social engagement when using VSM with preschool students with autism. Victor and colleagues (2011) demonstrated the effectiveness of VSM with participants diagnosed with high-functioning autism. Results indicated a rapid increase in social engaged time after one week of viewing a video of themselves engaging in socially appropriate behaviors. The gains were also found to be sustained following the withdrawal of the intervention, and the skills generalized to other settings within the school. Schultz, Little, and Akin-Little (2014) examined whether VSM could improve the length of time young children, ages 3 to 6, with ASD remained socially engaged with their sibling. All three children demonstrated significant gains in their verbal social engagement time and were able to maintain these gains once treatment was removed. Two of the three children made significant gains and one child made moderate gains in their gestural-based social engagement time. All three maintained these gains after the treatment ended. Finally, a meta-analysis of studies using VSM with children with ASD (Bellini & Akullian, 2007) indicated gains in functional skills ($n = 8$, M PND = 89%), social communication ($n = 15$, M PND = 77%), and social functioning

($n = 5$, M PND = 76%). Results of these studies and the meta-analysis have demonstrated that VSM is an effective behavioral intervention for children with ASD.

CONCLUSION

Having children with autism act as their own model via VSM potentially circumvents some of the problems typically associated with observational learning. First, VSM eliminates the problem of locating appropriate models, thus maximizing the characteristics that influence the effectiveness of modeling such as similarity to self, competence, and prestige. Second, self-modeling is an unobtrusive intervention that is easy to implement (Buggey, 2005; Hitchcock, Dowrick, & Prater, 2003). In other words, it does not require there to be any disruptions to the child's natural environment. The only requirement for implementation is the presence of an adult who can start the video and ensure that the child is attending. Third, VSM is a nonrestrictive intervention that has the potential to promote the inclusion of children with disabilities in general education classrooms (Buggey, 2005; Hitchcock et al., 2003). Finally, self-modeling is cost-effective (Hitchcock et al., 2003).

Buggey (2007) pointed out that although VSM has been found to be effective across a wide range of ages, diagnoses, and behaviors, it does not always work. For example, he pointed out a lack of positive results with individuals with more severe forms of autism, although more recent research (e.g., Schultz et al., 2014) has suggested that VSM can be an effective intervention with young children lower on the spectrum. Buggey also discussed issues with confidentiality and the importance that any children who may appear in a video have parental consent and student assent. Buggey cautioned that target behaviors must be developmentally appropriate. Care must be taken to ensure that the final edited video does not show the individual engaging in a task that is beyond his or her capabilities.

VSM also may alleviate many of the cultural issues associated with traditional modeling therapies. Research has shown that children are more likely to imitate models that are similar to themselves (e.g., in age, gender, race), are competent in the behaviors they are modeling, and have prestige (Bandura, 1977). Selecting appropriate models for children from diverse backgrounds with disabilities becomes difficult when these characteristics are considered. For example, finding an appropriate model for a young Asian American child with autism whose target behavior is initiating social interactions would require locating another Asian American child who is competent in social interactions (the hallmark of the disorder) who also has the prestige to keep the target child engaged. Finding such a model may prove to be very difficult, if not impossible. VSM eliminates this need as the individual serves as his or her own model.

REFERENCES

Aderka, I. M. (2009). Factors affecting treatment efficacy in social phobia: The use of video feedback and individual vs. group formats. *Journal of Anxiety Disorders, 23*, 12–17. http://dx.doi.org/10.1016/j.janxdis.2008.05.003

Ayala, S. M., & O'Connor, R. (2013). The effects of video self-modeling on the decoding skills of children at risk for reading disabilities. *Learning Disabilities Research & Practice, 28*, 142–154. http://dx.doi.org/10.1111/ldrp.12012

Banda, D. R., Copple, K. S., Koul, R. K., Sancibrian, S. L., & Bogschutz, R. J. (2010). Video modelling interventions to teach spontaneous requesting using AAC devices to individuals with autism: A preliminary investigation. *Disability and Rehabilitation, 32*, 1364–1372. http://dx.doi.org/10.3109/09638280903551525

Bandura, A. (1971). *Social learning theory*. New York, NY: General Learning Press.

Bandura, A. (1977). *Social learning theory*. Englewood Cliffs, NJ: Prentice Hall.

Bellini, S., & Akullian, J. (2007). A meta-analysis of video modeling and video self-modeling interventions for children and adolescents with autism spectrum disorders. *Exceptional Children, 73*, 264–287. http://dx.doi.org/10.1177/001440290707300301

Bellini, S., Akullian, J., & Hopf, A. (2007). Increasing social engagement in young children with autism spectrum disorders using video self-modeling. *School Psychology Review, 36*, 80–90.

Bellini, S., & McConnell, L. L. (2010). Strength-based educational programming for students with autism spectrum disorders: A case for video self-modeling. *Preventing School Failure, 54*, 220–227. http://dx.doi.org/10.1080/10459881003742275

Boudreau, J., & Harvey, M. T. (2013). Increasing recreational initiations for children who have ASD using video self modeling. *Education & Treatment of Children, 36*, 49–60. http://dx.doi.org/10.1353/etc.2013.0006

Buggey, T. (2005). Video self-modeling applications with students with autism spectrum disorder in a small private school setting. *Focus on Autism and Other Developmental Disabilities, 20*, 52–63. http://dx.doi.org/10.1177/10883576050200010501

Buggey, T. (2007). A picture is worth: Video self-modeling applications at school and home. *Journal of Positive Behavior Interventions, 9*, 151–158. http://dx.doi.org/10.1177/10983007070090030301

Buggey, T., & Ogle, L. (2012). Video self-modeling. *Psychology in the Schools, 49*, 52–70. http://dx.doi.org/10.1002/pits.20618

Buggey, T., Toombs, K., Gardener, P., & Cervetti, M. (1999). Training responding behaviors in students with autism: Using videotaped self-modeling. *Journal of Positive Behavior Interventions, 1*, 205–214. http://dx.doi.org/10.1177/109830079900100403

Charlop-Christy, M. H., Le, L., & Freeman, K. A. (2000). A comparison of video modeling with in vivo modeling for teaching children with autism. *Journal of Autism and Developmental Disorders, 30*, 537–552. http://dx.doi.org/10.1023/A:1005635326276

Cihak, D., Fahrenkrog, C., Ayres, K. M., & Smith, C. (2010). The use of video modeling via a video iPod and a system of least prompts to improve transitional behaviors for students with autism spectrum disorders in the general education classroom. *Journal of Positive Behavior Interventions, 12*, 103–115. http://dx.doi.org/10.1177/1098300709332346

Delano, M. E. (2007). Improving written language performance of adolescents with Asperger syndrome. *Journal of Applied Behavior Analysis, 40*, 345–351. http://dx.doi.org/10.1901/jaba.2007.50-06

Dowrick, P. W. (1999). A review of self modeling and related interventions. *Applied & Preventive Psychology, 8*, 23–39. http://dx.doi.org/10.1016/S0962-1849(99)80009-2

Dowrick, P. W. (2012). Self modeling: Expanding the theories of learning. *Psychology in the Schools, 49*, 30–41. http://dx.doi.org/10.1002/pits.20613

Farrer, L., Gulliver, A., Chan, J. K. Y., Batterham, P. J., Reynolds, J., Calear, A., . . . Griffiths, K. M. (2013). Technology-based interventions for mental health in tertiary students: Systematic review. *Journal of Medical Internet Research, 15*, e101. http://dx.doi.org/10.2196/jmir.2639

Gelbar, N. W., Anderson, C., McCarthy, S., & Buggey, T. (2012). Video self-modeling as an intervention strategy for individuals with autism spectrum disorders. *Psychology in the Schools, 49*, 15–22. http://dx.doi.org/10.1002/pits.20628

Hartley, E. T., Kehle, T. J., & Bray, M. A. (2002). Increasing student classroom participation through self-modeling. *Journal of Applied School Psychology, 19*, 51–63. http://dx.doi.org/10.1300/J008v19n01_04

Hitchcock, C. H., Dowrick, P. W., & Prater, M. A. (2003). Video self-modeling intervention in school-based settings: A review. *Remedial and Special Education, 24*, 36–45. http://dx.doi.org/10.1177/074193250302400104

Howard, J. S., Sparkman, C. R., Cohen, H. G., Green, G., & Stanislaw, H. (2005). A comparison of intensive behavior analytic and eclectic treatments for young children with autism. *Research in Developmental Disabilities, 26*, 359–383. http://dx.doi.org/10.1016/j.ridd.2004.09.005

Laposa, J. M., & Rector, N. A. (2014). Effects of videotaped feedback in group cognitive behavioral therapy for social anxiety disorder. *International Journal of Cognitive Therapy, 7*, 360–372. http://dx.doi.org/10.1521/ijct.2014.7.4.360

Lawrence, P. J., Davies, B., & Ramchandani, P. G. (2013). Using video feedback to improve early father infant interaction: A pilot study. *Clinical Child Psychology and Psychiatry, 18*, 61–71. http://dx.doi.org/10.1177/1359104512437210

Manz, C. C., & Sims, H. P., Jr. (1981). Vicarious learning: The influence of modeling on organizational behavior. *Academy of Management Review, 6*, 105–113. http://dx.doi.org/10.5465/amr.1981.4288021

Mazurek, M. O., & Wenstrup, C. (2013). Television, video game and social media use among children with ASD and typically developing siblings. *Journal of Autism and Developmental Disorders, 43*, 1258–1271. http://dx.doi.org/10.1007/s10803-012-1659-9

McGraw-Hunter, M., Faw, G. D., & Davis, P. K. (2006). The use of video self-modelling and feedback to teach cooking skills to individuals with traumatic brain injury: A pilot study. *Brain Injury, 20*, 1061–1068. http://dx.doi.org/10.1080/02699050600912163

Miller, K. M. (2013). *Examining the effects of self-regulated strategy development in combination with video self-modeling on writing by third grade students with learning disabilities* (Unpublished doctoral dissertation). University of Central Florida, Orlando.

Montgomerie, R., Little, S. G., & Akin-Little, A. (2014). Video self-modeling as an intervention for oral reading fluency. *New Zealand Journal of Psychology, 43*, 18–27.

Nemeth, D., & Janacsek, K. (2011). Are children with autism good or bad learners? *Proceedings of the National Academy of Sciences, 108*, E57–E57. http://dx.doi.org/10.1073/pnas.1101816108

Ortiz, J., Burlingame, C., Onuegbulem, C., Yoshikawa, K., & Rojas, E. D. (2012). The use of video self-modeling with English language learners: Implications for success. *Psychology in the Schools, 49*, 23–29. http://dx.doi.org/10.1002/pits.20615

Peters-Scheffer, N., Didden, R., Korzilius, H., & Sturmey, P. (2011). A meta-analytic study on the effectiveness of comprehensive ABA-based early intervention programs for children with autism spectrum disorders. *Research in Autism Spectrum Disorders, 5*, 60–69. http://dx.doi.org/10.1016/j.rasd.2010.03.011

Reddy, P. D., Desai, G., Hamza, A., Karthik, S., Ananthanpillai, S. T., & Chandra, P. S. (2014). Enhancing mother infant interactions through video feedback enabled interventions in women with schizophrenia: A single subject research design study. *Indian Journal of Psychological Medicine, 36*, 373–377. http://dx.doi.org/10.4103/0253-7176.140702

Sallows, G. O., & Graupner, T. D. (2005). Intensive behavioral treatment for children with autism: Four-year outcome and predictors. *American Journal on Mental Retardation, 110*, 417–438. http://dx.doi.org/10.1352/0895-8017(2005)110[417:IBTFCW]2.0.CO;2

Savard, J., Ivers, H., Savard, M.-H., & Morin, C. M. (2014). Is a video-based cognitive behavioral therapy for insomnia as efficacious as a professionally administered treatment in breast cancer? Results of a randomized controlled trial. *Sleep, 37,* 1305–1314. http://dx.doi.org/10.5665/sleep.3918

Schmidt, C., & Bonds-Raacke, J. (2013). The effects of video self-modeling on children with autism spectrum disorder. *International Journal of Special Education, 28,* 136–146.

Schultz, S., Little, S. G., & Akin-Little, A. (2014, March). *Increasing the amount of social engagement time young children with autism use with their siblings using video self-modeling.* Paper presented at the 4th annual meeting of the Association of Professional Behavior Analysts, New Orleans, LA.

Steele, M., Steele, H., Bate, J., Knafo, H., Kinsey, M., Bonuck, K., . . . Murphy, A. (2014). Looking from the outside in: The use of video in attachment-based interventions. *Attachment & Human Development, 16,* 402–415. http://dx.doi.org/10.1080/14616734.2014.912491

Stone, B. P. (2000). Videotape modeling interventions for selective mutism: A comparative research investigation. *Dissertation Abstracts International, 61,* 1744A.

Victor, H., Little, S. G., & Akin-Little, A. (2011). Increasing social engaged time in children with autism spectrum disorder using video self-modeling. *Journal of Evidence-Based Practices for Schools, 12,* 105–124.

Watson, T. S., & Watson, T. S. (2009). Behavioral assessment in the schools. In A. Akin-Little, S. G. Little, M. A. Bray, & T. J. Kehle (Eds.), *Behavioral interventions in schools: Evidence-based positive strategies* (pp. 27–41). Washington, DC: American Psychological Association. http://dx.doi.org/10.1037/11886-002

Wert, B. Y., & Neisworth, J. T. (2003). Effects of video self-modeling on spontaneous requesting in children with autism. *Journal of Positive Behavior Interventions, 5,* 30–34. http://dx.doi.org/10.1177/10983007030050010501

Williams, V. P., Bishop-Fitzpatrick, L., Lane, J. D., Gwyther, L. P., Ballard, E. L., Vendittelli, A. P., . . . Williams, R. B. (2010). Video-based coping skills to reduce health risk and improve psychological and physical well-being in Alzheimer's disease family caregivers. *Psychosomatic Medicine, 72,* 897–904. http://dx.doi.org/10.1097/PSY.0b013e3181fc2d09

Williamson, R. L., Casey, L. B., Robertson, J. S., & Buggey, T. (2013). Video self-modeling in children with autism: A pilot study validating prerequisite skills and extending the utilization of VSM across skill sets. *Assistive Technology, 25,* 63–71. http://dx.doi.org/10.1080/10400435.2012.712604

Woltersdorf, M. A. (1992). Videotape self-modeling in the treatment of attention-deficit hyperactivity disorder. *Child & Family Behavior Therapy, 14,* 53–73. http://dx.doi.org/10.1300/J019v14n02_04

16

TEACCH AND OTHER STRUCTURED APPROACHES TO TEACHING

LAURIE McLAY, SARAH HANSEN, AND AMARIE CARNETT

A number of classroom-based teaching approaches have been developed to enhance children's learning. Many of these approaches follow structured and clearly defined teaching methods, are individualized according to the learning needs and progress of each child, and incorporate data-based decision making. This includes the Training and Education of Autistic and other Communication Handicapped Children (TEACCH) structured teaching program, precision teaching, and direct instruction. The primary purpose of this chapter is to provide you with an overview of the TEACCH approach to structured teaching. However, other structured, classroom-based teaching approaches including precision teaching and direct instruction, will also be described. This will include a description of the historical and theoretical foundation of these approaches, the principles that underpin these approaches, strategies for implementing programs within the classroom context, and an evaluation of the underlying evidence base.

http://dx.doi.org/10.1037/0000126-017
Behavioral Interventions in Schools: Evidence-Based Positive Strategies, Second Edition, S. G. Little and A. Akin-Little (Editors)
Copyright © 2019 by the American Psychological Association. All rights reserved.

TEACCH

The TEACCH structured teaching program was developed in 1966 at the University of North Carolina (Schopler & Reichler, 1971). Division TEACCH was later established as a statewide program in 1972 (Schopler, 1994). Since its conception, strategies identified through the TEACCH program have been implemented throughout the United States and internationally, across a variety of settings. Division TEACCH developed a unique approach to working with children with autism spectrum disorder (ASD) and their families that recognized ASD as a developmental, rather than emotional, disorder. Structured teaching is a multidisciplinary teaching approach that was designed specifically for children with ASD, to more effectively align educational strategies with the unique features of ASD (e.g., difficulties with receptive and expressive language, attention, memory, social relationships, sensory stimulation in the environment).

Foundations of TEACCH

The structured teaching approach is underpinned by an eclectic combination of psychological theories, including cognitive-social learning theory and developmental psychology. The structured teaching approach recognizes both the value of external contingencies (e.g., rewards and punishments) as well as internal determinants of behavior (e.g., an individual's thoughts, expectations, understanding). Emphasis is also placed on understanding and responding to each individual's unique developmental profile, in recognition of the fact that children with ASD do not follow conventional developmental patterns. The structured teaching approach is also based on research evidence that has identified the unique neuropsychological differences of children with ASD, occasionally referred to as the "culture of Autism" (Mesibov & Shea, 2010, p. 571; Ozonoff, South, & Provencal, 2005; Tsatsanis, 2005). This includes executive functioning difficulties (e.g., difficulties with attention and memory); preferences for processing visual information; communication difficulties; preferences for, and aversions to, specific types of sensory input; preference for, and adherence to, routines and settings; generalization difficulties; problems understanding concepts of time; and intense and at times obsessive interests and preferences for activities that can be difficult for children to disengage from (Mesibov & Shea, 2010).

The TEACCH program is underpinned by a number of core values (Mesibov, Shea, & Schopler, 2005). Foremost is an understanding, appreciation, and respect for the culture of ASD. Structured teaching specifically recognizes the characteristic difficulties of ASD, as well as each individual's skills, talents, special interests, feelings, personality, quirks, and potential. According to Mesibov and Shea (2010), there are four key principles that underpin the TEACCH program. The first is to ensure that the environment is organized so that the sequence of events, increments of time, and teaching and learning spaces are clear, predictable, and easy to understand. This may involve making environmental modifications or providing supplementary external supports that meet the needs of children with ASD within the classroom (e.g., creating designated spaces within the classroom for set activities, such as low-stimulation spaces for relaxation). The second principle is to take advantage of the strengths and preferences of children with ASD for processing visual input (Panerai, Ferrante, & Zingale, 2002) by providing visual information to support children's understanding of expectations, to support engagement, and to minimize the likelihood of distress. This may include specific visual supports such as picture schedules or to-do lists, depending on the child's developmental level (Mesibov & Shea, 2010). The third is to use children's special interests to support learning (i.e., to support engagement and/or to reward achievement)—for example, if a child has an interest in trains, access to train stickers may be provided as reinforcement for completion of set activities. Similarly, if developmentally appropriate, train timetables may be used to teach children to tell the time. The fourth is to support children to initiate meaningful and functional communication by supporting them to develop a foundation of preverbal skills and receptive understanding as the foundation for development of functional, self-initiated language and communication. Communication objectives and strategies should also align with each individual's cognitive ability (Mesibov & Shea, 2010; Mesibov, Shea, & Schopler, 2005).

In addition to these core principles, the TEACCH program follows a child-centered approach in which the child and family's unique needs, interests, strengths, and goals are the focus of intervention. Within the TEACCH model the parents are viewed as an invaluable resource and a central component of successful treatment (Panerai et al., 2009; Schopler, 1994; Van Bourgondien & Schopler, 1996). As such, delivery of the TEACCH program relies on close collaborative relationships between professionals (e.g., teachers, therapists) and parents.

Finally, intervention goals, strategies, and supports are individualized for each child on the basis of assessment outcomes and in accordance with the aforementioned principles (Panerai, Ferrante, & Zingale, 2002). A central goal of the TEACCH program is to support individuals to learn skills that will assist them in all aspects of life, with the goal of maximizing children and young people's independence across contexts (Panerai et al., 2002; Schopler, Mesibov, & Hearsey, 1995).

Components of Structured Teaching

The TEACCH program is used with children and young people of all ages and developmental levels. TEACCH provides a framework for establishing educational programs that are ASD friendly; consider the cognitive skills, interests, and needs of children with ASD; and reduce support and enhance independence. Adaptations are made to the structure of the learning environment (e.g., physical organization of the environment, teaching space and activities) to accomplish these goals (Mesibov & Shea, 2010). This includes the structuring of daily events as well as specific tasks (Mesibov & Shea, 2010). Educational programs that are delivered using a structured teaching approach are based on four central components: physical structure, daily schedules, work systems, and visual structure and information (Mesibov, Howley, & Naftel, 2016).

Physical Structure and Organization

When using a structured teaching approach, it is essential that the classroom is organized based on our knowledge of the sensory difficulties and cognitive, developmental, and perceptual strengths and challenges of children with ASD. As such, the classroom environment should be clearly structured and include minimal distractions to facilitate task engagement and attention, convey expectations, and enhance independence. For example, depending on the needs of the child, the classroom may include designated spaces for play/leisure activities, snack time, and academic tasks, individual and whole-class activities, as well as low-stimulation or quiet areas that offer solitude if children and young people become overwhelmed (Mesibov, Howley, & Naftel, 2016). Within these spaces, available materials should be easily accessible.

Daily Schedules

Daily schedules provide children with representation of the activities that will take place that day and the sequence in which these events or activities will occur; for example, this may include symbols that represent morning circle time, library, writing, snack time, and so on. Presenting daily tasks using visual schedules can help children with ASD to understand and anticipate the daily expectations and routines and therefore can help to facilitate independent transitions between activities and across contexts (i.e., between the classroom and library). Furthermore, assisting children to understand expectations and routines can help to minimize anxiety and manage challenging behaviors in an environment that might otherwise be confusing or unpredictable. Daily schedules can be particularly important for children with ASD because of the challenges that many children with ASD have with receptive language, comprehension, and sequential memory and organization. Daily schedules can consist of photographs, pictures, drawings, or written words, depending on each child's level of understanding.

Work System

Work systems, also known as "schedules within a schedule" or "to-do lists," are often used alongside daily schedules to organize the structure of each specific activity. They are used to convey visually what each child or young person is expected to do, the number of tasks that must be completed, how the child will determine whether they are making progress and when the task is complete, and what they are expected to do when they have finished (Mesibov, Howley, & Naftel, 2016); for example, if a child is able to comprehend written language, then they could be presented with a written work system in which each task and corresponding set of materials are clearly labeled. These labels would correspond with the child's written list of tasks to complete. As the child completed each task, they could then cross it off or tick a box on a checklist to indicate that the task is completed and to see what to proceed to next. This list would provide visual representation of how many tasks the child is expected to complete and also what the child is required to do when they have finished all activities. Children may require repeated practice in using work systems before they are able to be used independently. However, ultimately, work systems are viewed as being essential to supporting children and young people in learning to work without adult support. Work systems are individualized according to the activities being undertaken by each child, though they can also be used during activities that are being completed in pairs or groups.

Visual Structure and Information

Visual structure and information refers to the organization, structure, and presentation of the tasks themselves. Visual clarity, visual organization, and visual instructions are seen as being critical to the organization and presentation of activities. Visual clarity means ensuring that important components of each task are clearly presented (e.g., large photographs might be placed on cabinets or drawers within the classroom to indicate where materials are located) and that the materials used to complete each task are clearly ordered, accessible, developmentally appropriate, and minimally stimulating (e.g., a multistep construction activity may be broken down so that each of the steps that need to be completed are presented on individual pages, with corresponding materials, spaced across the workstation). Finally, visual instructions, using images or written text, explain task requirements, including an indication of what is expected for a task to be completed.

Critics of TEACCH

Although structured teaching has been used extensively throughout the United States and internationally, critics of this approach identify some limitations. First, the TEACCH approach is typically implemented by staff who have an extensive knowledge of the core features of ASD, and the implications of this, and/or by staff who have experience in working with children with ASD (Panerai et al., 2002). It may be difficult for classroom teachers who lack this knowledge to effectively implement structured teaching strategies within the classroom. Second, it may be difficult to implement the TEACCH approach in inclusive settings (Panerai et al., 2009), particularly given the extent of the environmental adaptations and individualization required. Physically organizing an environment into set areas for specific activities, the extensive use of individualized visual supports and structures, and the individualization of communication strategies may be difficult in regular education settings (Panerai, Ferrante, & Zingale, 2002). Finally, in regular education settings, the structure and duration of activities and the classroom schedule is typically specified by the teacher or school and not to the needs of individual students (Panerai et al., 2002). Organizing the classroom schedule so that it is responsive to the needs of all students in the classroom would require significant amounts of flexibility that are not always possible with classrooms and schools.

Evidence Base That Underpins TEACCH

Several studies have been conducted since the initial introduction of the TEACCH program. The following sections discuss the evidence base that underpins the TEACCH program, its use across contexts, limitations of the current research base, and recommendations for future research.

Overall Evidence

The use of the TEACCH program has been frequently reported in the literature related to treatment programs for children with autism (Mesibov & Shea, 2010; Virues-Ortega, Julio, & Pastor-Barriuso, 2013). In two surveys, it was noted that between 18% and 30% of parents of children with ASD that were surveyed were using or had previously used the TEACCH program (Goin-Kochel, Mackintosh, & Myers, 2009; Green et al., 2006). For example, in a survey conducted by Goin-Kochel and colleagues (2009), 18.4% of parents of children with ASD reported trying the TEACCH program ($n = 479$). Of that group, 25% reported dramatic improvement, 43.2% reported some improvement, 12.5% reported no noticeable effect, and 11.4% reported that their child had become worse.

A growing body of literature continues to assess the efficacy and quality of this intervention (Virues-Ortega et al., 2013). Thus, recommendations have been made when evaluating the effectiveness of the TEACCH program that are based on controlled studies using the standards of evidence-based practices (EBP; D'Elia et al., 2014; Mesibov & Shea, 2010). In their review of the literature, Virues-Ortega and colleagues (2013) conducted a meta-analysis to evaluate this emerging practice. The authors evaluated 13 studies and found an overall mean effect size of .47, indicating a moderate effect (i.e., showed some effectiveness). In particular, authors noted a moderate-to-large effect when looking at social behavior and maladaptive behavior, compared with the small effect reported for perceptual, motor, verbal, and cognitive skills. Additionally, the authors noted a publication bias (i.e., publication of studies with only positive outcomes) and small study effects that impacted their findings. The authors concluded that further research should be conducted to evaluate outcomes of the TEACCH program and strengthen this evidence-base. Given the small effect size for certain skills and limitations noted in this meta-analysis, the degree of effectiveness of this treatment program remains unclear.

One of the most notable organizations, the National Autism Center, has published a comprehensive report evaluating the levels and quality of research for autism interventions (*National Standards Report* [National Autism Center, 2009]; *Findings and Conclusions: National Standards Project, Phase 2* [National Autism Center, 2015]). Here, structured teaching is listed as an emerging intervention for individuals who are under the age of 22, meaning there is some evidence of effectiveness. These types of interventions (i.e., structured teaching, structured work systems) were also evaluated by the National Professional Development Center on Autism Spectrum Disorder in their 2014 report on EBPs (Wong et al., 2015). Structured work systems were previously listed as an EPB in the initial report (1997) but was removed in the latest report (2014) because of a change in requiring more stringent criteria for evaluating the evidence. Thus, independent work systems is currently listed as having insufficient evidence (Wong et al., 2015). As such, additional high-quality research is needed to conclude the level of effectiveness.

Evidence Base for Use in Schools

Several studies have evaluated the use of the TEACCH program in school settings. The majority of this research has investigated the use of this intervention inside specialized classroom environments, such as a resource classroom or self-contained settings. For example, Mechling and Savidge (2011) investigated the use of a personal digital assistant (PDA) with multi-level prompts to increase novel structured tasks and transitions between tasks for three students (M age = 14 years) with autism. Procedures selected for this study used the elements of structured teaching under the TEACCH program model. Results of this study indicated that two of the three students had higher rates of task completion following intervention, and all students had an increase in between task transitions using the PDA.

Other school-based studies have used elements of the TEACCH program, such as individual work systems. For example, Hume and Odom (2007) evaluated the effects of a work system on independent work and play skills for three students with autism (ages 20, 6, and 7 years) within a public school system. Results of this study indicated that each participant showed increases in on-task behavior and the number of tasks completed (or play materials used). Additionally, these skills were maintained after a 1-month follow-up for each student.

In a similar study, Bryan and Gast (2000) investigated the use of a picture activity schedule and the effects of on-task behavior and on-schedule behavior for four students with high-functioning autism. The results of this study indicated increased levels of targeted behaviors (i.e., on-schedule and on-task behaviors) when the activity schedule was used compared with the reversal phase (i.e., no book). Further, these results generalized to novel tasks with minimal or no training. Future research investigating inclusion-based settings and other types of behaviors (i.e., social communication skills, academic tasks) would be beneficial to add more support to this emerging treatment package.

Evidence Base for Use in Early Childhood Education

Researchers have evaluated the use of the TEACCH program for children with autism in early childhood settings. For example, D'Elia and colleagues (2014) evaluated the potential benefits of a low-intensity version (i.e., 2 hours at home and 2 hours at school) of the TEACCH program in a longitudinal study. A total of 30 children participated and were divided into treatment groups (i.e., 15 children in the low-intensity TEACCH program and 15 children in a nonspecific approach group where traditional therapies were provided). During the study, children were assessed four times for autism severity, adaptive functioning, language skills, maladaptive behaviors, and parental stress. Results of this study indicated that the use of a low-intensity home and school TEACCH program may be beneficial as reduction in symptoms of autism, maladaptive behaviors, and parent stress were reported.

In a similar study, Ozonoff and Cathcart (1998) evaluated the effectiveness of the TEACCH-based home program for children from 2 to 6 years of age by comparing two matched groups of 11 children (i.e., treatment and control group). These programs ran about 10 weeks, and families met weekly with two therapists for about an hour. During these meetings, therapists provided skill modeling to the parent. Each family was encouraged to spend at least 30 minutes per day working with their child in their home; however, specific goals and skills were not reported. Results of the use of the TEACCH program indicated a significant improvement in a subtest (i.e., Psychoeducational Profile—Revised test; Schopler, Reichler, Bashford, Lansing, & Marcus, 1990) of imitation, motor, and nonverbal conceptual skills, as well as an increase in overall test scores.

Finally, Welterlin, Turner-Brown, Harris, Mesibov, and Delmolino (2012) evaluated the efficacy of the TEACCH-based home/parent training program. Data collected compared pre- and posttreatment scores on the Mullen Scales of Early Learning (Mullen, 1995) and the Scales of Independent Behavior–Revised (Bruininks, Woodcock, Weatherman, & Hill, 1996), and direct measures of behavior (i.e., independent functioning) were compared between the treatment and wait-list control groups. The findings of this study indicated improvements in the children's independent work skills and parents' ability to provide structured learning environments with effective prompts for the treatment group. The overall findings of this research suggest positive effects as a result of the TEACCH program; however, as previously stated, additional replication of these findings would be valuable to support the current evidence base.

Use in Residential Programs

Some research investigating the efficacy of the TEACCH program has been conducted in the context of residential programs. For example, Panerai, Ferrante, and Zingale (2002) evaluated the use of the TEACCH program by comparing treatment outcomes among children with autism in a residential facility and children with autism who attended regular schools. Authors reported a difference between the experimental group (i.e., children who received the TEACCH program) and the control group, indicating the TEACCH program was more effective than the standard services given to the control group.

Siaperas and Beadle-Brown (2006) also investigated the use of structured teaching for 12 adults with autism within residential homes using a repeated measures design. Results of this study indicated improvement in levels of personal independence, social abilities, and functional communication.

Use Across Cultures

One area of the research that is particularly noteworthy for the TEACCH program is the extent of research that extends across countries. For example, research on the efficacy of the TEACCH program has been evaluated in China (e.g., Tsang, Shek, Lam, Tang, & Cheung, 2007), Greece (e.g., Siaperas & Beadle-Brown, 2006), Italy (e.g., Panerai, Ferrante, Caputo, & Impellizzeri, 1998; Panerai, Ferrante, & Zingale, 2002; Panerai et al., 2009), Japan (e.g., Ichikawa et al., 2013; Sasaki, 2000), and the United Kingdom (e.g., Taylor & Preece, 2010). Although, findings are preliminary and warrant replication, the extension of this subject area across various countries adds to the potential value of structured teaching.

Limitations

Although the reviewed body of research indicates the potential benefits of the TEACCH program for children with autism, one obvious limitation is the need for further replication and extension to other types of disabilities. As an emerging research practice, there is also a need for replication to establish this intervention as an EBP.

One limitation of a treatment packaged intervention, such as the TEACCH program, is that it is difficult to analyze each treatment component (Virues-Ortega et al., 2013). As such, specific analysis on the various components of this treatment package and the specific treatment outcomes would be of great value to the existing body of literature and to the application of structured learning programs. In addition to the TEACCH program, two other structured approaches to classroom teaching have been identified for inclusion in this chapter. They are precision teaching and direct instruction.

PRECISION TEACHING

Precision teaching is a decision-making system used to evaluate and plan teaching skills based on measurement of students' behavioral fluency. Behavioral fluency can be defined as responding that is fast and accurate (Binder, 1996). Precision teaching was first proposed by O. R. Lindsley, a student of B. F. Skinner, in the early 1960s (Lindsley, 1964). Lindsley started applying the principles of precision teaching on the basis of his observations of free-operant learning in his research lab where he worked with children and adults with psychosis. Lindsley noted that recording rate of behavior was more sensitive to the change from interventions than most other measures. In 1965, Linsley moved this experiment into the classroom and began to focus on the application of his theory to the school setting. Lindsley was interested in the effects of implementing a precise measurement system in classroom settings that focused on rate, to guide teaching rather than attempting to manipulate teaching practices (Lindsley, 1992). Linsley and colleagues identified the tendency of educational measures to be based on percentage correct rather than rate to be a major barrier toward progress in education (Rogers & Skinner, 1956). Thus, he proposed to improve classroom learning by teaching students and teachers to use what he called the Standard Behavior Chart or Standard Celeration Chart, which was a logarithmic chart for recording behavior frequency and rate. When charted over the days and weeks of the school year, this system allowed for the generation of curves that demonstrated growth over time.

Lindsley taught teachers and students to implement these strategies themselves and use the results to make decisions about teaching practices implemented and curriculum taught (Lindsley, 1992). Successful use of rate measurement, as well as student and teacher charting of data, was demonstrated across school settings, such as Montessori classrooms for children with special needs (Fink, 1968), a first-grade classroom (Starlin, 1971), and others (Caldwell, 1966; Holzschuh & Dobbs, 1966). Typical data collection systems focused only on accuracy at the time (e.g., percentage of trials correct), whereas precision teaching was novel in its insistence on tracking accuracy and rate (Binder, 1988). As the field of precision teaching evolved, screening measures were developed to begin to identify children at risk for academic failure (Binder & Watkins, 2013). Precision teaching has since evolved into a data-based, decision-making framework that is appropriate for use with structured teaching practices (e.g., direct instruction; Binder & Watkins, 2013). Principles of precision teaching are used across settings, including adult learning (e.g., Say All Fast Minute Each Day Shuffled [SAFMEDS]).

Precision teaching is based on early understanding of the principles of behavior. There are direct influences from Skinner, Pavlov, and other pioneers of behaviorism. Precision teaching is grounded in behavioral theory. Specifically, precision teaching specifies the importance of behavioral fluency as the best metric to analyze responding rates and track learning over time. Behavioral fluency is theorized to be the best indicator of learning under the precision-teaching theory. The core concepts of precision teaching evolved from laboratory assessments of behavior that were precise and sensitive to changes from intervention.

There are four core principles of precision teaching. The first principle is that the learner knows best. Precision teaching recognizes the unique growth trajectory of the learner rather than their accuracy compared with others or to a developmental standard. In fact, original precision teaching theory stated that if the program of instruction was working for the child, then the data would reflect that, and if it did not, it was a problem with the program, not the student (Lindsley, 1991). A second core principle of precision teaching is a focus on directly measurable and observable behaviors. Focusing on observable behavior allows behaviors to be measured correctly, and accurate growth to be charted over time. This can include the use of a Celeration Chart to track student behavior over time. Lindsley noted that all the teachers he observed were using a different method for taking data on the children in their class, so communication of teaching methods or child progress for a child with multiple teachers was time consuming and burdensome. Lindsley developed a chart that allowed the use of a logarithmic scale to chart student improvement from day to year and also allowed multiple teachers working with the same child to chart progress in a uniform way. Lindsley focused on frequency (counts per minute) of the target behavior, which he thought to be the most sensitive and accurate data collection method (Lindsley, 1991).

Components of Precision Teaching and Implementation

Successful implementation of precision teaching requires three main steps. Primarily, practitioners must define and operationalize the behavior they want to chart (White, 1986). Lindsley suggested considering movement and repeatability when considering a behavior of interest (i.e., how easy will it be to capture the behavior in a class period, how observable is the behavior). The second core component is the charting of the behavior. Immediate charting of behavior on a standard celebration chart is core to precision teaching. Charting should be sensitive to unique pupil needs and be based on the outcome from focused pupil practice. Precision teaching calls for brief practice periods for data collection (e.g., frequency across a 10-minute practice period; Kubina, Morrison, & Lee, 2002). Finally, the evaluation of the chart is the final core component to precision teaching. Original writing about the precision teaching method simply stated that if there was curve to the student's data in the intended direction, leave the program alone, and if there was flatness in the student's data, then the program needs to be modified (West, Young, & Spooner, 1990). Since its origin, more complex decision rules have been built into precision teaching including other factors, such as student characteristics, reinforcement, performance and prerequisite skills, and curriculum or instruction being used (Haring, Liberty, & White, 1980).

Critics of Precision Teaching

Some critiques of precision teaching include concern about the content of teaching, even given accurate data collection, potential error patterns, and lack of mechanism to teach critical thinking or problem solving (Lauchlan, 2001). Additionally, some reviews of precision teaching packages have noted that much of the research on fluency-building methodologies do not control for the rate of reinforcement delivered (i.e., learner could be on a very thick reinforcement schedule, biasing responding). Further, this review notes that studies seldom report practice (i.e., if the student is reviewing content outside of the observation period, and if so, how frequently and with what results; Doughty, Chase, & O'Shields, 2004).

Evidence Base That Underpins Precision Teaching

Over time, precision teaching, and adaptations of precision teaching, have been used across academic areas and settings. For example, in a systematic review, Ramey and colleagues (2016) identified 55 studies using precision teaching and related strategies to teach children with developmental disabilities. Of these studies, 23 targeted literacy, 10 targeted math, and 17 targeted assorted skill acquisition targets (i.e., driving, sports). Authors of this review identified the use of precision teaching for children with developmental disabilities to be an emergent practice according to standards for evaluating evidence-based practices (Ramey et al., 2016). Specifically, results of this review indicate precision teaching to be emerging for literacy (seven out of 23 studies demonstrated conclusive evidence), emerging for math (four out of 10 studies reporting beneficial effects), and emerging for vocational skills (two out of six studies reporting beneficial effects). Other older literature reviews have supported these findings (e.g., Fuchs & Fuchs, 1986). Because of its focus on assessment and decision making rather than curriculum, precision teaching has been used with a variety of other targets, including motor skills (e.g., Eastridge & Mozzoni, 2005), attention span (e.g., Binder, Haughton, & Van Eyk, 1990), and driving skills (Bell, Young, Salzberg, & West, 1991), with varying levels of efficacy.

Precision Teaching for Literacy

Results of the most recent systematic review indicated 23 studies targeting literacy skills, the largest group of studies across domains (Ramey et al., 2016). For teaching literacy skills, precision teaching has been used to target a range of skills from sight words to storytelling. Precision teaching interventions on literacy use charting techniques packaged with a variety of teaching strategies including direct instruction, corrective feedback, and reading racetracks (Ramey et al., 2016) For example, Roberts and Norwich (2010) evaluated the effect of "enhanced" precision teaching to improve word reading skills in secondary students. When compared with a treatment-as-usual group, students showed more consistent acquisition of words as well as improved academic self-concept.

Precision Teaching for Numeracy

Results of the systematic review also indicated 10 studies targeting numeracy skills using precision teaching and related strategies (Ramey et al., 2016). Examples of numeracy skills that have been targeted using precision teaching include multiplication and math facts. Precision teaching has been paired with complementary strategies like flash cards, SAFMEDS, and corrective feedback (Ramey et al., 2016). For example, one study used precision teaching to develop fluency on multiplication fact knowledge. Results of this quasi-experimental study indicated that children receiving precision teaching outperformed their peers receiving typical classroom teaching on multiplication (Gallagher, 2006).

DIRECT INSTRUCTION

Direct instruction is a systematic teaching procedure based on principles of applied behavior analysis and focused on classroom teaching. The instructional components of direct instruction include a teacher-led focus, structured, and sequenced. Specifically, the teacher-directed instruction usually involves a lecture format with one teacher providing lecture and or demonstration content (Adams & Engelmann, 1996). Direct instruction was originally developed in the United States in the 1960s by Siegfried Engelmann and colleagues, who first tested their ideas about learning while teaching basic academic skills to children using a system of logical analysis and testing (Stein, Kinder, Silbert, & Carnine, 2005). The Bereiter-Engelmann preschool program at the University of Illinois at Urbana was the original testing ground for direct instruction and demonstrated dramatic gains in children living in poverty. This preschool program was based on the idea that with effective instruction, children at a disadvantage could make sufficient gains to reach the level of their peers (Engelmann, 1999). Direct instruction is unique in that it evolved out of programs like the Bereiter-Engelmann preschool program serving children at risk. Although direct instruction began as a philosophy of teaching rather than specific procedures, it soon developed into a system of curriculum design, teaching strategies, and classroom management tools (Adams & Engelmann, 1996).

Direct instruction has evolved considerably from its conception, until now. Engelmann and colleagues took findings from the original Bereiter-Engelmann preschool program and supported these practices with principles from behavior analysis. Direct instruction was originally developed as Direct Instruction System for Teaching Arithmetic and Reading (DISTAR). This included several programs and products: DISTAR Reading, DISTAR Arithmetic, and DISTAR Language I. Now, direct instruction refers to a group of interventions, including DISTAR and Language for Learning. As progression of direct instruction continued, these practices were synthesized, and Engelmann and colleagues began to research a specific set of procedures at the University of Oregon. These practices were evaluated as part of Project Follow Through, where positive effects of direct instruction strategies were found to be effective over large cohorts of children (CITE). Today, strategies from direct instruction are used across settings (e.g., special education classrooms, general curriculum, even adult learning opportunities).

Direct instruction is influenced by behavioral theory, structured teaching, and the concept that skills are best taught in sequence and broken down into small components. Direct instruction has similar components to discrete trial training (DTT; see Chapter 9, this volume), such as reinforcement of correct responses, correction, and prompting (Flores & Ganz, 2014). Further, direct instruction uses proven teaching practices such as modeling, prompting, and error correction to establish and sustain behavioral fluency (Engelmann, 1971). Direct instruction is based on parsimony and meant to contain little wasted instructional time (Ganz & Flores, 2009). There are three identified components of direct instruction. Primarily, the program design speaks to how content, teaching, and skill development are organized within a lesson, across content, and over time. Second, the organization of instruction is critical to effective direct instruction. Students are organized into groups on the basis of skill level to meet individual needs, time is carefully allotted to each section of the lesson to allow for effective teaching, and teaching is scripted to minimize off-task time or ineffective explanations (Engelmann & Carnine, 1982). Finally, the student-teacher interactions are a prescribed principle of direct instruction and involve carefully scripted lessons that allow for active student participation (individual and group), appropriate correction and motivation procedures, and teaching to mastery (Watkins & Slocum, 2004).

Components of Direct Instruction and Implementation

Direct instruction is based on extensive task analysis of the skill, which builds lessons that are predetermined and carefully sequenced by difficulty. Each skill is broken down into component skills, which are taught, in sequence, until mastered. These activities are delivered by a teacher to a small group on students, and concepts are built step-by-step and lesson by lesson. Lessons are fast paced and teacher directed without much input from students (Carnine & Fletcher-Janzen, 2013). Within lessons, activities are sequenced in terms of demonstration (i.e., modeling, explanation), guided practice (e.g., call and response with the class), and finally independent practice of the new material (e.g., worksheets). During the demonstration section of the lesson, the teacher is scripted and gives a clear and unambiguous presentation of curriculum. In the guided practice segment, teachers implement prompting and corrective feedback procedures, as well as feedback after the independent practice portion.

Critics of Direct Instruction

Direct instruction has a very clear philosophy and as such has gathered some distrust from certain groups of educators (Duffrin, 1996; Proctor, 1989). For example, those ascribing to a constructivist (child-led) theory of education tend to disagree with the teacher-directed lessons and pacing. Some theorize that the teacher-directed nature of direct instruction creates a power differential wherein the teacher has all the power and the child has no autonomy in directing their learning. Further, some feel that direct instruction deskills teachers because every lesson is predetermined and completely scripted to the point that anyone could pick up the script and deliver the lesson. This criticism of direct instruction infers that because teachers are given no autonomy in terms of content, instructional method, or pacing, there is little room for the creativity that individual teachers bring to teaching (McMullen & Madelaine, 2014).

In addition, some feel that the prescribed nature of direct instruction may mean that students do not get the opportunity to engage in culturally relevant or meaningful material (McMullen & Madelaine, 2014). Because of the lack of child input, some fear that the content may not always be meaningful enough to engage the learner or be respectful to multiple viewpoints or cultures. Additionally, some evidence suggests that direct instruction does not target more advanced cognitive skills such as critical thinking or empathy (Kuhn, 2007; Pressley et al., 1992).

Evidence Base That Underpins Direct Instruction

Despite several decades of research on direct instruction, there are varying reports of its efficacy across reviewers (e.g., Adams & Engelmann, 1996; Flores & Ganz, 2009; Hattie, 2009). Independent reviews have cited high levels of efficacy for direct instruction across instruction targets (i.e., literacy, math). For example, an early review found an effect size average of .97 across variables in 34 studies, indicating it was a strong intervention (Adams &

Engelmann, 1996). In a 2009 paper, Hattie conducted a mega-analysis of preexisting meta-analyses on achievement and identified direct instruction as one of the most effective strategies, with an overall average effect size across 304 studies of .59 (indicates a moderate effect, meaning it was mostly effective; Hattie, 2009). Other papers specific to intervention target have also found moderate to high effects of direct instruction (e.g., Przychodzin-Havis et al., 2005; Przychodzin, Marchand-Martella, Martella, & Azim, 2004) and for children with special needs (e.g., Finnegan & Mazin, 2016; Flores & Ganz, 2007, 2009; Spencer, Evmenova, Boon, & Hayes-Harris, 2014). However, the intervention report from What Works Clearinghouse (WWC; Kratochwill et al., 2010) noted insufficient evidence from rigorous studies to make conclusions about the efficacy of direct instruction. The WWC report goes on to note that the vast majority of studies providing evidence for direct instruction (and reading intervention in general) are of insufficient quality to provide evidence of the effectiveness of practices (WWC, 2010).

Direct Instruction for Literacy

There is some evidence that direct instruction has efficacy for literacy skills. A systematic literature review identified 25 studies using the direct instruction reading mastery program and concluded the program to be effective (Schieffer, Marchand-Martella, Martella, Simonsen, & Waldron-Soler, 2002). Direct instruction has been used across components of literacy. As an example, Flores and Ganz (2007) used direct instruction to teach statement inference, use of facts, and analogies to four students with developmental delays. Results of the multiple baseline design across skills indicated a strong effect of the intervention as demonstrated by change in level and trend postintervention for all participants and little overlapping data. This means that this intervention was effective at increasing these skills in the participants.

Direct Instruction for Math

Some meta-analyses have also found direct instruction to be an effective intervention for math. For example, in a systematic review of 12 studies, Przychodzin and colleagues (2004) concluded that 11 of the included studies demonstrated significant results. As with literacy, direct instruction has been used as an intervention on a variety of math concepts and targets. For example, one of the reviewed studies (Brasch, Williams, & McLaughlin, 2008) demonstrated the efficacy of direct instruction for instruction on multiplication fact mastery for two high school students with attention-deficit/hyperactivity disorder. Results of the multiple baseline design across problem sets indicated immediate change in level and maintenance of gains over time after the direct instruction intervention. This means that the intervention was effective at increasing multiplication fact mastery.

CONCLUSION

The TEACCH approach to structured teaching, precision teaching, and direct instruction are examples of structured approaches to teaching that can be used in classroom contexts. These approaches each follow set procedures and/or protocols that aim to support students learning. Each of these approaches are underpinned by a clear set of theoretical constructs, principles, and guidelines for their implementation. Although there is emerging evidence to demonstrate that these strategies can support students' learning, some of the components of these approaches may be difficult to implement in regular education settings. Therefore, it is important that teachers have a strong understanding of these strategies if they are to be implemented effectively, and with fidelity, across learners. Further research into each of these approaches is required to demonstrate the effectiveness of these approaches in classroom contexts.

REFERENCES

Adams, G. L., & Engelmann, S. (1996). *Research on direct instruction: 25 years beyond DISTAR*. Seattle, WA: Educational Achievement Systems.

Bell, K. E., Young, K. R., Salzberg, C. L., & West, R. P. (1991). High school driver education using peer tutors, direct instruction, and precision teaching. *Journal of Applied Behavior Analysis, 24*, 45–51.

Binder, C. (1988). Precision teaching: Measuring and attaining exemplary academic achievement. *Youth Policy, 10*(7), 12–15.

Binder, C. (1996). Behavioral fluency: Evolution of a new paradigm. *The Behavior Analyst, 19*, 163–197.

Binder, C., Haughton, E., & Van Eyk, D. (1990). Increasing endurance by building fluency: Precision teaching attention span. *Teaching Exceptional Children, 22*(3), 24–27.

Binder, C., & Watkins, C. L. (2013). Precision teaching and direct instruction: Measurably superior instructional technology in schools. *Performance Improvement Quarterly, 26*, 73–115. http://dx.doi.org/10.1002/piq.21145

Brasch, T. L., Williams, R. L., & McLaughlin, T. F. (2008). The effects of a direct instruction flashcard system on multiplication fact mastery by two high school students with ADHD and ODD. *Child & Family Behavior Therapy, 30*, 51–59. http://dx.doi.org/10.1300/J019v30n01_04

Bruininks, R., Woodcock, R., Weatherman, R., & Hill, B. (Eds.). (1996). *Scales of Independent Behavior—Revised*. Park Allen, TX: DLM Teaching Resources.

Bryan, L. C., & Gast, D. L. (2000). Teaching on-task and on-schedule behaviors to high-functioning children with autism via picture activity schedules. *Journal of Autism and Developmental Disorders, 30*, 553–567. http://dx.doi.org/10.1023/A:1005687310346

Caldwell, T. (1966). *Comparison of classroom measures: Percent, number, and rate* (Educational Research Tech. Rep.). Kansas City: University of Kansas Medical Center.

Carnine, D., & Fletcher-Janzen, E. (2013). *Direct instruction*. New York, NY: Wiley.

D'Elia, L., Valeri, G., Sonnino, F., Fontana, I., Mammone, A., & Vicari, S. (2014). A longitudinal study of the TEACCH program in different settings: The potential benefits of low intensity intervention in preschool children with autism spectrum disorder. *Journal of Autism and Developmental Disorders, 44*, 615–626. http://dx.doi.org/10.1007/s10803-013-1911-y

Doughty, S. S., Chase, P. N., & O'Shields, E. M. (2004). Effects of rate building on fluent performance: A review and commentary. *The Behavior Analyst, 27*, 7–23. http://dx.doi.org/10.1007/BF03392086

Duffrin, E. (1996). Direct instruction making waves. *Catalyst, 8*, 1–11.

Eastridge, D., & Mozzoni, M. P. (2005). Fluency and functional motor skills following brain injury. *Behavioral Interventions, 20*, 77–89. http://dx.doi.org/10.1002/bin.175

Engelmann, S. (1971). The effectiveness of direct verbal instruction on IQ performance and achievement in reading and arithmetic. *Control of Human Behavior, 3*, 69–84.

Engelmann, S. (1999). The benefits of direct instruction: Affirmative action for at-risk students. *Educational Leadership, 57*, 77–79.

Engelmann, S., & Carnine, D. (1982). *Theory of instruction: Principles and applications*. Stratford, NH: Irvington.

Fink, E. R. (1968). *Performance and selection rates of emotionally disturbed and mentally retarded preschoolers on Montessori materials* (Doctoral dissertation, University of Kansas, Lawrence).

Finnegan, E., & Mazin, A. L. (2016). Strategies for increasing reading comprehension skills in students with autism spectrum disorder: A review of the literature. *Education & Treatment of Children, 39*, 187–219. http://dx.doi.org/10.1353/etc.2016.0007

Flores, M. M., & Ganz, J. B. (2007). Effectiveness of direct instruction for teaching statement inference, use of facts, and analogies to students with developmental disabilities and reading delays. *Focus on Autism and Other Developmental Disabilities, 22*, 244–251. http://dx.doi.org/10.1177/10883576070220040601

Flores, M. M., & Ganz, J. B. (2009). Effects of direct instruction on the reading comprehension of students with autism and developmental disabilities. *Education and Training in Developmental Disabilities, 44*, 39–53.

Flores, M. M., & Ganz, J. B. (2014). Comparison of direct instruction and discrete trial teaching on the curriculum-based assessment of language performance of students with autism. *Exceptionality, 22,* 191–204. http://dx.doi.org/10.1080/09362835.2013.865533

Fuchs, L. S., & Fuchs, D. (1986). Effects of systematic formative evaluation: A meta-analysis. *Exceptional children, 53,* 199–208.

Gallagher, E. (2006). Improving a mathematical key skill using precision teaching. *Irish Educational Studies, 25,* 303–319. http://dx.doi.org/10.1080/03323310600913757

Ganz, J. B., & Flores, M. M. (2009). The effectiveness of direct instruction for teaching language to children with autism spectrum disorders: Identifying materials. *Journal of Autism and Developmental Disorders, 39,* 75–83. http://dx.doi.org/10.1007/s10803-008-0602-6

Goin-Kochel, R. P., Mackintosh, V. H., & Myers, B. J. (2009). Parental reports on the efficacy of treatments and therapies for their children with autism spectrum disorders. *Research in Autism Spectrum Disorders, 3,* 528–537. http://dx.doi.org/10.1016/j.rasd.2008.11.001

Green, V. A., Pituch, K. A., Itchon, J., Choi, A., O'Reilly, M., & Sigafoos, J. (2006). Internet survey of treatments used by parents of children with autism. *Research in Developmental Disabilities, 27,* 70–84. http://dx.doi.org/10.1016/j.ridd.2004.12.002

Haring, N. G., Liberty, K. A., & White, O. R. (1980). Rules for data-based strategy decisions in instructional programs: Current research and instructional implications. In W. Sailor, B. Wilcox, & L. Brown (Eds.), *Methods of instruction for severely handicapped students* (159–192). Baltimore, MD: Brookes.

Hattie, J. A. (2009). *Visible learning: A synthesis of 800+ meta-analyses on achievement.* Abingdon, England: Routledge.

Holzschuh, R., & Dobbs, D. (1966). *Rate correct vs. percentage correct* (Educational Research Tech. Rep.). Kansas City: University of Kansas Medical Center.

Hume, K., & Odom, S. (2007). Effects of an individual work system on the independent functioning of students with autism. *Journal of Autism and Developmental Disorders, 37,* 1166–1180. http://dx.doi.org/10.1007/s10803-006-0260-5

Ichikawa, K., Takahashi, Y., Ando, M., Anme, T., Ishizaki, T., Yamaguchi, H., & Nakayama, T. (2013). TEACCH-based group social skills training for children with high-functioning autism: A pilot randomized controlled trial. *BioPsychoSocial Medicine, 7*(1), 14. http://dx.doi.org/10.1186/1751-0759-7-14

Kratochwill, T. R., Hitchcock, J., Horner, R. H., Levin, J. R., Odom, S. L., Rindskopf, D. M., & Shadish, W. R. (2010). *Single-case designs technical documentation.* Princeton, NJ: What Works Clearinghouse.

Kubina, R. M., Jr., Morrison, R., & Lee, D. L. (2002). Benefits of adding precision teaching to behavioral interventions for students with autism. *Behavioral Interventions, 17,* 233–246.

Kuhn, D. (2007). Is direct instruction an answer to the right question? *Educational Psychologist, 42*, 109–113. http://dx.doi.org/10.1080/00461520701263376

Lauchlan, F. (2001). Addressing the social, cognitive and emotional needs of children: The case for dynamic assessment. *Educational and Child Psychology, 18*(4), 4–18.

Lindsley, O. R. (1964). Direct measurement and prosthesis of retarded behavior. *Journal of Education, 147*, 62–81.

Lindsley, O. R. (1991). Precision teaching's unique legacy from B. F. Skinner. *Journal of behavioral education, 1*, 253–266.

Lindsley, O. R. (1992). Precision teaching: Discoveries and effects. *Journal of Applied Behavior Analysis, 25*, 51–57.

McMullen, F., & Madelaine, A. (2014). Why is there so much resistance to direct instruction? *Australian Journal of Learning Difficulties, 19*, 137–151. http://dx.doi.org/10.1080/19404158.2014.962065

Mechling, L. C., & Savidge, E. J. (2011). Using a personal digital assistant to increase completion of novel tasks and independent transitioning by students with autism spectrum disorder. *Journal of Autism and Developmental Disorders, 41*, 687–704. http://dx.doi.org/10.1007/s10803-010-1088-6

Mesibov, G., Howley, M., & Naftel, S. (2016). *Accessing the curriculum for learners with autism spectrum disorders* (2nd ed.). New York, NY: Routledge.

Mesibov, G. B., & Shea, V. (2010). The TEACCH program in the era of evidence-based practice. *Journal of Autism and Developmental Disorders, 40*, 570–579. http://dx.doi.org/10.1007/s10803-009-0901-6

Mesibov, G. B., Shea, V., & Schopler, E. (2005). *The TEACCH approach to autism spectrum disorders.* New York, NY: Springer.

Mullen, E. M. (1995). *Mullen Scales of Early Learning: AGS edition.* Circle Pines, MN: American Guidance Service.

National Autism Center. (2009). *National standards report.* Randolph, MA: Author.

National Autism Center. (2015). *Findings and conclusions: National Standards Project, Phase 2.* Randolph, MA: Author.

Ozonoff, S., & Cathcart, K. (1998). Effectiveness of a home program intervention for young children with autism. *Journal of Autism and Developmental Disorders, 28*, 25–32. http://dx.doi.org/10.1023/A:1026006818310

Ozonoff, S., South, M., & Provencal, S. (2005). Executive functions. In F. R. Volkmar, R. Paul, A. Klin, & D. Cohen (Eds.), *Handbook of autism and pervasive developmental disorders: Vol. 1. Diagnosis, development, neurobiology, and behavior* (3rd ed., pp. 606–627). Hoboken, NJ: Wiley.

Panerai, S., Ferrante, L., Caputo, V., & Impellizzeri, C. (1998). Use of structured teaching for treatment of children with autism and severe and profound mental retardation. *Education and Training in Mental Retardation and Developmental Disabilities, 33*, 367–374.

Panerai, S., Ferrante, L., & Zingale, M. (2002). Benefits of the Treatment and Education of Autistic and Communication Handicapped Children (TEACCH) programme as compared with a non-specific approach. *Journal of Intellectual Disability Research, 46*, 318–327. http://dx.doi.org/10.1046/j.1365-2788.2002.00388.x

Panerai, S., Zingale, M., Trubia, G., Finocchiaro, M., Zuccarello, R., Ferri, R., & Elia, M. (2009). Special education versus inclusive education: The role of the TEACCH program. *Journal of Autism and Developmental Disorders, 39*, 874–882. http://dx.doi.org/10.1007/s10803-009-0696-5

Pressley, M., El-Dinary, P. B., Gaskins, I., Schuder, T., Bergman, J. L., Almasi, J., & Brown, R. (1992). Beyond direct explanation: Transactional instruction of reading comprehension strategies. *The Elementary School Journal, 92*, 513–555. http://dx.doi.org/10.1086/461705

Proctor, T. J. (1989). Attitudes toward direct instruction. *Teacher Education and Special Education, 12*(1–2), 40–45. http://dx.doi.org/10.1177/088840648901200107

Przychodzin, A. M., Marchand-Martella, N. E., Martella, R. C., & Azim, D. (2004). Direct instruction mathematics programs: An overview and research summary. *Journal of Direct Instruction, 4*, 53–84.

Przychodzin-Havis, A. M., Marchand-Martella, N. E., Martella, R. C., Miller, D. A., Warner, L., Leonard, B., & Chapman, S. (2005). An analysis of corrective reading research. *Journal of Direct Instruction, 5*(1), 37–65.

Ramey, D., Lydon, S., Healy, O., McCoy, A., Holloway, J., & Mulhern, T. (2016). A systematic review of the effectiveness of precision teaching for individuals with developmental disabilities. *Review Journal of Autism and Developmental Disorders, 3*, 179–195. http://dx.doi.org/10.1007/s40489-016-0075-z

Roberts, W., & Norwich, B. (2010). Using precision teaching to enhance the word reading skills and academic self-concept of secondary school students: A role for professional educational psychologists. *Educational Psychology in Practice, 26*, 279–298. http://dx.doi.org/10.1080/02667363.2010.495215

Rogers, C. R., & Skinner, B. F. (1956). Some issues concerning the control of human behavior. *Science, 124*, 1057–1066. http://dx.doi.org/10.1126/science.124.3231.1057

Sasaki, M. (2000). Aspects of autism in Japan before and after the introduction of TEACCH. *International Journal of Mental Health, 29*(2), 3–18. http://dx.doi.org/10.1080/00207411.2000.11449488

Schieffer, C., Marchand-Martella, N. E., Martella, R. C., Simonsen, F. L., & Waldron-Soler, K. M. (2002). An analysis of the Reading Mastery program: Effective components and research review. *Journal of Direct Instruction, 2*, 87–119.

Schopler, E. (1994). A statewide program for the treatment and education of autistic and related communication handicapped children (TEACCH). *Psychoses and Pervasive Developmental Disorders, 3*, 91–103.

Schopler, E., Mesibov, G., & Hearsey, K. (1995). Structured teaching in the TEACCH system. In E. Schopler & G. Mesibov (Eds.), *Learning and cognition in autism* (pp. 243–268). New York, NY: Plenum Press. http://dx.doi.org/10.1007/978-1-4899-1286-2_13

Schopler, E., & Reichler, R. J. (1971). Parents as cotherapists in the treatment of psychotic children. *Journal of Autism and Childhood Schizophrenia, 1*, 87–102. http://dx.doi.org/10.1007/BF01537746

Schopler, E., Reichler, R. J., Bashford, A., Lansing, M. D., & Marcus, L. M. (1990). *Psychoeducational Profile—Revised (PEP–R)*. Austin, TX: PRO-ED.

Siaperas, P., & Beadle-Brown, J. (2006). A case study of the use of a structured teaching approach in adults with autism in a residential home in Greece. *Autism, 10*, 330–343. http://dx.doi.org/10.1177/1362361306064433

Spencer, V. G., Evmenova, A. S., Boon, R. T., & Hayes-Harris, L. (2014). Review of research-based interventions for students with autism spectrum disorders in content area instruction: Implications and considerations for classroom practice. *Education and Training in Autism and Developmental Disabilities, 49*, 331–353.

Starlin, C. (1971). Peers and precision. *Teaching exceptional children, 3*, 129–132.

Stein, M., Kinder, D., Silbert, J., & Carnine, D. W. (2005). *Designing effective mathematics instruction: A direct instruction approach*. Upper Saddle River, NJ: Pearson.

Taylor, K., & Preece, D. (2010). Using aspects of the TEACCH structured teaching approach with students with multiple disabilities and visual impairment (Reflections on practice). *British Journal of Visual Impairment, 28*, 244–259. http://dx.doi.org/10.1177/0264619610374682

Tsang, S. K., Shek, D. T., Lam, L. L., Tang, F. L., & Cheung, P. M. (2007). Brief report: Application of the TEACCH program on Chinese pre-school children with autism—Does culture make a difference? *Journal of Autism and Developmental Disorders, 37*, 390–396. http://dx.doi.org/10.1007/s10803-006-0199-6

Tsatsanis, K. D. (2005). Neuropsychological characteristics in autism and related conditions. In F. R. Volkmar, R. Paul, A. Klin, & D. Cohen (Eds.), *Handbook of autism and pervasive developmental disorders: Vol. 1. Diagnosis, development, neurobiology, and behavior* (3rd ed., pp. 365–381). Hoboken, NJ: Wiley. http://dx.doi.org/10.1002/9780470939345.ch13

Van Bourgondien, M. E., & Schopler, E. (1996). Intervention for adults with autism. *Journal of Rehabilitation, 62*, 65–71.

Virues-Ortega, J., Julio, F. M., & Pastor-Barriuso, M. (2013). The TEACCH program for children and adults with autism: A meta-analysis of intervention studies. *Clinical Psychology Review, 33*, 940–953. http://dx.doi.org/10.1016/j.cpr.2013.07.005

Watkins, C. L., & Slocum, T. A. (2004). The components of direct instruction. In N. E. Marchand-Martella, T. A. Slocum, and R. C. Martella (Eds.), *Introduction to direct instruction* (pp. 28–65). Upper Saddle River, NJ: Pearson.

Welterlin, A., Turner-Brown, L. M., Harris, S., Mesibov, G., & Delmolino, L. (2012). The home TEACCHing program for toddlers with autism. *Journal of*

Autism and Developmental Disorders, 42, 1827–1835. http://dx.doi.org/10.1007/s10803-011-1419-2

West, R. P., Young, K. R., & Spooner, F. (1990). Precision teaching: An introduction. *Teaching Exceptional Children, 22*(3), 4–9.

White, O. R. (1986). Precision teaching—precision learning. *Exceptional Children, 52*, 522–534.

Wong, C., Odom, S. L., Hume, K. A., Cox, A. W., Fettig, A., Kucharczyk, S., . . . Schultz, T. R. (2015). Evidence-based practices for children, youth, and young adults with autism spectrum disorder: A comprehensive review. *Journal of Autism and Developmental Disorders, 45*, 1951–1966. http://dx.doi.org/10.1007/s10803-014-2351-z

III

COGNITIVE BEHAVIOR THERAPY

17

WHAT IS COGNITIVE BEHAVIOR THERAPY?

RAYMOND DiGIUSEPPE, RACHEL VENEZIA,
AND ROSEANNE GOTTERBARN

Cognitive behavior therapy (CBT) represents a form of psychotherapy used by school psychologists to resolve disturbed emotions and dysfunctional behavior in students by acknowledging the role of human learning and the effects of the environment, cognitions, and language in disturbance. At present, CBT serves as the overriding, generic term used to describe a wide range of approaches to psychotherapy that represent three distinct yet overlapping approaches to therapy: (a) behavior therapy, (b) cognitive therapies, and (c) mindfulness and acceptance therapies. These approaches are similar, but they conceptualize the mediation of dysfunctional behavior differently.

CBT originated within behavior therapy (BT) and remains committed to many of its values and traditions. The main professional and scientific organization that represents the field was originally known as the Association for the Advancement of Behavior Therapy, and in 2004 added the term *cognitive* to become the Association for Behavioral and Cognitive Therapies.

---

http://dx.doi.org/10.1037/0000126-018
Behavioral Interventions in Schools: Evidence-Based Positive Strategies, Second Edition, S. G. Little and A. Akin-Little (Editors)
Copyright © 2019 by the American Psychological Association. All rights reserved.

VARIATION WITHIN COGNITIVE BEHAVIOR THERAPY

Despite its popularity, CBT represents a variety of related yet different approaches. Some theorists use the metaphor of three waves to explain the differences between CBT theories. The first wave of CBT represents the behavioral tradition, based on the work of Skinner and Pavlov (Martin & Pear, 2015) and applied behavior analysis (Martin & Pear, 2015) and pragmatic behavior therapy (Fishman, Rotgers, & Franks, 1988). Learning principles formed the basis of this approach, and the major interventions included relaxation training; exposure; operant interventions; stimulus control; and the rehearsal of new, adaptive responses such as assertiveness training and social skills training.

The second wave emerged when some theorists became dissatisfied with the behavioral model. These behavior therapists recognized that human thought and language played a crucial role in learning and maintaining dysfunctional behavior. As the cognitive revolution occurred in BT, the number of such approaches increased rapidly. This group of theorists included Ellis's rational emotive behavior therapy (REBT), Beck's cognitive therapy, Meichenbaum's (1993) self-instructional training, and problem-solving skills training (Nezu, Maguth Nezu, & D'Zurilla, 2013).

The third wave included techniques based on Mindfulness and an approach to language and cognition called *relational frame theory* (RFT). RFT differs from previous cognitive therapies in that it does not recommend changing the content of clients' beliefs but instead attempts to break or change the connections between beliefs and emotions with dysfunctional behavior. RFT promotes teaching acceptance of negative thoughts and emotions and then learning to act flexibly and in one's best interests despite their occurrence.

The metaphor of the three waves fails to conceptualize these differences accurately. Waves come in a sequence. As a new wave arrives, the previous waves recede back into the ocean. The three waves of CBT did not occur in three distinct points in time. Each has roots in ancient philosophy and the history of 20th-century psychology. The first two waves have not relinquished their energy and faded into the undertow of science or clinical practice, as this metaphor would suggest. They remain active areas of research and practice with committed proponents. We think a better metaphor would be three branches of CBT as Darwin used the term in evolution. New species appear like branches on a bush, such as three groups of great apes: gorillas, chimpanzees, and bonobos. Each branch has common ancestors yet continues to exist and evolve on its own. None of the models of CBT has driven the others to extinction.

Even within these three major CBT groups, diversification exists. As early as 1993, Kuehlwein and Rosen (1993) identified 10 schools of CBT. Since that publication, more variants of CBT have appeared. In Table 17.1 we present a nonexhaustive list of the types of CBT approaches that we uncovered.

TABLE 17.1
Forms of Cognitive Behavior Therapy and Their Founders

Form of therapy	Reference
Applied behavioral analysis	Martin & Pear (2015)
Acceptance and commitment therapy	Hayes et al. (2011)
Behavior therapy	Wolpe (1969)
Pragmatic behavior therapy	Fishman et al. (1988)
Cognitive therapy	Beck (1976)
Cognitive analytic therapy	Ryle (2005)
Constructivist cognitive psychotherapy	Neimeyer (2009)
Dialectical behavior therapy	Linehan (1993)
Functional analytic psychotherapy	Kohlenberg & Tsai (1991)
Fixed role therapy	Kelly (1955)
Metacognitive therapy	Wells (2008)
Mindfulness-based interventions	Kabat-Zinn (2013)
Mindfulness cognitive therapy	Sigel et al. (2013)
Multimodal therapy	A. A. Lazarus (1981)
Parent training	Forgatch & Patterson (2010)
Problem-solving therapy	Nezu et al. (2013)
Rational emotive behavior therapy	Ellis (1962)
Rumination-focused CBT	Watkins et al. (2007)
Schema-focused cognitive therapy	Young, Klosko, & Weishaar (2003)
Self-instructional training	Meichenbaum (1977)
Trauma-focused CBT	Cohen (2006)
Trial-based cognitive therapy	de Oliveira (2016)
Wellness therapy	Fava (2016)

Note. CBT = cognitive behavior therapy.

These models share more similarities than differences and propose that different psychological processes mediate the relationship between environmental stressors and dysfunctional emotions and behaviors. Although these models incorporate many different interventions, their interventions are compatible with the other models. Hofmann, Asmundson, and Beck (2013) described CBT as a theoretically consistent model that addresses a wide range of clinical problems, yet each problem might require different intervention. Thus, CBT practitioners might use multiple procedures to accomplish change yet remain theoretically consistent using theoretical constructs that are discussed in this book.

Observing several professionals delivering CBT sessions might confuse a novice because she or he will see CBT practitioners doing different things with different problems. An example of this diversity within a theoretical consistence appears in O'Donohue and Fisher's (2009) book. They provide 74 chapters describing different CBT interventions to treat an array of clinical problems. Exhibit 17.1 highlights some of the interventions used in CBT. Despite this wide variety, CBT is eclectic in techniques but consistent in

EXHIBIT 17.1
Techniques Used in Cognitive Behavior Therapy

Assertiveness training
Assessing the client's emotions, thoughts, and behaviors that occurred when the client tried to implement a homework assignment
Assessing the presence of dysfunctional behaviors or emotions
Behavioral activation: increasing mastery and pleasuring experiences
Bibliotherapy
Challenging the client's negative automatic thoughts
Challenging the client's irrational beliefs
Changing the clients' underlying schema
Defusion
Decentering
Diagnostic interviewing
Distress tolerance
Exploring the adaptability of the client's emotions and behaviors
Exploring the adaptability of the client's belief system
Flooding
Graduate exposure
Habit reversal training
Harm reduction
Imaginal exposure
Mindfulness exercises
Modeling and role-playing new skills
Negotiating homework
Offering alternative rational beliefs and schema to replace the client's irrational beliefs and dysfunctional schema
Operant strategies
Opposite action
Parent training
Performing an ABC (Antecedents, Behaviors and Consequences) functional analysis of behavior.
Performing an ABC (Activating Event, Beliefs, and Emotional Consequences) analysis of thoughts.
Performing a comprehensive multimodal assessment of behaviors, affect, sensations, imagery, cognitions, interpersonal relationships, drugs, or biological influences
Performing a multimodal assessment
Relapse prevention
Relaxation procedures
Response chaining
Response prevention and exposure
Reviewing homework
Self-control procedures
Self-instructional training
Shaping
Social problem-solving
Helping the client generate alternative solutions to problems
Helping the client evaluate the consequences effectiveness of alternative solutions
Social skills training
Stimulus control procedures

EXHIBIT 17.1 (Continued)
Techniques Used in Cognitive Behavior Therapy

Teaching the B → C connection (i.e., explaining to clients that their beliefs, not just events, cause their emotional excesses)
Teaching the difference between irrational and rational beliefs
Token economies
Validating the client's emotions
Values and goals clarification

---

theory. A. A. Lazarus (1967) coined the term *technical eclecticism* to describe clinical practice that remains theoretically consistent in focusing on behavioral and cognitive concepts yet uses many methods to target the theoretical mechanism identified by one's orientation.

ASSUMPTIONS AND PRINCIPLES OF COGNITIVE BEHAVIOR THERAPY

Given these variations, readers might wonder what concepts unify them. Below we describe the four common assumptions, principles, and history that represent the foundation of CBT. First, the definition of *behavior* is broad and refers not only to the actions of striated muscles but also to the reaction of the sympathetic nervous system, thoughts, and emotions.

Second, CBT started with and remains committed to principles derived from the science of experimental psychology. Many CBT-based interventions evolved from scientific learning principles and lead to the field of applied behavior analysis (Martin & Pear, 2015) or to Wolpe's (1969) systematic desensitization and other exposure interventions. A strong behavioral tradition exists that focuses on learning theory principles to inform clinical practice (Fishman, 2016).

Third, as CBT grew, its practitioners discovered that variables besides operant and classical conditioning contributed to effective psychotherapy. Some practitioners shifted their emphases to developing therapies based on all scientific principles of human behavior (A. A. Lazarus, 1977). At present, learning, cognitive, social, and system principles all influence the practice of CBT.

Fourth, CBT has a commitment to researching the efficacy and effectiveness of its interventions. The gold standard of such research is the randomized clinical trial (RCT); however, single-subject designs and meta-analytic reviews of treatments remain a hallmark of CBT. Adherents of CBT have been responsible for setting the criteria for empirically supported treatments

(ESTs). A task force of scientists (American Psychological Association Presidential Task Force on Evidence-Based Practice, 2006) set the criteria for the degree and type of scientific support necessary for an intervention to be classified as an EST. On the basis of research reviews, two websites identify the interventions that meet these criteria. The ESTs for adult treatments have been posted and revised on a website by the Society of Clinical Psychology (APA Division 12; https://www.div12.org/), and the list of treatments for children and adolescents has been posted on a website maintained by the Society of Clinical Child and Adolescent Psychology (APA Division 53; http://www.apa.org/about/division/div53.aspx).

The originators (first branch) of BT held to some foundational assumptions and values (Fishman, 2016) that are also advocated by the other two branches (DiGiuseppe, David, & Venezia, 2016; Follette & Hazlett-Stevens, 2016). These principles included the following:

- All humans learn and maintain normal and abnormal behaviors by the same psychological principles.
- Abnormal behavior can be altered or changed through the scientifically established principles of social learning, including operant learning, classical conditioning, cognitive appraisal, and acquiring new responses to stressors.
- Practitioners state the goals of therapy in terms that can be objectively evaluated.
- Assessment of clients' problems remains a continuous process that informs case formulation, diagnosis, and the monitoring of clinical progress.
- Change methods are specified clearly so they can be replicated by all professionals.
- Outcome measures focus on behavior change in the real world across multiple situations and time.
- Practitioners describe clients' goals as concrete behaviors and emotions and not in hypothetical or theoretical constructs.
- A functional assessment of a client's problem leads to an individually designed treatment plan.
- The client and the practitioner jointly decide on the treatment goals and methods.
- Practitioners assesses clients' strengths and address change by increasing adaptive behaviors that are incompatible with the clinical problems.
- Change usually occurs in small steps.
- Behavioral flexibility is associated with coping and personal growth; therefore, therapy focuses on clients developing multiple adaptive behaviors.

- The connections between stimuli that precede maladaptive behaviors need to be changed.
- The consequences of a behavior are a powerful influence on the continuation of the behavior.

CBT practitioners share the above assumptions. Several other theoretical ideas have been added to the above list to reflect the contributions of Branch 2 approaches by Beck (1976) and Ellis (1994) via the cognitive revolution in BT. These were clearly identified by Dobson (2010) and DiGiuseppe, Doyle, Dryden, and Backx (2014), as follows:

- Cognitive activity affects behavior.
- Cognitions can be monitored and altered.
- Desired emotional and behavior change can occur through cognitive change.
- The active rehearsal of new incompatible adaptive cognitions to counter maladaptive cognitions affects change. CBT differs from psychodynamic therapy in that its practitioners believe that insight into the relationship between thoughts and emotions or into the irrationality or incorrectness of thoughts is usually not sufficient to bring about desired change.

THE THERAPEUTIC RELATIONSHIP IN COGNITIVE BEHAVIOR THERAPY

CBT differs from other theoretical orientations in that it does not claim that the therapeutic relationship functions as a causative factor that helps clients improve. It does not posit that acceptance by the psychotherapist is a curative component of treatment or that analysis of the client's relationship with the therapist is necessary for change. Because of this lesser emphasis on the therapeutic relationship as a curative factor, many professionals assume that CBT practitioners do not focus on the relationship or work to foster a strong connection between the therapist and client. Nothing can be further from the truth.

The source of this misperception goes back to a debate between Rogers (1950, 1957) and Ellis (1948/2000, 1959, 1962). Rogers (1957), in his client-centered therapy, proposed that unconditional acceptance by the therapist was a necessary and sufficient condition for human therapeutic change. By *necessary*, Rogers meant that change could not take place without unconditional acceptance, and by *sufficient*, Rogers meant that unconditional acceptance alone is all that is required for change. Ellis (1948/2000, 1959, 1962) responded by suggesting that unconditional acceptance was neither necessary nor sufficient for human change. It was not necessary because some people changed without it through bibliotherapy, attending lectures, modeling friends, and other experiences. Ellis contended that unconditional acceptance could not be sufficient because many clients experienced unconditional acceptance from their psychotherapist and do not achieve change. Ellis (1962) concluded that although unconditional acceptance by therapists was neither necessary nor sufficient for therapeutic change, it was still important. By *self-acceptance*, CBT practitioners mean that clients acknowledge the existence of their own faults, negative thoughts, and uncomfortable emotions without condemning themselves.

The active and directive nature of CBT also leads some to believe that CBT does not place importance on the therapeutic relationship. Modern research on the therapeutic relationship refers to the importance of the relationships as the *therapeutic alliance*. This concept is a multidimensional construct and includes three components: (a) agreement on the goals of therapy, (b) agreement on the tasks of therapy, and (c) an emotional bond between the client and therapist. Research dating back more than 40 years has demonstrated that behavior therapists establish equal or stronger therapeutic relationship with their clients than do psychodynamic therapists (Sloane, Staples, Cristol, & Whipple, 1975). However, the myth about the lack of attention paid to the development of the therapeutic alliance has persisted. Using a measure based on Rogers's model of the therapeutic relationship, DiGiuseppe, Leaf, and Linscott (1993) countered this claim. They found that clients receiving REBT or CBT had scores on the Therapy Relationship Questionnaire (Traux & Carkhuff, 1967) that were equal to or greater than those reported by clients in all studies conducted using that instrument. Norcross and Lambert (2011) reported that the therapeutic alliance is more strongly associated with a positive outcome in CBT than in other forms of therapy. They noted that clients would engage in CBT activities such as cognitive restructuring and exposure only if they had a good relationship with the psychologist.

It is common for a therapeutic alliance to rupture in CBT when clients are reluctant to engage in identifying or challenging their beliefs. Castonguay, Goldfried, Wiser, Raue, and Hayes (1996) found that attempts to resolve the rupture by persuading clients of the validity of the cognitive rationale were negatively correlated with outcome. These interventions worsened the alliance and thus potentially interfered with client change. In contrast, successful strategies to repair the relationship included inviting the client to explore the potential rupture, offering an empathic response by expressing concern about the client's emotional reaction toward the therapist or therapy, and disarming interventions such as exploring and validating some aspects of the client's perception of the therapist's contribution to the alliance rupture.

After discussing the alliance rupture, therapists can continue applying CBT techniques.

People seeking therapy have differing attitudes about change. The stages-of-change model (Norcross, Krebs, & Prochaska, 2011) identifies attitudes of change that span a continuum ranging from not thinking one needs change (the precontemplative stage) to thinking one is ready to take concrete action (the action stage). CBT is most useful when clients have reached the action stage of change because by nature CBT represents a set of action stage interventions. Unlike psychodynamic psychotherapy, CBT is not a treatment designed for exploration. Some CBT techniques, such as behavioral activation, or reinforcement sampling, could be used to increase clients' motivation for change and move them to the action stage. However, given CBT's predilection to action, asking clients to actively change their thoughts, feelings, and behaviors could cause a rupture in the therapeutic alliance if they have not reached the action stage and are ambivalent about change. Therefore, it is important to first assess clients' attitude and motivation to change to prevent the possibility of an alliance rupture. If the client has not reached the action stage of change, CBT practitioners can first use motivational enhancement interventions (Miller & Rollnick, 2012) until the client is motivated to change.

STATUS OF COGNITIVE BEHAVIOR THERAPY IN PSYCHOTHERAPY

The origins of BT date back to the 1950s with the development of Wolpe's (1958) book, *Psychotherapy by Reciprocal Inhibition* and the founding of the University of London's Maudsley Hospital under Hans Eysenck. The first use of the term *CBT* occurred at the First Conference on Cognitive Behavior Therapy in 1976, hosted and funded by the Albert Ellis Institute (Hollon & DiGiuseppe, 2011). Since that time, CBT has become a major force in psychotherapy. CBT has many specialty journals dedicated to theory, practice, and research, and articles on CBT appear in the most prestigious journals in counseling, clinical, and counseling psychology and psychiatry. Andersson and colleagues (2005) noted that CBT is acknowledged as an effective intervention for almost all psychiatric conditions and numerous somatic conditions and that it is difficult to find a psychological problem for which the efficacy of CBT has not been tested. For many conditions, CBT has become the treatment of choice. The commitment to research has fostered this legacy of CBT as a successful form of psychotherapy.

CBT has evolved into the major and most popular theoretical orientation to psychotherapy among practitioners and faculty members. In

September 2018, we conducted a PsycINFO literature search of the term "CBT" in the "abstract" of an article. We uncovered 28, 706 citations, which is evidence that CBT has attained a predominant position in the psychotherapy literature. This research emphasis garnered the support of CBT within the academic community, in particular among academic scholars who seek university positions and then train new generations of mental health professionals.

Several factors—at least six—could account for CBT's ascendance. First, advocates of CBT who strongly valued research emerged from BT. Using randomized clinical trials to test treatments has always been the hallmark of CBT because this type of research has strongly influenced the conversation about the effectiveness of psychotherapy to academics, practitioners, the public, and governments. The major CBT professional organization, the Association for Behavioral and Cognitive Therapists, continually provides resources to disseminate knowledge and practice of CBT interventions to all mental health professionals (DiGiuseppe, 2007). The dissemination of CBT has been extended to include training primary health care providers such as nurses and physicians (Mathieson et al., 2013).

Second, CBT theorists have stated their hypothetical construct in definitions that promote the measurement, testing, and falsification of their theories. The hypothetical constructs identified by CBT theories were more easily turned into self-report measures than were the constructs of psychodynamic theories. Automatic thoughts, underlying schemas, irrational beliefs, cognitive flexibility, defusion, and social problem-solving skills all spawned self-report measures that assess clients' thinking and test the models of CBT and help therapists and therapists assess what to target in therapy and how to assess change in these constructs over the course of treatment.

Third, all types of CBT prescribe relatively brief, structured treatments that easily fit in the cost-effective, managed-care, and evidence-based zeitgeist of the past several decades. Fourth, the structured nature of CBT theories and the clearly identifiable skills them makes them easy to teach; many treatment manuals are available for practitioners and graduate students to guide their training. An additional advantage is that CBT interventions are simple enough that live or video demonstrations of sessions can demonstrate the techniques to practitioners.

Fifth, CBT has achieved an integration of psychodynamic psychotherapy's focus on the internal experience, early BT's focus on observable behavior, and client-centered therapies' focus on forming therapeutic relationships. The focus on clients' present and conscious thoughts, emotions, and behaviors allows the therapist to access internal experiences and thoughts about past harmful events while at the same time maintaining the goals of assessing and changing something observable. The focus on both stream-of-consciousness thoughts and tacit, underlying beliefs and schema provide insights into the deeper aspects of the client's personality. Attaining a good working alliance with clients allows them to experience a healthy relationship with a helping professional. This integrative aspect of CBT allows practitioners to focus on the best aspects of the psychodynamic, humanistic, and behavior methods.

Sixth, strong personalities have historically dominated the field of psychotherapy. Charismatic personalities developed most variants of CBT. Each of them has been an inspirational speaker and teacher, has developed innovative theories, and been compassionate therapists and leaders of professional organizations and recipients of professional awards. In 2009, Cook, Biyanova, and Coyne surveyed more than 2,400 North American psychotherapists and therapists and asked them to identify the most prominent figures in the field of psychotherapy. Although Carl Rogers continued to hold the position as the most prominent theorist, three of the top 10 most prominent theorists represented CBT; Aaron Beck was second, and Albert Ellis was third. If that study were replicated now and extended beyond North America, there is no doubt even more CBT scholars would mostly likely be added to the top 10 most influential theorists.

HISTORY OF COGNITIVE BEHAVIOR THERAPY

When CBT emerged, psychoanalytic therapy dominated the field, and Rogerian client-centered therapy was a close second. The first generation of CBT therapists based their work on the learning theories of Pavlov and Watson (Martin & Pear, 2015). They believed that humans learned maladaptive behavior and emotional reactions from learning experiences. In some sense, there were always two arms or traditions in BT: (a) interventions developed on the basis of Pavlov's classical conditioning and (b) those based on Skinner's operant procedures. In classical conditioning, the feared stimuli are paired with painful or unpleasant stimuli. Therapy replaces them by having the client experience the stimuli without the presence of painful or unpleasant stimuli, or by pairing the feared stimulus with a new response, such as relaxation. Such work helped the treatment of fear and anxiety disorders. It has continued to grow, and exposure is still the treatment of choice for these disorders. The work of Watson and Skinner focused on operant conditioning paradigm, which addresses the important issues of the consequence of the behavior. Behavioral reactions are strengthened and increased if they are rewarded or reinforced. Reinforcement can be positive when the behavior is followed by something pleasant; however, behavior can also be reinforced if it is followed by the avoidance or removal of a negative stimulus, which is referred to as *negative reinforcement*. The stimuli that precede behavior are important because people learn that reinforcers for a behavior might come when only a certain stimulus or situation is present. The techniques involved withholding the reinforcers for maladaptive behavior, reinforcing adaptive behavior that was incompatible with the symptomatic behavior, and providing discrimination training whereby reinforcers followed behavior in some situations and not in others. These operant principles were quickly used to create reinforcement systems or token economies that were used to increase on-task academic behaviors in children, help children complete homework, reduce psychotic symptoms, and improve self-care or prosocial behavior in psychiatric hospital patients. Teaching clients to increase the number of rewarding activities in their daily activities became an early operant intervention for depression (Lewinsohn, Weinstein, & Alper, 1970) and is still considered the first-line intervention for depression today (Richards et al., 2016).

Operant principles can describe and change interpersonal relationships. Patterson (1975) described the interaction between disruptive children and their families as *coercive family process*. In such an interaction, one person's tantrums (i.e., the child's) are annoying to the other (the parent). As the parent gives in to the child's tantrums, the response positively reinforces the child's tantrums by providing a pleasurable reward, and negatively reinforces the parent by removing the unpleasant stimuli (the tantrum). The parent training procedures that developed from this model remain the most effective intervention for many child behavior problems (Skotarczak & Lee, 2015); however, they have been improved by adding cognitive procedures to increase the parent's compliance with the treatment (O. David & DiGiuseppe, 2016).

The first evidence-based paradigm in the psychotherapy field was BT (D. David, Lynn, & Ellis, 2010), which focuses on how the environment affects learned behaviors. The behaviorist school boasts such influential leaders as Eysenck, A. A. Lazarus, and Wolpe. Behaviorists sought to understand human behavior using a structured, empirical approach. BT went through a crisis when it faced the fact the many topics (e.g., the role of modeling in learning, the Skinnerian theory of language) could not be explained by behavioral principles. Thus, a new paradigm appeared: a cognitive paradigm, as an exposition of a cognitive revolution (e.g., Beck, 1976; Ellis, 1957). During this revolution, some behavior therapists challenged the emergence of CBT and claimed that cognitions were an epiphenomenon that played no role in the mediation of disturbance and that cognitive interventions added nothing to the effectiveness of psychotherapy. The founders of CBT who came from the behavioral tradition had to overcome a theoretical bias against even talking about private experiences such as beliefs, thoughts, or language. In the end, however, the new cognitive paradigm assimilated components of the behavioral paradigm and an integrated paradigm emerged:

CBT (e.g., Ellis, A. A. Lazarus, Mahoney, and Meichenbaum; see also Hollon & DiGiuseppe, 2011).

Many of the seminal figures in the second branch of CBT were originally trained in the behavioral tradition. These include Goldfried and Davison (1976), A. A. Lazarus (1977), Mahoney (1974), and Meichenbaum (1977). Goldfried and Davison's and A. A. Lazarus's seminal books provided the integration of cognitive and behavior approaches into a coherent practice. These pioneers integrated a cognitive perspective into their BT practices. Most CBT models incorporate behavioral principles, behavioral techniques, and include behavioral assignments between sessions. Although cognitive theories can explain the effectiveness of behavioral interventions (D. David, 2004), almost no approach to CBT uses cognitive interventions alone. This is because cognitions, emotions, and behaviors are interconnected aspects of human experience. Thoughts, emotions, and behavior have reciprocal relationships with each other; if one component is changed, the others are changed.

Other important seminal figures in CBT came from the psychodynamic field. Ellis (1962) and Beck (1976) both received their initial training in psychoanalytic therapy. Each of them broke with that approach to found schools of psychotherapy that emphasized the role of cognition in the etiology of distress and the process of change. Ellis (1957, 1962) and Beck (1970, 1976) had tremendous influences on this field and, once again, on the integrative influences on CBT. Although when compared with psychodynamic psychotherapies, CBT includes more activity on the part of the therapist and relies less on insight as a mechanism of change, both approaches are concerned with deep cognitions, such as schemas and assumptions, that are tacit or unconscious (Hollon & DiGiuseppe, 2011).

BASIC PRINCIPLES OF COGNITIVE BEHAVIOR THERAPY

Unlike psychodynamic and other insight-oriented approaches to psychotherapy, CBT focuses on changing what and how people think, behave, and feel in the present to reduce psychopathology and promote human growth. CBT does not focus on identifying unconscious drives but rests on the premise that people's thoughts and language influence their emotions and actions. CBT posits that certain types of cognitions lead to functional emotions and adaptive behaviors, whereas other types of cognitions generate dysfunctional emotions and maladaptive behavior, leading to psychological disorders.

The notion that thoughts connect to emotions, behavior, and disturbance has a long history in Western civilization in both philosophy and literature. The Greek Stoic philosopher Epictetus (90 BC/1996) summed up the theory in 90 BC in his now-famous quote, "People are not disturbed by things, but by the view they take of them" (p. 5). The Roman philosopher–emperor Marcus Aurelius (121–180 AD), wrote, "Very little is needed to make a happy life; it is all within yourself, in your way of thinking" (quoted in Rutherford, 1989, p. 168). Michel de Montaigne (1533–1592), an influential author of the French Renaissance and the father of modern skepticism, qualifies as an early CBT practitioner with his quote, "My life has been full of terrible misfortunes, most of which never happened" (de Montaigne, 1957, p. 47). CBT theory appears in the writings of the English language's most famous author, William Shakespeare (n.d.), whose character Hamlet says, "There is nothing either good or bad, but thinking makes it so" (p. 16).

Hamlet's statement alludes to CBT's distinction between knowing and appraising information. People process information by first making observations, extracting knowledge and, by evaluating this knowledge, determining whether it is relevant to the achievement of their goals. Next, people make appraisals of the facts that lead to aroused emotions (R. Lazarus, 1991). As Hamlet said, *appraisal* about facts makes things bad or good. CBT focuses on the link between knowledge and appraisal, and the arousal of emotions.

Cognitions

First, CBT focuses on processing information about the world. Information processing (i.e., cognitions) includes knowing, believing, and mental representations that people experience as thoughts and hold to be true, as well as various forms of implicit cognitions and mental representations in the form of implicit expectations and associations. CBT proposes that people aim to survive, procreate, and thrive, and that humans extract knowledge from their environment concerning the existence of any threats and the presence of resources, because this knowledge facilitates achieving life goals. Humans appraise knowledge about the environment for the purpose of evaluating goal significance, thus arousing emotions (R. Lazarus, 1991). Most CBT theories focus on this link between the knowledge extraction and appraisals of the knowledge with the arousal of emotional states.

CBT focuses mostly on articulated, conscious cognitions and automatic thoughts, which make up the *stream of consciousness*, a term coined by William James (1890), or *automatic thoughts*, the termed used by Beck (1976). Any taxonomy of cognitions within CBT needs to make this fundamental distinction between *knowing* (factual cognitions) and *appraising* (evaluative cognitions; Abelson & Rosenberg, 1958; D. David, Miclea, & Opre, 2004; D. David & Szentagotai, 2006). An example of a factual cognition is "I am stuck in traffic and will be late for class." This cognition consists of an observation and a neutral prediction of what will happen. It makes no judgment regarding whether this outcome will be positive or negative. Instead of being neutral, an evaluative cognition of this situation makes a judgment, such as "It is awful to be late for class." Evaluative cognitions can turn into schemas, which are less accessible to consciousness. These cognitions reflect broad ideas about the state of the world and interpersonal relationships. They are not in conscious experience but can be activated and made conscious by exploration.

Emotions

Emotions mobilize humans to respond to or to cope with environmental threats or a lack of resources (Darwin, 1872). Although emotions are a normal, necessary part of life, many forms of psychological disturbance involve excessive, prolonged, or extended emotional arousal. Alternatively, some forms of psychopathology result from a lack of appropriate emotions or emotions that are too mild in intensity or too short duration. Disturbed, unhealthy, or dysfunctional emotions are a barrier to adaptation if the high emotional arousal interferes with people's ability to function effectively. Changing beliefs helps people move from disturbed emotions to those that are more functional. Some critics of CBT falsely portray it as dismissing emotion, or as promoting an emotionless style of functioning. This is not true. Emotions provide internal cues to people that a problem exists in their environment that requires attention. The elimination of emotions would interfere with human adaptation because the absence of emotion would eliminate this important signaling system.

Once emotions have been generated, humans often evaluate them. These appraisals about one's internal emotional experiences can generate new, more intense and disruptive emotional reactions. These new emotional reactions can create anxiety about anxiety, depression about depression, or any subset of the possible permutations. CBT attempts to replace dysfunctional cognitions that lead to disturbed emotions with cognitions, which lead to more adaptive emotions that promote coping or help people circumvent dysfunctional beliefs and emotions and behave consistently with their goals and values despite the dysfunctional thoughts.

The various forms of CBT view the roles of beliefs and emotions differently. Some theorists think that emotions result from appraisal cognitions that could be conscious or unconscious (Ellis, 1962, 1994). Others view cognitions, behaviors, and emotions as influencing each other. Thoughts are only symptoms that are associated with emotions and behaviors. Changing any one of the three can change the other two. Cognitions are easily accessible through human language. One cannot directly affect emotions or behavior without the ability to present distress-causing stimuli or to change behaviors without access to reinforcers that are important to the client. However, through language, one can discuss thoughts about the stimuli and reinforcers and the evaluations of those things (e.g., cognitive therapy; Beck, 1976). Other theories view thoughts as linguistic covert responses that are linked to dysfunctional emotions and behaviors, and therapy is designed to break these connections and help the person learn to react flexibly, acting in his or her own best interest despite the arousal of the thoughts and emotions (acceptance and commitment therapy [Hayes, Villatte, Levin, & Hildebrandt, 2011] and mindfulness therapy [Kabat-Zinn, 2013]). For some of these theories, cognitions are the independent variables that change emotions, the dependent variables. For others, cognitions are the dependent measures that are provided by life experiences and are environmental in nature.

CBT requires some prerequisite abilities on the part of the client. It requires clients to have some awareness of their emotions. It assumes that clients have some ability to identify stream-of-consciousness thoughts that co-occur with their emotions. It assumes that clients can access and articulate tacit, nonconscious deeper beliefs from these stream-of-consciousness thoughts. CBT also assumes that clients can identify which desires are being thwarted to generate these emotions. Finally, CBT assumes that clients want to change the disturbed emotions that interfere with achieving their goals. According to the stages-of-change model, CBT represents an active stage intervention. CBT could fail with clients who are unaware of their emotions, cannot not identify which motives are being thwarted, cannot identify their stream-of-consciousness beliefs, cannot access their deeper tacit schema, or lack a desire to change. In such cases, the practitioner would do best to use other therapeutic strategies that address such issues before using CBT.

Understanding clients' emotions is crucial to effective CBT. Therapists cannot know which cognitions to target unless they know which emotions relate to their clients' problems. Therapists work to change cognitions that relate to disturbed, unhealthy emotions and help clients develop new cognitions that lead to more functional adaptive emotions and coping skills. By focusing on emotions, practitioners can identify which cognitions to focus on in treatment.

CBT focuses on the knowledge and appraisal processes that are involved in excessive or insufficient emotional arousal. Disturbed emotions or dysfunctional behaviors are hypothesized to occur because of some absent, erroneous, dysfunctional, incorrect, exaggerated, or extremely overevaluative appraisal of environmental threats, or rigid, inflexible ideas or habits that one must behave in a certain way.

CBT proposes that practitioners focus on both events and beliefs that are likely to arouse emotions. This emphasis on the information that people extract from the environment to ensure survival and adaptation is the key focus of CBT.

COGNITIVE MODELS

Understanding the convergent and distinctive features of the various CBT models will prepare readers to understand, practice, and research CBT. One tradition that influenced CBT is the *cognitive deficit model*, which involves teaching skills that clients can use to cue the desired behaviors and thus self-reinforce their occurrence. Such cognitive interventions involved teaching clients self-control skills and self-instructional statements for responding to stimuli outside of therapy sessions that are similar to the events that elicited maladaptive responses, which the client and therapist have discussed in session (Kanfer & Goldstein, 1975; Meichenbaum, 1977).

Cognitive Deficit Models

According to the *self-instructional training model*, well-adjusted people develop cognitive processes and structures that mediate or guide their adaptive behavior when they encounter novel stressful situations, whereas disturbed individuals do not successfully develop the skills to recall these adaptive cognitive processes. Teaching adaptive skills in psychotherapy requires a mechanism that will allow clients to recall new learned responses in novel, real-world situations. *Cognitive deficit model* interventions were originally intended for children with externalizing disorders and seriously disturbed clients; they include cognitive behavior modification, self-instructional training, stress inoculation methods (Meichenbaum, 1977, 1993), and problem-solving therapy (Spivack, Platt, & Shure, 1976).

Cognitive Dysfunction Models

The second tradition from which CBT emerged is the cognitive dysfunction model. This tradition can be divided into two groups of interventions: constructivistic-attributions models and incorrect-beliefs models. The early proponents of CBT credit Kelly's (1955) *psychology of personal constructs* as the first modern approach to cognitive psychotherapy. Kelly recognized that humans attempt to understand their world and have evolved and survived because of their ability to impose order on a seemingly chaotic universe. Individuals develop a system of dichotomous constructs to help make the world predictable. This system of constructs grows and changes as individuals interact with the world, and this construct system becomes the client's truth as she or he understand and experiences the world. The extent to which individuals can understand another's construct system represents an important measure of empathy. Therapy from a CBT perspective involves understanding clients' systems of constructs and helping them evaluate whether their constructs help them maneuver the world effectively. Kelly focused on helping clients become flexible (a recurrent theme in CBT), relinquishing ineffective constructs and developing effective ones. The idea that the person's own construction of reality played such an important role in disturbance led to the constructivist methods, which conceptualizes therapy as a task of understanding a person's world (Neimeyer, 2009). Compared with the objective reductionist models of the natural sciences, advocates of the constructivist approaches developed and adopted an epistemology and philosophy of science based more on phenomenology.

THEORY OF PERSONALITY AND PSYCHOPATHOLOGY

Theories of psychotherapy usually rest on well-defined psychological theories of personality, development, and psychopathology. Most CBT theorists do not articulate personality theories of normal function. However, the principles identified above in the Assumptions and Principles of Cognitive Behavior Therapy section provide a clear statement of a personality theory for CBT. Below we expand on these principles and identify some additional psychological processes that guide the CBT view of functioning that directly lead to interventions advocated in CBT.

Two Pathways to Emotions

All CBT approaches include both cognitive and behavioral interventions. Although they challenge, change, or teach new cognitions, they include behavioral activities in the session and behavioral assignments between them. Do the behavioral and cognitive interventions have the same neural pathways to connect to our emotions?

This issue goes back to a debate between Al Ellis, the founder of REBT, and Joe Wolpe, one of the most influential figures in BT. In 1974, Wolpe and Ellis went to Hofstra University to debate the role of cognition and conditioning in psychopathology and psychotherapy (see Hollon & DiGiuseppe, 2011). Wolpe, who spoke first, drew a human head on the blackboard and identified visual and auditory sensory brain centers, proposing that two pathways lead to anxiety. The first pathway runs from the senses to the lower levels of the brain (around the thalamus) and makes connections from there to the hypothalamus. He proposed that this pathway is learned through conditioning. Wolpe stated that this pathway accounted for about 90% of all anxiety disorders. Exposure interventions and systematic desensitization effectively treat disturbed anxiety mediated by this pathway. The second pathway involves information from the senses traveling to connections in the thalamus, then up through the cortex, and then back down the thalamus and into the hypothalamus. The reaction time for this pathway is slower and requires the person to learn through testing his or her faulty assumptions. Treatment of disturbed emotions that formed through this pathway involves testing and replacing disturbed thoughts and beliefs.

The audience expected Ellis to challenge Wolpe, but instead Ellis agreed with Wolpe's explanation of the two pathways mediating emotional disturbance. He disagreed, however, with Wolpe's idea of how much emotional disturbance was caused by each pathway. Ellis said the cognitive pathway mediated 90% of emotional disturbance and the conditioning pathway mediated 10%. This debate demonstrated that REBT, a type of CBT, clearly exists within the larger context of BT. CBT holds that there are multiple mechanisms of psychopathology, and different strategies are often required for effective therapy. This dual pathway theory identified by Wolpe and Ellis remains an active area of inquiry within CBT (Power & Dalgleish, 2008).

Two Competing Psychological Systems

Nobel Prize–winning psychologist Kahneman (2011) supports this view of human functioning in his book *Thinking, Fast and Slow*. His review of the research in cognitive psychology indicates that humans possess two information-processing systems. System 1 has fast thoughts that are automatic, irrational, and impressionistic. They draw inferences and quickly invent causes for events. Dysfunctional thoughts that lead to emotional disturbance usually have the characteristics of fast thoughts. In contrast, System 2 consists of slow thoughts that are rational and algorithmic. They require sustained attention and effort. These processes are susceptible to energy depletion (Baumeister, Vohs, & Tice, 2007) until they become overlearned. Luckily, the process of slow, rational thinking can override fast, irrational thinking. Psychotherapy teaches clients to use slow thoughts, which are more rational, to counter fast thoughts, which are irrational and automatic.

People without emotional or behavioral disturbance have more positive than negative thoughts. As the ratio of negative thoughts increases, people become more depressed (Schwartz, 1986; Schwartz & Garamoni, 1989). Several studies (Garamoni, Reynolds, Thase, Frank, & Fasiczka, 1992; Schwartz, 1997) have shown that clients receiving CBT improve as the ratio of positive to negative thoughts increases. Regardless of the clients' progress in psychotherapy, they will continue to experience some recurring negative thoughts. Clients sometimes erroneously infer from such experiences that they are not getting better or that treatment is not working and that they will remain disturbed. It is important to teach clients that negative beliefs are part of the human condition. Everyone has them, but once the thoughts occur, people have the choice of how to respond to them. They can give in to them, or they cope can with them by challenging them, accepting them, or moving on to activities that are more positive.

FUTURE DIRECTIONS

The amount of evidence supporting the efficacy and effectiveness for CBT is overwhelming. An examination of APA Division 12's (Society of Clinical Psychology) website demonstrates the degree to which CBT has produced successful forms of psychotherapy for almost every psychiatric disorder and clinical problem. All branches of the CBT tree clearly have strong empirical support and represent empirically based practice.

Although the research support for CBT is massive and impressive for each disorder and clinical problem, many clients still are not successful in responding to this form of psychotherapy. We think that clinical efficacy could improve with greater theoretical clarity. We often know that CBT can be effective for a clinical problem, but we still are not sure which strategy or combination of techniques will be the most effective for a particular client. In many CBT studies, books, and manuals, the authors describe focusing on dysfunctional cognitions. However, it often is unclear what exactly they mean by *dysfunctional cognitions* because the fact that such cognitions can manifest at different levels is often unacknowledged or unaddressed by "cocktail-like CBT," which instead mixes or confounds those levels. As a consequence, it is hard to incorporate these results into a coherent, complete, and integrated theory of CBT. Given all the different types of interventions that reside under the CBT tree, we usually do not know one will be best for a particular problem. CBT has not yet developed an assessment paradigm that will tell the clinician whether radical acceptance, assertiveness training, challenging irrational beliefs, or teaching problem solving is the best strategy for a particular client at that particular moment. Perhaps all the CBT techniques would do equally well, but it would be helpful to have an assessment strategy that led to prescriptive interventions. Furthermore, therapeutic benefits are likely to occur if we develop a clearer understanding of which types of cognitions mediate which emotional disturbances and which cognitive constructs are influenced by which interventions.

CONCLUSION

CBT is a multifaceted approach to therapy that has come to dominate the field of mental health. It has a long a long history that draws on ancient Western and Asian philosophies, scientific learning theories, and new research on cognitive processing. CBT includes a wide variety of interventions that fit most diagnoses and clinical problems. It is strongly supported by research. However, the reason we have stayed committed to CBT is because CBT is an evolving system that responds to external criticism and new research findings.

REFERENCES

Abelson, R. P., & Rosenberg, M. J. (1958). Symbolic psycho-logic: A model of attitudinal cognition. *Behavioral Science, 3,* 1–13. http://dx.doi.org/10.1002/bs.3830030102

American Psychological Association Presidential Task Force on Evidence-Based Practice. (2006). Evidence-based practice in psychology. *American Psychologist, 61,* 271–285. http://dx.doi.org/10.1037/0003-066X.61.4.271

Andersson, G., Asmundson, G. J., Carlbring, P., Ghaderi, A., Hofmann, S. G., & Stewart, S. H. (2005). Is CBT already the dominant paradigm in psychotherapy research and practice? *Cognitive Behaviour Therapy, 34,* 1–2. http://dx.doi.org/10.1080/16506070510008489

Baumeister, R. F., Vohs, K. D., & Tice, D. M. (2007). The strength model of self-control. *Current Directions in Psychological Science, 16,* 351–355. http://dx.doi.org/10.1111/j.1467-8721.2007.00534.x

Beck, A. T. (1970). Cognitive therapy: Nature and relation to behavior therapy. *Behavior Therapy, 1,* 184–200. http://dx.doi.org/10.1016/S0005-7894(70)80030-2

Beck, A. T. (1976). *Cognitive therapy and the emotional disorders.* New York, NY: Meridian.

Castonguay, L. G., Goldfried, M. R., Wiser, S., Raue, P. J., & Hayes, A. M. (1996). Predicting the effect of cognitive therapy for depression: A study of unique and common factors. *Journal of Consulting and Clinical Psychology, 64,* 497–504. http://dx.doi.org/10.1037/0022-006X.64.3.497

Cohen, J. A. (2006). *Treating trauma and traumatic grief in children and adolescents.* New York, NY: Guilford Press.

Cook, J. M., Biyanova, T., & Coyne, J. C. (2009). Influential psychotherapy figures, authors, and books: An Internet survey of over 2,000 psychotherapists. *Psychotherapy, 46,* 42–51. http://dx.doi.org/10.1037/a0015152

Darwin, C. (1872). *The expression of the emotions in man and animals.* London, England: John Murray. http://dx.doi.org/10.1037/10001-000

David, D. (2004). Beyond the behavioral approach-conclusions: Toward an evidence-based psychology and psychotherapy. *Journal of Clinical Psychology, 60,* 447–451. http://dx.doi.org/10.1002/jclp.10257

David, D., Lynn, S. J., & Ellis, A. (Eds.). (2010). *Rational and irrational beliefs: Research, theory, and clinical practice.* New York, NY: Oxford University Press.

David, D., Miclea, M., & Opre, A. (2004). The information-processing approach to the human mind: Basics and beyond. *Journal of Clinical Psychology, 60,* 353–368. http://dx.doi.org/10.1002/jclp.10250

David, D., & Szentagotai, A. (2006). Cognitions in cognitive-behavioral psychotherapies: Toward an integrative model. *Clinical Psychology Review, 26,* 284–298. http://dx.doi.org/10.1016/j.cpr.2005.09.003

David, O., & DiGiuseppe, R. (2016). *The Rational Parenting Program.* New York, NY: Springer. http://dx.doi.org/10.1007/978-3-319-22339-1

de Montaigne, M. (1957). *Complete works: Essays, travel journal, letters.* Stanford, CA: Stanford University Press.

de Oliveira, I. R. (2016). *Trial-based cognitive therapy: Distinctive features.* New York, NY: Routledge.

DiGiuseppe, R. (2007). Dissemination of CBT research results: Preaching to the uninterested or engaging in scientific debate. *Behavior Therapist, 30,* 117–120.

DiGiuseppe, R., David, D., & Venezia, R. (2016). Cognitive theories. In J. C. Norcross, G. R. VandenBos, & D. F. Freedheim (Eds.), *APA handbook of clinical psychology: Vol. 2. Theory and research* (pp. 145–182). Washington, DC: American Psychological Association. http://dx.doi.org/10.1037/14773-006

DiGiuseppe, R. A., Doyle, K. A., Dryden, W., & Backx, W. (2014). *A practitioner's guide to rational emotive behavior therapy* (3rd ed.). New York, NY: Oxford University Press.

DiGiuseppe, R., Leaf, R., & Linscott, J. (1993). The therapeutic relationship in rational-emotive therapy: Some preliminary data. *Journal of Rational-Emotive & Cognitive-Behavior Therapy, 11,* 223–233. http://dx.doi.org/10.1007/BF01089777

Dobson, K. S. (Ed.). (2010). *Handbook of cognitive behavioral therapies.* New York, NY: Guilford Press.

Ellis, A. (1957). Rational psychotherapy and individual psychology. *Journal of Individual Psychology, 13,* 38–44.

Ellis, A. (1959). Requisite conditions for basic personality change. *Journal of Consulting Psychology, 23,* 538–540. http://dx.doi.org/10.1037/h0049260

Ellis, A. (1962). *Reason and emotion in psychotherapy.* Fort Lee, NJ: Lyle Stuart.

Ellis, A. (1994). *Reason and emotion in psychotherapy: A comprehensive method of treating human disturbance, revised and updated.* New York, NY: Birch Lane Press.

Ellis, A. (2000). A critique of the theoretical contributions of non-directive therapy. *Journal of Clinical Psychology, 56,* 897–905. (Original work published 1948) http://dx.doi.org/10.1002/1097-4679(194807)4:3<248::AID-JCLP2270040308>3.0.CO;2-8

Epictetus. (1996). *The enchiridion* [E-book]. Boulder, CO: NetLibrary. (Original work published 90 BC)

Fava, G. A. (2016). *Well-being therapy: Treatment manual and clinical applications.* Buffalo, NY: Karger. http://dx.doi.org/10.1159/isbn.978-3-318-05822-2

Fishman, D. B. (2016). Behavioral theories. In J. C. Norcross, G. R. VandenBos, & D. F. Freedheim (Eds.), *The handbook of clinical psychology: Vol. 2. Theory and research* (pp. 79–118). Washington, DC: American Psychological Association. http://dx.doi.org/10.1037/14773-004

Fishman, D. B., Rotgers, F., & Franks, C. M. (Eds.). (1988). *Paradigms in behavior therapy: Present and promise.* New York, NY: Springer.

Follette, V. M., & Hazlett-Stevens, H. (2016). Mindfulness and acceptance therapies. In J. C. Norcross, G. R. VandenBos, & D. F. Freedheim (Eds.), *The handbook of clinical psychology: Vol. 2. Theory and research* (pp. 273–302). Washington, DC: American Psychological Association. http://dx.doi.org/10.1037/14773-000

Forgatch, M. S., & Patterson, G. R. (2010). Parent management training—Oregon model: An intervention for antisocial behavior in children and adolescents. In J. R. Weisz & A. E. Kazdin (Eds.), *Evidence-based psychotherapies for children and adolescents* (2nd ed., pp. 159–178). New York, NY: Guilford Press.

Garamoni, G. L., Reynolds, C. F., III, Thase, M. E., Frank, E., & Fasiczka, A. L. (1992). Shifts in affective balance during cognitive therapy of major depression. *Journal of Consulting and Clinical Psychology, 60,* 260–266. http://dx.doi.org/10.1037/0022-006X.60.2.260

Goldfried, M., & Davison, G. (1976). *Clinical behavior therapy.* New York, NY: Holt, Rinehart & Winston.

Hayes, S. C., Villatte, M., Levin, M., & Hildebrandt, M. (2011). Open, aware, and active: Contextual approaches as an emerging trend in the behavioral and cognitive therapies. *Annual Review of Clinical Psychology, 7,* 141–168. http://dx.doi.org/10.1146/annurev-clinpsy-032210-104449

Hofmann, S. G., Asmundson, G. J., & Beck, A. T. (2013). The science of cognitive therapy. *Behavior Therapy, 44,* 199–212. http://dx.doi.org/10.1016/j.beth.2009.01.007

Hollon, S. D., & DiGiuseppe, R. (2011). Cognitive theories of psychotherapy. In J. C. Norcross, G. R. VandenBos, & D. K. Freedheim (Eds.), *History of psychotherapy: Continuity and change* (2nd ed., pp. 203–241). Washington, DC: American Psychological Association. http://dx.doi.org/10.1037/12353-007

James, W. (1890). *The principles of psychology.* New York, NY: Henry Holt.

Kabat-Zinn, J. (2013). *Full catastrophe living: How to cope with stress, pain and illness with mindfulness mediation.* Boston, MA: Piatkus Books.

Kahneman, D. (2011). *Thinking, fast and slow.* New York, NY: Farrar, Straus and Giroux.

Kanfer, F. H., & Goldstein, A. P. (1975). *Helping people change: A textbook of methods*. Oxford, England: Pergamon Press.

Kelly, G. (1955). *The psychology of personal constructs* (Vol. 1). New York, NY: W.W. Norton.

Kohlenberg, R. J., & Tsai, M. (1991). *Functional analytic psychotherapy: Creating intense and curative therapeutic relationships*. New York, NY: Plenum Press. http://dx.doi.org/10.1007/978-0-387-70855-3

Kuehlwein, K. T., & Rosen, H. (Eds.). (1993). *Cognitive therapies in action: Evolving innovative practice*. San Francisco, CA: Jossey-Bass.

Lazarus, A. A. (1967). In support of technical eclecticism. *Psychological Reports, 21*, 415–416. http://dx.doi.org/10.2466/pr0.1967.21.2.415

Lazarus, A. A. (1977). Has behavior therapy outlived its usefulness? *American Psychologist, 32*, 550–554. http://dx.doi.org/10.1037/0003-066X.32.7.550

Lazarus, A. A. (1981). *The practice of multimodal therapy*. New York, NY: McGraw-Hill.

Lazarus, R. S. (1991). *Emotion and adaptation*. London, England: Oxford University Press.

Lewinsohn, P. M., Weinstein, M. S., & Alper, T. (1970). A behavioral approach to the group treatment of depressed persons: A methodological contribution. *Journal of Clinical Psychology, 26*, 525–532. http://dx.doi.org/10.1002/1097-4679(197010)26:4<525::AID-JCLP2270260441>3.0.CO;2-Y

Linehan, M. (1993). *Skills training manual for treating borderline personality disorder*. New York, NY: Guilford Press.

Mahoney, M. J. (1974). *Cognition and behavior modification*. Cambridge, MA: Ballinger.

Martin, G., & Pear, J. (2015). *Behavior modification: What is it and how to do it* (10th ed.). New York, NY: Routledge.

Mathieson, F., Collings, S., Dowell, A., Goodyear-Smith, F., Stanley, J., & Hatcher, S. (2013). Collaborative research: A case example of dissemination of CBT in primary care. *The Cognitive Behaviour Therapist, 6*, e4.

Meichenbaum, D. (1977). *Cognitive behavior modification: An integrative approach*. New York, NY: Plenum Press. http://dx.doi.org/10.1007/978-1-4757-9739-8

Meichenbaum, D. (1993). Changing conceptions of cognitive behavior modification: Retrospect and prospect. *Journal of Consulting and Clinical Psychology, 61*, 202–204. http://dx.doi.org/10.1037/0022-006X.61.2.202

Miller, W. R., & Rollnick, S. (2012). *Motivational interviewing: Helping people change* (3rd ed.). New York, NY: Guilford Press.

Neimeyer, R. A. (2009). *Constructivist psychotherapy: Distinctive features*. New York, NY: Routledge.

Nezu, A. M., Maguth Nezu, C., & D'Zurilla, T. J. (2013). *Problem-solving therapy: A treatment manual*. New York, NY: Springer.

Norcross, J. C., Krebs, P. M., & Prochaska, J. O. (2011). Stages of change. *Journal of Clinical Psychology, 67*, 143–154. http://dx.doi.org/10.1002/jclp.20758

Norcross, J. C., & Lambert, M. J. (2011). Psychotherapy relationships that work II. *Psychotherapy, 48,* 4–8. http://dx.doi.org/10.1037/a0022180

O'Donohue, W. T., & Fisher, J. E. (2009). *General principles and empirically supported techniques of cognitive behavior therapy.* Hoboken, NJ: Wiley.

Patterson, G. R. (1975). *Applications of social learning to family life.* Champaign, IL: Research Press.

Power, M. J., & Dalgleish, T. (2008). *Cognition and emotion: From order to disorder* (2nd ed.). New York, NY: Psychology Press.

Richards, D. A., Ekers, D., McMillan, D., Taylor, R. S., Byford, S., Warren, F. C., . . . Finning, K. (2016). Cost and outcome of behavioural activation versus cognitive behavioural therapy for depression (COBRA): A randomised, controlled, non-inferiority trial. *The Lancet, 388,* 871–880. http://dx.doi.org/10.1016/S0140-6736(16)31140-0

Rogers, C. R. (1950). A current formulation of client-centered therapy. *The Social Service Review, 24,* 442–450. http://dx.doi.org/10.1086/638020

Rogers, C. R. (1957). The necessary and sufficient conditions of therapeutic personality change. *Journal of Consulting Psychology, 21,* 95–103. http://dx.doi.org/10.1037/h0045357

Rutherford, R. B. (1989). *The meditations of Marcus Aurelius: A study.* New York, NY: Oxford University Press.

Ryle, A. (2005). Cognitive analytic therapy. In J. C. Norcross & M. R. Goldfried (Eds.), *Handbook of psychotherapy integration* (2nd ed., pp. 196–217). New York, NY: Oxford University Press.

Schwartz, R. M. (1986). The internal dialogue: On the asymmetry between positive and negative coping thoughts. *Cognitive Therapy and Research, 10,* 591–605. http://dx.doi.org/10.1007/BF01173748

Schwartz, R. M. (1997). Consider the simple screw: Cognitive science, quality improvement, and psychotherapy. *Journal of Consulting and Clinical Psychology, 65,* 970–983. http://dx.doi.org/10.1037/0022-006X.65.6.970

Schwartz, R. M., & Garamoni, G. L. (1989). Cognitive balance and psychopathology: Evaluation of an information processing model of positive and negative states of mind. *Clinical Psychology Review, 9,* 271–294. http://dx.doi.org/10.1016/0272-7358(89)90058-5

Shakespeare, W. (n.d.). *The tragedy of Hamlet, prince of Denmark.* Champaign, IL: Project Gutenberg, n.d. eBook Collection, EBSCOhost.

Sigel, Z. V., Williams, J. M. C., & Teasdale, J. D. (2013). *Mindfulness-based cognitive therapy for depression* (2nd ed.). New York, NY: Guilford Press.

Skotarczak, L., & Lee, G. K. (2015). Effects of parent management training programs on disruptive behavior for children with a developmental disability: A meta-analysis. *Research in Developmental Disabilities, 38,* 272–287. http://dx.doi.org/10.1016/j.ridd.2014.12.004

Sloane, R. D., Staples, F. R., Cristol, A. H., & Whipple, K. (1975). *Psychotherapy versus behavior therapy*. Cambridge, MA: Harvard University Press. http://dx.doi.org/10.4159/harvard.9780674365063

Spivack, G., Platt, J., & Shure, M. (1976). *The social problem-solving approach to adjustment*. San Francisco, CA: Jossey-Bass.

Traux, C., & Carkhuff, R. (1967). *Towards effective counseling and psychotherapy: Training and practice*. Chicago, IL: Aldine.

Watkins, E., Scott, J., Wingrove, J., Rimes, K., Bathurst, N., Steiner, H., . . . Malliaris, Y. (2007). Rumination-focused cognitive behaviour therapy for residual depression: A case series. *Behaviour Research and Therapy, 45*, 2144–2154. http://dx.doi.org/10.1016/j.brat.2006.09.018

Wells, A. (2008). *Metacognitive therapy for anxiety and depression*. New York, NY: Guilford Press.

Wolpe, J. (1958). *Psychotherapy by reciprocal inhibition*. Palo Alto, CA: Stanford University Press.

Wolpe, J. (1969). *The practice of behavior therapy*. New York, NY: Pergamon.

Young, J. E., Klosko, J. S., & Weishaar, M. (2003). *Schema therapy: A practitioner's guide*. New York, NY: Guilford Press.

18

COGNITIVE BEHAVIOR THERAPY WITH CHILDREN

MARK D. TERJESEN, TAMARA DEL VECCHIO, AND NORA GERARDI

Earlier chapters in this volume present the basic principles of cognitive behavior therapy (CBT) as well as the two original models of CBT: (a) the rational emotive behavior therapy approach developed by Albert Ellis and (b) the cognitive therapy approach developed by Aaron Beck. We briefly describe both models below with a greater focus of this chapter being on the adaptation of these models within a cognitive behavioral framework for working with youth in schools.

AN OVERVIEW OF COGNITIVE BEHAVIOR THERAPY

CBT is an amalgam of both cognitive and behavioral theories of human behavior (A. T. Beck, 1970/2016; Benjamin et al., 2011; Ertmer & Newby, 1993; Persons, 2012). The cognitive model posits that it is the way people

http://dx.doi.org/10.1037/0000126-019
Behavioral Interventions in Schools: Evidence-Based Positive Strategies, Second Edition, S. G. Little and A. Akin-Little (Editors)
Copyright © 2019 by the American Psychological Association. All rights reserved.

perceive a given situation (through automatic negative thoughts), instead of the situation itself, that predicts their subsequent emotional or behavioral reaction (A. T. Beck, 1976; J. S. Beck, 2011). In contrast, the behavioral model emphasizes the role of reinforcing or punishing consequences for behaviors as the mechanisms for learning and continuing emotional or behavioral responses (Benjamin et al., 2011; Ertmer & Newby, 1993; Persons, 2012; Staddon, 2014). CBT, which incorporates both cognitive and behavioral principles, posits the assumption that a person's cognitions, behaviors, and emotions reciprocally determine each other (Bandura, 1977; Friedberg & McClure, 2015); that is, change in any one of these elements is expected to produce changes in the others (e.g., if a student is able to challenge his or her negative automatic thoughts, then his or her mood will improve). A dynamic and complex system is formed, with interpersonal and environmental contexts, physiology, emotional functioning, behavior, and cognition interacting with each other (see Figure 18.1; Friedberg & McClure, 2015).

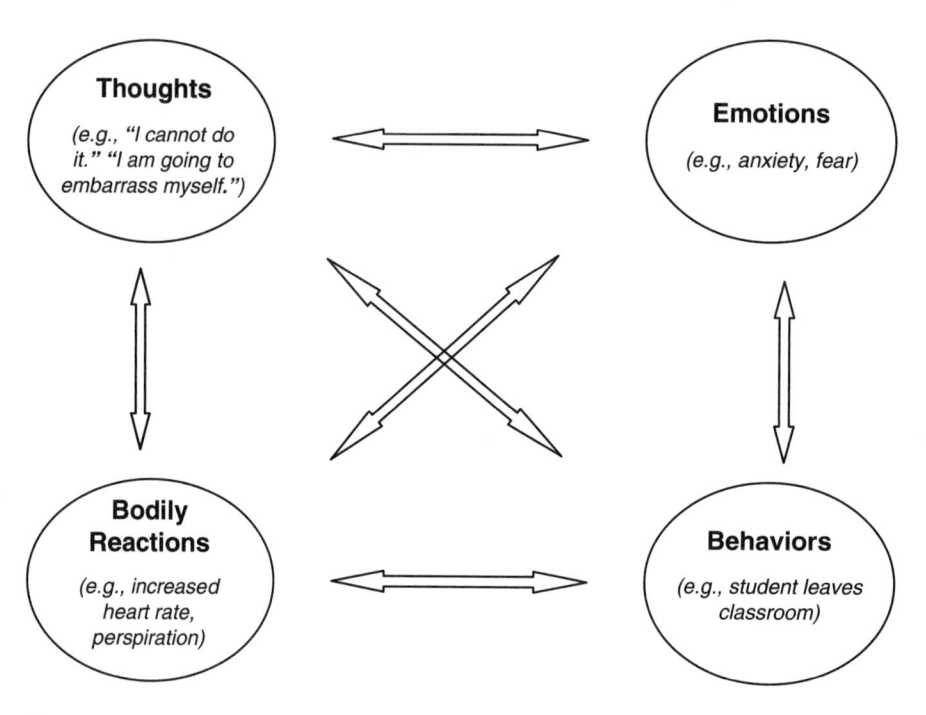

Figure 18.1. Cognitive Behavior Therapy Model.

CBT is a time-sensitive, structured, present-oriented psychotherapy that is problem solving in its orientation (Association for Behavior and Cognitive Therapies, 2017; A. T. Beck, 1976; J. S. Beck, 2011; Kendall, 2011; Persons, 2012). CBT is directed toward solving current problems and teaching clients skills to modify dysfunctional thinking and behaving; ultimately, CBT replaces ways of living that do not work with new ways of living that do work and are aligned with a client's values and goals (Association for Behavior and Cognitive Therapies, 2017; A. T. Beck, 1976; J. S. Beck, 2011). As such, core strategies in CBT include helping clients identify and evaluate their automatic thoughts. Through these core strategies clients can think more realistically and feel better emotionally and thus behave more functionally (A. T. Beck, 1976; J. S. Beck, 2011). Moreover, clients are encouraged to engage in more functional behaviors, which increases their likelihood of being reinforced for their adaptive instead of maladaptive behaviors.

Psychopathological symptoms in children and adolescents are treated by intervening to change the automatic thoughts and behaviors that cause unpleasant emotions (Persons, 2012). Components of CBT include psychoeducation and psychotherapy; *psychoeducation* involves teaching the client psychologically related concepts and information, and *psychotherapy* involves encouraging clients to use and generalize cognitive and behavioral skills (Friedberg & McClure, 2015). Basic behavioral tools used with children might include relaxation training (e.g., progressive muscle relaxation), social skills training, role playing and behavioral rehearsal, contingency management, the scheduling of pleasant events, and exposure techniques (Friedberg & McClure, 2015). Cognitive techniques focused on changing thought content might include de-catastrophizing, tests of evidence, and reattribution (e.g., responsibility pie; see Friedberg & McClure, 2015).

EVIDENCE FOR COGNITIVE BEHAVIOR THERAPY

Robust evidence supports the use of CBT for number of childhood disorders, including anxiety (Cartwright-Hatton, Roberts, Chitsabesan, Fothergill, & Harrington, 2004), depression (Arnberg & Öst, 2014), and aggression (Smeets et al., 2015). More recently, evidence that supports the use of CBT delivered in the schools is beginning to accumulate. Mental health treatment in the school can differ from clinic-based interventions in many ways. Perhaps most advantageously is the ability of schools to target individual symptomatic children as well as provide a broad delivery of services. School-based CBT is delivered at one of three levels of reach: *Universal* efforts are designed for all children, regardless of diagnosis or symptomology; *selective* programs are targeted to children considered at risk on the basis of individual student or family characteristics; and *indicated* programs are typically delivered to children with mild to moderate symptoms that may not yet qualify for a diagnosis.

School-based CBT has most prominently been used to treat students' anxious and depressive symptoms. In a meta-analytic review of the effectiveness of school-based CBT, Mychailyszyn, Brodman, Read, and Kendall (2012) found that CBT is moderately effective in reducing anxiety (pre–post Hedge's $g = 0.50$) and mildly effective in reducing depression (pre–post Hedge's $g = 0.30$). However, the effectiveness of CBT differs on the basis of level of delivery. For example, Neil and Christensen (2009) found that the proportion of significant effects were comparable across level of delivery, with 50% to 58% of the studies they reviewed reporting significantly lower levels of anxiety treatment condition participants versus those in the control condition. Yet this effect varied with universal programs evidencing effects ranging from a moderate ($d = 0.32$) to a very large ($d = 1.37$) effect size compared with selective programs that evidenced a small effect size ($d = 0.11$). For depression, in contrast, indicated treatment most often produced significant effect sizes, followed closely by universal treatments, then selective programs (Calear & Christensen, 2010); 40% to 55% of studies they reviewed reporting significant lower levels of depression in the treatment condition than control condition. For successful treatments, the strength the effect was comparable across treatment delivery models ($ds = 0.25–1.40$). Unfortunately, we were unable to locate a review of the school-based treatment of aggression. However, in a more general review of CBT treatment for aggression using a pretest–posttest control group design, Smeets et al. (2015) concluded that school delivery resulted in a very small effect ($d = 0.10$, based on four studies) compared with a medium effect size ($d = 0.61$) for clinic-based interventions.

The delivery of psychological interventions in the schools may vary, with group therapy with children and adolescents being a common approach in both clinical and school-based settings (Terjesen & Esposito, 2006). For reasons related to fiscal, practical, and presenting problems (e.g., social skills), implementing interventions in a group format appears to be preferable to individual treatment approaches (Hales, 2008). Unfortunately, much like the overall research on school-based interventions, the science behind group-based approaches is lacking (Corey, 2008; Forman, Olin, Hoagwood, Crowe, & Saka, 2009; Matta, 2014). Matta (2014) reported that reviews of group treatment approaches and interventions conducted in the school environment have produced varying results, and very often results are described qualitatively as opposed to quantitatively (Whiston & Quinby, 2009; Whiston & Sexton, 1998). However, in a review of 17 studies, Prout and Prout (1998) reported a group-based intervention effect size of 0.95, indicating that group-based approaches are an effective modality of treatment in the school environment. However, these results are not consistent with a review of school-based psychotherapy in which an analysis of 64 group treatments resulted in a smaller effect size of 0.47 (Reese, Prout, Zirkelback, & Anderson, 2010).

Despite the overall positive effect of school-based CBT, the outcomes vary greatly, with as many as 60% of treatment studies (Calear & Christensen, 2010) not yielding significant effects. It is perhaps not surprising that there is not support for a one-size-fits all treatment program; differences based on population or delivery method are expected. Much of the research on the effectiveness of school-based CBT is relatively recent. Because of an overall small number of studies have examined the effectiveness of school-based CBT, there is limited information available on whether moderators, such as gender, modulate treatment outcome. Although preliminary evidence suggests that CBT is more effective for children from middle to high socioeconomic class families, the data are limited to a small review of just six studies (Kavanagh et al., 2009). Thus, continued work in this area is needed to elucidate moderators and mediators (i.e., mechanisms) of treatment outcome.

These limitations notwithstanding, school-based CBT holds incredible promise. The intervention encompasses several effective treatment options that vary in intensity. Some programs could be easily imbedded into school settings. For example, universal prevention efforts, usually provided at the school or classroom level by teachers or school support staff (e.g., Promoting Alternative Thinking Strategies; Greenberg, Kusche, Cook, & Quamma, 1995). On the other hand, some programs can offer more individualized treatment and are generally provided one on one or in small groups by school counselors and school psychologists (e.g., Coping Cat; Kendall & Hedtke, 2006). Recent treatment research has begun to investigate adaptive interventions, which offer treatment professionals guidance about determining whether an intervention type or dosage should be altered in response to their clients' needs and progress in treatment (Almirall & Chronis-Tuscano, 2016), in contrast to a traditional one-for-all treatment approach. Although the research on adaptive interventions in response to other concerns is promising (Almirall & Chronis-Tuscano, 2016; Pelham et al., 2016), the extent to which adaptive treatments might be helpful for children in schools and the suitability of adapting treatments within a school setting is not yet known.

COGNITIVE BEHAVIOR THERAPY IN PRACTICE

It is important for school-based practitioners to consider a number of variables that may influence the efficacy of the delivery of CBT in the schools. These could be student specific (e.g., motivation to change) as well as how best from a practical standpoint to introduce the concepts that are core to the CBT process.

Building Motivating for Change

One challenge in delivery of any direct psychological intervention in the school may be the student's motivation to change. Children in school settings are often not self-referred and frequently are mandated to receive school-based counseling. As such, their motivation to engage in the counseling process may be minimal, and this constitutes a barrier to effective delivery of CBT in the schools.

When preparing for the provision of counseling, school-based clinicians may wish to consider what level of preparation for change the student may be in, as described in the stages of change model (Prochaska & DiClemente, 1983). Most nonreferred students arrive to school-based counseling in the pre-contemplation stages, where they are not actively considering change. In this case, to mitigate resistance, clinicians can validate their lack of readiness and clarify to students that ultimately the decision to change is theirs. To help promote the idea of change and to foster self-exploration, clinicians may encourage students to reevaluate their current behavior and its associated consequences. Highlighting the dissonance between desired outcomes and actual outcomes of behavior can help motivate students to seeking change. CBT may be very helpful in building motivation to change through use of motivational syllogism, proposed by DiGiuseppe and colleagues (DiGiuseppe, 1995; DiGiuseppe, Linscott, & Jilton, 1996). The four elements of motivational syllogism are as follows: (a) my present emotion is dysfunctional; (b) an acceptable alternative emotional script exists for this type of activating event; (c) giving up the dysfunctional emotion and working toward feeling the alternative one is better for me; and (d) my beliefs cause my emotions; therefore, I will work at changing my beliefs to change my emotions. As students move toward considering and preparing for change, the school-based clinician can identify obstacles to change and, in collaboration with the student, work to overcome these obstacles while promoting self-efficacy for change.

In child and adolescent therapy, the therapeutic working alliance has a small but reliable association ($r = .27$) with treatment outcomes (Shirk & Karver, 2003). School-based practitioners may wish to consider the three main components of the therapeutic working alliance as outlined by Bordin (1979): (a) agreement on the goals of therapy, (b) agreement on the tasks of therapy, and (c) working on the relationship bond. Taking a collaborative, nonargumentative stance is important in building a strong therapeutic working alliance. For example, Chu and Kendall (2004) found that child involvement in the development of treatment tasks is a significant predictor of clinical treatment gains. In addition, Creed and Kendall (2005) identified three therapist behaviors that may be related to a strong early (e.g., Session 3) therapeutic alliance with an anxious child receiving manualized CBT. The authors indicated that "collaboration" and "finding common ground" between therapist and child was predictive of higher child ratings of an alliance, while "pushing the child to talk" beyond their comfort level was predictive of lower child ratings of an alliance. Thus, early on, school practitioners may want to identify the factors that may contribute to a strong client–therapist alliance and recognize that these may vary depending on the client and the presenting problem.

WHY STUDENTS FEEL AND BEHAVE: A COGNITIVE–BEHAVIORAL CONCEPTUALIZATION

Treatment with CBT is derived from a cognitive formulation of the presenting symptoms and disorder; the beliefs and behavioral strategies that characterize a specific disorder inform treatment (J. S. Beck, 2011; see also https://www.beckinstitute.org). Cognitive formulations are informed by the *content-specificity hypothesis*, which postulates that affective states (e.g., anxiety, depression) can be discerned on the basis of the unique related cognitive content (A. T. Beck, 1976; R. Beck & Perkins, 2001). For example, depression is characterized by a negative cognitive triad such that depressed individuals tend to explain unfavorable events through a self-critical view of themselves (e.g., "I am stupid"), a negative view of their experiences and other people (e.g., "School is ruined," "None of my peers like me"), and a pessimistic view of the future (e.g., "I am never going to succeed in school," "I will never make friends"; A. T. Beck, 1976; J. S. Beck, 2011). As such, a depressed student might be observed to be inattentive in class, how a disinterest in class or other activities, and have low motivation. These behaviors may be influenced by cognitive symptoms, such as self-critical thoughts and a sense of hopelessness for the future, as well as emotions, such as sadness or apathy. Anxiety, in contrast, tends to be characterized by future-oriented worry thoughts and catastrophizing (A. T. Beck, 1976; Friedberg & McClure, 2015). An anxious student might be observed engaging in avoidance behaviors, such as skipping class or refusing to go to school. These behaviors would again by hypothesized as influenced by catastrophic thinking and emotions such as fear.

To best understand a student's unique presentation, a conceptualization is essential; conceptualizations involve an understanding of the individual student and his or her specific beliefs and patterns of behavior (A. T. Beck, 1976; J. S. Beck, 2011). The conceptualization includes the students'

EXHIBIT 18.1
Sample Case Conceptualization

Demographics:
  Age: 13
  Grade: 8
  Gender: Male

In childhood, John had difficulty with his academic success in school. His poor academic performance yielded automatic thoughts, including "I am not good enough," "I cannot succeed," and "I will disappoint others by never doing well in school." John formed a core belief that there was something wrong with him and that he would never being good enough. John's beliefs were recently activated when he was academically tested at school and subsequently diagnosed with a specific learning disability. As a result, John has experienced symptoms of depression, including ruminating on his past academic failures, disinterest in school, increased sadness, and low motivation to attend school. John currently experiences thoughts such as "I shouldn't bother going to school" and "Others think I am stupid." His depressive symptoms are now contributing to an even poorer academic performance. John lacks coping strategies to deal with his depression, and as a consequence his overall behavioral activation has decreased. John stays home from school, reporting physiological symptoms such as body aches and stomachaches. These symptoms likely are manifestations of his depression.

---

symptoms (including disorders and problems), hypotheses about the causes of the student's problems, precipitants of the current problems, and the origins of the causes (Persons, 2012). Understanding the unique characteristics of a given student, including the relationships among the student's thoughts, feeling, and behaviors, increases the therapist's ability to implement evidence-based CBT techniques. See Exhibit 18.1 for a sample case conceptualization.

INTRODUCING COGNITIVE BEHAVIOR THERAPY TO THE STUDENT

Although the different CBT models have some considerable conceptual overlap, variations exist in the intervention used in each (Hyland & Boduszek, 2012). Whereas the more traditional cognitive therapy models focus on the automatic thoughts or inferences that one may endorse about an event (e.g., "No one came to my party because they don't like me"), the rational emotive behavior therapy approach focuses on the evaluations of the event (e.g., "It is AWFUL that no one came. I am a loser!"). Although there are differences in these types of cognitions, the early steps for school-based practitioners are to help students understand the relations among what happened, what they think about that event, and their resulting emotions and behaviors. It is important that students realize that it is not the undesirable situations or events that *cause* them to experience unhealthy emotions and engage in specific behaviors but instead that their beliefs and cognitions about these events that may be unhealthy, irrational, or dysfunctional in nature such that they are at an increased risk for maladaptive emotional and behavioral responses. As we stated earlier, these beliefs may lead to either unhealthy or functional behavioral or emotional consequences. In Figure 18.2 we provide a model for conceptualizing the relationship among situations, cognitions, emotions, and behavior (Bernard, Ellis, & Terjesen, 2006). School-based practitioners and students who collaboratively complete a Happening–Thinking–Feeling–Behavior chart or similar activity can help students understand the role of cognitions in the development of emotions and behaviors.

When students understand the relationship between cognitions and emotions, it is important to help them distinguish between adaptive, healthy, and rational cognitions and beliefs and those that are unhealthy, dysfunctional, or irrational. School-based practitioners should endeavor to draw the distinction between patterns of thinking that are adaptive, realistic, healthy, flexible, logical, and empirically consistent with reality with those that are more inflexible, dysfunctional, and not consistent with reality (Hyland & Boduszek, 2012; Szentagotai & Freeman, 2007). When students respond to a negative experience with flexible, healthy, and logical cognitions they are more likely to experience healthy negative emotions (e.g., concern, disappointment, frustration, regret) and thus will handle stressors in a more adaptive manner (Hyland & Boduszek, 2012). Alternatively, students who

Happening →	Thinking →	Feeling →	Behavior →
Upcoming math exam	"I am going to fail! That would be terrible."	Anxious (9/10)[a]	Procrastination, lack of sleep
Girlfriend ended our relationship	"She was the one! No one will ever care about me. I am a loser."	Depressed (8/10)[a]	Avoidance of peers; lack of engagemen in enjoyable activities

Figure 18.2. Happening–Thinking–Feeling–Behavior (HTFB) Chart.
[a]The order of assessment questions using the HTFB framework is as follows: 1. Identify a specific Happening or event (day, place, person, task). 2. Assess different feelings the client had about the Happening and assess the intensity of each using the Emotional Thermometer. 3. Assess behavior reactions that accompany feelings. 4. Select one feeling at a time to work on. From "Rational-Emotive Behavioral Approaches to Childhood Disorders: History, Theory, Practice and Research," by M. E. Bernard, A. Ellis, and M. D. Terjesen, 2006, p. 455, in A. Ellis & M. E. Bernard (Eds.), *Rational-Emotive Behavioral Approaches to Childhood Disorders: Theory, Practice and Research*, New York, NY: Springer Science+Business Media. Copyright 2006 by Springer Science+Business Media. Adapted with permission.

respond to a negative event in an unhealthy, irrational manner they are more likely to experience the more extreme, maladaptive, unhealthy negative emotions (e.g., anger, anxiety, depression, guilt) and as a result be more likely to engage in maladaptive behavioral responses (Hyland & Boduszek, 2012).

Cognitive Restructuring of Unhealthy Thinking

School-based practitioners work with students to actively challenge and disprove unhealthy beliefs and help them develop a new belief system that is more adaptive, flexible, and rational in nature (Sava, Maricutoiu, Rusu, Macsinga, & Virga, 2011). As an example, we want to work with students to move from thinking, "This is the *worst* thing that could happen to me. I can't stand it!" which may lead to unpleasant emotions (e.g., anxiety, depression) and behaviors (e.g., avoidance, withdrawal), to having them believe "This may be bad, but not terrible, and I can deal with it!" which may lead to more adaptive emotions (e.g., concern, disappointment) and behaviors (e.g., perseverance, remaining in the situation). The challenging and subsequent replacement of these maladaptive thoughts with more healthy, functional beliefs have been linked to reduced emotional and behavioral difficulties in children and adolescents (David, Szentagotai, Eva, & Macavei, 2005; Esposito, 2009). See the Resources section at the end of this chapter for websites that can offer downloadable forms to educate students about the model.

Cognitive restructuring involves collaboratively working with students to debate or challenge the unhealthy cognitions they are endorsing while developing a newer, healthier belief system. A number of methods are used in cognitive restructuring to work toward identifying cognitive errors (e.g., all-or-none thinking, discounting the positive), helping students identify when they are distorting what actually occurred, and correcting faulty attributions related to an aversive situation (e.g., thinking, "It is my fault my parents are getting divorced"). Restructuring approaches can be cognitive, imaginal, and behavioral in nature (DiGiuseppe, Doyle, Dryden, & Backx, 2013), and we describe them below as they relate to specific beliefs students may endorse.

A number of core cognitive disputation techniques can be used to challenge automatic negative thoughts (e.g., "I am going to fail this test") and evaluative irrational beliefs (e.g., "If I fail this test it would be *awful*!") that school-based practitioners may wish to consider. School-based practitioners may work with students to analyze the situation and their accompanying cognitions, behaviors, and emotions and examining the evidence behind these unhealthy thoughts: "Where is the evidence to support your idea that she does not like you?" "Are my thoughts based on facts or just a 'feeling' you have?" "Am I misinterpreting the situation?" or "Is there evidence for and against my thoughts?" School-based practitioners may work with students to collect data about the accuracy of their belief and possibly design an "experiment" whereby they can test their thoughts (Terjesen, 2015). Students can then work on generating a new, healthier way to think to replace unhealthy thoughts, such as "Even though this is difficult, I can deal with this and work on it as best I can until it is completed."

Another approach to challenging unhealthy beliefs involves working with students to examine whether their beliefs make logical sense; that is, does the manner in which they are thinking about the situation or themselves make logical sense? An example of logically challenging of unhealthy thinking would be, "Just because you want to succeed at math, does it follow logically that it *must* happen?"

Another approach to restructuring unhealthy cognitions that are leading to emotional and behavioral responses (Terjesen, 2015) involves working with the students to provide an objective definition of their thoughts. For example, when a student describes rejection by peers as "terrible," the school-based practitioner would work with that student to come up with an agreed-on definition of *terrible* that may be more objective in nature. In other words, if others looked at the situation, would the vast majority assign a similar value or level of just how terrible this event is? If the student can define terrible as "one of the *very worst* things that could ever happen to me," this may provide him or her with a better understanding of how, although the event she or he has experienced may certainly be negative or undesirable, it may not meet the newly developed definition of something as being terrible. The development of an informal "awfulness scale" from 1 to 100, on which 100 represents the worst possible scenario (i.e., death of a loved one) can also help students gain perspective as to where their negative experiences would rate in comparison (Terjesen, 2015).

Challenging unhealthy thoughts by examining the disadvantages and dysfunctional nature of these thoughts—and, more specifically, how these irrational beliefs or automatic thoughts are in fact stopping them from working toward their goals—can be a very useful approach with students (Terjesen, 2015). If a student is experiencing social anxiety and considering not going to a party that he wants to attend because he is thinking, "If I go and say something stupid, they will all laugh at me and it would be awful!" the practitioner would collaboratively work with the student to challenge these ideas by asking, "How is it helping me if they keep thinking that I will say something stupid and they will laugh at me? I want to go to this party; how does it help me to attend by thinking it would be awful if I made a social mistake?" The answers to these questions will most likely help the student recognize that these cognitions actually do not help and in fact impede him from achieving his goal (i.e., going to the party). This then provides an educational opportunity for the clinician to reinforce the connection of thinking to emotion and behavior and work toward developing a new, healthy, adaptive, alternative way of thinking.

The use of visual aids or mnemonic devices also may assist in the development of cognitive restructuring with students and is often seen to be more hands on in comparison with work with older adults (i.e., beyond school age; Bernard & Pires, 2006; Ellis & Bernard, 2006). Consideration of the developmental level of the student when engaging in CBT is important given that it may affect the types of cognitive techniques used given that such techniques may vary on the basis of their developmental level (Bernard et al., 2006; Terjesen, 2015). Younger students may benefit from a greater focus on increasing their emotional vocabulary to help distinguish different emotional experiences as well as differentiate thoughts from feelings and clarifying the relationship between them. With younger students, cognitive restructuring may be above their developmental level and thus it may be better to focus on rehearsal of more healthy, adaptive ways of thinking instead of directly challenging automatic thoughts and disputing irrational beliefs (Terjesen, 2015). On the other hand, adolescents are often able to grasp more abstract concepts in cognitive restructuring (e.g., "Why must you succeed at everything important to you?") in comparison with younger students, with whom it is better to focus on more concrete examples (e.g., "Why must you succeed in sports?").

Increasing Adaptive Behaviors

Cognitive techniques are regularly integrated with behavioral ones, with the choice and focus of intervention contingent on the presenting problem and what has shown to be effective in the intervention research. The practitioner may integrate some direct behavioral activities to challenge unhealthy beliefs as well as reinforce the adaptive, healthy ways of thinking. Harrington (2011) offered a number of behavioral activities that involve clients performing specific behaviors that counter their irrational beliefs. These include encouraging students to challenge their avoidance tendencies by having them perform a behavior that is counter to avoidance (e.g., start a conversation with someone), having students expose themselves to an emotionally charged situation and not remove themselves until their emotional arousal subsides, and having them learn to tolerate the discomfort of making a mistake. We provide an outline below of common behavioral interventions used for youth in schools and discuss the role of cognitions in CBT.

Contingency management is an active component of CBT-based counseling. It is used to modulate the frequency of behavior. By adding something desired (positive reinforcement) or removing something undesired (negative reinforcement), practitioners can promote the adoption of new adaptive behaviors. The use of reinforcers will vary on the basis of the child's age and may include activities (e.g., 20 minutes of extra free time), social interactions (e.g., going to the park with friends), tangibles (e.g., access to a toy, edibles), and sensory stimuli (Terjesen, Rooney, Barnea, & Nicosia, 2017). Use of reinforcers may often involve collaboration with parents and teachers in both identifying and implementing appropriate reinforcers (Martin & Pear, 2016). Furthermore, school-based counselors may use reinforcement in sessions to steer a student desired behavior as well as for when the student completes behavioral homework between sessions.

In contrast to reinforcers, which increase a behavior, positive punishment (i.e., the addition of something undesired) and negative punishment (i.e., the removal of something desired) decrease the likelihood that that behavior will occur in the future. Although punishment can be effective in decreasing behavior (Kazdin, 2013), it focuses only on what *not* to do. Thus, we recommend using punishment sparingly and only in conjunction with positive techniques.

One such example of a technique that uses both reinforcement and punishment is a *token economy*, in which students are rewarded for performing desired behaviors with symbols or tokens that can subsequently be exchanged for desired rewards. Students may also lose tokens for engaging in undesired behaviors. In a school setting, these approaches are commonly used in classrooms to promote specific behaviors at the individual or classroom level. Token economies could regularly be used in CBT-based counseling sessions for promotion of desired in- and out-of-session behaviors. The eventual goal would be to fade out the use of tokens with more natural reinforcers (e.g., verbal praise) that are more common and that students will experience in the real world (Martin & Pear, 2016; Terjesen et al., 2017).

Relaxation Training

School-based counselors may regularly integrate relaxation training as part of their counseling approach. Clinicians may work with students to identify which parts of the body they wish to start with (e.g., "When you feel stressed or tense, where do you experience it in your body?") and then demonstrate the process of relaxation. This involves having the students create the experience of tension through possibly gripping something with their hand, holding it, and then letting it go. The school-based clinician will then point out the differences in physiological arousal (i.e., when the students create the tension and lets it go) and reinforce the idea that they can create and reduce the experience of tension. In the session, students will practice relaxation for 30 seconds to a minute on different muscle groups, with the clinician continuing to reinforce the fact that they are creating and letting go of the tension.

SYSTEMATIC DESENSITIZATION- AND EXPOSURE-BASED APPROACHES

Developed by Wolpe (1961) to break down anxiety response behaviors in a structured manner, *systematic desensitization* involves inducing a state of physiological arousal that inhibits anxiety through muscle relaxation (Terjesen et al., 2017). In school settings, children may experience anxiety across a number of different domains and contexts (Herzig-Anderson, Colognori, Fox, Stewart, & Warner, 2012). School-based clinicians will work with students in developing their muscle relaxation skills, constructing a hierarchy of anxiety stimuli to which they experience an anxious response and then having them practice relaxation while being systematically exposed to stimuli derived from the hierarchy. The counselor typically will expose the students to lower level anxiety-arousing stimuli for a few seconds. Students will learn to manage the anxiety through relaxation training and habituation. Students then are exposed to stronger levels of anxiety-provoking stimuli and are encouraged to use relaxation skills during each exposure.

BEHAVIORAL ACTIVATION

With depressed students, school-based clinicians may also seek to use *behavioral activation*. The goal is to have students monitor their daily mood and activities while increasing the number of pleasant activities they experience. School-based clinicians will work with students to create a schedule of activities that will increase their likelihood of experiencing a positive outcome or reward. By developing a list of reinforcing activities, students are rewarded for moving through this hierarchy. Students may also be asked to rate their mood both before and after they participate in the designated activity to demonstrate the rewarding component of engaging in these behaviors.

Homework

Homework plays an integral role in CBT treatment and should be reviewed at the beginning of each session. A recent meta-analytic review (Kazantzis et al., 2016) indicated that both the amount of homework completed and the quality of the homework completed (i.e., assessments of skill acquisition) were positively associated with symptom change in CBT. Homework encourages the practice of skills learned in session, allowing school-based clinicians to gauge the level skills acquired. Moreover, incomplete or incorrectly completed homework provides rich information to the clinician regarding areas in need of further clarification or practice. For example, a review of the

Happening–Thinking–Feeling–Behavior chart (see Figure 18.2), previously assigned as homework, can highlight areas of confusion regarding how the students' thoughts, feelings, and behaviors are associated. The ultimate goal of therapy is for a student to no longer require treatment. Homework assignments can foster generalization of skills learned in session to situations and events that occur in students' daily lives and help the clinician determine whether a particular student is able to use the skills taught without clinician involvement.

For these reasons, homework noncompliance is problematic and is expected to negatively affect treatment outcome. Homework noncompliance can result from many factors, including, but not limited to, a misunderstanding regarding what was expected as part of the homework assignment, whether the task was too emotionally or behaviorally challenging, and the student failing to find value in the assignment. As discussed previously, with respect to general motivational issues and the importance of the therapeutic alliance; a nonargumentative, collaborative stance; an agreement on the goals and tasks of therapy; and a strong bond are often helpful in avoiding homework noncompliance. However, when homework noncompliance occurs, positive reinforcement in the form of small rewards, such as stickers or an in-session game, can often increase motivation. For adolescents, pinpointing obstacles to homework completion and collaboratively identifying solutions to be explored can be helpful. For younger children, teacher or parent involvement in the form of prompts can increase skill practice.

SUMMARY AND CONCLUSION

The school setting—both the counselor's office and the classroom—may be the ideal environment in which to deliver many common CBT strategies (DiGiuseppe, 2009; Lochman, Powell, Whidby, & FitzGerald, 2012). Put more specifically, direct assessment of behavior and application of principles learned within counseling sessions is more feasible in the school setting, and the immediacy with which school-based counselors can work with students to identify and alter maladaptive cognitions, manage unhealthy emotions, and practice and offer reinforcement of positive cognitions and behaviors is a notable strength of school-based delivery of CBT. In the school setting students can practice new ways of interpreting events and rehearse new social problem-solving skills (Lochman et al., 2012); that is, there is an opportunity for data collection to test current unhealthy beliefs held as well as practice new ways of thinking and behaving. Furthermore, the CBT strategies that are often used in treating social–emotional difficulties among youth can be applied to prevention programs to facilitate the development of healthy cognitive schemas to offset future problems (Kendall, 2012; Lochman et al., 2012).

There is an interesting dichotomy between what school-based practitioners are being trained in and what they are practicing. Yates (2003) found, in a survey of 500 school psychologists, that the majority reported that they subscribed to a cognitive behavioral theoretical orientation, yet only 36.5% reported actually using CBTs. A number of variables may be important to consider when explaining that disconnect between training and practice. To begin, perhaps it is due to the fact that these evidence-based interventions for youth were developed and evaluated in settings other than schools (Ludwig, Lyon, & Ryan, 2015) and perhaps the transportability and application within the school setting is not practical. In addition, maybe the structure of the counseling environment in schools focuses more on behavioral change and building behavioral skills instead of looking at changing unhealthy cognitions that may influence on these emotions and behaviors.

Although considerable advances have been made in the development and application of CBT with youth, the research for school-based adaptations of CBT has lagged behind. It is important for school-based practitioners to be aware of where the CBT approaches are to be delivered and determine whether they are applicable within the school setting. As an example, treatment of school refusal behavior would involve both behavioral and cognitive strategies, depending on the function of the behavior, and can be facilitated by the school-based staff. However, treatment of trauma in the schools should be delivered only by a clinician trained in trauma-focused approaches and through coordination with the school staff and educators.

The application of CBT in the schools can assist youth in managing unhealthy behavioral and emotional patterns. Individual, group, and classroom-based approaches that promote an understanding of the relationship of cognitions with emotion and behaviors students will promote acceptance of responsibility for their own emotions and behaviors and may motivate them to work on changing these cognitions (Terjesen, 2015). The specific interventions described in this chapter offer a variety of cognitive, emotional, and behavioral strategies to promote healthy cognitions and, as a result, reduce students' unhealthy feelings and behaviors and increase their potential for academic, social, and personal success.

SUGGESTED READINGS AND RESOURCES

Websites

- Therapist Aid (http://www.therapistaid.com). This site provides resources including worksheets, videos, and articles related to general CBT techniques and disorder-specific interventions. Worksheets are available to be downloaded at no cost.

- Psychology Tools (http://www.psychologytools.com). Worksheets and handouts, including those related to case conceptualization and formulation, thought record, and cognitive restructuring handouts and worksheets are available for download at no cost. Scales/measures are also available.
- The Beck Institute for Cognitive Therapy (https://www.beckinstitute.org). The Beck Institute website provides a comprehensive overview of CBT as well as information about both online and in-person training in CBT.
- Academy of Cognitive Therapy (http://www.academyofct.org). The Academy of Cognitive Therapy has several professional resources available on its website, including rating scales, training resources, recommended CBT readings, and resources specific to CBT treatment for trauma.

Books

Beck, J. S. (2011). *Cognitive behavior therapy, second edition: Basics and beyond.* New York, NY: Guilford Press.

This book provides information about the basics and fundamentals of CBT practice. The book provides strategies for engaging clients, developing a sound case conceptualization, planning treatment, and structuring sessions effectively.

Friedberg, R. D., & McClure, J. (2015). *Clinical practice of cognitive therapy with children and adolescents, second edition: The nuts and bolts.* New York, NY: Guilford Press.

This book provides information for formulating and tailoring treatment to children. Case examples target specific emotional and behavioral problems as well as cultural issues.

Joyce-Beaulieu, D., & Sulkowski, M. L. (2015). *Cognitive behavioral therapy in K–12 school settings: A practitioner's toolkit.* New York, NY: Springer.

This book provides CBT resources tailored specifically to meet the needs and resources of schools.

Manassis, K. (2009). *Cognitive behavioral therapy with children: A guide for the community practitioner.* New York, NY: Taylor & Francis.

This book primarily focuses on child cognitive behavior therapy assessment and treatment for community practitioners.

Mennuti, R. B., Christner, R. W., & Freeman, A. (Eds.). (2012). *Cognitive-behavioral interventions in educational settings: A handbook for practice.* New York, NY: Taylor & Francis.

This book focuses on strategically creating and individualized intervention specific to the child's age, developmental level, and presenting problem.

Stallard, P. (2002). *Think good–feel good: A cognitive behaviour therapy workbook for children and young people.* New York, NY: Wiley.

This workbook provides 10 modules that can be completed as a program or individually as well as online resources. It offers a complaint section for clinicians and provides guidance regarding parent involvement and cognitive distortions as well as psychoeducational materials.

Woloshyn, L. (2009). *Mighty Moe: An Anxiety Workbook for Children*. Retrieved from http://www.cw.bc.ca/library/pdf/pamphlets/Mighty%20Moe1.pdf

This workbook is geared toward children ages 5 to 11 with anxiety.

Training and Courses

- The Association for Psychological Therapies (http://www.aptmentalhealthcoursesonline.com): The Association for Psychological Therapies provides online training making time and pacing convenient for individuals looking to gain introductory and specialized CBT training.
- Behavioral Health Associates, Inc. (http://www.behavioralhealthassoc.com): This training program is an intensive 10-week program (70 hours) that provides presentations, demonstrations, and practice in using cognitive techniques.
- Academy of Cognitive Therapy (http://www.academyofct.org): This group provides a list of training programs available, depending on geographical region.
- The Beck Institute for Cognitive Therapy (https://www.beckinstitute.org): Online and in-person trainings are available through the Beck Institute.
- Association for Behavioral and Cognitive Therapies (http://www.abct.org): This website provides information regarding its annual convention as well as continuing education opportunities by means of online webinars.
- The Albert Ellis Institute (http://albertellis.org/): Online and in-person externships and internships, trainings, and workshops are offered on this site.

REFERENCES

Almirall, D., & Chronis-Tuscano, A. (2016). Adaptive interventions in child and adolescent mental health. *Journal of Clinical Child and Adolescent Psychology, 45*, 383–395. http://dx.doi.org/10.1080/15374416.2016.1152555

Arnberg, A., & Öst, L. G. (2014). CBT for children with depressive symptoms: A meta-analysis. *Cognitive Behaviour Therapy, 43*, 275–288. http://dx.doi.org/10.1080/16506073.2014.947316

Association for Behavior and Cognitive Therapies. (2017). *What to expect from therapy*. Retrieved from http://www.abct.org/docs/factsheets/WHAT_TO_EXPECT.pdf

Bandura, A. (1977). *Social learning theory*. Englewood Cliffs, NJ: Prentice Hall.

Beck, A. T. (1976). *Cognitive therapy and the emotional disorders*. New York, NY: International Universities Press.

Beck, A. T. (2016). Cognitive therapy: Nature and relation to behavior therapy. *Behavior Therapy, 47,* 776–784. http://dx.doi.org/10.1016/S0005-7894(70)80030-2 (Original work published 1970)

Beck, J. S. (2011). *Cognitive behavior therapy: Basics and beyond*. New York, NY: Guilford Press.

Beck, R., & Perkins, T. S. (2001). Cognitive content-specificity for anxiety and depression: A meta-analysis. *Cognitive Therapy and Research, 25,* 651–663. http://dx.doi.org/10.1023/A:1012911104891

Benjamin, C. L., Puleo, C. M., Settipani, C. A., Brodman, D. M., Edmunds, J. M., Cummings, C. M., & Kendall, P. C. (2011). History of cognitive-behavioral therapy in youth. *Child and Adolescent Psychiatric Clinics of North America, 20,* 179–189. http://dx.doi.org/10.1016/j.chc.2011.01.011

Bernard, M. E., Ellis, A., & Terjesen, M. D. (2006). Rational-emotive behavioral approaches to childhood disorders: History, theory, practice and research. In A. Ellis & M. E. Bernard (Eds.), *Rational-emotive behavioral approaches to childhood disorders: Theory, practice and research* (pp. 3–84). New York, NY: Springer Science+Business Media. http://dx.doi.org/10.1007/0-387-26375-6_1

Bernard, M. E., & Pires, D. (2006). Emotional resilience in children and adolescence: Implications for rational-emotive behavior therapy. In A. Ellis & M. E. Bernard (Eds.), *Rational emotive behavioral approaches to childhood disorders: Theory, practice and research* (pp. 156–174). New York, NY: Springer Science+Business Media. http://dx.doi.org/10.1007/0-387-26375-6_5

Bordin, E. S. (1979). The generalizability of the psychoanalytic concept of the working alliance. *Psychotherapy: Theory, Research & Practice, 16,* 252–260. http://dx.doi.org/10.1037/h0085885

Calear, A., & Christensen, H. (2010). Systematic review of school-based prevention and early intervention programs for depression. *Journal of Adolescence, 33,* 429–438. https://dx.doi.org/10.1016/j.adolescence.2009.07.004

Cartwright-Hatton, S., Roberts, C., Chitsabesan, P., Fothergill, C., & Harrington, R. (2004). Systematic review of the efficacy of cognitive behaviour therapies for childhood and adolescent anxiety disorders. *British Journal of Clinical Psychology, 43,* 421–436. http://dx.doi.org/10.1348/0144665042388928

Chu, B. C., & Kendall, P. C. (2004). Positive association of child involvement and treatment outcome within a manual-based cognitive-behavioral treatment for children with anxiety. *Journal of Consulting and Clinical Psychology, 72,* 821–829. http://dx.doi.org/10.1037/0022-006X.72.5.821

Corey, G. (2008). *Theory and practice of group counseling* (7th ed.). Belmont, CA: Thomson.

Creed, T. A., & Kendall, P. C. (2005). Therapist alliance-building behavior within a cognitive–behavioral treatment for anxiety in youth. *Journal of Consulting and Clinical Psychology, 73*, 498–505. http://dx.doi.org/10.1037/0022-006X.73.3.498

David, D., Szentagotai, A., Eva, K., & Macavei, B. (2005). A synopsis of rational-emotive behavior therapy (REBT): Fundamental and applied research. *Journal of Rational-Emotive and Cognitive-Behavior Therapy, 23*, 175–221. http://dx.doi.org/10.1007/s10942-005-0011-0

DiGiuseppe, R. (1995). Developing the therapeutic alliance with angry clients. In H. Kassinove (Ed.), *Anger disorders: Diagnosis, assessment and treatment* (pp. 131–150). New York, NY: Taylor & Francis.

DiGiuseppe, R. (2009). Introduction to cognitive behavior therapies. In A. Akin-Little, S. G. Little, M. A. Bray, & T. J. Kehle (Eds.), *Behavioral interventions in schools: Evidence-based positive strategies* (pp. 95–109). Washington, DC: American Psychological Association. http://dx.doi.org/10.1037/11886-006

DiGiuseppe, R., Doyle, K., Dryden, W., & Backx, W. (2013). *A practitioner's guide to rational-emotive behavior therapy*. Oxford, England: Oxford University Press. http://dx.doi.org/10.1093/med:psych/9780199743049.001.0001

DiGiuseppe, R., Linscott, J., & Jilton, R. (1996). Developing the therapeutic alliance in child–adolescent psychotherapy. *Applied & Preventive Psychology, 5*, 85–100. http://dx.doi.org/10.1016/S0962-1849(96)80002-3

Ellis, A., & Bernard, M. E. (Eds.). (2006). *Rational emotive behavior approaches to childhood disorders*. New York, NY: Springer. http://dx.doi.org/10.1007/b137389

Ertmer, P. A., & Newby, T. J. (1993). Behaviorism, cognitivism, constructivism: Comparing critical features from an instructional design perspective. *Performance Improvement Quarterly, 6*, 50–72. http://dx.doi.org/10.1111/j.1937-8327.1993.tb00605.x

Esposito, M. A. (2009). REBT with children and adolescents: A meta-analytic review of efficacy studies. *Dissertation Abstracts International: Section B. Sciences and Engineering, 70*(5-B), 138.

Forman, S. G., Olin, S. S., Hoagwood, K. E., Crowe, M., & Saka, N. (2009). Evidence-based interventions in schools: Developers' views of implementation barriers and facilitators. *School Mental Health, 1*, 26–36. http://dx.doi.org/10.1007/s12310-008-9002-5

Friedberg, R. D., & McClure, J. M. (2015). *Clinical practice of cognitive therapy with children and adolescents: The nuts and bolts*. New York, NY: Guilford Press.

Greenberg, M., Kusche, C., Cook, E., & Quamma, J. (1995). Promoting emotional competence in school-aged children: The effects of the PATHS curriculum. *Development and Psychopathology, 7*, 117–136. http://dx.doi.org/10.1017/S0954579400006374

Hales, R. E. (2008). *The American Psychiatric Publishing textbook of psychiatry* (5th ed.). Arlington, VA: American Psychiatric Publishing.

Harrington, N. (2011). Frustration intolerance: Therapy issues and strategies. *Journal of Rational-Emotive & Cognitive-Behavior Therapy, 29*, 4–16. http://dx.doi.org/10.1007/s10942-011-0126-4

Herzig-Anderson, K., Colognori, D., Fox, J. K., Stewart, C. E., & Warner, C. M. (2012). School-based anxiety treatments for children and adolescents. *Child and Adolescent Psychiatric Clinics of North America, 21*, 655–668. http://dx.doi.org/10.1016/j.chc.2012.05.006

Hyland, P., & Boduszek, D. (2012). Resolving a difference between cognitive therapy and rational emotive behavior therapy: Towards the development of an integrated CBT model of psychopathology. *Mental Health Review, 17*, 104–116. http://dx.doi.org/10.1108/13619321211270425

Kavanagh, J., Oliver, S., Lorenc, T., Caird, J., Tucker, H., Harden, A., . . . Oakley, A. (2009). School-based cognitive-behavioural interventions: A systematic review of effects and inequalities. *Health Sociology Review, 18*, 61–78. http://dx.doi.org/10.5172/hesr.18.1.61

Kazantzis, N., Whittington, C., Zelencich, L., Kyrios, M., Norton, P. J., & Hofmann, S. G. (2016). Quantity and quality of homework compliance: A meta-analysis of relations with outcome in cognitive behavior therapy. *Behavior Therapy, 47*, 755–772. http://dx.doi.org/10.1016/j.beth.2016.05.002

Kazdin, A. (2013). *Behavior modification in applied settings* (7th ed.). Long Grove, IL: Waveland Press.

Kendall, P. C. (Ed.). (2011). *Child and adolescent therapy: Cognitive-behavioral procedures.* New York, NY: Guilford Press.

Kendall, P. C. (2012). Guiding theory for therapy with children and adolescents. In P. C. Kendall (Ed.), *Child and adolescent therapy: Cognitive-behavioral procedures* (4th ed., pp. 3–24). New York, NY: Guilford Press.

Kendall, P. C., & Hedtke, K. A. (2006). *Cognitive-behavioral therapy for anxious children: Therapist manual.* Ardmore, PA: Workbook.

Lochman, J. E., Powell, N. P., Whidby, J. M., & FitzGerald, D. P. (2012). Aggression in children. In P. C. Kendall (Ed.), *Child and adolescent therapy: Cognitive-behavioral procedures* (4th ed., pp. 27–53). New York, NY: Guilford Press.

Ludwig, K. A., Lyon, A. R., & Ryan, J. L. (2015). Anxiety in youth: Assessment, treatment, and school-based service delivery. In R. Flanagan, E. Levine, & K. Allen (Eds.), *Cognitive and behavioral interventions in the schools: Integrating theory and research into practice* (pp. 45–65). New York, NY: Springer. http://dx.doi.org/10.1007/978-1-4939-1972-7_3

Martin, G., & Pear, J. (2016). *Behavior modification: What is it and how to do it* (10th ed.). New York, NY: Routledge.

Matta, A. R. (2014). *Efficacy of school-based group therapy with children and adolescents: A meta-analytic review* (Unpublished doctoral dissertation). Department of School Psychology, St. John's University, Queens, NY. Retrieved from https://scinapse.io/papers/2523500700

Mychailyszyn, M. P., Brodman, D. M., Read, K. L., & Kendall, P. C. (2012). Cognitive-behavioral school-based interventions for anxious and depressed youth: A meta-analysis of outcomes. *Clinical Psychology: Science and Practice, 19*, 129–153. http://dx.doi.org/10.1111/j.1468-2850.2012.01279.x

Neil, A. L., & Christensen, H. (2009). Efficacy and effectiveness of school-based prevention and early intervention programs for anxiety. *Clinical Psychology Review, 29*, 208–215. http://dx.doi.org/10.1016/j.cpr.2009.01.002

Pelham, W. E., Jr., Fabiano, G. A., Waxmonsky, J. G., Greiner, A. R., Gnagy, E. M., Pelham, W. E., III, . . . Murphy, S. A. (2016). Treatment sequencing for childhood ADHD: A multiple-randomization study of adaptive medication and behavioral interventions. *Journal of Clinical Child and Adolescent Psychology, 45*, 396–415. http://dx.doi.org/10.1080/15374416.2015.1105138

Persons, J. B. (2012). *The case formulation approach to cognitive-behavior therapy.* New York, NY: Guilford Press.

Prochaska, J. O., & DiClemente, C. C. (1983). Stages and processes of self-change of smoking: Toward an integrative model of change. *Journal of Consulting and Clinical Psychology, 51*, 390–395. http://dx.doi.org/10.1037/0022-006X.51.3.390

Prout, S. M., & Prout, H. T. (1998). A meta-analysis of school-based studies of counseling and psychotherapy: An update. *Journal of School Psychology, 36*, 121–136. http://dx.doi.org/10.1016/S0022-4405(98)00007-7

Reese, R. J., Prout, H. T., Zirkelback, E. A., & Anderson, C. R. (2010). Effectiveness of school-based psychotherapy: A meta-analysis of dissertation research. *Psychology in the Schools, 47*, 1035–1045. http://dx.doi.org/10.1002/pits.20522

Sava, F. A., Maricutoiu, L. P., Rusu, S., Macsinga, I., & Virga, D. (2011). Implicit and explicit self-esteem and irrational beliefs. *Journal of Cognitive and Behavioral Psychotherapies, 11*, 97–111.

Shirk, S. R., & Karver, M. (2003). Prediction of treatment outcome from relationship variables in child and adolescent therapy: A meta-analytic review. *Journal of Consulting and Clinical Psychology, 71*, 452–464. http://dx.doi.org/10.1037/0022-006X.71.3.452

Smeets, K. C., Leeijen, A. A., van der Molen, M. J., Scheepers, F. E., Buitelaar, J. K., & Rommelse, N. N. (2015). Treatment moderators of cognitive behavior therapy to reduce aggressive behavior: A meta-analysis. *European Child & Adolescent Psychiatry, 24*, 255–264. http://dx.doi.org/10.1007/s00787-014-0592-1

Staddon, J. (2014). *The new behaviorism.* Hove, England: Psychology Press.

Szentagotai, A., & Freeman, A. (2007). An analysis of the relationship between irrational beliefs and automatic thoughts in predicting distress. *Journal of Cognitive and Behavioral Psychotherapies, 7*, 1–11.

Terjesen, M. D. (2015). Changing unhealthy patterns of thinking—An REBT approach. In R. Flanagan, K. Allen, & E. Levine (Eds.), *Cognitive and behavioral interventions in the schools* (pp. 232–237). New York, NY: Springer.

Terjesen, M. D., & Esposito, M. (2006). Rational-emotive behavior group therapy with children and adolescents. In A. Ellis & M. E. Bernard, *Rational emotive behavioral approaches to childhood disorders* (pp. 385–414). New York, NY: Springer. http://dx.doi.org/10.1007/0-387-26375-6_13

Terjesen, M. D., Rooney, T., Barnea, M., & Nicosia, V. (2017). Behavior therapy. In A. Vernon & K. A. Doyle (Eds.), *Cognitive behavior therapies: A guidebook for practitioners* (pp. 37–74). Alexandria, VA: American Counseling Association. http://dx.doi.org/10.1002/9781119375395.ch2

Whiston, S. C., & Quinby, R. F. (2009). Review of school counseling outcome research. *Psychology in the Schools, 46*, 267–272. http://dx.doi.org/10.1002/pits.20372

Whiston, S. C., & Sexton, T. L. (1998). A review of school counseling outcome research: Implications for practice. *Journal of Counseling & Development, 76*, 412–426. http://dx.doi.org/10.1002/j.1556-6676.1998.tb02700.x

Wolpe, J. (1961). The systematic desensitization treatment of neuroses. *Journal of Nervous and Mental Disease, 132*, 189–203. http://dx.doi.org/10.1097/00005053-196103000-00001

Yates, M. A. (2003). *A survey of the counseling practices of school psychologists.* Available from ProQuest Dissertations and Theses database. (UMI No. 3083522)

19

APPLICATION OF ALTERNATIVES FOR FAMILIES: A COGNITIVE BEHAVIORAL THERAPY TO SCHOOL SETTINGS

CARRIE B. JACKSON, LAUREL A. BRABSON,
AMY D. HERSCHELL, AND DAVID J. KOLKO

Alternatives for Families: A Cognitive Behavioral Therapy (AF-CBT; Kolko, Herschell, Baumann, & Shaver, 2009; Kolko & Swenson, 2002) is an evidence-based treatment developed for families to decrease the risk of physical abuse and caregiver–child conflict while improving family cohesion (Kolko, 1996a, 1996b; Kolko, Iselin, & Gully, 2011). More recent research has also supported the use of AF-CBT for reducing child externalizing symptoms (e.g., disruptive behaviors; Kolko et al., 2009; Kolko, Campo, Kelleher, & Cheng, 2010; Kolko, Campo, Kilbourne, & Kelleher, 2012). Families who do not receive services to improve family functioning and reduce the risk of physical abuse may be prone to long-term detrimental outcomes such as becoming entangled in a continuous cycle of physical abuse or using harsh discipline techniques (Wodarski, Kurtz, Gaudin, & Howing, 1990). Family conflict, physical abuse, and child externalizing behavior problems can also have significant negative long-term outcomes for children, including emotional and behavioral difficulties, aggressive behaviors, and deficits in social skills (Ackerman, Newton,

http://dx.doi.org/10.1037/0000126-020
Behavioral Interventions in Schools: Evidence-Based Positive Strategies, Second Edition, S. G. Little and A. Akin-Little (Editors)
Copyright © 2019 by the American Psychological Association. All rights reserved.

McPherson, Jones, & Dykman, 1998; Silverman, Reinherz, & Giaconia, 1996; Thabet & Vostanis, 2000). Therefore, it is necessary to make effective treatments available to families experiencing these difficulties.

To address these concerns, AF-CBT has traditionally been provided in clinic or community settings to strengthen overall family functioning; however, it may also be used in school settings to optimize treatment outcomes. A previous article by Herschell, Kolko, Baumann, and Brown (2012) outlined the AF-CBT model and provided clinical considerations for applying this model within a school setting. The current chapter builds on this previous article by incorporating more recent empirical support for AF-CBT as well as additional information on using this treatment model within schools. The three goals of the current chapter are to (a) describe the AF-CBT treatment model, (b) highlight empirical support for AF-CBT, and (c) discuss the applicability of the AF-CBT treatment model to school settings.

NAME CHANGE AND HISTORY

Since the initial development of AF-CBT, the content and name of the model has undergone several changes. AF-CBT, previously described as Abuse-Focused Cognitive-Behavioral Therapy, was originally developed by David J. Kolko in 1985 in collaboration with Sharon Hicks and through consultation from David Wolfe, James Alexander, and Art Robin (Kolko, 1996a). The name was changed to Alternative for Families: A Cognitive Behavior Therapy in 2007 to more closely align with the goals of AF-CBT in building family skill sets and helping children with a wide range of symptoms (e.g., aggression, disruptive behaviors), not limited to those who have experienced abuse. In addition, the term *abuse* was removed from the name because it was found to apply only to a small subset of families using AF-CBT, may stigmatize families seeking treatment, and might negatively affect the therapeutic relationship. In 2010, researchers began to examine the integration of AF-CBT with an associated model, PARTNERS CBT for Physical Abuse (Kolko et al., 2009). These two similar and related treatment models were integrated in an effort to increase the accessibility of these treatments to appropriate families. The efforts to integrate these two approaches are displayed in the current version of AF-CBT (3rd ed.; Kolko, Brown, Baumann, Shaver, & Herschell, 2013).

TARGETED POPULATIONS

AF-CBT is designed to address coercive family behavior patterns that often include verbal or physical aggression (or both) enacted by a caregiver, as well as behavioral or emotional problems experienced by the child.

Characteristics of families appropriate for AF-CBT include negative or coercive parenting, family conflict, negative perceptions about the child, heightened anger reactivity, and poor caregiver behavior management practices. Common consequences often seen in the children of these families include aggression, externalizing behaviors, emotional distress, and poor social skills. Revisions to the original AF-CBT model have helped increase the appeal and applicability for families who may have some of these characteristics and would benefit from treatment but who do not have a history of maltreatment.

To facilitate the identification of families for whom AF-CBT is appropriate, the AF-CBT team has published a set of eligibility criteria (see http://www.afcbt.org). These criteria include the following:

- child is between the ages of 5 and 17,
- at least one caregiver (offending or nonoffending) is willing to participate, and
- child and caregiver are both able to participate adequately (e.g., do not have very low intellectual functioning or severe or uncontrolled psychopathology) and may eventually be placed together in family sessions.

In addition, at least one of the following should be present in the caregiver:

- caregiver has an allegation or report of suspected physical abuse;
- caregiver has done something that resulted or could have resulted in injury or harm to the child;
- caregiver has likely used excessive or harsh physical discipline with the child; and/or
- caregiver and the child and family have conflicts and heated arguments, which may include caregiver verbal aggression and abuse.

If none of the previous caregiver criteria are met, at least one of the following child criteria may be met:

- displays a pattern of oppositional, argumentative, or explosive and angry behaviors;
- has been verbally or physically aggressive, or has exhibited other high-risk behaviors; and/or
- exhibits trauma symptoms related to physical discipline or physical abuse.

AF-CBT has been shown to be effective with families of diverse backgrounds. The original pilot trial of AF-CBT included families of diverse racial backgrounds (Kolko, 1996a). Despite this, the treatment session guide was further refined to promote greater adaptability for culturally diverse families (Baumann, Kolko, Jones, Sturdivant, & Smith, 2006). The current version has been successful with clients of varied racial and ethnic backgrounds, socioeconomic statuses, and religions and has been implemented in both urban and rural communities (Herschell et al., 2012). A unique component, which we describe in greater detail below, is the initial engagement and psychoeducation phase of AF-CBT. This phase includes numerous strategies designed to increase the retention and commitment of families throughout treatment. Such strategies include learning about the caregivers' own histories of being parented and disciplined as well as their viewpoints about physical discipline, including potentially relevant religious beliefs (Herschell et al., 2012). In addition, motivational interviewing techniques, which may differ for families of different backgrounds, are used to assess and mitigate potential conceptual and logistical barriers to treatment.

MODEL DESCRIPTION

AF-CBT was created to be applicable to families with a variety of presenting problems, from differing cultural backgrounds. The content and techniques used in AF-CBT were developed on a strong conceptual basis, as well as several treatment perspectives, to accomplish this goal.

Conceptual Basis

The AF-CBT model incorporates several conceptual paradigms in order to comprehensively address problems on the family, caregiver, and child levels. Some of these paradigms are used to conceptualize and understand family dynamics and characteristics. For instance, Patterson's (1982) coercion theory, which draws from the behavioral perspective, is often used to describe the pattern of child and caregiver aggression that is characteristic of many physically abusive situations. In addition, the theory of developmental victimology (i.e., harm that occurs to a person because of others who are violating social norms) helps elucidate the symptoms associated with trauma exposure at various levels of a child's development.

AF-CBT also draws on and incorporates several treatment perspectives into the treatment model. To be specific, social learning and functional analysis have been drawn from behavioral learning theory; cognitive restructuring and challenging misattributions and distortions are two strategies borrowed from cognitive theory; reframing functional skills has been drawn from family systems theory; and psychoeducation and planning to manage hostile reactions are borrowed from the psychology of aggression (Herschell et al., 2012). The use of these strategies and their underlying conceptual orientations has led to a strong emphasis in AF-CBT on the development of the intra- and interpersonal skills needed to maintain self-control, reduce negative or aggressive family interactions, and increase positive family interactions. These various strategies are combined within the three treatment phases of AF-CBT: Phase I (Engagement and Psychoeducation), Phase II (Individual Skill Building), and Phase II (Family Application), which we describe in detail below.

Assessment

As indicated by the eligibility criteria, AF-CBT is applicable for a variety of clinical concerns and is not designed to treat any one specific diagnosis; therefore, a thorough evaluation is a crucial first step in treatment. This evaluation phase should include multisource assessments (i.e., both caregiver and child report) and should help the provider identify the individual needs of the family that will become treatment targets. Although a number of useful and relevant measures exist (Herschell et al., 2012), four specific measures are currently recommended for use during the pretreatment evaluation: (a) the Alabama Parenting Questionnaire (Frick, 1991; Shelton, Frick, & Wootton, 1996), (b) the Brief Child Abuse Potential Inventory (Milner, 1986; Ondersma, Chaffin, Mullins, & Lebreton, 2005); (c) the Child PTSD Symptom Scale (Foa, Johnson, Feeny, & Treadwell, 2001), and (d) the Strengths and Difficulties Questionnaire (Goodman, Meltzer, & Bailey, 1998; see Table 19.1). Results from these measures should help the provider tailor the treatment to each specific family and evaluate outcomes at service termination.

The Alabama Parenting Questionnaire is a 42-item caregiver-report measure designed to assess a variety of parenting practices. It includes five subscales: Supervision and Monitoring, Positive Parenting, Consistency of Discipline, Corporal Punishment, and Involvement with Children. Several additional items ask about other discipline practices (e.g., removal of privileges, use of time out) and can be used on an item-by-item basis to inform treatment. These subscales can be used to identify parenting practices that are strengths and weaknesses for each caregiver. The Positive Parenting and Corporal Punishment subscales are especially relevant to the content of AF-CBT. Scores lower than 21 on the Positive Parenting subscale and higher than 7 on the Corporal Punishment subscale indicate clinically significant problems in using positive parenting practices and the use of corporal punishment with children, respectively.

The Brief Child Abuse Potential Inventory is a 33-item caregiver-report measure designed to assess for the risk of child maltreatment. Its seven subscales address different caregiver risk factors for child maltreatment, including

TABLE 19.1
Interpretation of Assessment Measures for Use in Alternatives for Families: A Cognitive Behavior Therapy

Name and acronym	Focus	Source	Scale	Subscales	Corresponding problem cutoff
Alabama Parenting Questionnaire (Frick, 1991)	Parenting practices and discipline	Caregiver	42 items	Parental Supervision Positive Parenting Inconsistent Discipline Corporal Punishment Involvement Other Discipline	≥ 18 ≤ 21 ≥ 18 ≥ 7 ≤ 35 —
Brief Child Abuse Potential Inventory (Ondersma et al., 2005)	Child abuse risk	Caregiver	33 items	Abuse Risk Family Conflict Happiness Persecution Distress Rigidity Loneliness Poverty	≥ 9 ≥ 2 — — — — — —
Child PTSD Symptom Scale (Foa et al., 2001)	Child posttraumatic symptoms	Child	26 items	PTSD Symptom Severity	≥ 15
Strengths and Difficulties Questionnaire (Goodman, 2001)	Prosocial behavior and conduct problems	Caregiver	25 items	Conduct Problems Prosocial Behavior Emotional Symptoms Hyperactivity/Inattention Peer Problems	≥ 4 ≤ 4 ≥ 5 ≥ 7 ≥ 4

Note. PTSD = posttraumatic stress disorder. From "Application of Alternatives for Families: A Cognitive-Behavioral Therapy to School Settings," by A. D. Herschell, D. J. Kolko, B. L. Baumann, and E. J. Brown, 2012, Journal of Applied School Psychology, 28, pp. 276–277. Copyright 2012 by Taylor & Francis. Reprinted with permission.

Abuse Risk, Happiness, Persecution, Family Conflict, Distress, Rigidity, Loneliness, and Poverty. The Abuse Risk and Family Conflict subscales can help identify potential problem areas for families appropriate for AF-CBT and can help in the development of safety plans. For the Abuse Risk subscale, at least nine endorsed items suggest that the caregiver may be at risk of child maltreatment. If two or more items are endorsed as "Agree" on the Family Conflict subscale, this suggests that the family is experiencing moderate levels of family conflict that should be a target of treatment.

The Child PTSD Symptom Scale is a 26-item child-report measure used to assess the presence and severity of posttraumatic stress disorder–related symptoms in youth ages 8 to 18 years. The scale consists of two items in which the child describes the traumatic event, 17 items related to the three PTSD diagnostic clusters, and seven items assessing functional impairment. This measure yields an overall PTSD symptom severity score that can help develop treatment targets specific to the child. Scores of at least 15 for overall PTSD symptom severity indicate a significant problem area and that treatment should seek to alleviate PTSD symptoms in the child.

Finally, the Strengths and Difficulties Questionnaire is a 25-item instrument used to assess a variety of behaviors in children ages 3 to 16 years. This questionnaire is available in both caregiver- and child-report formats, although the child report is able to be completed only by children age 11 years and older. This measure includes several subscales to assess Emotional Problems, Conduct Problems, Hyperactivity/Inattention, Peer Problems, and Prosocial Behavior. Results from this measure can help to identify problem areas specific to the child that may or may not reflect the clinical consequences of child maltreatment but that are still important to address during treatment. For AF-CBT, the Conduct Problems and Prosocial Behavior subscales are used to identify areas of difficulties and strength in the child; specifically, scores greater than 3 on the Conduct Problems subscale imply that the child is currently displaying a significant amount of conduct problems that should be targeted throughout treatment.

Treatment Structure

As demonstrated by the emphasis on careful and informative assessment, AF-CBT is designed to be individualized and adaptable for each family. The treatment itself is structured into three consecutive phases, with each phase covering several content areas that follow the ALTERNATIVES acronym (see Table 19.2, in which the first letter of each term of ALTERNATIVES is in boldface type). Although the phases are delivered in order, the topics may be delivered flexibly, according to the unique needs and goals of each family. Throughout each phase, and depending on the specific topic, sessions

TABLE 19.2
Phases and Key Topics in Alternatives for Families:
A Cognitive Behavioral Therapy

Phase	Key topics
I: Engagement and Psychoeducation	• Orientation (child and caregiver) • **A**lliance building and engagement (caregiver) • **L**earning about family experiences (child) • **T**alking about parenting and psychoeducation (caregiver)
II: Individual Skill Building	• **E**motion regulation (child and caregiver) • **R**estructuring thoughts (child and caregiver) • **N**oticing positive behavior (caregiver) • **A**ssertiveness and social skills (child) • **T**echniques for managing behavior (caregiver) • **I**maginal exposure—for posttraumatic stress disorder (child) • Preparation for clarification (caregiver)
III: Family Application	• **V**erbalizing healthy communication (caregiver and child) • **E**nhancing safety through clarification (caregiver and child) • **S**olving family problems (caregiver and child) • Graduation (caregiver and child)

Note. Letters in boldface spell out *ALTERNATIVES*. From "Application of Alternatives for Families: A Cognitive-Behavioral Therapy to School Settings," by A. D. Herschell, D. J. Kolko, B. L. Baumann, and E. J. Brown, 2012, *Journal of Applied School Psychology, 28,* p. 279. Copyright 2012 by Taylor & Francis. Reprinted with permission.

may be conducted with the child and the caregiver separately, or as joint sessions. The competencies within each phase should be met before treatment continues to the next phase.

In Phase I (Engagement and Psychoeducation), the overarching goals are engagement and psychoeducation. The focus in this phase is on understanding the family's unique needs, providing them with information about what treatment will involve, thereby enhancing their motivation and decreasing barriers to participation. Providers build rapport with the family by learning about the caregivers' experience of being parented and discussing their reason for referral. During this phase, the orientation session is typically conducted jointly, with both the caregiver and child. The topics of engagement, learning about family experiences, and psychoeducation are generally covered with the caregiver independently. The topic of learning about feelings and family experiences is examined in independent sessions with the child and focuses on teaching the child to identify feelings and to understand their perspective about their own family interactions. The mastery of each of these topics serves as a foundation for Phase II.

The goal of Phase II (Individual Skill Building) is to provide individual family members with the skills needed to promote positive and healthy family interactions. Most of the topics in Phase II are covered in separate individual sessions for the child and caregiver, in order to more directly address the needs of each individual. Children and caregivers learn emotion regulation skills for anxiety and anger. In addition, caregivers learn cognitive restructuring for maladaptive thoughts related to the use of physical force in response to their child's behavior. Children also learn cognitive restructuring for maladaptive thoughts related to self-blame or a dangerous home environment. Additional caregiver topics include noticing positive child behavior and behavior management techniques as alternatives to more negative and coercive practices. Providers also guide caregivers in drafting a clarification letter in which caregivers identify their role in the abuse, apologize to the child, and discuss strategies they will use to maintain safety for their child in the future. In addition, children are taught assertiveness and social skills to facilitate more positive child–caregiver communication. They also begin to process the abuse or hostility with their therapist through imaginal exposures. Similar to the caregiver's clarification letter, children develop a meaning-making statement that describes the causes and effects of abuse. Throughout this phase, psychoeducation is provided to ensure the family understands the overall effect of verbal and physical aggression and to clarify the roles of mandated reporters and Child Protective Services.

The goal of Phase III (Family Applications) is to bring the caregiver and child back together for joint sessions that focus on healthy communication, clarification, family problem solving, and relapse prevention. During the clarification session, the caregiver may share his or her clarification letter (as appropriate) and the child may share his or her meaning-making statement. Relapse prevention is an element of this phase and includes recommitment to family routines and the effective use of behavior management strategies learned in Phase II. Additional after-care plans or referrals may be provided as needed, once all skills and treatment goals have been mastered.

Empirical Support for Alternatives for Families: A Cognitive Behavioral Therapy

AF-CBT has garnered extensive research support for reducing family conflict, caregiver aggression, and child physical abuse. AF-CBT's combination of individual cognitive behavior therapy (CBT) and family therapy components were originally evaluated separately (two conditions) and compared with routine clinical services in a randomized trial (Kolko, 1996b). In this original outcome study, families involved in treatment were primarily referred because of concerns of physical abuse or harsh physical discipline practices.

Compared with routine clinical services, both the individual CBT and family therapy conditions demonstrated more positive family outcomes (e.g., reduced family conflict, increased cohesion), caregiver outcomes (e.g., reduced abusive behavior, reduced need for corporal punishment), and child outcomes (e.g., child-to-caregiver aggression, externalizing behaviors; Kolko, 1996a, 1996b; Mammen, Kolko, & Pilkonis, 2002; Mammen, Kolko, & Pilkonis, 2003). It is important to note that this initial outcome study demonstrated long-term benefits (up to 5 years) for families involved in treatment, including lower levels of recidivism, anger, anxiety, and increased social competence for families who completed treatment (Kolko et al., 2011). A second report of this study compared the outcomes of the two treatment conditions (CBT vs. family therapy). In this report, individual CBT was slightly more effective than family therapy at reducing caregiver anger and use of physical force in discipline (Kolko, 1996a, 1996b). During these initial outcome studies, AF-CBT (Version 1.0) was named Abuse-Focused CBT (Kolko, 1996a, 1996b).

Following this initial outcome study, the individual CBT and family therapy components were integrated into Version 2.0 of AF-CBT (Alternatives for Families: A Cognitive Behavioral Therapy). Although initially developed for families experiencing increased conflict or physically abusive behaviors, AF-CBT has also been found to be effective in reducing externalizing behaviors. Compared with children who received usual care in a primary care setting, children who received AF-CBT showed a reduction in clinically significant externalizing behavior problems (e.g., aggression, disruptive behaviors, hyperactivity), with many of the children no longer meeting diagnostic criteria for oppositional defiant disorder (Kolko et al., 2010; Kolko, Campo, Kilbourne, & Kelleher, 2012). These studies also demonstrated a reduction in parenting stress (Kolko et al., 2010; Kolko, Campo, et al., 2012, 2014). In addition, all three of these studies provided evidence for the long-term effectiveness of AF-CBT in reducing externalizing behavior problems for up to 5 years after treatment (Kolko et al., 2010; Kolko, Campo, et al., 2012, 2014). AF-CBT has also been found to reduce child behavior problems in both clinical and community settings (Kolko et al., 2009) and has demonstrated significant improvements in caregiver, child, and family functioning.

The evidence base for AF-CBT has led to the treatment model being considered an effective treatment for child abuse victims, and an evidence-based therapy according to several classification systems. The National Child Traumatic Stress Network has recognized AF-CBT as a "model" or "promising" treatment program (http://www.nctsn.org). The California Evidence Based Clearinghouse for Child Welfare (http://www.cebc4cw.org/program/alternatives-for-families-a-cognitive-behavioral-therapy/) has rated AF-CBT with a score of 3, indicating that it is a "Promising Practice." AF-CBT's growing evidence base has led to an increase in efforts to implement the treatment model in wider community settings where many families receive behavioral health services (Kolko, Fitzgerald, & Laubach, 2014). In comparison with commonly used training methods (e.g., reading treatment manuals), efforts to train community therapists in AF-CBT have proven more effective in increasing provider knowledge of CBT techniques, general therapy skills, and abuse-specific skills (Kolko, Baumann, et al., 2012). This research reflects a growing need to expand the reach of research-informed treatment to community settings for a broader public health impact.

APPLICATION OF ALTERNATIVES FOR FAMILIES: A COGNITIVE BEHAVIORAL THERAPY TO SCHOOL SETTINGS

A significant gap exists between the number of children who are in need of behavioral health services and the number of children who receive appropriate services (Perou et al., 2013). Outpatient behavioral health clinics are a commonly used setting; however, families seeking treatment often encounter a variety of barriers (Mojtabai et al., 2011). For children in need of behavioral health services, these settings often require reliance on caregivers who may be less willing to attend sessions because of transportation issues, inconvenience with scheduling, a reluctance due to the stigma associated with receiving behavioral health services, or some combination of these (Gulliver, Griffiths, & Christensen, 2010). Given the aforementioned challenges to families accessing treatment in outpatient behavioral health settings, in the following section we describe the advantages for providing AF-CBT in schools.

Advantages of School Settings

School settings represent unique opportunities to identify and treat children with behavioral health needs. In contrast to young children who are in frequent contact with their pediatricians (American Academy of Pediatrics [AAP], 2001), school-age children spend a majority of their time in school and therefore are in more frequent contact with school personnel. Thus, the burden for identifying school-age children in need of behavioral health services is more likely to fall on school personnel than any other professional (AAP, 2001). School personnel may be more likely to recognize when children are in need of behavioral health services because of unique symptom presentations in school settings, such as a decrease in academic performance, an increase in disruptive behaviors during class, and impairment in social interactions with peers and teachers (Fitzgerald & Cohen, 2012).

The school as a treatment setting has several benefits over a more traditional clinic setting. Some evidence has demonstrated that children and adolescents access school behavioral health services at a rate higher than outpatient services (Adelman & Taylor, 1998; Evans, 1999; Ringeisen, Henderson, & Hoagwood, 2003). This may be because common barriers, such as transportation and stigma, are often reduced in this setting (Adelman & Taylor, 1998; Evans, 1999). In addition to increasing the likelihood of families attending treatment sessions, providing services in schools also allows providers to target both home and educational issues (Fitzgerald & Cohen, 2012). Research has also suggested that school-based services are more cost-effective than traditional services, possibly given the increased number of sessions that children and adolescents are able to attend in comparison to clinic-based services (Flaherty, Weist, & Warner, 1996). Although research has not specifically addressed the cost-effectiveness of AF-CBT in schools, the ability to increase sessions attended while reducing costs for families to attend sessions is promising.

Clinical Considerations

Providing school-based behavioral health services represents a unique challenge to providers. The AAP's Committee on School Health (2004) issued a policy statement on school-based behavioral health services in 2004, and several of these challenges and recommendations are integrated within the context of AF-CBT treatment, as described below. Of utmost importance, before receiving treatment in the schools, is caregiver consent, which must be obtained (Evans, 1999). This process can be more challenging in the school than a clinic setting because the caregiver is not always available during the school day or able to travel to the school. One possible solution to this challenge is to schedule a separate consent session at an alternate location that is more convenient for the caregiver. However, this challenge is not unique to consent for treatment and may be present throughout the course of treatment.

Ongoing caregiver involvement in treatment is central to the goal in AF-CBT of improving family functioning. However, in comparison with outpatient settings, it is difficult to have the same level of caregiver involvement in school settings. AF-CBT's treatment model relies heavily on a mix of individual caregiver and child sessions to build specific skills before moving to joint family sessions to reduce family conflict and improve overall family functioning. Efforts should be made to incorporate the caregiver into school-based services by either including the caregiver in school sessions or by providing caregiver sessions in an alternate setting (e.g., outpatient clinic, home; Weist, 2005).

An additional issue that may arise during the consent process is the need to maintain the confidentiality and privacy of all services and health-related information. Whereas outpatient clinics generally have procedures in place to ensure that all client information is protected and secure, schools may be less familiar with legal requirements that must be followed for behavioral health records. Also, there may be a blurred division between what would be considered part of the student's educational record and what would be part of the behavioral health record. These distinctions ideally should be outlined before services begin, with clear guidelines in place to ensure that all documentation is maintained in accordance with the law. Such distinctions should also be elaborated to caregivers during the consent process. In addition, informed consent should include information on the degree to which providers can access student educational information in order to appropriately monitor treatment progress and ensure the most beneficial outcomes (Weist, 2005; Zirkelback & Reese, 2010).

Given the unique nature of the school setting, it is likely that there are differences in the referral process for children referred within the school compared with families referred for outpatient treatment (see AAP's, 2004, Recommendation 3 for Schools). To be specific, it is possible that school personnel would be more likely to refer children for AF-CBT because of concerns of disruptive behavior, given that those behaviors are often present in classrooms. Conversely, families receiving AF-CBT treatment in outpatient settings are often referred through the child welfare system because of concerns about harsh parenting. It is crucial that behavioral health providers working in the school understand these referral differences, because they may have to assess for child maltreatment and follow appropriate mandated reporting procedures more frequently than they would in the clinic setting (see AAP's, 2004, Recommendation 7 for Schools).

There are also several logistical obstacles to providing behavioral health services in the schools that are important to consider (see AAP's, 2004, Recommendations 1 and 8 for Schools). One such concern is that it may be difficult for providers to schedule sessions with children and adolescents that do not conflict with their academic schedule. This concern may manifest in two ways. First, simply removing a child from a classroom for a therapy session decreases the child's amount of instructional time. However, this concern can be alleviated by coordinating with teachers and administrators to find a time that would be least disruptive to the child's academic progress. Second, the sensitive and potentially distressing nature of topics discussed within AF-CBT sessions may be particularly disruptive to the student's ability to concentrate and attend to class content. Before the child returns to class, efforts should be made to reduce any distress that may occur during sessions. In addition to scheduling sessions around a child's academic schedule, finding a private space within the school that is available and confidential is essential. It may be particularly difficult to coordinate the student's schedule with the availability of a private room for sessions, and thus providers may require additional help from school personnel in organizing these logistics (Zirkelback & Reese, 2010).

One final consideration that may affect the ability to administer AF-CBT in a school setting relates to the nature of families who serve to benefit from the treatment. Although not pertinent to all families, some families undergoing AF-CBT treatment include offending caregivers. School personnel who are not familiar with the treatment model may be hesitant to allow an offending caregiver onto school grounds and wary of bringing the offending caregiver into session with the victim. Before family sessions begin, individual work with the child and the caregiver should be done to ensure the success of these joint sessions. Although school personnel may be cautious about family sessions occurring in the school setting, it is important for providers to emphasize their necessity to the family's treatment progress and the extensive individual work done before these sessions take place.

CONCLUSION

AF-CBT is an evidence-based therapy for families experiencing high levels of conflict, and it has also been shown to be effective in reducing externalizing behavior problems, caregiver anger and stress, and re-abuse rates (Kolko, 1996a, 1996b; Kolko, Fitzgerald, & Laubach, 2014). Schools offer an opportunity to identify and optimally treat children and adolescents experiencing difficulties deemed appropriate for AF-CBT treatment. AF-CBT may be successfully delivered in schools, reducing common barriers to treatment, such as transportation issues and reluctance to seek treatment because of perceived stigma. With the potential impact of delivering AF-CBT in a school setting, current research should focus on expanding its use in schools in an effort to reach a greater number of families in need of behavioral health services.

REFERENCES

Ackerman, P. T., Newton, J. E., McPherson, W. B., Jones, J. G., & Dykman, R. A. (1998). Prevalence of post traumatic stress disorder and other psychiatric diagnoses in three groups of abused children (sexual, physical, and both). *Child Abuse & Neglect, 22*, 759–774. http://dx.doi.org/10.1016/S0145-2134(98)00062-3

Adelman, H. S., & Taylor, L. (1998). Reframing mental health in schools and expanding school reform. *Educational Psychologist, 33*, 135–152. http://dx.doi.org/10.1207/s15326985ep3304_1

American Academy of Pediatrics. (2001). Developmental surveillance and screening of infants and young children. *Pediatrics, 108,* 192–195. http://dx.doi.org/10.1542/peds.108.1.192

American Academy of Pediatrics, Committee on School Health. (2004). School-based mental health services. *Pediatrics, 113,* 1839–1845. http://dx.doi.org/10.1542/peds.113.6.1839

Baumann, B. L., Kolko, D. J., Jones, H., Sturdivant, M., & Smith, W. (2006). *Improving the cultural relevancy of an evidence based intervention for physically abusive families.* Pittsburgh, PA: University of Pittsburgh.

Evans, S. W. (1999). Mental health services in schools: Utilization, effectiveness, and consent. *Clinical Psychology Review, 19,* 165–178. http://dx.doi.org/10.1016/S0272-7358(98)00069-5

Fitzgerald, M. M., & Cohen, J. (2012). Trauma-focused cognitive behavior therapy for school psychologists. *Journal of Applied School Psychology, 28,* 294–315. http://dx.doi.org/10.1080/15377903.2012.696037

Flaherty, L. T., Weist, M. D., & Warner, B. S. (1996). School-based mental health services in the United States: History, current models and needs. *Community Mental Health Journal, 32,* 341–352. http://dx.doi.org/10.1007/BF02249452

Foa, E. B., Johnson, K. M., Feeny, N. C., & Treadwell, K. R. H. (2001). The Child PTSD Symptom Scale: A preliminary examination of its psychometric properties. *Journal of Clinical Child & Adolescent Psychology, 30,* 376–384.

Frick, J. (1991). *The Alabama Parenting Questionnaire* (Unpublished instrument). University of Alabama.

Goodman, R. (2001). Psychometric properties of the Strengths and Difficulties Questionnaire. *Journal of American Academy of Child & Adolescent Psychiatry, 40,* 1337–1345.

Goodman, R., Meltzer, H., & Bailey, V. (1998). The strengths and difficulties questionnaire: A pilot study on the validity of the self-report version. *European Child & Adolescent Psychiatry, 7,* 125–130. http://dx.doi.org/10.1007/s007870050057

Gulliver, A., Griffiths, K. M., & Christensen, H. (2010). Perceived barriers and facilitators to mental health help-seeking in young people: A systematic review. *BMC Psychiatry, 10,* 113. http://dx.doi.org/10.1186/1471-244X-10-113

Herschell, A. D., Kolko, D. J., Baumann, B. L., & Brown, E. J. (2012). Application of alternatives for families: A cognitive-behavioral therapy to school settings. *Journal of Applied School Psychology, 28,* 270–293.

Kolko, D. J. (1996a). Clinical monitoring of treatment course in child physical abuse: Psychometric characteristics and treatment comparisons. *Child Abuse & Neglect, 20,* 23–43. http://dx.doi.org/10.1016/0145-2134(95)00113-1

Kolko, D. J. (1996b). Individual cognitive-behavioral treatment and family therapy for physically abused children and their offending parents: A comparison of clinical outcomes. *Child Maltreatment, 1,* 322–342. http://dx.doi.org/10.1177/1077559596001004004

Kolko, D. J., Baumann, B. L., Herschell, A. D., Hart, J. A., Holden, E. A., & Wisniewski, S. R. (2012). Implementation of AF-CBT by community practitioners serving child welfare and mental health: A randomized trial. *Child Maltreatment, 17*, 32–46. http://dx.doi.org/10.1177/1077559511427346

Kolko, D. J., Brown, E. J., Baumann, B. L., Shaver, M., & Herschell, A. D. (2013). *Alternatives for families: A cognitive behavioral therapy. Session guide (3rd ed.)*. Unpublished manuscript, University of Pittsburgh School of Medicine, Pittsburgh, PA.

Kolko, D. J., Campo, J. V., Kelleher, K., & Cheng, Y. (2010). Improving access to care and clinical outcome for pediatric behavioral problems: A randomized trial of a nurse-administered intervention in primary care. *Journal of Behavioral & Developmental Pediatrics, 31*, 393–404. http://dx.doi.org/10.1097/DBP.0b013e3181dff307

Kolko, D. J., Campo, J., Kilbourne, A. M., Hart, J., Sakolsky, D., & Wisniewski, S. (2014). Collaborative care outcomes for pediatric behavioral health problems: A cluster randomized trial. *Pediatrics, 133*, e981–e992. http://dx.doi.org/10.1542/peds.2013-2516

Kolko, D. J., Campo, J. V., Kilbourne, A. M., & Kelleher, K. (2012). Doctor–office collaborative care for pediatric behavioral problems: A preliminary clinical trial. *Archives of Pediatrics & Adolescent Medicine, 166*, 224–231. http://dx.doi.org/10.1001/archpediatrics.2011.201

Kolko, D. J., Dorn, L. D., Bukstein, O. G., Pardini, D., Holden, E. A., & Hart, J. (2009). Community vs. clinic-based modular treatment of children with early-onset ODD or CD: A clinical trial with 3-year follow-up. *Journal of Abnormal Child Psychology, 37*, 591–609. http://dx.doi.org/10.1007/s10802-009-9303-7

Kolko, D. J., Fitzgerald, M. M., & Laubach, J. (2014). Evidence-based practices for working with physically abusive families: Alternatives for families: A cognitive behavioral therapy. In R. M. Reece, R. F. Hanson, & J. Sargent (Eds.), *Treatment of child abuse: common ground for mental health, medical, and legal practitioners* (2nd ed., pp. 59–66). Baltimore, MD: Johns Hopkins University Press.

Kolko, D. J., Herschell, A. D., Baumann, B. L., & Shaver, M. E. (2009). *Alternatives for families: A cognitive-behavioral therapy for child physical abuse. Session guide v. 2.4 (8-1-09)*. Pittsburgh, PA: University of Pittsburgh School of Medicine.

Kolko, D. J., Iselin, A. M. R., & Gully, K. J. (2011). Evaluation of the sustainability and clinical outcome of alternatives for families: A cognitive-behavioral therapy (AF-CBT) in a child protection center. *Child Abuse & Neglect, 35*, 105–116. http://dx.doi.org/10.1016/j.chiabu.2010.09.004

Kolko, D., & Swenson, C. C. (2002). *Assessing and treating physically abused children and their families: A cognitive-behavioral approach*. Thousand Oaks, CA: Sage.

Mammen, O. K., Kolko, D. J., & Pilkonis, P. A. (2002). Negative affect and parental aggression in child physical abuse. *Child Abuse & Neglect, 26*, 407–424. http://dx.doi.org/10.1016/S0145-2134(02)00316-2

Mammen, O., Kolko, D., & Pilkonis, P. (2003). Parental cognitions and satisfaction: Relationship to aggressive parental behavior in child physical abuse. *Child Maltreatment, 8*, 288–301. http://dx.doi.org/10.1177/1077559503257112

Milner, J. S. (1986). *The Child Abuse Potential Inventory: Manual*. Odessa, FL: Psychological Assessment Resources.

Mojtabai, R., Olfson, M., Sampson, N. A., Jin, R., Druss, B., Wang, P. S., . . . Kessler, R. C. (2011). Barriers to mental health treatment: Results from the National Comorbidity Survey Replication. *Psychological Medicine, 41*, 1751–1761. http://dx.doi.org/10.1017/S0033291710002291

Ondersma, S. J., Chaffin, M., Mullins, S. M., & Lebreton, J. M. (2005). A brief form of the Child Abuse Potential Inventory: Development and validation. *Journal of Clinical Child & Adolescent Psychology, 34*, 301–311. http://dx.doi.org/10.1207/s15374424jccp3402_9

Patterson, G. R. (1982). *Coercive family process: Vol. 3*. Eugene, OR: Castalia Publishing Company.

Perou, R., Bitsko, R. H., Blumberg, S. J., Pastor, P., Ghandour, R. M., Gfroerer, J. C., . . . Huang, L. N. (2013). Mental health surveillance among children—United States, 2005–2011. *Morbidity and Mortality Weekly Report, 62*, 1–35. Retrieved from https://www.cdc.gov/mmwr/preview/mmwrhtml/su6202a1.htm

Ringeisen, H., Henderson, K., & Hoagwood, K. (2003). Context matters: Schools and the research to practice gap in children's mental health. *School Psychology Review, 32*, 153–159.

Shelton, K. K., Frick, P. J., & Wootton, J. (1996). Assessment of parenting practices in families of elementary school-age children. *Journal of Clinical Child Psychology, 25*, 317–329. http://dx.doi.org/10.1207/s15374424jccp2503_8

Silverman, A. B., Reinherz, H. Z., & Giaconia, R. M. (1996). The long-term sequelae of child and adolescent abuse: A longitudinal community study. *Child Abuse & Neglect, 20*, 709–723. http://dx.doi.org/10.1016/0145-2134(96)00059-2

Thabet, A. A., & Vostanis, P. (2000). Post traumatic stress disorder reactions in children of war: A longitudinal study. *Child Abuse & Neglect, 24*, 291–298. http://dx.doi.org/10.1016/S0145-2134(99)00127-1

Weist, M. D. (2005). Fulfilling the promise of school-based mental health: Moving toward a public mental health promotion approach. *Journal of Abnormal Child Psychology, 33*, 735–741. http://dx.doi.org/10.1007/s10802-005-7651-5

Wodarski, J. S., Kurtz, P. D., Gaudin, J. M., Jr., & Howing, P. T. (1990). Maltreatment and the school-age child: Major academic, socioemotional, and adaptive outcomes. *Social Work, 35*, 506–513. http://dx.doi.org/10.1093/sw/35.6.506

Zirkelback, E. A., & Reese, R. J. (2010). A review of psychotherapy outcome research: Considerations for school-based mental health providers. *Psychology in the Schools, 47*, 1084–1100. http://dx.doi.org/10.1002/pits.20526

20

TRAUMA-FOCUSED COGNITIVE BEHAVIOR THERAPY

STEVEN G. LITTLE AND ANGELEQUE AKIN-LITTLE

Trauma is not an uncommon experience among children and adolescents. Abuse, domestic and community violence, natural disasters, and grief are all examples of childhood traumatic experiences. Felitti and colleagues (1998) conducted a retrospective study of more than 17,000 adults and found that more than one half of their sample reported at least one adverse event in childhood. In a more recent study of 1,698 adult participants in the United Kingdom (Frissa et al., 2016), 72.1% reported at least one life event that met the criteria for trauma according to the *Diagnostic and Statistical Manual of Mental Disorders* (fifth ed. [DSM–5]; American Psychiatric Association, 2013). According to the Bureau of Justice Statistics (Truman & Morgan, 2016), 31.2 adolescents per 1,000 (ages 12–17) were victims of violent crimes (rape or sexual assault, robbery, aggravated assault, and simple assault), and 7.8 per 1,000 were victims of serious violent crimes (aggravated assault, rape, robbery, homicide), in 2015. In addition, more than 1 million people

http://dx.doi.org/10.1037/0000126-021
Behavioral Interventions in Schools: Evidence-Based Positive Strategies, Second Edition, S. G. Little and A. Akin-Little (Editors)
Copyright © 2019 by the American Psychological Association. All rights reserved.

were displaced at by Hurricane Katrina in 2005, with many still not having returned to their homes (Akin-Little & Little, 2008). Other natural disasters, such as the Haiti earthquake in 2010 and the Tōhoku earthquake and tsunami in Japan in 2011 killed thousands and left hundreds of thousands homeless. Hurricane Sandy in 2012 and Tropical Cyclone Ike in 2008, floods in Houston in 2015 and Louisiana in 2016, and the Texas wildfires of 2011 all left thousands of families homeless. It is clear that exposure to traumatic events is not uncommon in childhood and adolescence, and psychologists who work with children and in schools should have some training in how to meet the needs of this population.

Trauma is an emotional response to a terrible event, such as an accident, a rape, or a natural disaster. Immediately after the event, shock and denial are typical. Longer term reactions include unpredictable emotions; flashbacks; strained relationships; and even physical symptoms, such as headaches or nausea. Although these feelings are normal, some people have difficulty moving on with their lives. Psychologists can help these individuals find constructive ways of managing their emotions (see, e.g., http://www.apa.org/topics/trauma/).

According to *DSM–5*, directly experienced traumatic events include, but are not limited to, experiences such as exposure to war, threatened or actual physical assault and abuse, threatened or actual sexual violence and abuse, exposure to a terrorist attack, natural or human-made disasters, and severe motor vehicle accidents. For children, sexually violent events include developmentally inappropriate sexual experiences that do not involve physical violence or injury. Witnessed events include, but are not limited to, observing threatened or serious injury, unnatural death, physical or sexual abuse of another person, domestic violence, accident, war or disaster. Indirect exposure through learning about an event is limited to violent experiences that have affected close relatives or friends.

Symptoms that result from traumatic stressors can be grouped into four main categories: (a) affective, (b) behavioral, (c) cognitive, and (d) physical (Cohen, Mannarino, & Deblinger, 2006). Affective symptoms include fear, depression, and anger. Behavioral symptoms usually involve avoidance of reminders of the traumatic experiences, and cognitive symptoms involve distorted cognitions children may have about themselves, others, the event, or the world, with the main one being the belief that the event is their fault. Finally, physical symptoms are related to the chronic stress and include elevated pulse and blood pressure, increases in muscle tension, and hypervigilance. However, we should note that not every child exposed to a traumatic event will develop trauma symptoms. Many children demonstrate *resiliency*, the ability to thrive and excel even when exposed to severe stressors (Leckman & Mayes, 2007; Little & Akin-Little, 2013; Little, Akin-Little, & Somerville, 2011).

One intervention that has been empirically supported for use with children and adolescents experiencing symptoms as a result of trauma exposure is trauma-focused cognitive-behavioral therapy (TF-CBT; Cohen, Mannarino, & Deblinger, 2006). An extensive body of research has supported the efficacy of TF-CBT with sexually abused children (e.g., Cohen, Deblinger, Mannarino, & Steer, 2004; Cohen, Mannarino, & Knudsen, 2005), and an emerging literature indicates it can be just as effective for other types of trauma (Cohen, Mannarino, & Deblinger, 2006; Cohen, Mannarino, & Staron, 2006). A recent meta-analysis of interventions for children and adolescents with posttraumatic stress disorder (PTSD; Morina, Koerssen, & Pollet, 2016) indicated medium to large effect sizes when compared to wait list ($g = 1.44$) and active control conditions ($g = 0.66$). In addition, TF-CBT is one of only three trauma interventions for children and adolescents that have been identified as meeting the criteria as "Well-Supported by Research Evidence" by the California Evidence-Based Clearinghouse for Child Welfare (2017), and it is the only trauma treatment for children with a scientific rating of 1 (California Evidence-Based Clearinghouse for Child Welfare, 2017). TF-CBT is used with children and adolescents who have been exposed to trauma in an attempt to develop a collection of core skills that build on one another (Cohen, Mannarino, & Deblinger, 2006). Treatment is designed to match the needs of the individual child and family and, to be effective, must be consistent with the family's religious, community, and cultural values. In addition, the therapist must be flexible and creative; the family must be actively involved with treatment; and the therapist must model trust, empathy, and acceptance throughout the course of therapy. The goal of TF-CBT is an optimally functioning individual and family well after treatment has been terminated. To accomplish this, the therapist attempts to establish a sense of self-efficacy in the client's affect, behavior, and cognitions (Cohen, Mannarino, & Deblinger, 2006). We should note, however, that TF-CBT is contraindicated for children or caregivers who are experiencing psychosis, suicidality, or dangerous behaviors (Hanson & Jobe-Shields, 2017).

SPECIFIC COMPONENTS OF TRAUMA-FOCUSED COGNITIVE-BEHAVIORAL THERAPY

TF-CBT is a short-term treatment that involves individual sessions with both children and parents as well as joint parent–child sessions. The main components of TF-CBT include psychoeducation, parenting skills, relaxation, affective modulation, cognitive coping and processing, trauma narrative, in vivo mastery of trauma reminders, conjoint child–parent sessions, and enhancing future safety and development. In this chapter, we summarize these components; a more complete description of each component can be found in Cohen, Mannarino, and Deblinger's (2006) book *Treating Trauma and Traumatic Grief in Children and Adolescents.*

Psychoeducation is the initial component of TF-CBT and continues throughout therapy for both the child and parent. Information about trauma, its effects, and its treatment should all be included. It is important to individualize the information so that it is specific to the type of trauma that was experienced and the child's developmental level. Educating parents and children about treatment helps form expectations and prepares them for the types of activities that will be conducted during therapy. The second component is the development of *parenting skills*; these skills focus on helping parents deal with their child's behavior problems (Cohen, Deblinger, Mannarino, & Steer, 2004). Parenting skills taught include the use of praise, selective attention, time out, and contingency management. *Relaxation* techniques are taught to the child in an effort to help him or her reduce the physiological symptoms of stress and help the child sleep. No one relaxation technique in particular is recommended, but the developers of TF-CBT use a combination of focused breathing, meditation, and progressive muscle relaxation. Therapists who do not have a background in the use of relaxation techniques may want to consider referring to the relaxation program developed by Cautela and Groden (1978).

Affective modulation involves teaching children to manage their emotions and deal with their anxiety. Children who have experienced a traumatic event may find it hard to identify emotions, differentiate among emotions, or express their feelings appropriately. If a child is able to express and control his feelings, he may be less likely to use avoidance as a coping strategy. Techniques that are used during this component include thought interruption, positive imagery, positive self-talk, and social skills training. *Cognitive coping and processing* involves teaching children and parents about the relationships among thoughts, feelings, and behavior and helps them identify and correct maladaptive thoughts. Developing a narrative version of their traumatic experiences is believed to be an essential component of TF-CBT and is designed to help the client control intrusive and upsetting trauma-related imagery. The goal of the *trauma narrative* is to separate unpleasant associations between thoughts, reminders, or discussion of the trauma from overwhelming negative emotion. Over the course of several sessions the child is encouraged to describe what happened as well as their thoughts and feelings, before, during, and after the trauma in greater and greater detail. Eventually the child will share this narrative with their parents or caregiver.

In vivo mastery of trauma reminders is designed to help resolve generalized avoidant behaviors. Frequently innocuous cues in the environment can bring up unpleasant emotions and lead to avoidance of those cues. This does not mean you want to desensitize the child to all perceived trauma cues. Many are legitimate and serve to help the child from being retraumatized. Part of this component is getting the child to recognize important cues from innocuous, conditioned cues. TF-CBT also includes *conjoint child–parent sessions* to review information, read the trauma narrative, and facilitate communication. The goal is to get the child comfortable in talking her parent or caregiver about her traumatic experiences and other significant events that have happened. These sessions tend to occur toward the end of therapy because the child first needs sufficient time to cognitively process the trauma. The final component of TF-CBT is *enhancing future safety and development*. In many cases the child will be unlikely to face a similar trauma in the future. Although it is acceptable to stress this, the therapist should never assure any child that he will never experience trauma again; instead, the goal is to ensure that the child has the skills necessary to minimize the likelihood of future trauma and cope with trauma effectively should it occur again.

EMPIRICAL SUPPORT FOR TRAUMA-FOCUSED COGNITIVE-BEHAVIORAL THERAPY

TF-CBT has been empirically validated and is recognized by multiple sources as an empirically based intervention. TF-CBT has consistently been demonstrated as an efficacious treatment for PTSD, depression, anxiety, and other related symptoms. An abundance of evidence supports the efficacy of TF-CBT over treatments such as nondirective play therapy and supportive therapies for children who are the victims of sex abuse (Cohen, Deblinger, & Mannarino, 2004). In addition, although the majority of studies have focused on child sex abuse, evidence also suggests that it is effective for children who have been exposed to a wide range of other forms of trauma as well as children who have been multiply traumatized (Cohen, 2005; Hanson & Jobe-Shields, 2017).

Cohen and Mannarino (1996) conducted the first treatment outcome study for sexually abused children using TF-CBT and compared TF-CBT with a nondirective supportive therapy (NST) for sexually abused preschool children and their parents. Treatment consisted of 12 individual sessions for both the child and parent. The results indicated that the TF-CBT group demonstrated improvement on most outcome measures, whereas the NST group did not exhibit similar outcomes. In a follow-up to this study, Cohen and Mannarino (1997) evaluated treatment outcome 6 and 12 months after initial treatment. The results indicated that, over time, the TF-CBT group exhibited significantly more improvement than the NST group. The results also indicated the superior effectiveness of TF-CBT over NST in reducing sexually inappropriate behavior.

Cohen, Deblinger, Mannarino, and Steer (2004) compared the efficacy of TF-CBT with child-centered therapy (CCT) for the treatment of PTSD and related emotional and behavioral problems in children who had been sexually abused. Participants were randomly assigned to a manualized treatment consisting of TF-CBT or CCT. The results indicated that parents in the TF-CBT group reported lower levels on each of the outcome measures (except parental support) than those who received CCT; specifically, children and parents in the TF-CBT group reported improvement in PTSD symptoms, depression, shame, behavioral problems, and dysfunctional abuse attributions. The results also indicated that two times as many children in the CCT group continued to have PTSD based on *DSM–IV–TR* (American Psychiatric Association, 2000) criteria. TF-CBT also appeared to improve children's feelings of trust, perceived credibility, and shame. This study is important because it supports the use of a shorter version of TF-CBT.

Deblinger, Mannarino, Cohen, and Steer (2006) assessed the maintenance effects of TF-CBT and CCT of participants in Cohen, Deblinger, Mannarino, and Steer's (2004) study. Participants were followed for 6 additional months while attending booster sessions. The results indicated that children in the TF-CBT group maintained the gains made at posttreatment; that is, the children who received TF-CBT continued to show fewer PTSD symptoms and fewer symptoms of shame compared with children in the CCT group. In addition, parents in the TF-CBT group reported less emotional distress than did parents in the CCT group. This study is important because it provides support that a shortened version of the TF-CBT protocol has benefits that persist (at least for 6 months) after treatment has concluded. That children experienced less abuse-related shame during follow-up is also important given that shame may mediate the impact of sexual abuse and thus hinder long-term recovery.

Cohen, Mannarino, and Knudsen (2004) examined a 16-session (eight sessions trauma based and eight sessions grief based) TF-CBT for childhood traumatic grief (CTG). Traumatic grief occurs when trauma symptoms interfere with a child's ability to successfully deal with the normal grieving process. Their results indicated that children experienced significant improvements in CTG, PTSD, depression, and anxiety symptoms and a reduction in behavior problems. PTSD symptoms improved only during the trauma-focused treatment components, whereas CTG improved during both trauma-focused and grief-focused components. In addition, parents experienced significant improvement in PTSD and depressive symptoms. In a follow-up study, Cohen, Mannarino, and Staron (2006) examined the effectiveness of a 12-session cognitive behavior therapy–CTG model in treating trauma and grief symptoms.

Despite the relative effectiveness of the 16-session approach, this study sought to examine the impact of a shortened version of the CBT-CTG protocol used by Cohen, Mannarino, and Knudsen (2004). Participants included 39 children and adolescents who had experienced the loss of a parent or sibling due to accidental death, medical reasons, homicide, suicide, or drug overdose. Significant improvements in children's self-reported symptoms of CTG, PTSD, depression, and anxiety were reported. In addition, parents reported improvements in their child's PTSD, internalizing and externalizing symptoms, and total behavior problems, but they themselves did not report improvement in their depressive symptoms. Similar to Cohen, Mannarino, and Knudsen (2005)'s study, a decline in PTSD symptoms and improvement in adaptive functioning was observed only during the trauma-focused phase of CBT, whereas CTG symptoms improved for both the trauma- and grief-focused CBT interventions. The authors concluded that a trauma- and a shortened version of a grief-focused CBT protocol is effective in reducing PTSD and CTG as well as anxiety, behavioral problems, and depressive symptoms. This study has practical utility because it demonstrated that a shortened version of a trauma- and grief-focused CBT can be effective in improving childhood trauma and grief symptoms. This study also involved a collaborative approach with children and parents, so the information gained from therapy can be transferred between home and clinic and potentially improve generalization and maintenance.

Other studies have supported the efficacy of TF-CBT in community-based programs (Konanur, Muller, Cinamon, Thornback, & Zorzella, 2015), with spiritual modifications (Wang et al., 2016), adjudicated teens in a residential treatment facility (Cohen et al., 2016), and with adults with a mild intellectual disability (Kroese et al., 2016). However, only a few studies have been conducted in a school-based setting. Kataoka et al. (2003) used group TF-CBT with Latino immigrant students who had been exposed to community violence. Participants included 198 students in Grades 3 through 8 with trauma-related depression, PTSD symptoms, or both. The therapy was delivered in Spanish. The results indicated that students in the intervention group had significantly greater improvement in PTSD and depressive symptoms compared with wait-list controls at a 3-month follow-up. These findings suggest that this program can be implemented in a school setting and is associated with a decline in trauma-related mental health problems. Beehler, Birman, and Campbell (2012) used TF-CBT as part of a comprehensive, school-based mental health program for traumatized immigrant children and adolescents and found improved functioning in regard to PTSD symptoms.

CONCLUSION

Children and adolescents clearly are experiencing traumatic events. However, most psychologists working in schools are not receiving specific training in efficacious service delivery for these children. TF-CBT is an effective therapeutic technique that can be used in many different types of situations. In an attempt to provide additional training to psychologists, the National Crimes Treatment and Research Center at the Medical College of the University of South Carolina developed, with the help of a grant from the Substance Abuse and Mental Health Services Administration a 10-hour web-based, multimedia, distance education course for mental health professionals seeking to learn TF-CBT. The only requirements for participating in the training are that individuals have a master's degree or higher in a mental health discipline or are currently enrolled in a graduate training program in a mental health discipline. Interested individuals can find more information about the training program at http://tfcbt.musc.edu/ (Medical University of South Carolina, 2005).

REFERENCES

Akin-Little, K. A., & Little, S. G. (2008). Our Katrina experience: Providing mental health services in Concordia Parish, Louisiana. *Professional Psychology: Research and Practice, 39*, 18–23. http://dx.doi.org/10.1037/0735-7028.39.1.18

American Psychiatric Association. (2000). *Diagnostic and statistical manual of mental disorders* (4th ed., text rev.). Washington, DC: Author.

American Psychiatric Association. (2013). *Diagnostic and statistical manual of mental disorders* (5th ed.). Washington, DC: Author.

Beehler, S., Birman, D., & Campbell, R. (2012). The effectiveness of cultural adjustment and trauma services (CATS): Generating practice-based evidence on a comprehensive, school-based mental health intervention for immigrant youth. *American Journal of Community Psychology, 50*, 155–168. http://dx.doi.org/10.1007/s10464-011-9486-2

California Evidence-Based Clearinghouse for Child Welfare. (2017). *Trauma treatment—Client-level interventions (child & adolescent)*. Retrieved from http://www.cebc4cw.org/topic/trauma-treatment-client-level-interventions-child-adolescent/

Cautela, J. R., & Groden, J. (1978). *Relaxation: A comprehensive manual for adults, children, and children with special needs*. Champaign, IL: Research Press.

Cohen, J. A. (2005). Treating traumatized children: Current status and future directions. In E. Cardeña & K. Croyle (Eds.), *Acute reactions to trauma and psychotherapy: A multidisciplinary and international perspective* (pp. 109–121). New York, NY: Haworth Press. http://dx.doi.org/10.1300/J229v06n02_10

Cohen, J. A., Deblinger, E., & Mannarino, A. P. (2004, September). Trauma-focused cognitive-behavioral therapy for sexually abused children (pp. 109–121). *The Psychiatric Times, 21*(10), 109–121.

Cohen, J. A., Deblinger, E., Mannarino, A. P., & Steer, R. A. (2004). A multi-site, randomized controlled trial for sexually abused children with abuse–related PTSD symptoms. *Journal of the American Academy of Child & Adolescent Psychiatry, 43*, 393–402. http://dx.doi.org/10.1097/00004583-200404000-00005

Cohen, J. A., & Mannarino, A. P. (1996). A treatment outcome study for sexually abused preschool children: Initial findings. *Journal of the American Academy of Child & Adolescent Psychiatry, 35*, 42–50. http://dx.doi.org/10.1097/00004583-199601000-00011

Cohen, J. A., & Mannarino, A. P. (1997). A treatment study for sexually abused preschool children: Outcome during a one-year follow-up. *Journal of the American Academy of Child & Adolescent Psychiatry, 36*, 1228–1235. http://dx.doi.org/10.1097/00004583-199709000-00015

Cohen, J. A., Mannarino, A. P., & Deblinger, E. (2006). *Treating trauma and traumatic grief in children and adolescents.* New York, NY: Guilford Press.

Cohen, J. A., Mannarino, A. P., Jankowski, K., Rosenberg, S., Kodya, S., & Wolford, G. L., II. (2016). A randomized implementation study of trauma-focused cognitive behavioral therapy for adjudicated teens in residential treatment facilities. *Child Maltreatment, 21*, 156–167. http://dx.doi.org/10.1177/1077559515624775

Cohen, J. A., Mannarino, A. P., & Knudsen, K. (2004). Treating childhood traumatic grief: A pilot study. *Journal of the American Academy of Child & Adolescent Psychiatry, 43*, 1225–1233. http://dx.doi.org/10.1097/01.chi.0000135620.15522.38

Cohen, J. A., Mannarino, A. P., & Knudsen, K. (2005). Treating sexually abused children: 1 year follow-up of a randomized controlled trial. *Child Abuse & Neglect, 29*, 135–145. http://dx.doi.org/10.1016/j.chiabu.2004.12.005

Cohen, J. A., Mannarino, A. P., & Staron, V. R. (2006). A pilot study of modified cognitive-behavioral therapy for childhood traumatic grief (CBT-CTG). *Journal of the American Academy of Child & Adolescent Psychiatry, 45*, 1465–1473. http://dx.doi.org/10.1097/01.chi.0000237705.43260.2c

Deblinger, E., Mannarino, A. P., Cohen, J. A., & Steer, R. A. (2006). A follow-up study of a multisite, randomized, controlled trial for children with sexual abuse-related PTSD symptoms. *Journal of the American Academy of Child & Adolescent Psychiatry, 45*, 1474–1484. http://dx.doi.org/10.1097/01.chi.0000240839.56114.bb

Felitti, V. J., Anda, R. F., Nordenberg, D., Williamson, D. F., Spitz, A. M., Edwards, V., . . . Marks, J. S. (1998). Relationship of childhood abuse and household dysfunction to many of the leading causes of death in adults. The Adverse Childhood Experiences (ACE) Study. *American Journal of Preventive Medicine, 14*, 245–258. http://dx.doi.org/10.1016/S0749-3797(98)00017-8

Frissa, S., Hatch, S. L., Fear, N. T., Dorrington, S., Goodwin, L., & Hotopf, M. (2016). Challenges in the retrospective assessment of trauma: Comparing a checklist approach to a single item trauma experience screening question. *BMC Psychiatry, 16,* 20. http://dx.doi.org/10.1186/s12888-016-0720-1

Hanson, R. F., & Jobe-Shields, L. (2017). Trauma-focused cognitive–behavioral therapy for children and adolescents. In S. N. Gold (Ed.), *APA handbook of trauma psychology: Trauma practice* (pp. 389–410). Washington, DC: American Psychological Association. http://dx.doi.org/10.1037/0000020-018

Kataoka, S. H., Stein, B. D., Jaycox, L. H., Wong, M., Escudero, P., Tu, W., . . . Fink, A. (2003). A school-based mental health program for traumatized Latino immigrant children. *Journal of the American Academy of Child & Adolescent Psychiatry, 42,* 311–318. http://dx.doi.org/10.1097/00004583-200303000-00011

Konanur, S., Muller, R. T., Cinamon, J. S., Thornback, K., & Zorzella, K. P. M. (2015). Effectiveness of trauma-focused cognitive behavioral therapy in a community-based program. *Child Abuse & Neglect, 50,* 159–170. http://dx.doi.org/10.1016/j.chiabu.2015.07.013

Kroese, B. S., Willott, S., Taylor, F., Smith, P., Graham, R., Rutter, T., . . . Willner, P. (2016). Trauma-focused cognitive-behaviour therapy for people with mild intellectual disabilities: Outcomes of a pilot study. *Advances in Mental Health and Intellectual Disabilities, 10,* 299–310. http://dx.doi.org/10.1108/AMHID-05-2016-0008

Leckman, J. F., & Mayes, L. C. (2007). Nurturing resilient children. *Journal of Child Psychology and Psychiatry, 48,* 221–223. http://dx.doi.org/10.1111/j.1469-7610.2007.01743.x

Little, S. G., & Akin-Little, A. (2013). Trauma in children: A call to action in school psychology. *Journal of Applied School Psychology, 29,* 375–388. http://dx.doi.org/10.1080/15377903.2012.695769

Little, S. G., Akin-Little, A., & Somerville, M. P. (2011). Response to trauma in children: An examination of effective intervention and post-traumatic growth. *School Psychology International, 32,* 448–463. http://dx.doi.org/10.1177/0143034311402916

Medical University of South Carolina. (2005). *A web-based learning course for trauma-focused cognitive-behavioral therapy.* Retrieved from http://tfcbt.musc.edu

Morina, N., Koerssen, R., & Pollet, T. V. (2016). Interventions for children and adolescents with posttraumatic stress disorder: A meta-analysis of comparative outcome studies. *Clinical Psychology Review, 47,* 41–54. http://dx.doi.org/10.1016/j.cpr.2016.05.006

Truman, J. L., & Morgan, R. E. (2016). *Criminal victimization, 2015.* Retrieved from https://www.bjs.gov/content/pub/pdf/cv15.pdf

Wang, D. C., Aten, J. D., Boan, D., Jean-Charles, W., Griff, K. P., Valcin, V. C., . . . Wang, A. (2016). Culturally adapted spiritually oriented trauma-focused cognitive–behavioral therapy for child survivors of *restavek*. *Spirituality in Clinical Practice, 3,* 224–236. http://dx.doi.org/10.1037/scp0000101

INDEX

AAC (augmentative and alternative communication) systems, 276–279
AAP Committee on School Health, 386
ABA. *See* Applied behavior analysis
ABC. *See* Antecedent–behavior–consequence
ABC pattern of behavior, 246. *See also* Antecedent–behavior–consequence (ABC)
A-B-C (antecedent–behavior–consequence) recording, 28–29
ABIs (antecedent-based interventions), 276
ABLLS-R (Assessment of Basic Language and Learning Skills—Revised), 212, 272
Abuse-Focused Cognitive-Behavioral Therapy, 376, 384. *See also* Alternatives for Families: A Cognitive Behavioral Therapy (AF-CBT)
Academic engagement, problem classroom behaviors and, 68
Academic performance interventions, 143–161
  evidence-based, 144, 147
  in mathematics, 153–158
  in reading, 147–153
  by subject area, 145–146
  in writing, 158–161
Academic skills
  in children with ASD, 228–229
  teaching, 46
  VSM for students with ASD, 291–292
Acceptance
  self-, 332
  unconditional, 331–332
Acquisition of skills, 46
Acquisition tasks, 252
Across-activities choices, 64
Adaptive behavior
  assessing, for ASD, 197–198
  cognitive techniques for increasing, 362–363
  failure to develop, 228
  reinforcing, 336

Adaptive functioning, 198, 360
Adults as change agents, 171–184
  behavioral consultation, 173–178
  performance feedback, 180–183
  social influence, 178–180
AF-CBT. *See* Alternatives for Families: A Cognitive Behavioral Therapy
Affective modulation, in TF-CBT, 396
Aided AAC systems, 277–279
Akin-Little, A., 6, 119, 288, 292
Akullian, J., 292–293
Alabama Parenting Questionnaire, 379, 380
Alberto, P. A., 84
Alder, N., 67
Alexander, James, 376
Alicke, M. D., 5
Allen, R. F., 218
Almason, S. M., 219
Alphabet knowledge, 137, 147–148
Alternative behavior, differential reinforcement of (DRA), 81
Alternative replacement behaviors, 24–25
Alternatives for Families: A Cognitive Behavioral Therapy (AF-CBT), 375–388
  assessment, 379–381
  conceptual basis, 378–379
  content and name of model, 376
  eligibility criteria for, 377
  empirical support for, 383–385
  in school settings, 385–388
  target populations, 376–378
  treatment structure, 381–383
American Academy of Pediatrics (AAP) Committee on School Health, 386
American Psychological Association (APA)
  evidence-based practice policy of, 6–7
  Society of Clinical Child and Adolescent Psychology, 330
  Society of Clinical Psychology, 330
Andersen, P. M., 193
Andersson, G., 333

Antecedent-based interventions (ABIs), 276
Antecedent–behavior–consequence (ABC), 246. *See also* Three-term (reinforcement) contingency
   behavioral principles in context of, 44–49
   in CPRT, 250
   in FBA for ASD, 197
   modifying antecedent stimuli, 44–45
   strategies for modifying consequences, 47–49
   strategies for teaching behavior, 45–47
   in verbal behavior, 265
Antecedent–behavior–consequence (A-B-C) recording, 28–29
Antecedent modifications, 218
Antecedents, in instructional choices, 64–66
Antecedent stimuli, modifying, 44–45
APA. *See* American Psychological Association
Applied behavioral analysts, 133
Applied behavior analysis (ABA), 133–139, 246, 286
   application to young learners with ASD, 210–219
   for ASD, 205–220, 246–247, 263, 264
   behavior analysis organizations, 134–135
   and CBT, 326, 329
   competency in, 136–139
   defining characteristics of, 208–209
   design and implementation of, 4
   dimensions of, 136
   disseminating ABA services, 219
   in education, 135–136
   foundational research on treating children with ASD and related disorders, 209–210
   history and basic principles of, 206–208
   in PBIS, 43, 49–53
   as professional practice or discipline, 135
   for verbal behavior intervention with ASD, 273
Appraising, in CBT, 338, 339
Armstrong, A. B., 88–89

Arnberg, A., 6
ASD. *See* Autism spectrum disorder
Asmundson, G. J., 327
Assessment(s)
   in AF-CBT, 379–381
   for ASD, 194–199, 211–213
   behavioral vs. traditional, 16. *See also* Behavioral assessment
   of verbal behavior, 268, 271–272
Assessment of Basic Language and Learning Skills—Revised (ABLLS-R), 212, 272
Association for Behavioral and Cognitive Therapies, 325, 334
Association for Behavior Analysis International, 134
Association for the Advancement of Behavior Therapy, 325
Attention function, 217
Attention of child, in CPRT, 250
Augmentative and alternative communication (AAC) systems, 276–279
Augmenting, 266, 267
Autism spectrum disorder (ASD), 4, 191–200
   ABA and early intervention for, 205–220
   assessment of, 194–199
   behaviors associated with, 193
   classroom pivotal response training, 245–258
   communication deficits with, 264
   diagnosing, 191–195
   discrete trial training, 227–240
   efficacy of ABA for, 133
   increase in students with, 16
   prevalence of, 191
   structured teaching approaches, 299–316
   verbal behavior intervention, 263–279
   video-based interventions, 285–294
Autistic regression, 195–196
Automatic function, 217
Automatic thoughts, 338, 353, 361
AWARE (Project Advancing Wellness and Resilience Education) Grant Program, 36
Axe, J. B., 218
Axelrod, S., 126

Ayala, S. M., 291
Ayllon, T., 5
Azrin, N., 5

BACB (Behavior Analyst Certification Board), 135, 137
Backx, W., 331
Baer, D. M., 108, 208
Banda, D. R., 288
Bandura, A., 125, 286–287
Barkin, S., 85
Barriers interfering with interventions, 144, 146
Barrish, H. H., 5
Bases of power models, 178–180
Bates, J. A., 120–121
Battaglia, M., 6
Baumann, B. L., 376
BCBA–D (Board Certified Behavior Analysts at the doctoral level), 4
BCBAs. See Board Certified Behavior Analysts
Beadle-Brown, J., 307
Beck, Aaron T., 326, 327, 331, 335, 337, 338
Beehler, S., 399
Behavior(s)
  antecedent–behavior–consequence sequence, 44–49. See also Antecedent–behavior–consequence (ABC)
  with ASD, 193
  automatic, 353
  CBT definition of, 329
  CBT views of, 337, 339
  defining problem behaviors, 22–23
  desired, 24–25
  events surrounding, 25–26
  interactions of environment and, 17–18
  intraindividual analysis of, 17–18
  intrinsically motivated, 114
  natural variation in, 16–17
  pivotal, 247
  prioritizing target behaviors, 23–24
  replacement, 24–25
  strategies for teaching, 45–47
  as target for measurement and intervention, 16. See also specific interventions/treatments
  verbal, 264–265

Behavioral activation, 364–365
Behavioral analysts, 133
Behavioral assessment, 15–31
  and behavioral problem-solving, 18–19
  collecting narrative data, 22–26
  critical concepts, 16–18
  intervention development, 30–31
  referral, 20
  teacher interview, 20–21
Behavioral consultation, 173–184
  bases of power models, 179–180
  key assumptions in, 174
  outcome research on, 177–178
  performance feedback in, 180–183
  stages of, 174–177
  time and resources required for, 19
Behavioral contrast, 120–121
Behavioral fluency, 308, 309
Behavioral interventions. See also specific topics
  for academic performance, 143–161
  adults as change agents, 171–184
  development of, 30–31
  efficacy of, 5–6
  generalization and maintenance of, 97–110
  low-intensity strategies for classroom management, 64–71
  positive and preventive approaches to, 7
  reductive procedures, 77–90
  school-wide PBIS, 35–55
Behavioral learning theory, 378
Behavioral momentum, 78–79, 86
Behavioral problem-solving
  and behavioral assessment, 18–19
  collaborative, 30
  narrative reports and recordings for, 15–30
Behavioral research, on reinforcer–reward effects, 118–120
Behavioral Stream Interview, 20
"Behavioral Treatment and Normal Educational and Intellectual Functioning in Young Autistic Children" (O. I. Lovaas), 209–210

Behavior analysis
    applied. *See* Applied behavior analysis (ABA)
    defined, 134
    organizations in field of, 134–135
    as a profession, 16
    science and practice of, 134
    Skinner's introduction of, 206
Behavior Analyst Certification Board (BACB), 135, 137
Behavior–environment interactions, 17–18
Behaviorism, 5, 135
    basic tenets of, 43–44
    in context of three-term contingency, 44–49
    radical, 135
The Behavior of Organisms (B. F. Skinner), 206
Behavior therapy (BT)
    arms/traditions in, 335
    cognitive revolution in, 326
    and emergence of CBT, 325, 336
    as first evidence-based paradigm, 336
    foundational assumptions and values in, 330–331
    origin of, 333
    rational emotive behavior therapy in, 343
Bellini, S., 288, 292–293
Belotti, R., 6
Bereiter-Engelmann preschool program, 312
Bergan, John R., 19, 20, 173–174
Berkeley, S., 151
Berman, J. S., 5
Bijou, S. W., 5
Birkan, B., 104–105
Birman, D., 399
Birnbrauer, J. S., 5
Biyanova, T., 335
Blending strategies, 109
Board Certified Behavior Analysts (BCBAs), 133, 136–139, 211, 219
Board Certified Behavior Analysts at the doctoral level (BCBA–D), 4
Bogschutz, R. J., 288
Bondy, A. S., 277
Bordin, E. S., 356
Bradford, D. C., 16

Brady, M. P., 215
Braithwaite, K. L., 217–218
Bray, M. A., 89
Bribery, 126–127
Brief Child Abuse Potential Inventory, 379–381
Briesch, A. M., 6
Briesch, J. M., 6
Brodman, D. M., 354
Brodsky, G., 5
Brown, E. J., 376
Bryan, L. C., 306
Bryant Shaw, J., 198
BT. *See* Behavior therapy
Buggey, T., 292, 294
Bureau of Justice Statistics, 393
Burns, M. K., 150, 151
Burton, B., 89
Busse, R. T., 177

California Evidence Based Clearinghouse for Child Welfare, 385
Cameron, J., 114, 116–117, 121–125
Campbell, R., 399
Cantwell, E. D., 66
Cariveau, T., 107
Carr, J. E., 219
Carton, J. S., 121–122
Casey, R. J., 5
Castonguay, L. G., 332
Cathcart, K., 307
CBT. *See* Cognitive behavior therapy
CCC (cover–copy–compare), 154
CCT (child-centered therapy), 398
Centers for Disease Control and Prevention (CDC), 195
Cerasoli, C. P., 125
CET (cognitive evaluation theory), 116–117, 124
Chaining, 46, 86
Charlop-Christy, M. H., 288
Child-centered therapy (CCT), 398
Child PTSD Symptom Scale, 380, 381
Choices, instructional, 64–66
Chomsky, N., 264
Christensen, H., 354
Chu, B. C., 356–357
Clark, E. C., 89
Classical conditioning, 335

Classroom contextual factors
  in assessing behaviors and
    interventions, 26–28
  in shaping strategies for
    interventions, 18–19
  in TEACCH program, 302
  and teacher interviews, 21
Classroom management, 61–72
  and classroom structure, 63
  instructional choices, 64–66
  low-intensity strategies for, 64–71
  opportunities to respond, 66–69
  precorrection, 69–71
Classroom pivotal response teaching
  (CPRT), 245–258
  components of, 250–255
  foundations of, 246–250
  implementation of, 255–257
Classroom structure, 63
Codding, R. S., 154
Coercion theory, 378
Coercive family process, 336
Coercive power, 178, 179
Cognitions
  in CBT, 338–340
  cognitive restructuring, 360–362
  dysfunctional, 344
  emotions and, 359–360
Cognitive behavioral interventions,
  efficacy of, 5–6
Cognitive behavior therapy (CBT), 4,
  325–345
  AF-CBT, 375–388
  assumptions and principles of,
    329–331, 337–341
  behavioral activation, 364–365
  with children, 351–366
  cognitive models in, 341–342
  conceptualization of students'
    feelings and behavior in,
    357–358
  evidence for, 353–355
  exposure-based approaches, 364
  future directions for, 344
  history of, 335–337
  introducing CBT to students,
    358–363
  overview of, 351–353
  readings and resources, 366–368
  in school-based practice, 353–357

status within psychotherapy,
  333–335
systematic desensitization, 364
techniques used in, 328–329
and theory of personality and
  psychopathology,
  342–344
therapeutic relationship in,
  331–333
trauma-focused, 393–400
variation within, 326–329
waves within, 326
Cognitive coping and processing,
  in TF-CBT, 396
Cognitive deficit model, 341
Cognitive dysfunction models,
  341–342
Cognitive evaluation theory (CET),
  116–117, 124
Cognitive functioning assessment,
  for ASD, 197
Cognitive research, behavioral
  criticisms of, 120–125
Cognitive restructuring, 360–362
Cognitive theory, 378
Cognitive therapy (Beck), 326,
  351–352
Cohen, J. A., 6, 396–399
Colvin, G., 69, 70–71
*Common Core State Standards for
  Mathematics*, 153
Common stimuli, programming for,
  105–106
Communication. *See also* Verbal
  behavior intervention in ASD
  ABA-based interventions for
    ASD, 273
  assessing, for ASD, 198, 212–213
  receptive and expressive, 265
  in TEACCH program, 301
Computational skills, 153–158
  cover–copy–compare, 154
  explicit timing, 155
  incremental rehearsal, 155
  performance feedback, 155–156
  taped problems technique,
    154–155
Confidentiality, 387
Conjoint child–parent sessions,
  in TF-CBT, 397

Consequences
    in antecedent–behavior–
        consequence sequence, 44.
        See also Antecedent–behavior–
        consequence (ABC)
    negative punishment, 48
    negative reinforcement, 47–48
    positive punishment, 48
    positive reinforcement, 47
    strategies for modifying, 47–49
    in Tier 1 PBIS, 52
Consultation
    behavioral, 19, 173–178
    human services, 172–173
    problem-solving, 175
Content-specificity hypothesis, 357
Contingency management, 362–363
Contingent reinforcement, 229–230, 254
Conyers, C., 80
Cook, J. M., 335
Coonrod, E. E., 194
Copple, K. S., 288
Correction, 69–70
Cover–copy–compare (CCC), 154
Coyne, J. C., 335
CPRT. *See* Classroom pivotal response teaching
Creed, T. A., 357
Cueing
    in CPRT, 250, 252–254
"Culture of Autism," 300

Daily schedules, in TEACCH program, 302–303
Dart, E. H., 80, 239
Data
    for ASD interventions, 215–216, 218–219
    culturally valid, in PBIS, 38–40
    from direct observation, 29–30
    in precision teaching, 309, 310
Davidovitch, M., 196
Davis, C. A., 198–199
Davison, G., 337
Deblinger, E., 396, 398
Deci, E. L., 114–117, 124
Delano, M. E., 292
D'Elia, L., 306
Delmolino, L., 307

Delprato, D. J., 236
De Martini-Scully, D., 89
De Montaigne, Michel, 338
DePalma, V., 105
Developmental victimology theory, 378
Diagnostic and Statistical Manual of Mental Disorders (fifth ed.; DSM–5), 191–192, 198, 263, 264, 394
Diagramming, 157
Dickinson, A. M., 115–116, 121
Didden, R., 6
Differential reinforcement, 80–81, 207
Differential reinforcement of alternative behavior (DRA), 81
Differential reinforcement of incompatible behavior (DRI), 81
Differential reinforcement of low rates of behavior (DRL), 80
Differential reinforcement of other behavior (DRO), 80–81
DiGiuseppe, R. A., 331, 332, 356
Direct instruction
    components and implementation of, 313–314
    critics of, 314
    evidence base underpinning, 314–316
    for students with ASD, 312–316
Direct Instruction System for Teaching Arithmetic and Reading (DISTAR), 313
Direct observation, 19
    of learners with ASD, 216
    misleading data from, 29–30
    naturalistic, 26–30
    reasons for conducting, 26–27
Direct reinforcement, 254
Discrete trial training (DTT), 227–240, 247
    application and evaluation of, 237–238
    characteristics of, 232–233
    components of, 229–232
    and more naturalistic training approaches, 235–237
    sequencing the delivery of, 234–235
    for students with ASD, 213–214
    training instructors to use, 239

for verbal behavior intervention
    with ASD, 273, 274
Discriminative stimulus (S^D), 207
DISTAR (Direct Instruction System
    for Teaching Arithmetic and
    Reading), 313
Distributed trial sequencing, in DTT,
    234–235
Dittrich, G. A., 80
Dixon, D. R., 213
Dobson, K. S., 331
Dodson, K. G., 105–106
Downs, A., 237–239
Downs, R. C., 237–239
Doyle, K. A., 331
DRA (differential reinforcement of
    alternative behavior), 81
Drabman, R., 5
DRI (differential reinforcement of
    incompatible behavior), 81
Drills (math), 155
DRL (differential reinforcement of low
    rates of behavior), 80
DRO (differential reinforcement of
    other behavior), 80–81
Dryden, W., 331
DSM–5. *See Diagnostic and Statistical
    Manual of Mental Disorders*
    (fifth ed.)
DTT. *See* Discrete trial training
Ducharme, J. M., 218
Duhon, G. J., 105–106
Dukes, C., 215
Dunlap, G., 19, 65
Durand, V. M., 103
Dvorsky, M., 8, 9
Dysfunctional cognitions, 344
D'Zurilla, T. J., 173

Early intensive behavioral intervention
    (EIBI)
    for ASD, 210, 219
    for verbal behavior intervention
        with ASD, 273
EBDs. *See* Emotional or behavioral
    disorders
EBPs. *See* Evidence-based practices
Eccles, C., 80
Echoic, 266, 267
Educator's Practice Guides for Writing, 159

Edwards, R. P., 20–21
Effectiveness research, 237, 329
Efficacy research, 237, 329
Egeland, J., 193
EIBI. *See* Early intensive behavioral
    intervention
Eisenberger, R., 116–117, 121
Ekinci, O., 196
Elaborative interrogation, 151
Elliott, S. N., 177
Ellis, A., 326, 331–332, 335, 337, 342,
    343
Emergent reading skills, 147–149
Emotional or behavioral disorders
    (EBDs)
    and classroom structures, 63
    instructional choice strategy, 64–66
    opportunities to respond strategy, 67
    precorrection strategy, 70
Emotions
    in CBT, 339–341
    cognitions and, 359–360
    pathways to, 342–343
    in response to trauma, 394
Empirically supported treatments
    (ESTs), 329–330
Engelmann, Siegfried, 312, 313
Enhancing future safety and
    development, in TF-CBT, 397
Ennis, R. P., 71
Environment. *See also* Classroom
    contextual factors
    classroom structures, 63
    interactions of behavior and, 17–18
    and socially significant behaviors,
        208
    for TEACCH, 301, 302, 304
    in verbal behavior approach, 268
EO (establishing operation), 207
Epictetus, 338
Erchul, W. P., 179–180
Escape function, 217
ESSA (Every Student Succeeds Act),
    97
Establishing operation (EO), 207
ESTs (empirically supported
    treatments), 329–330
Evaluative cognitions, 338, 339
Event recording, 218
Everett, G. E., 85

Every Student Succeeds Act (ESSA), 97
Evidence-based practices (EBPs), 6–7
   academic performance interventions, 144, 147
   AF-CBT, 383–385
   behavioral consultation, 177–178
   CBT, 329–330, 353–355
   for children with ASD, 245–246
   direct instruction, 314–316
   DTT, 237–238
   in mathematics, 153–158
   PBIS, 36
   performance feedback, 182–183
   precision teaching, 311–312
   PRT, 246
   in reading, 147–153
   TEACCH, 304–308
   TF-CBT, 397–399
   in using ABA for students with ASD, 219
   verbal behavior intervention with ASD, 268–271, 273–276
   video-based interventions with ASD, 291–293
   video modeling, 287–288
   in writing, 158–161
Exclusionary time-out, 85
Exemplars, sufficient, 104–105
Expert power, 178–180
Explicit instruction, in mathematics, 153–154
Explicit timing, in math computational skills, 155
Exposure-based approaches, in CBT, 364
Expressive language, 265
Extinction, 48–49, 82–83, 206–207
Extinction burst, 82
Extrinsic motivation, 114–116
Extrinsic reinforcement effects on intrinsic motivation, 113–127
   behavioral criticisms of cognitive research, 120–125
   best practices in using reinforcement procedures, 125–127
   theories and investigations of reinforcer–reward effects, 116–120
Eysenck, Hans, 333, 336

Factual cognitions, 338–339
Fallon, L. M., 183
Family systems theory, 378
Farley, M., 89
FBA. *See* Functional behavior/behavioral assessment
FCT (functional communication training), 217–218, 275
Feedback
   performance, 155–156, 180–183
   video, 285, 291
Feedforward modeling, 288–290
Feinberg, R., 117, 123
Felitti, V. J., 393
Ferrante, L., 307
Field, C. E., 89
Finch, S., 85
Fisher, J. E., 327
Fleury, V. P., 219
Flora, D. B., 120
Flora, S. R., 114, 118, 120, 121
Flores, M. M., 315
Fluency, 46
Ford, M. T., 125
Fossum, M., 237–238
Fowler, J., 8, 9
Freeman, K. A., 288
French, J. R. P., 178–179
Frissa, S., 393
Frost, L. A., 277
Functional Assessment Informant Record—Teacher, 20–21
Functional behavior/behavioral assessment (FBA)
   advances in, 16
   for ASD, 195–197
   goals of, 18, 103
   of problem behavior, 216–217
   specific information in, 22
Functional behaviors, 103
Functional communication training (FCT), 217–218, 275
Function-based interventions, 217–218
Function-based reinforcement, 53
Furlow, C. M., 239

Ganz, J. B., 315
Garcia, D., 215
Gast, D. L., 306
Geiger, K. B., 237

General case programming, 104–105
Generality, 98
Generalization of interventions, 97–110
    blending strategies, 109
    instructional phase strategies, 103–107
    planning phase strategies, 101–103
    programming for, 100–109
    requesting, 108
    response generalization, 99
    stimulus generalization, 98–99
    temporal generalization, 99–100
    transfer phase strategies, 107–109
Generalization of learning, 46, 47
Getty, K. C., 180
Glick, L., 196
Glynn, S. M., 84
Goal setting
    for reading fluency, 150
    for writing, 160
Goin-Kochel, R. P., 304–305
Goldfried, M. R., 173, 332, 337
Goldstein, S., 85
Gould, E., 213
Graham, S., 159
Gray, K., 105
Greene, D., 118
Gresham, F. M., 18, 24, 78–80
Griffith, C., 71
Groen, A. D., 210
Guess, D., 235
Guided practice, 159
Gunter, P. L., 67

Hackenberg, T. D., 83–84
Hale, A., 153
Hall, V., 123
Handheld computing technology, as SGD, 279
Happening–Thinking–Feeling–Behavior (HTFB) chart, 359, 365
Harrington, N., 362
Harris, K. R., 159
Harris, S., 307
Harrison, J. R., 6
Harsh bases of power, 179
Hartmann, D. P., 16
Hattie, J. A., 315
Hawkins, R. O., 153
Haydon, T., 68

Hayes, A. M., 332
Hayes, S. C., 266
Herrnstein, R. J., 24
Herschell, A. D., 376
Hicks, Sharon, 376
Himle, M., 80
Hockersmith, I., 105
Hofmann, S. G., 327
Holtzman, G., 196
Homework, in CBT, 364–365
Hoogsteder, L. M., 6
Hopf, A., 292
Horcones, C. L., 115
Horner, R. H., 50
Hovik, K. T., 193
How to Kill Creativity (National Education Association), 125
HTFB (Happening–Thinking–Feeling–Behavior) chart, 359, 365
Human services consultation, 172–173
Hume, K., 306
Hypermedia, 152

IDEA (Individuals With Disabilities Education Act), 35, 191
Incidental teaching approaches, 106, 214
Incompatible behavior, differential reinforcement of (DRI), 81
Incremental rehearsal, of computational skills, 155
Indicated school-based CBT, 354
Indiscriminable contingencies, 107
Individuals With Disabilities Education Act (IDEA), 35, 191
Individuals With Disabilities Education Improvement Act of 1990, 136
Informant reports, 19, 20, 24
Informational power, 178–180
Institute of Education Sciences, 159
Instructional choices, 64–66
Instructional hierarchy, 144
Instructional phase intervention strategies, 101–107
Intellectual disability, with ASD, 197, 198, 228
Interdisciplinary teams, BCBAs on, 139
Interests of children with ASD, in TEACCH program, 301
Intermittent reinforcement, 107

Interpersonal influence, power/
  interaction model of, 179–180
Interval recording, 218–219
Interviews
  for behavioral assessment, 19–26
  in behavioral consultation, 175–177
  in diagnosing ASD, 195
  semistructured, 20–21
Intraindividual analysis, 17–18
Intraverbal, 266, 267
Intrinsic motivation
  defined, 114–116
  effect of extrinsic reinforcement on,
    113–127
In vivo mastery of trauma reminders,
  396–397
Ip, E. H., 85
Isolation time-out, 85
Iwata, B. A., 5, 82

JABA (Journal of Applied Behavior
  Analysis), 135, 208
James, William, 338
Jenson, W. R., 89
Johansen, M., 237–238
Johnson, B. M., 107
Journal of Applied Behavior Analysis
  (JABA), 135, 208
The Journal of Behavioral Assessment, 16
Journal of Organizational Behavior
  Management, 135
Journal of the Experimental Analysis of
  Behavior, 134–135

Kahneman, D., 343
Kataoka, S. H., 399
Kazdin, A. E., 83, 84
Kehle, T. J., 89
Kelly, A. N., 218
Kelly, G., 341–342
Kendall, P. C., 354, 356–357
Kern, L., 19, 64
Kidder, J. D., 5
Klotz, M., 5
Knowing, in CBT, 338–339
Knudsen, K., 398, 399
Kodak, T., 107, 211–212
Koegel, B. L., 232
Koegel, L. K., 232, 233, 235
Koegel, R. L., 232

Kohn, A., 122–123
Kolko, D. J., 376, 383–384
Kopp, B., 80
Korzilius, H., 6
Kostewicz, D. E., 65
Koul, R. K., 288
Kratochwill, T. R., 177
Kuehlwein, K. T., 326

Lacy, L., 235
LaFleur, L. H., 182
Lambert, M. J., 332
Lane, D. M., 198
Lane, K. L., 66, 71, 89–90
Language assessment, for children with
  ASD, 212–213
Language development, 264
Language for Learning, 313
Language theory, 264, 265
Laprime, A. P., 80
Lazarus, A. A., 329, 336, 337
Le, L., 288
Leaf, J. B., 238
Leaf, R., 332
Learned helplessness, 248
Learning
  by children with ASD, 228
  phases of, 46
  social learning theory, 286–287
  vicarious, 287
Least restrictive alternative, 87–88
Legitimate power, 178–180
Lensbower, J., 105
Lepper, M. R., 118, 123
Lerman, D. C., 82, 228, 233
Lewis, T. J., 70–71
Lindsley, Ogden R., 5, 308–310
Ling, S., 153
Linscott, J., 332
Listener behavior, 266–267
Literacy skills
  direct instruction for, 315
  precision teaching for, 311–312
Litow, L., 5
Little, S. G., 6, 86–87, 119, 288, 292
Lopata, C., 194
Lorah, E. R., 279
Lovaas, O. I., 5, 209–210
Love, J. R., 219
Loveland, K. A., 198

Low rates of behavior, differential reinforcement of (DRL), 80

Maag, J. W., 83, 88–89
MacKenzie-Keating, S. E., 85
Maguire, R. W., 218
Mahoney, M. J., 337
Main idea strategy instruction with self-monitoring, 151–152
Maintenance
    of interventions, 97–110
    of learning, 46–47
    response, 99–100
Maintenance tasks, 252
Mancil, G. R., 68
Mand, 266, 267, 275
Mannarino, A. P., 396–399
Marcus Aurelius, 338
Martens, B. K., 86
Massed trial sequencing, in DTT, 234, 235
Mathematics
    common core standards for, 153
    computation interventions, 145–146, 153–158
    direct instruction for, 315
    precision teaching for numeracy, 312
Matta, A. R., 354
Mawhinney, T. C., 115–116
McClelland, S. S., 6
McConnell, L. L., 288
McDaniel, C. E., 29
McDaniel, H., 8, 9
McDonald, L., 85
mDRO (momentary DRO), 80
Mechling, L. C., 306
Mediation strategies, 108–109
Medway, F. J., 177
Meichenbaum, D., 326, 337
Mesibov, G. B., 301, 307
Mesmer, E. M., 105–106
Messenger, M., 66
Miller, K. M., 291–292
Miltenberger, R., 80
Mindfulness techniques, 326
Mintz, C. M., 120
Modeling, 159
    in discrete trial training, 231–233
    feedforward, 288–290
    positive self-review, 288–289
    video, 285, 287–288
    video self-modeling, 285–293
Momentary DRO (mDRO), 80
Montgomerie, R., 288, 291
Morgan, P. L., 149–151
Mortenson, B. P., 182
Motivating operations (MOs), 207, 265–267
Motivation
    for change, in CBT, 356–357
    intrinsic and extrinsic, 113–127
    as pivotal behavior in ASD, 247–249
Mulligan, M., 234, 235
Mychailyszyn, M. P., 354

NAC (National Autism Center), 273, 305
Najdowski, A. C., 213
Narrative reports and recordings
    advantage of, 20
    behavioral assessment and behavioral problem-solving, 18–19
    and behavioral assessment concepts, 16–18
    collecting narrative data, 22–26
    informant reports, 19, 20
    naturalistic direct observation, 19, 26–30
    sufficient data to support strategies, 19
    teacher interview, 19–21
National Autism Center (NAC), 273, 305
National Child Traumatic Stress Network, 385
National Education Association, 125–126
National Governors' Association Center for Best Practices, Council of Chief State School Officers, 153
National Professional Development Center on ASD (NPDC), 273, 305
National Reading Panel, 149
National Standards Project (NSP), 273
National Technical Assistance Center on PBIS (TA Center on PBIS; OSEP Center on PBIS), 35, 36, 40

Natural environment teaching (NET)
  for students with ASD, 214
  for verbal behavior intervention for ASD, 273
Naturalistic behavioral interventions, 247
  discrete trial training compared to, 235–237
  PRT, 246, 247, 249
Naturalistic direct observation, 19, 26–30
Naturalistic interventions (NI), 274
Naturalistic teaching strategies (NTS), for verbal behavior intervention for ASD, 273–275
Neef, N. A., 105
Negative punishment, 48, 207–208
Negative reinforcement, 47–49, 82, 206, 335–336
Neil, A. L., 354
Neisworth, J. T., 292
Ness, E. J., 239
NET. *See* Natural environment teaching
Nevin, J. A., 78
Newton's second law of motion, 79
New Zealand schools, 4
Ng, O., 218
NI (naturalistic interventions), 274
Nicklin, J. M., 125
Nisbett, R. E., 118
Noell, G. H., 86, 182, 183
Nondirective supportive therapy (NST), 397–398
Nonexclusionary time-out, 85
Norcross, J. C., 332
Norwich, B., 311–312
NPDC (National Professional Development Center on ASD), 273, 305
NSP (National Standards Project), 273
NST (nondirective supportive therapy), 397–398
NTS (naturalistic teaching strategies), for verbal behavior intervention for ASD, 273–275
Nuernberger, J. E., 80
Numeracy, precision teaching for, 312

O'Connor, R., 291
Odom, S., 306
O'Donohue, W. T., 327
Ogliari, A., 6
Øie, M., 193
O'Leary, K. D., 5
Olympia, D., 89
O'Neill, K., 6
O'Neill, R. E., 104
Operant conditioning, 246
Opportunities to respond (OTRs), 66–69
Organizational behavior management, 135
OSEP Center on PBIS. *See* National Technical Assistance Center on PBIS
Osnes, P. G., 100–101, 107
Öst, L. G., 6
Other behavior, differential reinforcement of (DRO), 80–81
OTRs (opportunities to respond), 66–69
Outcomes, culturally equitable, 38, 39
Overcorrection, 84–85
Overjustification hypothesis, 118, 120
Owens, J. S., 180
Ozonoff, S., 307

Panerai, S., 307
Parenting skills, in TF-CBT, 396
Partington, J. W., 214
PARTNERS CBT for Physical Abuse, 376
Patching, B., 69
Patterson, G. R., 5, 336, 378
Pavlov, I., 326
PBIS. *See* Positive Behavioral Interventions and Supports
PBS (positive behavioral supports), 88
Pearson, D. A., 198
PE (picture exchange) communication, 277, 278
PECS (picture exchange communication system), 277–278
Peer assistance
  discrete trial training for, 239
  in writing, 160–161
Peer-assisted learning strategies, 152
Peer influence, 90
Peer tutoring, for computational skills, 156
Performance feedback, 180–183
  defined, 155, 181
  math computational skills, 155–156
Perin, D., 159

Personality theory, 342–344
Peters-Scheffer, N., 6
Petursdottir, A. I., 219
Phonemic awareness, 137, 148
Phonics, 137, 148–149
Piasta, S. B., 148
Picture exchange (PE) communication, 277, 278
Picture exchange communication system (PECS), 277–278
Pierce, W. D., 114, 117, 122–124
PII (problem identification interview), 175
Pitchford, M., 80
Pivotal behaviors, 247
Pivotal response training (PRT), 275
Pivotal response treatment (PRT), 246–250. *See also* Classroom pivotal response teaching (CPRT)
P.L.A.N. strategy, 159
Plan implementation stage (behavioral consultation), 176, 180–183
Planning phase intervention strategies, 101–103
Pliance, 266, 267
Positive Behavioral Interventions and Supports (PBIS), 35–55
  behavioral principles applied throughout tiers of, 49–53
  behavioral principles underlying, 43–49
  critical elements of, 38–41
  enhancements to, 53–54
  implementation of, 40–43
  tiers of support in, 37–38
Positive behavioral supports (PBS), 88
Positive interventions, 87–88
Positive-practice overcorrection, 86
Positive punishment, 48, 49, 207
Positive reinforcement, 47, 49, 51, 52, 206
Positive self-review, 288–289
Poulson, C. L., 104
Power bases, 178–180
Power/interaction model of interpersonal influence, 179–180
Practices
  culturally valid, in PBIS, 38–40
  evidence-based. *See* Evidence-based practices (EBPs)

Pragmatic behavior therapy, 326
Precision teaching
  components and implementation of, 310
  critics of, 310–311
  evidence base underpinning, 311–312
  for students with ASD, 308–312
Precorrection, 69–71
Preference assessment, for children with ASD, 211–212
Prewriting, 161
Privacy, 387
Proactive interventions, 88–90
Problem analysis stage (behavioral consultation), 176
Problem evaluation stage (behavioral consultation), 176–177
Problem identification interview (PII), 175
Problem Identification, Problem Analysis, and Plan Evaluation Interviews, 20
Problem identification stage (behavioral consultation), 175
Problem-solving consultation, 175
Problem-solving skills training, 326
Professional and Ethical Compliance Code for Behavior Analysts, 137
Programming for generalization, 100–109
Project Advancing Wellness and Resilience Education (AWARE) Grant Program, 36
Project Follow Through, 313
Project Prevent Grant Program, 36
Prompt fading, 214–215, 232
Prompting, in DTT, 214, 230–232
Proper interventions, 88
Prout, H. T., 354–355
Prout, S. M., 354–355
PRT (pivotal response training), 275
PRT (pivotal response treatment), 246–250. *See also* Classroom pivotal response teaching (CPRT)
Przychodzin, A. M., 315
Psychoeducation, 353
  in AF-CBT, 378, 382, 383
  in TF-CBT, 396
Psychology of aggression, 378
Psychology of personal constructs, 341–342

INDEX   415

Psychotherapy
  in CBT, 353
  status of CBT within, 333–335
  theories of, 342
Psychotherapy by Reciprocal Inhibition (J. Wolpe), 333
Pumroy, D. K., 5
Punishment, 79, 83–87, 207–208
  in CBT, 363
  defined, 83, 246
  negative, 48, 207–208
  overcorrection, 84–85
  positive, 48, 49, 207
  response cost, 83–84
  time-out, 85–87

Quality-dependent rewards, 116
Questions About Behavioral Function (QABF), 196–197
Quiroz, D. R., 5–6

Radical behaviorism, 135
Radley, K. C., 239
Ramey, D., 311
Rational emotive behavior therapy (REBT), 326, 332, 343, 352
Raue, P. J., 332
Raven, B. H., 173, 178–180
Ray, A. G., 179
Read, K. L., 354
Reading fluency, 149
Reading interventions, 145, 147–153
  emergent reading skills, 147–149
  reading comprehension, 151–153
  reading fluency, 149–151
REBT. *See* Rational emotive behavior therapy
Receptive language, 265
Reductive procedures, 77–90
  and behavioral momentum, 78–79
  positive, proper, and proactive considerations with, 87–90
  punishment, 83–87
  and reinforcement, 79–83
Reeve, K. F., 104
Reeve, S. A., 104
Referent power, 178–180
Referrals
  for behavioral assessment, 20
  reasons for making, 23
  from within schools, 387

Reinforcement, 79–83
  of alternative behavior, 81
  of attempts, 254–255
  best practices in using, 125–127
  in CBT, 362–363
  contingent, 229–230, 254. *See also* Three-term (reinforcement) contingency
  in CPRT, 254–255
  in DTT, 233
  and extinction, 48–49, 82–83, 206–207
  extrinsic, 113–127
  function-based, 53
  of incompatible behavior, 81
  intermittent, 107
  of low rates of behavior, 80
  negative, 47–49, 82, 206, 335–336
  of other behavior, 80–81
  in PBIS, 51–53
  positive, 47, 49, 51, 52, 206
  quality, rate, and immediacy of, 25, 26
  for reading fluency, 150–151
  recruiting, 108
  reductive procedures and, 79–83
  schedule thinning, 107
Reinforcement contingency, 229–230. *See also* Three-term (reinforcement) contingency
Reinforcer–reward effects
  behavioral investigations, 118–120
  cognitive evaluation theory, 116–117
  overjustification hypothesis, 118
  theories and investigations of, 116–120
Reiss, S., 120
Relational frame theory (RFT), 326
Relaxation training, 363, 396
Relevance of behavior rule, 101
Repeated readings, 150
Replacement behaviors, 24–25
Resiliency, 394
Resistance to intervention, 78–79
Response classes, 99
Response cost, 83–84
Response generalization, 99
Response maintenance, 99–100
Restitutional overcorrection, 85–86
Reward power, 178, 179

Rewards
    concern over use of, 113–114
    and intrinsic motivation. *See*
        Extrinsic reinforcement effects
        on intrinsic motivation
    reinforcer–reward effects, 116–120
    task-contingent and quality-
        dependent, 116
    verbal, 124
RFT (relational frame theory), 326
Rhymer, K. N., 29
Richardson, I., 85
Richdale, A. L., 217–218
Ringdahl, J. E., 80
Risley, T. R., 208
Rispoli, M., 218
Roberts, W., 311–312
Robin, Art, 376
Rogers, Carl R., 331, 335
Romaniuk, C., 80
Roper, B. L., 16
Rosen, H., 326
Royer, D. J., 66, 71
Rummel, A., 117, 123
Ryan, R., 114–117

Safir, M. P., 196
Sancibrian, S. L., 288
Sandall, S. R., 198–199
Saunders, M., 5
Savidge, E. J., 306
Scaini, S., 6
Schedule thinning, 100, 107
Scheindlin, B., 85
Schema instruction, for computational
    skills, 157
School Climate Transformation Grants
    (SCTG) Program, 36
School psychologists, 4
Schreibman, L., 235
Schultz, S., 292
Scott, J., 215
Script fading, 220
SCTG (School Climate Transformation
    Grants) Program, 36
S^D (discriminative stimulus), 207
Self-acceptance, 332
Self-efficacy, 287
Self-generated mediation strategies,
    108–109
Self-instructional training, 326, 341

Self-modeling
    in social learning theory, 287
    video, 285–293
Self-monitoring, 109, 151–152,
    159–160
Self-regulated strategy development
    (SRSD) model, 159–160
Semistructured behavioral interviews,
    20–21
Sequential modification, 106–107
SGDs (speech-generating devices),
    278–279
Shakespeare, William, 338
Shaping, 46, 207
Shared control, in CPRT, 252–253
Shea, V., 301
Sheeley, W., 153
Shogren, K. A., 66
Siaperas, P., 307
Sigafoos, J., 236
Sign language, 277
Skerbetz, M. D., 65
Skinner, A. L., 89
Skinner, B. F., 5, 97, 135, 206, 212,
    264–266, 326, 335
Skinner, C. H., 18–19, 27, 29, 89
Skogli, E. W., 193
Smeets, K. C., 354
Smith, M. N., 213
Smith, S. C., 70
Smith, T., 210
Soares, D. A., 6
Social influence, 178–180
Social learning theory, 286–287
Social skills
    assessing, for ASD, 213
    in children with ASD, 228–229
    teaching, 46
Society of Clinical Child and
    Adolescent Psychology
    (APA Division 53), 330
Society of Clinical Psychology
    (APA Division 12), 330
Soft bases of power, 179, 180
Solomon, B. G., 182–183
"Some Current Dimensions of Applied
    Behavior Analysis" (Baer, Wolf,
    and Risley), 208
Spaced trial sequencing, in DTT,
    234, 235

Speech-generating devices (SGDs), 278–279
Splett, J. W., 8, 9
SRSD (self-regulated strategy development) model, 159–160
Stage, S. A., 5–6
Stages-of-change model, 333, 340
Stahmer, A. C., 249
Staron, V. R., 398–399
State, T. M., 64
Steege, M. W., 20
Steer, R. A., 398
Stefanatos, G. A., 195
Stimulus, defined, 246
Stimulus control, 207
Stimulus generalization, 98–99
Stokes, T. F., 100–101, 107
Stone, W. L., 194
Stormont, M. A., 70
Strategy instruction
    defined, 151
    for mathematics, 153–154, 157
    for reading comprehension, 151–152
    for writing, 158–160
Stream of consciousness, 338
Strengths and Difficulties Questionnaire, 380, 381
Structured teaching approaches for ASD, 299–316. *See also individual approaches*
    components of, 302–305
    direct instruction, 312–316
    discrete trial training, 227–240
    precision teaching, 308–312
    TEACCH, 300–308
Sturmey, P., 6, 229
Sugai, G., 50, 69–71
Sundberg, M. L., 214
Sushinsky, L. W., 120
Sutherland, K. S., 67, 68
Swanson, H. L., 154
Systematic desensitization, 364
Systems, in PBIS, 40

TA Center on PBIS. *See* National Technical Assistance Center on PBIS
Tact, 266, 267
Tague, C. E., 5
Tang, S., 123
Tangible function, 217
Taped problems technique, 154–155
Tarbox, J., 197, 213
Task analysis
    in direct instruction, 313–314
    in teaching self-help skills, 215
Task-contingent rewards, 116
Taylor, L. A., III, 115–116
TEACCH. *See* Training and Education of Autistic and other Communication Handicapped Children
Teachers
    behavioral assessment interviews with, 19–21
    and direct instruction, 314
    forming effective working relationships with, 21
    training for. *See* Training for professionals
Teaching loosely, 106
Teach to mastery strategy, 103–104
Teaming, in PBIS, 40
Technical eclecticism, 329
Technological descriptions, in ABA, 208–209
Tekin-Iftar, E., 104–105
Temporal contiguity, 122
Temporal generalization, 99–100
Text enhancements, for reading comprehension, 152
Text structure analysis interventions, 152
Textual, 266
TF-CBT. *See* Trauma-focused cognitive behavioral therapy
Tharp, R. G., 173
Theodore, L. A., 89
Therapeutic alliance, 332
Therapeutic relationship, in CBT, 331–333
Think Before You Read, While Reading, and After Reading, 152
Thinking, Fast and Slow (D. Kahneman), 343
Thomas, C. J., 198–199
Thompson, J. L., 219
Three-term (reinforcement) contingency, 44–49, 229–230, 246. *See also* Antecedent–behavior–consequence (ABC)

additional components with, 230, 231
in discrete trial training, 230, 231
modifying antecedent stimuli, 44–45
in PBIS, 49
strategies for modifying consequences, 47–49
strategies for teaching behavior, 45–47
Tier 1 supports, 37–38, 40, 41, 50–52, 62
Tier 2 supports, 38, 40–42, 50, 52, 62
Tier 3 supports, 38, 40–42, 50, 52–53, 62
Tiered systems, 62
Time-out, 85–87
Tirosh, E., 196
Token economy, 363
Tomanik, S. S., 198
Toussaint, K. A., 211–212
Townsend, D. B., 104
Tracking, 266
Training and Education of Autistic and other Communication Handicapped Children (TEACCH), 300–308
components of, 302–305
critics of, 304
evidence base underpinning, 304–308
foundations of, 300–301
for use across cultures, 308
for use in early childhood education, 306–307
for use in residential programs, 307
for use in schools, 305–306
Training for professionals
in ABA, 136–137
in ABA with children with ASD, 219
BCBAs, 137
in behavior and classroom management, 126
in CPRT, 255–256
in DTT, 239
in PBIS, 41–42
in TF-CBT, 400
Transcriptive, 266
Transfer phase intervention strategies, 101, 102, 107–109
Trauma
defined, 394
prevalence of, 393–394
symptoms resulting from, 394

Trauma-focused cognitive behavioral therapy (TF-CBT), 393–400
empirical support for, 397–399
specific components of, 395–397
Trauma narrative, 396
Traumatic grief, 398–399
Treating Trauma and Traumatic Grief in Children and Adolescents (Cohen, Mannarino, and Deblinger), 396
Treatment fidelity, 256, 257
Treatment integrity, 181
Treatment × Skill interaction, 135
Triadic relationship, 173
Troutman, A. C., 84
Turner-Brown, L. M., 307

Unaided AAC systems, 277
Unconditional acceptance, 331–332
Universal school-based CBT, 353–354
Updyke, J. F., 177

Vance, M. J., 80
Van Loan, C., 68
Vannest, K. J., 6
Vargo, K. K., 80
VBIs for ASD. *See* Video-based interventions for ASD
VB-MAPP (Verbal Behavior Milestones Assessment and Placement Program), 212–213, 272
Verbal behavior, 264–265
Verbal Behavior (B. F. Skinner), 212
Verbal behavior intervention in ASD, 263–279
assessing verbal behavior, 268, 271–272
augmentative and alternative communication, 276–279
evidence-based practices for, 273–276
Skinner's verbal behavior, 264–265
verbal operants, 265–271
Verbal Behavior Milestones Assessment and Placement Program (VB-MAPP), 212–213, 272
Verbal operants, 265–271
multiply controlled, 267–268
speaker and listener, 265–267
Verbal rewards, 124
Vernon, T. W., 232

VF (video feedback), 285, 291
Vicarious learning, 287
Victor, H., 292
Video-based interventions (VBIs) for ASD, 285–294
    empirical support for, 291–293
    theoretical foundation for, 286–287
    types of, 287–291
Video feedback (VF), 285, 291
Video modeling (VM), 285, 287–288
Video self-modeling (VSM), 285–293
Virues-Ortega, J., 305
Visual clarity, 303
Visual instructions, 303–304
Visual organization, 303
Visual structure and information, in TEACCH, 301, 303–304
Vladescu, J. C., 211–212
VM (video modeling), 285, 287–288
Vocabulary preview, 152–153
Voice output communication aids (VOCAs), 278
Volker, M. A., 194
VSM (video self-modeling), 285–293

Wagner, D., 150, 151
Wagner, R. K., 148
Wang, H. T., 198–199
Watson, J. B., 5, 335
Watson, T. S., 20
wDRO (whole-interval DRO), 80
Wehby, J. H., 68, 89–90
Weiss, B., 5
Weist, M. D., 8, 9
Weisz, J. R., 5

Welterlin, A., 307
Wert, B. Y., 292
Wetzel, R. J., 173
What Works Clearinghouse (WWC), 315
Whichard, S. M., 179
Whole-interval DRO (wDRO), 80
Wiersma, U. J., 123
Wilson, C. L., 215
Wilson, K. E., 179–180
Wiser, S., 332
Within-task choices, 64
Witt, J. C., 86, 182
Wolf, M. M., 5, 208
Wolfe, David, 376
Wolpe, J., 333, 336, 342–343, 364
Wong, C., 219
Word problem solving, 156–157
Work systems, in TEACCH program, 303
W.R.I.T.E. strategy, 159
Writing interventions, 146, 158–161
WWC (What Works Clearinghouse), 315
Wynn, J. W., 210

Yates, M. A., 366
Young Autism Project of the University of California Los Angeles, 209

Zero responding, differential reinforcement of, 80
Zettle, R. D., 266
Zimmerman, B. J., 115
Zingale, M., 307

ABOUT THE EDITORS

Steven G. Little, PhD, is currently on the clinical psychology faculty at Walden University. Dr. Little earned his PhD in school psychology from Tulane University in 1987 and has taught and directed programs at various universities in the United States and New Zealand. He has published extensively in the school psychology and applied behavioral analysis (ABA) literature, served as president and is a Fellow of Division 16 (School Psychology) of the American Psychological Association. He has served on the editorial boards of numerous journals as diverse as the *Journal of Social Psychology* to school psychology and ABA journals. His main research and practice interest is in behavioral interventions with children in homes and schools, with a specific focus on video self-modeling and holistic approaches to behavioral interventions with children. Dr. Little is also assistant director of the Svarcanas Centre, which is dedicated to research and practice in the area of healing through asanas, meditation, and pranayama practice.

Angeleque Akin-Little, PhD, is director of the Svarcanas Centre and president of Akin-Little and Little Behavioral Psychology Consultants, PLLC. She earned her PhD in school psychology from the University of Southern Mississippi in 1999 and is a licensed psychologist and board-certified behavior analyst (BCBA-D). She has served on the faculty at a number of universities in the United States and New Zealand and is a Fellow of Division 16 (School Psychology) of the American Psychological Association. Her main research and practice interests are in the area of behavioral interventions in homes and schools, particularly, applied behavior analysis with children with autism spectrum disorder and holistic approaches to behavioral interventions with children. She is also a certified yoga instructor (200 hours).